DATE DUE

MAR 2 '89			
OCT 26 '92			
NOV 1 4 '96			
OCT 3 0 2013			

CHRIST AND THE FINE ARTS

CHRIST
AND THE FINE ARTS

REVISED AND ENLARGED EDITION

*AN ANTHOLOGY
OF PICTURES, POETRY, MUSIC, AND STORIES
CENTERING IN
THE LIFE OF CHRIST*

BY CYNTHIA PEARL MAUS

Fully Illustrated

HARPER & ROW, PUBLISHERS

New York and Evanston

TO

LOVERS OF ART

AND THE ARTISTIC

✦

CONTENTS

A detailed contents page will be found preceding each of the several sections listed below

CHRIST AND THE FINE ARTS

INTRODUCTION

THE preparation of this anthology on *Christ and the Fine Arts* has been a remarkably compensating bit of service. The author is perhaps no better fitted than many another lover of beauty to perform this task, except in the fact that since January 1932 she has had, for the first time in a busy, active life, the opportunity to make an unhurried study of the life of Christ as He is portrayed by the four major fine arts—pictures, poetry, music and stories. That this work of love needed to be done by someone is evident since, so far as the author knows, no other such a life of Christ has hitherto been made available.

This anthology has been prepared primarily for youth and leaders of youth, although its author hopes that adults will also find it stimulating and challenging. Twenty years of service with young people and their adult leaders, as an editor, author, and continent-wide superintendent of Young People's Work for the churches of Christ, plus an inborn love of the beautiful constitute the background of experience out of which this volume has grown.

It is the conviction of the compiler of this anthology that if the youth of today, or for that matter of any day, are to get a clear vision and grasp of the contribution which Jesus Christ has made and is making through the centuries to the development and enrichment of human life, that vision and grasp will be better attained by looking at Christ through the eyes of the artist as he portrays the ideal against the background of the real than in any other way.

There is in every heart a love of the beautiful. We are made so that we respond to the ideal and the infinite even though we cannot and do not fully comprehend either. Through the ages men's intellects have been unable to agree about what and who Christ is; but human hearts in every generation have united in love for this matchless personality in whom the ideal of all men individually and collectively is realized. With the poet, Sidney Lanier, we find our own hearts singing:

> But Thee, but Thee, O sovereign Seer of Time,
> But Thee, O poet's Poet, Wisdom's Tongue,
> But Thee, O man's best Man, O love's best Love,
> O perfect life in perfect labor writ,
> O all men's Comrade, Servant, King, or Priest—
> What *if* and *yet*, what mole, what flaw, what lapse,
> What least defect or shadow of defect,
> What rumor, tattled by an enemy,
> Of inference loose, what lack of grace
> Even in torture's grasp, or sleep's, or death's—

1

> Oh, what amiss may I forgive in Thee,
> Jesus, good Paragon, thou Crystal Christ?

This anthology, therefore, is dedicated to youth and lovers of youth, who, through the fine arts, wish to *see*, to *feel*, and to *discover* with the eyes of the spirit, the Christ of the centuries, the Friend, the Comrade, the Consoler of men through the ages.

Recently some unknown writer speaking of the influence of Jesus through nineteen hundred years of Christian history said:

"Here is a man who was born in an obscure village, the child of a peasant woman. He grew up in another village, and that a despised one. He worked in a carpenter shop for thirty years, and then for three years He was an itinerant preacher. He never wrote a book. He never held an office. He never owned a home. He never had a family. He never went to college. He never put His foot inside a really big city. He never traveled, except in His infancy, more than two hundred miles from the place where He was born. He had no credentials but HIMSELF.

"While still a young man, the tide of popular opinion turned against Him. His friends ran away. One of them betrayed Him. He was turned over to His enemies. He went through the mockery of a trial. He was nailed upon a Cross between two thieves. His executors gambled for the only piece of property He had on earth, His seamless robe. When He was dead, He was taken down from the cross and laid in a borrowed grave through the courtesy of a friend. Nineteen wide centuries have come and gone, and today Jesus is the centerpiece of the human race, and the leader of all human progress.

"I am well within the mark when I say that all the armies that ever marched, all the navies that were ever built, all the parliaments that have ever sat, and all the kings that have ever ruled *put together* have not affected the life of man upon this earth like this one solitary personality.

"All time dates from His birth, and it is impossible to understand or interpret the progress of human civilization in any nation on earth apart from His influence. Slowly through the ages man is coming to realize that the greatest necessity in the world is not water, iron, gold, food and clothing, or even nitrate in the soil; but rather Christ enshrined in human hearts, thoughts and motives."

More poems have been written, more stories told, more pictures painted, and more songs sung about Christ than any other person in human history, because through such avenues as these the deepest appreciation of the human heart can be more adequately expressed.

The purpose of the fine arts is to help us to see, to feel, and to appreciate the world in which we live. They are concerned, not with prosaic facts, but with the poetic joy of discovering beauty wherever it may be found. In the landscape, the sea, the sky, the human soul and many another source, the fine arts discover and picture for those of us who would otherwise be inarticulate, the love, the light, the beauty of God so richly incarnate in Jesus Christ. With the ancient prophet Isaiah, the fine arts say: "When we see Him, really see Him as He is, there is no beauty we can desire in Him." All the fine arts proclaim the Ever-

Present Christ to be the world's masterpiece,—the great classic in human character by which all progress toward a perfected humanity is being measured.

> He built no temple, yet the farthest sea
> Can yield no shore that's barren to His place
>   For bended knee.
>
> He wrote no book, and yet His words and prayer
> Are intimate on many, myriad tongues,
>   Are counsel everywhere.
>
> The life He lived has never been assailed,
> Nor any precept, as He lived it, yet
>   Has ever failed.
>
> He built no kingdom, yet a King from youth
> He reigned, is reigning yet; they call His realm
>   The Kingdom of the Truth.[1]

There are six major parts in this anthology on *Christ and the Fine Arts*, and each part, save one, has several sections. In order to make this volume more readily useful in planning worship services, devotional and special day programs and features of various types, a general table of Contents is provided giving the page number of the introductory articles, major parts and sections. Then each section begins with a detailed table of Contents listing the page number of all the poetry, pictures, music and stories related to the section as designated, thus making this comprehensive volume on the life of Christ from the viewpoint of the four great arts more usable in program building.

Immediately following the general Introduction four brief articles will be found. These are designed to help young people and adults to acquire an increased appreciation of the contribution which each of the fine arts makes toward understanding the influence of Christ through the centuries. Brief suggestions are given also in regard to the most effective ways of using the *fine arts* in program building. The spiritual and cultural value of any great poem, picture, story or song may be neutralized, indeed, entirely destroyed in the hands of an unappreciative blunderer, who will not pay the price through study and effort to make the fine arts *artistic*.

The author sends out this, her fifth volume, in the hope that it will make a permanent and lasting contribution through the years in helping young people and adults to discover the immeasurable beauty, joy, love and light that are inherent in the life of the Christ of the ages. After all it is only as we acquire the art of embodying in our own day-by-day living something of the matchless beauty, poise, purity, power and strength which He possessed that we are able to become torch-bearers in that realm to which the Master referred when He said: "Ye are the light of the world."

Armored not only with a knowledge of the fine arts, but also with the abil

[1] "The Man Christ," Therese Lindsey. From *The Master of Men*, Clark. Used by permission.

ity to make them *live* for folk in beautiful and rugged simplicity, you and I may become His torch-bearers to yet unborn generations:

> Hold high the torch of beauty, truth and love!
> You did not light its glow—
> 'Twas given you by other hands, you know.
> 'Tis yours to keep it burning bright,
> Yours to pass on when you no more need light;
> For there are other feet that we must guide,
> And other forms go marching by our side;
> Their eyes are watching every tear and smile,
> And efforts which we think are not worthwhile,
> Are sometimes just the very helps they need,
> *Actions* to which their souls would give most heed;
> So that in turn they'll hold it high, and say,
> "I watched someone else carry it this way."
> If brighter paths should beckon you to choose,
> Would your small gain compare with all you'd lose?
> Hold high the torch of beauty, truth and love!
> You did not light its glow—
> 'Twas given you by other hands, you know.
> I think it started down its pathway bright,
> The day our Maker said: "Let there be light."
> And He once said, who hung on Calvary's tree—
> "Ye are the light of the world." Go! . . . Shine—for me.[2]

May something of the richness of *beauty, truth* and *love* that was incarnate in Him be builded in you as you use the material in this anthology—this is the fervent wish of the author and compiler.

Cynthia Pearl Maus

Autumn 1958
Los Angeles, California

[2] Adapted from a poem entitled "Hold High the Torch" by Nelle D. Bradley, published in the April, 1923, issue of *The Youth's Companion*. Reprinted by permission of Mrs. Nelle D. Bradley, Interlaken, N. Y.

MY MASTER'S FACE

No pictured likeness of my Lord have I;
He carved no record of His ministry
    On wood or stone.
He left no sculptured tomb nor parchment dim,
But trusted for all memory of Him
    Men's hearts alone.

Who sees the face but sees in part; who reads
The spirit which it hides, sees all; he needs
    No more. Thy grace—
Thy life in my life, Lord, give Thou to me;
And then, in truth, I may forever see
    My Master's face!

                            —*William Hurd Hillyer*

✦

USING PICTURES IN TEACHING RELIGION

PRINCIPAL FORSYTH says: "The principle of art is the incarnation of God's eternal beauty: The principle of religion is the incarnation of God's eternal human heart. Neither can do the other's work, yet their work is complimentary, and I wish the divorce between them—art and religion—were more nearly healed. I wish the artists felt more of the need which art can never fill; and I wish the religious felt more of the need that art alone can fill."

Never was there a time, when the educational value of great religious art was more generally recognized than it is today. This is partly due to the fact that *time* is more valuable *now* than ever before, and pictures are *time-savers*. They present to the eye what it would take much longer to tell to the ear. This mental economy is a real service, for the less time and strength it takes to get an idea, the more time will be left in which to use and enjoy it.

The use of great pictures in teaching religious concepts rests upon the sound educational principle that a truth which reaches the mind through the eye-gate and the ear-gate at the same time doubles the impression. Psychologists tell us that sense impressions received through sight are of a higher order than those received through any other sense. Thus we say, "In one ear and out the other," but we never say, "In one eye and out the other."

In the long ago art rendered religion an incalculable service. From the Edict of Milan to the Reformation, the church was the patron saint of art. In the days when the populace was for the most part illiterate, the sacred story of the

Christian religion was told in the universal language of the painter and the sculptor. And for the masses the artist's brush taught the story of Christianity more convincingly than the pen of the theologian. Works of art were the people's Bible.

But the Puritanism of the Reformation divorced art from religion, and as in Greece *art* killed *religion*, so in Christian Europe *religion* killed *art*. The Puritan protest against art was made in the heat of conflict, and was, as a result, one-sided and prejudiced. Religious people today have regained and are regaining a truer perspective and a saner judgment. They see that the abuse of a thing is no sufficient reason for its disuse altogether. They see that to present truth in the form of beauty is not a hindrance but a help to truth. They see that the Bible has been denied the aid of the imagination and that its value has been lessened as a consequence. They know that the function of art is to render visible the Divine, and that it is not a foe, but the friend of religion.

The Christian world is beginning to turn to art with a new spirit of appreciation due largely to the ease with which the public may now have access to at least reproductions of great masterpieces of art at a comparatively nominal cost. Just as the printing-press ushered in the democracy of learning, so the camera ushered in the democracy of art; and pictures that were once found only in the great cathedrals and art galleries, or in the homes of the rich, are now found everywhere in reproductions.

In every great picture there are two elements, the *idea* and its *expression*. There ought never to be any disparity between these two elements, for in proportion as an artist values the thought he portrays, he will spare no pains in perfecting his technique in the presentation of that thought.

If great religious masterpieces of art are to render a real service as *moral teachers* it is important to keep in mind the distinction made by Henry Turner Bailey, between a *view* and a *picture*. A view is taken directly from nature, while a picture is composed to embody an idea. Views are valuable aids in creating mental images of places outside of one's experience. It must be remembered, however, that views give only the mere externals. For illustration, a view of Jacob's well, as it is today, has value only as verifying the fact that this well still exists. It has no value in teaching the truth about the *water* of *life*. Pierre Mignard's picture (see page 211) of "Christ and the Woman of Samaria" is vastly more important than any facts about the well. Truth is always more important than facts. The photograph or view gives one the external facts only; the artist's picture interprets for one the inward spiritual meaning behind these facts.

Art does not deal with things as they are in themselves. Science does that. Art, particularly religious art, deals exclusively with things as they affect the human soul. Tennyson once asked Watts his notion of what a true portraitist should be. Watts' reply so impressed the poet that he wrote it out in the beautiful lines, which afterwards appeared in the poem "Elaine" in *The Idylls of the King*:

> As when a painter, gazing on a face,
> Divinely thro' all hindrance, finds the man
> Behind it, and so paints him that his face,
> The shape, and colour of a mind and life,
> Lives for his children ever at its best.

It is the artist's function to portray what the camera cannot give and what the eyes of others often do not see. A woman looking once with the English painter, Turner, at one of his marvelous landscapes, said to him, "Mr. Turner, I cannot see in nature what you put into your pictures." The artist, with quiet dignity, replied: "Don't you wish you could, Madam?" Precisely this is the artist's mission, to help all of us to see, in nature and in human life, what the physical eye, unaided, could never discern. No painter is an artist who merely puts on canvas what any man can see with his own eyes. The artist's function is to show us something we have not seen, or have only imperfectly realized. Thus the artist becomes an interpreter, a teacher.

Classical religious paintings render at least two great services. One is to impress deeply on the mind and heart some great truth or Biblical scene which has made only a slight impression before. Such a service is rendered by Holman Hunt's "The Light of the World," or by Hofmann's "Christ and the Rich Young Ruler." The other great service which classical pictures render is to call our attention to a side of some truth which we have never before noticed. Browning says this is one of art's greatest functions.

> For don't you mark? We're made so that we love,
> First when we see them painted, things we have passed
> Perhaps a hundred times, nor cared to see.
> And so they are better painted, better for us,
> Which is the same thing. Art was given for that.
> God uses us to help each other so,
> Lending our minds out.

Clementz' picture of "The Boy Christ in the Temple" renders just that service for us. It embodies a dozen or more passages of Scriptures from Deuteronomy to John, and sums up in a small compass all the facts in relation to that story, many of which have passed unnoticed before.

Even more important is the service art renders in opening up some side of a great spiritual truth which we have never before fully realized. Thus Holman Hunt's "The Light of the World" helps us to understand and apply to ourselves Jesus' words: "Behold, I stand at the door and knock; if any man hear my voice, and open the door, I will come in to him, and will abide with him, and he with me." When we look upon this marvelous picture, we understand, as we have not understood before, the meaning of Christ's words. He, the unseen, though ever-present guest, is standing just outside the door to every human heart seeking entrance. But the latch is on the inside. He cannot come in to be the "shepherd of our souls" until we lift the latch and bid Him to come in and abide with us.

We are so accustomed to thinking of beauty as merely decorative and orna-
mental that we forget that beauty is a moral necessity. God wrought beauty
into the structure of the universe. Beauty is the highest form of righteousness.
Beauty and *truth* are not separated in God's world, and they ought not to be
in human thought. God, who gave as much care to painting a lily as to forming the eternal hills, joined truth and beauty in holy union; and what God
has joined together, man ought not attempt to put asunder, because beauty
has a moral value for truth.

This universal love of beauty is one of the resources of human life that
Christianity ought to pervade with its spirit and claim as its own. It is to this
instinctive love of the beautiful that the artist makes his appeal, and gets,
therefore, a wider hearing for the truth he presents in this universally loved
form.

Art is the interpretation of the great eternal realities of life, and as soon as
the artist tries to embody the greatest feelings and aspirations of the human
soul, he gets on Biblical ground, for there is no great interest or aspiration of
man which the Bible has not treated. It is for this reason that great artists
have dealt so largely with Biblical themes. Painting and the Bible could not be
kept separate. They are congenial companions, because they have one common characteristic: both deal, not with the immediate and material, but with
the eternal and spiritual. The function of art is to embody the *universal* and
the *eternal*. The function of religion is to help man to discover that his *selfhood* (soul) is *eternal*, that he is building it day by day; and that "as a man
soweth, so shall he also reap." The chief characteristic of the Bible and art is
the same. They belong together.

As a preparation for the interpretation of the great religious masterpieces of
art included in this anthology may we be conscious always of the definite
spiritual value of great pictures as moral teachers; and of our obligation and
responsibility to become so familiar with and so appreciative of the best in
art that we will never mar the message which every great picture, artistically
presented, contains.

The masterpieces of art included in this anthology have been selected because they present an eye-gate story of the Christ of the centuries. They hint
at some connection between the everyday world in which Christ lived and
wrought, and the unseen spiritual world that was all about Him. Jesus lived
so continuously and fully in both these worlds that no artist can depict His life
without reminding us of His words, "The kingdom of God is within you."
Both these elements (the visible and the invisible) were present in varying degrees in the story of His birth, His growth and maturity, His call to specific
service, His friendships and labors, His successes and disappointments, His
tragic end, and His triumphant resurrection.

Dr. Albert Edward Bailey says, "Take out of these human happenings the
spiritual element of joy and peace, of love and sacrifice, of consciousness of a
mission, of pity for suffering, of hatred of sin, of tolerance with selfishness in
high places, of devotion to truth; take out faith and the ever-present conscious-

ness of God in which all these elements are rooted, and you have nothing left worthy of an artist's time to depict."

The compiler of this anthology believes that if young people and adults will pay the price to make great masterpieces of religious art live, through an artistic presentation of the artist's message in story, accompanied with music and a reproduction of the picture, they may become co-workers with Christ in making truth and beauty so attractive that the unseeing will be led to follow Him, whom to know aright is life abundant here and life eternal hereafter.

Whenever possible couple with the art interpretations in *Christ and the Fine Arts* visible, eye-gate reproductions of the one hundred pictures contained in this revised, enlarged edition. Kodachrome slides 2 x 2 of the art reproduced in this volume may be obtained from the Office of Visual Education Service, The Divinity School, Yale University, 409 Prospect Street, New Haven, Conn.

Link with these oral interpretations of great religious art not only the visual presentation of the pictures, but whenever possible either vocal or instrumental music of some of the great hymns and spirituals that suggest the same message to human hearts.

It is not important that the interpreter of the picture be *seen*. It is important that he or she shall be *heard* and that he shall infuse into this oral interpretation of the picture such an appreciation of its message as will make it live in the minds and hearts of those who see the masterpiece and hear its story.

Many a devotional service, special day program, club and church service has been redeemed from mediocrity through the intelligent and artistic use of "great pictures as moral teachers."

WHAT IS POETRY?

"Poetry is that impassioned arrangement of words, whether in verse or prose, which embodies the exaltation, the beauty, the rhythm and the truth of life."
—Richard Le Gallienne

"Poetry is the grouping of words, phrases and ideas that have always loved each other, but never got together in that combination before."
—Author Unknown

"Poetry is the expression—under the light of the imagination—of the unfamiliar beauty in the world, the beauty that is 'the smile upon the face of truth.' Poetry is the revelation of the strange in the familiar, of the eternal in the transitory. It is the impassioned cry of the heart in the presence of the wonder of life."
—Edwin Markham

✢

POETRY

Mere words, but O, how crystal-clear they shine,
How like the chime of silver bells they are!
A voice for those who have no voice at all,
A song sung in the dark, and heard afar.

The Psalmist sang, and men have listened long;
From countless hearts the old loved hymns are cried:
"Lead kindly Light, amid th' encircling gloom,"
"Abide with me; fast falls the eventide."

Words set to music, thus great hymns are wrought.
From poetry that stirs the hearts of men:
Sheer poetry that lifts us up to heaven,
And draws Christ down to walk the earth again.
—Grace Noll Crowell

TRUTH PICTURED THROUGH POETRY

No LIFE of Christ as portrayed through the fine arts would be complete that ignored the contribution which poets and poetry make in helping us to appreciate the power and passion, the truth and beauty, the sacrifice and selflessness of Him, who, for countless thousands of people of every nation, race and clime, is the "Magnificent Obsession" of the centuries.

What is poetry? Dr. Theodore G. Soares in *Finding God through the Beautiful* has given us one of the best brief interpretations of what poetry is. He says: "Poetry is thought, sometimes philosophy, sometimes argument, but always *emotion*. The poet wants to tell us how he feels about his subject. It is an experience rather than a proposition. So poetry belongs to those realms of life where we feel most deeply. Love must be poetic. Heroism is poetic, and especially when we say what heroism means to us must we sing the song of the heroes. Sorrow is poetic—the dirge and the elegy. The fierce passions of war express themselves in battle-songs. Not a little of the Old Testament poetry came from the book of the wars of Jehovah. Especially is religion poetic. Religious experience, the concepts and practices of religion shot through with feeling of their values—reach out naturally to poetry as its most fitting vehicle of expression."[1]

To present-day critics who predict that poetry is doomed to perish, that it will eventually be sponged out by the hand of science, one might well answer that it would be just as true to prophesy that poetry would some day obliterate science. Both statements are erroneous. Poetry and science each stands on its own ground, separate and secure, co-equal and eternal.

And to those who confess that they do not understand or enjoy poetry, and that it will eventually be exhausted by the poets, themselves, because there will be nothing new left to see or to say, we venture to suggest that poetry will live as long as love, as beauty, and as truth exist, because poetry is the expression in beautiful, artistic form, of man's highest and most cherished ideals.

No, poetry will never perish. Poetry has existed in the world from the dawn of creative genius until now, and it will continue throughout all time. In the dim, distant centuries of the world's beginnings, the poet appeared as the impassioned seer. Religion, itself, in the Vedas, the Eddas, and the Scriptures descended as a song, as a poetic vision of the Creative Man.

Edwin Markham says: "The poet is a dweller between two worlds, the Seen and the Unseen; he beholds objects and events in their larger outline and deeper mystery. He never rests with the sensual, the apparent. He frees us from the tyranny of the moment. His mission is an eternal quest for the absolute reality and veracity behind the veil of the senses."

[1] Used with permission of the author and publishers.

And Sir Philip Sidney says: "Of all the writers under the sun, the poet is the least a liar." Precisely as the soul needs the body to give it visible identity, so the Fact needs the Ideal to give it genuine reality. The *ideal* completes the *fact* by giving it a new and larger significance. The fact, standing alone, is often a liar because it is only part of truth. The ideal rounds it out into the full circle of clarity and reality. Poets fulfill for us that ancient Scripture saying: "We look, not at things which are seen and temporal, but at things which are not seen and eternal."

The poet is forever pressing onward through the superficial, the things that show, to the significant, the permanent, the universal truth behind the facts. He is forever ignoring the mere outward shell, giving us instead the inner spirit. For this very reason the poet's pictured truth is "deeper than science and truer than history."

Through the mind's eye of the poet we escape from the hard monotony of our daily lives, from the despotism of the actual to the ideal, the spiritual. That which Novalis says of philosophy is equally true of all great poetry: "She can cook no bread; but she can procure for us God, freedom and immortality."

And throughout all time the ideal must be preserved even at the cost of martyrdom, for when ideals perish from the earth, the home will shrivel to a house, the grave to a pit, the nation to a rabble, and the world to chaos.

The poet, dwelling as he does in exalted heights, comes into our conscious life to judge the world as it is, in the light of the world as it ought to be. He comes to infuse into the hearts of men the loftier courage of life; to create for their consolation and joy that nobler, "wilder beauty than earth supplies" as he brings to us poems that face the sordid, tragic facts of life in the light of the spiritual forces that are available for its purging and renewal.

With strange and unfamiliar beauty of ideas and ideals he chastens our souls by disturbing our lazy optimism with a bugle cry of battle for the hard right as over against the easy wrong. He stirs us to a noble discontent and a divine impatience with things as they are. Into a world of the imperfect he sends not peace but a sword bathed in the beauty of the perfection of Heaven. He points the way, away from the immediate and ephemeral, to the abiding and the eternal. He constantly challenges us with his pronouncements "that to *be something* is more important than to *get something*; that to *make a life* is more worthy than to *make a living*"; that the demands of love, honor, purity, justice and service are the highest interests and values that human life can attain.

If such be the function of poets and poetry, no look at the life of Christ through the fine arts would be complete that did not include some of the choice treasures in verse that have been the contribution of poetic sages through all the centuries.

In this anthology on *Christ and the Fine Arts* the compiler has endeavored to bring together poems from both the older classical authors and the newer and more modern "free verse" exponents in presenting this composite view of Christ through pictured truth. The limitations of space, of course, make it impossible to include many poems that are worthy of a place in any poetic picture of the Christ of the centuries.

As with the story, so it is with poetry—artistry in interpretation may be enhanced to a very great degree by the use of musical accompaniment. This fact is daily attested by the musical mosaics that artists of the radio and screen bring to us constantly. Care must be taken, however, to use music that fits the rhythm of the poetry. Both the musical accompaniment and the human voice must fuse together in a perfect articulatory and emotional blending. The music must never be so dominant that it drowns out the speaking voice, and the rhythm of the music and poem must complement each other in producing a single, definite emotional impression.

Very often stereopticon slides of great religious masterpieces of art may be linked with music and poetry in creating a more vivid and pleasing emotional impression than would otherwise be possible. The reader or poetic interpreter in such instances should be as inconspicuous as possible so far as "being seen" is concerned. It is much more important that he or she shall be clearly *heard* and *felt*, than seen.

In the oral interpretation of poetry a rich and varied quality of voice as well as the discreet use of stress, pause and pitch in reading is of vital importance. Be sure, first of all, that you both understand and appreciate the message which the poem contains. Look up the pronunciation of every unfamiliar word. Read the poem aloud many times using a variety of tone quality to stress significant words and phrases. The skillful use of the *pause* before words or phrases that should stand out significantly adds effectiveness in interpretation. Cultivate the habit of memorizing poems that are worthy to live forever in your sub-conscious mind. Acquire the habit, in the public reading of poetry, of using different ranges of pitch—the elevation or depression of the voice. Nothing is more deadly to the poet's message than a monotone quality of voice. And above all, in your interpretation of poetry, be sure that your own emotional appreciation of the author's message is felt by your hearers because your appreciation is genuine, and because of the skillful way in which you use the pause, pitch and stress.

Nothing adds greater effectiveness in worship services, in special day programs, and in brief talks and addresses than the wise use of poetry that fits the message and the occasion. These brief bits of poetic truth will remain in the memory-stream of your hearers long after your prosaic affirmations have been forgotten, for this is the distinctive contribution which poetry contributes to the enrichment of our prosaic, everyday lives.

STORY-TELLING ONE OF THE OLDEST ARTS

SEUMAUS MACMANUS says: "Story-telling is one of the oldest arts in the world—and one of the most joy-giving. Story-telling, when it was in its prime, developed its own artists—and few artists were more loved or more in demand. In the greatest story-telling country in the world, Ireland, the professional story-teller, called in the Gaelic language, the Shanachie, took rank with princes. He travelled over the land with a great retinue in his train, and was welcomed with festive joy in both court and cot—where his session usually held from candle-light till cock-crow. And still, thank God, we have the beautiful story-teller in the glens among the hills of Ireland.

"The art carries with it and fosters community feeling, the brotherhood of man, fireside magic, home influence, and joy. . . . The story-teller is as the Promised Land, alluring, fruitful, joy-giving—his mind a blessed region flowing with milk and honey. The story-teller refreshes the weary, rejoices the sad, and multiplies the joy of those who are already glad. He is a God-gift to the community. Welcome him, nurture him, cherish him."—From: Foreword, 1924-25 *Year Book*. National Story Teller's League. Used with special permission.

MAKING SPIRITUAL VALUES CREATIVE
THROUGH STORIES

THROUGHOUT the six major sections of this anthology on *Christ and the Fine Arts* a large number of both prose and poetic stories will be found, that have been gleaned from the world's storehouse of great literature. The compiler has deliberately sought to include not only good telling stories, but stories that are worthy to live forever because of their intrinsic emotional and literary merit.

Knowledge of the facts of the Bible alone will not conserve the values of religion. Religious ideas and ideals must be diffused with emotion. Whether or not the stories included in this anthology, therefore, are to *live* and to become great *moral teachers* depends, not only on the author of each particular story, but on the ability of every person using these stories to tell them in a vitally interesting and artistic way.

Many people think of the story only as a vehicle for teaching little children. The story method of making truth live, however, is not limited in its use to childhood; because the story is a universal teaching method—it is the vehicle by which truth for any and every age may be most graphically shared.

Throughout the history of mankind the story has been one of the greatest factors in the making of the history of nations and peoples; because in stories are mirrored the feelings and emotions, the passions and purposes, the loves and hatreds, the justices and injustices, the defeats and victories of mankind. And in all the yet unborn tomorrows, the story will continue to be the great *dynamic,* vital, life-renewing molder of hearts and of motives, especially when the story is thought of in terms of an art, and skill acquired by those who would inspire others through the art of story-telling.

G. Stanley Hall says: "Of all the things a teacher ought to know *how* to do, the most important, without exception, is to be able to tell stories." And then he adds that, "any person who will master the art of telling a half dozen or more great stories, will, in the process, have set for himself such a standard of excellence in telling as will forever-after redeem him from mediocrity." Story-tellers are not *born*, they are *made*; and any person may acquire this ability who will pay the price that skill in any art requires—tireless study and practice over a continued period of time.

When Jesus associated with people *something happened*, not so much because of what He said, but because of what He was—the fullness of God, walking the highways of the world with a sympathetic understanding of men, their passions and purposes, their aspirations and disappointments, their tragic successes, and their sublime failures.

Because the compiler of this anthology believes that through stories (and no book in all the world contains or has inspired more great stories than the

Bible) we are able to catch the true meaning of what the *mind* and *soul* and *heart* of *God* is like, as we see Him incarnate in Jesus Christ, a generous number of great stories that have had their inspiration in the life of Christ are included in this volume.

Stories help us to *see* and to *feel* what the friendship and companionship of Jesus did to people. For a story is not what you *say*, but what you *see*; not what you *hear*, but what you *feel*. It is the best method of sharing experiences with others, because it is the only painless process of teaching known. If you can be taught at all by any method, you are taught by the time you reach the end of the story, for whatever you have *seen* and *felt* in the deepest recesses of your own heart as a result of that shared experience is its permanent, abiding spiritual enrichment to you. And if the story has been well told, you have become so absorbed in its imaginative appeal that you have been unconscious of effort, either mental or emotional, during this sharing process.

Many stories are couched in poetic form. You will find a number of such stories in this anthology. Skill in telling either prose or poetic stories will become your developed ability only through constant study and practice. Analyze each story as you would a painted picture, for as Margaret W. Eggleston says: "A story is a mind picture painted by the human voice instead of the human hand. A story is a great life-message that passes from one soul to another. It steals as quietly as a canoe into the hidden places where naught else can go; it is as soothing as a song sometimes and at other times it cuts like a two-edged sword. It is quickly given, but it lasts in life through eternity. It has power to bless and it has also power to curse."[1]

Look up the meaning of every unfamiliar word; visualize every separate episode or incident in the story. Try to imagine that you are the person or persons to whom the incidents in the story were, at one time, a living experience. This will help you to bring to the telling of the story the emotional response that was present when the episodes in the story were a first-hand, living experience for the personalities involved in it.

Read the story again and again. Tell it aloud repeatedly, criticizing your own ability to make others *see* and *feel* the message for which the story was written. Speak in a clear, well-modulated voice and be unhurried in your manner, save where the action in the story requires another type of interpretation. *Tell*, do not *read* your stories. The human eye, face and voice are the mediums through which you are to share the rich experiences of the story with others. If you thrust a book or paper between yourself and your listeners, you hamper your own ability to bring the message in the story in an artistic way. And if you would tell stories well, practice the art of visualization of each episode until it becomes habitual so to do.

Artistry in telling stories may be heightened by the use of musical accompaniment. This is particularly true of poetic stories. The violin, the cello, the marimba, the harp, and in some instances even the piano and pipe-organ may

---

[1] From *The Use of the Story in Religious Education*. Used with permission of Harper & Brothers, publishers.

be used. Care must be exercised, however, on the part of both the accompanist and the teller to see that the musical accompaniment is not too loud so that it drowns out the changing inflections of the human voice; and that the rhythm of the speaking voice and the accompanying instrument fuse together in perfect emotional and articulatory blending.

Throughout this anthology footnote suggestions indicate musical selections that are ideal for use with particular poems and stories, and which are easily obtainable, locally, in sheet music or other form.

Above all, we need to remember in the use of any of the fine arts that it takes both an *artist* and an *art* to make *truth live*. No cheap substitute or makeshift on the part of either the artist or the art vehicle may be used without destroying the message which the poem, song, story or picture contains.

MUSIC

Let me go where'er I will
I hear a sky-born music still:
It sounds from all things old,
It sounds from all things young,
From all that's fair, from all that's foul,
Peals out a cheerful song.

It is not only in the rose,
It is not only in the bird,
Not only where the rainbow glows,
Nor in the song of woman heard,
But in the darkest, meanest things
There alway, alway something sings.

'Tis not in the high stars alone,
Nor in the cup of budding flowers,
Nor in the red-breast's mellow tone,
Nor in the bow that smiles in showers,
But in the mud and scum of things
There alway, alway something sings.

—Ralph Waldo Emerson

✢

As they sang—
Of what I know not, but the music touched
Each chord of being—I felt my secret life
Stand open to it as the parched earth yawns
To drink the summer rain; and at the call
Of those refreshing waters, all my thoughts
Stir from their dark and secret depths, and burst
Into sweet, odorous flowers, and from their wells
Deep calls to deep and all the mystery
Of all that is, is laid open.

—Anonymous

TEACHING RELIGION THROUGH MUSIC

RELIGION has much to learn from music, for religion deals with life, and music is the most perfect symbol of life. In the words of the poet:

> God is its author, and not man; he laid
> The keynote of all harmonies; he planned
> All perfect combinations, and he made
> Us so that we could hear and understand.

John Harrington Edwards says: "The art and science of music by no means reveal all that God is. But the boundless realm of melodious and accordant sound does indicate a Creator, whose nature is full to ceaseless overflow of the love of audible beauty. The Being thus disclosed provides in the structure of the universe and of man for the making of melody and harmony in this, and probably in all, worlds. 'Everything that the sun shines on, sings,' and sings of the Great Musician."

Before men developed the art of either oral or written language by which to communicate with one another, it is probable that they sang imitatively. The first articulate sounds by which mind communicated with mind were, in all probability, musical echoes or imitations of melodious sounds heard in nature. Language and the art of music grew from the same common stem; and, as with all other arts, music was born out of the perhaps unconscious attempt to express what was strongly and pleasantly felt.

Think of what music means to the human soul and what it can do. It cannot be merely a soulless form of physical energy—or the result of mechanical evolution the only purpose of which is to stimulate the nerves. It is rather a door opening into the Infinite. It is a medium of communication between spiritual beings. God, Himself, speaks to His children through music.

Some unknown author has said of music:—"Servant and master am I; servant of those dead, and master of those living. Through me spirits immortal speak the message that makes the world weep, and laugh, and wonder, and worship.

"I tell the story of love, and the story of hate; the story that saves, and the story that damns. I am the incense upon which prayers float to Heaven. I am the smoke which palls over the field of battle where men lie dying with me on their lips.

"I am close to the marriage altar, and when the grave opens, I stand nearby. I call the wanderer home, I rescue the soul from the depths, I open the lips of lovers, and through me the dead whisper to the living.

"One I serve as I serve all; and the king I make my slave as easily as I subject his slave. I speak through the birds of the air, the insects of the field, the crash of waters on rock-ribbed shores, the sighing of wind in the trees, and I am even heard by the soul that knows me in the clatter of wheels on city streets.

"I know no brother, yet all men are my brothers; I am the father of the best that is in them, and they are fathers of the best that is in me; I am of them, and they are of me; for I am the instrument of God. I Am Music."

It is this capacity to express and reflect the spiritual moods of men that gives music its right to be included among the "fine arts." One of the clearest-seeing teachers of our time champions music's claim to fine arts' ranking by saying: "We have not only a mortal body, with wants in the supplying of which coarse and arbitrary words are well enough; but we have also an enduring spirit with lasting emotions, and these emotions, which belong to the nature of spirit, have specific sounds which are their natural expression. Here, arises music, the eldest, if not the divinest of the fine arts."

The songs of a people keep alive their spiritual aspirations. They cheer, comfort, refine and elevate. They furnish the atmosphere and wings by which mortals can, for a little time at least, get almost free of matter, and rise as on wings to the realm of pure beauty. And thus, by the aid of music, they may be lifted, if they will, nearer God; or it may raise them from the earth just enough to give them freedom and excitation for the evil that clings also to their baser nature.

The human body is especially fitted for musical response. Brain, nerves, ears, throat and hand are marvelously fashioned and correlated to produce real music. One of the greatest Christian leaders of today says: "Music is demanded by Christian thought because it is the creation of God. Into everything moulded by His creative hands, music has passed from God's finger-tips. I know of nothing which is so much the creation of God as music. Man does not create it; he only finds it out. Man does not create truth; he only finds it out and brings it into his life as a purifying power. God creates truth. Man does not create electricity. He merely discovers it and uses it. Now music is as much the creation of God as truth or electricity. God has put music everywhere. I believe that the very core and center of God's own being is a sweet song of infinite love."

And Celia Thaxter, the poetess, says:

> If God speaks anywhere, in any voice,
> To us his creatures, surely here and now
> We hear him, while the great chords seem to bow
> Our heads, and all the symphony's breathless noise
> Breaks over us, with challenge to our souls!
> Beethoven's music! From the mountain peaks
> The strong, divine, compelling thunder rolls;
> And "Come up higher!" are the words it speaks,
> "Out of your darkened valleys of despair;
> Behold, I lift you up on mighty wings

Into Hope's living, reconciling air!
Breathe, and forget your life's perpetual stings,—
Dream, folded on the breast of Patience sweet;
Some pulse of pitying love for you may beat."[1]

It is upon this power of self-expression that the active element in love depends; and it is the very life of both God and man. There is in every human heart a divine craving to bridge the void between spirit and Spirit. God has manifested Himself, in part, in the beauties and wonders of nature and in human life; and man has responded with the "fine arts." For all the arts and sciences are but the stammering efforts of the finite mind to think God's thoughts after Him, and to commune with the inventive, creative, teaching, inspiring Mind which is at the center of all good.

John Harrington Edwards says: "Christianity is the religion of spiritual song. It inherited a magnificent psalmody, but it has also given birth to an invaluable hymnology, as well as the art of harmony to which modern music owes the greater part of its boundless wealth. Outside Christendom, religious music has hardly shed the primitive, animistic character of rhythmic noise, and children's songs are almost unknown. But the Christian religion found in music a congenial ally, ready to aid its progress in the individual heart, and in the world's history. The thought of God, of Christ and His cross, of the Christian graces, and of immortal life is entirely consonant with musical expression.

"Hebrew psalmody and Christian hymnology have served as wings to bear the Gospel far and wide over the earth. Every upward movement of Christianity has been marked by a fresh outburst of lyric fervor which has added to it both expulsive and impulsive force. This spiritualized *art element* in evangelism drives out seductive evil by the higher joy and purer ministry of sacred song. Reformation and Revival have always owed a great measure of their power to the inspiring and truth-conveying aid of music.

"Music is not mere expression of feeling. It calls for the cooperative activity of imagination, understanding and purposive will. . . . Nothing but *soul* can put *soul* into *music*, and the soul is God's work. The more of God there is in the composer or performer, the loftier and purer the strain. . . . Unbelief does not praise. The real Author of melody and harmony keeps these priceless boons, in their best forms, for the special favor of those who take the Giver with the gift."

Music which interprets the deepest feelings of the human heart is understood and appreciated by people of all nationalities, classes and grades of culture. It is inherently *democratic*; and democracy needs music to refine it, to humanize it, and to elevate it. Music of the best grade always has this effect; therefore, we should discriminate in the character of the music used.

Music for young people should always be of the very best, because it is during the adolescent years that it has its greatest natural appeal. Charles Kingsley says: "There is something very wonderful in music. Words are wonderful

[1] "The Voice of God," from *The Christian Century*. Used with permission.

enough, but music is more wonderful. It speaks not to our thoughts as words do; it speaks straight to our hearts and spirits, to the very core and root of our souls. Music soothes us, stirs us up; it puts noble feelings into us; it melts us to tears, we know not how. It is a language by itself, just as perfect in its way as speech, as words; just as divine, just as blessed."

Music is one of the mightiest factors in human life in its influence on ideas, moods and ideals. G. Stanley Hall says: "For the average youth there is probably no other such an agent for educating the heart to love God, home, country and for cadencing the whole emotional nature, as *music*."

Music is *religious* or *irreligious* according to the set of emotions it stirs. Therefore jazz tunes, music with syncopated time, music that makes its chief appeal to the heels instead of the head and heart, has no place in building artistic worship services, special day, and other types of cultural programs.

No life of Christ from the viewpoint of the "fine arts" would be complete that did not include an introduction, at least, to some of the great hymns, spirituals and oratorios that have had their inception in the Christian religion. Therefore throughout the six major parts of this anthology a generous number of such interpretations will be found.

The *musical score* for the spirituals, hymns and oratorios whose interpretations are included in this volume have been purposefully omitted, first because the size of the book is too extensive to make their inclusion feasible, and second because the musical score for any and all of them may be found in almost any good church or church-school hymnal or in sheet music form.

We need to remember in the use of hymns, spirituals and special music, as in the use of pictures, poetry and stories, that it takes both an *art* and an *artist* to achieve the finest results. Soft, harmonious tones, clear enunciation of words, and a real inner appreciation of the message which the music contains are essential to its interpretation.

Whenever possible correlate the message in the music with that of some great poem or picture that makes a similar appeal. This two-fold emphasis doubles the strength of the impression. Remember that the Creator "hath made everything beautiful in its time"; and that artistic appreciation and presentation are keys to the character of both the individual and group. It is true that "music hath charms to still the savage breast"; it is equally true that the one who interprets music for others, conditions in a large measure just how much *charm* the selection is to provide.

Since "the sound of music that is born of human breath, comes straighter from the soul than any strain the hand alone can make," pay the price through private preparation to make your rendition of any hymn, spiritual, or special musical number in itself a work of art. When you are to contribute music in any worship service, special day or other cultural program, sit near the front of the room and your accompanying instrument, so that there will be no long waits when the time for your contribution arrives. Take your place quietly, and inconspicuously, and if the musical number needs an introduction make it briefly and artistically.

SONGS OF THE SPIRIT
(Negro Spirituals)

WHETHER conscious of it or not, the people of the United States are under lasting gratitude to the Negroes of the Southland in pre-Civil War days for some of the most beautiful, touching and truly characteristic folk-songs that our nation knows—Negro Spirituals, or "Songs of the Spirit" as someone has beautifully called them. Most of these spirituals possess a distinctly religious character, and grew out of a deep yearning in the heart of the Negro to understand God and to be reconciled to the hardness of his lot.

That the Negro is devoutly and incurably religious no one can doubt, who will take the time and trouble to study sincerely these beautiful and touching "songs of yearning" that this enslaved people gave to the world. "Swing Low, Sweet Chariot," "Standing in the Need of Prayer," "I Couldn't Hear Nobody Pray," "All of God's Chilluns Got Shoes," and many another stir the deepest emotions in the hearts of all truly religious people, and make them yearn with the Negro for the time when justice and righteousness shall prevail among all nations and peoples everywhere.

I shall never forget the first time I heard a great Negro baritone sing with heart-rending pathos that beautiful spiritual: "He Never Said a Mumblin' Word." It painted for me the suffering of Jesus for the sins of mankind, as no other song I have ever heard.

Nearly all of these spirituals tell a story; and this one reveals the saddest story which this old world of ours knows—the story of the Master of Men, who set His face steadfastly toward Jerusalem, even when He knew that it meant persecution and death. He would drink the cup of human suffering to its bitterest dregs that men might forever afterwards know what the brooding, everlasting love of God is like.

My tears flowed freely as the verses of this great spiritual moved toward its dramatic, heart-searching climax. Only a race that had lived and loved and suffered could write such a song; and only those who understand in some measure, at least, what the love of God is like can.sing these spirituals with real understanding and appreciation.

One has to be prepared to say with the poet:

> "I should be able His death to die,
> If I were but able His life to live."

in order to sing such spirituals as "The Crucifixion" and "Were You There?" with real understanding. These songs, once heard, are unforgettable in their appeal.

No life of Christ in the *fine arts* would be complete that omitted from its pages some of the best loved of these "songs of yearning" that have come down to us through the years from the inmost heart of the Negro. The compiler of this anthology, as well as its users, is under lasting gratitude to Mrs. Rosa Page Welch, a cultured Negro musician of ability and training, for the sincere interpretations of the beautiful Negro spirituals included in this volume.

Among the best collections of Negro folk-songs is the *Old Songs Hymnal* by Dorothy G. Bolton and Harry T. Burleigh, published by the Century Company, New York City. *The Abingdon Song Book* published by the Abingdon Press, New York City, also contains a splendid collection of these Negro spirituals.

PART I

THE NATIVITY AND CHILDHOOD OF JESUS

CONTENTS

PART I   SECTION I

THE ANNUNCIATION

---✠---

"And thou shalt call his name JESUS; for it is he that shall save his people from their sins."—MATTHEW 1:21

---✠---

THE NATIVITY OF JESUS: IN PROPHECY

"But thou, Beth-lehem Ephrathah, which art little to be among the thousands of Judah, out of thee shall one come forth unto me that is to be ruler in Israel. . . . And he shall stand, and shall feed *his flock* in the strength of Jehovah, in the majesty of the name of Jehovah his God: and they [the flock] shall abide; for now shall he be great unto the ends of the earth."—MICAH 5:2, 4

✛

"For unto us a child is born, unto us a son is given; and the government shall be upon his shoulder: and his name shall be called Wonderful, Counsellor, Mighty God, Everlasting Father, Prince of Peace. Of the increase of his government and of peace there shall be no end, upon the throne of David, and upon his kingdom, to establish it, and to uphold it with justice and with righteousness from henceforth even for ever."—ISAIAH 9:6-7

"ECCE ANCILLA DOMINI"

("Behold, the Handmaid of the Lord")

By

Dante Gabriel Rossetti

(Interpretation)

AMONG the many beautiful paintings of the Annunciation few, if any, possess greater spiritual appeal than Rossetti's "Behold, the Handmaid of the Lord."

In the days when Rome was the mistress of the world, and Roman soldiers made the power of her might felt throughout the world, there lived, in the little village of Nazareth in Galilee, a humble peasant girl. Her name was Mary, and she was betrothed to a young man named Joseph. We know almost nothing more about the girl. One day a marvelous thing happened to this maiden, whose marriage to the village carpenter was not far distant. A Divine messenger visited her and told her that she had been chosen by God to become the mother of a child who should be the Saviour for whom the Jewish people had been looking for many centuries.

This beautiful story of the Divine Messenger's appearance to Mary, Rossetti has attempted to tell us in this beautiful painting of "Ecce Ancilla Domini." The original, now in the Tate Gallery in London, was painted when Rossetti was but twenty-one years old. Rossetti was one of a group of artists who dedicated their lives to the interpretation of great experiences.

Study the center of interest in this picture, and note how the artist has succeeded in making Mary the more prominent of the two figures. It is said that Rossetti painted the face of his own sister Christina as the virgin in this picture. He knew that Mary of Nazareth was not an English girl, but he wanted his picture to interpret the experience, not to be merely the photograph of a Jewish maiden.

Mary is not looking at the angel. She does not seem to know he is there. Think about this dreamy-eyed girl. How does it happen that she of all the young women of the world is chosen for this experience? God has waited until this time to make a more complete revelation of Himself to the people of the world. He is going to send His only Son into the world to establish a kingdom of love and righteousness and peace. He can send Jesus in any wonderful way He may choose, but He will send Him as a little child to live in a human home. If this is to happen, there must be a mother for the child, and Mary is to be that mother. What will God look for in the young woman He chooses to be the mother of the Christ-child? Does He require a woman of wealth? of great beauty? of special education? No, He just needs a womanly woman.

"ECCE ANCILLA DOMINI"—*ROSSETTI*

What characteristics of real womanhood can we discover from Rossetti's interpretation of Mary in this picture? Symbolism helps us. In the original painting, the curtain behind Mary's head is a soft blue, suggesting to us the ideal of truth which has been preparing Mary to be a fine woman since her girlhood. At the foot of her bed is a hand loom on which she has been weaving her dreams, and the color is red, the symbol of Divine love. The pattern woven shows pure white lilies, which tell of the purity of her thoughts and deeds. The angel is holding out to her a spray of beautiful lilies, which would seem to emphasize this characteristic. The neatness and purity of the room suggest the womanly duties with which Mary has occupied her time.

To us, the girls and women of today, this picture interprets the great ideal which we should hold before us, and which we admire in every fine woman. We may see her best in our own mothers or grandmothers, or in a woman who has never been a mother but who is womanly in her ways. To this womanly girl in every generation comes the responsibility for creating beauty and giving sympathy with generous measure. As we look at this picture let us think of some of the character traits that we need to be cultivating as we enjoy the freedom of our modern world. As we weave our dreams on the loom of life, let us prepare for a woman's place in helping to build God's Kingdom of Love on the earth.[1]

> King's Daughter!
> Wouldst thou be all fair,
> Without—within—
> Peerless and beautiful,
> A very Queen?
>
> Know then;—
> Not as men build unto the Silent One—
> With clang and clamor,
> Traffic of rude voices,
> Clink of steel on stone,
> And din of hammer;—
> Not so the temple of thy grace is reared.
> But—in the inmost shrine
> Must thou begin,
> And build with care
> A Holy Place,
> A place unseen,
> Each stone a prayer.
> Then, having built,
> Thy shrine sweep bare
> Of self and sin,
> And all that might demean;
> And, with endeavor,
> Watching ever, praying ever,

[1] Adapted from *Christian Worship for American Youth*, by Laura Armstrong Athearn. Published by the Century Company, New York City. Used with permission.

Keep it fragrant—sweet, and clean:
So by God's grace, it be fit place—
His Christ shall enter and shall dwell therein
Not as in earthly fane—where chase
Of steel and stone may strive to win
Some outward grace—
Thy temple face is chiseled from within.[2]

—John Oxenham

✛

THE IMMACULATE CONCEPTION

By

Bartolomé Esteban Murillo

(Interpretation)

THE Immaculate Conception by Bartolomé Esteban Murillo is one of the most beautiful pictures known to the field of religious art, and included among the world's Twelve Great Paintings. It was painted for a hospital in Seville, taken to France during the Napoleonic wars, and later bought by the French government for $117,200, and placed in the Louvre in Paris, where it now hangs.

This picture presents Murillo's conception of the mystery of the Incarnation. He pictures Mary as standing upon the clouds with the crescent moon beneath her feet, and the earth nowhere in evidence.

In Murillo's conception it is as though Mary was caught up into the third heaven about which Paul speaks, and is there seeing things that it is impossible for human lips to utter.

The most distinctive feature in this remarkable picture, perhaps, is its matchless coloring. Mary's robe is as blue as the sky in May after a drenching rain. It is an exquisite blue. The faces of the angelic cherubs that cluster about Mary shine with a heavenly radiance. They seem almost to palpitate with life and motion, as if to urge upon Mary the power and mystery of this God-conceived Child that she is destined to bring into the world of men.

Mary's folded hands and upraised eyes would seem to indicate her quiet surrender to the will of God. Dr. Bailey says: "Her wonderful eyes do not see the glories above; they are no longer organs of vision, but of expression. They are windows through which we may look into a woman's soul at its supreme moment. And this moment is not for her a revelation of divine truth to the intellect; it is a mystical union of the finite and the infinite in her heart. Two super-charged potentials have here found contact and the result is a flash of blinding emotion. . . . The word has been made flesh.

"Is this a unique experience, happening only once in human history? Let the theologians decide that as they will—for doubtless they know the precise limits

God has set for himself, the precise boundaries of the human soul. They can tell where dead matter leaves off and life begins; where life ceases to be animal and becomes human; at what point human life becomes divine; and how our bodies can become 'temples of the Holy Ghost' without interfering with the chemical, the physical, the sub-human and the human forces that are already tenanted there."[3]

Poets, however, are often wiser than the theologians, and such world-famous poets as Tennyson, speaking of the birth of his own son in "De Profundis" says with conviction:

> Out of the deep, my child, out of the deep,
> From that great deep before our world begins,
> Whereon the spirit of God moves as He will—
> Out of the deep, my child, out of the deep,
> From that true world within the world we see,
> Whereof our world is but the bounding shore—
> Out of the deep—thou comest, darling boy!

And so Mary as she gazes into this heavenly light and blinding emotion becomes conscious of her union with spiritual forces, and that through this immaculate conception God's Child of Promise is to come into the world through her.

"In the fullness of time," God sent His own Son to a virgin betrothed to a carpenter of Galilee, with angelic cherubs attending His conception, angels and shepherds His birth in the lowly stable in Bethlehem, and a wondrous new star to guide the Wise Men from their far-away homes in the East to the place where the Christ Child was born.

And the knowledge of all these things Mary hid in her heart, suffering the shame and misunderstanding of relatives and friends; but faltering not in the divine ministry of mothering the only begotten Son of God, who came in the flesh that He might walk the highways of man's world for the inspiration and guidance of the races of men on their upward climb.

✠

THE ANNUNCIATION

By

Arthur Hacker

(Interpretation)

THE original of this wonderful painting by Arthur Hacker hangs in the Tate Gallery in London, England. A very large part of the impressiveness of the original of this wonderful masterpiece, regarded by many as the most etherrcally beautiful of all the Annunciation paintings, is lost in half-tone reproductions.

[3] From *The Gospel in Art*, Albert Edward Bailey. Published by the Pilgrim Press, Boston, Mass. Used with permission of the author and publishers.

THE IMMACULATE CONCEPTION—*MURILLO*

THE ANNUNCIATION—*HACKER*

To appreciate it in all its matchless beauty one must see the color of the original —the ethereal blue of the angel's robe, the brilliant copper glow of the water-pitcher, the dainty green of the grass, the radiant beauty of the early spring irises, the strength of the Syrian sunlight flooding the white walls till they gleam through the very body of the angel and throw a sheen of luster on the spotless robes of the Virgin.

The marvelous color of this painting by Hacker of "The Annunciation" arrests at once the attention of visitors even in a gallery noted for its preëminent color. As one gazes on this picture, however, one finds a deeper source of emotion in the intensity of the angel's expression, who appears to have suddenly swept down upon this girlish daydreamer, in the mystic shadows in Mary's eyes, for while these shadows veil her thought, they reveal her emotion.

As your gaze rests on Mary, you begin to love this sweet womanly girl, so young and pure, standing here in the midst of her task like one of the radiant lilies of her garden. As you look at the beautiful white lily stock which the angel holds beside her, you realize that it is meant to suggest a translation of your own feeling about Mary. This tall, stately, peasant girl in her flowing Oriental robes is just like that lily stock, though she knows it not—a beautiful opening flower with a heart of gold. Could man or God want anything more than this beautiful, pure, chaste girl of perhaps sixteen or seventeen as the mother of the "only begotten of the Father, full of grace and truth?"

We are indebted to the artist, Hacker, for having given us in this picture one of the most beautiful of all the Annunciation paintings.

✢

THE SISTINE MADONNA

By

Sanzio Raphael

(Interpretation)

TRAVELERS in Europe who come to Dresden, Germany, will find that there art is supreme. In the Royal Gallery are many treasures of surpassing value, the lovely work of vision-led men. Raphael's masterpiece, "The Sistine Madonna," is to be found in this gallery. It was originally painted for a church in the village of Piacenza, Italy. Now it occupies a room by itself in this famous center of art. It is a symphony in color. It casts a spell upon the beholder that subdues and quiets. It invokes reverence and prayer. Voices in this room are seldom raised above a whisper. It is as though one visited a shrine. Those who come to admire remain to worship.

What is the message of this great picture? It illustrates the preservative power of religion. Raphael lived in a period of intellectual awakening. Invention and discovery were quickening the life of the world. It was a time of expanding frontiers. The fifteenth century was one of the most remarkable of the Christian era for the impetus given to creative thinking, invention, and discovery.

Back of all these activities was a religious motive. Caxton built his press in order that the Bible might be printed. Columbus sailed westward in the hope that he might win converts to the cross as well as find a shorter way to India. Michelangelo wrought on Saint Peter's Cathedral. In a similar way the artist Raphael was moved by spiritual impulse. And the work which these men did has entered into the religious heritage of the world.

"All passes—art alone remains" is a quotation to be seen above the door of the Fine Arts Building in Chicago. Without entering into controversy in this matter we know that some things do pass away and some things have power to abide. Because Raphael sought to glorify God in the painting of his picture of the Sistine Madonna, it has come to a place in the world's life that survives the passing of the centuries.

This picture suggests also the ministry of a little child. Critics have said that the artist sought to express, in the figures which are presented, the cardinal virtues of *faith, hope,* and *love.* Saint Sixtus is the embodiment of *hope,* and he looks with eagerness to Christ as he points to a needy world. Saint Barbara, kneeling and with face averted from the glory of this divine revelation, expresses the attitude of *love.* The cherubs recall the "Inasmuch as ye did it not to one of the least of these." Mary and her Child in sacred relationship portray *faith.* It is not blind and unintelligent faith, but one which is open-eyed, honest, and ready to accept the commission of God to a waiting world.

When Jesus "set the child in their midst" he expressed the genius of Christianity. The training of the child life of any generation is not only the most statesman-like procedure for securing the spread of faith, but the spirit of a little child is the qualification for discipleship. In saving the child to Christian life and service we are helping to shape the destiny of the world to Christian ideas.[4]

This picture suggests also the mystery of incarnation. This mystery is delicately expressed in the following poem:

> A tired old doctor died today, and a baby boy was born—
> A little new soul that was pink and frail,
>   and a soul that was gray and worn.
> And—halfway here and halfway there
> On a white, high hill of shining air—
> They met and passed and paused to speak
>   in the flushed and hearty dawn.
>
> The man looked down at the soft, small thing,
>   with wise and weary eyes;
> And the little chap stared back at him,
>   with startled, scared surmise,
> And then he shook his downy head—

[4] "The Cradle Song" by Brahms provides excellent musical accompaniment for this interpretation; it should be begun at this point.

THE SISTINE MADONNA—*RAPHAEL*

"I think I won't be born," he said;
"You are too gray and sad!" And he shrank
from the pathway down the skies.

But the tired old doctor roused once more
at the battle-cry of birth,
And there was memory in his look, of grief
and toil and mirth.
"Go on!" he said. "It's good—and bad:
It's hard! *Go on!* It's ours, my lad."
And he stood and urged him out of sight,
down to the waiting earth.[5]

Raphael's masterpiece expresses that dramatic moment when the veil between heaven and earth has been parted. The curtains are drawn aside and Mother and Child are looking out upon the world with wonder, amazement, and surprise.

All the critics give Raphael the credit for having painted the most wonderful Christ Child to be found upon any canvas. There is in the face a combination of that which is human and divine. It is the same type of face that Hofmann later painted in his pictures of "Christ and the Doctors" and "Christ and the Rich Young Ruler," but growing older with the passing of the years.

In Raphael's conception it is as though the mystery of His mission had just broken across their consciousness. It is as though they were appalled by the awaiting task. They come—these two, Mother and Child—treading diaphanous clouds with angel faces innumerable about them, recalling the Scripture, "Which things the angels desire to look into," the splendors of heaven pouring its radiance upon the earth.

What is the spiritual significance of this picture to us? "The word was made flesh, and dwelt among us." God became *man* that men might learn to live in a Godlike way. He took residence on the earth that earth might be more like heaven. He showed us in His own Son that flesh need not be a devilish thing, but full of grace and truth.

This historic event is the symbol of a process. It is ever God's purpose that the Word shall be made flesh, that the physical shall be filled with His glory, that truth shall connect with life, that virtue shall get into action and conduct, that the world shall be a continual incarnation of spiritual forces in human form. God writes His truth not in flaming letters on the sky, nor does He cast them in bronze or chisel them in marble for the guidance of the race. He writes His truth in *human life.* "I beseech you, therefore, brethren, by mercies of God, that ye present your bodies a living sacrifice, holy, acceptable unto God, which is your reasonable service. And be not conformed to this world: but be ye transformed by the renewing of your mind, that ye may prove what is that good, and acceptable, and perfect will of God."[6]

From *Sermons on Great Paintings*, by Harold Francis Branch. Published by H. M. Shelley, Philadelphia, Pa. Used with permission.

[6] Adapted from *Pictures That Preach*, by Charles Nelson Page. Published by the Abingdon Press, New York City. Used by permission.

THE DOOR

"He that entereth in by the door is the shepherd of the sheep."

He came to us
Himself a Star!
He spoke to us
Himself a Song!

The entrance to His place of birth
  Was by a little Door,
So humble all might find Him there,
  The wise, the rich, the poor.

A little Door, where cows had passed,
  Opened to a King!
The Shepherds and the Wise Men bent
  To see so fair a thing.

The talking trees upon the Door
  Their chequered shadows cast
"Ah, who shall know, and who shall know,
  How He will go at last?"

Somewhere upon a far-off hill
  At Christmas time,
  At Christmas time,
A little Door creaks open still,—
  It opens still.

—*Helen Slack Wickenden*

HIS CRADLE

It rocked and rocked for joy,
  This battered world,
When Mary's little boy
  Up in it curled,
    Despite its chill.
    O may He fill
Today His chosen bed,
  Through you and me,
Who love and help to spread
  Simplicity.

—*Herbert Seymour Hastings*

CHRISTMAS CAROL

As Joseph was a-wurkin',
  He heard an angel sing,
"This night shall be the birth-night
  Of Christ our heavenly King.

"His birth-bed shall be neither
  In housen nor in hall,
Nor in the place of paradise,
  But in the oxen's stall.

"He neither shall be rocked
  In silver nor in gold,
But in the wooden manger
  That lieth in the mold.

"He neither shall be washen
  With white wine nor with red,
But with the fair spring water
  That on you shall be shed.

"He neither shall be clothèd
  In purple nor in pall,
But in the fair, white linen
  That usen babies all."

As Joseph was a-wurkin',
  Thus did the angel sing,
And Mary's Son at midnight
  Was born to be our King.

Then be you glad, good people,
  At this time of the year;
And light you up your candles,
  For His star it shineth clear.

                              —*Anonymous*

SONG OF THE LITTLE CHILD

The night the little Child was born
  I wonder how it seemed
To lie in a hay-bright manger
  With all His dreams undreamed. . . .
Perhaps He felt how safe and warm
It was upon His mother's arm.

I wonder how it seemed to Him
    To have the Wise Men there,
Kneeling before His little feet
    With frankincense and prayer. . . .
Perhaps He but the closer pressed
His lips upon His mother's breast.

I wonder if He raised His eyes
Up to a splintered beam
Through which the light of a waiting star
    Shone in a long white stream,
And if an angel twined it round
In halos, so His head was crowned. . . .
Perhaps he thought the light was there
To shine on His mother's braided hair.

—*Louise Ayres Garnett*

CHRISTMAS EVE

The door is on the latch tonight,
    The hearth fire is aglow;
I seem to hear soft passing feet—
    The Christ Child in the snow.

My heart is open wide tonight,
    For stranger, kith, or kin;
I would not bar a single door
    Where love might enter in.

—*Anonymous*

THE ANNUNCIATION

God whispered, and a silence fell; the world
    Poised one expectant moment, like a soul
Who sees at heaven's threshold the unfurled
White wings of cherubim, the sea impearled,
    And pauses, dazed, to comprehend the whole;
Only across all space God's whisper came
And burned about her heart like some white flame.

Then suddenly a bird's note thrilled the peace,
    And earth again jarred noisily to life
With a great murmur as of many seas.
But Mary sat with hands clasped on her knees,
    And lifted eyes with all amazement rife,
And in her heart the rapture of the spring
Upon its first sweet day of blossoming.

—*Theodosia Garrison*

THE BIRTH OF CHRIST IN PROPHECY
AND GOSPEL

(Prophecy—MICAH 5:2, 4; ISAIAH 9:6-7)

BUT thou, Beth-lehem Ephrathah, which art little to be among the thousands of Judah, out of thee shall one come forth unto me that is to be ruler in Israel; whose goings forth are from of old, from everlasting.

And he shall stand, and shall feed *his flock* in the strength of Jehovah, in the majesty of the name of Jehovah his God; and they [the flock] shall abide; for now shall he be great unto the ends of the earth.

For unto us a child is born, unto us a son is given; and the government shall be upon his shoulder: and his name shall be called Wonderful, Counsellor, Mighty God, Everlasting Father, Prince of Peace.

Of the increase of his government and of peace there shall be no end, upon the throne of David, and upon his kingdom to establish it, and to uphold it with justice and righteousness from henceforth, even for ever.

(The Annunciation—LUKE 1:26-33, 38)

Now in the sixth month the angel Gabriel was sent from God unto a city of Galilee, named Nazareth, to a virgin betrothed to a man whose name was Joseph, of the house of David; and the virgin's name was Mary. And he came unto her, and said, Hail, thou art highly favored, the Lord *is* with thee.

But she was greatly troubled at the saying, and cast in her mind what manner of salutation this might be.

And the angel said unto her, Fear not, Mary: for thou hast found favor with God. And behold, thou shalt bring forth a son, and shalt call his name JESUS. He shall be great, and shall be called the Son of the Most High: and the Lord God shall give unto him the throne of his father David: and he shall reign over the house of Jacob for ever; and of his kingdom there shall be no end.

And Mary said, Behold, the handmaid of the Lord; be it unto me according to thy word. And the angel departed from her.

(The Magnificat—LUKE 1:46-55)

And Mary said, My soul doth magnify the Lord,
And my spirit hath rejoiced in God my Saviour.

For he hath looked upon the low estate of his handmaid: for behold, from henceforth all generations shall call me blessed.

For he that is mighty hath done to me great things; and holy is his name.

And his mercy is unto generations and generations on them that fear him.

He hath showed strength with his arm; he hath scattered the proud in the imagination of their heart.

He hath put down princes from *their* thrones, and hath exalted them of low degree.

The hungry he hath filled with good things; and the rich hath he sent empty away.

He hath given help to Israel, his servant, that he might remember mercy (as he spake unto our fathers) toward Abraham and his seed for ever.

(The Nativity[7]—LUKE 2:1-7)

Now it came to pass in those days, there went out a decree from Cæsar Augustus, that all the world should be enrolled. This was the first enrolment made when Quirinius was governor of Syria.

And all went to enrol themselves, every one to his own city.

And Joseph also went up from Galilee, out of the city of Nazareth, into Judæa, to the city of David, which is called Bethlehem, because he was of the house and family of David; to enrol himself with Mary, who was betrothed to him, being great with child.

And it came to pass, while they were there, the days were fulfilled that she should be delivered.

And she brought forth her first-born son; and she wrapped him in swaddling clothes, and laid him in a manger, because there was no room for them in the inn.

(The Visit of the Shepherds—LUKE 2:8-20)

And there were shepherds in the same country abiding in the field, and keeping watch by night over their flock.

And an angel of the Lord stood by them, and the glory of the Lord shone round about them: and they were sore afraid.

And the angel said unto them: Be not afraid; for behold, I bring you good tidings of great joy which shall be to all the people: for there is born to you, this day in the city of David a Saviour, who is Christ the Lord. And this *is* the sign unto you: Ye shall find the babe wrapped in swaddling clothes, and lying in a manger.

And suddenly there was with the angel a multitude of the heavenly host praising God, and saying,

Glory to God in the highest,

And on earth peace among men in whom he is well pleased.

And it came to pass, when the angels went away from them into heaven, the shepherds said one to another, Let us now go even unto Bethlehem, and see this thing that is come to pass, which the Lord hath made known unto us.

And they came with haste, and found both Mary and Joseph, and the babe lying in the manger.

[7] The effectiveness of this correlated Christmas story from the Bible may be heightened by having three Christmas hymns played softly on the piano, organ or violin or both, beginning with this Nativity section. Use "O Little Town of Bethlehem" with The Nativity section; "While Shepherds Watched Their Flocks" with the section The Visit of the Shepherds; and "We Three Kings of Orient Are" with the section The Visit of the Wise Men.

And when they saw it, they made known concerning the saying which was spoken to them about this child.

And all that heard it wondered at the things which were spoken unto them by the shepherds. But Mary kept all these sayings, pondering them in her heart.

And the shepherds returned, glorifying and praising God for all the things that they had heard and seen, even as it was spoken unto them.

(The Visit of the Wise Men—MATTHEW 2:1-12)

Now when Jesus was born in Bethlehem of Judæa in the days of Herod the king, behold, Wise-men from the east came to Jerusalem saying, Where is he that is born King of the Jews? for we saw his star in the east, and are come to worship him.

And when Herod the king heard it, he was troubled, and all Jerusalem with him. And gathering together the chief priests and scribes of the people, he inquired of them where the Christ should be born. And they said unto him, In Bethlehem of Judæa: for thus it is written through the prophet,

> And thou Bethlehem, land of Judah,
> Art in no wise least among the princes of Judah:
> For out of thee shall come forth a governor,
> Who shall be shepherd of my people Israel.

Then Herod privily called the Wise-men, and learned of them exactly what time the star appeared. And he sent them to Bethlehem, and said, Go and search out exactly concerning the young child: and when ye have found *him*, bring me word, that I also may come and worship him.

And they, having heard the king, went their way: and lo, the star, which they saw in the east, went before them, till it came and stood over where the young child was.

And when they saw the star, they rejoiced with exceeding great joy. And they came into the house and saw the young child with Mary his mother; and they fell down and worshipped him; and opening their treasures they offered unto him gifts, gold and frankincense and myrrh.

And being warned *of God* in a dream that they should not return to Herod, they departed into their own country another way.

THE VIRGIN'S STORY

(As Told by Mary, His Mother)

WE ARE on the way to the feast again and camped near the Holy City. The road is thronged with people. Joseph's tent is near ours. I am so glad Joseph's tent is near. Oh, how beautiful the Temple is with the morning sun gilding it! City set on a hill, crown of all the nations.

. . . . .

One of the rabbis in the Temple today read from the prophet Isaiah about the wonderful child who was to rule upon a throne like David's, and of whose government there would be no end. How my soul kindled under his portrayal of coming glory! Through all her humiliation that hope sustains Israel.

We are on the way home. Mother asked me last night about Joseph, and I fell into her arms and told her I loved him. Then she said, "Joseph is a good man."

. . . . .

Joseph and I are betrothed. What beautiful days! Life passes like a dream. Joseph comes much to talk with father and mother about the hopes of Israel.

. . . . .

My heart is in a tumult. I tremble. I know not what to think; for as I knelt at my evening prayer an angel appeared to me and told me I was to be the mother of the Messiah. Seeing my confusion, he hastened to assure me: "And you shall call his name JESUS; and he shall be great; he shall be a King, like David; and his Kingdom will have no end."

. . . . .

"I am a virgin yet in my father's house," I pleaded; "it cannot be."
"There is no cannot with God," he said, and vanished, leaving me alone.

. . . . .

O my soul; my soul is in an ecstasy! Oh, words too large for my tongue to frame. Can it be? It cannot be! It is a dream! It could not come to one in such humble station. To be the *mother* of the Messiah; oh, that is an honor for only the rich and the great!

What? the secret of our nation between God and me! Shall I go up to Jerusalem to the High Priest? But I would be laughed to scorn. To whom may I go? Who would understand?

. . . . .

I yearned to tell mother this morning, but could not, it seemed so pre-sumptuous, so unbelievable, yes, impossible. And Joseph—how can Joseph understand?

.   .   .   .   .

My secret oppresses me. If there was one to whom I could unburden myself, one who could understand!

.   .   .   .   .

I could bear it no longer and am on my way to Hebron to see my cousin Elizabeth. We have heard wonderful stories about Elizabeth. Perhaps she will understand. To her I may pour out my soul.

Elizabeth met me at the door, and before I had spoken she broke into rapture, calling me the mother of the Messiah and pronouncing blessings on me. It has been revealed to her, she said.

.   .   .   .   .

Three months with Elizabeth. Blessed days! We lived in another world—a world far removed from this—and unburdened to each other our bursting hearts. Two babes were to change the face of the world and those babes would call us *mother*.

I am leaving for home today. Farewell, Elizabeth. I am loth to leave; you only can understand. I must go now to the outside world—where explanations will be asked and no one will believe—perhaps not even mother.

Home in Nazareth. Joseph is coming tonight with his friend. I am afraid to meet Joseph tonight.

.   .   .   .   .

I fled to my room and wept. Mother came in and wept with me. I did not see Joseph. Mother tried to explain, but could not. He went away in great distress, while I lay under the heaviest burden womankind ever bears. O my God, time will vindicate me, but meantime what? I am troubled; my heart panteth; my strength faileth. Lover and friend hast thou put far from me; my friends stand aloof; my confusion is continually before me, and the shame of my face is covered.

Joseph is planning to send me away. How long wilt thou forget me, O Lord? How long wilt thou hide thy face from me? Consider and hear me, O Lord, my God; lighten my eyes lest I sleep the sleep of death.

.   .   .   .   .

Blessed be God; he has heard my cry. Joseph came to me, bowing low and imploring forgiveness; he made obeisance, declaring his unworthiness.

"Then you understand," I said.

"An angel appeared to me in a dream," he answered, "saying 'Joseph, thou son of David, fear not to take unto thee Mary, thy betrothed; for that which is conceived in her is of the Holy Spirit. And she shall bring forth a son, and thou shalt call his name JESUS; for he shall save his people from their sins.' "

Together we bowed in silence; then Joseph prayed brokenly: "Return unto thy rest, O my soul; for thou, Lord, hast dealt bountifully with us, and we shall walk uprightly before thee all our days."

.   .   .   .   .

Our wedding day. Elizabeth came—and her angel-promised child. Elizabeth and Joseph talked much together, and Joseph looked long into the face of her babe.

.   .   .   .   .

Elizabeth and Joseph and I are trying to understand the prophecies concerning the Messiah. We pondered over and over that Scripture that tells of a virgin that should bear a son and that his name should be called "God-with-us."

Joseph looked tenderly at me and said, "It seems so plain now."[8]

✠

WHEN CHRISTMAS COMES

ONLY God could have thought of Christmas. Its beauty is beyond the wit of mortals, so simple in its sublimity, so homey, yet so heavenly. On a tapestry woven of stable straw and starlight it unveils a picture to soften and purify the heart and to bring us back from a wisdom that is not wise, because it is hard, unholy, and unhopeful. Man would have made this event a pageant, its stage directions as follows:—

> Array of Great Ones
> The Army marches by
> Fanfare of trumpets
> Enter the King!

Man-made pageants pass and fade, but God works in slower and more secret ways. He blows no trumpet; He rings no bell. He begins within, seeking His ends by quiet growth, and by a strange power men call weakness, a wisdom often mistaken for folly. Man has *one answer* to every problem—*force*; but that is not the way of God. He did not send an army to conquer the world; He sent a babe to make a woman cry. The divine method is different: Instead of noise and parade there was—

> The crowded Inn
> A Mother and a Babe
> No cradle, just a manger
> A man stunned by wonder
> A wandering Star.

[8] From *His Mother, A Story of Our Lord*, by G. M. Anderson. Published by the Bethany Press, St. Louis, Mo. Used by special permission of the heirs and the publishers.

Such wisdom bends the knee; such beauty breaks the heart—and mends it. It is a scene to sanctify the world, as if to teach us that God enters the life of man by lowly doors, attended by starry ideals and simple shepherd sentiments— the birth of Jesus, just "one of the children of the year." They are *wise men* who bow at such a shrine, linking a far-off pilgrim star with the cradle of a little child. By such faith, men are truly wise, knowing that no hope is too high, no dream too holy to be fulfilled—even the hope and dream of "peace on earth among men of good-will."

. . . . .

Must we admit that Christmas is only a fairy story, heart-woven and dream-spun, and that the gray shadows which life casts over us are the grim truth? Is it no more than a figment of fancy, tender and lovely, fragrant with old memories, enshrined in the love and armored with the wonder of child- hood—a day of make-believe tugging at our hearts, with the pull of play- time? . . .

No, Christmas is both a fact and a faith; but even if it were only a brief season of good-will, a holiday from our forgetfulness of others, or just a family festival, it would be welcome. At least it is a day of poetry in the midst of drab days of prose. . . .

If man is a being in whom God can dwell, as Christmas affirms, if his soul may even be a cradle of the Eternal Love, then our highest social visions have hope of fulfillment. Then, indeed, we have not only a Divine Ally work- ing with us, but also a hidden ally, potential and prophetic, in "the better angels of our nature," to which we do not appeal in vain. . . .

For Christmas is the theology of a civilization yet to be. Like the early Christians, we must live in an air of expectancy, as of something immense, impending, of a profound change to take place. . . . Men of spiritual aware- ness in all lands feel that a time has come in the history of man when he must take a step into a higher range of being, or else lose and slip back. . . . To save his life he must reverse the old order of the brute, and assert the diviner law of love, not as a poetic faith, but as the actual basis of his life. Only so can our wounded world be lifted out of the shadow of strife and cruelty into the light of justice and joy. . . .

Christmas is a prophetic day, looking not so much backward, as forward. It is a history of the future, of an order of life not yet attained, of a religion not yet realized. To our dull eyes it seems visionary; but to God it is a vision of a world yet to be. . . .

> God abides in a terrible patience
> Unangered and unworn,
> And still for the child that was taken
> A child is born.

Over an armed camp, in a hard old Roman world, the song of the angels rang out, proclaiming "Peace on earth among men of good-will." How far off it must have seemed on that night! How far off it seems today! Yet it will come true. It is not a myth; it is not a mockery. Surviving ages of slaughter, it still haunts us, proving its immortality. It is not a mortal melody, but a divine symphony. Because it is far off we know that it is not our music, but was sent into the soul of man by ONE who is as far above us as the stars are above the mists.

It is a song out of the heart of God for a hungry world. It means much that we can hear it, despite gray fears and grim facts, forever singing above the din of strife; and, hearing it, take up its strain in the busy world of today. Not in our day, not in many days perhaps, but at last it will be fulfilled. The world will fill up with men of good-will who keep step with its music and live by its law—men who know that man was made for love, because God is love, and that *love* and *joy* must blend in the final note of the great world-song.[9]

✛

JOY TO THE WORLD

No HYMN resounds more clearly the message of joy and praise over the birth of the King of Kings, than the one written by Isaac Watts in 1719, entitled, "Joy to the World, the Lord Is Come."

Watts lived at a time when religion in England was at "low ebb"; yet he prophesied the rule of the Lord. Preaching was very formal and frigid in his day, yet this hymn was marked with enthusiasm and joy. Though the great missionary movement of the century had not yet begun, he wrote in the present tense.

This hymn, first published by Watts in his *Psalms of David Imitated in the Language of the New Testament*, paraphrases these verses from the ninety-eighth Psalm.

> Make a joyful noise unto the Lord, all the earth;
> Break forth and sing for joy, yea, sing praises.
> Let the sea roar, and the fullness thereof:
> The world, and they that dwell therein:
> Let the floods clap their hands;
> Let the hills sing for joy together
> Before the Lord; for he cometh to judge the earth:
> He will judge the world with righteousness,
> And the people with equity.

The tune, taken from Handel's "Messiah," was arranged by Lowell Mason.

[9] Briefed from "When Will Christmas Come?" by Joseph Fort Newton, in *The Atlantic Monthly*, December, 1925. Used by permission of the author and publishers.

He seems to have taken the arrangement, however, from the English Collection by Clark of Canterbury.

> Joy to the world, the Lord is come:
> Let earth receive her King;
> Let every heart prepare him room,
> And heaven and nature sing.
>
> Joy to the world, the Saviour reigns;
> Let men their songs employ;
> While fields and floods, rocks, hills and plains,
> Repeat the sounding joy.
>
> No more let sins and sorrows grow,
> Nor thorns infest the ground;
> He comes to make his blessings flow
> Far as the curse is found.
>
> He rules the world with truth and grace,
> And makes the nations prove
> The glories of his righteousness,
> And wonders of his love.
>
> —*Isaac Watts, 1719*

✠

O COME, ALL YE FAITHFUL

ALTHOUGH the authorship and the century in which this hymn was written are unknown, it is definitely established that the hymn is of Roman Catholic origin. More than forty different English translations have come from the original Latin writing; but the one most commonly used is a translation made by Reverend Frederick Oakley (1808-1880). Reverend Oakley was educated at Christ Church, Oxford, and served the Church of England for nineteen years. Then he decided to enter the priesthood of the Roman Catholic Church. He later became a canon of the district of Westminster.

Some scholars believe that the music originally used with this poem was a primitive chant used by the early churches, while others hold that "A Portuguese Hymn"—the tune with which we are all familiar—has always been associated with this poem. The tune[10] was arranged by Vincent Novello, an organist at the Portuguese Chapel in London, where the tune was probably heard, in its present form, for the first time. The composer of the tune is almost as uncertain as the author of the words.

> O come, all ye faithful, joyful and triumphant,
> O come ye, O come ye to Bethlehem;
> Come and behold him, born the King of angels:

[10] Tune: "Adeste Fideles" or "A Portuguese Hymn."

Refrain

O come, let us adore him,
O come, let us adore him,
O come, let us adore him, Christ the Lord.

Sing, choirs of angels, sing in exultation,
O sing, all ye citizens of heaven above;
Glory to God, all glory in the highest:

Refrain

Yea, Lord, we greet thee, born this happy morning,
Jesus, to thee be all glory given;
Word of the Father, now in flesh appearing:

Refrain

—*trans. by Frederick Oakley*

✠

I HEARD THE BELLS

SELDOM do we think of Henry Wadsworth Longfellow (1807-1892) as a
hymn-writer, for with the mention of his name come thoughts of "the village
smithy," "the chestnut tree," "three doors left unguarded," and the stair
clock tirelessly ticking away "Forever—never! Never—forever!"

The hymn "I Heard the Bells" was written by him at a time when the
thought of peace weighed heavily upon his mind. Christmas 1863, the time
at which this hymn was penned, found the United States in the midst of
bloody turmoil. The Civil War was at its climax. This beloved American
poet must have been much concerned, for in every stanza there is an emphasis
on "peace on earth, good-will to men."

Longfellow was born in Portland, Maine. After graduating from Bowdoin
College, he spent four years in study and travel; and then returned to his
alma mater as Professor of Modern Languages. He spent six years as a professor at Bowdoin, and then became Professor of Modern Languages at
Harvard.

The tune most commonly used with this hymn is "Waltham," composed by
John Baptiste Calkin.

> I heard the bells on Christmas day
> Their old familiar carols play,
> And wild and sweet the words repeat
> Of peace on earth, good-will to men.
>
> And thought how, as the day had come,
> The belfries of all Christendom
> Had rolled along the unbroken song
> Of peace on earth, good-will to men.

And in despair I bowed my head:
"There is no peace on earth," I said:
"For hate is strong, and mocks the song
Of peace on earth, good-will to men."

Then pealed the bells more loud and deep
"God is not dead, nor doth He sleep;
The wrong shall fail, the right prevail,
With peace on earth, good-will to men."

Till, ringing, singing on its way,
The world revolved from night to day,
A voice, a chime, a chant sublime,
Of peace on earth, good-will to men.[11]

—*Henry Wadsworth Longfellow, 1863*

✛

THERE'S A BEAUTIFUL STAR

AMONG the more recent Christmas hymns, none is more rhythmical and beautiful than "There's a Beautiful Star," by the Mining Engineer Rossiter Raymond (1840-1918).

Indeed, it is interesting to note how many Christian laymen have won fame as hymn-writers. The following are a few only of the names of those who have won distinction through their hymn contributions:

Robert Grant (Governor of Bombay), "O Worship the King."

John Byrom (Inventor of shorthand), "Christians, Awake."

John Hay (Secretary of State), "Not in Dumb Resignation."

Edward Osler (Surgeon), "Praise the Lord, Ye Heavens, Adore Him."

Harriet Beecher Stowe (Novelist), "Still, Still with Thee."

James Edmeston (Architect and Surveyor), "Saviour, Breathe an Evening Blessing."

James Montgomery (Editor), "Hail to the Lord's Anointed."

Fortunatus (Troubadour), "Welcome, Happy Morning."

President Wilson (Professor of English at Princeton University), read manuscript and assisted in editing "In Excelsis," published by *The Christian Century*, New York City.

Like "We Three Kings of Orient Are," this beautiful Christmas hymn, "There's a Beautiful Star," lends itself to dramatization, for it, too, tells the story of the journey of the Wise Men from the East following the star to the birth-stall of the Manger Child in Bethlehem.

It may also be used as the processional hymn for all those in the assembly who would bring their "white gifts" to the altar for the needy of every land.

[11] From *Longfellow's Complete Poetical Works.* Used by permission of and arrangement with Houghton Mifflin Company.

There's a beautiful star, a beautiful star,
That weary trav'lers have followed afar;
Shining so brightly all the way,
Till it stood o'er the place where the young Child lay.

Refrain

Star, star, beautiful star!
  Pilgrims weary we are;
To Jesus, to Jesus,
  We follow thee from afar.

In the land of the East, in the shadows of night,
We saw the glory of thy new light;
Telling to us, in our distant home,
The Lord, our Redeemer, to earth had come.

Refrain

We have gold for tribute and gifts for prayer,
Sweet incense, myrrh, and spices rare;
All that we have we hither bring,
To lay it with joy at the feet of the King.

Refrain

—Rossiter Raymond

CONTENTS

PART I   SECTION II

THE NATIVITY

✠

"Let us go now even unto Bethlehem, and see this thing
that is come to pass."—LUKE 2:15

✠

THE NATIVITY OF JESUS: IN GOSPEL

"Now it came to pass in those days, there went out a decree from Cæsar Augustus, that all the world should be enrolled. . . . And all went to enrol themselves, every one to his own city. And Joseph also went up from Galilee, out of the city of Nazareth, into Judæa, to the city of David, which is called Bethlehem, because he was of the house and family of David; to enrol himself with Mary, who was betrothed to him, being great with child. And it came to pass, while they were there, the days were fulfilled that she should be delivered. And she brought forth her first-born son; and she wrapped him in swaddling clothes, and laid him in a manger, because there was no room for them in the inn."—LUKE 2:1, 3-7

THE ARRIVAL AT BETHLEHEM

By

Luc Olivier Merson

(Interpretation)

"The Arrival at Bethlehem" as first shown in the Paris Salon in 1885, was a tiny picture only a few inches square. It is now privately owned. When it was first exhibited the *Gazette des Beaux-arts* said, in referring to it (col. 31, p. 492): "It is a charming and delicate thing. The composition, the color, the feeling, accord so exquisitely with the spirit of the naïve complaint (of the old Christmas carol); a little too much insistence on any single trait and the spell is broken, but that word, 'too much' the artist has not said."

Whether or not Merson got his inspiration from the ancient carol, "Another Street," is not known; but the picture harmonizes so perfectly with this carol that it is quoted here for the sake of comparison. This carol is in the form of an imaginary conversation between Joseph, Mary, and the hostess of the little Inn in Bethlehem that turned these two away on the night of the birth of the Christ Child.

St. Joseph:
  "Another street we'll try,
   A courtyard there may be
  Here, before mine eye
   Is this grand hostelrie."

Mary, the Virgin:
  "Prithee, of your grace,
   No further can I go.
  Alone seek you a place;
   My strength it faileth so."

St. Joseph:
  "Hostess dear and kind,
   Pray, of your great pitie,
  Some little corner find,
   To lodge my faint ladie!"

The Hostess:
  "Common folks and poor
   In here we never keep.
  Try that other door;
   'Tis there such people sleep."

Whether the experience described in this carol was actual or not we do not know; but from the Gospel story we do know that Joseph had difficulty in

Photo by Braun et Cie. Courtesy E. S. Herrmann, New York C

THE ARRIVAL AT BETHLEHEM—*MERSON*

"TIDINGS OF GREAT JOY"—*PLOCKHORST*

finding a place in which he and Mary could lodge for the night; and that in their desperate plight they were directed to a stable near the inn in which the Christ Child was born.

Judging from Merson's conception of the arrival at Bethlehem, the entire village must have been asleep when Joseph and Mary arrived. Joseph knew, too, that he must make haste in finding a place for his young wife to rest. In his haste he doubtless knocked louder than usual; for he seems to have awakened the neighborhood dogs shown in the picture, and their barking seems also to accentuate the need of haste.

Mary's weary and suffering face is turned away from the door to the inn, yet does not seem to feel unkindly toward the inn hostess in her refusal. Perhaps she shakes her head as she hears the innkeeper's refusal, "the inn is full," saying softly to herself, "Blessed are the merciful, for they shall obtain mercy." Or perhaps in her suffering and fright she may be uttering a prayer that her soon-to-be-born Son, the Messiah, may teach folk of this and other towns the meaning of *love* and *kindness* and *mercy* to those in distress, no matter how lowly their station in life may be.

You feel, as you gaze at this picture, that Merson has felt all this. Dr. Bailey in *The Gospel in Art* says: "It matters not that his Bethlehem with its unpaved street, its houses of plaster and thatch, looks more like Brittany, than Palestine; the setting is only a background for a very human story that concerns three people—helpless and desperate Mary, helpless and exasperated Joseph, and a hard-hearted woman. It is the eternal conflict of human need and human selfishness that has been exemplified a thousand times before this night and a thousand times since, even to this day of grace. It is the sort of situation that Christ's religion is trying to make impossible. 'Blessed are the merciful' is one of the persistent and heavenly overtones in the music of the Gospel. 'Who hath this world's goods and beholdeth his brother in need and shutteth up his compassion from him, how doth the love of God abide in him?' "[1]

We feel, as we look at this picture, that "the hope and fears of all the years" are met here, and the testimony of all the succeeding centuries shows that this hour was a fateful one. "He came to his own, and his own received him not." They knew not the time of their visitation.

This picture in a way symbolizes our own blindness. So often, even today, people surfeited with worldly goods forget to show mercy to those in dire need from one cause or another, and thereby fail to entertain angels unawares. Many times those who are rich in "things" are poor in thoughts of love and in deeds of mercy to the less fortunate. Like the innkeeper in this scene, who, blindly desiring to serve only the rich and the great, missed his chance to achieve the honor of providing the birthplace of the world's greatest King, we, too, often fail to show in our own lives the attributes of the King of Kings—*love, mercy, justice,* and *kindness* to "his little ones," and our lives are poor and squalid indeed.

[1] From *The Gospel in Art*, Bailey. Published by the Pilgrim Press, Boston, Mass. Used by permission of the author.

"TIDINGS OF GREAT JOY"

By

Bernard Plockhorst

(Interpretation)

OF ALL the artists who have attempted to paint the angelic announcement of "Glad tidings of great joy" to the shepherds, the one by Bernard Plockhorst, the German painter, seems to me to outrank all others in beauty and naturalness.

Instead of the traditional five or six shepherds, which most of the artists portray, Plockhorst has chosen only three, a father, a wife and mother, and an almost-grown son. These three with a shepherd dog, the familiar shepherd's crook, and a group of startled, bewildered sheep huddling in the corner of a sheep-cot constitute the background of this beautiful and arresting painting.

Tradition indicates that this scene took place on a hillside a mile and a half, perhaps two miles, southeast of the little village of Bethlehem. In the distance may be seen the mosque-like dome and roofs of a few scattered buildings; while above them and shining directly down upon them is the luminous star which guided not only the shepherds, but also the wise men who came from the East in search of this new-born King.

In the upper right-hand corner and almost over a winding stream at the foot of the hillside is the gorgeous heavenly visitor with wings fully spread and hands outstretched—one seeming to point toward Bethlehem, while in the other is the olive branch of peace. About the graceful flowing robes and clouds that all but hide the angel's feet are the small winged cherubs, about which the Scriptures say, "These do always behold their heavenly Father's face."

One of these cherubs seems to be gazing directly into the young man's face, his tiny baby hand clinging to the angel's form, as if to say the long-expected Messiah is not unlike me in beauty and heavenly joy. The others are gazing with raptured faces at the angelic messenger whose attendants they are, as if they, too, were listening to his words:

"Fear not, for behold I bring you *glad tidings of great joy* which shall be unto all peoples: For unto you, this night, in the city of David is born a Saviour which is Christ the Lord. And this shall be a sign unto you: Ye shall find the babe wrapped in swaddling clothes and lying in a manger."

There is grace and beauty in every line of this heavenly visitor's form and of his cherub-like attendants. There is strength and ruggedness in the artistic grouping, and in the bodily and facial expression of these worshiping shepherds in the foreground.

The light from the star, which also proclaims the birth of a new kind of King, floods with effulgent glory not only this angelic heavenly host, and the startled, yet reverent shepherds, but also the entire hillside, near and far, with a brilliance almost of the noonday sun.

Soon this heavenly messenger will disappear, leaving only the star to guide their feet. Yet we feel that the shepherds will hurriedly select from the fold a "wee ewe lamb without spot or blemish" as their offering and hurry away into Bethlehem "to see this thing which has come to pass" and of which the angels sang: "Glory to God in the highest, and on earth, peace among men of good-will." Meanwhile this faithful shepherd dog will be left to guard the flock until their return.

✛

THE ARRIVAL OF THE SHEPHERDS

By

Henri Lerolle

(Interpretation)

ALTHOUGH little is known of the life of Henri Lerolle, the French landscape and portrait painter, some of his works are very popular. The artist was born of wealthy parents in the city of Paris in 1848. He early achieved the distinction of at least two medals in addition to the decoration of the Legion of Honor, and was exhibiting his work as early as 1888.

Some of the critics have denied him great *creative ability*. They agree that his works show the influence of Millet and others, utilizing their methods and effects with remarkable intelligence, much as a clever musician might arrange the score of a grand opera for the piano, but without a great deal of real creative ability.

*"The Arrival of the Shepherds," while comparatively a modern painting, is one of the best loved and most realistic of all the Nativity pictures; and shows the artist's ability to enter deeply into the feeling of the scene.[2]

The background of the picture is a huge, dimly-lighted cave. The trunks of great trees serve as rafters, and these rest on rugged tree columns that seem to sustain a none-too-substantial roof. Their untouched ruggedness and irregular placement aid in producing the feeling that these people are simple, unlearned folk.

Great stones together with the débris of the hill above have almost blocked the opening to the cave. Since no other opening is evident, one imagines that the shepherds have entered through a doorway somewhere behind them. On one side is to be seen some pitchforks and a supply of fodder. On the other are some feeding-tubs, animals, and sheaves of ripened grain.

There is a realism about this Nativity picture that grips one. It is the result

[2] The hymn "O Little Town of Bethlehem" is effective played as a musical accompaniment to this interpretation. It should begin with the paragraph marked with the asterisk.

THE ARRIVAL OF THE SHEPHERDS—LEROLLE

Photo by Braun et Cie. Courtesy E. S. Herrmann, New York City

of an effort on the part of the artist to paint this scene as true to life as it must have been. It embodies the critical attitude of the nineteenth century toward anything that is superfluous. In harmony with nineteenth-century theology the artist has eliminated the appearance of angels with their majestic wings, robes, and crowns. He has pictured the shepherds in their scant fur pelts, made of Joseph and Mary simple peasant parents, stripped the baby of all tinsel and transferred the light from the baby to the mother.

The only suggestion of the supernatural that appears in Lerolle's "The Arrival of the Shepherds" is this highlight, and even it does not result from an attempt to elevate the Virgin higher than her Son, or in any way to support the dogma of the "Mother of God." It seems to be merely the artist's device to paint in sharp, clear-cut outlines the face of Mary, while at the same time it emphasizes the profound significance of spiritual motherhood in the world.

Lerolle seems to have thought this out correctly. This Child of Promise needs no halo. Whatever glory He possesses was not born with Him. Rather it was created by Him as He grew from normal infancy to divine adulthood. Jesus Himself made no claim to miraculous birth or unusual powers of growth and development. The crown of light that surrounds Mary, however, is rightly due with the birth of her first-born Son. It is a symbol of that glory that is hers eternally as the perfect mother.

The shepherds present in their attitudes another bit of critical realism. If we today had heard the midnight song of the angelic host, and like these shepherds had followed the star until it came and stood over where the young Child lay, I doubt if we would have rushed up to the manger in a hurried, familiar way. Like these rugged shepherds, in all probability we would have approached with fear and reverence to gaze from behind the screen of friendly pillars on the fulfillment of the angel's prophecy. Note how one shepherd has raised his hand in awe, while another has dropped upon his knee. The younger one in the rear has raised himself on tiptoe that he may see this tiny Child of Promise about which the angels sang. These shepherds are not unlike us today in the presence of the fulfillment of one of the glorious providences and mysteries of God.

There is about this crude stable with its rough upright and crossed tree beams, the peasant parents and the worshiping shepherds, an atmosphere that is native to their lowly station in life; yet withal a reverence of feeling that profoundly moves those of us who gaze upon it to a reverent devotion to this new-born King.

The lights and shadows in this picture are unique. The painting grows upon you. To see it once is to want to see it again and again. There is about it the fulfillment of the angel's song: "Ye shall find the babe wrapped in swaddling clothes, and lying in a manger."

The original of this picture is privately owned. It hangs in the Carcassonne Museum in Paris. It is without doubt the best loved of all the Nativity ictures.

THE FLIGHT INTO EGYPT

By

Eugene Girardet

(Interpretation)

IN THIS painting by the French artist, Eugene Girardet, of the middle of the nineteenth century, we have one of the most artistic portrayals of that long and wearisome journey which Joseph and Mary made into Egypt, fleeing in the night from the wrath of Herod the King, who had sent forth an edict that would have meant the death of this new-born Child of Promise had they not heeded the Heavenly Messenger's warning.

The artist has chosen the sandy desert of Egypt as the background for this study in fatigue and weariness, which the parents of the Christ Child must have undergone in that long, slow, and perilous journey to a land of safety for their first-born Son.

These two weary travelers have long since left behind the land of their nativity, and are journeying over the interminable desert of sand that intervenes between Palestine and the flourishing Valley of the Nile toward which they are slowly wending their way. That they are approaching the end of that long journey is evident from the distant pyramids in the background.

The artist, true to the desert custom, shows these weary footsore immigrants as traveling by night to avoid the burning rays of the desert sun. The starless sky would seem to indicate that the dawn of another day is close at hand. Beside the patient donkey walks the aged Joseph. With one hand he clasps the bundle of their precious burden of gold, frankincense, and myrrh, while, with his staff plunged into the soft sand, he trudges silently the weary miles that still separate them from the peace and protection of Egypt.

Every line of the faces and figures of Mary and Joseph, as well as of the posture of their faithful burro, indicate the fatigue and weariness of body, mind, and heart that have resulted from this hurriedly-prepared-for, secret journey into this distant, unknown land. As we look at the pyramids in the background, we cannot help but wish that they were nearer, for that would mean that this long journey is nearer its end than it otherwise can be. Neither shrubbery, trees, nor water relieve the barrenness of that stretch of sand that must yet be traversed before they reach the fertile Valley of the Nile.

As we look at Girardet's picture we cannot but feel that the end of that long perilous journey is near. Perhaps it is early morning of the last day. At least the stars have disappeared and Mary has released her mantilla and thrown it up over both her own head and that of the sleeping child as though to shield them both from the heat of the returning dawn. Even the donkey seems to sense the fact that the end is near at hand, as with head down and ears thrown back

THE FLIGHT INTO EGYPT—*GIRARDET*

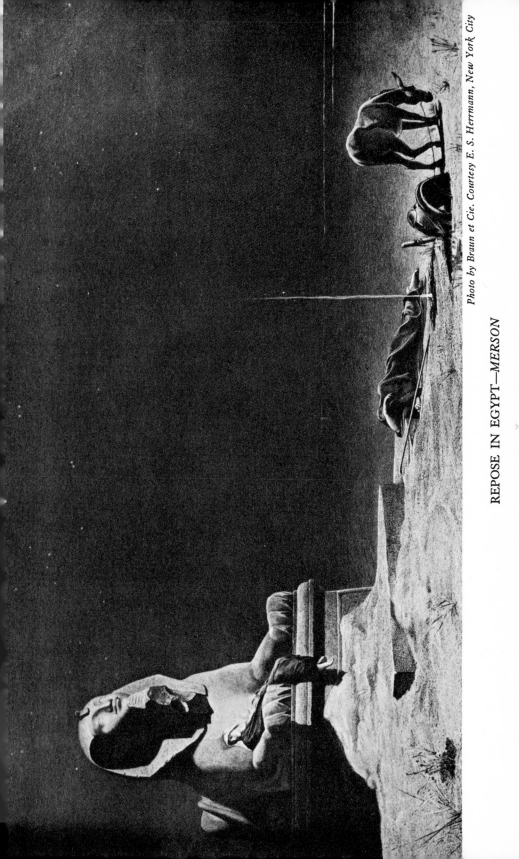

Photo by Braun et Cie. Courtesy E. S. Herrmann, New York City

REPOSE IN EGYPT—MERSON

he pushes sturdily on through the last wearisome miles to the shelter of the trees along the Valley of the Nile. Joseph, too, seems to be able to walk and carry a portion of the family's pack with just the aid of his staff. The scarf partially covering his face also indicates an effort to protect his eyes from the glare of daytime traveling in desert lands.

As we study Girardet's "The Flight into Egypt," we feel like sounding forth a song of joy because just over the raise that separates them from the nearest pyramid is Egypt. Soon it will be reached and the perils of the desert, at least, for this family of the line of David will be over. The warning of the angel to "Take the young child and flee into Egypt" will have been heeded; and this first-born Child of Promise will be permitted to grow up under the protection of the land of the Sphinx and the pyramids, until such time as the Holy Family can, with safety, return to their native land.

✢

REPOSE IN EGYPT

By

Luc Olivier Merson

(Interpretation)

THE original of Merson's "Repose in Egypt" is about four by six feet. It was painted in 1879 and twice thereafter. One, at least, of the three original paintings is owned in the United States by Dr. George Kennedy of Hyde Park, Massachusetts.

Luc Olivier Merson was born in Paris in 1846. He was the son of a distinguished art critic. He became a painter of historical-religious themes, though in somewhat eccentric style. His honors consist of a Grand Prix at Rome, medals in 1869 and 1873, and the Legion of Honor in 1882. The works by which he is best known in this country are "The Arrival at Bethlehem" and "Repose in Egypt." His title to consideration lies in his faculty for humanizing Scriptural characters.

The "Repose in Egypt" is a very unusual composition. The center of gravity of the picture seems, at first, to be on the extreme left; but if you will observe yourself while you observe the picture you will find that the moments of force equalize themselves when your eye rests somewhere between the Sphinx and the fire.

On the one side is the mass of the monument, on the other the sharply defined though smaller masses of the streak of river, the donkey, and the smoke stream. At a point between these your interest hovers, and while there it becomes infused with the influence of two powerfully suggestive infinities, the *desert* and the *sky*.

The lines of composition, it is true, center in Mary and the Child: toward them converge the edges of the Sphinx's head-dress, the edges of the sand-drifts, the left paw of the Sphinx, Joseph's staff and recumbent form, which in turn continue the lines to the saddle and tethering-rope. But the message of the picture is greatly enhanced by the undefinable suggestiveness of the two infinities. It is they that give the emotional undertone to the rest, that add *majesty* and *awe* and *silence*, and conjure forth the powerful fancies that are imprisoned in the magic name of Egypt.

The coloring of the original also contributes to the feeling-tone: the night is violet-gray, and the stars are so weirdly created that those of the second and third magnitudes come out only as you gaze long at the sky. And while it is the moon that lights the scene, an orange glow, radiating from the sleeping Child, diffuses about the Sphinx's heart a warmth as of love in a desolate world.[3]

. . . . .

*You are in Egypt at night, and alone except for the sleepers. The wind that by day has piled the sand in drifts now has ceased its play. The smoke from the little fire rises straight as a sword-blade against the background of the darkness. Not a leaf of the scant herbage trembles, not a sound pulses across the waiting air. The desert stretches away illimitably, dead and still. Unruffled the moonlight sleeps upon the narrow mirror of the Nile. The patient donkey, relieved of his saddle, stands by his peg and dreams, too somnolent to bite the spear of grass beneath his nose. Joseph has forgotten his long and anxious tramp across interminable deserts—his bed the sand, his pillow, a stone. The Baby sleeps in the heaven of His mother's bosom; Mary sleeps in the arms of the sleepless and immemorial Sphinx. The whole world is waiting, waiting, waiting.

"Ah, Sphinx of the countless years, tell me your dreams! You front the level moon with a face that baffles me, with eyes that see yet do not reveal, with lips that smile so faintly that while one says, 'Lo, there!' the smile becomes a question and the question vanishes. What thoughts dwell in your mind of stone? What hopes or fears flit through the adamantine chambers of your bosom? Are you, too, waiting? and for what?"

"I am the Genius of the Unexplained, the symbol of the Eternal Mystery. I am waiting between the two eternities for him who shall solve my riddle."

"O Sphinx, the world is full of riddles. What is thine?"

"I would know the meaning of Man. Out of the gray dawn of the world he came, and as the centuries fall I have seen his generations file down the long valley, sowing and reaping, dreaming and building, with laughter and tears; till each in his turn reaches the borders of my desert, gazes into my face a moment and vanishes over the horizon of the setting sun. I would know the whence and whither and the all-between—the fountain whence they spring, the river that makes green their footsteps, and the ocean whither they flow."

[3] This interpretation of Merson's "Repose in Egypt" will be rendered more effective if read to the music—"Tenderly Sleeping." The music should begin with the paragraph marked with the asterisk.

"Thy vigil is ended, O Sphinx! In thine own bosom lies the answer. This little Child is He who shall teach Man his meaning. Out of the fountain of Immortal Love He came, into the deep of Immortal Love shall He go; and all between—the shadow valley of the sowing and the reaping, of the dreams and labors, of the laughter and the tears—is watered by the river of Immortal Love!"[4]

Something of all this Merson is trying to tell us in his "Repose in Egypt." Like his "Arrival at Bethlehem," once seen, it is an unforgettable picture.

✛

HOW FAR TO BETHLEHEM?

"How far is it to Bethlehem town?"
Just over the Jerusalem hills adown,
Past lovely Rachel's white-domed tomb—
Sweet shrine of motherhood's young doom.

It isn't far to Bethlehem town—
Just over the dusty roads adown,
Past Wise Men's well, still offering
Cool draughts from welcome wayside spring;
Past shepherds with their flutes of reed
That charm the woolly sheep they lead;
Past boys with kites on hill-tops flying,
And soon you're there where Bethlehem's lying,
Sunned white and sweet on olived slopes,
Gold-lighted still with Judah's hopes.

And so we find the Shepherd's field
The plain that gave rich Boaz yield;
And look where Herod's villa stood.
We thrill that earthly parenthood
Could foster Christ who was all-good;
And thrill that Bethlehem town today
Looks down on Christian homes that pray.
It isn't far to Bethlehem town!
It's anywhere that Christ comes down
And finds in people's friendly face
A welcome and abiding-place.
The road to Bethlehem runs right through
The homes of folks like me and you.
                                    —*Madeleine Sweeny Miller*

[4] Adapted from *The Gospel in Art*, by Albert Edward Bailey. Published by the Pilgrim Press, Boston, Mass. Used by permission of the author.

THE SHEPHERD SPEAKS

Out of the midnight sky a great dawn broke,
And a voice singing flooded us with song.
In David's city was He born, it sang,
A Saviour, Christ the Lord. Then while I sat
Shivering with the thrill of that great cry,
A mighty choir a thousandfold more sweet
Suddenly sang, Glory to God, and Peace—
Peace on the earth; my heart, almost unnerved
By that swift loveliness, would hardly beat.
Speechless we waited till the accustomed night
Gave us no promise more of sweet surprise;
Then scrambling to our feet, without a word
We started through the fields to find the Child.

—John Erskine

THE CONSECRATION OF THE COMMON WAY

The hills that had been long and lean
Were pricking with a tender green,
And flocks were whitening over them
From all the folds of Bethlehem.

The King of Heaven had come our way,
And in a lowly stable lay:
He had descended from the sky
In answer to the world's long cry—
Descended in a lyric burst
Of high archangels, going first
Unto the lowest and the least,
To humble bird and weary beast.
His palace was a wayside shed;
A battered manger was his bed:
An ox and ass with breathings deep
Made warm the chamber of his sleep.

Three sparrows with a friendly sound
Were picking barley from the ground:
An early sunbeam, long and thin,
Slanted across the dark within
And brightened in its silver fall
A cart-wheel leaning to the wall.
An ox-yoke hung upon a hook:
A worn plow with a clumsy crook
Was lying idly by the wheel.

And everywhere there was the feel
Of that sweet peace that labor brings—
The peace that dwells with homely things.

Now have the homely things been made
Sacred, and a glory on them laid,
For He whose shelter was a stall,
The King was born among them all.
He came to handle saw and plane,
To use and hallow the profane:
Now is the holy not afar
In temples lighted by a star,
But where the loves and labors are.
Now that the King has gone this way,
Great are the things of every day!

—*Edwin Markham*

WHO ARE THE WISE MEN?

Who were the Wise Men in the long ago?
Not Herod, fearful lest he lose his throne;
Not Pharisees too proud to claim their own;
Not priests and scribes whose province was to know;
Not money-changers running to and fro;
But three who traveled, weary and alone,
With dauntless faith, because before them shone
The Star that led them to a manger low.

Who are the Wise Men now, when all is told?
Not men of science; not the great and strong;
Not those who wear a kingly diadem;
Not those whose eager hands pile high the gold;
But those amid the tumult and the throng
Who follow still the Star of Bethlehem.[5]

—*B. Y. Williams*

THE INN THAT MISSED iTS CHANCE

(The Landlord speaks—A.D. 28)

What could be done? The inn was full of folks:
His honor, Marcus Lucius, and his scribes
Who made the census; honorable men
From farthest Galilee, come hitherward
To be enrolled; high ladies and their lords;

---

[5] From *House of Happiness*. Reprinted by permission of the author.

The rich, the rabbis, such a noble throng
As Bethlehem had never seen before
And may not see again. And there they were,
Close-herded with their servants, till the inn
Was like a hive at swarming-time, and I
Was fairly crazed among them.

    Could I know
That *they* were so *important? Just the two,*
No servants, just a workman sort of man,
Leading a donkey, and his wife thereon
Drooping and pale,—I saw them not myself,
My servants must have driven them away;
But had I seen them,—how was I to know?
Were inns to welcome stragglers, up and down
In all our towns from Beersheba to Dan,
Till He should come? And how were men to know?
There was a sign, they say, a heavenly light
Resplendent: but I had no time for stars,
And there were songs of angels in the air
Out on the hills; but how was I to hear
Amid the thousand clamors of an inn?

Of course, if I had known them, who they were,
And who was He that should be born that night—
For now I learn that they will make him King,
A second David, who will ransom us
From these Philistine Romans—who but he
That feeds an army with a loaf of bread,
And if a soldier falls, he touches him
And up he leaps, uninjured?—Had I known,
I would have turned the whole inn upside down,
His honor, Marcus Lucius, and the rest,
And sent them all to stables.

So you have seen him, stranger, and perhaps
Again may see him? Prithee say for me
I did not know; and if he comes again,
As he will surely come, with retinue,
And banners, and an army—tell him my Lord
That all my inn is his to make amends.

          (*Exit* Traveler)

Alas, alas! to miss a chance like that!
This inn that might be chief among them all—
The birthplace of the MESSIAH,—had I known![6]

                          —*Amos R. Wells*

[6] From *Teaching the Youth of the Church,* Maus. Used with permission of the author and publisher.

KINGS AND STARS

As they came from the East
Following a star,

One said:
The sun burns,
The moon changes,
Stars are faithful.

One said:
They shine in all tongues,
Every heart knows them,
By starlight there are no borders.

One said:
The world widens
By starlight,
The mind reaches;
Stars beget journeys.

—*John Erskine*

EVERYWHERE, EVERYWHERE, CHRISTMAS TONIGHT

Everywhere, everywhere, Christmas tonight!
Christmas in lands of the fir tree and pine,
Christmas in lands of the palm tree and vine,
Christmas where snow peaks stand solemn and white,
Christmas where cornfields lie sunny and bright,
Everywhere, everywhere, Christmas tonight!

For the Christ Child who comes is the Master of all,
No palace too great and no cottage too small;
The angels who welcome Him sing from the height,
"In the city of David, a King in his might."
Everywhere, everywhere, Christmas tonight!

Then let every heart keep its Christmas within,
Christ's pity for sorrow, Christ's hatred for sin,
Christ's care for the weakest, Christ's courage for right,
Christ's dread of the darkness, Christ's love for the light,
Everywhere, everywhere, Christmas tonight!

—*Phillips Brooks*

THE INN OF LIFE

"As it was in the beginning.
Is now
And . . . ?"

Anno Domini 1.

"No room!
No room!
The inn is full,
Yea—overfull,
No room have we
For such as ye—
Poor folk of Galilee—
Pass on! Pass on!"

"Nay then!
Your charity
Will ne'er deny
Some corner mean
Where she may lie unseen,
For see,
Her time is nigh."

"Alack! And she
So young and fair!
Place have we none:
And yet—how bid ye gone?"

"Stay then!—out there
Among the beasts
Ye may find room
And eke a truss
To lie upon!"

Anno Domini 1929.

"No room!
No room!
No room for Thee,
Thou man of Galilee!
The house is full,
Yea, overfull,
There is no room for Thee—
Pass on! Pass on!

"Nay—see!
The place is packed.
We scarce have room
For our own selves;
So how shall we
Find room for Thee,
Thou man of Galilee—
Pass on! Pass on!

"But—if Thou shouldst
This way again,
And we can find
So much as one small corner
Free from guest,
Not then in vain
Thy quest.
But now—the house is full,
Pass on!"

Christ passes
On his ceaseless quest,
Nor will He rest
With any—
Save as Chiefest Guest.[7]

—*John Oxenham*

[7] From *Selected Poems of John Oxenham*. Used by permission of the author.

WHEN THE KING CAME

THE truth is that there never was any Christmas till the year One!

Year after year, and year after year, the evergreen trees grew in the woods and nobody came to get them. Nobody thought of lighting them up with candles or loading them down with candies and ornaments. The holly berries glowed red, the mistletoe gleamed white in the treetops, but no one paid any attention to them. The twenty-fifth day of December came and went like the twenty-second and the twenty-ninth without any thought of a celebration. Boys and girls grew up into men and women with never a Christmas carol, a Christmas tree, or a Christmas gift—because that was before the King came.

But God saw the sin and sorrow that were upon the earth. He heard little children and even grown men and women weeping because they were trying to be good and knew not how. So He decided to make Himself known in a new way. He decided to come to the earth, not in His royal robes of splendor, not with Holy angels with Him; but as a little child—to be born, grow up, and live among the people and so teach them how to live.

Thus it happened that in the Year One, out of Nazareth came Joseph, the carpenter, and with him came Mary, his wife. Down they came, over hill and dale, along the way which led to Bethlehem, for it was the time of a census. When they arrived in Bethlehem there was no place where they might stay, except a common stable strewn with hay, and with dusty cobwebs hanging from the rafters. So there, accordingly, they went.

And there, while angels sang on the hillsides, and the great white light from a beautiful star above the stable streamed into the night, the King came. He came as a little child, and Mary wrapped Him in swaddling clothes, as the way is with babes, and laid Him in the manger.

The same night on the hills outside the town there were shepherds keeping their flock through the darkness. All at once a great and wonderful light began to shine, and out of the central shining there appeared an angel, gleaming like a flame of fire. The shepherds were afraid, but the angel said unto them:

"Fear not, for behold, I bring you good tidings of great joy. For unto you is born this day in the city of David, a Saviour which is Christ the Lord. Yonder in Bethlehem you will find him, sleeping in a manger."

And suddenly there was with the angel a multitude of the heavenly host praising God and saying, "Glory to God in the highest, and on earth, peace, good-will toward men."

Then the music ceased, the heavenly visitants departed, and the night was dark again. But one star stood above the little town of Bethlehem, and ever its rays streamed brighter and farther, until the whole sky throbbed with its radiance. And the shepherds cried, "We will follow the star; for there lies the King!"

Forward on the frosty road and into the silent night the shepherds hastened. And ever their breath streamed white behind them, and ever their eager feet struck aside the stones from their pathway, till they came to Bethlehem; and there, in the stable, above which stood the star, they found the Babe lying in a manger.

Thus was kept the first Christmas, with carols by the angels in heaven, and God's own Son, the Saviour of the world, coming as a Christmas gift for all mankind.[8]

✚

THE ANGEL AND THE SHEPHERDS

A MILE and a half, it may be two miles, southeast of Bethlehem there is a plain separated from the town by an intervening swell of the mountain. . . .

At the side farthest from the town, and close under a bluff, there was an extensive *mârâh*, or sheep-cote, ages old. In some long-forgotten foray the building had been unroofed and almost demolished. The inclosure attached to it remained intact, however, and that was of more importance to the shepherds who drove their charges thither than the house itself. . . .

There were six of these men, omitting the watchman, and after a while they assembled in a group near the fire, some sitting and some lying prone. . . .

They rested and talked; and their talk was all about their flocks, a dull theme to the world, and yet a theme which was all the world to them. . . .

While they talked, and before the first watch was over, one by one the shepherds went to sleep, each lying where he had sat.

The night, like most nights of the winter season in the hill country, was clear, crisp, and sparkling with stars. There was no wind. The atmosphere seemed never so pure, the stillness was more than silence; it was a holy hush, a warning that heaven was stooping low to whisper some good thing to the listening earth.

By the gate, hugging his mantle close, the watchman walked; at times he stopped, attracted by a stir among the sleeping herds, or by a jackal's cry off on the mountain-side. The midnight was slow in coming to him; but at last it came. His task was done; and now for the dreamless sleep with which labor blesses its wearied children! He moved toward the fire, but paused; a light was breaking around him, soft and white, like the moon's. He waited breathlessly. The light deepened; things before invisible came into view; he saw the whole field, and all it sheltered. A chill sharper than that of the frosty air—a chill of fear—smote him. He looked up; the stars were gone; the light was dropping as from a window in the sky; and as he looked it became a splendor; then, in terror, he cried,

[8] Adapted by Annie L. MacKinnon from the Bible and "When the King Came," by Hodges. Used with permission of the author and adapter.

"Awake, awake!"

Up sprang the dogs, and, howling, ran away.

The herds rushed together, bewildered.

The men clambered to their feet, weapons in hand.

"What is it?" they asked in one voice.

"See!" cried the watchman, "the sky is on fire!"

Suddenly the light became intolerably bright and they covered their eyes and dropped upon their knees; then as their souls shrank with fear, they fell upon their faces, blind and fainting, and would have died had not a voice said unto them:

"Fear not!"

And they listened.

"Fear not; for behold, I bring you good tidings of great joy, which shall be to all people. For unto you, this day, in the city of David, is born a Saviour, which is Christ the Lord! And this shall be a sign unto you, ye shall find the babe wrapped in swaddling clothes and lying in a manger."

The voice in sweetness and soothing more than human, and low and clear, penetrated all their being and filled them with assurance. They rose upon their knees, and looking worshipfully up, beheld in the center of a great glory the appearance of a man, clad in a robe intensely white; above its shoulders towered the tops of wings shining and folded. A star over its forehead glowed with a steady luster, brilliant as Hesperus. Its hands were stretched toward them in blessing; its face was serene and divinely beautiful.

The herald spoke not again; his good tidings were told; and yet he stayed awhile. Then suddenly the light, of which he seemed the center, turned roseate and began to tremble; and then up, as far as the men could see, there was a flashing of white wings, and a coming and going of radiant forms, and voices as of a whole multitude chanting in unison,

"Glory to God in the highest, and on earth, peace, good-will toward men!"

Not once the praise, but many times.

Then the herald raised his eyes as seeking the approval of one afar off; his wings stirred, and spread slowly and majestically, on their upper side white as snow, in the shadows vari-tinted, like the mother-of-pearl. He rose lightly and, without effort, floated up out of view, taking the light up with him. And long after he was gone, down from the sky in measures mellowed by distance fell the refrain:

"Glory to God in the highest, and on earth, peace, good-will toward men."

Then the shepherds said one to another, "Come, let us take a wee ewe lamb from the fold, and go yonder into Bethlehem, and see this thing which has come to pass. The priests and doctors have been a long time looking for the Christ. Now He is born, and the Lord has given us a sign by which to know Him. Let us go and worship Him."

And they followed the light until it came and stood over where the young Child lay. And they went in, and found Mary and Joseph and the Child, asleep in the sweet-smelling hay. And they worshiped him, leaving the wee ewe lamb without spot or blemish as their offering; and returned again to their flock on the hillside, believing anew the words of their prophets.

"For unto us a Child is born. Unto us a Son is given. And the government shall be upon His shoulders; and of the increase of His Kingdom there shall be no end. And his name shall be called, 'Wonderful Counselor, the Mighty God, the Everlasting Father, the Prince of Peace.' "[9]

✢

THE SHEPHERD'S STORY

"Bring hither that sheepskin, Joseph, and lay it down on this bank of dry earth, under this shelving rock. The wind blows chilly from the west, but the rock will shelter us. The sky is fair and the moon is rising, and we can sit here and watch the flock on the hillside below. Your young blood and your father's coat of skins will keep you warm for one watch, I am sure. At midnight, my son, your father, Reuban, and his brother James will take our places; for the first watch the old man and the boy will tend the sheep."

"Yes, grandfather; you shall sit in that snug corner of the rock, where you can lean back and take your comfort. I will lie at your feet. Now and then I will run and see whether the sheep are wandering, and that will warm me, if I grow cold."

"Have you never been out on the hills at night with your father?"

"Never, grandfather. I have often begged him to let me come; but he kept saying that I must wait until I was twelve years old. On the last full moon was my birthday, and today, when he returned from Bethlehem to the flock, he brought me with him."

"So this is the lad's first night with the sheep in the fields, and the old man's last night, I fear," said the aged shepherd, sadly. "It is not often in these days that I venture out to keep the watches of the flock; but this one night of the year I have spent upon these hills these many years, and I always shall as long as I have strength to walk so far."

"Was your father, too, a shepherd?"

"Yes, and all his fathers before him for many generations. On these hills my ancestors have kept their sheep for I know not how long. . . .

"Do you know, my boy, that this is the night of the year on which the Lord Christ was born?"

"Oh yes," answered the lad. "My father told me as we were walking hither today, but I had forgotten it. And you were with the sheep that night?"

"Aye."

[9] Adapted from Chap. XI of *Ben Hur*, by Lew Wallace. Published by Harper & Brothers, New York City. Used by special permission.

"Where was it?"

"Here, on this very spot."

The boy's eyes began to grow and fill with wonder and there was a slight tremor in his voice as he hurriedly plied the aged man with his eager questions. Stephanus drew his shepherd's cloak around him, and leaned forward a little, and looked out upon the silent moonlit hills, and then up into the sky.

"How long ago was that, grandfather?"

"Just fifty years ago this night."

"And how old were you then?"

"Fourteen, and a stout boy for my age. I had been for two years in the fields with my father, and had tasted to the full the hardships and dangers of the shepherd's life."

"Who were you with on that night?"

"My father and his brother James, and Hosea, the son of John, a neighbor and kinsman of ours. On that year, as on this year and often, there came in the mid-winter a dry, warm season between the early and latter rain. We had driven forth our flock from Bethlehem and were dwelling by night in the shelter of the tower on the hillside yonder, watching and sleeping, two and two. My father and I were wont to keep the earlier watches. At midnight we would call James and Hosea, and they would watch till morning. But that night, when the sun went down and the stars came out we were all sitting here, upon this hillside, talking of the troubles of Israel and the promises of deliverance spoken of by the prophets; and James and Hosea were asking my father questions, and he was answering them, for he was older than they, and all the people of Bethlehem reverenced him as a wise and devout man.

·   ·   ·   ·   ·

"Suddenly I saw my father rise to his feet. Then the other men sprang up, with astonishment and wonder upon their faces. It had grown light all at once, lighter than the brightest moon; and as I turned my face in the direction in which the others were looking I saw, standing there upon that level place, a figure majestic and beautiful beyond the power of words to describe."

"Were you not afraid, grandfather?"

"Indeed I was, my boy. My heart stopped beating. The others were standing, but I had no power to rise. I lay there motionless upon the earth. My eyes were fixed upon that wonderful face, upon those clear, shining eyes, upon that brow that seemed to beam with the purity of the soul within. It was not a smile with which that face was lighted. It was something too noble and exalted to call by that name. It was a look that told of power and peace, of joy and triumph."

"Did you know that it was an angel?"

"I knew not anything. I only knew what I saw was glorious, too glorious for mortal eyes to look upon. Yet while I gazed, and in far less time than I have now taken to tell you of what I saw, the terribleness of the look began

to disappear, the sweetness and grace of the soul shone forth, and I had almost
ceased to tremble before the angel opened his mouth. And when he spoke,
his voice, clearer than any trumpet and sweeter than any lute, charmed
away all my fears.

" 'Be not afraid,' he said, 'for behold I bring you good tidings of great joy
which shall be to all people. For there is born to you this day, in the city of
David, a Saviour, which is Messiah, the King. And this is the sign unto you.
Ye shall find a Babe wrapped in swaddling clothes and lying in a manger.'

"Oh, that voice, my boy! It makes my heart beat now to remember its
sweetness. It seemed to carry these words into our innermost hearts; to print
them on our memories, so that we never could forget one syllable of what he
said. And then, before we had time to make reply, he turned aside a little and
lifted his face toward heaven, and in a tone far louder than that in which he
had spoken to us, but yet so sweet that it did not startle us at all, came forth
from his lips the first strain of that great song:

" 'Glory to God in the highest!'

"When he had uttered that he paused a moment, and the echoes, one after
another, from the hills that were near and the hills that were far away, came
flying home to us; so that I knew for once what the prophet meant when he
said that all the mountains and the hills should break forth into singing. But
before the echoes had all faded we began to hear other voices above our heads,
a great chorus, taking up the strain that the first angel had sung. At first it
seemed dim and far away; but gradually it came nearer and filled the air,
filled all the earth, filled all our souls with the most entrancing sweetness.
'Glory to God in the highest!'—that was the grandest part. It seemed as though
there could be no place so high that the strain would not mount up to it, and
no place so happy that that voice would not make it thrill with new gladness.
But then came the softer tones, less grand, but even sweeter—'Peace on earth,
good-will toward men.' "

"Did you see the choir of angels overhead, grandfather?"

"Nay, I saw nothing. The brightness was too dazzling for mortal eyes. We
all stood there, with downcast eyes, listening spellbound to the wonderful
melody, until the chorus ceased, and the echoes, one after another, died away,
and the glory faded out of the sky, and the stars came back again, and no
sound was heard but the faint voice of a young lamb calling for its mother.

"The first to break the silence was my father. 'Come,' he said in a solemn
voice. 'Let us go at once to Bethlehem, and see this thing which is come to
pass, which the Lord hath made known unto us.'

"So the sheep were quietly gathered into the fold at the tower and we
hastened to Bethlehem. . . . It was midnight when we climbed the hill of
the little town of Bethlehem; the constellation of Cesil, called by the Greeks,
'Orion,' was just setting in the west. We knew not whither to go. We had only
the sign of the angel by which we should know the infant Messiah. He was to
be wrapped in swaddling clothes and lying in a manger.

" 'Let us go to the inn,' said my father. 'It stands on the very spot where King David was born. Peradventure we shall find Him there.'

"Over the entrance to the court of the inn a lantern was swinging from a rope stretched across from post to post. Guided by its light, we entered, and found the courtyard full of beasts of burden, showing that the inn was crowded with travelers. In the arched shelter of the hostelry as many as could find room were lying; some who could not sleep were sitting up and waiting drearily for the morning. Two aged women near the entrance were talking in a low voice.

" 'Peace be unto you!' said my father.

" 'The Lord be gracious unto thee,' answered the oldest woman in a solemn voice, as she looked upon my father's white beard; 'but,' she quickly added, 'there is scanty cheer in this place for late comers.'

" 'We seek not lodging,' said my father; 'but know you whether among the guests is an infant born this day?'

" 'Verily there is,' answered the aged dame; 'a Man Child more beautiful than any my eyes have ever beheld. He is lying in a manger there in the cave that serves for the stable.'

"We hastened to the mouth of the cave; and there beheld our King. The oxen and the asses were lying near, and a strong man, with a grave benignant face, was leaning on his staff above the manger. A beautiful young mother lay close beside it, her cheek resting on her hands that were clasped over the edge of the rock-hewn crib. Into this a little straw had been thrown, and over it a purple robe had been cast, whereon the Infant lay. A lamp, set upon a projection of the wall of the cave, burned brightly near. The great eyes of the wonderful Child were wandering about the room; His hand touched His mother's lips. I waited to hear Him open His mouth and speak.

"There was a moment of silence after we entered the cave. My father broke it with his salutation:

" 'Hail, thou blessed among women!' he cried. 'This child of thine is a Prince and a Saviour.'

"And then we all bowed low upon our faces before Him and worshiped Him with praise and gladness.

.   .   .   .   .

"Then my father told them all the things that we had heard and seen—the message of the angel, the song in the air, the glory of the Lord that had appeared to us—and how we had quickly come to Bethlehem and had found the things as the angel had told us. 'And it is even,' he cried, 'as the prophet himself hath spoken: 'Thou, Bethlehem, though thou be little among the thousands of Judah, yet out of thee shall He come forth unto me that is to be the ruler in Israel, whose going forth hast been of old, even from everlasting.'

"And all that heard were full of astonishment—all save the mother. I saw no wonder on her face; the great things that my father told caused her no astonishment; she listened with a quiet and solemn joy, like one who was saying in her heart, 'I knew it all before.'

"When my father had finished speaking, we all bowed low again before the young Child; and the mother lifted Him in her arms and placed His cheek against her own, smiling graciously on us, but uttering no word. And we came forth from the stable and stood again beneath the stars in the courtyard of the inn.

· · · · ·

"In the early morning we came back again to our pastures and our flock, rejoicing to stand again in the place where the glory of God had shone and the music of heaven had filled the air."[10]

✢

THE STAR

Once upon a time in a country far away, there lived a little girl named Ruth. Ruth's home was not at all like our houses, for she lived in a little tower on top of the great stone wall that surrounded the town of Bethlehem.

Ruth's father was the hotelkeeper—the Bible says the "innkeeper." This inn was not at all like our hotels of today. There was a great open yard, which was called the courtyard. All about this yard were little rooms and each traveler who came to the hotel rented one.

This inn stood near the great stone wall of the city, so that as Ruth stood one night, looking out of the tower window, she looked directly into the courtyard. It was truly a strange sight that met her eyes. So many people were coming to the inn, for the king had made a law that every man should return to the city where his father used to live, to be counted and to pay his taxes.

Some of the people came on the backs of camels, with great rolls of bedding and their dishes for cooking upon the back of the beast. Some came on little donkeys, and on their backs, too, were the bedding and the dishes. Some people came walking—slowly, for they were very tired.

As Ruth looked down into the courtyard she saw camels being led to their places by their masters, she heard the snap of the whips, she saw the sparks shoot up from the fires that were kindled in the courtyard, where each person was preparing his own supper; she heard the cries of the tired, hungry little children.

Presently her mother, who was cooking supper, came over to the window and said, "Ruthie, thou shalt hide in the house until all those people are gone. Dost thou understand?"

[10] Abridged from a longer story by Washington Gladden in *Christmas Stories and Legends*, by Phoebe A. Curtis. Published by the Meigs Publishing Company, Indianapolis, Indiana. Used by special permission.

"Yes, my mother," said the child, and she left the window to follow her mother back to the stove, limping painfully, for little Ruth was a cripple. Her mother stooped suddenly and caught the child in her arms.

"My poor little lamb. It was a mule's kick, just six years ago, that hurt your poor back and made you lame."

"Never mind, my mother. My back does not ache today, and lately, when the light of the strange new star has shone down upon my bed my back has felt so much stronger and I have felt so happy, as though I could climb upon the rays of the star up, up into the sky and above the stars!"

Her mother shook her head sadly. "Thou art not likely to climb much, now or ever, but come, the supper is ready; let us go and find your father. I wonder what keeps him?"

They found the father standing at the gate of the courtyard, talking to a man and woman who had just arrived. The man was tall, with a long beard, and he led by a rope a snow-white mule, on which sat the drooping figure of the woman. As Ruth and her mother came near, they heard the father say, "But I tell thee that there is no more room in the inn. Hast thou no friends where thou canst go to spend the night?" The man shook his head. "No, none," he answered. "I care not for myself, but my poor wife." Little Ruth pulled at her mother's dress. "Mother, the oxen sleep out under the stars these warm nights and the straw in the caves is clean and warm; I have made a bed there for my little lamb."

Ruth's mother bowed before the tall man. "Thou didst hear the child. It is as she says—the straw is clean and warm." The tall man bowed his head. "We shall be very glad to stay," and he helped the sweet-faced woman down from the donkey's back and led her away to the cave-stable, while little Ruth and her mother hurried up the stairs that they might send a bowl of porridge to the sweet-faced woman, and a cup of new milk, as well.

．　．　．　．　．

That night when little Ruth lay down on her bed the rays of the beautiful new star shone through the window more brightly than before. They seemed to soothe the tired, aching shoulders. She fell asleep and dreamed that the beautiful bright star burst and out of it came countless angels, who sang in the night:

"Glory to God in the highest, peace on earth, good-will toward men." And then it was morning and her mother was bending over her, saying, "Awake, awake, little Ruth. Mother has something to tell thee." Then as her eyes opened slowly her mother said, "Angels came in the night, little one, and left a Baby to lay beside your little white lamb in the manger."

．　．　．　．　．

That afternoon Ruth went with her mother to the fountain. The mother turned aside to talk to the other women of the town about the strange things heard and seen the night before, but Ruth went on and sat down by the edge of the fountain. The child was not frightened, for strangers came often to the well; but never before had she seen men who looked like the three who now came toward her. The first one, a tall man with a long white beard, came close to Ruth and said, "Canst tell us, child, where is born He that is called King of the Jews?"

"I know of no king," answered Ruth, "but last night while the star was shining the angels brought a baby to lie beside my little white lamb in the manger." The stranger bowed his head. "That must be He. Wilt thou show us the way to Him, my child?" So Ruth ran and her mother led the three men to the cave, "and when they saw the Child, they rejoiced with exceeding great joy, and opening their gifts, they presented unto Him gold and frankincense and myrrh," with wonderful jewels, so that Ruth's mother's eyes opened with wonder, but little Ruth saw only the Baby, which lay asleep on its mother's breast.

"If I might only hold Him in my arms," thought she, but she was afraid to ask.

· · · · ·

After a few days, the strangers left Bethlehem, all but the three—the man, whose name was Joseph, and Mary his wife, and the Baby. Then, as of old, little Ruth played about the courtyard and the white lamb frolicked at her side. Often she dropped to her knees to press the little woolly white head against her breast, while she murmured: "My little lamb, my very, very own. I love you, lambie," and then together they would steal over to the entrance of the cave to peep in at the Baby, and always Ruth thought, "If I might only touch His hand." But she was afraid to ask.

One night as she lay in her bed she thought to herself: "Oh, I wish I had a beautiful gift for Him, such as the wise men brought; but I have nothing at all to offer and I love Him so much." Just then the light of the star, which was nightly fading, fell across the foot of the bed and shone full upon the white lamb which lay asleep at her feet—and then she thought of something.

The next morning she arose with her face shining with joy. She dressed carefully and with the white lamb held close to her breast went slowly and painfully down the stairway and over to the door of the cave. "I have come," she said, "to worship Him, and I have brought Him—my little white lamb." The mother smiled at the lame child, then she lifted the Baby from her breast and placed Him in the arms of the little maid who knelt at her feet.

· · · · ·

A few days later an angel came to the father, Joseph, and told him to take the Baby and hurry into the land of Egypt, for the wicked king wanted to do it harm; and so these three—the father, the mother and the Baby—went by night to that far country of Egypt. And the star grew dimmer and dimmer and passed away forever from the skies over Bethlehem; but little Ruth grew straight and strong and beautiful as the almond trees in the orchard, and all the people who saw her were amazed, for Ruth was once a cripple.

"It was the light of the strange star," her mother said; but little Ruth knew it was the touch of the blessed Christ Child, who was once folded against her heart.[11]

✛

O LITTLE TOWN OF BETHLEHEM

"O Little Town of Bethlehem" was written by Bishop Phillips Brooks. From early childhood he loved and memorized hymns. By the time he had reached college age he could repeat from memory more than two hundred of them. He never forgot them, and often used them in his sermons.

While he was rector of the Holy Trinity Church in Philadelphia, his parishioners sent him abroad for a year. In December his travels took him to the Holy Land, where he retraced the steps of his Master. On Christmas Eve he went to the little town of Bethlehem. As he stood in the old church close to the spot where Jesus was born, where worshipers were singing praises to God in hymns, Phillips Brooks was moved with emotion. The memories of that evening so filled his soul that, two years later, he echoed his experiences to the people of America in the Christmas hymn, "O Little Town of Bethlehem." It was first used by the children of his Sunday school at their Christmas service in 1868.

The lovely tune was written by Mr. Lewis H. Redner, who was the organist for the Holy Trinity Church. Almost a quarter of a century passed before churches sensed the immortal beauty of this Christmas hymn.

> O little town of Bethlehem,
> How still we see thee lie!
> Above thy deep and dreamless sleep
> The silent stars go by;
> Yet in thy dark streets shineth
> The everlasting Light;
> The hopes and fears of all the years
> Are met in thee tonight.
>
> For Christ is born of Mary,
> And, gathered all above,
> While mortals sleep, the angels keep
> Their watch of wond'ring love.
> O morning stars, together
> Proclaim the holy birth!
> And praises sing to God the King,
> And peace to men on earth.

[11] "The Star," by Florence M. Kingsley. Published by Henry Altemus Company. Used by special permission.

How silently, how silently
  The wondrous gift is given!
So God imparts to human hearts
  The blessings of his heaven.
No ear may hear his coming;
  But in this world of sin,
Where meek souls will receive Him still,
  The dear Christ enters in.

O holy Child of Bethlehem,
  Descend on us, we pray;
Cast out our sin, and enter in,—
  Be born in us today.
We hear the Christmas angels
  The great, glad tidings tell;
O come to us, abide with us
  Our Lord Emmanuel!

—Phillips Brooks, 1868

✦

SILENT NIGHT, HOLY NIGHT

"And there were shepherds in the same country, abiding in the field, and keeping watch by night over their flock. . . . And they came with haste, and found Mary and Joseph, and the babe lying in the manger."—Luke 2:8, 16.

This ageless story has always been the source of inspiration, and Joseph Mohr (1792-1848) found that it was to him. In 1818, when he was assistant pastor of Oberdorf, near Arnsdorf, he attended a Christmas Eve meeting at the Arnsdorf schoolhouse. He was greeted by Franz Gruber, a schoolmaster, organist, songwriter, and intimate friend. As the Christmas celebration progressed, Mohr withdrew from the room. Later when recalled to participate in the service, he brought with him a folded paper, a gift to Franz Gruber. Gruber opened it and read aloud, "Silent Night, Holy Night," the poem which has become the best-loved of all the Christmas hymns.

So touched was he by this beautiful poetic gift that a sudden inspiration seemed to come to him. A short time after Mr. Mohr had retired that evening he heard his poem being sung to the beautiful tune, "Stille Nacht." Mr. Gruber had composed the melody! Thus, on that memorable eve in 1818, the richness of the Christmas thought and spirit found expression in:

Silent night, holy night,
All is calm, all is bright,
Round yon Virgin Mother and Child,
Holy Infant so tender and mild,
Sleep in heavenly peace,
Sleep in heavenly peace.

Silent night, holy night,
Darkness flies, all is light;
Shepherds hear the angels sing,
"Alleluia! hail the King!
Christ the Saviour is born,
Christ the Saviour is born."

Silent night, holy night,
Guiding star, lend thy light;
See the Eastern wise men bring
Gifts and homage to our King!
Christ the Saviour is born,
Christ the Saviour is born.

Silent night, holy night,
Wondrous stars, lend thy light;
With the angels let us sing
Alleluia to our King!
Christ the Saviour is born,
Christ the Saviour is born.

—Joseph Mohr, 1818

✛

HARK! THE HERALD ANGELS SING

It is difficult to speak of the works of Charles Wesley without coupling his efforts with those of his brothers, John and Samuel. Four thousand hymns were published in the lifetime of the Wesleys and about twenty-five hundred were left in manuscript form.

Although Charles Wesley was considered the greatest hymn-writer ever produced by the Church of England, only one of his hymns—"Hark! the Herald Angels Sing"—was admitted to their *Book of Common Prayer* for many years. This hymn first appeared in *Hymns and Sacred Poems,* a joint hymnal published by John and Charles Wesley in 1739. When first printed it began:

Hark, how all the welkin rings,
Glory to the King of Kings.

Several revisions have been made in the original words, but it has always re-mained the most widely published hymn of Charles Wesley. No doubt its popularity has lived because of the clear, beautiful and joyous manner in which the story of Christ's birth and mission are revealed.

More than a century passed before the poem became associated with any fixed tune. Dr. Cummings, principal of the Guild Hall School of Music discovered this tune in Mendelssohn's "Festgesang."

Hark! the herald angels sing,
"Glory to the new-born King;
Peace on earth, and mercy mild,
God and sinners reconciled."
Joyful all ye nations, rise,
Join the triumph of the skies;
With th' angelic host proclaim,
"Christ is born in Bethlehem!"
Hark! the herald angels sing,
"Glory to the new-born King!"

Christ, by highest heaven adored,
Christ, the everlasting Lord!
Come, Desire of Nations, come,
Fix in us thy humble home.
Veiled in flesh the Godhead see;
Hail th' Incarnate Deity,
Pleased as man with men to dwell;
Jesus, our Emmanuel;
Hark! the herald angels sing,
"Glory to the new-born King!"

Hail, the heaven-born Prince of Peace!
Hail, the Sun of Righteousness!
Light and life to all he brings,
Risen with healing in his wings;
Mild he lays his glory by,
Born that man no more may die,
Born to raise the sons of earth,
Born to give them second birth;
Hark! the herald angels sing,
"Glory to the new-born King!"

—Charles Wesley, 1739

✛

IT CAME UPON A MIDNIGHT CLEAR

THE words of this hymn were American-born. Edmund Hamilton Sears (1810-1876) wrote the lyric poem in 1849. He was born in Sandisfield, Massachusetts. His lineage dates back to the Colonial days, for he was a descendant of Richard Sears, a Hollander who joined the Plymouth Colony in 1630.

After graduating from Union College in New York, Edmund Sears began to study law. A call to the ministry seemed to interest him more than his law study, however, so he entered Harvard Divinity School. After completing his work at Harvard he held several small pastorates in the central part of

Massachusetts. He was of Unitarian faith, but believed in the divinity of Christ and preached it in his pulpit.

The hymn tune, "Carol," which is associated with Sears' words, was composed by Richard Storrs Willis. Mr. Willis was a brother of Nathaniel Parker Willis, the poet, and son of Deacon Nathaniel Willis, the founder of *The Youth's Companion.*

It is a pity that this hymn is sung only at the Christmas season, for it bears a message of social service, effective at all seasons of the year.

> It came upon a midnight clear,
> That glorious song of old,
> From angels bending near the earth,
> To touch their harps of gold;
> "Peace on the earth, good-will to men,
> From Heaven's all-gracious King";
> The world in solemn stillness lay,
> To hear the angels sing.
>
> Still through the cloven skies they come,
> With peaceful wings unfurled;
> And still their heavenly music floats
> O'er all the weary world;
> Above its sad and lowly plains
> They bend on heavenly wing,
> And ever o'er its Babel sounds
> The blessed angels sing!
>
> And ye, beneath life's crushing load,
> Whose forms are bending low,
> Who toil along the climbing way
> With painful steps and slow,
> Look now! for glad and golden hours
> Come swiftly on the wing;
> O rest beside the weary road,
> And hear the angels sing.
>
> For lo! the days are hastening on,
> By prophet-bards foretold,
> When, with the ever-circling years
> Comes round the age of gold;
> When peace shall over all the earth
> Its ancient splendors fling,
> And the whole world give back the song
> Which now the angels sing.
>
> *—Edmund H. Sears, 1849*

AS WITH GLADNESS MEN OF OLD

ALTHOUGH this hymn is not as popular as many that herald the Christmas story, yet it contains a very beautiful message. An expression of joy and gladness permeate the words and a personal petition to God is found in every stanza.

This hymn was written by William Chatterton Dix (1837-1898) when he was twenty-three years old. He was recovering from a very serious illness at the time, hence his longing for joy and happiness found expression in this hymn.

William Dix was born in Bristol, England, and was the son of a surgeon. He trained himself for a business career and for many years held the managership of a Marine Insurance Company in Glasgow.

He wrote about forty hymns, the more popular of which are "Come unto Me, Ye Weary" and "As with Gladness Men of Old."

The tune was arranged by Mr. Dix from a German chorale, written in 1838. He protested when the tune was named after him, for he disliked it and never felt it quite suitable to his words; nevertheless this association of words and music lived and, no doubt, will continue to do so.

> As with gladness men of old
> Did the guiding star behold;
> As with joy they hailed its light,
> Leading onward, beaming bright;
> So, most gracious Lord, may we
> Evermore be led to thee.
>
> As with joyful steps they sped
> To that lowly manger-bed
> There to bend the knee before
> Him whom heaven and earth adore;
> So may we with willing feet
> Ever seek Thy mercy seat.
>
> As they offered gifts most rare,
> At that manger rude and bare,
> So may we with holy joy,
> Pure and free from sin's alloy,
> All our costliest treasures bring,
> Christ, to Thee, our heavenly King.
>
> Holy Jesus, every day
> Keep us in the narrow way;
> And, when earthly things are past,

Bring our ransomed souls at last,
Where they need no star to guide,
Where no clouds Thy glory hide.
—*William Chatterton Dix, 1861*

✛

WHILE SHEPHERDS WATCHED THEIR FLOCKS

FOR a century and a half before the writings of Nahum Tate, worshipers of the English Church had been singing an "old version of the Psalms of David." Thus, when a "new version" of the Psalms appeared in 1696, written by Nahum Tate and Nicholas Brady, much opposition arose. Many thought of the "old version" as being God-inspired, while, on the other hand, they regarded the newer compositions as "human" and sacrilegious. Nevertheless, the "new version" lived. Later (1703) Mr. Tate wrote a supplement of sixteen hymns, one of which was "While Shepherds Watched Their Flocks." It is interesting to note that this supplement was one of the early efforts of English poets to provide hymns for the Church distinct from the Psalms of David.

Nahum Tate, the son of an Irish clergyman, was born in Dublin in 1652. He was a friend and literary associate of the great poet Dryden, and was appointed poet-laureate of England by King William III.

Many tunes are used in connection with this hymn, the most beautiful of which is "Teignmouth."

While shepherds watched their flocks by night,
All seated on the ground,
The angel of the Lord came down,
And glory shone around.
"Fear not," said he, for mighty dread
Had seized their troubled minds;
"Glad tidings of great joy, I bring
To you and all mankind.

"To you, in David's town, this day,
Is born of David's line,
The Saviour, who is Christ the Lord;
And this shall be the sign;
The heavenly Babe you there shall find
To human view displayed,
All meanly wrapped in swaddling bands,
And in a manger laid."

Thus spake the seraph—and forthwith
Appeared a shining throng
Of angels, praising God, and thus
Addressed their joyful song:

"All glory be to God on high,
   And to the earth be peace;
Good-will henceforth from heaven to men
   Begin, and never cease."

— *Nahum Tate, 1703*

✣

WE THREE KINGS OF ORIENT ARE

AMONG the beautiful carols that have had their inception in the Bible stories about the birth of Jesus, none is more beautiful than "We Three Kings of Orient Are," by John H. Hopkins.

Our New Testament tells us (Matthew 2:1-16) that when Jesus was born in Bethlehem of Judea, three wise men came to Jerusalem and later to Bethlehem, seeking this new-born King. We know also that they were guided by a wonderful new star that appeared in the sky.

We do not know just what countries they may have come from, probably small kingdoms on the other side of the great desert which separated their homes from the place where Jesus was born; but we do know that they came from the East, doubtless mounted on picturesque camels, whose padded hoofs could easily withstand the burning heat of desert lands.

If you will listen to the music of "We Three Kings of Orient Are," you will note that its rhythm suggests the swaying movements of the camels and that its minor tones indicate its Oriental strain.

Out of the East these wise men came bearing rich gifts for this Child of Promise, whose star of announcement they had seen. Crossing fertile fields, passing waterfalls and rivers, they followed on through rugged mountain passes and barren, waste desert lands, guided by this strange new star which seemed to lead them.

The first king brought *gold*, doubtless for a crown with which to honor this new uncrowned King of a new kind of Kingdom.

The second king brought *frankincense*, a very sweet, spicy perfume which, when it is burned, makes a spiral smoke that rises heavenward. The people of the Old Testament times used it in their services of worship, because it helped them to think of the nearness of their Heavenly Father. Since Jesus was the Father's best gift to men, this wise man from the East brought a gift which made him think of Jesus as God's best gift to humanity.

The third king brought *myrrh*, a spice always used in the burial service in the East. This gift of myrrh prophetically reminds us that Jesus was to give His life for those He loved and for others who knew not the *will* and *spirit* of His Heavenly Father.

This Christmas carol is particularly fitting for use by young people because it lends itself to dramatization. As it is being sung by a trio or quartette, three young men, richly gowned, may enter the auditorium from various entrances and make their way, with stately, kingly tread to the platform where the birth-scene of the manger Child is being presented in the form of drama or tableau.

Stereopticon slides No. 1612, "The Gifts of the Wise Men (Hofmann); No. 20136, "The Worship of the Magi"; No. 16748, "The 'Worship of the Wise Men"; No. 8711, "The Wise Men before Herod"; and No. 18192, "The Wise Men and the Star" (Taylor)—all obtainable from the Victor Animatograph Corporation, Davenport, Iowa—will also help to make meaningful the message of this, one of the most beautiful and symbolic of all the Christmas carols.

We three kings of Orient are;
Bearing gifts we traverse afar
Field and fountain, moor and mountain,
Following yonder star.

Refrain

O star of wonder, star of night,
Star with royal beauty bright,
Westward leading, still proceeding,
Guide us to thy perfect light.

Born a King on Bethlehem's plain,
Gold I bring to crown Him again,
King forever, ceasing never,
Over us all to reign.

Refrain

Frankincense to offer have I,
Incense owns a Deity nigh;
Prayer and praising all men raising,
Worship Him, God on high.

Refrain

Myrrh is mine, its bitter perfume
Breathes a life of gathering gloom:
Sorr'wing, sighing, bleeding, dying,
Sealed in the stone-cold tomb.

Refrain

        —John H. Hopkins, 1857

Glorious now behold Him rise,
King and God and Sacrifice;
Al-le-lu-la, Al-le-lu-la!
Sounds thro' the earth and skies.

        —John H. Hopkins, 1857

PART II

THE YOUTH OF JESUS

CONTENTS

PART II

THE YOUTH OF JESUS

✠

"And Jesus advanced in wisdom and stature, and in favor with God and men."—LUKE 2:52

✠

97

THE YOUTH OF JESUS

"And the child grew, and waxed strong, filled with wisdom: and the grace of God was upon him.

"And his parents went every year to Jerusalem at the feast of the passover. And when he was twelve years old, they went up after the custom of the feast; and when they had fulfilled the days, as they were returning, the boy Jesus tarried behind in Jerusalem; and his parents knew it not; but supposing him to be in the company, they went a day's journey; and they sought for him among their kinsfolk and acquaintance: and when they found him not, they returned to Jerusalem, seeking for him. And it came to pass, after three days they found him in the temple, sitting in the midst of the teachers, both hearing them, and asking them questions: and all that heard him were amazed at his understanding and his answers. And when they saw him, they were astonished; and his mother said unto him, Son, why hast thou thus dealt with us? behold, thy father and I sought thee sorrowing. And he said unto them, How is it that ye sought me? knew ye not that I must be in my Father's house? And they understood not the saying which he spake unto them. And he went down with them, and came to Nazareth; and he was subject unto them: and his mother kept all *these* sayings in her heart.

"And Jesus advanced in wisdom and stature and in favor with God and men."—LUKE 2:40-52

THE WORKSHOP AT NAZARETH—*BRIGGS*

THE WORKSHOP AT NAZARETH

By

Main Briggs

(Interpretation)

For an artistic presentation of the paternal love and care of Joseph for Jesus, the Child of Promise, none is more satisfactory than this modern painting of "The Workshop at Nazareth," by Main Briggs. This picture portrays a child of somewhat younger years than "The Holy Family," by Grosso, or "The Return to Nazareth," by Millais. Indeed, this lad appears to be some five or six years old as over against the youth in his early teens portrayed in other pictures of the workshop of Nazareth.

Joseph also is shown as a younger, and less toil-worn, man. I like to think that Briggs in his "The Workshop at Nazareth" is portraying one of those periods of confidential sharing that must have come, now and then, between father and son, perhaps at the end of a busy day or week. Mary is absent in Briggs' conception of the workshop of Nazareth, probably busying herself in the preparation of their evening meal.

Father and Son look as though they might have finished their work for the day, and to have tidied up both themselves and the shop in preparation for the Sabbath day that in every devout Jewish home began with sundown on Friday. As they busied themselves with last-minute tasks, Joseph may have recalled for the lad that commandment dear to every Jewish heart, "Remember the Sabbath day to keep it holy," which through the centuries has been so strictly observed and held in reverence by devout Jews everywhere. Or they may have been thinking together about what it takes to make, not only the Sabbath day, but every day, a *holy* day.

The Child, dressed in his soft clinging white tunic and sash, stands between his father's knees, one hand resting affectionately on Joseph's arm, while the other hand, clutching three nails dear to his boyish heart, is uplifted and rests near his sash. Joseph still has his mallet in his hand, as though he had not quite finished some last-minute task; and yet felt that he must sit down and answer as best he could the strange and discerning questions which this first-born and best-loved Son of his so often asked.

They may have been discussing some of the ancient prophecies of the Jewish faith in regard to the promised Messiah who was to build again the throne of David, and to reign eternally thereon.

As you gaze into the open face of this remarkably beautiful Christ Child in the Nazareth workshop, you have the feeling that as he looks steadfastly into heaven, he is seeing things unseen to mortal eyes. No doubt this young

Son has just said something so profound and significant about the character of the Kingdom that he is to build, that Joseph, bending forward, looks at him with deep concern in his fatherly face.

Jesus has what the artists call the far-seeing eyes, that seem to speak of truth beginning to be discerned, perhaps for the first time, of a Kingdom not made with nails and hammers, but springing eternally in the hearts and lives of men when they come to understand what the love of God is like.

I like to feel that Joseph, too, comprehends something of the unusual contribution that this gifted Son is to make toward the building of that spiritual Kingdom in the hearts of men everywhere, as, with the poet, he says silently in his heart:

> None shall make a yoke or plow
>   Better than mine own,
> But this child, whose sunlit brow
> Holds the kiss of angels now—
>   He will build a throne.
>
> Mine to teach his little hands;
>   He shall learn the whole
> Craft the workman understands;
> But in this and wider lands
>   He will guide the soul.
>
> I shall show him tricks of birds,
>   Where the sparrows build their nests,
> Teach him lore of fleecy herds;
> But his heart will hold the words
>   Hid in sages' breasts.
>
> Mine to teach the lower ways,
>   Little secrets of the sod;
> His to guide in later days,
> Where celestial torches blaze,
>   In the light of God.[1]

[1] "The Song of Joseph—," Mary Brent Whiteside. From *Christ in the Poetry of Today*. Used with permission of the author.

THE SON OF A CARPENTER—LAFON

THE SON OF A CARPENTER

By

François Lafon

(Interpretation)

AMONG the many artists who have attempted to portray Jesus as a lad working in his father's carpenter shop in Nazareth, none has given us a more beautiful and life-like interpretation than the picture by the French painter François Lafon, the original of which is in Jerusalem.

Mary, the Virgin mother, is seated on a rough bench, her folded hands resting quietly in her lap. She seems to be in one of those remembering moods so natural to the mother who "kept all these sayings in her heart."

The Christ Child in a simple white tunic, his dark hair falling to his shoulders, stands, with unsandaled feet, behind his father's workbench, evidently in the act of measuring with his eye the place where the cross-piece should be nailed. Like any healthy boy, his mouth is pursed up as though he was whistling happily as he worked.

Joseph, his father, with his saw in one hand, and the other resting on the workbench, is watching intently to see if the lad's decision as to where the cross-piece should be placed is accurate. There is pride in Joseph's face as he watches this first-born Son, who even in his early youth gives promise of becoming one of the best carpenters in all Galilee. Work, to this unusual Son. of his, is a joy. Unlike many of the village boys, his Son finds his greatest happiness, not in fishing or strolling along the hillsides of Nazareth, but in fellowship with his mother and father as together they answer the calls of the villagers for workmanship that only carpenters can supply.

Near to Mary's feet two doves, symbols of peace and good-will, have alighted to gather the crumbs from among the shavings and litter that have fallen at the end of the workbench. Behind her a stairway leads to the main living quarters above the workshop, that tradition says was built along the hillside. Through the door or opening behind Joseph one can see trees and shrubbery.

There is a natural beauty and repose about this homely everyday scene in the workshop at Nazareth that pleases the eye. The family are at peace with one another and with their world. The storm of antagonism that is to block the pathway of this Child of prophecy later, when He sets Himself seriously to the accomplishment of His heavenly Father's will, has not yet cast its shadow over the peace, serenity, and industry of this humble carpenter's home.

There is just a veiled suggestion that Jesus may be making a cross, and that Mary's dreaming forebodings sense the later impending sorrow that is to come to this her first-born Son by way of the cross; but I prefer to think of the boyhood life of Jesus as a normal, happy child life unmarred by the impending danger which characterized His later years of service and sacrifice.

THE HOLY FAMILY

By

Giacomo Grosso

(Interpretation)

ONE naturally thinks of the return of the Holy Family to Nazareth as an idyllic scene that should have inspired many artists. Among the early painters, however, this incident was rarely ever pictured. On the whole, pictures of the Holy Family in the carpenter's shop at Nazareth are quite modern.

Among these modern paintings "The Holy Family," by the French artist, Giacomo Grosso, is among the best. It portrays the carpenter shop in Nazareth not only with Mary, Joseph, and the Christ Child present but with some neighbors in the doorway present also.

The father has evidently been at work on an unfinished chest, but has paused in his labors to listen with rapt attention to the words of wisdom that fall with rare charm and grace from the lips of this youthful village lad who is destined to become one of the world's greatest teachers.

Mary, the Virgin mother, sits in the background. She is dressed simply in a dark robe with a spotlessly white scarf over her head and shoulders. Across her lap is some unfinished garment on which she has been working. One arm rests on a near-by projecting wall in front of which hangs a sheer white curtain, evidently there for the purpose of barring out the blinding sunlight of the large open arch. She, too, has stopped her work to listen to this gifted Son. Her dark eyes are peering intently at the youthful Christ, while her left hand, slightly raised, is directly in front of her heart, seeming to suggest "But Mary kept all these sayings in her heart."

In the doorway sit and lean a group of neighbors—a woman and two or three men who have stopped to listen to the eloquent words of this lad of the carpenter shop whose intelligence and yearning after righteousness have already won for him the respectful consideration of Nazareth neighbors.

Christ is the center of interest, standing, as he does, in the foreground of the picture. He is dressed in a simple tunic bound about the waist with a sash. One hand, relaxed, hangs at his side, the other, upraised and outward, seems to include the whole world in the concept of the heavenly Father's Kingdom about which he is earnestly telling his listeners.

The profile view of the face of Jesus is strong and well molded, and the eyes are the eyes of a prophet and seer, that behold the things of the spirit as if they were actually present.

With poise, dignity, and unaffected naturalness he stands, holding the rapt attention of his audience, small though it may be, as he tells them of a God of Love who is the heavenly Father of all mankind, of every race, class, and kind the world around. There is wonder and admiration in the eyes of Joseph and Mary, who love this unusual and gifted Son with a reverence bordering on worship.

The doorway friends also are lost in their admiration for and interest in the message which he brings to them. You can almost hear them think aloud, "Can this be Jesus, the carpenter's son? Whence, then, hath he these unusual gifts?"

This comparatively modern painting is reverent and beautiful in every respect, reminding us that even in his youth Jesus must have been conscious that he should always be "about my Father's business."

✛

THE BOY CHRIST IN THE TEMPLE

By

Hermann Clementz

(Interpretation)

WE CANNOT know just how Jesus looked as a boy. In Luke's Gospel we read that when Mary and Joseph had "performed all things according to the law of the Lord, they returned into Galilee to their own city of Nazareth. And the child grew and waxed strong in spirit, filled with wisdom, and the grace of God was upon him."

Of all the artists who have attempted to portray the scene of Jesus' visit to the Temple at twelve years of age, and of his tarrying behind in conversation with the learned doctors of the law, three only have won outstanding recognition: "Finding the Boy Christ in the Temple," by the English painter Holman Hunt, the original of which hangs in the Birmingham Gallery in England; "The Boy Christ in the Temple," by the German painter Hermann Clementz, the original of which is privately owned in Europe; and "Christ and the Doctors," by Johann Heinrich Hofmann, also a German artist. His picture of this incident is perhaps most universally known.

Even though we cannot know just how Christ looked as a boy, this beautiful picture of "The Boy Christ in the Temple," by Clementz, approaches perhaps nearest to our ideal of the youthful Christ. The face of the boy Jesus, in its ideal beauty, is almost without a fault. It radiates all that is good and pure and true. Fine features, an open countenance, a commanding presence, all express divine intelligence. God's light and truth and goodness are shining in his wonderful dark eyes. His dress, a simple white tunic, is a fitting symbol of his own personal purity.

In all three of these paintings of Christ in the Temple at twelve, Jesus naturally forms the center of the group. He not only attracts attention, but appears to be holding the attention of these learned doctors of the law. With

THE HOLY FAMILY—GROSSO

THE BOY CHRIST IN THE TEMPLE—*CLEMENTZ*

modesty, yet with wisdom, he seems to be answering the most difficult questions. The power of his clear, earnest voice stirs the hearts of his hearers, and they marvel at the wisdom of his speech.

"The Boy Christ in the Temple," by Clementz, is perhaps more rugged than either of the other two. It also portrays more of the inner Temple area, and sets the boy Christ a bit more apart from the learned doctors of the law, who seem to be listening intently, as they shrewdly watch to discover any error in the words of this young boyish teacher. Clementz also adds an aged rabbi near the opening leading to the Temple court, which reveals Mary and Joseph parting the curtains as they end their three-day search for this lovely and unusual Son, who has been missed from the home-going caravan of travelers returning from the annual Passover pilgrimage.

Again and again we find our eyes turning to the supreme attraction of the picture, the Christ Child, who in His divine loveliness stands in the midst of these sages with a kingly presence, a calm dignity, and the conscious assurance that He is in His Father's house and about His Father's business. His earnest words must have been like messages direct from God to those listening rabbis.

Although Clementz' picture of "The Boy Christ in the Temple" is not so well known as Hofmann's "Christ and the Doctors," it is growing in popularity and appreciation as the years go by. The Boy Christ is more boyish; and the picture is more satisfying in its portrayal of the entire Gospel incident.

✠

HIS MOTHER IN HER HOOD OF BLUE

"When Jesus therefore saw his mother ——"

When Jesus was a little thing,
  His mother, in her hood of blue,
Called to Him through the dusk of spring:
  "Jesus, my Jesus, where are you?"

Caught in a gust of whirling bloom,
  She stood a moment at the door,
Then lit the candle in the room,
  In its pink earthen bowl of yore.

The little Jesus saw it all—
  The blur of yellow in the street;
The fair trees by the tumbling wall;
  The shadowy other lads, whose feet

Struck a quick noise from out the grass;
  He saw, dim in the half-lit air,
As one sees folk within a glass,
  His mother with her candle there:
    "Jesus! Jesus!"

When He a weary man became,
    I think, as He went to and fro,
He heard her calling just the same
    Across the dusk of long ago,
        "Jesus!"

For men were tired that had been bold—
    And strange indeed this should befall—
One day so hot, one day so cold—
    But mothers never change at all.
        "Jesus!"

                    —*Lizette Woodworth Reese*

LIKE OTHER BOYS

He was a boy like other boys,
    And played and sported with the rest;
He had His troubles and His toys,
    And strove for mastery with the best.

He was a very boy, and had
    His little faults—like other boys;
But he was always gay and glad,
    And eager in His small employs.

With all the rest He went to school,
    But gave His lessons more concern,
And school to Him was never dull,
    He had so keen a wish to learn.

He loved all birds and beasts and flowers
    And in the hills spent happy days
Lying unseen in cunning bowers
    Where He could watch their curious ways.

He was great-hearted, tender, true,
    And brave as any boy could be,
And very gentle, for He knew
    That Love is God's own Chivalry.

He was a boy—like you—and you—
    As full of jokes, as full of fun,
But always He was bravely true,
    And did no wrong to anyone.

And one thing I am sure about—
He never tumbled into sin,
But kept himself, within, without,
As God had made Him, sweet and clean.[2]

—*John Oxenham*

IN GALILEE

Erect in youthful grace and radiant
With spirit forces, all imparadised
In a divine compassion, down the slant
Of these remembering hills He came, the Christ.

Should not the glowing lilies of the field
With keener splendor mark His footprints yet?
Prints of the gentle feet whose passing healed
All blight from Tabor unto Olivet?

—*Katharine Lee Bates*

A BOY WITH A GREAT DREAM

O Jesus, once a Nazareth boy,
And tempted like as we,
All inward foes help us destroy
And spotless all to be.
We trust Thee for the grace to win
The high victorious goal,
Where purity shall conquer sin
In Christ-like self-control.

—*Anonymous*

THE YOUNG WORKMAN

Yes, I believe He loved them, too,
The songs of saw and plane,
And the rhythmic ring of hammers;
Perhaps they called again
From out the Nazareth workshop,
Where once He used to be,
As He sat or walked with fisher-folk
And gazed on Galilee.
Perhaps for loads of timber,
Not souls, His young arms yearned,
For labor that, accomplished,
Was accepted and not spurned.

[2] From *Gentlemen—The King.* Published by the Pilgrim Press, Boston, Mass. Used by permission of the author.

Perhaps the love of building
  Grasped His hands, that folded lay
Or gently gestured as He talked
  About the Living Way—
Grasped them, made them fairly tingle
  With the energy to build,
Until the house not made with hands
  His earthly longings stilled.
Just as Galilean waves and fears
  Were quiet when He willed.
O Thou, our Master Builder,
  In our grime and sweat and soil
Let us ever honor Thee as Thou
  Didst ever honor toil.

—Mary Dillingham Frear

THE CHRISTMAS SYMBOL

Only a manger, cold and bare,
  Only a maiden mild,
Only some shepherds kneeling there,
  Watching a little Child;
And yet that maiden's arms enfold
  The King of Heaven above;
And in the Christ Child we behold
  The Lord of Life and Love.

Only an altar high and fair,
  Only a white-robed priest,
Only Christ's children kneeling there
  Keeping the Christmas feast;
And yet beneath the outward sign
  The inward Grace is given—
His Presence, who is Lord Divine
  And King of earth and heaven.

—Author Unknown

ALL THE ROAD TO EGYPT

All the road to Egypt
  Sang to see them pass,
The Child asleep on Mary's arm,
Old Joseph, shielding them from harm,
The Angel, beautiful as hope,
Leading by a twist of rope
  The little, gray-coat ass.

All the road to Egypt
  Knelt to see them pass,
The Child's dear head haloed gold,
Madonna's robe in many a fold
Of changing blue like shimmering wave,
Whose falling grace a glory gave
  Even to the dusty ass.

All the road to Egypt
  Danced to see them pass,
Old Joseph's cloak of cinnamon,
The Angel's restless wings that shone
Green as the trees of Paradise,
And like some curious, chased device
  A little silver ass.

All the road to Egypt
  Bloomed to feel them pass,
So raced the sap in stem and root
The withered fig tree sprang to fruit;
The palm and olive bowed their load
To Mary's lips; that purple road
  Bore thistles for the ass.

Still the road to Egypt,
  While the centuries pass,
Remembering that sweet caravan,
Mother and Child, their guardian
Following on staff of sandalwood,
And serving them in brotherhood
  God's angel and God's ass.

                        —*Katharine Lee Bates*

THE HOLY FAMILY

So sweetly through that humble home
  The rippling laughter went
That Mary felt the world's blue dome
  Too small for her content;

And careful Joseph, while he held
  The boy in grave caress,
Wist not what tender thrill dispelled
  His workday weariness.

The crown sat softly, only rings
  Of baby hair agleam
With lusters dropt from angels' wings
  And starlight down a dream.

The thorn tree was a seedling still,
  And with laughter's frolic chime
The Christ Child did His Father's will,
  As when, of elder time,

A ruddy lad in Bethlehem
  Was keeping sheep and played
Blithe music on his harp to them
  Before the psalms were made.

—Katharine Lee Bates

THE CARPENTER

Silent at Joseph's side He stood,
And smoothed and trimmed the shapeless wood.
And with firm hand, assured and slow,
Drove in each nail with measured blow.

Absorbed, He planned a wooden cask,
Nor asked for any greater task.
Content to make, with humble tools,
Tables and little children's stools.

Lord, give me careful hands to make
Such simple things as for Thy sake.
Happy within Thine House to dwell
If I may make one table well.

—Phyllis Hartnoll

✛

STRANGE HAPPENINGS TO THE YOUNG CHILD
(As Told by Mary, His Mother)

Out of the hundreds of babies taken to the Temple by their mothers in compliance with the law, ours was identified today as the Messiah. An old man, who gave his days and nights to prayer, said the Lord had revealed it to him that this was the Christ and that the Child would cause the rise and fall of many in Israel.

An aged prophetess, who also spent much time in prayer in the Temple, took the Babe out of the old man's arms and held Him up and showed Him to the people, telling them that it was He that would bring redemption to Israel.

. . . . . .

Back in Bethlehem. Joseph came to me with awe in his face. "Mary," he said, "what did the old prophet in the Temple mean when he said 'that a sword would pierce your own heart'?"

"I do not know, Joseph," I answered; "but if this is the Messiah He cannot fail; it cannot mean that."

. . . . .

A caravan of learned men from the far East drew up at our door today, led, they said, by a star; and dismounting, made obeisance as they approached; then, falling down before the Child, they worshiped and called him King of the Jews and poured out at his feet costly presents. They quoted our prophets who had foretold the birth of the King in Bethlehem.

When the Wise-men had gone, we looked at each other, and then at the gifts, and were lost in wonder.

Joseph borrowed a roll and we read over and over the Scripture that led the Wise-men to our door.

"God did not forget, did he, Joseph?" I said. "We forgot."

Little Bethlehem, they shall sing of thee in days to come. Thou shalt live because this Child was born in thee.

. . . . .

Joseph came to me trembling today.

"What is it, Joseph?" I said.

"Herod plots to kill the Child," he said, "and what can humble people like we are do to foil the king?"

I thought of the sword that was to pierce my heart. Was this it? But God could foil the king.

"It will be all right, Joseph," I said. "Fear not."

. . . . .

I knew it would be all right. God did keep us in mind; he came to us in a dream last night and told us to flee into Egypt; that Herod is bent on destruction. We had our hearts set on going back to Nazareth, but the joys of home cannot now be ours. For the Child's sake we will gladly be exiles. God leads.

. . . . .

In Egypt. Lonely days. Everybody and everything is strange. But there are many Jews here and Joseph finds work; yet we are praying for the day when we can return. We say nothing about who the Babe is, but when we are by ourselves we are full of questions that neither of us can answer.

. . . . .

Two years in Egypt and now we are going home. Blessed be God—we are going home! They are removed who sought the Child's life. Oh, how delightful to get home!

. . . . .

Home! Home in Nazareth. God is good. The Child is safe.

. . . . .

Jesus was walking before we left Egypt. And now He is trying to talk. I cannot get used to it. Who am I to be teaching the Messiah to walk and talk? But, oh, it absorbs me!

. . . . .

I watch for signs as He grows. It is so wonderful to be living in a state of expectancy, not knowing what might break forth at any moment. Sometimes I am perplexed.

. . . . .

Thoughts of who He is have overwhelmed me today. I am under restraint. With what discipline shall a mother guide such a child? That Holy Thing that shall be born of thee shall be called the Son of God, declared the angel. Son of God! And here am I rearing the Son of God!

Jesus is twelve years old and we are taking Him up to the feast at Jerusalem. We are wondering if He will do just as other boys do at the feast; we wonder if He knows who He is. We say little things sometimes to test Him, but cannot be sure from his answers how much He knows.

. . . . .

In Jerusalem. As far as we can see He is taking it just as other boys, greatly enjoying it, respectful and reverent. There are no signs.

. . . . .

There was a sign today. He was the center of attraction in the Temple. The rabbis gathered around Him and listened to His questions and answers, and wondered.

. . . . .

He had been lost from us three days and we had been searching for Him everywhere, fear torturing our hearts that some evil had befallen Him. How we upbraided ourselves for having brought Him up to Jerusalem!

And when we found Him, there he stood in the Temple surrounded by a great company of people, and apparently unconcerned about our anguish.

When we asked Him why He had not been more considerate, He said:

"Why, had you not considered that I must be about my Father's business?"

I am storing that up in my heart. Some day I may understand what it means.[3]

[3] From *His Mother, A Story of Our Lord*, by G. M. Anderson. Published by the Bethany Press, St. Louis, Mo. Used by special permission of the heirs and publishers.

HOME AGAIN IN NAZARETH

By

Cynthia Pearl Maus

YEARS had passed since that night when Joseph and Mary entered the strange land of Egypt, sent thither by Jehovah's warning to find refuge from the jealous hatred of King Herod.

You remember that Herod, angered because the Wise-men had departed into their own country without returning to Jerusalem to tell him where the new-born King might be found, sent his soldiers out with an edict to put to death all the male children in Palestine that were "two years old or under." In this cruel way he sought to rid himself and his country of the claims of this prophetic Boy King to the throne of Israel.

When this foul edict had been accomplished Herod felt secure. He did not know that the Baby King he sought to kill was far away in the strange land of Egypt, learning there to walk, and talk, perhaps, now and then, even a word of the land that was sheltering Him from the wrath of a wicked and cruel king.

Here in this strange land Jesus learned also to speak the mother tongue of His own race, the language of His mother and father, and of the land to which He would some day return. How long the Holy Family remained in Egypt is not accurately known. It is estimated, however, that Jesus was perhaps three or four years old when the voice of an angel came again to Joseph, saying:

"Arise, now, and take the young Child and his mother, and go into the land of Israel, for they are dead that sought the young Child's life."

What exciting, happy days must have preceded that homeward journey! There was no need for secrecy or a hurried departure this time, such as had attended the flight of the Holy Family into Egypt. "Going home!" How good these words sounded to Mary and Joseph; and how happy they were as they set out with their little Son to return to their native land.

Leaving Egypt in the company of a caravan of merchants who were bound for far-away Syria, Joseph had planned to leave the caravan when he came to the boundary line of Palestine—to go first to the Holy City, Jerusalem, there to worship once more in the Temple. When he reached the border of Israel, however, he learned that Archelaus reigned in his father Herod's place. And being afraid for the safety of the young Child, he continued with the caravan along the road of the level plain which bordered on the Great Sea.

After several days of journeying northward, the road turned sharply east, and they began to ascend the slopes of Galilee. "Almost Home!" was the reply that Joseph frequently made to this little Son who was seeing for the first time the springtime beauty of His native land.

"See," said Joseph. "Yonder on the left is the rocky top of Mount Carmel, jutting out into the sea. And yonder are the foothills of the summit of higher hills and mountains which surround Nazareth, where we are to live." Thus Joseph pointed out to the boy Jesus and his travel-weary mother, important landmarks along the way as they continued steadily on toward their journey's end.

Up and up wound the road toward Nazareth, which is built on the west slope of a bowl-shaped valley encircled by hilltops. Soon they reached the plain of Esdraelon, a famous battle-ground of Hebrew history; and before long they found themselves at the outskirts of the village.

It was the evening hour when they arrived, and as of old, Mary noted that the women were coming down to the well to draw water for the evening meal. The caravan came to a halt so that the travelers and animals alike might be refreshed, while two maidens stepped out and offered their jars of water to the weary strangers, as is the custom even unto this day in Oriental lands.

In the confusion of the scene the movements of Joseph and Mary and the young Child passed unnoticed; but as Joseph reached up to help Mary dismount from her donkey, the shy yet fearless face of their beautiful young Son attracted attention, and soon they were surrounded by a group of eager kinsmen and friends who welcomed them home.

There was no lack of invitations for places to stay during those first days in Nazareth, until Joseph could repair the old home, which had fallen into decay during their absence. After the first greetings were over the travelers passed on through the village streets, escorted by the women water-carriers, who paused, now and then, at the doorways of old friends to call greetings and to share with them the good news that Joseph and Mary had returned.

The lamps in the homes in which they remained as guests during those first few nights burned longer than usual, as Mary and Joseph greeted other neighbors who called, and shared with them some of the strange and thrilling experiences that had been theirs during their flight into Egypt, their sojourn in that distant land, and their caravan journey homeward with the merchants bound for Syria.

After the first general excitement caused by their return had died away, the family settled down in their repaired home to the regular duties of everyday living, happy to be back again safely with the friends and kinsmen of other years.

There were many trips which Jesus made with His mother to the fountain to the East of the village for water. Meanwhile Joseph worked again at his carpenter bench as of old, making things not only to supply the needs of his neighbors, but also, in his leisure time, things that would make the keeping of their humble home happier and lighter for Mary.

Occasionally Jesus went with His mother or father to the market place, which to His boyish eyes was a most interesting spot with its small shops and stalls where goods of every kind and sort might be bartered for.

And on the Sabbath day He went with his mother and father to the synagogue for worship and the reading of the law. But His happiest hours were spent in the hills surrounding Nazareth. There He often went with His mother and father, or with some neighbor lad toward the end of the day to watch the sun as it sank to rest in a gloriously colored sky. And when He grew older He was allowed to picnic there with other of the village boys as they gathered wild fruits and berries for friends and family.

On cold and rainy days He worked with His father in their small carpenter shop, where He learned to shape the oxen's yokes and plows. As He grew older He attended the village synagogue school, where at the feet of the rabbi He learned not only to read and understand the law of His people, but also to write the language of His native land. And thus in the work and play of happy, care-free childhood He grew, as Luke tells us, "in wisdom, and stature, and in favor with God and men."

✣

"CAN ANY GOOD THING COME OUT OF NAZARETH?"

INTO the little carpenter's shop with its saws and hammers and planes, smelling of fresh new lumber, there came many kinds of people on many errands.

All of the rich and educated Jewish people who lived in the cities, or even in other parts of Palestine, despised and made fun of Nazareth for no better reason, perhaps, than that it was small and poor and out of the way. There was a saying among outsiders like this, "Can any good thing come out of Nazareth?"[4] It was always said with a smile and a wise shrug, as though to say: "Of course not. Why expect any?"

And yet life in Nazareth went on much as it did in other places. Caravans from far-off places passed through and sometimes stopped for water or food; travelers on foot or on donkey or camel often stopped, and quite often there came peddlers, story-tellers, or teachers with their small group of followers who would stop overnight and talk with anyone who was interested in what they had to say. In fact there was a guest-room[5] in Nazareth, a room furnished and kept clean and attractive for the chance traveler. If a guest came, the whole of little Nazareth was like to stand around and gossip and watch and listen to all that went on, in the hope that something might be learned or, perhaps, out of pure curiosity. . . .

Sometimes a wheel was broken on the rocky road or a saddle must be mended. Then a carpenter was needed and the owner of the wheel or saddle

---

[4] For the prevailing opinion see John 1:45-46.
[5] Hospitality was considered a great privilege and duty. See Mark 14:14.

came to father Joseph's shop. The little boy Joshua[6] had a fine chance to see and hear all that went on, for He could stand close to father Joseph and hand him a tool now and then.

Once, the little boy remembered when He was a man, it was a poor Jewish man who came with a broken yoke complaining bitterly that he had been robbed and beaten by tax-collectors who had overtaken him, and, declaring that their horses needed fodder, had taken all that he had and left him beaten and half dead by the roadside.

"They said," cried the man, wiping the blood and dust from his face with his arm, "that a dog of a Jew is fit to be kicked, and they struck me with my own ox-yoke rather than touch me with their hands."

"Did you not tell them," cried father Joseph, "that you had already paid your full tax to Cæsar and that nothing more was due the government from you for another year?"

"What cared they for what I could say or for what is just and right? God smite them," he cried, fiercely, lifting his clenched hands. "God curse ——"

"Speak not of God's vengeance in this place," father Joseph said, sternly, glancing at the little Boy. "Run, lad, and tell your mother that one is here who needs her balsams and healing lotions and stay you with the little ones while she comes to this poor man's help. He has been cruelly treated and needs pity and care."

Joshua ran quickly, glad to escape to the sweet peace of the little house, from the sight of the angry, bloodstained man whom the arrogant Publicans had beaten and robbed. Later, when the man was sleeping, father Joseph told Him some things that helped Him to understand and filled His heart with a great longing and desire to help all men everywhere to be merciful and just.

"We—I mean the Jews—my Boy," father Joseph had said, "are ruled by the Romans. There was a time, hundreds of years ago, when we lived happily in this beautiful country and were ruled by our own kings. The country was ours. But we were too few and too weak, too quarrelsome and proud, too wicked and forgetful of God if the truth were told, to resist our enemies and they swept down on us from the north in all the savagery of cruel warfare and carried away our people into slavery. That was but the beginning of our troubles. First came the Assyrians, those bold, fierce, fighting-men who plundered our cities and drove before them like cattle our bravest and best men and women. Less than half of our people remained in their own country. Then, as if God had altogether forgotten us, came the Persians, who, having conquered the Assyrians, our conquerors, destroyed our sacred city of Jerusalem and the Temple and drove before them into captivity all whom the Assyrians had left.

"It is a sorrowful story. Perhaps you would rather not know it," said father Joseph, seeing the little Boy's wide eyes fill with tears and His lips tremble.

"No, no! Tell me all!" He cried. "They are my people. I must know how to understand."

[6] The little boy's name was Joshua ben Joseph. This means the son of Joseph. Joshua when translated into our language becomes Jesus.

"The Persians were kinder to us than the Assyrians had been," father Joseph went on. "True, we were slaves and they exacted labor and tribute from us, but after a long time some of our most loyal people were allowed to come back and begin to rebuild the Temple and the wall about Jerusalem. All might have gone well had not the Greeks, under Alexander the Great, conquered the Persians in battle more than three hundred years ago and so become our masters."

Joshua listened to His father without a word, but with such quiet intentness that He seemed to understand not just the words but all that the terrors of such merciless warfare had meant to His people. But His face was pale and His eyes shone with tears. When father Joseph paused He cried, "What, then, are we still slaves?"

"The Greeks permitted us to live in our own land but exacted from us such tribute in money and labor that we were helpless. They did worse even than that. They tried by every means in their power to destroy our faith in God and compelled us to worship their gods. They even placed a statue of their god, Jupiter, before the most holy altar of the living God in our Temple and compelled men and women to bow down to it and worship it. In this terrible trouble God helped us for He raised up a courageous Jew to defy the Greeks. This was Mattathias. He utterly refused to worship Jupiter and, together with his five brave sons, escaped to the hills and resisted the Greeks until freedom was won. Then once more, for a hundred years Israel had her own kings who ruled our people with wisdom and justice."

There was silence in the little shop broken only by the tap, tap of hammer on wood. Then Joshua said, "But these were Roman tax-collectors who beat and robbed the poor fellow yonder. How came they to be our masters?"

"Our little country, my Boy, is like the grain between the upper and the nether millstones for we lie between the great countries which are always quarreling and fighting to see which shall rule the world; the Persians, the Greeks, or the Egyptians. But after a while a new race of fighting-men challenged all of these powers. The Romans with their wealth, their skill, and their arrogant spirit came. They have an emperor whom they call Cæsar. Now Cæsar rules the world. And we, to whom God gave the land, pay tribute to him. Just now our country is divided into three parts. Each part is ruled by one of King Herod's sons under the Emperor Augustus Cæsar, who dwells in Rome. Our ruler in Galilee is Herod Antipas, the Tetrarch, a cunning, cruel coward, who has a palace not far away from this small town in the city of Sepphoris.

"We are allowed to have a governing body of our own called the Sanhedrin and our own courts, but in all large and important questions Herod Antipas is our law and master. It seems that we are permitted to live," father Joseph went on, bitterly, "that we may make money to pay taxes to the Romans, and that our young men may fill their armies with slaves and soldiers. We suffer always such treatment as this poor man has suffered and we are powerless. We who were once so great and glorious! We who are God's chosen people!

O God! Our God!" father Joseph prayed with the tears streaming down his cheeks, "send us a Saviour to lead us out of this bondage. Forsake us not but remember Thy people how they suffer. Fulfill Thy promises in us, Our Gracious Jehovah.

"Yes," he added in a calmer tone to the wide-eyed little Boy, "God has promised us a Messiah who will right our wrongs and help us to take our true place and power in the world. When He comes, all wrong shall be righted and we shall dwell in peace and happiness."

No more was said for a long time. The little Boy seemed to be thinking too deeply to ask any more questions. When evening came the poor man wakened and seemed much happier. Mother had washed his wounds, bound them with clean strips of cloth, and given him food. He was almost cheerful. "It is good," he said, "almost worth being robbed and beaten, to find such kind and generous friends. I shall never forget, and sometime if I can serve you in return I shall do so."

"Leave the yoke," said father Joseph. "I will mend it and my work shall cost you nothing."

"The God of our fathers forfend and bless thee. The Lord bless thee and keep thee," said the man, earnestly.

That evening when they were sitting in the twilight upon the roof of their small home Joshua crept close to His mother and whispered. "When I am a man I shall help the poor and the sick, as you do. But why does God let us suffer so? Why does He let us be hurt?"

"I know not, little Son, except that He wishes us to learn to be pitiful and tender-hearted."[7]

✤

THE TEMPLE BEAUTIFUL

By

Edna Madison Bonser

IT WAS very early when the little Boy awoke. Only a faint glow in the eastern sky showed that it was morning. A sweet coolness and quiet lay over the crowded city that, with the full coming of the day, would hum with the voices of the joyous pilgrims to the Feast of the Passover.

It had been dark when the group from Nazareth had reached Jerusalem. Father Joseph, mother, and the little Boy had gone at once to the home of a kinsman, where, after bathing and eating, they had slept, tired from their long hard journey.

For days and days the little Boy had been thinking of the Temple. But when at last they had climbed the hills beyond Bethany, where in daylight the first

[7] From *The Little Boy of Nazareth*, Edna Madison Bonser. Copyright 1930. Published by Harper & Brothers. Reprinted with special permission.

glimpse of its snowy marble walls and golden turrets might be caught, it had been quite dark, a deep, soft engulfing blackness through which they walked slowly, for the road was crowded with travelers.

Too weary for dreams, the little Boy slept through long hours, but awoke with the thought, "Today I shall see the Temple, the house of God, the wondrous, holy Place of Peace." There was no more sleep for Him.

He had lain close to father Joseph through the night, and now, as He stirred and sat up, father Joseph woke also and said, softly, "What is it, Son? Is it morning so soon?"

"The sky is growing bright," answered the little Boy. "It will soon be full day. Couldn't we creep softly down and be the first to enter the Temple of worship?"

"A priest is standing on the highest pinnacle of the Temple, watching for the first rays of the sun that he may give the signal to the trumpeters. When we hear the silver trumpet's call we shall know that the great gates of the Temple will swing open and we may go in. Let us wait here for the call. From this roof we can see the sunlight as it strikes the pinnacles of the Temple and the white-robed priests as they go about their duties. The sound of the chanting will come to us here also. Then, when it is fully day, we may go together to worship."

So while the dawn strengthened and the shadows of darkness disappeared, the little Boy and father Joseph watched and waited.

"Long, long ago," father Joseph almost whispered so that he might not disturb others who were sleeping, "our people built the first Temple in the wilderness. They had but lately escaped from Egypt and were poor and without suitable building-material, but God directed them. Only such as were wise and willing-hearted were permitted to help build that first place for worship as though God would have no grudging, selfish service." . . .

While they talked together the light had grown stronger. The sky was full of a soft, clear radiance. A little breeze stirred the trees and vines from which came the first low calls and twitter of sleepy birds. The tips of the spires of the Temple shone like imprisoned stars. A little stir and murmur rose from the streets.

"What became of that Tabernacle?" asked the little Boy.

"In a few years our people reached the Promised Land, and built their homes and worshiped at many altars, in high places, under oak trees and beside streams. I do not know what became of the Tabernacle. It had been built so that it could be taken down and carried to a new location. So I have no doubt it was used for many years. But after many years our greatest king, King Solomon, the wise, built in Jerusalem another Temple like the first but larger and more costly. . . .

"For more than five hundred years our people worshiped there in peace, but it was destroyed at last; its walls were burned; its golden vessels and sacred symbols, the Ark and the tables of the law, destroyed or left a smoking desolation while they who had kept it with such loving devotion were driven away to exile and slavery, to years of untold suffering in foreign lands.

"For long years it lay so. Then the good King Cyrus allowed a few of the most loyal Hebrew people to return to Jerusalem and set, as best they could, its ruined walls in place and establish once more a Temple worship. This was called Zerubbabel's Temple."

"Is it the same as this Temple we now have?" asked the little Boy.

"The Temple of Zerubbabel was almost destroyed in battle when Pompey laid siege to Jerusalem and captured it for the Romans. But upon its ruins Herod the Great built this for us. He has spared no expense. Its walls are of marble and its steps and pinnacles of gold. But none who see it may fail to note the golden eagles of Rome emblazoned in the banner that floats over it, and few there are who trust or honor Herod, he who hated the Jews yet sought to win their tolerance by such costly gifts. Even the house of God must exist with Rome's permission. But hark! The trumpets! The watchman has seen the sun before its first rays have reached us. Now we may go in."

As the little Boy and mother and father Joseph made their way through the narrow steep streets of Jerusalem to the first service they were overtaken and carried along by a joyous crowd of people all in their holiday best, all eager and glad to see old friends from the country, all full of happy plans for feasting and games and gossip once the sacrifices should be made and the prayers said. But to the little Boy, the prayers, the songs, and the sacrifices were the things of greatest importance.

Leaving the dark streets, they entered the Temple through the Gate Beautiful and immediately the noise and clamor died away. A sweet peace and quiet lay over all, broken only by the chanting of the priests and the music of harps and cymbals. Looking upward from the gate was like looking up the golden ladder into heaven, the little Boy thought as He stood for a moment and gazed about Him. Before them lay the fifteen golden steps on which the singers stood, while back of these, leading up and up, were more golden steps before the most holy place. On a golden altar the smoke of a sacrifice ascended into the blue of the sky, while priests repeated the sacred prayers, and the people, kneeling with their faces toward the altar, joined their voices in the deep responses.

The little Boy dropped to His knees beside father Joseph and at once forgot everything except that He was here at last where He had longed to be, in the house of His Heavenly Father, the place where one might speak with God. He was only a little country lad, up for the first time from the village of Nazareth. He had never seen a sacrifice or heard any service other than the simple prayers and readings of the synagogue, but He felt as one who had been on a long journey and had at last come home.

Almost at once He recognized the words of the prayers, and with a glad little cry of surprise began to repeat them, His child's voice lost in the deep voices of the men, but His spirit mingling and lost in the prayers of all. What to many gathered there was but a form was to Him the actuality and reality of His being. What others *talked about, He was.* "With great love has thou loved us.

O Lord our God, and with much overflowing pity hast thou pitied us, our Father and our King. For the sake of our fathers who trusted in thee . . . have mercy upon and teach us. Enlighten our eyes in thy law; and cause our hearts to cleave to thy commandments; unite our hearts to love and fear thy name. . . . Thou hast chosen us from among all nations and tongues and hast in truth brought us near to thy great name . . . that we may lovingly praise thee and thy oneness. Blessed be the Lord who in love chose his people Israel."[8]

He knew also the creed which followed. Had not father Joseph taught it to Him almost the first words that He could speak? Reverently He repeated it. "Hear, O Israel, Jehovah our God is one Jehovah. And thou shalt love Jehovah thy God with all thy heart and with all thy soul and with all thy might. And these words which I command thee shall this day be upon thy heart."[9]

Then with faces hidden they listened to the priestly benediction so beautiful and comforting, "Jehovah bless thee and keep thee. Jehovah make His face to shine upon thee and be gracious unto thee. Jehovah lift up His countenance upon thee and give thee peace."[10]

The service was ended. The people passed out of the Temple, but the little Boy went out only to return again and again. This was what He had hungered for. This was the beginning of desire and a clear purpose that grew in Him until the end.[11]

✝

THE HIDDEN YEARS AT NAZARETH

"THE hidden years," as Jesus' boyhood days are commonly called, have found expression in this hymn by Allen Eastman Cross. The words are addressed directly to the "soul of youth," and challenge him to live for truth.

Dr. Cross was born in Manchester, New Hampshire, in 1864. After studying at Phillips Andover, Amherst College, and the Andover Theological Seminary, he became the associate pastor of the Old South Church at Boston; and later still the pastor of the First Congregational Church at Milford, Massachusetts, serving there for eleven years. In 1925, after a slow journey around the world, Dr. Cross returned to his ancestral home in Manchester, where he has since remained, devoting his time to writing.

Speaking of the circumstances that contributed to his writing the hymn "The Hidden Years at Nazareth," Dr. Cross says: "I had always meditated on

[8] *The Prayer.* The words of the prayer used here are quoted from *Sketches of Jewish Life*, Edersheim, page 269.

[9] *The Shema.* This was called the Jewish creed. See Deuteronomy 6:4-9.

[10] *The Benediction.* The words of this benediction could be spoken only by a priest of the tribe of Aaron—Numbers 6:24-26.

[11] From *The Little Boy of Nazareth*, by Edna Madison Bonser. Copyright 1930. Used with permission of Harper & Brothers, publishers.

the unrecorded life of Jesus. It seemed to me pathetic that we knew so little of the youth of one whom we so loved. When I was in Palestine, the most challenging places to my imagination were not the monumental shrines of tourist debate, but the open hills and waters of Galilee; and most of all the little green cup of Nazareth, high up in the hills.

"I first saw it from my camp at Jenin, across the old war plain of Esdraelon. And then it seemed like a chalice of peace. And the more, since our Prince of Peace lived there!

"Wordsworth says that 'poetry is emotion remembered in tranquillity.' The emotion of this sacrament came as I wandered through the old streets, and up the hill above the town, and found red anemones looking out from among the rocks, as the Boy Jesus must have seen them.

"But the tranquillity for expression did not come till years afterward. President Earl Harper of Evansville had urged me to write a new hymn on the youth of Jesus. Then as I brooded on those unrecorded years, my first communion of the heart at Nazareth came back, and the words to express it were given to me."

The tune "Nazareth," which is associated with this hymn, was composed by H. S. Harts in 1927.

> The hidden years at Nazareth,
> How beautiful they seem,
> Like fountains flowing in the dark
> Or waters in a dream!
> Like waters under Syrian stars
> Reflecting lights above,
> Repeating in their silent depths
> The wonder of God's love!
>
> The hidden years at Nazareth!
> How marvelous they lie,
> As open to the smile of God
> As to the Syrian sky!
> As open to the heart of man
> As to the genial sun,
> With dreams of high adventuring,
> And deeds of kindness done!
>
> The hidden years at Nazareth!
> How radiant they rise,
> With life and death in balance laid
> Before a lad's clear eyes!
> O soul of youth, forever choose
> Forgetting fate or fear,
> To live the truth, or die with God,
> Who stands beside thee here![12]

—Allen Eastman Cross, 1927

[12] From *The New Hymnal for American Youth.* Copyright by Allen Eastman Cross. Used by permission of the author.

BRIGHTEST AND BEST OF THE SONS OF THE MORNING

THIS great devotional hymn by Reginald Heber is evidently based on the Scripture, Revelation 22:16, which refers to Jesus not only as the offspring of David, but as "the bright, the morning star."

In this hymn Mr. Heber thinks of Jesus as the "brightest and best of the sons of the morning" and invokes Him to "dawn on our darkness and lend us thine aid," as he thinks of the distance men must yet reach in their upward climb toward God.

The second stanza emphasizes how vain are the gifts men may offer to this uncrowned King of a new and different kind of Kingdom than men have yet known. While the third stanza stresses how vain are any of the offerings that humanity can bring as by bribes of homage or earthly riches they seek to secure the favor of the King of Kings.

Jesus did not leave the riches of His heavenly Father's home to come to this earth that men might merely pay homage to Him as a great king. He came as the humblest of men, His birthplace the stall of beasts, that men might know how great is the love of God for the humblest of His creation; and knowing God's love pour out their souls' adoration in righteous living. Only by such adoration can Jesus become to all men the "brightest and best of the sons of the morning."

> Brightest and best of the sons of the morning,
> Dawn on our darkness and lend us thine aid,
> Star of the east, the horizon adorning,
> Guide where our infant Redeemer is laid.
>
> Say, shall we yield Him, in costly devotion,
> Odors of Edom and offerings divine,
> Gems of the mountain and pearls of the ocean,
> Myrrh from the forest, or gold from the mine?
>
> Vainly we offer each ample oblation,
> Vainly with gifts would His favor secure;
> Richer by far is the heart's adoration,
> Dearer to God are the prayers of the poor.
>
> Cold on His cradle the dewdrops are shining,
> Low lies His head with the beasts of the stall;
> Angels adore Him in slumber reclining,
> Maker and Monarch and Saviour of all.
>
> —*Reginald Heber, 1811*

O THOU LABORER IN THE WORKSHOP

IN THE complete poem of this beautiful hymn there are four stanzas. Each stanza is a prayer uttered in behalf of some group of people. Strength is sought, in the first stanza, for men who toil—for those who work in mill and mine; for those who follow field and forest. In the next stanza, an unswerving purpose for the Church is petitioned, so that the lives of forgotten men may once more be touched.

The last two stanzas are seldom printed in hymnals, but the prayers set forth in them are none the less gripping. The third stanza asks that comfort be given to the tired hands of burdened women. And the last thought of the poem pleads for courage for the Church that it may buffet the storms day by day.

This beautiful hymn was written by William Watkins Reid, who was born in Ballinasloe, Ireland, in 1890. He received the Bachelor of Science and Master of Arts degrees from the New York University. He has served as Director of the News Service for the Board of Foreign Missions of the Methodist Episcopal Church; and as president of the Religious Publicity Council. He is now living in New York City.

The tune "Balducci," which is used with Mr. Reid's poem, was composed by A. H. Mann. If this great hymn is unfamiliar to you, make it a familiar friend by learning and singing it frequently. Number 27 in *The Abingdon Hymnal.*

> O thou Laborer in the workshop,
> Carpenter of Galilee,
> Thou hast wearied in the noon-heat,
> Thou hast hewn the stubborn tree;
> Strengthen, Lord, Thy brother toilers,
> Those who work in mill and mine,
> Those who follow field and forest
> Threshing grain and felling pine.
>
> O Thou Traveler on the highway,
> Without place to lay Thy head,
> Thou wast often footsore, weary,
> Hungry for Thy daily bread.
> Hearten, Lord, despairing wanderers,
> Men forgot by fellow men,
> Give Thy Church unswerving purpose—
> Life to touch their lives again.

Son of God and born of woman,
  Thou didst know a mother's care;
Mother love Thy footsteps guarded,
  Mother lips first taught Thee prayer;
Comfort, Lord, the burdened woman,
  Toiling, worn, in poverty;
Her whose tired hands still labor
  For a little child like Thee.

O Companion of the boatmen,
  Fishermen had faith in Thee,
Thou didst calm the angry waters
  On yon Galilean Sea;
Grant, O Lord, Thy Church the courage
  Storms to buffet day by day,
May she pilot through life's maelstrom
  Vessels that have lost the way.[13]

—William Watkins Reid, 1927

✠

SHEPHERD OF TENDER YOUTH

"Shepherd of Tender Youth" is an old, old hymn, dating back to the second century. It was written, tradition says, by Clement of Alexandria. For years it was lost to the Western Church, and then in 1846 it was discovered and translated by Henry M. Dexter.

Though not so familiar as some other hymns. it is nevertheless challenging, meaningful, and beautiful, and growing in popularity among the young people of today.

It emphasizes the shepherding character and quality of Jesus for the young in all lands and in all ages, and stresses the answering response that the "shepherd's tender care for the young" naturally begets in the hearts of youth everywhere.

The tune to which it is most frequently sung was composed by Edward Bunnett in 1887.

Shepherd of tender youth,
Guiding in love and truth,
  Through devious ways;
Christ, our triumphant King,
We come Thy name to sing;
Hither our children bring
  To sound Thy praise.

[13] Words reprinted by permission of the author.

Thou art our holy Lord,
The all-subduing Word,
   Healer of strife;
Thou didst Thyself abase,
That from sin's deep disgrace
Thou mightest save our race,
   And give us life.

Ever be Thou our guide,
Our shepherd and our pride,
   Our staff and song;
Jesus, Thou Christ of God,
By Thy perennial word,
Lead us where Thou hast trod,
   Make our faith strong.

So now, and till we die,
Sound we Thy praises high,
   And joyful sing;
Let all the holy throng
Who to Thy church belong,
Unite and swell the song
   To Christ, our King.
           —*Clement of Alexandria, 220 A.D.*

✠

YOUNG AND RADIANT, HE IS STANDING

In this new and beautiful hymn we have one of the best of our present-day challenges to youth. It portrays Jesus as "young and radiant" as indeed He was to win the lifetime devotion of men in all ranks of life.

We feel, as we ponder the words to the first and second stanzas, that the author must have had in mind Jesus' visit to the Temple in His twelfth year and His tarrying behind there that He might learn more of His heavenly Father's will as He conversed with the learned doctors of the law; and also His return with His parents to humble Nazareth that He might there grow to manhood "in wisdom, in stature, and in favor with God and men."

The motif of the third and fourth stanzas carries us on through the incident of the cleansing of the Temple, which the priests had made a den of thieves and robbers, to His unseemly death on the cross for the ideal of God's "kingdom of love."

The words of this beautiful hymn were written as late as 1921 by Allen Eastman Cross. The tune was provided the same year by Louis Adolphe Coerne.

Young and radiant, He is standing
  As He stood at Salem's shrine;
Just a lad, a lad forever,
  With a look and grace divine.
"Tell me, how it is ye sought Me?
  Wist ye not My Father's plan?
I must be about His business,
  Would I be a Son of Man."

I can see Him humbly kneeling,
  As He knelt upon the hill;
While the waters hushed their music,
  And the night grew bright and still:
"Brothers, tell Me why ye sought Me?
  Wist ye not My Father's plan?
He must grow in grace and wisdom,
  Who would be a Son of Man."

Like a flame His soul is striking
  In His wrath at greed and shame;
"Ye have made a den of robbers
  Of the Temple to His name;
Know ye not His equal justice?
  Wist ye not My Father's plan?
He must bathe His sword in heaven
  Who would be a Son of Man."

I can see Him dying, loving
  Unto death on Calvary;
His dead hands still pleading, praying,
  Worn and torn for you and me!
"Brothers, will ye scorn and leave Me?
  Wist ye not My Father's plan?
He must wear a crown of sorrow
  Who would be a Son of Man."[14]

—*Allen Eastman Cross, 1921*

[14] Words copyrighted by the author. Used by permission.

PART III

JESUS, THE MAN

CONTENTS

PART III   SECTION I

A LOVER OF CHILDREN

✠

"Suffer the little children to come unto me, and forbid them not."—LUKE 18:16

✠

A LOVER OF CHILDREN

"And he took a little child, and set him in the midst of them: and taking him in his arms, he said unto them, Whosoever shall receive one of such little children in my name, receiveth me: and whosoever receiveth me, receiveth not me, but him that sent me."—MARK 9:36-37

✠

"Then were there brought unto him little children, that he should lay his hands on them, and pray: and the disciples rebuked them. But Jesus said, Suffer the little children, and forbid them not, to come unto me: for to such belongeth the kingdom of heaven. And he laid his hands on them, and departed thence."—MATTHEW 19:13-15

CHRIST BLESSING THE CHILDREN

By

Bernard Plockhorst

(Interpretation)

IN PLOCKHORST's "Christ Blessing the Children" we have another of those paintings that are rich in detail and pleasing to the eyes in both its foreground and background. Far in the background are the distant mountains. A bit nearer on the hillside is the faint outline of an Oriental village, while nearer a group of women, great water-jars on their heads or shoulders, come to this wayside pool for the daily supply of fresh water that must be available for their household tasks.

When you look at this picture you think always of Mark 9:36-37; 10:13-16, and of Luke 18:15-17. There are no more beautiful and revealing pictures of Jesus anywhere than these meager glimpses into His busy life of teaching, preaching, and healing; when, for a time at least, He set aside the weightier tasks of the day to receive, fondle, and bless the children.

Mothers are not likely to forget that children are nearer heaven than anyone else, for they deal with them daily in all the sweet and intimate relationships of motherhood and the home. But men, in every generation, engrossed in the outside cares of the day, often forget that the heart of a child, more truly than anything else in this world, reflects what the *mind* and *heart* of *God* is *like*. Men are prone to forget the "one thing needful," *childlike faith and love,* which Jesus made the badge of discipleship for His "kingdom of love."

Plockhorst, with true artistic instinct, pictures Jesus as sitting on the edge of a wayside pool. Just behind him is a shepherd whose flock of sheep have crowded to the pool for a drink of this cool, refreshing water.

In the background in front of Jesus are some of His disciples, one or two of them interested and understanding, the others wondering why He wastes His precious time on a bunch of children. In front of these men are the mothers, looking, with loving eyes, at this Great Teacher, who has taken time to bless their offspring. Some unknown author paid motherhood a great compliment when he said that "God couldn't be everywhere, and so He made mothers." What the races of men might have become without their refining love and influence is too gruesome even to imagine.

In front of the Master of Men are the children which men, in their haste and self-importance, so often forget. Some of them have already left their mothers and crowded close to the feet and arms of this great Lover of Childhood. Notice how the artist emphasizes Jesus' love and care for even "the least of these." All eyes, even those of the distant water-carriers, are toward or

CHRIST BLESSING THE CHILDREN—*PLOCKHORST*

JESUS AND THE CHILDREN—*COPPING*

pointing to the Master of Men; and in the near foreground what a lesson in love can be gained as one gazes into the faces of these mothers whose children the Great Teacher is so fondly caressing.

Jesus has just lifted "the least of these" into His arms, stretching out, at the same time, His free hand to the flaxen-haired child that crowds close to His knee for her share of attention and affection. No doubt this golden-haired cherub has just lisped in her childish accent, "I love you." Note the eager-eyed expression of the one at His right, who has raised her tiny hand to clasp the Master's outstretched arm, and thus assure Him that she loves Him too, and would like a little loving in return.

The one crouching by his mother's side as she sits seems to be saying, "I picked these flowers for you, mother; but I should like to give them to Him. May I?" The out-thrust of his little arm toward Jesus speaks eloquently of the love and admiration of his childish heart.

Even the tiny infant that one of the younger mothers has raised to her shoulder is stretching out his hand as though to reach and touch this Friend of Little Children.

As we look into the sweet, trusting faces of these children our own reverence for the love, beauty and purity that are childhood's gifts to the world increases, and with gladness we say with the Master of Men, "Of such is the Kingdom of Heaven."

✣

JESUS AND THE CHILDREN

By

Harold Copping

(Interpretation)

IN "JESUS and the Children," by the English painter Harold Copping, the original of which is owned by the Dayton, Ohio, Council of Religious Education, we have one of the most beautiful of all the modern paintings of this particular incident in the life of Jesus.

Except for the long, flowing robes of the Master, and His Oriental sandals, the setting of this picture might be in or about the streets of almost any modern city or town. In the center stands the Master of Men, holding in His arms a typically modern schoolgirl of kindergarten or first-grade age. By her side is an older girl with her school-bag in her hand. She looks intently into the Master's face and one hand is slightly outstretched as though she might be in the act of asking Him a question or contributing a bit of information that she possesses about the matter under discussion.

Directly in front of the Great Teacher are two newsboys. The older one seems to have disposed of his papers; but the younger one still has a quantity to sell. Perhaps, like many of the newsboys of today, they may have been arguing about which street corner is theirs, or of an unfair advantage that one has taken in swiping a customer belonging to the other. Whatever the problem is, we have the feeling that the Great Teacher has stopped to talk with them about the fundamental character issues involved.

Again, boylike, these two may have been teasing the little girl in the arms of Jesus. If so, she has dried her tears in the Master's protecting arms and is looking out at us with an expression that seems to say, that He, the Lover of Children, is making things all right. The boys will understand, now, why they must not tease her any more because she is timid and afraid.

The face of Jesus is a masterpiece; kindly, searching, He looks directly into the face of the younger boy, who has evidently been the aggressor, while His hand rests affectionately on the shoulder of the older boy. Whatever Jesus is saying has caught not only the interest and attention of the boys, but also of the older girl as well, for her eyes are fixed upon Him. Then, too, there is an expression, not only about her face, but her bodily position and outstretched hand, that seems to say: "The Great Teacher is right. If all of us would act toward each other as He suggests, there would be no tears or heartache for anyone. Instead, all would be happy and full of joy."

The children in this picture are not the children of wealth. They represent a host of average boys and girls of the great middle class, for they are neither poorly dressed nor richly gowned. They are just average children, such as might be found on the street corner of any city or town today.

Whatever the problem may be that they are facing together, it is of absorbing interest to the three and satisfactory, at least, to the littlest one, who may not understand all that is being said, but who, nevertheless, feels that things are all right now since the Children's Friend has talked it through the boys.

As we look at this modern painting of "Jesus and the Children" we feel that if Jesus were to walk the streets, in person, of any of our cities or towns, as He did in the long ago, He would gather the children about Him and would be sincerely interested in every problem that affected their health, their happiness, and their growth in character.

THE TRIUMPHAL ENTRY

By

Bernard Plockhorst

(Interpretation)

AMONG the many beautiful paintings of "The Triumphal Entry" of Jesus and his disciples into Jerusalem at the height of His popularity none is more attractive than this one by the German painter, Bernard Plockhorst.

THE TRIUMPHAL ENTRY—PLOCKHORST

R. Plockhorst.

The event so beautifully portrayed in this picture occurred near the close of the third year of His active ministry. The fame of Jesus as a teacher, and as a worker of miracles, had spread throughout all Galilee and Judæa. Multitudes crowded about Him, and everywhere not only His disciples, but others less closely associated with Him, expected daily to see this Kingdom of God about which Jesus talked so freely and frequently, immediately established.

Luke says (19:11): "And as they heard these things, he added and spake a parable, because he was nigh to Jerusalem, and because they supposed that the Kingdom of God was immediately to appear."

After sharing with the multitude this parable of the pounds, Jesus sent two of His disciples into the village of Bethphage, telling them that there they would find a colt tied, and to release it and bring it to Him. He indicated to them that if the owners of the colt remonstrated they were simply to say, "The Lord hath need of him."

The colt was brought. They threw their garments upon it, and Jesus mounted it and sat thereon. As they drew near to the descent from the Mount of Olives just outside Jerusalem, the whole multitude began to rejoice and to praise God with a loud voice for all the mighty works which they had seen, saying, "Blessed is the King that cometh in the name of the Lord: peace in heaven and glory in the highest."

Plockhorst pictures for us this group of the disciples and followers of Jesus, which has grown into a great multitude, with palm branches in their hands, and waving them high in the air, as with joy they sing the praises of their Messiah on His way to establish the Kingdom of God. John, the beloved, with staff in hand, is leading the colt on which Jesus rides as he looks with love, adoration, and anticipation into his Master's face.

It was in the youth of the year. The children are dancing along in front of their Friend and Teacher, as they join in the song of joy and praise and strew their freshly gathered flowers in the way. Mothers, in the exuberance of their joy and forgetful of the cost, are casting before Him, as He rides, the lovely Oriental rugs that their hands have woven with such care. All around this close inner group of disciples and women that followed the Great Teacher may be seen the faces of a host who did not know Him so well, but who pushed into the foreground that they might see His face and perchance touch the hem of His garments as He rode along the highway.

In the background women, their water-bottles on their heads, may be seen crowding in to get a look at this Master Teacher whose fame has spread throughout the land.

Men have climbed into niches in the great archway through which He has just passed on His way to the city, that they might get a closer view. It was in connection with this very journey into Jerusalem that Zacchæus, the man of small stature, climbed up into a sycamore tree and was later rewarded by hearing the Master say: "Zacchæus, make haste and come down; for today I must abide at thy house." And we know that Zacchæus hastened to comply with that request, and that as a result of the visit of Jesus in his home he, too, experienced "salvation come to his house."

The hateful Pharisees crowded near to urge Jesus to rebuke his disciples for this public display of loyalty in proclaiming Him to be the Messiah, sent of God. But Jesus answered them saying: "If these shall hold their peace, the very stones will cry out."

Somehow, as we think of the sorrow and suffering that later came to the Son of God, and which forever tarnished the glory of Jerusalem, the capital city of the Jews, we find ourselves rejoicing with these disciples that this much recognition, at least, of the greatness of the Master of Men came to Him. Soon the shadows caused by the evil plotting of members of the Sanhedrin were to close in upon Him and to blot out forever this close human fellowship with those who loved Him and whom He loved.

When the dark hours of disgrace, ignominy, and shame that later overwhelmed Him came, He had, at least, the memory of this day of devotion, when, in the spontaneity of their joy, His friends proclaimed Him King of Kings, and Lord of Lords.

The face of Jesus is particularly beautiful in this painting, as is also the love, admiration, and expectancy on the face of John, the beloved. Happiness and smiles, love and adoration, are everywhere apparent on the faces of His disciples and the women who followed Him and who loved Him with an undying devotion. Joyously the children march and sing as they strew their freshly picked wayside flowers along His pathway.

Less than a week will pass ere the shadows of the cross will darken His way, bringing sorrow, heartache, and remorse to each and every one of them; but this *day of rejoicing* is unmarred with sorrow; and, save for the Resurrection morn, was the happiest day that He and His followers were to know.

✛

HEALING THE SICK CHILD

By

Gabriel Cornelius Max

(Interpretation)

GABRIEL CORNELIUS MAX is an Austrian painter who was born at Prague in 1840. He was the son of a sculptor, and studied at the Academies of Prague, Vienna, and Munich. In 1867, at Munich, he first exhibited his painting entitled, "The Christian Martyr," the picture of a young girl crucified. It caught the public attention immediately, and from that time on the artist enjoyed a steadily increasing fame. He traveled over most of Europe, won many medals, and in 1879 was made Professor of Art at the Munich Academy. Many of his pictures are on religious subjects. He has been called the "Soul-painter," because of his interest in the psychologic, the weird, and the poetic.

Among the best known and admired of his religious paintings is this one that shows Christ in the act of healing a sick child. There is a simplicity about all of Max's pictures that attracts immediate attention. He gives comparatively little heed to the background, which is nearly always severely plain, concentrating his effort rather on the faces and bodily posture of his subjects.

The background of this painting, "Healing the Sick Child," is unusually plain. No trees, flowers, rich draperies or beautifully arched porticoes relieve the severity of the scene. Just the rough and rugged stone of a walled city with a partially revealed arched entrance, or it may be the wall of some humble home near which an exhausted mother and child have come in the hope of securing a cooling breeze for the child's fevered brow.

The relaxed arms and body of the child, his slightly inclined head, all indicate a feverish sleep. He is too ill to know or care much about what is going on around him. The child is not young, perhaps two or three years old, and therefore in his fever-exhausted sleep a heavy burden for this young mother to carry far. Her posture would seem to indicate a temporary respite only from the weight of the burden she has so lovingly borne to this spot. Perhaps she has heard that the young Rabbi who has the power to heal is to pass this way, and has hurriedly taken her place near this entrance, in the hope that when the Rabbi comes He may heal the child of this ravaging fever.

There is a look of expectancy in the face of this young and beautiful mother. If He fails, all hope is gone. He must not—He cannot—fail to cool the fevered brow of this her only child, and to bring to his spent little body the glow of normal health and happiness.

The face of the Master is not upon the young mother, beautiful though she is, but rather upon the fever-stricken child, now in a semiconscious sleep as he reclines against his mother's breast and arm.

The center of interest in this picture is the Master's face and outstretched arm. He will bring healing to this little one because it is not His Father's will that even the least of these should perish. Notice the gracefully poised head and shoulders of the Christ. They are not the face and head of a weak Christ, but of One who bore men's sorrows and healed their distresses. One can almost feel the healing power surging through arm and hand as the Great Physician puts His outstretched hand upon the feverish brow of this sick child.

The mother's loving faith in Him shall be rewarded. Soon the fever will leave the hot brow and fever-parched lips of her little one; and he will again run and skip and play in the gay happiness that only little children know; and the mother in grateful remembrance of the healing strength of this Rabbi will teach her little boy to follow the Master Teacher in helpful service to others as the years of his childhood and youth slip by.

Somehow we feel the beauty and healing sympathy of this Galilean peasant Teacher as we look at this simple setting of three people near the city's wall—a loving and faith-driven mother, a desperately sick child, and the Rabbi, sent of

Photo by courtesy Kunstverlag-Trowitzsch & Sohn, Germany

HEALING THE SICK CHILD—*MAX*

God, who went about throughout all Galilee, Judæa and Samaria, healing the sick, raising the dead, giving sight to the blind and hearing to the deaf; but best of all teaching men, women, and little children both by word and example that the life abundant is a life of service to needy ones in all lands and under all conditions of life.

✠

BARLEY BREAD

"We have here but five loaves and two fishes."—Matt. 14:17

As I was going down the street to sell my loaves of barley,
A crowd of men were following the Man of Nazareth,
  And I in wonder followed too,
  Outside the town where lilies grew,
  And cyclamen, and bells of blue—
I ran till out of breath.

"Barley bread, barley bread! Who will buy my barley?
Sweet and crisp as any from the oven in the square,
  Buy my loaves of bread and fish
  Freshly caught as one could wish"—
I followed them beyond the town and found Him waiting there.

A hollow place among the hills was filled with many people,
  And there upon the trodden grass He made the men sit down,
A long way from the gates it was, and we were tired and hungry,
  A crowd of hungry people big enough to fill a town.

They came with jingling silver then, and bought my bread and fishes;
He broke them there in sight of all, and lifted up His hands.
  And everyone had food to eat—
  My fish as good as any meat,
  And barley bread, so brown and sweet,
Enough for His demands.

My heart was strangely stirred within, to see Him feed the people;
I looked and loved Him, standing there, the sunlight on His head;
  And as the sun set on the hill,
  And all the men had had their fill,
We gathered up the fragments, and went home at last to bed.

O Teacher out of Nazareth, if I have aught to give You,
Take, take the little that I have, just as you took my food,
  For till today I never heard
  A thing so moving as your word;
So take my loaves of barley bread and feed the multitude.

—Hilda W. Smith

A POET LIVED IN GALILEE

A Poet lived in Galilee,
  Whose mother dearly knew Him—
And His beauty like a cooling tree
  Drew many people to Him.

He loved the speech of simple men
  And little children's laughter,
He came—they always came again,
  He went—they followed after.

He had sweet-hearted things to say,
  And He was solemn only
When people were unkind—that day
  He'd stand there straight and lonely

And tell them what they ought to do:
  "Love other folk," He pleaded,
"As you love Me and I love you!"
  But almost no one heeded.

A Poet died in Galilee,
  They stared at Him and slew Him. . . .
What would they do to you and me,
  If we could say we knew Him?

—*Witter Bynner*

THE CHRISTMAS STREET

Red of holly, swirl of snow,
  Scurry of passing feet,
Jumble of people, high and low—
  This is the Christmas street.
White man, black man, bishop, Jew—
Christ was born for all of you!

Cherished children, a hungry tot,
  Sad little face and eye;
Chinaman, Negro, polyglot,
  Tramp and tramping by.
Rich man, poor man, beggar man, too—
Christ has died for all of you!

Santa Claus and mistletoe,
　Newsboy, fakir, cheat,
Drab and virgin, on they go—
　This is the Christmas street.
Pass and pass, O motley crew—
Christ He lives in all of you!
—Margaret Prescott Montague

THE SILENT STARS GO BY

O Little Child of Bethlehem,
　Why do your young eyes grieve?
What do your outstretched arms implore
　Of us this Christmas Eve?

"Look! In the dark streets shineth
　No Everlasting Light.
Hearts, crucified by daily fears,
　Watch through the silent night.

"Their arms hold tight to little ones,
　Tear-blinded eyes turn East,
Too tired to ask for more than crumbs,
　Dropped from My Christmas Feast."

O Little Child of Bethlehem,
　Descend to us, we pray,
And show our hearts how best to share
　With these, on Christmas Day.[1]
—Harriet Hartridge Tompkins

TO A CHILD I KNOW

Dear little child with eyes
　Like violets glowing,
And face all dimpled with
　Enchanting smile,
You have a beauty which is
　Innocently flowing
Unhindered yet by any
　Thought of guile.
Your soul is breathing
　Peaceful as a flower,
And loving me keeps me
　In touch with love.

[1] From *World Call*, December, 1934. Used by permission.

Before the world steps in
   I prize each precious hour,
That lifts my soul through you
   To God above.[2]

—J. M. Ballantyne

THE TEACHER AND HIS TASK

"O God!" I cried. "Why may I not forget?
These boys and girls entering life's battle
Throng me yet,
Am I their keeper? Only I—to bear
This constant burden for their good and care?
So often have I seen them led in paths of sin—
Would that my eyes had never open been!"
The thorn-crowned and patient One replied,
"They thronged Me, too; I, too, have seen."

"So many others go at will," I said,
Protesting still.
"They go, unheeding; but these boys and girls,
Wilful and thoughtless, yes, and those that sin,
Drag at my heart. For them I serve and groan.
Why is it? Let me rest, Lord. I have tried."
He turned and looked at me, "But I have died."

"But, Lord, this ceaseless travail of my soul!
This stress! This often fruitless toil
These souls to win!
They are not mine."
He looked at them—the look of one divine!
Then turned and looked at me: "But they are Mine."

"O God!" I said, "I understand at last.
Forgive! and henceforth I will bondslave be
To thy least, frailest little ones;
I would not more be free."
He smiled and said, "It is to Me."[3]

—Lucy Rider Meyer

[2] From *The Front Rank*. Used by permission.
[3] From *Teaching the Youth of the Church*, Maus. (Adapted from "My Burden," by Lucy Rider Meyer.)

"AS YE DO IT UNTO THESE"

In little faces pinched with cold and hunger
　　Look, lest ye miss Him! In the wistful eyes,
And on the mouths unfed by mother kisses,
　　Marred, bruised, and stained His precious image lies!
And when ye find Him in the midnight wild,
　　Even in the likeness of an outcast child,
O wise men, own your King!
　　Before His cradle bring
Your gold to raise and bless,
　　Your myrrh of tenderness,
For, "As ye do it unto these," said He,
　　"Ye do it unto Me."

　　　　　　　　　　　　　　　—*Author Unknown*

✛

"SUFFER THE CHILDREN TO COME UNTO ME"

By

Cynthia Pearl Maus

THERE are no more beautiful stories in the New Testament than those that tell us about Jesus' love for and appreciation of childhood. To understand this affection for children one needs to read not only Mark's and Luke's story of Jesus blessing the "little ones," but also His many miracles of healing performed for childhood's sake.

Some unknown writer has suggested that Jesus' unusual concern, not only for the temporal welfare of the children of his day, but also for their spiritual unfoldment as well, may have arisen out of the memory of the tragedy to the male children of Bethlehem that occurred at the time of His own birth.

Not in all history is there a more diabolical monster than the wicked Herod who ruled Palestine with an iron hand at the time those wise men from the East, came seeking the uncrowned King as they followed His star in the sky. One of Herod's worst manias was his senseless jealousy of any and every possible claimant to the throne which he so vilely disgraced. Everyone who came his way, anyone who crossed his fancy as a possible pretender was immediately slain. Priests, nobles, members of the Sanhedrin, political suspects, even the members of his own family—those he feared, those he loved, and those he hated all fell indiscriminately before his cruel will. He smote, he starved, he strangled, he tortured and he burned the innocent and the guilty alike.

Whether or not the memory of the incident His own mother had told Him, of Herod's wicked slaying of all the male infants two years and under at the time of His birth, had anything to do with Jesus' love and care for children we may only surmise; but we do know by various accounts that He loved them, as they loved Him; that He took them in His arms, gave them His richest blessing, and used them as a type of the qualities of character that His followers must come to possess, if they were to become worthy representatives of God's "kingdom of love."

Mark (9:33-37) gives us an interesting picture of what happened to the disciples immediately following that marvelous experience of the Transfiguration, which we may easily reconstruct by reading between the lines. He says: They (Jesus, Peter, James and John) came down from the Mount of Transfiguration. At the foot of the mountain they joined the other disciples, and they wended their way into the city of Capernaum. When they were in Capernaum and in the house, Jesus turned to His disciples and said, "What were ye reasoning about on the way?" And they hung their heads, for they knew that they had been arguing, the one with the other, as to who should be *greatest* in this Kingdom about which Jesus talked so frequently.

Then Jesus sat down and called His disciples to Him, and said: "If any man would be first, he shall be last of all, and the servant of all." And He took a little child, just an ordinary child, and set it in their midst. Then taking it in His arms He said unto them: "Whosoever shall receive one of such little children in my name, receiveth me, and he that receiveth me, receiveth not me, but him that sent me."

And again in the tenth chapter of that same Gospel, Mark tells us about the mothers bringing their children to Jesus that He might bless them; and how these same quarreling disciples rebuked them. But Jesus, when He saw what they were doing, was angry, and said unto them: "Suffer the children to come unto me; and forbid them not: for to such belongeth the Kingdom of Heaven. Verily, I say unto you, Whosoever shall not receive the Kingdom of God as a little child, he shall in no wise enter therein. And he took them in His arms, and blessed them, laying His hands upon them."

This incident takes on even greater significance when we remember that it occurred when Jesus was busiest, for He was on His way to Jerusalem to suffer and die for the redemption of mankind.

Evidently some mothers had been standing on the edge of the crowd that thronged Jesus, listening to His words and watching what He did. He was so good, and strong, and brave, and pure that they felt they would like to have this kind-faced Rabbi lay His hands in blessing upon their children. They talked it out among themselves, got together in a little group, and began to push forward toward Jesus, leading their children by the hand and carrying the little ones in their arms.

When the disciples saw what was happening they hurried forward and began to say to these mothers that the Master was too busy and preoccupied with great things pertaining to the Kingdom to be bothered with children. Then Jesus, looking around, saw what was happening, and how quickly His disciples had forgotten the object lesson He had given them a day or two before about "being the servant of all." His eyes flashed. "Let the children come to Me," He said, sweeping his disciples aside. "Do not hinder them. For the heavenly Father's Kingdom belongs to those who are childlike in spirit."

The children and mothers hurried forward at the Rabbi's command, and He stooped down and took them up, one by one, and gave them His blessing.

When the children had had their share of the Master's love and benediction, He rose up immediately, turned His face toward Jericho and Jerusalem; toward the enemies that were plotting His death; toward all the struggle and agony that lay ahead of Him; but in His heart He held the memory of the happy, care-free faces of these "littlest ones," through which His Father's "Kingdom of Love" was to be builded the world around.

✛

THE MOTHER OF THE LAD WITH THE LOAVES AND FISHES

It was late sunset beside the Sea of Galilee. Peace and beauty lay all around, but there was no peace in the heart of the woman who walked hurriedly past Bethsaida and Capernaum to a rock commanding a view of the sea. For Miriam, the wife of Jonas the fisherman, was hopeless and bitter to the point of despair. She was still a young woman, but her youth showed only occasionally in her dark eyes. She threw herself upon the rock and began to weigh the years of her life in the balance, beginning with the old days in Capernaum.

She and Lois, orphaned early, made their home with their Aunt Hannah, where had been quiet and beauty which they had sensed even as children. From their aunt they learned tapestry-making, and the two girls grew to womanhood happy and busy. Sitting alone in the court one day, Miriam looked up and saw a young man standing in the gateway. He was a fisherman, carrying a large reed basket.

"We do not wish anything today," she said. But he did not go away, simply stood awkwardly, looking at her. Finally he said: "I am Jonas of Bethsaida. What is thy name?" "Miriam," she answered proudly. "We make fine tapestry for sale." Jonas said, "I have my own house and soon I shall buy a boat and catch only large fish." Then he went away. She thought of how she would tell Hannah and Lois when they returned from market, and how they would all laugh together; but somehow when they returned, she said nothing. After that, Jonas came every week to stand in the gateway, but always when she was alone. Once he said, "I fear thou would'st find my house too small and dark for thee."

Meanwhile Miriam became more skillful with her needle and Hannah watched with pride. Then the stroke fell and Aunt Hannah did not answer when they called. When they returned from the burial a man awaited them who said Hannah had once borrowed money from him, and while she had repaid most of it, there was still some due and he would have to take all her personal belongings. They were helpless in his hands. Then it was that Lois announced her intention of going to Tiberias to work with Annas, who made fine embroidery for royalty and nobles. Miriam would not go, for she saw only horror and sin in the city of Herod. Then she said to Lois, "I can marry," and told her of Jonas.

So Lois went alone to Tiberias and Miriam married Jonas, the poor fisherman who lived in such a rudely built house of only two rooms, the only furniture being a battered clay lamp, the mill at the doorway, a table, a pallet, and a stool. But Miriam kept the hut clean and then sat down at her embroidery-frames, hoping for happiness and joy. But bitterness came instead. Her work became endless—water to carry, meal to grind, fish to clean for the market, until there was no time and her fingers became too rough for the fine silks.

So time passed, and before Jonas could buy his own boat there were hungry mouths to feed and grim, biting poverty came. The children were sound and strong; Jonas looked upon them with pride, but Miriam had but a weary, passive affection for them. Once in a while she would see the sails upon the sea and would gaze toward Tiberias, wondering about her sister Lois. She had never come back, so it must have been as beautiful as she had dreamed.

As soon as little Mark, the eldest, was old enough Jonas took him in the boat, and when he was twelve years old he was allowed to go to Capernaum to sell fish. One evening he came running home quite excited. "I could hardly sell my fish. Nobody was at home. And then all at once I saw the crowd before Simon's house. They were standing away out in the street. I tried to get in, but no one else could get near the door. And just then I saw four men carrying a pallet. They went close to me and I could see the sick man upon the bed. He had palsy. They tried to get in to the Rabbi, but the people were so crowded they could not move them, so the bearers went up the outside stairs to the roof and lifted some tiles and let the sick man right down in front of the Rabbi. In a few minutes he came out, walking. The Teacher had healed him."

"Come, eat your supper, Mark," Miriam said, wearily. It had been a hard day. But Jonas was curious. "What does the Rabbi look like?" "I do not know. I could not see Him." Some time later he had another strange story to tell them, when he told of the healing of the nobleman's son in Capernaum. "I should like to see the Rabbi," he said.

But it was of something different, more strange and important to Miriam, that she had to think about this evening. She had heard from Lois, who was well and happy and prosperous. She had never married and still worked with Annas. Would not her sister come to her? It was not yet too late. So Miriam fought her battle, thinking of all the comforts and of the ease that might be hers, but there were Jonas and the children. So she wrestled with her problem, but could reach no decision. Perhaps tomorrow she could think more clearly.

She worked all morning and at noon little Mark came running in and threw his basket down. "Mother," he cried, "the Rabbi I told thee of—the one who healed the palsied man and the nobleman's son, is over there, across the sea on the mountain-side, and everyone from Capernaum and Bethsaida is going over to see Him and hear Him teach. Mother, wilt thou let me go? I must see Him." His voice was passionate with eagerness. "Thou must eat first," said Miriam. "But I am not hungry. Mother, I dare not wait! I must overtake the crowds now. If I tarry I may miss Him!" "Still, thou must eat," Miriam replied, firmly. "Here," taking a handful of the barley cakes she had just baked and two of the small fish on the table, "take these with thee. Thou canst eat them on the way. But be not later than sundown returning."

The afternoon passed, Miriam still busy, still preparing, still warding off the last surrender. The sun began to go down and Mark had not returned. She started to find him, and came to the shore where the boats were for crossing, and asked for help. Soon she was on the eastern bank and went up the way directed, where the boatman said there must have been thousands following the Rabbi. At last she reached the crest of the hill and stopped, for she saw a great multitude seated, listening to a Man who stood before them. The sunset light rested upon His face as He spoke. She crept closer and saw suffering there, longing, a lonely sorrow that does not speak. Also love and sympathy, infinite strength. Stronger than all, there was the rare light of sublime and holy joy, of the peace that passeth understanding.

He stopped speaking and several men drew near Him and they talked together. Miriam could not hear what they said. Suddenly one of them turned and pointed behind him. It was then she saw Mark. He sat in the front row of people, his dark eyes riveted on the Rabbi's face. In one hand he absently clutched his open basket. Miriam could see that the food she had placed there was still in it. The eager, foolish lad; he had taken no time to eat. But all at once Miriam's eyes grew large with wonder. The young men were going among the people, separating them into groups, making paths between them. Then one of them went up to Mark and after a word took the basket from the boy's willing hand and, turning, gave it to the Rabbi. The Master gazed steadfastly toward Heaven, then beckoned to the men. They came bearing large empty baskets. There was a sudden straining forward on the part of the multitude, for out of Mark's tiny basket, held directly in their view, He was filling the others. Heaping them with loaves and fishes. Then the disciples went among the people, distributing the food, and returned to have the baskets refilled again and again. Miriam was on her knees, trembling. This Man, the Master, had taken her poor food from the hands of her own little lad, and with it had wrought a miracle. It was as if God, Himself, had reached down from His heavenly place to touch her humble hand.

At last she raised her head. The Master was watching her with clear, searching, asking eyes. With a cry she stretched forth her hands. "Master," she whispered, "thou hast opened my eyes. I will be faithful." He smiled and turned to look upon Mark, who still sat rapt, his eyes raised to the Master's face in worship. Her little lad! And she had never seen the beauty of his soul.

She rose and ran quickly over the path by which she had come. Mark came and she heard his passionate talk of wonder. She listened lovingly and the child, warmed by her new interest, showed her the adoration of his heart.

At last they were asleep and Miriam walked out by the sea. Tiberias? The old temptation was broken. Freedom! Never had she felt so free. Tapestries? Oh, blind, blind, that she had been. To her had been given tapestries of tender flesh and blood upon which to embroider the fair patterns of the soul.

Miriam knew that out of the common daily elements which her heart had so despised, there would come to her evermore now the miracle! She knew that in each day of lowly, wearing, faithful toil, she would see again the face of the Master of Men.[4]

✛

THE TEACHER'S DREAM

By

Amos R. Wells

A SUNDAY-SCHOOL teacher was dreaming. You say there is nothing strange about that. Teachers dream often and sometimes their dreams are nightmares. But this dream was different in that it contained the Lord Jesus. He was standing before this dreaming teacher with His arms oustretched, and an eager look in His eyes.

"Where are the souls of My children?" He asked the teacher.

"Here are their bodies," the teacher was able to reply. "They come to school very regularly and promptly."

Jesus took their bodies in His hands, and, lo! they turned to dust before the teacher's eyes.

"Where are the *souls* of My children?" Christ insisted.

"Here are their manners," faltered the teacher. "They are quiet and very respectful; they listen very carefully. Indeed, they are beautifully behaved."

Jesus took their manners, and they also turned to ashes in His hands.

Again the Lord repeated His question, "Where are the *souls* of My children?"

"I can give you their brains," the teacher answered. "They can name all the books of the Bible, forward and backward; they can repeat the list of the Hebrew kings. They know in order the seventy events in Your life here on earth; and they can recite the Sermon on the Mount from beginning to end. Really they are excellent scholars."

Jesus took their brains, and, lo! they dissolved into vapor and a puff of wind blew them away.

[4] By Agnes Sligh Turnbull in *Woman's World*, New York, N. Y. Used by special permission of the author.

"But WHERE are the SOULS of My children?" urged the Master, with sorrowful longing.

Then the teacher was filled with an agony that broke the bonds of slumber. "Alas!" cried the teacher, "I have done much for my children; but it is all as nothing, because I have not done the ONE THING needful. Henceforth my teaching, though it traverse many ways, shall have the ONE GOAL, and perhaps it will be given me to dream that dream again."[5]

✣

SING THEM OVER AGAIN TO ME

THIS gospel song will forever be associated in my mind with a happy experience in my own childhood. We lived for a period of time in Creston, Iowa, and there my older sister studied music under Mr. Ferguson, who for many years traveled professionally with P. P. Bliss, the great hymn-writer and evangelist, as his accompanist.

All three of us girls sang. My older sister was an alto, I a mezzo-soprano, and my younger sister a lyric soprano. Even in our childhood there was enough difference in the range of our voices that we harmonized splendidly as a trio; and as a result we were often called upon to sing for special occasions in the church.

On one such occasion Mr. Ferguson heard us sing this great Gospel song, "Sing Them Over Again to Me," as a trio; and afterwards he came up to us and told us that we had given him unusual pleasure in singing one of P. P. Bliss's favorite songs, and one that he frequently called for in revival services. Mr. Bliss felt that men needed to have the story of Jesus as the *word of life* sung to them again and again; and so he put that message into a song with its frequently recurring phrase "Wonderful words of Life." For to one who has never heard the story of Jesus, or who, through sin, has lost his way, the story of the redeeming love of our Saviour will always be "Wonderful words of Life."

> Sing them over again to me,
> Wonderful words of Life;
> Let me more of their beauty see,
> Wonderful words of Life.
> Words of life and beauty,
> Teach me faith and duty;
>
> *Refrain*
>
> Beautiful words, wonderful words,
> Wonderful words of life . . .
> Beautiful words, wonderful words,
> Wonderful words of Life.

[5] From *Missionary Tidings*, March, 1917. Used with permission of the author and publishers.

Christ, the blessed One, gives to all
Wonderful words of Life;
Sinner, list to the loving call,
Wonderful words of Life.
All so freely given,
Wooing us to heaven,

Refrain

Sweetly echo the gospel call,
Wonderful words of Life;
Offer pardon and peace to all,
Wonderful words of Life.
Jesus, only Saviour,
Sanctify forever,

Refrain

—*P. P. Bliss*

✠

FAIREST LORD JESUS

PRAISE and adoration permeate the thought of this beautiful hymn. One cannot read or sing its words without acquiring a deeper appreciation of nature and a greater glorification of Jesus Christ.

"Fair are the meadows," and "fairer still the woodlands," but Jesus is fairer and purer than either of these. "Fair is the sunshine," and "fairer still the moonlight," and the twinkling stars, but Jesus shines brighter and purer than any of these.

The last two stanzas, which are seldom printed in hymnals, make a vivid conclusion to this superlative exaltation of Jesus.

All in all, one finds in the words of this hymn a steadfast conviction; for just as surely as one witnesses around him the meadows, the sun, the moon, and the stars in their robes of splendor, just so surely is he convinced that the Son of Man shines forth in greater glory.

Although this hymn is known as the "Crusaders Hymn," it is doubtful that the Crusaders ever sang it. The words were written in 1677; and Richard Storrs Willis (1819-1900) translated the original German in which it was written and published the hymn in America in 1850.

The tune "Crusader's Hymn" was arranged by Professor Willis from a Silesian folk-song which appeared in a collection of folk songs in 1842.

Richard Willis was a musician and a newspaper man. He graduated from Yale University, and then spent some time in New York, where he edited *The Musical World* and wrote books of both sacred and secular music.

Fairest Lord Jesus,
Ruler of all nature,
O thou of God and man the Son!
Thee will I cherish,
Thee will I honor
Thou, my soul's glory, joy and crown.

Fair are the meadows,
Fairer still the woodlands,
Robed in the blooming garb of spring;
Jesus is fairer,
Jesus is purer,
Who makes the woeful heart to sing.

Fair is the sunshine,
Fairer still the moonlight,
And all the twinkling starry host;
Jesus shines brighter,
Jesus shines purer,
Than all the angels heaven can boast.

All fairest beauty,
Heavenly and earthly,
Wondrously, Jesus, is found in thee:
None can be nearer,
Fairer, or dearer
Than Thou, my Saviour, art to me.

Beautiful Saviour;
Lord of all nations;
Son of God and Son of man.
Glory and honor,
Praise, adoration,
Now and evermore be thine.
                    —*Seventeenth-century German hymn*

✛

ALL THINGS BRIGHT AND BEAUTIFUL

How beautifully and simply a childlike conception of God is set forth in this poem. Surely the author, Cecil F. Alexander (1823-1895) must have been a "lover of little children." She states in her lyric story how the Lord God made "all things bright and beautiful—all creatures, great and small—all things wise and wonderful," and then gave us eyes to see them and lips to tell about them. She must have known that a child's first response to anything he has seen is to tell someone else about it.

Mrs. Alexander was the wife of Archbishop Alexander, Primate of Ireland. Although handicapped by excessive shyness and nearsightedness, she was a woman of wide influence. She aided the sick and needy in her husband's parish by supplying them with food and clothing and medicine. She kept a garden, ran their farm, and served the whole world through her writing of poetry.

More than a quarter of a million copies of her *Hymns for Little Children* were sold in twenty years. Some of her best-known hymns are: "Once in Royal David's City," "There Is a Green Hill Far Away," "All Things Bright and Beautiful," and "Jesus Calls Us o'er the Tumult."

The tune often associated with "All Things Bright and Beautiful" is known as "Keats." It was written by William H. Monk (1823-1899). No doubt the most famous hymn tune credited to Monk is "Eventide," the melody of that beautiful hymn, "Abide with Me."

All things bright and beautiful,
  All creatures great and small,
All things wise and wonderful,
  The Lord God made them all.

Each little flower that opens,
  Each little bird that sings,
He made their glowing colors,
  He made their tiny wings.

The cold wind in the winter,
  The pleasant summer rain,
The ripe fruits in the garden,
  He made them every one.

The tall trees in the greenwood,
  The meadows where we play,
The rushes by the water
  We gather every day;

He gave us eyes to see them,
  And lips that we might tell
How great is God Almighty,
  Who has made all things well.

—Cecil F. Alexander, 1848

I THINK WHEN I READ THAT SWEET STORY OF OLD

THIS hymn was written by Jemima Thompson Luke in 1841—sixty-five years before her death. Like many hymns, it was inspired by a tune—a Greek melody or folk-song called "Athens"—which she had heard at the Normal Infant School at Gray's Inn Road. The pathos of the tune appealed to her fancy, and she searched many hymnals in vain to find words suited to the music.

Some time later, as she was riding in a stage-coach, she recalled the melody. On the back of an old envelope she scribbled the first stanzas of this hymn.

Referring to her composition, she once said: "It was a little inspiration from above, and not in me, for I have never written other verses worthy of preservation." The last two stanzas were added as an afterthought to make the hymn suitable for missionary usage. The entire hymn follows:

I think when I read that sweet story of old,
    When Jesus was here among men,
How He called little children as lambs to His fold,
    I should like to have been with them then.

I wish that His hands had been placed on my head,
    That His arm had been thrown around me,
And that I might have seen His kind look when He said,
    "Let the little ones come unto Me."

Yet still to His footstool in prayer I may go,
    And ask for a share in His love;
And if I thus earnestly seek Him below,
    I shall see Him and hear Him above.

In that beautiful place He has gone to prepare
    For all who are washed and forgiven;
And many dear children shall be with Him there,
    For of such is the kingdom of heaven.

But thousands and thousands who wander and fall
    Never heard of that heavenly home.
I wish they could know there is room for them all,
    And that Jesus had bid them to come.

I long for the joy of that glorious time,
    The sweetest, the brightest, the best;
When the dear little children of every clime
    Shall crowd to His arms and be blest.

—Jemima T. Luke, 1841

JESUS, FRIEND OF LITTLE CHILDREN

THIS hymn, "Jesus, Friend of Little Children," was written at Edinburgh, Scotland, in May, 1882, just after its author, Reverend Walter J. Mathams, had completed a trip to the Holy Land. It is one of the best known and used of all the children's hymns.

The Baptist Committee desired a new children's hymn to be included in their *Psalms and Hymns for School and Home*, then on press. The request which they sent to Mr. Mathams was so urgent that he felt at first that he could not complete it in so short a time. However, at the request of his sweetheart he went into a room alone, and in a short time six stanzas were written.

The fact that it was written just following his return from the Holy Land probably contributed unconsciously to its rich devotional character. For speaking of this subconscious influence, Mr. Mathams says, "I went through Palestine with vivid scenes of Christ and the children amongst the flowers and birds. I saw Him as the living Christ for all children of all lands and ages. Not 'above the bright blue sky,' but here on the dusty rugged road of human life, I saw Him then and I see Him now, leading all His lambs toward the infinite life. A very present Help is He."

Only three of the original six stanzas of this hymn appear in the average church and church-school hymnals. The popular musical setting is by J. H. Maunder. This hymn should always be sung in a spirit of reverent devotion.

> Jesus, Friend of little children,
>   Be a friend to me;
> Take my hand and ever keep me,
>   Close to Thee.
>
> Teach me how to grow in goodness,
>   Daily as I grow;
> Thou hast been a child,
>   And surely Thou dost know.
>
> Never leave me, nor forsake me,
>   Ever be my Friend;
> For I need Thee, from life's dawning
>   To its end.
>
>   —*Walter J. Mathams, 1882*

CONTENTS

PART III   SECTION II

THE MASTER TEACHER

—✠—

"And they were astonished at his teaching: for he taught them as having authority, and not as the scribes."—MARK 1:22

—✠—

THE MASTER TEACHER

"And Jesus went about in all Galilee, teaching in their synagogues, and preaching the gospel of the kingdom, and healing all manner of disease and all manner of sickness among the people."—MATTHEW 4:23

✛

"And seeing the multitudes, he went up into the mountain: and when he had sat down, his disciples came unto him: and he opened his mouth and taught them, saying,
"Blessed are the poor in spirit: for theirs is the kingdom of heaven.
"Blessed are they that mourn: for they shall be comforted.
"Blessed are the meek: for they shall inherit the earth.
"Blessed are they that hunger and thirst after righteousness: for they shall be filled.
"Blessed are the merciful: for they shall obtain mercy.
"Blessed are the pure in heart: for they shall see God.
"Blessed are the peacemakers: for they shall be called sons of God.
"Blessed are they that have been persecuted for righteousness' sake: for theirs is the kingdom of heaven.
"Blessed are ye when *men* shall reproach you, and persecute you, and say all manner of evil against you falsely, for my sake. Rejoice, and be exceeding glad: for great is your reward in heaven: for so persecuted they the prophets that were before you."—MATTHEW 5:1-12

CHRIST GOING THROUGH THE WHEAT-FIELDS

By

Johanan R. Wehle

(Interpretation)

AMONG the artists who have attempted to picture for us the story of Jesus going through the wheat-fields with His disciples on the Sabbath day, the one by Johanan R. Wehle, the German painter, is distinctive in its charm and naturalness.

Looking at this painting, one knows immediately that the artist had in mind Luke's story of Jesus and His disciples going through the wheat-fields on the Sabbath day (Luke 6:1-5). It is high noon, and the disciples, being hungry, have plucked some of the full heads of grain as they journeyed, and crushing out the kernels by rubbing it in their hands have satisfied their hunger by eating the ripened grain.

Certain of the Pharisees who constantly dogged the Master's steps for the purpose of finding fault with Him have taken the Teacher to task for this violation of the Jewish law of complete rest (except for attendance upon the services of the synagogue and Temple), saying: "Why do ye that which it is not lawful to do on the Sabbath day?"

Jesus answered them, you will remember, by calling their attention to the fact that David, with whose history every devout Jew was familiar, had even entered into the House of God on the Sabbath, eaten of the showbread of which it was lawful only for the priests to eat, in order to satisfy his hunger, and that he had invited those who were with him to partake also.

Again and again the Great Teacher stressed in the hearing of these scribes and Pharisees the fact that men and their needs were more important than institutions and their rituals. Nevertheless, certain of the Jews persecuted Jesus because He performed miracles of healing on the Sabbath, and allowed His disciples to violate the ordinances which they had written into the law prescribing in detail what men might or might not do on the Sabbath day.

Patiently Jesus argues the accusations through with them, closing or summing by the discussion by saying, "My Father worketh until now, and I work," and again, "The Sabbath was made for man, and not man for the Sabbath."

The full waving heads of grain in this picture, waist-high, bear eloquent testimony to the fact that the harvest-time is near at hand. One can see that John, the beloved disciple, is reaching out his hand for another head of this rich, ripened grain, notwithstanding the look of disapproval on the face of the Pharisee in the foreground, who is rebuking Jesus for His laxity in thus allowing His followers to violate the sacred laws of the Jews.

CHRIST GOING THROUGH THE WHEAT-FIELDS—WEHLE

CHRISTUS AND NICODEMUS—VON UHDE

The thoughtful, downcast eyes of the Master, as well as His caressing touch on His accuser's arm, bear evidence to the fact that He is honestly trying to answer the accusation in such a way as to help His accuser to understand that men are more important in the eyes of God than *laws* and *things.*

That this short-cut through the field of grain is not easy traveling can be seen by Peter's use of his staff as an aid in clearing a path through this densely grown field of wheat. Note how the standing grain seems to close in immediately after each person, indicating that this route provided no already cleared pathway for man or beast.

We are indebted to this German artist for illuminating for us a busy day of preaching, teaching, and healing in the life of this man who constantly "went about doing good."

✠

CHRISTUS AND NICODEMUS

By

Fritz von Uhde

THERE is no more beautiful story in all the New Testament than the one which John tells (3:1-21) of the coming of Nicodemus, a Pharisee and a Ruler of the Jews, to Jesus by night, seeking to understand this Kingdom of God idea about which the Master of Men spoke so frequently and realistically.

That not all the Pharisees were hypocrites is evident from John's story of the midnight visit of Nicodemus to Jesus. "The Unknown Disciple" pictures Nicodemus as a quiet but fair-minded man, who had no passion but for justice, and who in all his dealings with his fellows was himself just to a bone.

Why he came to Jesus by night we do not know. Perhaps it was because he was too much occupied, as a Ruler among the Jews, during the day to see Him then. Or he may have felt that the seriousness of the questions that were troubling his mind about the Rabbi's teachings concerning the Kingdom of God could not be adequately discussed amid the multitudes that constantly crowded about Jesus.

Tradition says that Nicodemus did become a follower of Jesus, if not openly during his lifetime on earth, then secretly, at least, from the hour of his midnight conversation with the Master of Men. And we do know from John's Gospel (7:50) that Nicodemus defended Jesus before the Pharisees; and that he brought spices for his burial (John 19:39) at the time of His crucifixion.

Certain it is that "The Unknown Disciple" pictures Nicodemus as among the admirers of Jesus, if not one of his open followers. And somehow as we look into the face of this man of years and wisdom, as von Uhde portrays him, we feel that it must be so. His is the open face of an honest seeker after truth and righteousness.

In von Uhde's painting the two are alone, "Christus and Nicodemus," probably in an upper room of some home in which Jesus may have been a guest while in Jerusalem. The room is simply furnished—a chair, a table, and perhaps a stool on which Nicodemus sits, an open book and some leaves of a parchment, which Nicodemus may have brought with him when he came to confer with Jesus and to try to square His teachings with the Jewish law, which as Ruler of the Jews he often had to propound.

We see but the profile of each man's face, yet that is sufficient to indicate the earnest effort which Nicodemus seems to be making to understand; and the eloquent upward pointing hand of the Master, when he says, "Verily, I say unto thee, Except one be born of water and the Spirit, he cannot enter the kingdom of God."

Fritz von Uhde, the painter of this wonderful, though comparatively modern, painting was born at Wolkenburg, Saxony, in 1848. He was an army officer until 1877, and then his passion for art led him to become a pupil of Munkacsy's. Very shortly he became the chief representative of this new, realistic school of painting; and was one of the most successful painters of religious themes in our day. He lived to a ripe old age as professor in the Academy of Art at Munich, Germany. His "Christus and Nicodemus" is regarded by art critics as among his best paintings.

✠

CHRIST TEACHING FROM A BOAT

By

Johann Heinrich Hofmann

(Interpretation)

AMONG all the beautiful pictures that cluster around the teaching ministry of Jesus, Hofmann's "Christ Teaching from a Boat" is, to me, the most beautiful.

In Jesus' lifetime the shores of this busy lake were densely populated. What is now ruins and uninhabited stretches of waste land was then teeming with the life of simple peasant people, who earned their living at modest tasks in and about the shores of blue Galilee. The beauty of the lake and the shore-line with green trees flourishing in the background present to us a truly typical lake-side scene during the lifetime of Jesus.

The rugged fishermen of the boat in which Jesus is standing, the group assembled on the beach and sitting on great boulders along the sandy shore of the lake, present just such a company as might have been drawn together at almost any hour of the day to listen with interest to the new Rabbi, whom many of them knew as the Carpenter of Galilee.

The children playing in the shallow water of the lake, the women resting from their daily toil as with folded hands and upturned faces they listen, His fishermen disciples in this and other near-by boats, together with a group of curious, questioning scribes who, with folded arms and piercing looks, now and then interrupt this comparatively unknown Teacher—all these constitute the audience of the Master of Men in Hofmann's picture.

To the right of the group of scribes and Pharisees standing on the lake shore is a rich young man, very similar in dress and posture to the young Jew who later came to Jesus, saying, "Master what good thing must I do to inherit eternal life?"

Blindness was a very prevalent disease in Palestine in Jesus' time, as it is in Oriental countries at all times, due to the heat and glare of the sun and the lack of adequate care and sanitation. At the extreme left-hand side of the picture we may dimly see the form of such a one who is being guided to Jesus for healing, perhaps.

Just what Jesus may have been talking about on this particular occasion, we do not know, for He often taught the people from a boat on the lake; but in Mark's Gospel (4:3-9) he indicates that on one such occasion Jesus shared with the multitude that followed Him the parable of the Sower:

"Behold, a sower went forth to sow; and it came to pass, as he sowed, some seed fell by the wayside, and the birds came and devoured it. And other fell on rocky ground, where it had not much earth; and straightway it sprang up, because it had no deepness of earth: and when the sun was risen, it was scorched; and because it had no root, it withered away. And other fell into the good ground, and yielded fruit, growing up and increasing; and brought forth, thirty-fold, and sixty-fold, and a hundred-fold. And he said: Who hath ears to hear, let him hear."

Whatever may have been His particular message on this day, we know that the common people heard Him gladly, because He taught them simply, yet with authority, and not as the scribes.

We know also that such a day of healing and teaching was an exhausting experience for Jesus, for near the end of the day He often sent the people away, while He and His disciples went away in the boat to another side of the lake, or He off on the mountain-side to pray.

Reverend Harold Francis Branch says: "The individual who thinks that it is easy to come in contact with men, to listen and sympathize with their troubles, to pray with them in their illnesses, to take upon his heart their burdens, to mourn with them in loss and in sin, has never thought deeply. It is exhausting work. But it is the crown and glory of our Holy Religion. . . . Every minister who is doing his work knows that it is. But it is the work of our Saviour. It is the work which Christ is doing in this picture. If the pulpit, if the church of Christ, if the ministry of Christ, retires and walks in paths removed from the multitude, then it is doomed. The tragedy of Russia is due in a large part to the spirit of aloofness and of withdrawal which for the last three hundred years has been permeating the Greek Orthodox Church. Drawing their robes in holy(?) disdain about them, the priests passed, in lofty superiority, among the people, utterly removed from them. Because of that Christ has brought the Greek

CHRIST TEACHING FROM A BOAT—*HOFMANN*

Orthodox Church of Russia down to the dust in humiliation, and has set upon her the red heel of Bolshevism."[1]

Our Saviour in Gethsemane prayed not that the Heavenly Father should take His disciples out of the world, but that He should keep them unspotted from the world, while they went about their tasks of preaching and teaching and healing all manner of diseases and heart-sicknesses.

Surely the message of "Christ Teaching from a Boat" to our hearts is, not to separate ourselves from the people and their needs, but rather to live among the people in helpful ministry to all, as by our words and deeds we testify to His love and mercy and goodness to the children of men.

✤

CHRIST AND THE FISHERMEN

By

Ernst Karl Zimmermann

(Interpretation)

OF ALL the pictures that have ever been painted to portray the influence of Jesus as a teacher, none are more impressive or beautiful than this one "Christ and the Fishermen," by the German artist, Ernst Karl Georg Zimmermann.

The artist was born in Munich, Germany, in 1852. He studied art with his father in the Munich Academy, and later perfected himself by travel and study in Belgium and Italy. He won several medals for the excellence of his work as a colorist; and in 1886 became a member of the Munich Academy of Art. He died in 1899.

If you would understand the winsomeness that Christ had for men, and the reciprocal attraction that men were to the Great Teacher, you will find it richly illustrated in this beautiful study of the sympathy, the kindliness, the understanding that Jesus embodied in his dealing with men of all ages and classes.

The setting of the picture is the shore of the Sea of Galilee. One day Jesus, passing that way, saw two stalwart young men with their aged father Zebedee in a near-by fishing-boat. Something in their faces, in their rugged, honest industry, or perhaps a chance word must have revealed to Jesus that these men were the sort of followers he needed in building His concept of God's Kingdom of Love into the hearts of men.

He spoke to them, and something in the simplicity of His unusual personality attracted them. They left their boats to a servant seen in the background, and with their father they came and sat on the shore to listen to Jesus. It is evident from the picture that the aged father brought with him some of the fishing nets,

[1] From *Christ's Ministry and Passion in Art*. Published by Harvey M. Shelley, Philadelphia, Pa. Used with permission of the author and publishers.

thinking, no doubt, to mend them while this attractive young Rabbi conversed with him and his sons.

As you look at this group, you are attracted most by the intent expression on the father's face. His mending has been forgotten for the time being, as he leans forward and looks with deep yearning into the Master's face. He is old and this gospel of love, of "turning the other cheek" is hard for him to understand. Years of a different type of thinking are not easily erased. The words of Jesus sound beautiful to his ears. He wishes that the message were all true; but how can he reconcile this new concept of a kingdom of "peace on earth and good-will toward men" with the bickering struggles that daily menace his dealing with people? On every hand the unscrupulous take advantage of those who try to be upright in their transactions.

Looking at the younger men, it is easy to distinguish John, the younger, from James. He is leaning forward, and with eager eyes searches the face of this young Rabbi. While he does not fully understand the scope of this new teaching, he is eager to learn more and to follow. We feel, as we look at John, that his eager spirit of inquiry will continue until Jesus leads him into the fullness of all truth.

James, the older brother in the background, seems to be the one slower to grasp the deeper meaning of this strange, new gospel. The artist has placed his face and form in the shadows, as if to further emphasize his inability to grasp the meaning of the Master's words.

The face of Jesus is strong, arresting, and beautiful. There is a majesty in the calm assurance of His face and figure that impels men to feel that they can safely follow Him anywhere. He is not looking at the young men, strong and virile as they are, but straight into the eyes of this aged father, as with infinite patience and kindliness the Great Teacher seeks to help him to a fuller understanding of truth. Note how His right hand seeks the wrist of the older man, while His other closes over the roughened, toil-worn fingers of the fisherman's left hand, as if to assure him that he, too, can be the recipient of this new Gospel of the Kingdom of Love.

Some one has said that "Christianity is a transaction between two personalities, that of the believer and that of Jesus Christ." How true that is. Jesus is the very heart, the center, and the source of all faith, and one's love and devotion to Him, reliance upon Him, and service to others in His name is the essence of the Christian religion.

It is difficult to escape the question, "Why should there be such personal devotion to Him on the part of men?" As we study His relationships with men and women, we come to understand that it was the confidence of Jesus in people that revealed to them qualities of character that even they did not know they possessed.

Jesus saw stability in Cephas, the shifting-sand type of fisherman, and in response he became Peter, the man of rock-like stability. He saw purity in Mary Magdalene, the harlot, and she rewarded that confidence by a life of clean, pure, unselfish devotion nowhere surpassed. In Matthew, the crafty tax-gatherer, sit-

CHRIST AND THE FISHERMEN   ZIMMERMANN

CHRIST AND THE TRIBUTE MONEY—*VAN DYCK*

ting at the receipt of customs, Jesus saw Matthew the just and flaming evangel of truth, returning to every man that he had defrauded tenfold and the author of a Gospel that will live throughout all time.

And in this picture of "Christ and the Fishermen" Jesus' confidence in these simple, slow-to-grasp fishermen was rewarded by a willingness on the part of Zebedee to dedicate these Sons of Thunder as followers of the lowly Nazarene. His servants could catch fish, that they, his sons, might leave all and become "fishers of men." So great was the confidence of Jesus in the innate and undeveloped goodness of men and women that He called forth the best in them; and qualities unsuspected on their part flowered into life-enriching fullness at the touch of His hand.

And throughout all the ages that have intervened since this wayside visit of Christ and the Fishermen, Jesus, in every generation, has called to young and old alike to "leave all and follow Him." Like these simple but sturdy fishermen of the long ago, we do not always understand fully either the Master's call or the purposes of His Kingdom of Love; but if and when we follow, there comes to us, as to these in the long ago, as a rich and compensating reward for following "in his steps," a growing understanding of what God's Kingdom of Love is, and the development of undreamed-of talents and abilities as we dedicate ourselves in service to the world's greatest Teacher, the Christ of Galilee.

With the Greeks of old, we answer in the words of the poet:

> We would see Jesus, in the early morning,
> Still as of old He calleth, "Follow me";
> Let us arise, all meaner service scorning,
> Lord, we are thine, we give ourselves to Thee.[2]
>
> —*J. Edgar Park*

✦

CHRIST AND THE TRIBUTE MONEY

By

Anton Van Dyck

(Interpretation)

JESUS, the Master Teacher, not only taught by example, by precept, by parable, by projects and object lessons, but He also taught by the direct method of questions and answers. Some Religious Educator has said, of Jesus and His teaching, that he was probably the first and only great teacher who was able to use with equal skill any and every teaching method known to the learning process.

During the latter part of His ministry, particularly, the Chief Priests and Pharisees were constantly trying to snare Jesus into saying or doing something by which they might bring Him into judgment. They were afraid to openly

[2] From *Worship and Song*, by Winchester and Conant. Copyright, the Pilgrim Press. Used with permission.

attack Him because the people followed Him in multitudes, for His ministry of healing had spread His fame, not only as a teacher, but also as a Worker of Miracles throughout all Palestine.

His growing popularity served but to increase the hatred and rancor of the priests and Pharisees; and so Matthew tells us that one day they took counsel together that they might ensnare Him in His public teaching and thus trap Him into saying something that might be interpreted as treason against the Roman Empire, under whose galling control Palestine was at that time.

Having worked out a plan by which they were sure Jesus might be trapped into apparent treachery against the Roman government, they sent to Jesus, one day, some of their own disciples with the Herodians for an audience, saying, with hypocritical falsity: "Teacher, we know that thou art true, and teachest the way of God in truth, and carest not for any one: for thou regardest not the person of men. Tell us therefore, What thinkest thou? Is it lawful to give tribute unto Cæsar, or not? But Jesus perceived their wickedness, and said, Why make ye trial of me, ye hypocrites? Show me the tribute money. And they brought unto him a denarius. And he saith unto them, Whose is this image and superscription? And they say unto him, Cæsar's. Then saith he unto them, Render therefore unto Cæsar the things that are Cæsar's; and unto God the things that are God's. And when they heard it, they marvelled, and left him, and went away" (Matthew 22:16-22).

It is this incident in the ministry of Jesus that the Dutch painter, Anton Van Dyck, has so fittingly portrayed in his "Christ and the Tribute Money."

Note the sharp, clear-seeing look in the Master's eyes. It is evident that He sees through their cunning perfidy. The artist has seen fit to depict, in addition to Jesus, only the faces of the two questioners sent forward by the chief priests and Pharisees to bait their trap. While the others cannot be seen in the picture, it is evident that they are not far away in the background.

The look of baffled surprise and wonder on the faces of these two, perhaps innocent tools of the priests and Pharisees, when Jesus answers their apparently innocent question so wisely and well, is arresting. They cannot take their eyes from the Master's wise and clear-seeing, though penetrating gaze. The Master's fingers may be pointing upward toward God to whom they are also to render their just tribute of praise and good works; but His eyes seem to be looking deep into their very souls.

Stunned, perhaps, with the simplicity and clarity of his reply, it is dawning on them, as well as on the chief priests and Pharisees in the background, that while He has answered their question fully and adequately, He has not supplied them with any treasonable word that may be used against Him. On the other hand, he has deliberately instructed them to pay to Cæsar and to Rome whatever tribute money may be imposed upon them by the Roman government under whose protection they live.

The light and lines of this masterpiece all center on Jesus, who in every teaching situation is constantly searching the hearts of men who are honest seekers after truth and God. It is not His will that any should perish, but that all may come to abundant life. And so with kindly yet searching eyes He looks deep into the souls of these two, who are being used by the hypocritical scribes and Pharisees to entrap Him.

✛

"MARY HATH CHOSEN THE BETTER PART"

By

Hermann Seegar

(Interpretation)

JUST as Bethlehem holds the honor of being the Master's birthplace, and despised Nazareth His earthly home, so little Bethany, under the shadow of Jerusalem, the capital city of the Jews, holds the honor of being known as the "home of His heart." For was it not here in the home of Mary, Martha, and Lazarus that Jesus loved to rest as He trudged the long weary miles from Galilee to Judæa? It was here that He spent the nights of His last week on earth, at least up until the time of His betrayal and arrest.

No story in New Testament annals has been more widely and variously interpreted than this incident which Hermann Seegar, the German artist, makes the theme of his painting "Mary Hath Chosen the Better Part." This picture visualizes for us a typical house-top veranda adjacent to the upper room usually used as the guest-chamber in an Oriental home. Near-by may be seen other typical Oriental houses snuggling at the foot of the Mount of Olives.

Seegar portrays the Master as sitting on a low stool near a small table on which one may see fruits for the refreshment of their distinguished guest. Near Him Mary, the younger sister, sits on the low projecting coping of the outer wall, her hands resting idly in her lap as she listens to the words of truth that fall from the gracious lips of the Master as He talks to her about the Kingdom of God, which, unlike any other kingdom, is to be builded in the inmost heart of all those who would live abundantly here and hereafter.

Into this quiet scene comes the bustling Martha, the good housekeeper, her basket under her arm. She pauses for a moment in her busy hurrying to and fro. Her attention is momentarily arrested by the Master's words; but she may not tarry without delaying the hour of their evening meal beyond its accustomed time. Seeing Mary so interested, cool, and refreshed, a pang of jealousy causes her to blurt out: "Lord, dost thou not care that my sister did leave me to serve alone? Bid her, therefore, that she help me."

Note the downcast eyes of Mary who is ashamed that her sister should thus openly accuse her of shirking and neglect to do her full share of the household tasks, that she might play the hostess in the Master's sight. A gracious hostess would at least have called quietly to the younger sister if she felt the need of additional assistance in preparing the evening repast.

"MARY HATH CHOSEN THE BETTER PART"—SEEGAR

To inject the censure of deliberate shirking in the Master's presence is cruel indeed.

But the Master, who sees clearly the hearts of both sisters, raises stern eyes to Martha as he says: "Martha, Martha, thou art anxious and troubled about many things; but one thing is needful: for Mary hath chosen the good part, which shall not be taken away from her."

The world is full of people who spend all their lives busily fussing about material things; and then alibi their lack of spiritual development on other members of their family or of society in general. After all, all of us choose the way in which we are to invest our time. And Martha, too, might have found time for a quiet visit with her Lord and Master after, if not before, the meal, without reflecting unkindly on her sister's inmost desires and motives.

"Man does not live by bread [material substance] alone"; there is a manna of spiritual discovery to be had by all those who hunger and thirst after righteousness. This is the message of Seegar's "Mary Hath Chosen the Better Part," a message which we all need to take to heart.

✛

CHRIST TEMPTED BY SATAN

By

Georg Cornicelius

(Interpretation)

MANY artists have attempted to paint the picture of the temptation of Jesus in the wilderness of Judæa following His baptism. To me the one by Georg Cornicelius, the German artist, is by far the most pleasing.

The artist was born at Hanau, Germany, in 1825. After a brief period of schooling, he worked first in a jewelry factory, and later in a pottery where he painted the designs. When he was fifteen he painted his first portrait, and about the same time began his art studies in the Academy. Later he traveled to Antwerp that he might both study and copy some of the great paintings in the art galleries there; and still later to Dresden, Paris, and Italy with the same purpose in mind. In 1888 he was named "Professor of Art" by the Russian crown-prince. His special interest was in religious paintings, in which he excelled as a colorist and in portraying spiritual experiences. He died in 1898. His best-known paintings are all on religious themes, and among them his "Christ Tempted by Satan" has achieved high ranking.

The appeal in this painting lies not so much in the form or even the face of Jesus, attractive as they are, nor in the shadowy, evil face that is lifting a man-made crown above Christ's head; but in the unusual expression in the wonderful eyes of the Master. The whole subtle mystery of the Temptation story is not explained, but portrayed, as Dr. Bailey suggests, in the expression of the eyes of Jesus. They seem to look, not at you, not through you, but past you into infinite abysses, as His mind judges, weighs, and tests the principles and conclusions that throughout future years are to direct His actions and conduct.

In the original of this remarkable painting the eyes are *red* with lack of sleep, not black, as they appear in reproductions. His hair is a bit disheveled by the wind, because for days, now, He has not thought of food, or sleep, or His personal appearance. And while His face rests upon His right hand, as one often instinctively does in deep thought, His left hand has gripped His wrist with a muscular tension that indicates something of the intensity of His absorbing inner struggle.

"If thou art the Messiah" is the problem that Jesus took with Him when He was driven by the Spirit into the wilderness for self-discovery and self-mastery, following that unusual experience at His baptism, when a voice out of Heaven said, "This is my beloved Son in whom I am well pleased."

Jesus knew that He had unusual powers that His brothers, His parents, and other men and women in Galilee did not possess. That His mother and family were also aware of this is evident in the story of the first miracle at Cana in Galilee. How should He use these powers for Himself? Should he make bread of stone? Should he extricate Himself by the use of these unusual powers from all sorrow, suffering, and excruciating experiences? Should He claim the temporal throne of David, and reinstate through the use of His miraculous powers, perhaps the most glorious and victorious reign that any Jewish king had ever known?

It took forty days of deep thinking and clear seeing to think Himself through all the entanglements involved in these momentous questions and decisions. No wonder He was unconscious of hunger or of the need of rest.

"This is my beloved Son in whom I am well pleased." How should an "only begotten" and "beloved son" behave? He was the Messiah, sent of God, and His work was to establish God's Kingdom of Love on earth. What were the principles and the motives that must guide Him if He was to reflect the *mind* and *soul* and *heart* of *God* to His fellow men?

In this painting Jesus does not see the Tempter. His sinister, shadowy face and the uplifted crown are for us. The artist has taken the inner struggle of Jesus with principalities and powers and objectified it for us. It is as though the eyes of Jesus were lenses through which we are to see the inner struggle that is going on in His own consciousness. The devil is an experience, not a person; and he is more often with us, as we struggle with evil forces within and without our conscious selves.

Some one has said that "character is what you are when you are dead sure no one else is looking." The bitterest battles are fought, won or lost, within personality, and not outside of it. Like Jesus, all of us fight our greatest battles with the evil forces that are all about us, alone, and within our own inner selves.

Jesus came through that harrowing experience in the wilderness spent physically and mentally; but He came out victorious. He would never use His

Photo by courtesy Review Pictures, Washington, D.C.

CHRIST TEMPTED BY SATAN—*CORNICELIUS*

Messianic power for His own personal glory or gratification. He would never make a spectacle of Himself to gain popularity. He would rule only in the inner throne-room of the human heart as in love and lowly service to mankind He teaches us that true greatness, as well as true happiness, comes through investing oneself, unselfishly for others. And coming through that experience in the wilderness of Judæa as well as in the wilderness of His own inner selfhood victorious, He could teach His disciples later with a conviction born of experience—"Yea, fear him who hath power to cast both your soul and body in hell."

Simply and beautifully the artist Cornicelius has portrayed for us not only the struggle of our Master for victorious inner righteousness; but something also of the struggle and victory that must be ours if we are to walk the highways of the world reflecting within ourselves the *grace* and *purity* and *truth* that we find incarnate in the Master of Men.

✠

JUDEAN HILLS ARE HOLY

Judean hills are holy . . .
    Judean hills are fair,
For one can find the footprints
    Of Jesus everywhere.

One finds them in the twilight
    Beneath the singing sky,
Where shepherds watch in wonder
    White planets wheeling by.

His trails are on the hillsides,
    And down the dales and deeps;
He walks the high horizons
    Where vesper-silence sleeps.

He haunts the lowly highways
    Where human hopes have trod
The Via Dolorosa . . .
    Up to the heart of God.

He looms, a lonely figure,
    Along the fringe of night,
As lonely as a cedar . . .
    Against the lonely light.

Judean hills are holy . . .
    Judean hills are fair,
For one can find the footprints
    Of Jesus everywhere.

                            —*William L. Stidger*

MY YOKE IS EASY

The yokes He made were true;
Because the man who dreamed
Was too an artisan,
The burdens that the oxen drew were light.
At night He lay upon his bed and knew
No beast of His stood chafing in a stall,
Made restless by a needless gall.

The tenets of a man
May be full fine,
But if he fails with plumb and line,
Scorns care, smooth planing,
And precision with the square,
Some neck will bear
The scar of blundering!

                            —*Gladys Latchaw*

HE LOVED A LAKE

We idled where the bank was blue
    With strange flowers in a good young land,
Where new-born bracken reached to us
    The closed sweet of her baby hand.

And over us in benison
    The dogwood held her Grecian cross
White while we marveled, and our feet
    Were silent in the carmine moss.

Our hearts were silent. Surely here
    The very God revealed His face,
And Jesus silent stood with us
    And with dear silence blessed the place.

Then came the murmur of a wind;
    A thrush sang in a hidden brake;
We were by Galilee, or here
    The Master with us by this lake!

He loved a lake! A little deep
  Whose shores sing with a breezy surf,
Where tiny foam in opal drift
  Is piled within each pebbled kerf.

And here He stood with us awhile
  And bent the dogwood—even now!
We know His peace within our souls,
  His holy cross upon our brow.

                              —Bennett Weaver

INTIMATE STRANGER

The stranger had a way with Him,
  The time He tarried in our place;
The children ran to play with Him,
  And something in His storied face
Made old folk wish to stay with Him
  Whose memory with their tales kept pace.

Not one but did confide in Him
  The inmost thought He ever had;
The wayward owned a guide in Him,
  To lead them out of mazes mad;
It seemed there was a side in Him
  For wise or wild, for sad or glad.

He lived apart—was near to us,
  Was intimate and stranger, too;
He ever grew more dear to us;
  Yet, only when He bade adieu.
The secret was made clear to us!
  And we, at last, The Poet knew!

                              —Edith M. Thomas

A LOST WORD OF JESUS

Here a word that Jesus spake
  Eighteen hundred years ago,
  Where the crimson lilies blow
Round the blue Tiberian lake:
There the bread of life He brake,
  Through the fields of harvest walking
  With His lowly comrades, talking
  Of the secret thoughts that feed
  Weary souls in time of need.
Art thou hungry? Come and take;

Hear the word that Jesus spake!
'Tis the sacrament of labor; bread and wine
divinely blest;
Friendship's food and sweet refreshment,
strength and courage, joy and rest.

Yet this word the Master said,
Long ago and far away,
Silent and forgotten lay
Buried with the silent dead,
Where the sands of Egypt spread,
Sea-like, tawny billows heaping
Over ancient cities sleeping,
While the River Nile between
Rolled its summer flood of green,
Rolled its autumn flood of red:
There the word the Master said,
Written on a frail papyrus, scorched by fire,
wrinkled, torn,
Hidden in God's hand, was waiting for its
resurrection morn.

Now at last the buried word
By the delving spade is found,
Sleeping in the quiet ground.
Now the call of life is heard:
Rise again and like a bird,
Fly abroad on wings of gladness
Through the darkness and the sadness
Of the toiling age, and sing
Sweeter than the voice of spring,
Till the hearts of men are stirred
By the music of the word;
Gospel for the heavy-laden, answer to the
laborer's cry;
*"Raise the stone, and thou shalt find me; cleave the
wood, and there am I."*[3]

—*Henry van Dyke*

OUT OF NAZARETH

Out of Nazareth came a Prophet,
A soul on fire with primeval force,
A Master of the cosmic mysteries,
A kingly Man who made His throne a cross.

[3] From *The Poems of Henry van Dyke*; copyright, 1920. Published by Charles Scribner's Sons. Used by permission.

A Democrat, who loved the common people,
  A Rebel, sensitive to every wrong,
A Teacher of the Truth that love must triumph,
  He fought the old injustice all life long.

He was a Radical of fiery faith
  Because He dug down deep to divine wells,
Because the thing that tore His loving heart
  Was suffering and sorrow in earth's hells.

He stood high up upon the hills of light
  Where few indeed have had the strength to stand;
He dared grief, pain, death, a criminal's fate
  That He might make this world a fairer land.
                              —*Vincent G. Burns*

THE CONTINUING CHRIST

Far, far away is Bethlehem,
  And years are long and dim,
Since Mary held the Holy Child
  And angels sang for Him.
But still to hearts where love and faith
  Make room for Christ in them,
He comes again, the Child from God,
  To find His Bethlehem.

Beyond the sea is Galilee
  And ways which Jesus trod,
And hidden are those high hills
  Where He communed with God;
Yet on the plains of common life,
  Through all the world of men,
The voice that once said, "Follow me,"
  Speaks to our hearts again.

Gethsemane and Calvary
  And death and bitter loss,
Are these but echoes drifting down
  From a forgotten cross?
Nay, Lord, for all our living sins
  Thy cross is lifted up,
And as of old we hear Thee say,
  "Can ye, too, drink My cup?"

O Life that seems so long ago,
  And yet is ever new,
The fellowship of love with Thee,
  Through all the years is true.
O Master over death and time,
  Reveal Thyself, we pray,
And as before amongst Thine own,
  Dwell Thou in us today!

                    —*W. Russell Bowie*

FISHERMEN

Once in quiet Galilee
Jesus walked beside the sea,
  Walked with fishermen.
Sometimes in a little boat,
Lightly on the waves afloat,
He sat with men, talked with men,
  Fishermen.

"Leave your fishing nets," said He.
"Come, let Me your Master be;
  Seek not fish, but men.
Draw them with a net of love,
Seek them for the Home above,
And follow Me, follow Me,
  Fishermen."

Lord, let us Thy fol'wers be,
Like the men of Galilee,
  Be Thy fishermen,
Faithful to each little task,
Glad to do what Thou shalt ask,
To follow Thee, follow Thee,
  Fishermen.

                    —*Mary Dillingham Frear*

SISTERS

By

Eleanor B. Stock

Mary's loveliness was twin sister to the dawn. She took the road to the village well, and as she walked, Life sang in her heart.

Life—she saw it all about her—in the sun, whose strong hands pushed the mist aside and clutched the little white houses standing in huddled groups along the road, and in the very road itself stretching so comfortably before her.

Life—she felt it within her—surging up in her healthy young body, filling her with complete and unshadowed happiness. Life was so splendid a thing! Did it not hold Martha, and Lazarus, and Jesus, their Friend, who even now would be taking the road to Bethany that He might break bread with them at sundown?

As she pondered these things she lifted her face with a little gesture of expectancy, and as though she had received a command, she stood perfectly still, poised and attentive. Soon a smile of welcome illumined her face. They had come—the great unseen wings! She felt their gentle touch upon her cheeks. Always, when she thought of the Master and His Kingdom, they came. Sometimes they flew past, brushing against her lightly and quickly, leaving her filled with a great buoyancy, a great radiance of spirit; but at other times, when she was tired, when in the early evening she sat in the doorway and watched the stars, they folded and upheld her and filled her with a great peace!

She had never spoken about them to Martha. Dear, practical Martha would not understand. But the Master—*He* would understand. Very shyly she had told Him.

"It is as the wings of a dove, covered with silver, and her pinions of yellow gold," He had answered her, quoting the words of the Sweet Singer of Israel. "God has gifted you with the sense of His presence."

This morning Mary felt their touch more vividly than ever, and her walk to the village wayside well became a pilgrimage to the Source of Life. And because she was young, her mind and body full of health, she reveled in feeling the graceful play of muscles bending effortlessly to their task of drawing and filling her water-jar. . . .

．　．　．　．　．

Noon came out of the dawn. Yet Mary lingered. Rebecca had a new scarf to show, Vashti a story to tell, old Hannah a heart to unburden, for her son Adoniram was ill. Little Marian, and still smaller David had hands and feet that longed to play. And, as always, Mary took these old familiar, everyday needs and held them close against her understanding heart, while time slipped by unheeded, *and Martha waited.*

When at last Mary lifted the latch of her door, the crisp fragrance of freshly baked loaves silently reproached her tardiness. She smiled ruefully. "I'm so sorry; I forgot it was our day to use the public oven." Mary put her arms around Martha. "But life's so big, dear, and, after all, tasks are so little—like ants, hundreds and hundreds of them, one after another, in a long line from morning until night. Oh, Martha, you ought to step over them once in a while —really you ought—and just forget them, the way I do. But you're tired, dear. Go and rest now, and don't worry about preparing the evening meal; just leave it all to me."

Martha smiled dubiously and patted her younger sister in much the same manner as one pets a charming but willful child.

With the first shadows of evening Mary stood in the doorway, watching for Jesus. It was not long before she saw Him coming along the road. A little child ran to Him and tugged at His garments. Mary saw that Jesus stopped and took it in His arms, and spoke graciously to it. Then old Hannah came seeking Him, and He turned aside and went with her to suffering Adoniram. Mary felt a sudden sense of awe. This Man, in whom Life was so vital, so unfettered and free, this great Man with the simple, courteous manners, this Poet of a Kingdom that lay hidden within the human heart, was Lazarus' Friend, and Martha's Friend, and hers!

To sit in the doorway with Him and listen to some story of the Kingdom was Mary's greatest delight. But tonight she would keep her promise and stay indoors, helping Martha with the evening meal.

He was there! The morning's vivid experience of the coming of the unseen wings, the great, beautiful, silent wings, demanded to be shared. Her tasks lay unheeded, her resolution forgotten; and Mary sat in the doorway, talking with the Master.

"You have healed Adoniram?" And, even as she asked, her voice held a note of joyful assertion.

"It is as you say, Mary. Did you doubt?" He asked, smiling quietly.

She grew serious at that, and shook her head. "How could I doubt—you? But tell me, Master, was he very ill? Hannah was much troubled about him."

"He whose heart is full of hate is always sick unto death, Mary."

"Yes, I know," she said, thoughtfully. "When there is anger or resentment in my heart, the unseen wings shun me, and no matter how I long for them they do not come. But they never fail to hear the call of my joy, or even of my sorrow, and when I think of the Kingdom that You say is within us, they draw very close."

"The wings of a dove—have you felt them today?"

"Yes; they seemed nearer than ever before. But how did You know?"

"The story of their coming is written in your eyes."

Mary and Jesus talked on and on. Busy Martha caught the hum of their voices. Now and then, passing the doorway as she went about her tasks, her eyes grew wistful. A whole radiant world lay open to them that somehow was locked and barred to her. She tried to enter in. Could it be that she was exiled because of some subtle difference between herself and Mary? The thought pressed upon her like a dull pain.

Her back ached as she bent to lay the mats; her hands felt heavy and thick as they took up their tasks. Usually she delighted in preparing some favorite dish for the Master, and took joyful pride in acting as hostess; but tonight, weariness drained her of all joy. After all, it didn't seem quite just that Mary should always be the one to sit talking to the Master, while she, Martha, did the work.

Looking at them, Martha saw that He too, had entered into that strange land from which she seemed exiled. The ache in her heart became unbearable. "Master, Master," she said, and her voice was almost a sob, "don't you care that I do all the work alone? Tell Mary to come in and help me."

Mary was startled. Martha's words fell like stones into the quiet pool of her thinking, inopportunely recalling her promise. She was about to answer Martha, to make the usual excuses, when Jesus said, His voice full of compassion: "Martha, you are troubled with many things. Mary has chosen the better part, that shall not be taken from her."

Instantly the cloud that crossed Mary's eyes gave way to an expression of relief. "That's just what I keep telling Martha. Why, if I always remembered to do the things Martha says need to be done, I would be stirring up such a noisy business, clattering pots and swishing brooms, that the beautiful wings would fly by, ever so softly, far off, in some quiet place on a little pathway, or a hillside open to the sky."

Jesus laughed. "Yes, Mary, you have chosen the better part, but there is only one way to keep it."

"How?"

"I need not tell you, for you already know."

Mary scanned His face, that of a seer and a poet; then she looked at His hands, strong and brown from having worked at countless tasks in the little carpenter shop in Nazareth; and she caught a glimpse of the working methods of Life, ever creating through dreams, and dreaming through deeds. "I believe I understand now," she said. "They are sisters, not strangers."

"Who?"

"Being and doing," she said, then rose and went in.

And in a little while Martha came out and sat with Jesus.[4]

[4] From *The Classmate*, May 9, 1931. Used with the special permission of the author.

THE MAN WHO WAS LET OFF

(Matthew 19:16-22; Mark 10:17-22; Luke 18:18-23)

Arranged by Cynthia Pearl Maus

No ONE of the Gospel stories has provided a greater challenge to young people than this story of the "Great Rejection," as some one has fittingly called the episode of Christ and the Rich Young Ruler, which Matthew, Mark, and Luke all tell in one form or another.

It is evident, by reading the context of this thrice-told Bible story, that this young man who followed Jesus was not only rich and cultured, but also *good* as far as conformity to the Jewish law of righteousness was concerned. It is also evident that he had been following Jesus closely enough not only to hear, but to covet, this abundant and eternal life about which the Son of Man spoke so frequently and convincingly.

Finally, one day, he sought the Master out, saying: "Good Teacher, what shall I do that I may inherit eternal life?"

And Jesus answered him in this wise: "Why callest thou me good? None is good, save one, even God." Then observing that he was a well-dressed young Jew, He continued: "Thou knowest the commandments: Do not kill, Do not commit adultery, Do not steal, Do not bear false witness, Do not defraud, Honor thy father and mother. Keep the commandments and thou shalt live."

And the young man, with a ring of justifiable pride in his voice, answered: "All these things have I observed from my youth up. What lack I yet?"

Then Mark says that "Jesus looked at him; and looking at him loved him"— loved him for his youth, loved him for his personal purity, loved him for his ability to make a great contribution to the day and generation of which he was a part; and loving him, said: "If thou wouldest be perfect, go, sell that which thou hast, and give to the poor . . . and come—follow me."

"But when the young man heard this saying, he went away sorrowful; for he was one that had great possessions."

"He wanted the goods, but the price staggered him. He was asked to give the whole; but he couldn't trust his heavenly Father's care. He missed his chance by not being game. He stood shivering on the shore of a great ambition; but he feared to take the plunge from which he would have come up in a tingle of new life. He might have traveled day by day in the company of Jesus, with the Master's words in his memory, his eyes upon Him, His friendship coaxing every good thing in the man's heart up and out. He might have become an apostle, one of the guiding spirits of the young Church, handling growing responsibilities, seeing the world, facing kings and mobs, tasting the fullness of life. His name might today be a household word wherever the Gospels are read, and millions of boys might have been named after him as after Peter and James and John. Instead— Oh! he probably lived and died as the richest man of his little Galilean town, carrying in his frozen heart the dead seed of a great life, unless, indeed, some Roman official squeezed him dry, or the Jewish wars did for him by force what he would not do freely for himself."[5]

Yes, the rich young ruler was "let off" from sacrifice and service; but he was also let off from the reward—developed Christ-like personality—walking the highways of the world with Jesus in helpful service to his fellow men.

✠

JESUS TEACHES FROM A BOAT

By

Cynthia Pearl Maus

THE popularity of Jesus as a teacher grew very rapidly, not alone because of the simplicity and directness of His address, but also because of the poetic beauty of the stories He told and the homely, familiar illustrations He used.

Crowds came pouring in from all sides to hear this new and comparatively unknown Rabbi from despised Nazareth. So much so that He was forced to get into a boat belonging, no doubt, to one of His disciples, and to push out into the lake. Along the shore of the Sea of Galilee, eastward from Capernaum, there is a lovely little bay shaped like a horseshoe. Many thousands of people can sit on the shore at this spot and hear clearly a man speaking from a boat in the middle of this curve in the bay.

From this vantage-point, one day, Jesus began to say to the multitude that gathered on the shores: "Behold, a sower went forth to sow. And as he sowed some seed fell along the path, and the birds came and soon pecked it up. Other seed fell on rocky ground, where there was but little soil. It shot up quickly, but because there was no depth of soil, it soon withered away under the scorching rays of the noonday sun. Still other seed fell among the thorns and brambles and they stifled it so that it yielded no crop."

Every growing lad on the beach could understand that kind of teaching; for had not they seen, many times, the thorny little plants, whose names are legion in Palestine, crowd out the good seed?

"But," continued Jesus, "some seed fell on good ground, and yielded a bountiful crop. It grew and increased and gave for the labor of the sower sometimes thirty- or sixty- or even a hundredfold." Then He added, "All of you that have ears to hear, listen! and profit by the wisdom of the careful sower."

Again we find Jesus using simple, wayside, growing things by which to illustrate what God's Kingdom of Love is like. His listeners knew that the mustard seed was, comparatively speaking, one of the smallest and most bountiful of all seeds. It grows in abundance in and around the Sea of Galilee and along the Jordan Valley.

One day He said to them, "The Kingdom of God is like the mustard seed,

[5] From *Some Men and Women of the Bible*, Binford. Used with permission.

which is the smallest of all seeds." The mustard plant, particularly in the Jordan Valley, where it is often cultivated, is very pungent and penetrating, and when crushed makes not only seasoning for foods, but healing for the skin as well.

It grows annually to a height of from eight to ten feet, often towering above the smaller herbs; and the birds—goldfinches and linnets—flock to perch on its branches and to feast on its tiny seed. It is a wonderfully productive plant, not only beautifying the garden with its rich yellow blossoms, but also producing each year tens of thousands of black seeds.

Doubtless because of both its beauty and its productiveness, and certainly because of its familiarity, Jesus used this plant to illustrate for His disciples and the multitude gathered on the shores of Galilee, what God's Kingdom of Love is like. Just a little of the spirit of God hidden deep in the soil of the human heart leavens and makes beautiful and useful the whole of one's life. But stony hearts, hard hearts, hearts that are interested in the trivial things of life, are unproductive soil for God's Kingdom of Love.

Again and again we find Jesus using homely, familiar things with which His hearers were well acquainted to picture for them what God's Kingdom of Love was like. He said, "The Kingdom of Heaven is like the yeast that a woman mixes into flour, for it ferments until the whole loaf is lifted up and it is ready for the baking."

Again Jesus likened the Kingdom of God to a farmer who sowed good seed in his field. During the night, while he slept, an enemy came and over the good seed sowed darnel or thorns. The Arabs spoke of it as a poisonous grass-weed, since it caused no end of trouble. Once it has been sown it is well-nigh impossible to weed it out. Instead it must be allowed to grow and mature with the wheat.

This parable was somewhat harder for the disciples to understand, and so at the end of the day, when the multitude had gone to their homes, they said, "Master, explain to us the parable of the darnel sown in the wheat field."

And Jesus answered: "The sower of the good seed is the Son of Man. The field is the world. The good seed, the sons of the Kingdom of God; the darnel, the sons of the evil one. The enemy who sowed the darnel is the devil. The harvest is the close of the age; the reapers are angels, messengers of God."

Seeing that His disciples still seemed a bit confused about the hidden, deeper meaning of the parable of the mustard seed, Jesus added: "What the sower sows is the word of God. Those who are like the seed that falls along the foot-path are those who, as soon as they hear the word, let Satan come and carry it off. In the same way those who receive the seed on rocky places are those who accept it enthusiastically, but they have no depth of character and soon let other things—sorrow and persecution—overthrow their good intentions. Those who receive the seed among thorns are those who, having heard the message, let lesser interests—the cares of the world, their enjoyment in being wealthy or the pursuit of happiness—choke out the Message so that it becomes unfruitful in their lives. But the good ground are those who, having heard the message, act on it so that it produces in them the fruit of God's spirit of love."

It is small wonder that His disciples liked to sit with Him in a boat at the end of a busy day of teaching, now and then rowing off to the other side of the lake, to listen to the rich cadences of His voice as He explained to them the deeper meaning of His parables and sayings often lost by the multitudes who in increasing number flocked to hear this Teacher who "taught with authority" —the authority of sincerity and truth—"and not as the scribes."

Much of Jesus' teaching was poetic in form. This is particularly true of the Lord's Prayer.[6] Translated back into Aramaic the Lord's Prayer is a poem with rhythm and rhyme.

So also is His parable of the foolish man who built his house on the sand, which one day Jesus used to end His teaching for that day. Basil Mathews in his *A Life of Jesus* puts it in this wise:

> Everyone, now, who listens to these my teachings,
> And acts upon them,
> Will be like the wise man
> Who built his house on the rock;
> And the heavy rain poured down;
> The swollen streams swirled along;
> And the winds blew and beat on that house.
> But it did not fall, for it was founded on rock.
>
> Everyone, however, who listens to these words of mine
> And does not act on them
> Will be like the stupid man
> Who built his house upon the sand.
> The heavy rain poured down;
> The swollen streams swirled;
> The winds blew and beat upon the house
> And it fell—with a mighty crash![7]

✠

THE KINGDOM OF MEN'S HEARTS

Now, Nicodemus was a ruler amongst the Jews, and I had known him from my childhood. He was a quiet man, but fair-minded above all other men. He had no passion but for justice, and in his dealings with his fellows he was himself just to the bone. I determined that I would go to him.

By this time it was midday and I found Nicodemus in his house, about to

[6] See page 308 for the poetic form of the Lord's Prayer.
[7] See page 200 of *A Life of Jesus*, Mathews. Published by Harper & Brothers.

sit down to eat. He asked me to join him, and when food had been put before us, I told him why I had come.

"Sadoc says you have become a follower of Jesus, and that He is preaching a kingdom not of the Romans," I said.

"Sadoc is a fool," said Nicodemus. "It is true that I have been to see Jesus, but it is not true that He preaches against Roman rule or that I have become his disciple."

"What is this talk of His Kingdom?" I asked. "Sadoc says it is more dangerous than that preached by John."

"I have heard John preach," said Nicodemus. He was a wild, unbalanced man. He preached repentance and denounced all men. It was teaching, look you, fitted to make men think upon their sins, but not to govern their lives. Jesus is greater than John."

"What, then, is this Kingdom?" I asked.

Nicodemus pondered a moment.

"It is hard to explain," he said. "It has long been in the minds of men of our nation that one day God would rule over us in an earthly kingdom. Jesus is well learned in the law, so He knows of that hope. But His doctrine is that that Kingdom is here already."

"But where," I cried, "seeing the Romans rule all Judæa?"

"I think He means that it is in men's hearts, and has nothing to do with their governors. But let me tell you of what He said to me," said Nicodemus. "I went to Him by night, for, indeed, it was the only way to see Him alone, and I asked Him of this Kingdom, and He said no man could see the Kingdom unless he was born again; and when I wondered, asking if a man could be born again when he was old, He said unless a man was born of the Spirit he could never enter the Kingdom."

"Then it is not a real kingdom?"

"Yes, it is real," he said at last, "but He seemed to think that what was meant by our prophets was that if you change men's hearts you will also change their governments. He spoke out of an inner certainty and with authority. When I questioned Him as to how a man could be born of the Spirit, He said that when He spoke of what He knew, men would not accept His statements; and if they would not believe when He spoke of earthly things, how could they believe if He spoke of heavenly?"

"What did He mean by that?" I asked.

"His meaning, I think, was that if He tells men the way to enter the Kingdom, and they won't believe Him, how can He expect them to believe Him if He tells of the mysteries of the Spirit? That, at least, was how I understood Him. He has the root of the matter in Him, and His teaching is certainly of God."

"And yet you have not become His follower?" I said.

"I cannot do as others have done, and throw up all to follow Him. I have taken too many duties upon me," he answered.

"Well, Nicodemus," I said, as I rose up to go, "I have it in my mind that

I may become a follower of Jesus. I go to seek Him now, to ask of this Kingdom." And Nicodemus answered sadly:

"You are young, and I am old. I do not say that if I were thy age, and not
a ruler of Israel, I would not do likewise. Go, and God be with you."[8]

✝

THOU DIDST TEACH THE THRONGING PEOPLE

THIS hymn emphasizes in a beautiful way not only the oral teaching of the
Master of Men, but also His ministry of teaching through healing, through
overcoming temptation, and through object lessons like stilling the storm on
turbulent Galilee.

It is true that people thronged about the Master, so much so that in self-
protection He found it necessary on more than one occasion to get into a boat
with His disciples and push out into the sea, where at least He might have quiet
and repose about Him as he taught the thronging multitude along the shore.

This Man who "taught with authority and not as the scribes" seems to have
been the master of varying methods by which truth may be shared with others;
He used many methods on many occasions, all with apparently equal skill.

And so the author in each verse of this hymn refers to different skills which
Jesus used to make truth live and ties each up with a petition for the needs of
Christians of today.

> Thou didst teach the thronging people
>   By blue Galilee;
> Speak to us, Thy erring children;
>   Teach us purity.
>
> Thou whose touch could heal the leper,
>   Make the blind to see;
> Touch our hearts and turn from sinning,
>   Into purity.
>
> Thou whose word could still the tempest,
>   Calm the raging sea,
> Hush the storm of human passion,
>   Give us purity.
>
> Thou didst sinless meet the tempter.
>   Grant, O Christ, that we
> May o'ercome the bent to evil,
>   By thy purity.
>
> —*Jemima Luke, 1841*

[8] From *By an Unknown Disciple*. Published by Harper & Brothers. Used by special permission.

BREAK THOU THE BREAD OF LIFE

THIS beautiful, devotional hymn, which has been sung by countless thousands of youth groups all over America and the world, was written by Mary Artemisia Lathbury, who through her poetry and hymns has become known as the "Laureate of Chautauqua."

The background of inspiration for this hymn is the shores of Lake Chautauqua in western New York, where, ever since 1873, thousands of young people and adults have come annually for study and prayer. The lake and its beautiful surroundings, the Chautauqua program and its rich devotional experiences, are reflected in this hymn, which through the years has become one of the favorites of youth groups everywhere.

At Lake Geneva, Northfield, Winona, Chautauqua, and other summer conferences held on the shores of quiet lakes, this great devotional hymn has recalled to young people something of the rich experience that the disciples of Jesus had with their Lord and Master by the waters of blue Galilee.

Its author was the daughter of the manse, and although not so prolific a hymn-writer as Frances Ridley Havergal, she had much in common with her in the mystical devotion to Jesus Christ, which her beautiful hymns express.

The tune was composed by William F. Sherwin. It is dignified and stately, yet simple, voicing throughout a sense of reverence in the presence of God. Through yet unborn generations this beautiful hymn will continue to enrich and bless the life of young people everywhere as they quest for the life abundant in Christ Jesus.

> Break Thou the bread of life,
> Dear Lord, to me,
> As Thou didst break the loaves
> Beside the sea;
> Beyond the sacred page
> I seek Thee, Lord;
> My spirit pants for Thee,
> O Living Word.
>
> Bless Thou the truth, dear Lord,
> To me, to me,
> As Thou didst bless the bread
> By Galilee;
> Then shall all bondage cease,
> All fetters fall,
> And I shall find my peace,
> My all in all.[9]

—Mary A. Lathbury, 1880

[9] Copyrighted by the Chautauqua Press. Used with permission.

SAVIOUR, LIKE A SHEPHERD LEAD US

IN "SAVIOUR, Like a Shepherd Lead Us" we have another of those hymns that emphasize the tender, shepherding quality and character of the Master of Men.

Not only was the birth of Jesus in Bethlehem of Judæa attested by humble shepherds who had heard the angel's song and prophetic message; but the Master of Men likened Himself to the shepherd of the sheep, the One who came to seek and to save that which was lost.

The name of the author of the words of this beautiful hymn has been lost to us; but the words and melody live on in memory, because it expresses the deep-seated longing of every devout follower of the Master Teacher.

"All we, like sheep, have gone astray," and we know that to live abundantly as Jesus did, we must have the constant and tender shepherding care of the Great Shepherd of the sheepfold—humanity.

The music was composed by William B. Bradbury.

> Saviour, like a shepherd lead us;
>   Much we need Thy tender care;
> In Thy pleasant pastures feed us,
>   For our use Thy folds prepare.
> Blessed Jesus, Blessed Jesus,
>   Thou hast bought us, Thine we are;
> Blessed Jesus, Blessed Jesus,
>   Thou hast bought us, Thine we are.
>
> We are Thine; do Thou befriend us,
>   Be the Guardian of our way;
> Keep Thy flock, from sin defend us,
>   Seek us when we go astray.
> Blessed Jesus, Blessed Jesus,
>   Hear the children when they pray;
> Blessed Jesus, Blessed Jesus,
>   Hear the children when they pray.
>
> Thou hast promised to receive us,
>   Poor and sinful though we be;
> Thou hast mercy to relieve us,
>   Grace to cleanse, and pow'r to free.
> Blessed Jesus, Blessed Jesus,
>   Early let us turn to Thee;
> Blessed Jesus, Blessed Jesus,
>   Early let us turn to Thee.

Early let us seek Thy favor;
Early let us do Thy will;
Blessed Lord and only Saviour,
With Thy love our bosom fill.
Blessed Jesus, Blessed Jesus,
Thou hast loved us, love us still;
Blessed Jesus, Blessed Jesus,
Thou hast loved us, love us still.

—Anonymous

✧

SAVIOUR, TEACH ME DAY BY DAY

IN THIS song we have another of those great hymns of the Church that place distinct emphasis on the teaching ministry of the Christ of Galilee.

It was written by Jane E. Leeson in 1842, and is usually sung to an older melody composed by Carl M. von Weber in 1826.

The peculiar emphasis in this hymn is not so much on Jesus teaching us, His followers of the present age, as on the motive of *love* which must permeate all the thoughts and actions of the Christian who would follow his Lord and Master in abundant Christ-like living in a world that is, as yet, Christian only in spots.

The need of the present-day followers of Christ for keeping close to Christ in loving, childlike following is the particular strain that the author of this beautiful hymn has sought to emphasize. That we shall learn is evident in the author's mind, if we follow close in loving service this great Teacher of the race.

Saviour, teach me day by day,
Love's sweet lesson to obey;
Sweeter lesson cannot be—
Loving Him who first loved me.

With a childlike heart of love,
At Thy bidding may I move;
Prompt to serve and follow Thee—
Loving Him who first loved me.

Teach me all Thy steps to trace,
Strong to follow in Thy grace;
Learning how to love from Thee—
Loving Him who first loved me.

Love in loving finds employ,
In obedience all her joy;
Ever new that joy will be—
Loving Him who first loved me.

—Jane E. Leeson, 1842

THE LORD IS MY SHEPHERD

THIS great hymn of the Church finds its inspiration in the Twenty-third Psalm, one of the most widely known and quoted of all these "poems of passion," as some one has beautifully called these poetic outbursts of David, the shepherd king.

You are conscious, as you read or sing the verses of this song, that the author had in mind the content of the "Shepherd's Psalm," as it is often referred to, because each verse recalls certain lines of the Twenty-third Psalm. Indeed, the resemblance is so apparent that, allowing for poetic license, the verses of this hymn seem almost to be a paraphrase of the Psalm itself.

The words of this hymn were written by James Montgomery in 1822, and the melody to which it is most frequently sung, and which fits the rhythm of the verses perfectly, was composed by Thomas Koschat in 1862.

The Lord is my Shepherd, no want shall I know,
I feed in green pastures, safe folded I rest;
He leadeth my soul where the still waters flow,
Restores me when wandering, redeems when oppressed,
Restores me when wandering, redeems when oppressed.

Through the valley and shadow of death though I stray,
Since Thou art my Guardian, no evil I fear;
Thy rod shall defend me, Thy staff be my stay;
No harm can befall, with my Comforter near,
No harm can befall, with my Comforter near.

In the midst of affliction my table is spread;
With blessings unmeasured my cup runneth o'er;
With perfume and oil Thou anointest my head;
Oh, what shall I ask of Thy providence more?
Oh, what shall I ask of Thy providence more?

Let goodness and mercy, my bountiful God,
Still follow my steps till I meet Thee above;
I seek by the path which my forefathers trod,
Through the land of their sojourn, Thy kingdom of love,
Through the land of their sojourn, Thy kingdom of love.

—James Montgomery, 1822

CONTENTS

PART III   SECTION III

A FRIEND OF PUBLICANS AND SINNERS

✠

"I came not to call the righteous, but sinners."—MARK 2:17

✠

A FRIEND OF PUBLICANS AND SINNERS

"And he entered and was passing through Jericho. And behold, a man called by name Zacchæus; and he was a chief publican, and he was rich. And he sought to see Jesus who he was; and could not for the crowd, because he was little of stature. And he ran on before, and climbed up into a sycamore tree to see him: for he was to pass that way. And when Jesus came to the place, he looked up, and said unto him, Zacchæus, make haste, and come down; for to-day I must abide at thy house. And he made haste, and came down, and received him joyfully. And when they saw it, they all murmured, saying, He is gone to lodge with a man that is a sinner. And Zacchæus stood, and said unto the Lord, Behold, Lord, the half of my goods I give to the poor; and if I have wrongfully exacted aught of any man, I restore fourfold. And Jesus said unto him, To-day is salvation come to this house, forasmuch as he also is a son of Abraham. For the Son of man came to seek and to save that which was lost."—LUKE 19:1-10

THE LOST SHEEP—*SOORD*

THE LOST SHEEP

By

Alfred Soord

(Interpretation)

NOWHERE in the field of modern religious art is there a more vivid presentation of Luke's story (Luke 15:3-7) of the lost sheep, than this picture by Alfred Soord, of the Contemporary British School of Art, who died in 1916.

As Dr. Bailey says: "The trouble with most of the 'Good Shepherds' is that they are good for nothing. The theme has been handled over and over again from the time of the Catacombs down, but usually one sees the same type of picture, the figure of a pretty man holding a lamb in his bosom. To one who has seen shepherds in Palestine there is something particularly repugnant in such a representation. No real shepherd ever wore the elegant draperies that adorn these artists' models. . . . When you come upon a real shepherd in the shepherds' country something is apt to grip your heart and your throat. Shepherding there is a man's job! There you see the rough jacket made of a fleece turned wool side in; the bare, bronzed bosom; the bare legs scratched with thorns; rough shoes of rawhide; the great club of oak with its knot on the end, heavy enough to fell a bear; the high-stepping stride and the muscles like steel that endure the tramps over rocky country, the fearless eye that can face danger alone; and you often see a lamb in the strong arms. Such is the person Jesus had in mind when he said 'I am the Good Shepherd.' "[1]

It is that kind of shepherd that Alfred Soord has painted for us in his "The Lost Sheep." No shepherd would have deliberately led his flock to a wild rock-ribbed, thorn-infested mountain steep like this one pictured by Soord. Perhaps the sheep herself is responsible for the situation in which she finds herself. Too much self-confidence; too adventuresome a spirit; ignorance of the precipices and of the danger of the eagles circling high and waiting for her to die; or it may have been an unconscious wandering away from the shepherd's protecting care that has brought this lonely, unprotected sheep to this steep mountain precipice. Whatever the cause, here she is clinging helplessly and hopelessly to the edge of nothing, with the night and a storm shutting in and the hungry eagles circling nearer and nearer to their unfortunate prey.

Into this desperate situation comes the good shepherd, to which Jesus likened Himself, seeking to save that which was lost and ready to die. As he digs the point of his shepherd's crook into the mountain's rocky side to sustain him while he reaches with the other outstretched arm for his lost sheep we feel a will and strength like unto the *will* and *strength* of the Master Shepherd of the

[1] From *The Gospel In Art,* Bailey. Used by permission of the author and publishers.

race, who came "to seek and to save that which was lost" and who is not willing that "even the least of these shall perish."

We feel that Soord has caught the spirit of Jesus' teaching. No soul, however poor, unfortunate or lost in degradation and sin, is beyond the outreach of Christ's shepherding love. Was it not for this purpose that He left the sheepfold of His heavenly Father to reside for a while with men that they might know something of what the loving heart of God is like? Our Christ is a seeking Shepherd. He came, "not to call the righteous who need no repentance"; but to provide a way by which men and women lost in sorrow, suffering, and sin might find again the sure-footed path of pure, virtuous, highminded living.

As we gaze at this picture we feel the struggle of the lost man and woman, the heart-break of the slave-driven, the sorrow of the under-privileged, the desperateness of the sinner who feels that now not even God knows or cares what is to become of him. And as this good shepherd gathers this lost sheep to his bosom, we too feel as if we would like to say, as Luke portrays Jesus saying, "Rejoice with me, for I have found my sheep which was lost."

✛

CHRIST THE WELCOME GUEST

By

Fritz von Uhde

(Interpretation)

THE conception of Jesus in the home of the lowly has been a favorite theme with artists through the centuries. None, however, has pictured it for us more simply, realistically, or beautifully than Fritz von Uhde, the German artist, in his "Christ the Welcome Guest." The original of this wonderful painting hangs in the National Art Gallery in Berlin.

This picture is not an old painting. The artist lived and wrought during the years from 1848 to 1911, and most of his religious paintings are modern in conception. We feel, however, as we look at this picture, that the artist has caught the spirit of the Master and of this home.

In the foreground is the Christ whom the common people heard gladly. He has just entered this humble home through the unlatched and partly open door in the rear, and is approaching the table with outstretched hand. Near Him in the left foreground is the workaday husband in his peasant clothes and wooden shoes. The gesture of his toil-worn hand indicates that he is inviting the Master of Men to dine with them, simple and frugal as is their evening meal. To the right is the busy housewife glancing up from the large bowl of gruel which she is just in the act of placing in the center of the table

CHRIST THE WELCOME GUEST—VON UHDE

to add, by her gracious smile, her invitation also to this uninvited though ever-welcome Teacher of the People.

In the background are the children, three of them, watching with shy interest and reverence this new, unexpected arrival in their home, while the fourth, the tiniest tot, is peeking up over the table to see, if possible, the appetizing dish that mother is so carefully placing in the center of the plainly-set table.

Farther away in the background are the grandmother and grandfather with heads slightly bowed and hands clasped as if waiting for the Master Teacher to express for them all some simple and suitable words of thanksgiving before they seat themselves for their evening repast.

There is nothing in the way of costly furnishings in this peasant home—just an old cabinet, a few chairs, and the family table. No rugs adorn the floor, no pictures the wall. One lamp only casts its mellow light over the center of the room from its suspended ceiling drop. But there is a generous welcome here, notwithstanding the meagerness of things that bespeak the comforts of the rich. There is a welcome here of people who are in the habit of sharing whatever they have with strangers and guests who happen to come their way and who live daily as though they believed and relied on their heavenly Father's protecting care. They are not idlers. It is evident by their toil-worn garments that they do their best; and their heavenly Father, who "knows what things they have need of," supplies the rest. Health, happiness, togetherness, and the habit and spirit of sharing with others make this humble peasant's home a paradise for the Man "who went about doing good, and who had not where to lay His head" except as it was supplied by those with whom He lived and taught and wrought.

Better a crust of bread with heartfelt hospitality, than the riches of Simon's palace, and the invitation to dine in it that came, perhaps, out of sheer curiosity. Something of the blessing of toil and of the integrity of simple living von Uhde is portraying for us in his picture of "Christ the Welcome Guest." This Man of the people is at home here. He, too, knew toil and the pinch of hunger.

✛

CHRIST AND THE ADULTERESS

By

Johann Heinrich Hofmann

(Interpretation)

WHILE the story of Christ and the adulteress is of somewhat doubtful origin (it is not in the original Gospel of John, where it is now found); yet the incident is no doubt historically true and presents a side of Jesus' nature that shows his remarkable insight into men's hearts and motives. Guilty persons usually throw up a smoke screen to protect themselves from being discovered in iniquity.

Just when this incident so artistically painted by Hofmann may have happened we do not know, probably on the last day of Jesus' public ministry as He taught in the Temple courts. A few months previous to this occurrence, Jesus had confessed to His disciples that the scribes and Pharisees were classing Him with the glutton and the wine-bibber, and a friend of men and women of shady background. As recent, perhaps, as yesterday He had allowed an abandoned woman to make a spectacle of Him by publicly washing His feet as He reclined at dinner in the home of Simon the leper, at Bethany.

Such a man was certainly bad himself, reasoned His accusers, and should be discredited as soon as possible in the presence of the multitude that followed Him constantly. The best way to do this was to confront Him with some one who had violated the law of Moses, and thus reveal whether or not he would stand by the Mosaic law or uphold sin and the sinner.

It is precisely this moment, when the hypocritical scribes and Pharisees brought this outcast woman to Jesus, that Hofmann has so graphically portrayed in his "Christ and the Adulteress." She is doubtless no worse than many of her accusers; but she is a sinful woman in a world of man-made laws, and as a violator of the Mosaic law, a good example by which to make a public test of this Rabbi who taught with authority, and therefore threw them into the background so far as the limelight was concerned.

Note how much Hofmann reveals of Jesus' attitude toward sin and sinners by His down-pointing hand and arm. His eyes are not upon the woman, though there is still much of beauty about her with which to attract the eyes of sin-bent men. Instead the Master's eyes search diligently the eyes of the men who would condemn her, while at the same time they make the law of Moses a smoke screen to hide their own moral and spiritual laxity.

Jesus is the center of interest. The two chief accusers in both the right and left foreground balance the picture. Their eyes are focused on Jesus. Nothing more than idle curiosity as to the woman's fate is evidenced by those in the background, with the exception of John only. The face of the beloved disciple between Jesus and the accused is an interesting study. There is real sympathy in it. He is turning over in his mind what must have happened to this beautiful girl in the past to bring so fair a woman to this despised estate. Even the men whose bodily lust she has satisfied feel no sympathy over thus publicly humiliating her.

The sinner is of secondary importance. Only four of the company are looking at her. They are all waiting with suspended attention to hear what the Rabbi's condemnation is to be. Into that calm and breathless moment comes the Master's clear-toned reply: "He that is without sin among you let him cast the first stone at her." With these words the defender of the law on the right unconsciously draws back a little. He knows that he is caught in the web of his own cunning. The other, on the left, tries to cover his chagrin by a pious, prayerful attitude of hands. He, too, must slink away in the presence of such a test. Neither of these accusers is interested in public morality. If these zealous guardians of righteousness had been they would have captured the woman's partner for whom the law prescribed the same penalty.

In the face of Jesus, Hofmann has painted a look of sorrow for sin and the sinful woman; but an even greater sorrow that men, supposedly guardians of the law of Moses, should sink so low as to stoop to this type of hatred, deceit, and trickery.

When they have all slunk away in chagrined embarrassment, this clear-visioned interpreter of the Mosaic law by which they claimed to regulate their lives, will say to the woman: "Neither do I condemn thee. Go and sin no more."

Dr. Bailey says: "Some one with dramatic insight has suggested that Jesus wrote on the ground: 'Jonas defrauded a poor man of a pair of shoes'; 'Eleazer stole a widow's house'; 'Asaph brought false accusation against his neighbor'; naming in each case one of the woman's accusers; and when each read in the sand the revelation of his guilt, in shame he withdrew from the presence of the righteous judge. This at any rate is the teaching of the incident: it is a graphic parable on the words 'Thou hypocrite, cast out first the beam out of thine own eye, and then shalt thou see clearly to cast out the mote out of thy brother's eye'; and an equally graphic parable on the redemptive power of sympathy and forgiveness."[2]

✛

CHRIST AND THE WOMAN OF SAMARIA

By

Pierre Mignard

(Interpretation)

THE picture of Christ by the wayside well near the ancient city of Sychar is an episode in the life and ministry of Jesus favored by many artists.

The Samaritans were fragments of colonies of different races that had been established by Assyrian power. In spite of the strictness of the Jewish laws with respect to intermarriage with alien races, much of it went on. The more ortho-dox Jews looked down upon this mixed race and hated them, and in return were hated by them.

As our Lord crossed this land of Samaria, he stopped at this wayside well near the gates of this ancient city, and being weary, sat down on the edge of the well to rest, while his disciples went on into the city to buy food.

While Jesus was resting, a woman of Samaria came up to draw water. Jesus opened the conversation by making a simple request of this strange woman, as she raised a bucket of cool, fresh water to the surface of the well.

"Give me to drink."

[2] From *The Gospel in Art,* Bailey. Used with permission of the author.

CHRIST AND THE ADULTERESS. HOFMANN

CHRIST AND THE WOMAN OF SAMARIA—*MIGNARD*

She hesitated, and in surprise asked how it was that he, being a Jew, should ask drink of her, a woman and a Samaritan.

And Jesus answering, said unto her: "If thou knewest the gift of God, and who it is that saith unto thee, 'Give me to drink,' thou wouldst have asked of him, and he would have given thee living water."

The woman, seeing that he had nothing with which to draw water, replied: "Sir, thou hast nothing to draw with, and the well is deep; from whence, then, hast thou this living water? Art thou greater than our father Jacob, which gave us the well and drank therefrom himself, and his children and his cattle?"

And Jesus answered her, saying: "Whosoever drinketh of this water shall thirst again: but whosoever drinketh of the water that I shall give him shall never thirst; but the water that I shall give him shall be in him a well of living water, springing up into everlasting life."

By this strange statement He aroused the curiosity of this Samaritan woman, who, according to her neighbors, was none too respectable, and she answered, quickly: "Sir, give me this water, that I thirst not, neither come all this way hither to draw."

Then Jesus replied with a brief but revealing statement, "Go, call thy husband, and come hither."

And the woman, surprised and perhaps embarrassed by his apparently intuitive knowledge of her secret life, replied, "I have no husband."

But this Prophet-Teacher probed still further into the woman's inner life by answering, "Thou saidst well, I have no husband: for thou hast had five husbands; and he whom thou now hast is not thy husband; in that saidst thou truly."

Already the woman had discovered that this stranger by the well had unusual powers, and she replied: "Sir, I perceive that thou art a prophet"; and then seeking to divert his attention from the things in her own life that were not complimentary, she said, adroitly: "Our fathers worshiped in this mountain; and ye say [the Jews] that in Jerusalem is the place where men ought to worship."

Jesus, with direct simplicity, replied: "Woman, believe me, the hour cometh, when neither in this mountain, nor yet in Jerusalem, shall ye worship the Father. Ye worship ye know not what: we know what we worship, for salvation is of the Jews. But the hour cometh, and now is, when the true worshipers shall worship the Father in spirit and in truth; for the Father seeketh such to worship Him. God is spirit, and they that worship him must worship him in spirit and in truth."

Then the woman, with true humiliation, replied: "I know that the Messiah cometh, which is called Christ; and when He is come, He will tell us all things."

And Jesus, in deep sincerity, answered, "I that speak unto thee am He."

Thereupon His disciples appeared with the provisions they had purchased in the near-by town, and were surprised to observe that He had been talking with this strange woman, yet no one of them dared to say, "What seeketh Thou?" or, "Why talkest Thou with her?"

At their approach the woman hurriedly left her water pot and went on her way into the city, and as she met men and women on the way she told them of the strange happening that had occurred to her by Jacob's well, saying: "Come, see a man which told me all things that ever I did. Can this be the Christ?"

Immediately the women and men with whom she shared her unusual experience hurried out to the well and came upon Jesus and His disciples.

As soon as the woman had disappeared the disciples urged Jesus to partake of food, saying, "Master, eat." But He replied, "I have meat to eat that ye know not of."

His disciples, thinking, no doubt, that the woman or some other passing traveler had fed Him, answered: "Hath any man brought Him aught to eat?"

And Jesus, observing their misunderstanding of His words, replied, "My meat is to do the will of Him that sent me, and to accomplish His work."

Of all the artists who have tried to paint this picture, and their name is legion, I prefer this one, "Christ and the Woman of Samaria," by the French painter Pierre Mignard, who lived from 1610 to 1695.

Beautifully, though not richly, gowned in Oriental robes and sandal-shod feet, Jesus sits on a stone by this wayside well. His face is young and exquisitely lighted against the somber darkness of his outer robe. One hand is reaching outward in gesture toward the woman; the other, with index finger pointing upward, seems to say "God is spirit, and they that worship Him must worship Him in spirit and in truth."

The profile of the woman's face as she looks intently into the face of Jesus is beautiful, also, though her garments are clearly those of the lower class. There are grace and beauty in every line of her body. The artist has made her an attractive, interested, not brazen, tempter of men. One arm rests on the water-jar, while with the other she has caught up the folds of her dress that she may hurry away into the city as soon as He ceases speaking, to spread the news as she goes of this prophetic Messiah, who told her "all the things that ever she did."

Behind the Master are the approaching disciples, while farther away against the background of a day well-nigh spent is the arched entrance of an ancient walled city.

This marvelous painting is beautiful in the simplicity of its intention, yet dignified. As we look into the face of the Master, so intent in His desire to share truth with even this common woman of the Samaritan streets, our hearts, too, respond: This is the Messiah, the Christ, sent by our heavenly Father to teach mankind the abundant way of life—a beautiful way of living even though it does make imperative, from day to day, the choosing of the hard right as over against the easy wrong.

THE MAGDALENE—*GUERCINO*

THE MAGDALENE

By

Giovanni Francesco Barbieri

(Interpretation)

GIOVANNI FRANCESCO BARBIERI, commonly known as Guercino, painted two pictures of Mary Magdalene, the harlot out of whom Jesus cast seven devils, both with the same motive—"deliverance through love." One is in Rome. The other, reproduced here, is in the National Museum at Naples. The reproduction shown here is from a photograph by Alinari, Florence, Italy.

Almost no other heroine of the Bible has been so often represented by artists as Mary of Magdala. That this is so is not strange. For one of the most beautiful and pathetic chapters in Christ's life is the story of his relation to Mary Magdalene. She followed Him from the city of Magdala, through Galilee, Samaria, and Judæa to Jerusalem. She was the last at the cross, the first at the grave. She first brought spices to the grave on Sunday morning to perform her task of reverential love to the Master's body, and when she was robbed of this task her wild grief deprived her of the power to recognize His voice or form. Of the action of the two Marys at the cross, it has been said that the Magdalene's grief was the wild grief of a lover; the other Mary's the unselfish love of a mother. If the Magdalene's strange love for Jesus had in it something of selfishness, in some respects it was a love deeper than anyone else had.

The place that Mary Magdalene occupies in Christian thought is not due, however, to her strange deep love for Jesus, but rather to what was wrought in her by Christ's love for her. It was Christ's love for her that delivered her from her past and made her what she became. This is the center of interest in the Magdalene's life. This central fact Guercino, with the true instinct of the artist, has seized and portrayed. In the picture two symbols are so used as to express one idea. Mary in her own person is made by the artist to symbolize her past life. The crown of thorns at which she is looking is the symbol of the love through which she was delivered. Her deliverance through the love of Him who wore the crown of thorns is the thought at which she is weeping as she now looks at it and remembers the price He paid to redeem sinners such as she.

This picture thus represents the central truth for which Mary's life has come to stand, that it is possible to be delivered, through love, from the lowest depths to the shining heights where dwelleth God; that there is a method by which soot can be washed from the soul's wings and they be made white as snow.

Magdalene is an outstanding illustration of the great fact of human experience, that "To whom much is forgiven, the same loveth much." What she was delivered from regulated her love for Christ. Magdalene will always remain a prominent illustration of the creative power of love. It is a creative power because it leads the loved one to look upon himself as the loving one looks upon him. Love idealizes its object. That is what love is for. By so doing it creates the hope and inspires the effort in the loved one to live up to that ideal. Christ's love led Mary Magdalene to see in herself the possibilities which He saw in her. This is the explanation of the profound statement, "We love Him because He first loved us." God's love idealizes men. The man or woman who feels as Mary Magdalene felt—

> That all I could never be,
> All that men ignored in me,
> That I was worth to God,

has the secret by which he will become other than what he is. It matters much what he thinks God thinks about him.

Love is said to be blind. No statement is more untrue, for nothing is so keen-eyed as love. If you want to know a man's defects, ask his wife. Love is blind only in the sense that it deliberately shuts its eyes to defects, and centers its attention on the possibilities in order to help them to grow and crowd out the defects. Only so can one be delivered either from ignorance or from moral weakness; only so was Mary Magdalene delivered; only so can deliverance of any kind come.

Men's thought of the possibilities which God's love sees in them is the *greatest creative power* in human life, for by it men are delivered from what they are, as Mary Magdalene was delivered through the idealizing love of Jesus. This is Guercino's message to us in his picture of "The Magdalene."[3]

✣

"DER VERLORENE SOHN"

(The Forlorn Son)

By

Eugene Burnand

(Interpretation)

THE parable of the "Prodigal Son," or the "forlorn son" as this Swiss artist so graphically paints him, and about which Luke tells us (15:11-32), would be incomplete without some picture of the home-coming and glorious reunion of the overjoyed father and the forlorn and disconsolate son. It has not been as frequently painted by artists as many other incidents in the teachings of Jesus. This one by the Swiss artist, Eugene Burnand, is among the most challenging.

[3] Adapted from *Great Pictures as Moral Teachers*, by Henry E. Jackson. Published by the John C. Winston Company, Philadelphia, Pa. Used with permission.

The surroundings in this painting are rather bleak. There is a suggestion only of the father's mansion in the right background. It is dimly seen because it is unimportant. The artist wants to show us, instead, something of both the tragedy and the joy of that long-hoped-for reunion, which he does by the close embrace on the part of the father of his long-lost son. His own robe well-nigh covers the scantily clothed, bent, bedrabbled form of this younger son who left his father's house with such high hopes and confidence, and who now returns as an outcast feeder of swine.

The face of the son is lost in the protecting and sheltering embrace of the father, as if to blot out all that the intervening years have written there. The yearning, brooding love of the father for this son that the artist wants us to feel he has put in the deep-set, anxious eyes of this aged father, and in the strength of the embrace with which he has gathered this well-loved son into his arms.

"Love never faileth," that is what the artist wants us to feel as we gaze into the eyes of this aged father and feel the throb of joy in his heart over the return of this son, long mourned as dead.

The artist wants us to feel that God's love is like that which we see pictured here in the father's face. His children often trample under the dust of their feet God's many and gracious kindnesses to them. They forget so fully and so frequently that they are a part of God, that "in Him we live and move and have our being." They forget that they are flesh of His flesh and bone of His bone; that they were created by His loving hands for the companionship that ought always to exist between fathers and sons. Yet they so often go their wayward, selfish ways, well-nigh destroying even the image of the Father in whose likeness they are made. But God never forgets His children. He stands, as does this father, in the foreground of the universe, waiting with deep-set, patient eyes and a never-give-up spirit of forgiveness for the sons and daughters who pilgrim into far countries and there waste themselves and their substance in unrighteous living.

Writing of this parable, Dr. Bailey says: "Try, if you please, to invent a different ending for this story. Make the old man rebuff the boy at first; have him stand on his dignity and require of the rascal proofs of his change of heart; let him read him a sermon on wild oats before the forgiving kiss is bestowed; have him take the penitent at his word—as he richly deserves to be taken—and try him out with the slaves for a year or two, till the family pride, or outraged justice, is satisfied. Imagine, in short, *any possible ending but this,* and you have destroyed the noblest picture of redeeming grace ever created, and lowered God to the level of man's virtue. Heathen religions in plenty, and some versions of the Christian religion, furnish us with the alternatives suggested above, or worse; Christ alone shows us the suffering Father who saves by forgiving."[4]

[4] From *The Gospel in Art,* p. 173. Published by the Pilgrim Press, Boston, Mass. Used by special permission of the author.

"DER VERLORENE SOHN"—*BURNAND*

TEMPTED

Into the wilderness
Straightway our Lord was driven of the Spirit;
Swept by that stress
Of rapture, sun and stars were but one shining
Till forty days had passed
And, Son of Man though Son of God, He hungered.

Why should He fast
With power to make stones bread; why fear, with succor
Of angels at His call;
Why fail, when all the world was to His Father
A golden ball,
One of many, but a little present
For a Beloved Son?

Ecstasy, faint with its own bliss, encountered
The scorpion
Of self, love's enemy. For love is holy
In loving; love is safe
Only in saving; love, despised, rejected,
The world's white waif,
Needs nothing that this earth can give of glory,
For love dwelleth in God.

So Christ's immortal rose above His mortal
And on it trod.
                              —*Katharine Lee Bates*

COMRADES OF THE CROSS

I cannot think or reason,
I only know He came
With hands and feet of healing
And wild heart all aflame.

With eyes that dimmed and softened
At all the things He saw,
And in his pillared singing
I read the marching Law.

I only know He loves me,
Enfolds and understands—
And, oh, His heart that holds me,
And oh, His certain hands—

The man, the Christ, the soldier,
Who from His cross of pain
Cried to the dying comrade,
"Lad, we shall meet again."

—Willard Wattles

JESUS

Jesus, whose lot with us was cast,
Who saw it out, from first to last:
Patient and fearless, tender, true,
Carpenter, vagabond, felon, Jew:
Whose humorous eye took in each phase
Of full, rich life this world displays,
Yet evermore kept fast in view
The far-off goal it leads us to:
Who, as Your hour neared, did not fail—
The world's fate trembling in the scale—
With Your half-hearted band to dine,
And chat across the bread and wine:
Then went out firm to face the end,
Alone, without a single friend;
Who felt, as Your last words confessed,
Wrung from a proud unflinching breast
By hours of dull ignoble pain,
Your whole life's fight was fought in vain:
Would I could win and keep and feel
That heart of love, that spirit of steel.

—Author Unknown

FROM NAZARETH HE COMES

From Nazareth He comes, the carpenter
Who knows of hammering and blows that break
The worker's hands. From Galilee He comes,
The fisherman who walks upon the lake.

Through fields of harvest, ripe for plucking grain;
Along the dusty roads that go beside
The vineyards, Christ, the noble carpenter,
Goes to the city to be crucified.

Jerusalem's streets are filled with those
Who cry "Hosanna!" and others, "Crucify!"
For all of these He hangs upon the cross
That lifts itself into the purple sky.

For all of these the Master lived and died.
His lamp is tall and bright; our lamps are dim,
But we can see the way ahead of us,
For where the Master goes we go with Him.

                              —*Raymond Kresensky*

WHAT OUR LORD WROTE IN THE DUST

We have saved the soul of the man who killed,
    We have turned to shrive the thief;
We restored the pride of the man who lied
    And we gave him our belief;
But for her who fell we have fashioned hell
    With a faith all stern and just—
It was so of old; and no man hath told
    What our Lord wrote in the dust.

We have sighed betimes for our brothers' crimes
    And have bade them be of cheer,
For the flesh is weak, and the soul grown meek
    May yet read its title clear.
But we draw away from the one astray
    As the truly righteous must,
She is cursed indeed—and we did not read
    What our Lord wrote in the dust.

For the men who thieved, and who killed and lied—
    Who have slain the woman's soul—
We have worked and prayed, and have seen them made
    All clean, and pure and whole;
But we drive her out with a righteous shout
    In our Pharisaic trust,
So the man goes free—but we do not see
    What our Lord wrote in the dust.

                              —*Author Unknown*

I AM THE DOOR

A traveler once, when skies were rose and gold
With Syrian sunset, paused beside the fold
Where an Arabian shepherd housed his flock;
Only a circling wall of rough, gray rock—
No door, no gate, but just an opening wide
Enough for snowy, huddling sheep to come inside.
"So," questioned he, "then no wild beasts you dread?"
"Ah yes, the wolf is near," the shepherd said.

"But"—strange and sweet the words Divine of yore
Fell on his startled ear, *"I am the door!*
When skies are sown with stars, and I may trace
The velvet shadows in this narrow space,
I lay me down. No silly sheep may go
Without the fold but I, the shepherd, know.
Nor need my cherished flock, close-sheltered, warm,
Fear ravening wolf, save o'er my prostrate form."
O word of Christ—illumined evermore
For us His timid sheep—"I am the door!"

—Author Unknown

ONE OF THE MULTITUDE

O Nazarene, we would not be deceived,
  We simple folk who follow, some for the healing,
  More for the loaves, a few for the revealing
Of God in whom our spirits have believed,
Even when his cruel world our hearts bereaved
  Of joy, our hearts that bear not even the dealing
  Of wild beast with its prey. Yet mercy, kneeling
To the Mercy whence it sprang, finds Him not grieved,
The Omnipotent, not grieved, enough to end
  Terror and ravage. Gentle Master, you
Have said He notes the sparrow's fall. Strange Friend,
To look and leave them fluttering in the snares!
  Two sparrows for one farthing, five for two
We purchase. Does it help them that He cares?

—Katharine Lee Bates

YET ANOTHER OF THE MULTITUDE

The very fellow that I saw yestreen
  Sharing his loaf with dogs! One whimpering cur
  Held up a bloody paw. Without demur
'Twas wrapt in dewy herbs, made whole and clean.
And you would hold that this mild Nazarene
  Is the Messiah, he whose voice shall stir
  Tabor and Carmel, so the scribes aver,
To blend their crowns and all that lies between
Into one summit for the Temple, whither
  He shall go up in majesty, all red
    With Roman blood! Ha, then, saith Zephaniah,
A crashing from the hills! His wrath shall wither
  Moab to nettles. But your man gives bread
    To outcast dogs. A milksop our Messiah!

—Katharine Lee Bates

THE POWER OF PURITY AND LOVE

THE women of the party were not inclined to dispute, and, indeed, we saw little of them, for they occupied themselves with serving. But sometimes Mary of Magdala, who, having been a harlot, was accustomed to talk to men, came and talked with us. I mind me that on one of these days there was a sharp discussion amongst the disciples. It was the first time that I had seen Mary since our start. Jesus had gone aside up the mountain to pray, and we waited in the shadow of an oak grove till He should return and we start again. I sat on the edge of the grove, somewhat apart, and when I saw a woman coming I did not at first see that it was Mary, for she was dressed like a woman of the people in a coarse blue garment. Her hair was plainly braided, and there was no paint on her face. She was beautiful still, but the change was so great that for a moment I stood aghast, and Mary laughed.

"You see I am no longer clad like a king's daughter," she said.

"But your clothes were beautiful, Mary," I answered with somewhat of regret.

"Yes; but their beauty was branded. Some day I shall wear as beautiful, but till the Kingdom comes I wear this," and she touched her coarse garment.

"Is not the Kingdom here already?" I asked.

"Not for me," she answered, sadly, so that I asked, hastily:

"Are you not happy, Mary?"

"How can I be happy till my soul is clean? My tears have but washed the paint from my face," she replied.

Some of the others, seeing us talking, had drawn near, for Mary was like wine to men and they still sought her. Even now, when she no longer wished to rouse their bodily desires, she stirred and excited their minds, and till her death she held them.

Peter, hearing the sadness in her voice, said in his hasty way, with something of self-importance in his tone:

"Men do not condemn you, Mary."

Whereupon Mary, with a flash of her old temper, answered, "It matters not to me whether men condemn me or not. What sins I committed they shared. I know men too well to value their judgment."

"Jesus did not come to condemn the world, but to save it," said John.

"Jesus did not condemn me," said Mary. "I condemn myself. My punishment for having lived a dirty life is to see the beauty of a clean one, and He showed me that. It is enough."[5]

[5] From *By an Unknown Disciple*. Published by Harper & Brothers, New York City. Used by special permission of the publishers.

JESUS, AS SEEN BY JOHANAN, COLLECTOR OF TAXES AT MAGDALA

(A Letter written to Zacchæus, Commissioner of Taxes at Jericho)

By

W. Russell Maltby

DEAR ZACCHÆUS:

I have just had Jesus, the prophet of Nazareth, to dinner today, and a number of our friends came to meet Him. I promised to let you know what happened, but I promised too much. I will tell you what I can but it is only an hour since He went, and He has left me full of thoughts.

As you know I was rather nervous about the whole affair. First thing this morning I would have given a good deal to stop the dinner altogether. You and I often say that our sort of people are no worse than other folk; but when I went over the invitations in my mind, I couldn't help feeling that we were a queer company for such a Man as Jesus. I wondered what would happen if Reuben began talking the way he does sometimes, and I meant to give him a hint before the meal began. However, I did not get an opportunity, and as it happened there was no need. Reuben wasn't himself today.

Well, Jesus came. What is He like? If you had asked me halfway through the dinner, I should have said that He was the nicest Man I had ever met. But now I think—oh, I don't know what I think, except that I am not fit to touch the latchet of His shoes. Of course we were all very anxious to hear Him talk. Reuben was hoping that He would give the Pharisees a dressing down, and made an opportunity for Him. But Jesus never mentioned the Pharisees, and to tell the truth I believe we all forgot that there were such people. He seemed just as ready to listen as to talk. And what a listener He is! I never met anyone who listens as He does.

I happened to mention my boy Benjamin, for we are wondering what trade to put him to, and of course we are rather anxious, as there are not many openings for a publican's son. Jesus was interested immediately, and asked me questions about the lad. He told me something, too, about His own boyhood. I began to feel rather ashamed at last, for you know it is very strange to meet some one who understands your own lad better than you do yourself. But Jesus does understand boys.

I cannot tell you all the things we talked about. They were much the same kind of things you and I might speak of, but there was a difference. I found myself talking to Him as though I had known Him all my life. I began telling Him—I can't think how I did it, now—about how I got into this business of ours, and I was explaining our difficulties and how impossible it is always to keep straight when everybody is trying to take advantage of you; and especially in these times when the future is so uncertain and one must make provision while one can for wife and family. He just listened, and looked straight into my face as though He understood all I said—and all I didn't say, as well—and as though He were sorry for us. He didn't interrupt, or argue with me, but the more I looked at Him, the more I wished I had never got into the cursed business, and the more I wished I could get out and begin again.

You will think it ridiculous, but as He sat there, I wondered why we were not all like Him. We are all sick; he alone is well. I remembered the time when you and I were boys together, and I felt that we had missed the road. If I had been alone with Him, I think I should have made a clean breast of it and asked Him what to do. He could see that my feelings were getting out of hand—they say in the town that Johanan has no feelings, and I half believed them until today. But really the tears were in my eyes, and I had such a longing, and felt so helpless. And Jesus said to me, as though He understood everything, "Don't be afraid, Johanan. Think it all over again, and remember your heavenly Father knows what you need. Don't lose your life trying to save it." Do you see what He meant?

Well, the meal ended, and I was bidding Him goodbye at the door, when the girl, Rachel—the harlot; you know her trade—came up to the door, and I felt the blood rush to my cheeks, lest she should show that she knew me. But she had eyes only for Jesus. Some of His friends drew back, also, when they saw her; but Jesus himself gave her a look which I shall never forget, went straight up to her, and said only this, "Don't do it any more, Rachel." She stood gazing after Him as He went, and then covered her face with her hands, and ran down the street after Him, crying. As for me, I watched Him till he was out of sight, and I had hard work not to run after Him, too. He is on His way to Jerusalem. He is to pass through Jericho. I mentioned you to Him. Be sure you see him. Don't let anything stop you.

Peace be unto you.

P. S.—Benjamin has just come in. You would love that boy, Zacchæus. I must be a better father to him. Do you remember the first time you and I went up to the Temple together? We were just Benjamin's age—twelve years old. Do you remember how we sang as we went up—

> Who shall ascend into the hill of the Lord?
> He that hath clean hands and a pure heart.

We have missed our way, Zacchæus. But I think, since Jesus was here, that God has not altogether cast us off. Do you think that we two could begin again?

JESUS, AS SEEN BY ZACCHÆUS, COMMISSIONER OF TAXES AT JERICHO

(Letter written to Johanan, Collector of Taxes at Magdala)

By

W. Russell Maltby

DEAR JOHANAN:

You have made Zacchæus a poor man. The half of all that I had gathered these many years went at one stroke, and the rest seems likely to follow. It was your letter that did it, and I shall leave you to do the repenting, for I cannot. I am too contented for any grieving.

You told me that I must not miss seeing Jesus, but I nearly did. It was seven days ago when I heard that He had entered Jericho, and I made off to see the Man who had made such a difference to you. But there was already a great crowd about Him, and being smaller than most, and not in the way of having favors shown me, I could not get near, do what I would: So I tried another plan. I ran on ahead and clambered on to the bough of a tree, and waited there, sure of a good view.

I saw Him in the distance. I watched Him as he came near, and I thought to see Him pass and leave me behind. He came within three paces of me and stopped. He looked me in the face and said, as though I were a friend, "Zacchæus, make haste and come down. You must give Me a home today."

Was I glad? I have asked myself a hundred times why those words quivered all through me. But is it nothing, Johanan, after so long a time, to be treated like a man? He gave me His friendship. Outcasts must make friends with outcasts, for we have no others, but what need had He of me?

I lost no time. I tumbled from my perch and gave Him the best welcome I knew how and turned to lead the way to our house. Then my trouble began. I had not gone twenty paces before I knew that something was wrong, and of course I should have foreseen it. The weather had changed, Johanan. The chatter of the crowd ceased. The very boys went quiet. There was a horrible silence. The light went out of men's faces and I saw round me nothing but anger and contempt.

You will say that we have seen all that many a time before. Yes, we have; but if we had not earned it, you and I, at least we paid them back for it. But was I to drag *Him* down into the mud I was in myself? It seemed as though He had lost all his friends at one stroke, and lost them all for me. Then the voices began again. They gave me all the usual names, but they were not aiming them at me this time. "Going *there* to eat!" said one; and I heard the answer, "Oh yes! he knows how to choose his table," "And his wine," said a third. He heard it, too, as well as I.

I wondered whether He repented of having involved Himself with me, and while I was wondering He drew a little nearer to me as we walked, and said, "You will have room for these other friends of mine?" and He pointed to the young men who were with Him. I answered, "Yes," but I was at my wit's end and could no longer play my part. Indeed, Johanan, all my armor was gone. If I could have turned upon them and said, "These men slander me. Publican as I am, my hands are clean!" But I could not say so. For once they spoke the truth when they said that my house was no place for Him. I looked at Him and my eyes were opened. Beside Him, we are all common and unclean. My ears were burning and my thoughts were in a maze; but still I found myself saying, "He must not come to my house in vain"; and just as we reached the house the light broke on me and I knew what to do.

I turned at the porch and stripped. "Listen," I cried, "I will give half of my fortune to the poor, and if I have defrauded any man of anything, I will pay him back forefold." Then my tongue failed me and I looked to Him to see if He could help me out. I could not read His thoughts, but there was a smile upon His face, and I became content. He lifted His hand as though to bless my house, and said, "Salvation has entered this house today. Zacchæus, too, is a son of Abraham."

Yes, He said it; those were His words. He said I was not an outcast, and I have found, Johanan, that a son of Abraham may call upon the God of Abraham. "Son of man," He said—did he call Himself by that name when you met Him?—"The Son of Man came to seek and save the lost." Strange that I did not know I was lost until I was found. He came in and stayed with us. All I can tell you is that we shall never be the same again. Old as I am, I have begun again. He has gone on to Jerusalem, where, I fear, He has many enemies. I have heard bad rumors; so tomorrow I am going up to Jerusalem, for I must know.

About the money! We leave this house in a month's time. Zacharias, our old servant, will remain with us, for he is not willing to leave us; but the rest will go. I have gone around making restitution as I promised. It was not easy, but it was easier than I expected, and I think I am near the end of it now. Some thought me mad, but they took the money and took it quickly, lest I should recover my senses in time. Some seemed to understand and were unwilling to receive so much, and some of them gave me the blessing of God and their tears. Old Issachar was nearly the occasion of my fall. He had over-reached me once, passing nineteen chests of balm when he had only paid on nine. So when my chance came I got even. He came to ask for restitution but offered none on his part. I was angry and told him that we were more than quits. He turned away and said, "Soon tired of being a son of Abraham, Zacchæus! Now that your new Friend is gone! I should have hurried and taken my chance while the fit lasted." I called him back. I counted out the money and gave it to him,—"I thank you, Issachar, for reminding me. For my new Friend's sake, take the money and welcome; and may the Great God be as kind to you as Jesus was to me."

Peace be with you!

JESUS, AS SEEN BY MARY MAGDALENE

It was in the month of June when I saw Him for the first time.[6] He was walking in the wheat-field when I passed by with my handmaidens, and He was alone.

The rhythm of His step was different from other men's, and the movement of His body was like naught I had seen before. Men do not pace the earth in that manner. And even now I do not know whether He walked fast or slow.

My handmaidens pointed their fingers at Him and spoke in shy whispers to one another. And I stayed my steps for a moment, and raised my hand to hail Him. But He did not turn His face, and He did not look at me; and I hated Him. I was swept back into myself, and I was cold as if I had been in a snowdrift; and I shivered.

That night I beheld Him in my dreaming; and they told me afterward that I screamed in my sleep and was restless upon my bed.

It was in the month of August that I saw Him again, through my window. He was sitting in the shadow of the cypress tree across my garden, and He was as still as if He had been carved out of stone, like the statues in Antioch and other cities of the North Country.

My slave, the Egyptian, came to me and said, "That man is here again. He is sitting there across your garden."

And I gazed at Him, and my soul quivered within me, for He was beautiful. His body was single and each part seemed to love every other part.

Then I clothed myself with the raiment of Damascus, and I left my house and walked toward Him.

Was it my aloneness, or was it His fragrance, that drew me to Him? Was it a hunger in my eyes that desired comeliness, or was it His beauty that sought the light in my eyes? Even *now* I do not know.

I walked to Him with my scented garments and my golden sandals, the sandals the Roman captain had given me, even these sandals. And when I reached Him, I said, "Good-morrow to you."

And He said, "Good-morrow to you, Miriam."

And He looked at me, and His night eyes saw me as no man had seen me before. And suddenly I was as if naked, and I was shy. Yet He had said only, "Good-morrow to you."

Then I said to Him, "Will you not come to my house?"

And He said, "Am I not already in your house?"

I did not know what He meant then, but I know *now*.

[6] This story will be more effective if portrayed in costume. Use a plain white Grecian robe with red sari about the head and shoulders. The teller should be seated at a small table. The following Introduction is suggested: "Paul, you would know how I, Mary Magdalene, came to know and love Jesus. Well, sit ye here, and I will relate my story to you."

And I said, "Will you not have bread and wine with me?"

And He said, "Yes, Miriam, but not now."

"Not now, not now," He said. And the voice of the sea was in those two words, and the voice of the wind and the trees. And when He said them unto me, *life* spoke to *death*.

For, mind you, my friend, I was dead. I was a woman who had divorced her soul. I was living apart from this self which you now see. I belonged to all men, and to none. They called me harlot, and a woman possessed of seven devils. I was cursed, and I was envied.

But when His dawn eyes looked into my eyes all the stars of my night faded away and I became Miriam, only Miriam, *a woman lost to the earth she had known, and finding herself in new places.*

And now again I said to Him, "Come into my house and share bread and wine with me."

And He said, "Why do you bid me to be your guest?"

And I said, "I beg you to come into my house." And it was all that was sod in me, and all that was sky in me, calling unto Him. Then He looked at me, and the noontide of His eyes was upon me, and He said, "You have many lovers, and yet I alone love you. Other men love themselves in your nearness. I love you in yourself. Other men see a beauty in you that shall fade away sooner than their own years. But I see in you a beauty that shall not fade away, and in the autumn of your days that beauty shall not be afraid to gaze at itself in the mirror, and it shall not be offended.

"I, alone, love the unseen in you."

Then He said in a low voice: "Go away now. If this cypress tree is yours and you would not have Me sit in its shadow, I will walk my way."

And I cried to Him and I said: "Master, come to my house. I have incense to burn for you, and a silver basin for your feet. You are a stranger, and yet not a stranger. I entreat you, come to my House."

Then He stood up and looked at me even as the seasons might look down upon the field, and He smiled. And again He said: "All men love you for themselves. I love you for yourself."

And then He walked away. But no other man ever walked the way He walked. Was it a breath born in my garden that moved to the east? Or was it a storm that would shake all things to their foundations?

I knew not, but on that day the sunset of His eyes slew the dragon in me, and I became a woman—I became Miriam, Miriam of Migdel—Mary, the Magdalene, a *slave* in *His kingdom of love.*[7]

---

[7] From *Jesus,* by Kahlil Gibran. Published by Alfred A. Knopf, New York City. Used with special permission of the publishers.

THE NINETY AND NINE

THIS great Christian hymn found its inspiration in the parable of the "Lost Sheep." Read Luke 15:3-7 and note the similarity between the story of the "Lost Sheep" as it is found in the Gospel and this hymn that attempts to tell the same story in poetic verse.

The story, as we find it in the hymn, has been elaborated in such a way as to emphasize the discomfort and peril which this search for the lost sheep must have cost the Master. Its dramatic quality has also been heightened by the conversational form into which the hymn is cast; but the essence of the story is the same in the song and the parable as given by Luke.

Jesus referred to Himself not only as the good shepherd, but also as the door to the sheepfold, which men must use if they would enter into life abundant.

This great hymn, picturing as it does the shepherd's love and care for even the least of the sheep, has a distinct appeal to young people because of its dramatic, emotional form and its personalized question-and-answer style. We feel the tragic *need* of the *lost sheep* much more strongly in this song than we do in reading this brief parable in Luke's Gospel.

> There were ninety and nine that safely lay
>   In the shelter of the fold,
> But one was out on the hills away,
>   Far off from the gates of gold;
> Away on the mountains wild and bare,
> Away from the tender Shepherd's care,
> Away from the tender Shepherd's care.
>
> "Lord, Thou hast here Thy ninety and nine;
>   Are they not enough for Thee?"
> But the Shepherd made answer: "This of Mine
>   Has wandered away from Me;
> And although the road be rough and steep
> I go to the desert to find My sheep,
> I go to the desert to find My sheep."
>
> But none of the ransomed ever knew
>   How deep were the waters crossed;
> Or how dark was the night that the Lord passed through
>   Ere He found His sheep that was lost.
> Out in the desert He heard its cry—
> Sick and helpless, and ready to die,
> Sick and helpless and ready to die.

"Lord, whence are those blood-drops all the way
   That mark out the mountain's track?"
They were shed for one who had gone astray
   Ere the Shepherd could bring him back.
"Lord, whence are Thy hands so rent and torn?"
"They are pierced tonight by many a thorn,
They are pierced tonight by many a thorn."

But all through the mountains, thunder riv'n,
   And up from the rocky steep,
There rose a cry to the gate of heav'n,
   "Rejoice! I have found My sheep."
And the angels echoed around the throne,
"Rejoice, for the Lord brings back His own!
Rejoice, for the Lord brings back His own!"

                          —*Elizabeth C. Clephane*

✤

O LOVE THAT WILT NOT LET ME GO

THIS great hymn was written by Dr. George Matheson, one of Scotland's ablest preachers and one of the world's greatest writers of devotional literature. It was written on the day of his sister's wedding, and not immediately following his rejection by his *fiancée*, as many suppose. For this reason it breathes the spirit of enduring pain rather than the sudden, poignant grief which accompanied his broken engagement because of blindness.

In spite of the fact that Mr. Matheson became totally blind soon after he entered the University of Glasgow, he graduated when he was nineteen and entered the ministry of the Church of Scotland in 1866. His first parish was Innellan, on the Firth of the Clyde, where he remained for eighteen years, winning the hearts of all by his gracious and attractive personality, and growing in power as a preacher and great devotional leader.

When he was forty-four and in the height of his power, he was called to St. Bernard Parish Church in Edinburgh. While in this pastorate he reached the zenith of his power and influence. His services were attended by great crowds, and here he also wrote some of his most famous devotional and theological works.

Speaking of the inspiration of the hymn "O Love That Wilt Not Let Me Go," Dr. Matheson said: "Something had happened to me which was known only to myself and which caused me the most severe mental suffering. This hymn was the fruit of that suffering. It was the quickest bit of work I ever did in my life. I had the impression of having it dictated to me by some inward voice rather than of working it out myself. I am quite sure that the whole work was completed in five minutes and equally sure that it never received at my hands any retouching or correction."

The tune to which this great hymn is sung was composed by Dr. Albert Lister Peace, then organist of Glasgow Cathedral and musical editor of *The Scottish Hymnal of 1885.*

O Love that wilt not let me go,
    I rest my weary soul in thee;
I give thee back the life I owe,
That in thine ocean depths its flow
May richer, fuller be.

O Light that followest all my way,
    I yield my flickering torch to thee;
My heart restores its borrowed ray,
That in thy sunshine's blaze its day
May brighter, fairer be.

O Joy that seekest me through pain,
    I cannot close my heart to thee;
I trace the rainbow through the rain,
And feel the promise is not vain
That morn shall tearless be.

O cross that liftest up my head,
    I dare not ask to fly from thee;
I lay in dust life's glory dead,
And from the ground there blossoms red
Life that shall endless be.
                              —George Matheson, 1882

✛

IMMORTAL LOVE, FOREVER FULL

THIS great Christian hymn by John G. Whittier is one of the richest hymns of the Church in its devotional message to our hearts. Its theme is the constant, never-ending, abundant love and mercy of our Lord and Master that cannot be exhausted or depleted by the selfishness and short-sightedness of men.

Christ, the abundant, is ever ready, ever available for the healing of the hurt of the world, when we, His needy and wayward children, turn to Him in love and filial devotion. He does not force Himself or His unfailing love upon us. The urge to seek Him and His aid in abundant living must come from within the human heart; but His majesty, love, and power are forever about and with us in the world to be claimed when in sincerity and truth our hearts reach out for His guidance and care.

Immortal Love, forever full,
  Forever flowing free,
Forever shared, forever whole,
  A never-ebbing sea.

We may not climb the heavenly steeps
  To bring the Lord Christ down;
In vain we search the lowest deeps,
  For Him no depths can drown.

But warm, sweet, tender, even yet
  A present help is He;
And faith has still its Olivet,
  And love its Galilee.

The healing of His seamless dress,
  Is by our beds of pain;
We touch Him in life's throng and press
  And we are whole again.

O Lord and Master of us all,
Whate'er our name or sign,
We own Thy sway, we hear Thy call,
  We test our lives by Thine.

  —*John G. Whittier, 1866*

✠

LORD, SPEAK TO ME THAT I MAY SPEAK

THIS familiar hymn was written by Frances Ridley Havergal, one of the most prolific hymn-writers of the nineteenth century. As one reads the verses of this great hymn-poem, one can well believe the author's words, "For me writing is praying" for every verse is an intensely personal prayer challenge.

Miss Havergal was the daughter of a minister, who himself was a gifted musician and a skilled poet. She began to write verse at the tender age of seven, and devoted her entire life, forty-three years, to the musical service of her church. In a very real sense she became a "minister of music," giving voice in this and other hymns from her pen to her rich background of Christian heritage and experience.

The theme of this great prayer-hymn, "Lord, Speak to Me That I May Speak," is found in Miss Havergal's use of four significant words—"speak" . . . "teach" . . . "fill" . . . and "use," as in each succeeding verse the author searches the hearts of young people and adults alike, challenging them to lives of sincere devotion and service.

The tune melody to which this great hymn is usually sung is by Robert Schumann, a truly great musical composer, who also began to compose before his seventh year.

> Lord, speak to me, that I may speak
> In living echoes of Thy tone;
> As Thou hast sought, so let me seek
> Thy erring children lost and lone.
>
> O teach me, Lord, that I may teach
> The precious things Thou dost impart;
> And wing my words, that they may reach
> The hidden depths of many a heart.
>
> O fill me with Thy fullness, Lord,
> Until my very heart o'erflow
> In kindling thought and glowing word,
> Thy love to tell, Thy praise to show.
>
> O use me, Lord, use even me,
> Just as Thou wilt, and when and where;
> Until Thy blessed face I see,
> Thy rest, Thy joy, Thy glory share.
>
> —*Frances R. Havergal, 1872*

✠

LOVE THYSELF LAST[8]

THIS great poem, "Love Thyself Last," from the pen of Ella Wheeler Wilcox, 1855-1919, has been set to music so that it is available as a hymn as well as a beautiful challenging poem.

Its theme is couched in the first half of the first line of each stanza as well as in the title of the poem itself, "Love Thyself Last"; and is in perfect accord with the selfless love of the Master of Men, who literally poured out His life and energy for others, taking no thought whatever for Himself or his own comfort or convenience.

Every verse of this great hymn is a challenge to Christians today to forget themselves in their service to Christ's needy ones along life's highway. When sung with reverence, sincerity, and feeling it provides one of those purifying challenges that send the Christian out to live everyday the life of service that marks the pathway of every truly devout follower of the sinless, selfless Christ.

It is usually sung to the tune "Morning Star," composed by John P. Harding in 1861.

[8] From *Poems of Power*, copyright by W. B. Conkey Company. Used with permission.

Love thyself last; look near, behold thy duty
  To those who walk beside thee down life's road;
Make glad their days by little acts of beauty,
  And help them bear the burden of earth's load.

Love thyself last; look far and find the stranger
  Who staggers 'neath his sin and his despair;
Go, lend a hand and lead him out of danger
  To heights where he may see the world is fair.

Love thyself last; the vastnesses above thee
  Are filled with spirit forces, strong and pure;
And fervently these faithful friends shall love thee,
  Keep thy watch over others and endure.

Love thyself last; and thou shalt grow in spirit
  To see, to hear, to know and understand;
The message of the stars, lo, thou shalt hear it,
  And all God's joys shall be at thy command.

                              —*Ella Wheeler Wilcox*

✣

TELL ME THE OLD, OLD STORY

"Tell Me the Old, Old Story" and "I Love to Tell the Story" were written in 1866 by Katherine Hankey. As she was convalescing after a long serious illness at her home in England, she wrote a poem of fifty stanzas upon the life of Christ. The hymns mentioned above were later taken from this longer poem.

So grateful was she for the story "that satisfies my longing," as she expressed it, that she spent much time in meditation; and as a result she wrote the words of these beautiful and well-beloved hymns.

Her mention in the first stanza of "For I am weak and weary, and helpless and defiled," no doubt referred to her own frail physical condition at that time.

The music was written by Dr. Doane, a well-known composer, who first heard the poem read at an international convention of the Young Men's Christian Association, held in Montreal. He obtained a copy of the words and later set them to the familiar tune that we all love. Both of these hymns are popular the world over and are sung in many different tongues.

Tell me the old, old story,
  Of unseen things above,
Of Jesus and His glory,
  Of Jesus and His love.

Tell me the story simply,
  As to a little child,
For I am weak and weary
  And helpless and defiled.

Tell me the story slowly,
  That I may take it in—
That wonderful redemption,
  God's remedy for sin.
Tell me the story often,
  For I forget so soon;
The early dew of morning
  Has passed away at noon.

Tell me the story softly,
  With earnest tones, and grave;
Remember! I'm a sinner
  Whom Jesus came to save.
Tell me that story always,
  If you would really be,
In any time of trouble,
  A comforter to me.

Tell me the same old story
  When you have cause to fear
That this world's empty glory
  Is costing me too dear.
Yes, and when that world's glory
  Is dawning on my soul,
Tell me the old, old story:
  Christ Jesus makes me whole."

                   —*Katherine Hankey, 1866*

CONTENTS

PART III   SECTION IV

THE MASTER WORKMAN

✠

"My Father worketh even until now, and I work."—John 5:17

✠

---✠---

THE MASTER WAS A WORKER

"Now there is in Jerusalem by the sheep *gate* a pool, which is called in Hebrew Bethesda, having five porches. In these lay a multitude of them that were sick, blind, halt, withered. And a certain man was there, who had been thirty and eight years in his infirmity. When Jesus saw him lying, and knew that he had been now a long time *in that case*, he saith unto him, Wouldest thou be made whole? The sick man answered him, Sir, I have no man, when the water is troubled, to put me into the pool: but while I am coming another steppeth down before me. Jesus saith unto him, Arise, take up thy bed, and walk. And straightway the man was made whole, and took up his bed and walked.

"Now it was the sabbath on that day. So the Jews said unto him that was cured, It is the sabbath, and it is not lawful for thee to take up thy bed. But he answered them, He made me whole, the same said unto me, Take up thy bed, and walk. They asked him, Who is the man that said unto thee, Take up *thy bed*, and walk? But he that was healed knew not who it was; for Jesus had conveyed himself away, a multitude being in the place. Afterward Jesus findeth him in the Temple, and said unto him, Behold, thou art made whole: sin no more, lest a worse thing befall thee. And the man went away, and told the Jews that it was Jesus who had made him whole. And for this cause the Jews persecuted Jesus, because he did things on the sabbath. But Jesus answered them, My Father worketh even until now, and I work."—JOHN 5:2-17

THE WEDDING AT CANA—*VERONESE*

THE WEDDING AT CANA

By

Paolo Veronese

(Interpretation)

Among the hundreds of beautiful paintings that hang in the Louvre in Paris, none, perhaps, attracts greater attention than "The Wedding at Cana" by Paolo Veronese (pronounced Vay-ro-nay-sy), who was born in Verona in 1528. Among all the artistic works of Veronese, the most celebrated is this great banquet scene, first because of its size: it measures twenty feet high by thirty feet wide, and is one of the largest in the Louvre or, for that matter, in the world; and second because of its gorgeous costumes and beautiful coloring. No black and white or brown print can ever do justice to the richness of color in the original.

"It is impossible to look at this picture without astonishment," writes Mr. W. M. Rossetti; "it enlarges one's conception of what pictorial art means and can do. The only point of view from which it fails is that of the New Testament narrative; for there is no more relation between the Galilean wedding and Veronese's court banquet than between a portrait of Lazarus and a portrait of Dives."

Of all of these great compositions of Veronese, a recent critic writes, "In spite of their sacred titles, they are, in reality, merely reproductions of those sumptuous banquets and festive entertainments in which the wealthy Venetians took delight and which were marked with an ever-increasing degree of state ceremonial. . . . Christ and his disciples are but insignificant accessories in the scene." Only a portion of the original painting is shown in this reproduction. Much of the blue sky, luminous atmosphere, and palatial architecture of the original has been eliminated, so that the facial expression of the guests might be seen with greater clarity.

Veronese in his conception of "The Wedding at Cana," which incident happened early in the ministry of Jesus, has seen fit to picture men and women seated together at a sumptuous banquet table in a magnificently palatial home. This, of course, is painter's license, for in a typical wedding feast of Bible times women would not be reclining at a table with men, although in humbler homes they frequently served as assistant hostesses in serving the bridegroom and his guests. An adjoining room was provided for the bride and her women friends, where they might hear the singing, laughing, and jesting. They would not, however, be seated at the table with men, but served apart in their own banquet-room.

The center of interest in the portion of this banquet scene shown in this print is not alone in the face of Jesus, although He does occupy a central place at the feast; but rather in the look of surprise and wonder on the face of one of the guests who has just been served some of the new wine and who says to the ruler of the feast, who had already been told by the servants that the wine was exhausted: "How is this, every man when he maketh a feast doth serve the good wine and then when men have drunk their fill, he serveth that which is worse? But thou hast kept the good wine until now!"

The relieved host near the end of the table does not understand what has happened any more than his guests; but he has been saved from public humiliation and from a disgrace that would have branded him and his household for all time as stingy and ungracious, and his relief shows plainly in his mysterious, puzzled face and eyes.

This story of the Wedding at Cana, which only John tells (2:1-10), with its apparently purposeless miracle, has bothered many followers of Jesus. They can understand why and how Jesus would use His miraculous power in sickness, death, and the healing of all kinds of infirmities; but they cannot quite fathom why or how He should thus come to the rescue of an improvident host, by turning water into wine, just to save the groom's family chagrin and embarrassment at a wedding feast.

A better understanding of the importance of the Oriental wedding ceremony, as the Jews conceived it, will help; as will also the seriousness of running out of wine on such an occasion, and the resulting disrespect and humiliation that such an accident would inevitably bring to the bridegroom and his family.

Then, too, Mary, the mother of Jesus, was probably among the women especially honored on this occasion by being an assistant hostess. How else would Mary have known of the disaster that had come in the midst of this gay wedding ceremony?

It is true that Jesus never used His miraculous power for Himself or for selfish purposes; but He did use it freely for others, as in the case of the feeding of the five thousand, no one of whom would have perished from hunger even if the disciples, at His instruction, had sent them away into the city to buy bread.

An Oriental wedding feast is an important ceremony. To fail with wine at such a time would be comparable to the bridegroom of today failing or forgetting to provide a ring for the ring ceremony in a church wedding. Shame and humiliation would rest not alone upon the bridegroom and his family but upon the bride as well.

Then, too, the failure of the wine to last throughout the feast, was, on this occasion, doubtless one of those unexplainable mistakes which, now and then, do occur in even the best regulated of households, and often due to no fault of the meticulous host.

That Jesus had not planned to use His unusual powers in any spectacular way at this feast is evident by His reply to his mother's tragic information, "They have no wine." For He said: "Woman, what have I to do with thee? mine hour is not yet come." Nevertheless, in response to her faith in both

His power and His graciousness in times of distress and humiliation, she turned to the servants and said: "Whatsoever he saith unto you, do it." Such faith in the genuineness of both His ability and His courtesy could not go unrewarded at a time of such impending disaster.

Into His mind may have come the words of Mordecai to Esther in the long ago: "Who knoweth whether thou art not come to the kingdom for such a time as this?" At any rate, Jesus turned to the astonished servants and said: "Fill the water-pots with water," and when they were filled to the brim, and without even rising from His place at the banquet table, He continued, "Draw out now, and bear to the ruler of the feast."

As, in the background of this picture, we see servants bearing to the ruler of the feast and his guests quantities of this last and "best wine," we feel that we, too, would like to join in a song of thanksgiving because this public humiliation of the bridegroom and his family has been thus happily averted. "Blessed are the happy in spirit, for theirs is the Kingdom of Heaven," is in entire accord with the spirit of the miracle of the wedding in Cana of Galilee.

✠

FEEDING THE FIVE THOUSAND

By

Bartolomé Esteban Murillo

(Interpretation)

THE story of the life of Murillo, who was born at Seville, Spain, in 1617, is as unusual as are his paintings. Little is known of his childhood except that his parents died when he was eleven. He studied art with his uncle and soon outdid him in skill. He had a desperate struggle with poverty and walked all the way to Madrid, where he was befriended by Valasquez, then the court painter. For approximately three years he grew under the guidance of this noted artist, and then returned to Seville, where he obtained his first commission to paint from a Franciscan monastery.

From this time on his rise to fame and affluence was rapid. His time was fully occupied with orders from religious bodies and nobles. He was admitted to the highest circle of society and worshiped by the people. In 1648 he married a lady of noble birth and his home became a resort for the distinguished. Only once did he leave Seville until the time of his death in 1682. Murillo was a very devout Catholic, as all of his pictures imply. He often painted the same picture over and over until satisfied with the portrayal of the conception that was in his mind.

His painting, "Feeding the Five Thousand," while not so familiar as his "The Immaculate Conception" and others, is regarded as one of the best of this scene. It was painted for the Hospital de la Caridad at Seville.

FEEDING THE FIVE THOUSAND—*MURILLO*

Just where the miracle of the Feeding of the Five Thousand occurred, we do not know. Matthew tells us that it was in "a desert place apart," and that the multitude followed Jesus on foot from the cities. "When Jesus saw that the multitude had followed Him even into this desert place, He had compassion on them and healed their sick" in spite of His own personal weariness and need of rest. Later that day, when evening was come, the disciples came to Jesus saying: "The place is desert, and the time is already past; send the multitude away, that they may go into the villages, and buy themselves food."

But Jesus replied: "They have no need to go away; give ye them to eat." John tells us that Philip answered: "Two hundred shillings' worth of bread is not sufficient for them, that every one may take a little." To this Andrew replied: "There is a lad here, who hath five barley loaves, and two fishes: but what are these among so many?"

Jesus answered: "Make the people sit down," so the men sat down, in number about five thousand, not counting the women and children. Then Jesus took "the five loaves, and brake; and gave to His disciples to set before the multitude. And they ate, and were filled; and there was taken up of that which remained over to them of broken pieces, twelve baskets."

Note the barrenness of this desert place somewhere outside the City of Bethsaida. Murillo pictures it as the rocky foothills of near-by mountains. Note also the naïve charm of the little lad in the foreground, offering his platter of two small fishes to Peter, who in turn will hand them to Jesus. Andrew, the just, who discovered and brought the lad to Jesus, is already placing the five barley loaves in the Master's lap. Jesus, Who sits on a boulder, has already lifted one of the loaves in His hand, as He raises His eyes to the Heavenly Father, and lifts His voice in a prayer of thanksgiving for daily food.

The disciples who are to serve the multitude are standing near Jesus in interesting groupings. They have already succeeded in their task of getting the people seated, and now, in silent yet interested attention, they wait to see what His purpose and plan may be. Observe how many faces, here and there among the multitude, are turned in the Master's direction. Perhaps they anticipate another of His marvelous stories as they sit thus on the hillside at the close of a busy afternoon of healing of diseases and infirmities.

What is the message of this beautiful painting to human hearts? Jesus not only gives healing for sick bodies, and bread for daily hunger; but Himself, "the Bread of Life," in a spiritual sense to all those who follow Him in lowly service. Was not this the meaning of the Last Supper in that upper room in Jerusalem, and of the *communion sacrament* which His followers, even unto this day, share with Him? Later these disturbed and anxious disciples are to hear Him say, as He broke the bread of their farewell meal together: "This is My body, broken for you. Take, eat; as often as you do this, you do show forth my death until I come again."

Bread is not the all-important thing in life; but it is important to the physical well-being and happiness of men. Now and then, during the ministry of Jesus, those who were ill with sickness and infirmity needed special care and healing; but in this instance all those who followed Him were tired and hungry. The children especially would have to go unfed hours longer than was their usual custom, unless this daily need was supplied. Therefore Jesus made Himself, and through prayer His heavenly Father, also, one with their daily needs by His miraculous multiplication of the five small loaves and the two scant fishes provided by the little lad. These were distributed freely by His disciples to a waiting and hungry multitude, who in their eagerness for healing from bodily ills had followed the Master even into this desert place apart.

A lesson in courtesy and thoughtfulness of others is here portrayed, as indeed it was in all the miracles of Jesus. Abundant life He came to bring as the priceless boon of His heavenly Father to the children of men—life physically, mentally, socially, and spiritually, which even these unlettered disciples came, more and more, to understand as the days of His ministry on earth went by.

Many times in the years that followed His ascension His disciples would recall this eventide miracle of the Feeding of the Five Thousand. They would have been willing to send the multitude away hungry; but the Master sent them away physically refreshed that they might ponder, with deeper faith and understanding, over the love and care of their heavenly Father for even the least of these, His children.

✤

RAISING THE DAUGHTER OF JAIRUS

By

J. F. Repin

(Interpretation)

THIS scene, "Raising the Daughter of Jairus," the ruler of the synagogue at Capernaum, has been a favorite with artists. Yet none has given us a picture of richer beauty and coloring than the German artist, J. F. Repin, of the Petersburg Academy of Art.

The death-chamber is perhaps the guest-room of this home of wealth and comfort. In the left background is a richly canopied bed, while directly to the right of the death-couch the rich Oriental rug has been hastily rolled aside and the water jar and basin stand in readiness, no doubt, for the embalming.

In the porticoed entrance may be dimly seen the form of a servant waiting to respond to his master's slightest command. While near and in front of this servant stands the mother with tear-stained face and hopeless, downcast eyes. This Rabbi in whom they had placed so much faith stopped along the way to heal others, and now their lovely daughter is dead, and with her death hope also died in the watch-weary heart of this lonely mother.

RAISING THE DAUGHTER OF JAIRIS. REPIN

Jairus in his rich robes stands with clasped hands and a look of hope in his face as the Rabbi approaches the death-couch on which reclines his beautiful and well-beloved daughter. Behind Jairus are two disciples, perhaps Peter and John the beloved, standing quietly with their eyes riveted on the Master of Men. They have seen Him heal the lame, the halt, and the blind. Can he bring back *life* from the grave also, is the question which, in astonishment, they are asking themselves.

On the death-couch in the foreground lies the body of this beloved daughter of the ruler of the synagogue. The soft glow of light from the threefold candlestick at the head of the couch casts its mellow, golden glow on the head-rest, pillow, and flowers that loving hands have placed just above the head of this dead girl. Her lovely dark hair duskily frames her face; very young and very beautiful it is now as she reclines in death-like repose in the clean white winding-sheet of burial.

Jesus, Himself, standing alone in the foreground, is the center of interest. Quietly He has reached His right hand to clasp the pulse of this beautiful daughter of Jairus whom death has already claimed. His eyes are not upon the girl, but closed in prayer as he bears his petition for the restoration of the life of this lovely girl to His heavenly Father's throne. The rich, mellow light of the candelabra shines with a soft glow upon His face, His beard and the auburn hair that falls in graceful rings to the shoulder line of His blue robe. Note the strength of His left hand and wrist against the bluish folds of His outer robe. It is the hand of a man of toil and labor, as well as of blessings and deeds of mercy.

As we look at this picture we are conscious that the artist has made us aware of certain values often overlooked. As Dr. Bailey says: "We feel the pathos and the tragedy of death that cuts off the hopes of youth in their flower; of wealth powerless to stay the hand of fate; of hearts breaking with their load of irremediable grief. In the figures of Jairus and his wife we feel the strength of the love that has bound this family together so closely and that was the compelling power behind the father's search and behind his cry, 'Come, lay thy hand upon her that she may live!' What value did Jairus set now upon all his wealth? The touch of death upon one he loved brought out the true perspective in life, leveled the structures of pride and power his hands had reared, and showed LOVE standing out clear and alone, the one radiantly beautiful and supremely desirable thing in all the world. . . .

"Over against these emotions the artist has set Christ, the one Who Himself carried our griefs and Whose heart was touched with the feeling of our woe. He is one Who never resisted the God-given impulse to help when He saw human need. He will give back to Jairus his daughter for no other reason than pity for a breaking heart. . . . Simple love and pity are here incarnate and operative. He has come to the maiden's funeral couch just to set His seal on human affection. And how tenderly and beautifully He has done it! as if the privilege of thus restoring love to its own were a sacrament that made Him and the Father one. This is one of the supreme lessons of the life of

Jesus: that ministry to human need is a sacrament. It makes sacred not only the act, but the doer, because through the act and the doer God himself is expressing His love "[1]

✛

"CHRIST, HAVE MERCY UPON US"

By

A. Deitrich

(Interpretation)

AMONG the many beautiful and challenging pictures that have been painted to portray the healing ministry of the Master of Men, none is more realistic and appealing than this one by the German artist, A. Deitrich, 1833-1908.

In the foreground the world's Great Physician stands, His hands outstretched in the merciful miracle of healing the emaciated form of this slowly dying wife, whose husband's arms enfold her with such loving care. Prostrate on the stones at the Master's side weeps a broken-hearted daughter, while in the background kneels a full-grown son. His beseeching hands, clasped in prayer, speak eloquently for the life of the mother he loves.

This picture might well be called "the tragedy of love," because for those whom we love we suffer more acute agony than for anyone else in the world, not even excepting the pain of disease that may, now and then, wrack our bodies. It is evident that this family of four have come to the Great Physician as a last, hopeless resort. Every line of the frail, emaciated form of this slowly dying mother indicates this, as do the downcast head and eyes of the husband and father, and the sob-wracked body of this nearly grown daughter. In the eyes of the dying woman only is there any hope expressed. That hope is met by a searching, smiling tenderness in the Master's face as He stretches out His hands in healing ministry.

Behind these four who occupy the foreground of the picture come a host of the sick and lame, the halt and blind, the deformed and diseased, each begging mercy for himself in his misery and discomfort. Others carry in their arms sick children that are dearer to them than even life itself. Down the incline of this shaded hillside they come, as far as the eye can reach, their bodies weakened by sickness, sin, and disease.

As we look upon the white-robed Christ, standing there with outstretched arms, we feel somehow that His strength will not fail until the last of these needy ones has felt the touch of His healing ministry of love and mercy.

The picture has been well named "Christ, Have Mercy upon Us," and recalls to our minds the host of Untouchables who followed at a distance the Master of Men along the crowded waysides of Galilee, calling out, "Jesus

[1] From *The Gospel in Art*, pp. 108-109. Published by the Pilgrim Press. Used with permission of the author.

"CHRIST, HAVE MERCY UPON US"—DEITRICH

of Nazareth, have mercy on me," in the hope that He would turn and still forever the ravages of leprosy in their rotting, disintegrating bodies.

In the midst of this magnificent scene of green, leafy foliage, the intertwining boughs of whose giant trees form a canopy of shade; how out of harmony with the life-giving health of nature's sun and shadow are the broken, emaciated forms of these disease-ravaged victims. No wonder the Great Physician often found Himself spent at the end of weary days of life-giving healing to the sons of men.

And yet as He stands there in quiet, sympathetic dignity we feel assured that His power will be sufficient unto the hour. To us He seems, as He doubtless did to them, the exhaustless Christ—the Great Physician Who, more fully and completely than any other individual who has ever lived, literally poured out the riches of His own strength and vitality in service to the needy, whether sick of body, mind, or soul.

✧

THE TRANSFIGURATION

By

Sanzio Raphael

(Interpretation)

"THE Transfiguration" which now hangs in the Vatican Gallery in Rome was originally painted by Raphael on the order of Cardinal Giuliano de' Medici as an altarpiece for the cathedral at Narbonne, France. It was Raphael's last work. He died in 1520, before he had hardly completed "The Transfiguration." The canvas was exhibited above his coffin as he lay in state; and it accompanied the huge procession of mourners to the Pantheon, where the painter's body was interred.

Following Raphael's death, it was decreed that this magnificent painting should never leave Rome, but should be kept there as a memorial to the artist's fame and to the artistic service that he had rendered to the Roman Catholic Church. Notwithstanding this edict, however, it was carried to Paris in 1797 along with other artistic loot which Napoleon appropriated during his wars. In 1815 it was returned to Rome, where it now adorns the Vatican. A marvelous copy of "The Transfiguration" in beautiful mosaic adorns St. Peter's Church also.

"The Transfiguration" is among Raphael's most dramatic compositions. It is so rich in color, lights, shadows, and imagery that the first impression one receives in looking at it is that of *contrasts*; for there are rich contrasts in color, in composition, in spirit, and in imagery.

The three distinct levels shown in the picture have been likened by some art critics to the three stages of man. The upper level with Christ in the center suspended in billowy clouds. Moses the lawgiver on the right, and Elijah the prophet on the left, represent man in his glorified, redeemed state. The second group or level composed of John the beloved, James, who was destined later to martyrdom, and Peter, the stone man, comprise the inner circle of the disciples and represent mankind in the process of redemption through the law, the prophets, and the Christ-revealed truth of God's own Son. While the third group, on the lowest level of the picture, including the other disciples and the friends and relatives of the demoniac boy, represent the nations who are to be brought into the redeeming process of the Kingdom of God which Jesus came to establish on earth.

The Reverend Harold Francis Branch indicates that one message of this picture, at least, is "the transforming power of prayer." He says: "The Transfiguration occurred not only while Jesus prayed, but as He prayed. Prayer is the great transformer. Matthew in his account says, 'His face did shine as the sun.'. . . Exodus 34:29-35 describes the shining of Moses' face as he came down from the mount after his interview with God. Compare also Acts 6:15, where the transfiguration of Stephen's face, on the occasion of his trial, is described, and it is declared that 'his face was as the face of an angel.' The Greek word which Matthew uses and which is translated 'transfigured,' is one which denoted an *inward* change, not merely an outward one. It is to say that Christ's deity shone through the veil of His flesh. . . . While John in his Gospel does not tell about the Transfiguration, he does speak of the vision of the glorified Saviour in the Revelation (1:13-16), which must have reminded the aged apostle of the scene on Mount Hermon.[2]

Prayer still has transforming power. More beautiful words describing the transforming power of prayer were never penned than those written by Archbishop Trent:

> Lord, what a change within us one short hour
>   Spent in Thy presence will avail to make!
>   What heavy burdens from our bosoms take;
> What parched grounds refresh, as with a shower!
> We kneel, and all around us seems to lower;
>   We rise, and all the distant and the near
>   Stands forth in sunny outline, brave and clear!
> We kneel, how weak! we rise, how full of power!
> Why, therefore, should we do ourselves this wrong,
> Or others, that we are not always strong;
>   That we are ever overborne with care;
>   That we should ever weak or heartless be,
> Anxious or troubled, when with us is prayer,
>   And joy and strength and courage are with Thee?

Speaking of this painting, Dr. Bailey says: "All of these figures are disposed about the figure of Christ with a skill and a beauty that Raphael alone commands. Discordant and confused as the lower half of the picture seems, it is

[2] From *Sermons on Great Paintings*, pp. 115-116. Copyright by Harvey M. Shelly, Philadelphia, Pa. Used by permission of the publishers.

THE TRANSFIGURATION—*RAPHAEL*.

nevertheless subtly related to its own center and to the upper half. Its leading lines and lights point upward in sinuous curves to Christ, as if subconsciously men knew that their true center was in Him. Note in detail how this is so, from the book and Andrew's arm on the left to the father's fallen mantle on the right. 'For there is none other name given under heaven among men whereby we must be saved.' And just as truly the secondary line points to human need. Either by look or gesture the disciples refer to the boy, while the boy is the actual as well as the logical center of the family group. By this means Raphael unifies the picture: he points to the boy as the problem and to Christ as the solution. . . .

"The face of Christ is an absolutely adequate embodiment of the meaning of the Transfiguration. The Master is not here dealing with men; He is not relieving human need, teaching with authority, nor denouncing scribes and Pharisees. He is revealing to His chosen friends His inmost character in the presence of defeat and impending death. A study of the original or of a detailed reproduction will show what Raphael conceived the basis of that character to be: it is an absolute and loving surrender of his personal will to the will of His Father. Hence a beauty in this face that defies the most cunning phrases: it is the beauty of a perfect soul. And it is at the same time, in some marvelous way, 'the face of that divine child of the Sistine, matured, perfected, transfigured.'

"This picture is Raphael's masterpiece. It is not only a supreme composition and a supreme work of character-interpretation, but an expression of the deepest truth of life. And what is that truth? That man needs a Saviour; and that to save us God in His love has given us Christ, a realization of transfigured and redeemed humanity."[3]

✛

THE CARPENTER

This He was then—
A workman among working men.

He knew the orchards of Gennesaret;
The circled vineyards that were set
Like living cinctures, branch and root,
And jeweled with their purple fruit.
The somber olives, wide of limb,
Had sheltered Him
At noontide, when He had to pass
Beneath a sky of shimmering brass.
He knew the almond trees, that spread
Frail rosy clouds above His head;

[3] From *The Gospel in Art*, pp. 244-245. Published by the Pilgrim Press, Boston, Mass. Used by permission of the author.

The groves of oak and terebinth,
And where the fruit of colocynth
Ran tangled through the scarlet fires
Of lilies and anemones,
And where, above the walnut trees,
The tall firs lifted pointed spires.

He knew the miracle of night; the throbbing gold
Of eastern stars, merging in wistful rose
Of day, that lingers here as though to hold
The blended glories, and reluctant, goes
Down the wide hills at last, and toward the sea.
These things He knew, and all the majesty
Of planets set on height ascending height—
Vistas and terraces of light,
As though divided by a single breath,
Were God—and Nazareth.

Here were no dark misgivings, and no doubt.
All night He lived a greater prayer than words,
Until the dawn He saw the fishing-fleets go out
Like a low flight of birds.
He watched the hillslopes lightly sprayed with gold;
The olives etched in radiance, that were dark.
He saw the sheep come bleating from the fold,
And in the air, a lark.
While down the road, between the hills at last,
With tinkling bells, a train of camels passed.
With rhythmic steps, He saw them go
Upon their way to Jericho,
And in His shop, He knew, were good,
Red cedar boards and olive wood,
Where waiting for His fingers, were
The labors of a carpenter.

A night of stars and God—and then
A workman's toil with working men.

                 —*Mary Brent Whiteside*

WORK

Work! That makes the red blood glow,
Work! That makes the quick brain grow.
   Plough and hammer, hoe and flails,
   Ax and crowbar, saw and nails—
     A splitter of rails,
Lincoln was never a snob or a shirk,
   Thank God for work!

Toil that binds mankind together,
Day by day in every weather.
　Pen and distaff, needle and thread,
　Visions of wonder over her head,
　　A toiler for bread,
Joan of Arc was a peasant child
　On whom God smiled.

Labor that God Himself has blest,
Honest endeavor that earns good rest.
　Bench and hammer, nails and cord,
　Hammer and chisel, plane and board—
　　Christ our Lord
Had a carpenter's thorny hands,
　He understands.

—Abbie Farwell Brown

IN THE CARPENTER SHOP

I wish I had been His apprentice,
　To see Him each morning at seven,
As He tossed His gray tunic about Him,
　The Master of earth and of Heaven.
When He lifted the lid of His work-chest,
　And opened His carpenter's kit,
And looked at His chisels and augers,
　And took the bright tools out of it;
When He gazed at the rising sun tinting
　The dew on the opening flowers,
And He smiled at the thought of His Father
　Whose love floods this fair world of ours;
Then fastened the apron about Him,
　And put on His workingman's cap,
And grasped the smooth haft of His hammer
　To give the bent woodwork a tap,
Saying, "Lad, let us finish this ox yoke,
　The farmer must finish his crop."
Oh, I wish I had been His apprentice
　And worked in the Nazareth shop.

But, still as of old we may serve Him,
　For did not the Carpenter say,—
"Inasmuch . . ." as ye aid my littlest one,
　Ye do it, my friend, for me.
His poor we have always with us
　The lonely, the sick, and the driven
To these we may give of our succor,
　For of such is His Kingdom of Heaven.

The drive of our world is terrific,
  There are many who fall by the way,
We may find them in the street and the alley,
  Of our cluttered-up cities today.
They feed on the crumbs from the table
  As did dogs in the Master's day;
Yet we live in plenty and comfort,
  Nor drop them a crumb by the way.
If the Carpenter's yearning for others
  Lived in our hearts, we'd hear Him say—
"Give! Give! do not hoard, my brother,
  For this is the abundant way."

—Author Unknown

QUESTIONS

Is this a tribute to the Nazarene,
  Beloved of children, brother of the poor,
  The peasant teacher turned from door to door;
Without a home save on God's friendly green?
This mitered pomp, these gilded lords of pride,
  These surging peoples awed by thronging priests,
  By old tradition, storied fasts and feasts—
Is this for Him who on a rude cross died?
How great His gain, who now commands such zeal,
  Such loyalty, beyond His fairest thought!
  In His high name what wonders have been wrought!
How proud His Kingdom—this we see today!
If He were here—who walked a pilgrim way—
If He were here . . .

—Thomas Curtis Clark

THE CHRIST OF COMMON FOLKS

I love the name of Christ the Lord, the Man of Galilee,
Because He came to live and toil among the likes of me.
Let others sing the praises of a mighty King of Kings;
I love the Christ of common folks, the Lord of common things.

The beggars and the feeble ones, the poor and sick and blind,
The wayward and the tempted ones, were those He loved to find;
He lived with them to help them like a brother and a friend,
Or like some wandering workman finding things to mend.

I know my Lord is still my kind of folks to this good day;
I know because He never fails to hear me when I pray.
He loves the people that He finds in narrow dingy streets,
And brings a word of comfort to the weary one He meets.

My job is just a poor man's job, my home is just a shack,
But on my humble residence He has never turned His back.
Let others sing their praises to a mighty King of Kings;
I love the Christ of common folks, the Lord of common things.

—George T. Liddell

SONG OF CHRISTIAN WORKINGMEN

Our Master toiled, a carpenter
  Of busy Galilee;
He knew the weight of ardent tasks
  And ofttimes, wearily
He sought, apart, in earnest prayer
For strength, beneath His load of care.

He took a manly share of work,
  No thoughtless shirker He.
From dawn to dusk, before His bench,
  He labored faithfully.
He felt just pride in work well done
And found rest sweet, at setting sun.

His father worked, and he rejoiced
  That honest toil was His—
To whom was given grace to know
  Divinest mysteries:
And shall not we find toiling good
Who serve in labor's brotherhood?

—Thomas Curtis Clark

AS HE WALKED WITH US

Calm, strong, and gentle Man of Galilee,
  Whose heart by every human voice is stirred;
  By whom are plaintive cries of creatures heard;
Whose eye escapes no tracery of tree,
Or modest wayside flower; alert to see
  The fantasy of cloud, the flight of bird;
  Whose ear can catch the faintest note and word
Of wind and stream, and distant western sea;
When I am treading on the open space,
  Or threading slowly through the crowded marts,
Skilled Craftsman of the woods and market place,
  Companion of all life and human hearts,
I crave, Thou unseen, understanding Guide,
To find Thee, silent, walking by my side.

—Harry Webb Farrington

OUR DIM EYES SEEK A BEACON

Our dim eyes seek a beacon,
And our weary feet a guide,
And our hearts of all life's mystery
Seek a meaning and a key;
But a cross shines on our pathway,
On it hangs the Crucified,
And he answers all our longings
With the whisper, "Follow me."

Life is a duty—dare it;
Life is a burden—bear it;
Life is a thorn-crown—wear it;
Though it break thy heart in twain,
Though the burden bear thee down,
Close thy lips and stand the pain,
First the cross, and then the crown.

—Author Unknown

LIKE JESUS

To earn daily bread with the work of your hands,
To be one with the low of all classes, all lands,
To stand for the truth when no one else stands,
This is to be—like Jesus!

To spurn the parade and the pomp of the scribe,
To throw off the fetters of temple and tribe
And win the free soul that laughs at each jibe,
This is to be—like Jesus!

To leaven the life with the unselfish deed,
To hoard not a treasure but scatter like seed
That will grow to be harvests which multitudes feed,
This is to be—like Jesus!

To prefer the pain of the heavier load,
To follow the rougher and steeper highroad,
Where the outcast and sinner have made their abode,
This is to be—like Jesus!

To endure discomfort and poverty's lack,
To live with the friends who are foes to your back
And welcome the torture of tyranny's rack,
This is to be—like Jesus!

To pity the wealthy, the sleek, and the great,
To give kindness for cruelty, forgiveness for hate,
And then gladly accept the criminal's fate,
This is to be—like Jesus!

To turn from success with its glamour and gloss,
To lose the world's honor, and welcome the loss,
To turn down the triumph and take up the cross,
This is to be—like Jesus!

—Vincent G. Burns

BLIND BARTIMEUS

Blind Bartimeus at the gates
Of Jericho in darkness waits;
He hears the crowd—he hears a breath
Say, "It is Christ of Nazareth!"
And calls in tones of agony,
"Jesus, have mercy now on me!"

The thronging multitudes increase;
Blind Bartimeus, hold thy peace!
But still, above the noisy crowd,
The beggar's cry is shrill and loud:
Until they say, "He calleth thee!"
"Fear not; arise, He calleth thee!"

Then saith the Christ, as silent stands
The crowd, "What wilt thou at my hands?"
And he replies, "O give me light!
Rabbi, restore the blind man's sight."
And Jesus answers, "Go in peace
Thy faith from blindness gives release!"

Ye that have eyes yet cannot see,
In darkness and in misery,
Recall those mighty Voices Three,
"Jesus, have mercy now on me!"
"Fear not, arise, and go in peace!
Thy faith from blindness gives release!"[4]

—Henry Wadsworth Longfellow

[4] This poem was written November 3, 1841. Mr. Longfellow writes under that date to Mr. Ward: "I was reading this morning, just after breakfast, the tenth chapter of Mark in Greek, the last seven verses of which contain the story of blind Bartimeus, and always seemed to me remarkable for their beauty. At once the whole scene presented itself to my mind in lively colors—the walls of Jericho, the cold wind through the gateway, the ragged, blind beggar, his shrill cry, the tumultuous crowd, the serene Christ, the *miracle*; these things took the form I have given them above. . . . I think I shall add to the title, 'supposed to be written by a monk of the Middle Ages,' as it is in the legend style."

MIRACLES

Thy miracles in Galilee
When all the world went after Thee
To bless their sick, to touch their blind,
O Gracious Healer of Mankind
But fan my faith to brighter glow!
Have I not seen, do I not know
One greater miracle than these?
That Thou, the Lord of Life, shouldst please
To walk beside me all the way,
My Comrade of the Everyday.

Was I not blind to beauty, too
Until Thy love came shining through
The dark of self and made me see
I share a glorious world with Thee?
Did I not falter till Thy hand
Reached out to mine? Did I not stand
Perplexed and mute and deaf until
I heard Thy gentle "Peace, be still,"
And all the turmoil of my heart
Was silenced and I found my part?

Those other miracles I know
Were far away, were long ago,
But this, that I may see Thy face
Transforming all the commonplace,
May work with Thee, and watch Thee bless
My little loaves in tenderness;
This sends me singing on my way,
O Comrade of the Everyday!

—Molly Anderson Haley

ALONE INTO THE MOUNTAIN

All day from that deep well of life within
    Himself has He drawn healing for the press
Of folk, restoring strength, forgiving sin,
    Quieting frenzy, comforting distress.

Shadows of evening fall: importunate still
    They throng Him, touch Him, clutch His garment's hem,
Fall down and clasp His feet, cry on Him, till
    The Master, spent, slips from the midst of them

And climbs the mountain for a cup of peace,
Taking a sheer and rugged track untrod
Save by a poor lost sheep with thorn-torn fleece
That follows on and hears Him talk with God.

—*Katharine Lee Bates*

THE MASTER'S TOUCH

"And he touched her hand, and the fever left her; and she arose and ministered
unto them."—MATTHEW 8:15.

"He touched her hand, and the fever left her."
He touched her hand as He only can,
With the wondrous skill of the great Physician,
With the tender touch of the Son of Man,
And the fever pain in the throbbing temples
Died out with the flush on brow and cheek;
And the lips that had been so parched and burning
Trembled with thanks that she could not speak;
And the eyes, where the fever light had faded,
Looked up—by her grateful tears made dim;
And she rose and ministered to her household—
She rose and ministered unto Him.

"He touched her hand, and the fever left her."
Oh blessed touch of the Man Divine!
So beautiful then to rise and serve Him
When the fever is gone from your life and mine;
It may be the fever of restless serving,
With heart all thirsty for love and praise,
And eyes all aching and strained with yearning
Toward self-set goals in the future days;
Or it may be a fever of spirit anguish,
Some tempest of sorrow that dies not down
Till the cross at last is in meekness lifted
And the head stoops low for the thorny crown;
Or it may be a fever of pain and anger,
When the wounded spirit is hard to bear,
And only the Lord can draw forth the arrows
Left carelessly, cruelly rankling there.

Whatever the fever, His touch can heal it;
Whatever the tempest, his voice can still;
There is only joy as we seek His pleasure;
There is only a rest as we seek His will—
And some day after life's fitful fever,
I think we shall say in the home on high:
"If the hands that He touched but did His bidding
How little it matters what else went by!"

Ah, Lord! Thou knowest us altogether,
  Each heart's sore sickness, whatever it be.
Touch Thou our hands! Let the fever leave us—
  And so shall we minister unto Thee!

—Author Unknown

THE GOSPEL OF LABOR

Yet often the King of that country comes out from His tireless host,
And walks in this world of the weary as if He loved it the most;
And here in the dusty confusion, with eyes that are heavy and dim,
He meets again the laboring-men who are looking and longing for Him.

He cancels the curse of Eden, and brings them a blessing instead:
Blessed are they that labor, for Jesus partakes of their bread.
He puts His hand to their burdens, He enters their homes at night:
Who does His best shall have as a guest the Master of life and light.

And courage will come with His presence, and patience return at His touch,
And manifold sins be forgiven to those who love Him much;
The cries of envy and anger will change to the songs of cheer,
The toiling age will forget its rage when the Prince of Peace draws near.

This is the gospel of labor, ring it, ye bells of the kirk!
The Lord of Love came down from above, to live with the men who work.
This is the rose He planted, here in the thorn-curst soil:
Heaven is blest with perfect rest, but the blessing of earth is toil.[5]

—Henry van Dyke

JESUS THE CARPENTER

If I could hold within my hand
  The hammer Jesus swung,
Not all the gold in all the land,
Nor jewels countless as the sand,
  All in the balance flung,
Could weigh the value of that thing
Round which His fingers once did cling.

If I could have the table Christ
  Once made in Nazareth,
Not all the pearls in all the sea,
Nor crowns of kings or kings to be
  As long as men have breath,
Could buy that thing of wood He made—
The Lord of Lords who learned a trade.

[5] From *The Toiling of Felix*, Chosen Poems. Copyright Charles Scribner's Sons. Used by permission.

Yea, but His hammer still is shown
  By honest hands that toil,
And round His table men sit down;
  And all are equals, with a crown
    Nor gold nor pearls can soil;
The shop of Nazareth was bare—
But brotherhood was builded there.

             —Charles M. Sheldon

ACCORDING TO ST. MARK

The way was steep and wild; we watched Him go
  Through tangled thicket, over sharp-edged stone
  That tore His feet, until He stood alone
Upon the summit where four great winds blow;
  Fearful we knelt on the cold rocks below,
  For the o'erhanging cloud had larger grown,
  A strange still radiance through His body shone
Whiter than moonlight on the mountain snow.

Then two that flamed amber and amethyst
  Were either side of Him, while low thunder rolled
  Down to the ravens in their dark ravine;
But when we looked again, as through a mist
  We saw Him near us.—Like a pearl we hold
  Close to our hearts what we have heard and seen.

             —Thomas S. Jones, Jr.

✢

JESUS, THE MIRACLE MAN

(As Told by Mary, His Mother)

TEN thousand people—men, women and children—followed Him out into the desert today, and stayed with Him all day, and they had no food. He took the lunch a little lad had brought for himself, prayed, and as He prayed it multiplied till there was enough for all, and some left.

When the multitude saw that He knew the secret of producing food without waiting for seasons, they were moved to great hopes for His Kingdom and immediately wanted to make Him king, but for some reason He turned away, and when they would have forced Him, He resisted and went up into the mountain apart where He spent the time in prayer.

    ·   ·   ·   ·

There is much disappointment that Jesus did not let Himself be made king; it seemed like a good time, but perhaps He knew better.

    ·   ·   ·   ·

The disciples were rowing across the Sea of Galilee at night and Jesus came to them walking on the water. They cried out in fear, not knowing it was Jesus. Then He made himself known to them and stepped aboard.

.　.　.　.　.

The disciples have spread the story of the feeding of the ten thousand and the walking on the water, and the town is filled with wonder. They cannot understand why such a man would not let Himself be made king.

"How could they starve out His armies in a siege?" some are saying.

"Nor could they drown them in the sea!" declare others.

.　.　.　.　.

I talked today with the mother of the little girl Jesus had brought back to life yesterday. How she clung to me, blessing me for being the mother of such a son! The child was with her, and the people gathered around them, listening to her story, which she never tired of telling.

.　.　.　.　.

Jesus stopped a funeral procession today, spoke to the bearers, and a young man arose alive. He was the only son of a widow. Poor thing, how she fell at Jesus' feet and poured out her gratitude in tears!

"Could not such a king raise up soldiers as fast as they fell?" suggested one of the company.

"Or make harmless the darts before they struck?" exclaimed another.

Our dear friend, Lazarus, is dead, and poor Mary and Martha are weeping out that they thought Jesus did not care, since He had not come at their request to heal him.

I told them that Jesus could raise him up; but they said it was impossible since he was now decomposing.

"Will He come yet?" they kept weeping. "Oh, why did He not come? He loved Lazarus. And He loved to come to our house. But what good will it do now? Yet His very presence would bring cheer."

.　.　.　.　.

Jesus did come. Mary and Martha fell weeping at His feet.

"We thought you would have come sooner," they sobbed; "we thought—we thought ——"

Then Jesus wept, and weeping cried, "I will raise him up."

"Impossible!" they cried; "he is decaying."

"Where have you laid him?" He groaned. "Come, he will live again."

By this time a large company had gathered and together they moved toward the tomb.

"What will He do?" they whispered. "He might have kept him from dying, but ——"

When they came to the place, Jesus prayed, then told Lazarus to come out, and he came out—ALIVE!

They brought him home and there was such a mingling of excitement and pathos and joy as is rarely experienced on earth.[6]

✠

THE HILL ROAD

By

Eleanor B. Stock

GOD had a song He wanted to sing, and when He had finished it He created a man to sing it. You see, it was a mighty song and needed a Godlike singer. And the man was Jesus, a carpenter of Nazareth. He went up to Jerusalem, and as He walked up and down its narrow, crowded streets, God's song swept across the hearts of people.

Some ran to meet it, it was so full of strength and beauty. But others ran from it, trembling with fear. And these were they who dreaded lest it rend the hate and uproot the falsehood in which their lives were so comfortably grounded.

When the rulers of Israel—priests, scribes, and Pharisees—heard it, they shuttered the windows of their souls and barred the gates of their mind against it; that is, all of them except Nicodemus and one or two others who, when they heard it, stopped to listen.

Nicodemus was no longer a young man, and at first he listened with the gentlemanly indifference of one who is tired of life. But a day came when the swift, clean words cut through the mist of indifference and with a lightning flash revealed Nicodemus to himself. . . .

That night he took the hill road to the Mount of Olives. He had heard that Jesus was in the habit of spending His nights there. In his eagerness he hurried. But it was not long before his footsteps faltered, heavy with weariness. He swayed with fatigue, caught hold of a rock, and sat down to rest. His hands trembled as he wiped the sweat from his face. But his soul's need was more urgent than that of his body, and it was not long before his determined tread fell softly upon the silence and Nicodemus was on his way again.

The road became a friendly path, ending abruptly among a clump of olive trees, as though it knew that Nicodemus could not possibly take another step.

As he stood looking down upon Jerusalem, he felt the presence of long-forgotten memories, and the tall, broad-shouldered dreams of his boyhood seemed to rise from the city of pinnacles and towers lying there so quiet and

[6] From *His Mother, A Story of Our Lord*, by G. M. Anderson. Published by the Bethany Press, St. Louis, Mo. Used by special permission of the heirs and the publishers.

clean in the white radiance of the Eastern night. Unconsciously he lifted his face toward heaven and stretched out his hands, palms upward, in prayer. In the light of the moon and stars his thin, tired face was like an exquisite cameo of old ivory, carved against the onyx shadows of the olive trees.

Jesus saw him thus. The beauty and pathos of the old man tugged at His heart and quietly, lest He break in upon the prayer, Jesus came and stood beside him. He watched the labored rise and fall of the old man's breathing, the throbbing pulse in the thick veins on his forehead, and at once sensed the courage and endurance it had cost Nicodemus to come out alone and by night up the hill road.

Nicodemus looked up. "You are here. I am so glad."

"Yes, during the time I am in Jerusalem I almost always spend my nights up here. Wide, unwalled places are good to refresh oneself in after being jostled the whole day long in the narrow crowded streets. But you are very tired." Jesus put out His hand to steady Nicodemus and, suiting His pace to that of the older man, led him to a spot under an olive tree.

Several minutes passed before either of them spoke. Now that he was face to face with the young Teacher, Nicodemus was at a loss for words. . . . How could he tell Jesus that for an old man to seek the comradeship of a younger, and for a ruler of Israel, a Hebrew of the Hebrews, a member of the Sanhedrin, to have any dealings whatsoever with a Sabbath-breaking Nazarene was not only flagrantly undignified, but dangerously unconvential. But Jesus came to his relief, sensing with instinctive kindliness the older man's difficulty.

"I understand perfectly. It is a bitter experience to be scorned by one's own, an experience from which we may well shrink unless we live so near to God that we are filled with His life."

No sooner had the word *life* been spoken, than Nicodemus found the words for lack of which he had been unable to make his need known. Now he spoke slowly, hesitatingly:

"You are a teacher come from God. . . ."

"Are you sure, Nicodemus?" And there was both sadness and a smile in the Master's voice, which Nicodemus was quick to catch.

"You may well ask that. We priests and Pharisees have so often tried to bait you with those very words, but I speak them in all sincerity. Only *You* can tell me, and my need is too great to be denied—how I, an old man, may find life, *eternal life*. . . ."

Jesus put his hand on that of the old man. "By knowing the God within you, by catching a vision of His Kingdom."

"But it is so long since I have felt God within me—and the eyes of my soul have grown too dim to see so divine a thing as His Kingdom. Surely you realize that I cannot do these things. And if I could—how?"

"There is only one way; you must be born anew."

Nicodemus shook his head and answered with bitter irony: "How can a man be born when he is old? Can he enter his mother's womb over again, and be born?"

"Do not wonder, Nicodemus, at My telling you that you must be born again, spiritually. The wind blows wherever it chooses, and you hear the sound thereof, but you do not know where it comes from or where it goes. This is the way with everyone who owes his birth to the Spirit."

"But how can that be?" Nicodemus asked, bewildered.

"You are a teacher of Israel and yet ignorant of this? I speak of that which I know, and of that which I have seen. You remember how it is told that Moses in the desert lifted the serpent up in the air—even so the Son of Man must be lifted up, so that everyone who believes in Him may have life. Don't you see, Nicodemus? You said your soul seemed to you like a barren, hemmed-in plain. Break down its barriers, widen its horizons, let God's light flood it, and even as the spring sunshine makes the fields blossom, so His light will make your soul alive with new interest, new hope, new joy, new life, life in its fullest sense. Lift up the Son of man within you, and this new life will be life eternal. That's what it means to be born again, Nicodemus, not once, but every day and every hour."

As Jesus spoke these words, night gave place to dawn. The untrammeled song of a lark swept over the hillside and lost itself in the immensity of life waking everywhere.

"It is as though that song had come out of my heart," Nicodemus began. He wanted to say more, to make some expression of gratitude, but he could not find the right words. "I came to you in the night," he hesitated, "a soul seemingly without life; now in the dawn I go back—reborn."

They arose and walked arm in arm to the edge of the hillside and stood looking down upon Jerusalem. The last star slipped away, and the moon faded from sight in a sky of rose and amber. Nicodemus turned thoughtfully homeward to march forward in an ever-broadening spiritual experience.[7]

✢

HEALING THE DAUGHTER OF JAIRUS

By

Elizabeth Stuart Phelps

JESUS was at home once more, but He was not permitted to rest. Crowds larger than He had left received Him. He was surrounded and overwhelmed. It seemed as if all the invalids in Galilee were moaning after Him. In the heart of His busiest and weariest hour an urgent demand came. He was wanted for a life-and-death case. An officer of the Jewish church, an important person, Jairus by name, had a little daughter, dearly cherished. She was scarcely

[7] From *The Classmate*, August 8, 1931. Used with the special permission of the author.

twelve years old, just at the lovely age, not yet past her play-days, but already with the dainty airs of a little woman—a winsome maid, her father's darling. She lay at the point of death, and in hot haste messengers had been sent for the Nazarene.

At the feet of Jesus, Jairus flung himself down like a slave, and such an agony went up in his face and attitude as a cold man could not easily have resisted. Jesus, melting with sympathy, tenderly reassured the father, and started at once in the direction of the ruler's house.

But what a throng! When He tried to pass through the people, they closed like a round wall about Him. Such a mass of humanity pressed upon Him that it was impossible to move.

At that moment, stealing past the push and rush of the thoughtless throng, a timid hand touched the fringe of his garment, then, terrified, withdrew instantly.

"Who touched me?" Jesus asked, quickly. No person in the crowd replied. "Strength goes out of me," insisted the Master. "Who was it?" And the crowd marveled that He even felt it, so great was the press of the multitude.

Jesus and Jairus walked together to the ruler's house. The father did not speak again. He was afraid of offending the rabbi. After those first hot words, the first wild moment, what could he do? When the servant came, weeping, and told him that it was too late, not to trouble the Master, for the little maid was gone—his heart had broken in one mad outcry. This great Healer, this mysterious man, so famous for his tenderness, so marvelous for his pity, must needs fail him, *him,* Jairus, out of all Palestine, and that in the hour of his terrible need! For the fact could not be denied that Jesus had stopped on the way to a dying patient to cure an old, chronic case.

That woman could have been healed just as well tonight, tomorrow, or next week. But He had lingered. And the child was dead.

"Do not be afraid," said Jesus, tenderly; "only believe!" But His face was very grave. And by a single motion of His expressive hand he ordered all his disciples back but three—Peter, James, and John, His dearest. The group entered the ruler's house.

The house was not silent. Oriental mourners had already taken possession of it. Obtrusive wails and groans, mingled with genuine sobs and tears, filled the place. Jesus seemed surprised at the condition in which He found the family.

"The child is not dead," He said, decidedly. Some of the neighbors, who did not altogether believe in the famous Healer, began to laugh. It was a derisive laugh, a cold sound in that house of woe, and it did not please Him. A keen rebuke shot from His mild eyes at the unseemly scorn.

"Nay," He repeated, "she is not dead. She is asleep."

He spoke in the tone of a man who was not to be gainsaid. . . . He went into the sick-room and looked at the child.

"This is sleep," he persisted. . . . The father's sobs had ceased. The mother lifted her face, discolored with tears, worn with watching, and piteously raised her hands. The three friends of the rabbi stood reverently wondering.

Jesus silently regarded the little maid. She lay unconscious and was quite rigid.

Jesus looked at her with a strange expression. His eyes seemed to say: "It is between Me and thee, little maid. We understand."

He was known to be very fond of children, and they of Him. He was sometimes seen with them climbing over His lap and laughing, as they put their arms about His neck with the unerring identification of those whom they can trust, which only children and dogs possess. Mothers brought their babies to Him for His blessing, and it is recorded how lovingly He gave it.

Now He looked at the little girl with the tenderness that is only to be expected of those in whom the love of children is profound and genuine.

She seemed to quiver beneath His look, but her color and her attitude did not change. Then He took her by the hand.

Her little wasted fingers lay for a few moments in His nervous and vital grasp; then He felt them tremble. . . . Who sees the instant when the lily blossoms? Who could have detected the moment of time in which the child began to stir? Was it His hand that moved, or hers that directed His slowly upward till it reached her pillow, and so came upon a level with her face?

It did not seem sudden or startling, but only the most natural thing in the world, when the little girl laid her cheek upon His palm. . . .

"Give her something to eat," said the Healer, quite in His ordinary tones. This sensible and commonplace order restored their senses to the excited household. But Jairus remembered how he had thought of Jesus, perhaps how he had spoken to Him, when the Nazarene stopped to cure the chronic case; and the father felt ashamed; but he did not know how to say so. And the little arms about his neck were warm! How could he think of anything else in the world? Jesus seemed to take this, too, as a matter of course. That was the wonderful, beautiful thing. Jairus felt as if he could worship the rabbi.

The whole countryside rang with the story.

"Death! A second time! Why, He cheats the grave, as another may cheat in war or a bargain! Who is this Man who does the deeds of the living God? But Jesus had denied that the child was dead. And He never retracted the denial.[8]

✛

THE MIRACLE OF CANA

ELIZABETH woke suddenly in the full morning light. A long band of gold slanted across the floor and burnished the silken wings of the white doves on

[8] From *The Story of Jesus Christ.* Published by Houghton Mifflin Company, Boston, Mass. Used with permission of the publishers.

the tapestry screen at the foot of her bed. This meant that the sun was already well up above the Galilean hills. A confusion of cheerful, homely sounds came from the village street; little John calling to his goats as he took them to pasture; the ring of Obed's hammer as he worked at the new house across the way; the slow grating of old Joanna's millstones next door; and the high, clear, teasing laughter of Dorcas and Esther as they went to the well.

Elizabeth sat up, her eyes full of a startled wonder. Another yesterday had slipped off into the long tale of years past. A new day was here. Tomorrow she was to marry Philip. *Tomorrow!* She rose quickly and dressed. The day would be full. There was a little more sewing, a few last arrangements to make for the transference of her goods from her house to Philip's; there would be many, many interruptions from the friendly, gossiping neighbors who would be stopping at her house all day long; the gay banter of the excited girls who would walk in the bridal procession: all this and much more would fill the new day.

And yet instead of being eager, Elizabeth felt curiously loath to begin its duties. The heavy apathy which had lain upon her spirit for the last weeks still clung to her. It was as though all the fires of her heart, once so warm and bright, had died.

Dorcas and Esther passed again with their water-jars on their shoulders. Vivid, gay young things in the first fresh bloom of youth. The sight of them tortured Elizabeth, for it turned her dull heaviness to sharp pain. That was what she had lost. Her youth. The beautiful golden years when love beat high in her breast, when she could have been a glowing, joyous bride, had been stolen from her. "The wedding of the old lovers," they were calling it in Cana, and without resentment Elizabeth accepted the words from her neighbors' lips. For it was the truth. She was twenty-nine years old; Philip was thirty-five. All the others of their ages had been married these twelve or fourteen years, and had many children now playing about their doors.

It was when Elizabeth was fifteen, a rosy, laughing girl, that Philip, twenty-one then, and very strong and manly, had asked for her in marriage. She remembered their meeting at the old well. Philip's flushed, handsome face bending above her as he spoke of his love.

But the next year, before they could be married, was the beginning of their troubles. It seemed, indeed, as though life had turned into an invisible archer who hurled dart after dart upon them from ambush.

Philip's search for work did not prosper. His very eagerness was against him. He changed nervously from this to that during the year. He wanted a little home for Elizabeth, for his father's house was already overcrowded. But at the end of twelve months he had failed miserably. They must wait another year.

But before the new year was gone, sorrow had come to the home of Elizabeth. Her mother, a little, quiet, busy woman, succumbed to fever. At sixteen Elizabeth had upon her shoulders the care of a big family. It was to her now that everyone turned: her father in his grief, the garrulous grandmother who was almost blind, the younger brothers and sister who crowded about her, crying and frightened. She had no time for her own tears. She took up the burden which her mother had laid down. She was changed overnight from a care-free girl to a serious woman. It puzzled her. She felt like a child who, after receiving nothing but love all its life, is suddenly struck a cruel blow.

When Philip found her, later, by the old well, where she had run blindly in her anguish, he kissed her white cheeks back to warmth. "If Jehovah wills," Philip said, "we must wait. But I shall still have thee for my wife. Many waters cannot quench love, neither can floods drown it!"

And so the years went on. Elizabeth spent the wealth of her womanliness upon the motherless household. Her days were crowded with heavier work than she had ever known. She learned to serve patiently and to give without thought of return. She learned to sing when her heart was heavy, and to make laughter for others when her own voice broke later in a sob. She learned the great woman's secret of taking four walls and divers human beings and making of them *a home*. Her father grew content again with his lot. Little Sarah and baby Enoch were tenderly cared for. Above them the row of brothers small and larger, that reached up to Elizabeth herself, grew and flourished.

She did not see Philip so often now. Her father thought their frequent meetings improper when no one knew when the wedding could be.

Sometimes when they were together Elizabeth wore a flower in her smooth, dark hair and talked in her old bright fashion. Sometimes they sat quiet, thinking of all that might have been. For Philip was doing well now in his work. He had bought a piece of land for himself near the village.

Ten years passed. Ten long, slowly-moving years. The waiting of Philip and Elizabeth became a byword in Cana. But at the end of the tenth year, as it often happens, the big household suddenly scattered. The older boys left home—one to sea, two to Jerusalem, one to be a soldier under the Empire, one to Damascus. And little Sarah, at fourteen, all laughter and eagerness and hopeful plans, was wed to a young innkeeper at Nazareth and had taken Enoch with her to help them.

At the end of two more years Elizabeth was alone in the old house. First the grandmother had gone, and a few months later her father had followed. She was at last free.

"And so thou canst say *tomorrow* at last?" began an old woman. "Who would ever have thought it could come! They say that Philip's father hath invited all Cana and half Nazareth to the wedding supper. There are twelve women asked to serve besides the servants he hath hired. But thou canst not blame him. Philip waited nearly fifteen years! It is a pity thou hast lost all thy color. Thou wouldst have made a lovely bride at sixteen. They say that Philip hath had thy wedding-dress sent from Jerusalem! Is that true? How many jewels hast thou for thy veil?"

"Wilt thou have these cakes?" Elizabeth asked, pressing her breakfast upon the visitor. "I find I cannot eat them. There are Dorcas and Esther at the door. I must open to them."

All through the day there was much coming and going at the house of

Elizabeth; but it seemed to her that in each attempted kindness, each curious question, each laughing congratulation, there was a little shaft, a goad, a tiny barb to pierce her heart. They were all her neighbors and she loved them, but their interest in the wedding, she knew, had in it something of pity for her and Philip and something of—if not contempt, at least a mild, amused superiority.

Even the display at the wedding supper, which Philip's father was bent upon making, would elicit only friendly jests.

Elizabeth tried bravely to put aside such thoughts. She tried to feel buoyant, excited, happily eager for the morrow. But as the day wore on she gave it up. The dull sense of having outlived her youth and its warmth of feeling persisted. She felt only a great passivity.

When Philip came that evening to walk with her for the last time before they were husband and wife, Elizabeth marveled at the change in him. He seemed to have lost his slight stoop. He was erect now, his eyes flashing as they did in the old days. His hands shook a little as they touched hers. He had forgotten the years of waiting. He had suddenly become the young lover again.

He talked with touching eagerness of the preparations for the feast. Elizabeth listened quietly, unstirred. He spoke of the guests and she feigned an interest she did not feel until suddenly she raised her head.

"Didst thou say Mary of Nazareth?" she asked.

"Yes," Philip answered. "Father hath invited her to be one of the twelve to assist with the serving. And he hath also bidden her oldest son, Jesus, and some of His friends to the feast."

"I am glad," Elizabeth answered, quickly. "Mary hath been kind to Sarah, and this son, this Jesus, is beginning Himself to teach, they say. Sarah knows Him and she thinks He has strange powers. I saw Him once. It was when Sarah's baby came. I had left old Joanna here with father and grandmother and had gone to Nazareth. I worked all night over Sarah; but in the morning, when everything was over, and there was no more need of me, I said good-by and started home. I have never known such despair as I felt that day. Sarah was so happy and the baby so sweet, and it seemed as though disappointment was ever to be my portion. And then, on the road, I met this Son of Mary's, this Jesus. He only looked at me and smiled and passed on, but somehow——"

She paused hesitant. "Thou wilt think me foolish. But somehow as He looked on me I felt different. I grew brave and quiet again, and able to go on— waiting."

Philip's answer was to draw her to him. "But it's over now! All the waiting. Over at last! And tomorrow we shall have a wedding that will surpass any ever seen in Cana! And the wedding-dress! Wait till thou seest it! No city bride will ever look finer than thou."

Elizabeth rose and dressed carefully the next morning. Some time during the morning would come the ceremonious entrance of the messengers from Philip bearing her bridal dress and ornaments and the ointment and perfumes.

There was no breakfast to make, for she must fast until evening. But there were the prayers of Atonement with which her mind must be occupied most of the day. She knelt facing Jerusalem and recited softly the solemn, stately words of the confession.

Later the messengers arrived. The bridal gown with all its expensive ornaments was spread upon the bed. She smiled tenderly at Philip's extravagance. He had sent perfumes enough for a lifetime.

In the early evening, while the neighbors swarmed about the rooms, trying to be helpful, Elizabeth stood before her mirror and let down her long black hair until it fell about her shoulders as a maiden bride's must hang.

They helped her into her bridal dress, exclaiming at its beauty. With her own hands Elizabeth adjusted the "attire" about her waist and the crown of fresh myrtle leaves that she had preferred to the golden imitation. Then over all was thrown the long white veil of betrothal that would not be raised until Philip's own hands lifted it in the hush of the bridal chamber. Elizabeth was ready.

The early dusk had grown swiftly to darkness. The young girls who had been running in and out were gone hastily to their own homes to don their last bit of finery for the procession.

A shout came from the doorway. "Here they come! Look! Thou canst see the torches! And the flutes! Dost thou hear them? Oh, it will be a great procession. Call Elizabeth. Tell her they have started!"

The sounds came clearly through the night. Philip and his groomsmen were on their way to her. The neighbors were all thronging the streets. The maidens were waiting, ready to circle about her when she emerged from the house. All at once the shouting increased deafeningly. The torches again became a confused glare. They had reached her house. Elizabeth felt herself conducted through lines of laughing, bowing men and women on to the doorway, where Philip met her and drew her inside.

He led her proudly to the room reserved for the women and seated her on the soft-rug-covered dais prepared for her. The other women and maidens who were invited to the house crowded in and found seats on the floor and cushioned ledges. Through the door which led into the room where the feast was spread for the men, and where the singing and dancing would take place, Elizabeth could see the women who were to serve, carrying food to the table and chatting importantly to each other as they worked. She watched the form of Mary of Nazareth as she came and went. So gentle in her movements, so quiet of speech, so tender and smiling as she looked upon the group that clustered round the bridegroom.

Then Terenth came in with refreshments for the women. "There are many strangers," she commented, excitedly. "Four men are sitting with Nathanael, and he keeps calling one of them Rabbi. He is Mary's Son from Nazareth, but I didn't know He was a rabbi! Philip's father is so excited. We can't bring things in fast enough to please him. He is mightily lavish with

the wine. Philip will have to go clear to the new vineyards for more for tomorrow night. Thou shouldst see how the guests eat!"

She ran out, laughing, but it seemed only a moment until she was back with
blanched face. *"The wine is gone!"* she gasped. "There isn't another drop and
the feast but barely begun! We thought there were two more vats of it and
they are empty! What can we do?"

At the first words Elizabeth had started in surprise. Now she sat tense with
hands gripped together. No more wine! The feast begun in riotous plenty
was to end in poverty and disgrace. Was this the last master-stroke of fate
against their plans—hers and Philip's?

"Tell Mary of Nazareth!" she whispered. "She is always calm and wise.
She will know *how* to tell the governor and the rest when it has to be known."

When Terenth had rushed away and the chatter of awed comment and criticism and speculation was in full flow about her, Elizabeth sat speechless and
stunned behind her veil.

This was no small calamity that was about to fall upon them. It was a life-
long disgrace for Philip and his father. Never again could they hold up their
heads in the village. No matter whose mistake it had been, the burden of
reproach would rest upon them. And no one would ever let them forget it.
This flagrant breach of hospitality, this unprecedented failure to make good
the promise of their lavish invitations. No apology could be offered or accepted. There would be only the ugly fact to speak for itself. There would be
a little while of forced merriment and then the guests would go. And Philip
and his father would be left amid the ruins of the feast and the bitterness of
their disgrace.

Suddenly she noticed that the women and maidens had stopped talking.
A silence had fallen upon the feast-room, too. Elizabeth caught her breath.
Some one must be telling Philip and his father now. For a long second the
strange hush lasted. And then everything was as it had been before. The
talking, the laughter, the women running to and fro with their platters and
pitchers. And high above the other voices rose the strong tones of the governor
of the feast.

"How is this, Philip?" he was demanding. "Every man when he maketh
a feast doth first serve the good wine, and then when men have well drunk,
he serveth that which is worse. But thou hast kept the *good* wine until now!"

The governor sounded well pleased. Then Philip replied, his voice still
vibrant with pride and joy: "But, governor, is the best not worth waiting for
always?"

Then overwhelmingly rose the shouts: "To the bridegroom! Fill your cups
and drink again to the bridegroom! Joy to Philip and his bride!"

One of the maidens leaned cautiously toward the door of the feast-room.
"They *have* wine! They are drinking it now. Terenth is silly and excitable.
Alarming us for naught. Wait till she comes again! We shall teach her a
lesson."

But Terenth was already there. "There had been a *miracle*! There is a man of God in this house!" Then, before the excited gasps of wonder had become coherent, Terenth went on: "*There was no wine.* Any of the women or the servants will tell you that. I did as Elizabeth bade me. I asked Mary of Nazareth to break the news to Philip and his father. I was just behind her as she entered the room. Instead of going to the end of the table she stopped beside her Son. I heard her whisper to Him: 'They have no wine'—only that. But she looked at Him beseechingly. Her Son looked grave for a moment and then He smiled a little and said in the gentlest voice: 'Woman, what have I to do with thee? Mine hour is not yet come.' But she smiled back at Him and touched His shoulder—they must love each other deeply, those two—and signed to a servant. 'Do whatever He telleth thee,' she said.

"Then this Jesus told the servant to fill the six big water-jars in the hallway, full of water. When it was done He said quietly: 'Draw out now and bear to the governor of the feast!'

"And as we drew, *the water was changed to wine!* They are drinking it now."

In the midst of it all, Elizabeth sat withdrawn, apart, trying to sense the awesome thing she had just heard. Under this roof, Philip's roof, which was now her home, *water had been changed into wine!* That quiet guest in the other room had wrought a *miracle!* God was dwelling in this place. She trembled. Then her fear of the unknown power lifted. She felt only the gentle sympathy of this Son of Mary whom she had met that day on the Nazareth road. It enfolded her as though His spirit had left the table of feasting to commune with hers. She seemed to feel His eyes upon her, revealing great riches of truth illuminating her soul.

For suddenly, as she looked back over the years that stretched behind her, she saw a light upon them. Water into wine? Why, that was but the eternal miracle of service and sacrifice! Pouring out from one's own cup to fill another's. Changing the flat, stale water of life into a glowing chalice of joy for thirsty lips. She herself had done that. For little Sarah, for the boys, for her father and the blind grandmother, she had held out the overflowing cup which her unselfish love had sweetened.

And now, in her own great hour, to which her worn-out heart and body seemed unable to rise, there had been poured out for her the very wine of God!

Suddenly the voices of the women became audible to her ears. "Elizabeth! How canst thou sit so quiet? Hast thou no *feeling? It is a miracle!* Who hath heard of such things since the days of the prophets! At thy wedding! *A miracle!* It will be remembered as long as Cana stands. And thou dost sit there without speaking. Dost thou not *believe* it?"

"Yea, I believe it. It hath been wrought *in me!*" she answered.

For through her veins fresh life seemed to be coursing. It welled up within her, rich and strong. All the ardor of her young girlhood seemed to return to her. Before her stretched the years for which she and Philip had waited.

A glory lay upon their unlived days. Would always lie upon them. The glory of the Miracle. Water into wine at the divine touch of love.

She bowed her head in adoration. Some day she would look into the eyes of the Wedding Guest of Nazareth and tell Him she understood.[9]

✣

O MASTER WORKMAN OF THE RACE

FROM beginning to end, one finds in the words of this magnificent hymn a challenge to noble work. In the first stanza we are reminded that Jesus began at the early age of twelve to do His Father's will. The second stanza portrays the Carpenter of Nazareth as a Builder of Life Divine, as a worker who spent Himself. The words of the third stanza carry a petition for a bold and good conscience, a true purpose, and a great joy in doing the Father's work.

The words of this beautiful hymn-poem were written by Jay Thomas Stocking (1870—), a prominent Congregational minister, now serving as pastor of the Pilgrim Congregational Church in St. Louis, Missouri. He was graduated from Amherst in 1895, later took a theological course at Yale Divinity School, and then studied in the University of Berlin. He is the author of "The Golden Goblet," "The Dearest Spot on Earth," and "The City That Never Was Reached."

"Materna," the hymn tune to which we sing "America, the Beautiful," is often used with the words of Dr. Stocking's poem. It was composed by Samuel Ward.

Another tune sometimes associated with this poem is "Amesbury," by Uzziah Christopher Burnap. And still another tune sometimes used is one written by John Stainer.

> O Master Workman of the race,
>   Thou Man of Galilee,
> Who with the eyes of early youth
>   Eternal things did see,
> We thank Thee for thy boyhood faith
>   That Shone Thy whole life thro';
> "Did ye not know it is my work
>   My Father's work to do?"
>
> O Carpenter of Nazareth,
>   Builder of life divine,
> Who shapest man to God's own law,
>   Thyself the fair design.
> Build us a tower of Christ-like height,
>   That we the land may view,

[9] From *Far above Rubies* by Agnes Sligh Turnbull. Published by Fleming H. Revell Company. Used with special permission of the author and publishers.

And see like Thee our noblest work
Our Father's work to do.

O Thou Who dost the vision send
And givest each his task,
And with the task sufficient strength,
Show us Thy will, we ask;
Give us a conscience bold and good,
Give us a purpose true,
That it may be our highest joy
Our Father's work to do.[10]

—*Jay T. Stocking, 1912*

✤

MY MASTER WAS A WORKER

JESUS came, saying, "My Father worketh until now, and I work." As we look about us, we see the constant evidence of God's spirit at work in the world. The universe itself testifies to the fact that the Creative Spirit behind it not only *was* but *is* a worker.

We cannot read the story of the life of Jesus without coming to appreciate the fact that He was one of the busiest of men. In less than thirty-three years He accomplished a record of *things done* and *movements initiated* that has become the wonder and admiration of men in all succeeding ages. Yet the Master of Men never seemed to be in a hurry. He knew how to labor, but He also knew how to find repose of spirit and release from the press of things seen, by silent meditation and communion with the great Unseen Spirit of the Universe Whose child He was.

This thought of Jesus as a worker, William George Tarrant put in one of the most beautiful and challenging hymns of the church. We cannot be idlers in a world that needs to have so many things made right and hope to be followers of the "Master Workman of the Race" as Dr. Stocking in another hymn calls Jesus.

My Master was a worker,
With daily work to do,
And he who would be like Him
Must be a worker too;
Then welcome honest labor,
And honest labor's fare,
For where there is a worker,
The Master's man is there.

[10] Words copyright, 1912, by the Congregational Sunday School and Publishing Society. Used by permission.

My Master was a comrade,
   A trusty friend and true,
And he who would be like **Him**
   Must be a comrade too;
In happy hours of singing,
   In silent hours of care,
Where goes a loyal comrade,
   The Master's man is there.

My Master was a helper,
   The woes of life He knew,
And he who would be like Him,
   Must be a helper too;
The burden will grow lighter,
   If each will take a share,
And where there is a helper
   The Master's man is there.

Then, brothers brave and manly
   Together let us be,
For He, who is our Master,
   The Man of men was He;
The men who would be like Him
   Are wanted ev'rywhere,
And where they love each other
   The Master's men are there.
           —William George Tarrant, 1853

✢

JESUS, THOU DIVINE COMPANION

In "Jesus, Thou Divine Companion" by van Dyke we have another of those great hymns of the Church that places major emphasis not only on Jesus as a worker, but on His divine companionship with the children of men.

In all ages, men and women who have opened up their lives to the sunlight of Jesus' love and purifying influence have found in Him an intimate and all-sustaining comradeship—a peace and repose of spirit that passes all understanding.

Something of what the coming of this lowly child of manger-birth, Who associated Himself with the path of labor and Who lived His life out among the common people, means, Henry van Dyke has put into this beautiful poem, "Jesus, Thou Divine Companion." This poetic hymn was written in 1909. It is usually sung to a much older tune composed by George F. Le Jeune in 1872.

Jesus, Thou divine Companion,
　By Thy lowly human birth
Thou hast come to join the workers,
　Burden-bearers of the earth.
Thou, the Carpenter of Nazareth,
　Toiling for Thy daily food,
By Thy patience and Thy courage
　Thou hast taught us toil is good.

They who tread the path of labor,
　Follow where Thy feet have trod:
They who work without complaining
　Do the holy will of God.
Thou, the Peace that passeth knowledge,
　Dwellest in the daily strife;
Thou, the Bread of Heaven, art broken
　In the sacrament of life.

Every task, however simple,
　Sets the soul that does it free;
Every deed of love and kindness,
　Done to man is done to thee.
Jesus, thou divine Companion,
　Help us all to work our best;
Bless us in our daily labor,
　Lead us to our Sabbath rest.

—Henry van Dyke, 1909

✛

HARK! THE VOICE OF JESUS CALLING

"HARK! the Voice of Jesus Calling" is one of the great missionary hymns of the Church that found its inspiration in the appeal of Jesus for workers, as found in John 4:35-36, when He said to His disciples, "Say not ye, there are yet four months, and then cometh the harvest? Behold, I say unto you, Lift up your eyes, and look on the fields, that they are white already unto harvest." This Scripture, coupled with Isaiah's reply, "Here am I, O Lord, send me," provides the message and motive for this, one of the most challenging of all the missionary hymns of the church.

Daniel March, the author of the words of this hymn, would have us realize that work for the Master is ever present, waiting to be done by willing hands and hearts. We need "not cross the ocean" to become missionaries of the Cross, or in some other special way dedicate ourselves to full-time Christian service. Always and everywhere about us there are souls in need, distracted and undone by circumstances that surround them. They need the calming influence of the Christ, the world's great Burden-bearer. You and I have the opportunity daily to introduce them to the Christ, whose life and personality enrich and make abundant every life that is open to His transforming influence.

Hark! the voice of Jesus calling—
"Who will go and work today?
Fields are white, the harvest waiting—
Who will bear the sheaves away?"
Loud and long the Master calleth,
Rich reward He offers free:
Who will answer, gladly saying,
"Here am I, O Lord: send me"?
Who will answer, gladly saying,
"Here am I, O Lord; send me"?

If you cannot cross the ocean,
And the other lands explore,
You can find the needy nearer,
You can help them at your door;
If you cannot speak like angels,
If you cannot preach like Paul,
You can tell the love of Jesus,
You can say He died for all.
You can tell the love of Jesus,
You can say He died for all.

While the souls of men are dying,
And the Master calls for you,
Let none hear you idly saying,
"There is nothing I can do."
Gladly take the task He gives you,
Let His work your pleasure be;
Answer quickly when He calleth,
"Here am I, O Lord: send me."
Answer quickly when He calleth,
"Here am I, O Lord: send me."

—*Daniel March, 1868*

✠

BE OF GOOD CHEER, THE MASTER SAID

IN THIS hymn-poem by Dr. Earl Marlatt, which is of comparatively recent authorship, we have another of those great Christian hymns that are based on the idea of work and of the interdependence of the Master Workman and His helpers as portrayed in the parable of the vine and branches, one of the most suggestive and beautiful of all the stories of Jesus. Read John 15:1-8.

It is usually sung to a tune known as St. Agnes, which was composed by John B. Dykes in 1866.

Each verse of this hymn begins with those significant words of Jesus, "Be of Good Cheer," and is then linked up with some teaching or action on the part of the Master of Men that should be a constant source of inspiration to the followers of Christ to be the most cheerful and optimistic people in all the world.

> Be of good cheer, the Master said.
>   I am the Vine of life,
> Ye are the branches bearing fruit,
>   Ripe for the wine-press strife.
>
> Be of good cheer; the strife is not
>   Man against man or God.
> Rather must spirit vanquish grass,
>   Souls rise above the sod.
>
> Be of good cheer, the Master said,
>   Each one of you, a world,
> Shines with a more enduring glow
>   Than planets sunward hurled.
>
> Be of good cheer. My Father works
>   In and through all of you.
> I am His Son and ye His sons,
>   Brothers in work to do.[11]

—Earl Marlatt, 1926

✣

O SON OF MAN, THOU MADEST KNOWN

AMONG the more recent beautiful hymn-poems written about the theme of Christ as a worker, none is more beautiful than this one by Milton S. Little-field, titled "O Son of Man, Thou Madest Known."

The author thinks of Jesus as teaching us not only in words, but also by His daily example the "sacredness of common things." He challenges us to think of Jesus going about His daily tasks in the humble carpenter shop in Nazareth, and later with His disciples throughout all Judæa, Galilee, and Samaria, teaching and healing the people; and in thinking of Jesus thus to appreciate to the fullest the opportunities to bless the lives of others, which the common everyday human tasks provide.

This hymn-poem emphasizes the same thought which another of our present-day poets—John Oxenham—stresses in his "The Pilgrim Way":

[11] Words copyright by the author. Used by permission.

But once I pass this way,
And then—and then the silent **Door**
  Swings on its hinges—
  Opens—closes—
  And no more
  I pass this way.
  So while I may
  With all my might
  I will assay
  Sweet comfort and delight
To all I meet upon the Pilgrim way,
For no man travels twice
  The Great Highway
That climbs through darkness up to light,
  Through night
  To day.

The tune to which Dr. Littlefield's hymn-poem is most frequently sung was composed by Thomas B. Southgate in 1855.

O Son of Man, Thou madest known,
Through quiet work in shop and home,
The sacredness of common things,
The chance of life that each day brings.

O Workman true, may we fulfill,
In daily life the Father's will;
In duty's call, Thy call we hear
To fuller life through work sincere.

Thou Master Workman, grant us grace
The challenge of our tasks to face;
By loyal scorn of second best,
By effort true, to meet each test.

And thus we pray in deed and word,
Thy kingdom come on earth, O Lord;
In work that gives effect to prayer
Thy purpose for Thy world we share.[12]

                    —Milton S. Littlefield, 1916

[12] Words copyright by Milton S. Littlefield. Used by permission.

CONTENTS

PART III   SECTION V

A MAN OF PRAYER AND ACQUAINTED WITH GRIEF

✠

"Sit ye here, while I go yonder and pray."—MATTHEW 26:36

✠

A MAN OF PRAYER AND ACQUAINTED WITH GRIEF

"And he came out, and went, as his custom was, unto the mount of Olives; and the disciples also followed him. And when he was at the place, he said unto them, Pray that ye enter not into temptation. And he was parted from them about a stone's cast; and he kneeled down and prayed, saying, Father, if thou be willing, remove this cup from me: nevertheless not my will, but thine, be done. And there appeared unto him an angel from heaven, strengthening him. And being in an agony he prayed more earnestly; and his sweat became as it were great drops of blood falling down upon the ground. And when he rose up from his prayer, he came unto the disciples, and found them sleeping for sorrow, and said unto them, Why sleep ye? rise and pray, that ye enter not into temptation." Luke 22:39-46

✛

"Simon Peter saith unto him, Lord, whither goest thou? Jesus answered, Whither I go, thou canst not follow me now; but thou shalt follow afterwards. Peter saith unto him, Lord, why cannot I follow thee even now? I will lay down my life for thee. Jesus answereth, Wilt thou lay down thy life for me? Verily, verily, I say unto thee, The cock shalt not crow, till thou hast denied me thrice." John 13:36-38

CHRIST IN GETHSEMANE—*HOFMANN*

CHRIST IN GETHSEMANE

By

Johann Heinrich Hofmann

(Interpretation)

THE picture of "Christ in Gethsemane" which Johann Heinrich Hofmann has painted for us is one of the most beautiful as well as one of the most widely known paintings in all the world. Perhaps no other single scene in the life of Christ has been more frequently copied than this one. This is true, no doubt, because of the fact that the artist has portrayed the *ideal* against the background of the *real* for us in a masterly way.

The Garden of Gethsemane which is located upon the Mount of Olives was, in all probability, the private garden of some friend of the Master's, and a place where He frequently went to meditate and to pray. It was a lonely spot then, as it is today. This Garden is now owned by the Franciscan Order of the Roman Catholic Church. It came into their control in 1681. In the garden today there are eight giant olive trees, the circumferences of which range from twenty-four to thirty feet. The Moslems have never levied a tax upon this ground, perhaps because the Franciscan monks as well as the inhabitants of Jerusalem and of Palestine venerate this garden and its giant olive trees as the most holy and hallowed ground in all the world. One of these giant olive trees is designated as "The Tree of the Agony," and is supposed to be the one under which the Master suffered and prayed.

In the background of this midnight scene of suffering as Hofmann portrays it, may be dimly seen the forms not only of Peter, James, and John, but also the faint outline of Jerusalem on a distant hill almost directly below the only break in the cloudy sky.

Earlier in the night, Jesus had left eight of the disciples at the entrance of the garden, taking with Him into its deeper recesses the three who, on more than one occasion, had entered into a deeper fellowship with Him. But in this, the hour of His deepest suffering, He has withdrawn from even these three and is facing the crisis *alone*.

Here, in one of the loneliest spots that could possibly be found, the artist portrays Jesus kneeling with outstretched, clasped hands before a barren rock, that glaringly hurls back the reflection of heavenly light. The upturned face of the Master in this midnight vigil is illuminated by a light that seems to come down from above. It is the only light in the picture save that which the artist has used as a halo about the head of Christ to suggest His spiritual struggle against the evil forces in the world.

Some one has likened the thorny bush with its dead branches and savage thorns to the curse of sin which is in the world as a result of man's disobedience to God's will in another garden in the long ago. Here in the Garden of Gethsemane the Sinless Christ begins the agonizing process of man's redemption from sin by bringing his will into complete harmony with that of His Heavenly Father's.

How like the experience of the Master of Men in this midnight hour is the deepest one we know. Every great soul knows what it means, not only to be lonely, but to be alone. To a certain degree this is the experience of all men. Alone we are born, alone we die. In the last analysis, every great crisis of our lives must be faced *alone*. There are times when the advice and companionship of friends will not avail. The decision is too great, too momentous, to be shared. It must be met and solved alone with God. The poet puts it thus:

> His heart craved sympathy,
>   But He was alone.
> He was fighting the battle for all the race,
>   And He was alone.
> He was pitted against all the powers of hell,
>   And He was alone.
> He was lonely—desperately lonely,
>   And He was alone!

He was alone with a *decision* and a *dedication* so crucial and so far-reaching that it could be shared only with God.

Speaking of this picture, Dr. Bailey says: "Hofmann has given us a thoroughly emotional treatment of the incident. We feel the beauty of it, the serene self-surrender of it, the transfiguring glory of it after the crisis of the struggle has passed. This experience was the most terrible that Jesus ever passed through. He had had moments of anxiety before, moments of storm and stress, moments of personal danger. He had undergone forty days of conflict in the wilderness so severe that it had to be pictured in symbolic language. But never has the scripture said of Him that He was in agony or that His sweat seemed like blood. Such language hints at a spiritual struggle too intense for description. . . .

"The struggle of Jesus in Gethsemane was the endeavor to harmonize His personal human will with the fate that now seemed to be His Father's will. It was to accept a course of events the good purpose of which he could not fathom; it was to avoid not the tortures of the cross but drinking the cup of failure bitterer than death. If He died, what would become of that sublime vision of a regenerated social order that apparently He alone had seen? What would become of His disciples who had hardly absorbed as yet the first principles of the Kingdom of Righteousness? From the distance of the Mount of Transfiguration a martyr's death had seemed to have a place in the great scheme of things, but now when death was at hand the tragedy to His cause seemed irreparable. Death simply could not be! Yet the outcome of His struggle was a victory of faith over sight, a surrender of His entire personal interests and the interests of the Kingdom into the Father's keeping. Henceforth He could face death or life with the calm consciousness which had been His in former days, 'I do always the things that please Him.' His attitude toward the Father was precisely what Tennyson has declared ours must be toward Him who by His midnight victory showed Himself to be the 'Strong Son of God' and our Master and Lord."[1]

> Strong Son of God, immortal Love,
>   Whom we that have not seen Thy face,
>   By faith, and faith alone, embrace,
> Believing where we cannot prove;
>
> Thou seemest human and divine,
>   The highest, holiest, manhood, thou:
>   Our wills are ours, we know not how;
> Our wills are ours, to make them thine.

✝

THE LAST SUPPER

By

Leonardo da Vinci

(Interpretation)

THE story of the wonderful life and accomplishments of Leonardo da Vinci reads like a fairy tale. From childhood he attracted attention because of his passion for learning. Greatly beloved, handsome, athletic, with muscles so powerful that he could bend iron and tame wild horses, he was, nevertheless, so tender-hearted that he would purchase little caged birds just for the pleasure of setting them *free* again.

He was born in the Castle Vinci between Florence and Pisa; he was brought up in Florence, where he lived until he was twenty-four. At fifteen he entered the studio of Verocchio. From the first, this brilliant and gifted youth won general favoritism, and soon proved the superior of his Master.

Leonardo da Vinci is said to have been the *greatest genius* that ever lived. Painting was only *one* of the many activities in which his talents were displayed. He was illustrious alike as a sculptor, an architect, an engineer, philosopher, writer, and musician. He designed the most remarkable bridges and warships of his day. In the *Renaissance in Italy* this comment on his inventive genius was made before the day of assured flying-machines. "His designs of wings to fly with symbolize his whole endeavor. He believed in solving the insolvable, and nature had so richly endowed him in the very dawn of discovery that he was almost justified in this delusion."

Da Vinci holds a unique place in the history of art. Up to the sixteenth

---

[1] From *The Gospel in Art*, by Albert Edward Bailey. Published by the Pilgrim Press, Boston, Mass. Used by permission of the author.

THE LAST SUPPER—*DA VINCI*

century very little had been done in the art of the world worth noting, except in Italy, and that was very crude. But during the sixteenth century Italy produced, all at once, a number of the world's greatest artists, including Raphael, Michelangelo, Titian, Correggio, and Leonardo da Vinci.

Da Vinci and Michelangelo are called the giants of the Florentine Renaissance. But da Vinci stands alone in:

1. The universal character of his genius.

2. The rare perfection of the high intellectual qualities of his art.

3. The extraordinary influence he exerted upon his contemporaries.

When "The Last Supper" was completed in 1498 Raphael was fifteen years of age, and Michelangelo was but twenty-three.

THE LAST SUPPER

No scene in the life of Christ has been painted more often than that of "The Last Supper," but no other attempt can compare with this wonderful painting of Leonardo da Vinci.

It is the ideal representation of a dramatic moment the delineation of the effect of a single word "betray" upon the twelve men most closely associated with Jesus during His life and ministry.

The scene is the night of the Passover supper. In a small upper room in a house in Jerusalem, Jesus, surrounded by his disciples, is breaking the bread of their farewell meal.

Christ is the center of all interest. He has just said, "One of you will betray me." *Love, terror, grief,* and *amazement* find expression in the cry of his disciples, "Lord, is it I?"

This picture was painted on the walls of a convent dining-room in Milan, Italy. The appropriate setting of the picture adds much to its charm. Seated at their meal, the brothers of the monastery could look upon the table of Christ, as if He were their guest. It is said to be an exact copy of the table, linen, and dishes used by the monks.

Christ is the central figure. The disciples sit in four groups of three each. In their bewilderment the disciples have drawn away for the moment, so that Christ sits alone.

Each disciple is expressing his feelings in his own way. There is no repetition of an action or a figure. Each gesture represents an individual type of character, yet all harmonize in directing thought toward Christ, the central figure, effecting unity as the motive of the scene.

At the Master's right, in broken-hearted silence, sits John the Beloved. Impulsive Peter leans forward, touching John's shoulder, and seems to be urging him to ask the Master who the traitor is.

There can be no doubt as to the real betrayer. In contrast to the gentle features of John is the dark, cunning face of Judas, who clutches the money-bag and looks at Jesus in alarm, as if fearful that He will indicate who His betrayer is.

Behind Peter is Andrew with upraised hands, then James the younger, and at the end Bartholomew, leaning forward in his eagerness to catch the words of the others.

To the left of Christ is Thomas with raised finger, seeming to say, "Lord, is it I?" In front of him, James the elder, expressing in face and gesture his horror at such a thought. Philip, bending over his companions with deep regret in his fine face, seems to say: "Thou seest my heart, Lord. Is it I?" Next to Philip, in the last group are Matthew, Thaddeus, and Simeon.

We are touched by the face of the Saviour, sad, submissive, forgiving, as though He were hopeful that Judas might even yet repent his action before it is too late. We read that the artist spent months on his conception of this one face, and left it, in his own mind, incomplete.

Notice how much da Vinci has expressed of the human and the divine in Christ's gestures. One hand, with palm downward, seems to say, "If it be possible, let this cup pass from me." The other, upturned, receptive, suggests the words, "Not my will, but thine be done."

The original of da Vinci's "The Last Supper" is nearly lost to us. Its history is a sad one. Being painted in oil, it suffered serious injury from the dampness of the plastered walls. Not many generations had passed before it began to fade. In the seventeenth century a door was cut into it. During Napoleon's invasion this hall was used as a military camp, and it is said the soldiers amused themselves by throwing bricks at the figures.

At one time the French king, Francis I, was so impressed with this painting that he bargained for its removal to France. An attempt was made, but the plaster began to crumble and the work of removal was abandoned.

Fortunately, Leonardo da Vinci's pupils made many copies of this masterpiece in the earlier years of its history, so that we have complete knowledge of it, and many attractive prints are available.

It is recognized as da Vinci's masterpiece, and is one of the *twelve paintings* called *world pictures*.

✢

"FOR HE HAD GREAT POSSESSIONS"

By

George Frederick Watts

(Interpretation)

GEORGE FREDERICK WATTS, the English portait-painter, was born in London in 1817. He was the son of a piano-tuner, and began to draw almost before he could walk or talk. By the time he was twelve years old he was a prolific illustrator and at fifteen began to study art seriously. When he was twenty he won a *first prize* of $1,500 for a design for decorating the Houses of Parliament, which money he used for the purpose of continuing his art study in Italy.

"FOR HE HAD GREAT POSSESSIONS"—*WATTS*

In 1847 he again won a first prize of $2,500 in a similar competition which assured his position as an artist.

From 1860 on he devoted his time largely to painting pictures that express the great truths of life, many of which are now permanently housed in the Tate Gallery in London. He was also a prolific portrait-painter, many of the most renowned men of England having sat for him. In 1867 he was elected a member of the Royal Academy, received degrees from the English universities, the Order of Merit from King Edward, and the cross of the Legion of Honor from France. He was also made a knight of the Order of San Luigi by Italy, and twice declined a Baronetcy.

While modest and self-effacing in personality, he had nevertheless an earnest desire to serve humanity through his art. Speaking of his motive in painting, Mr. Watts said: "My intention has not been so much to paint pictures that will charm the eye as to suggest great thoughts that will appeal to the imagination and the heart, and kindle all that is best and noblest in humanity."

Among the masterpieces of religious art painted by this great English artist with the purpose of expressing in an objective way some of the great truths of life, none ranks higher, perhaps, than this one portraying the rich ruler of whom both Matthew and Mark say, "He went away sorrowful; for he was one that had great possessions."

We cannot look at the bowed head and drooping shoulders of this richly gowned and jeweled man of wealth without recalling Dante's famous phrase, "One who made through cowardice the great refusal." Life, without the armor of riches, he has not the nerve to face. Already he has become the slave, not the master, of material things.

The face of the man is entirely hidden in this three-quarter-length figure, so that it is not easy to judge the man's age, refinement, character, or intellect. We must, therefore, refer to the Gospel stories as told by Matthew (19:16-26), Mark (10:17-27), and Luke (18:18-30) for the qualities which Jesus saw in him, and seeing, loved.

Judging from the silk sleeves, velvet and fur-trimmed mantle of the man, we know he was rich in this world's goods. The rings upon his fingers and the massive chain about his shoulders would seem to indicate also that he was vain enough to love outward adornment.

We are forced, however, by the very indefiniteness of this picture to interpret the character of this man largely by the one grasping hand which may be seen. It is a large hand, and seemingly alive. It is a grasping hand, but not a lovely one. "The fingers spread like talons; somewhat relaxed, to be sure, for this one moment of vain regret; but presently they will come together like a vise never again to open except to grasp some new object of desire."

Speaking interpretably of this picture, Dr. Albert Edward Bailey says: "The love of money, failing as it does to appreciate the worth of personality, brings upon the soul that it owns the loss of its own personality. The man is swallowed up of his passion. All that gives him distinctiveness as a soul, as a member of society, as God's image, dies out, and only the elemental function of grabbing remains. This is why Watts does not show the man's face. . . .

"When the love of money takes possession of the soul, one by one the virtues leave and the vices arrive. First, the fountains of sympathy are stopped; then the pride of life looks out at the windows—one sees the 'high-brow' and the 'automobile face'; then arises the will to dominate rather than to serve; and last, that worst abuse of riches, 'when it disjoins remorse from power.' Jesus knew the whole tragic devolution of the type; and he sounded to His disciples the clearest notes of warning: 'Lay not up for yourselves treasure upon the earth. . . . Ye cannot serve God and Mammon.' "[2]

✠

CHRIST WASHING PETER'S FEET

By

Ford Madox Brown

(Interpretation)

FORD MADOX BROWN, the son of a British naval officer, was born at Calais in 1821. His talent for painting developed early and he was given the best art education which Flanders afforded. A series of family tragedies, however, which culminated with the death of his wife in 1845 and the loss of his own health, made any great amount of productive work impossible. When he finally did begin to exhibit his paintings, his work became the subject of much negative criticism and even of derision on the part of art critics. Notwithstanding this adverse criticism, his work brought to him Rossetti as a pupil in 1848, and from that time on Brown became one of the inspirers of the Pre-Raphaelite Brotherhood, although he, himself, was never a member.

There is little doubt that Brown as an artist was ahead of his time. And while art critics scorned him and his work, his pictures began to sell, and in the years that followed he secured the recognition which should have come much earlier. His strongest qualities are *invention, composition,* and *color*; and to him we owe the startling change that came over British art in the middle of the nineteenth century. He was engaged in painting a series of mural decorations for the Town Hall of Manchester, when he died in 1893.

We are indebted to Ford Madox Brown for one of the most realistic of all pictures of that scene which occurred in the upper room in Jerusalem on the night of the betrayal and arrest of Jesus. While the heads of only nine of the disciples, not counting Peter in the foreground, are visible in this painting, the incident followed immediately their farewell meal with the Master in the upper room, and the other two may have been engaged in the task of settling up with the man of the house, whose upper room was used on this occasion.

[2] From *The Gospel in Art*, pp. 261-262. Published by the Pilgrim Press, Boston, Mass. Used by permission of the author.

Brown's presentation of this picture is a sermon on the text: "The Son of Man came, not to be ministered unto, but to minister, and to give his life a ransom for many." And how graphically and realistically he has painted the central figures of Jesus and Peter. The Master has just girded himself with a towel, and is here doing the menial work of a slave, and He looks the part. He has laid aside the outer mantle which lends so much dignity to Oriental clothes, has knelt before Peter with the gleaming copper water-basin near by, and is now in the act of drying one of Peter's feet with the free end of the towel which girds His waist.

The varying expressions of interest, confusion, and embarrassment on the part of the nine whose heads are more or less dimly seen above the table is an interesting study. John, at the extreme right, is watching with absorbed interest the service His Master is, in such great humility, performing. Regret that he had not first performed this humble task is clearly in the face of the man at the center-back of the table. While another on the left clutches his head with both hands as if to indicate that it is utterly impossible to understand this strange act and attitude on the part of their Teacher and Friend. At the extreme left end of the table, the artist has, with true traditional insight, painted Judas as red-haired and in the act of replacing his sandals on feet that have already been bathed by the Master they all profess to love and serve. His scheming look would seem to indicate that Satan has already entered into his heart. He will leave the company soon, for the words of Christ, "Now are ye clean, but not all," have already made him feel uncomfortable. Then, too, he has already made his bargain with the high priests to betray Christ with a kiss, and knows, in his inmost self, that he is out of harmony with the faithful little group who have just ended their farewell meal with the Master.

Peter and Jesus are the center of interest in Brown's conception of this incident, however, and what a study Peter's downcast head and eyes are! When Jesus began to perform this menial act toward him, Peter's indignation flared as usual, as his words clearly show—"Thou shalt never wash my feet." But when the Master, with calm dignity, explained to him that he could have no fellowship with Him in great things unless he had the humility to allow his Master's will to be supreme in the small, Peter's vehement response flew to the opposite pole, and he replied: "Not my feet only, but also my hands and my head!" Whatever humiliation had to be undergone, nothing must stand in the way when it came to being reckoned among Christ's trusted friends.

In this picture, Brown shows us a Peter whose pride has suddenly collapsed. He does not fully understand the meaning of this act of lowly service as yet; he only knows that it is his Master's will, and as such he accepts it. Note how expressive his concurrence is portrayed by his tightly clasped hands and his head deeply sunk on his chest. The light in his eyes, intensely fixed, would seem to indicate that the fire of humiliation still burns within him, although he has already brought his will under subjection to the Master's, even though he does not fully understand the lofty and incomprehensible character of his Teacher and Friend.

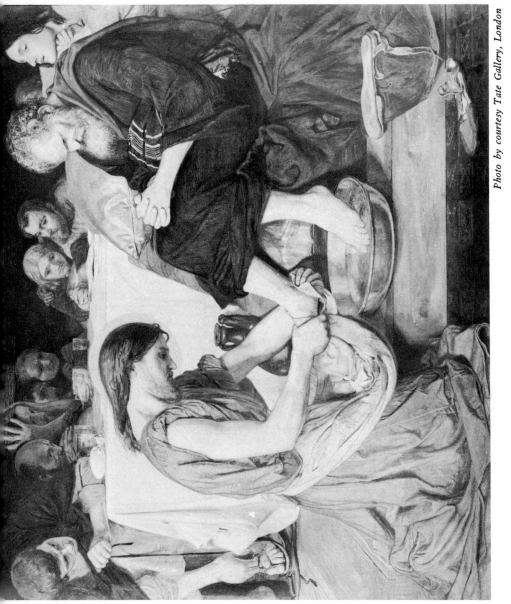

CHRIST WASHING PETER'S FEET—BROWN

Photo by courtesy Kunstverlag-Trowitzsch & Sohn, Germany

CHRIST AND THE RICH YOUNG RULER—CLEMENTZ

Christ's head, like Peter's, is sunk upon His breast, but the spirit that emanates from Him is in direct contrast with Peter's. His disciples had carried their jealousies over the "chief seats" even into this solemn hour and place. If each of them had not stood upon his self-conceived dignity and prestige, it is probable that one of them, at least, would now be performing this humble act of service for the others. The only way that Jesus could teach them the futility— yes, the downright wickedness—of their preferring-self-to-others attitude was by this servant act. The Master of Men therefore assumes not only the garb of a servant, but the spirit of one, that He may thereby teach them that any service is better than "place," and that among His followers, if one has not at all times and in all places the *spirit of service*, he does not belong among those who call themselves followers of the lowly Nazarene.

Brown's love of color, detail of composition, and inventiveness is nowhere more clearly shown than in this painting of "Christ Washing Peter's Feet." The deep red of the floor covering, the spotless white of the linen tablecloth, the rich tans, brown, maroon-red and green provide an arresting picture for the eyes; while the rich details of sandals, water-basin and pitcher, dishes, and even the money-bag near Judas' arm add to its distinctive charm.

This picture has a humbling message for believing Christians everywhere. "The servant is not above his Master, nor the Master above his servant" is the clear message that this beautiful painting so realistically portrays.

✛

CHRIST AND THE RICH YOUNG RULER

By

Hermann Clementz

(Interpretation)

OF ALL the artists who have attempted to portray on canvas the incident of Christ's conversation with the Rich Young Ruler to me the one by the German artist, Clementz, seems to be the greatest. This beautiful painting gives us the spiritual tragedy of a great refusal in the briefest compass of time.

The scene is novel and attractive. It is the outer room or portico of a house of wealth in which Jesus has been talking to His disciples and others on His way to Jerusalem about God's Kingdom of Love. This scion of the aristocracy, whom Jesus is addressing, has no doubt seen other noted Pharisees and scribes listening in on the revolutionary teaching of this new Rabbi, and has stopped to learn what this new teaching is all about. His colorful turban, brocaded coat, and brilliant sash are indicative of wealth, leisure, and material possessions.

It is easy to see how Jesus, looking upon such a young man, might love him for his youth, for his purity, and for his ability to make a great contribution to the day and generation of which he was a part; and, loving him, might have shared with Him the way by which one inherits eternal life.

Answering the youth's affirmation that he had kept the law, Jesus draws back the curtain to the portico leading to the street, and pointing to his Jewish brethren who slave as burden-bearers at animal carts says: "How can you say, 'I have kept the Law from my youth up. What lack I yet?' Behold, these thy brethren, sons of Abraham, live in dirty rags, slave as animal burden-bearers, and die of hunger, while your house is full of the material wealth that would bring to them release and a fighting chance at happiness."

That Jesus' words have made some impression on this young Jew is evident. With his chin resting on his hand he seems to be thinking through Christ's challenge to "Go, sell all that thou hast, distribute to the poor, and come and follow me."

The issue is clearly drawn in Jesus' mind; and His eyes are searching and unequivocal as with gesture He says: "Here are these needy folks who till the soil and create your wealth. There is no heaven for you till you deal justly with them."

Speaking of this incident, Dr. Bailey says: "Notice how the eyes of Jesus are searching the young man's soul. They are kindly eyes, but they are the eyes of One who knows life. They see the issues that are involved here; not so much the difference it will make to the poor if the riches are divided, but the difference it will make in the life of this youth. It will mean no more fine clothes, no more fine dinners, no more gay companions, no more idleness, no more comfortable feeling of security in hard times, no more sense of power; but on the other hand it will mean freedom from the *slavery of things*, an opportunity to know what the great human needs are, a chance to invest life where its returns will compound themselves not only in blessings to the poor and the despairing; but in heavenly riches for himself through all eternity.

"The antithesis of this picture is a constant one. On the one hand is poverty and wretchedness, crime and ignorance and degradation; on the other self-satisfied or proudly aggressive wealth. Between these two stands the Christ with His hands pointing to the world's needs and His heart wrestling with the youth of each generation in the hope that some few among them may break their golden chains and go down to help. Now and then one sees the vision and responds; but usually they go away sorrowful, and Christ turns again with a sigh, saying, "How hardly shall they that have riches enter into the kingdom of God.

"One does not have to be a Socialist to see the righteousness of this demand. But it had taken Christendom nearly two thousand years to get an inkling of the tremendous social reconstructions that are implicit in that word. And the cause of the tardiness of Christian insight and endeavor lies in the tardiness of the Christian heart to love as Christ loved. The fault is not all on one side, by any means. It is harder for the poor to love the rich than for the rich to love the poor; but love each other they must if either is to inherit eternal life. And when they begin to *love*, the problems of wealth and of poverty will both disappear."[3]

[3] From *The Gospel in Art*, Bailey, p. 260. Used by permission of the author.

TEMPTATION

They took Him to a mountain-top to see
Where earth's fair kingdoms flung their golden net
To snare the feet and trick the souls of men.
With slimy craft and cynic guile they said:
If He but sees the glory and the pride,
The pomps and pleasures of this tinsel world,
He will forget His splendid, futile dreams;
And so they took Him up and tempted Him.

They pointed far across their level earth,
East to the fabled empires of the Ind,
Whose rulers' power was as the power of gods,
Where caravans with tinkling camel-bells
Brought silks and perfumes, pearls and ivory,
And tribute from far humbled provinces;
South to the magic kingdom of the Nile,
To Nubia and Abyssinia,
Jungle and desert kingdoms, rude but rich
With slaves and gems and golden yellow sands;
Northward to barbarous lands but dimly seen,
Savage but surging with unmeasured strength;
West where Rome's empire sent her legions forth,
Conquering, building, ruling with wise force,
The mighty mother of an unborn brood
Of nations which should rise and rule the world.

All this they spread before Him, tempting Him,
And watched to see ambition light His eye,
The lust of power darken His bright face,
And avarice crook His hands to clutch the gold.

But from the mountain peak He raised His eyes,
And saw the deep, calm sky, the stars, and God.

—Winfred Ernest Garrison

IN THE GARDEN

My sins, my sin, my Saviour!
    Their guilt I never knew
Till with Thee in the desert
    I near Thy passion drew;
Till with Thee in the garden
    I heard Thy pleading prayer,

And saw the sweat-drops bloody
That told Thy sorrow there.

—*J. B. S. Monsell*

GETHSEMANE

There is a way which man hath trod
  For, lo, these thronging, countless years;
It is the way of life, of God;
  It is the way of night, of tears;
Its winding we may not foresee;
  It is the way—Gethsemane.

It is the way whereby we know
  Life's larger meanings and its claims,
The fellowship of human woe,
  Our partnership with others' pains.
It is the way which seems to be
Life's only way—Gethsemane.

—*Charles Russell Wakeley*

THE WAY

Pass not too near these outcast sons of men
Where walked your Christ ahead! lest you, too, share
The rabble's wrath; in time, take heed! Beware
The shame—the bitter woe of Him again.
Your flaming zeal speak not so rash—so loud!
Pass on your prudent way within the crowd.

What if they mark you of His band, and cry:
"Behold this one, as well!" Ah, you should know
The jeers, the stones, for all that with Him go!
Have caution, fool! let others yearn and die;
These broken ones you love with hot heartbreak
Can save you not! Be warned by His mistake!

Remember how He scorned the risk and loss!
Remember how they nailed Him to a cross!

—*Laura Simmons*

DESPISED AND REJECTED

Homeless!
The Living Bread
Hungered
While all beside were fed.
To their warm holes the foxes ran,
Birds flew to nest when the west was red,
But the Son of Man
Had not where to lay His head,

Open Door
Henceforth for all
Hungers,
Hearth and Banquet Hall
For hurt and loneliness is He
Thrust from Nazareth to roam,
Vagabond of Galilee,
Who is every outcast's Home.

—*Katharine Lee Bates*

THE PHARISEE

Two men went up into God's place to pray,
The one a Pharisee. He stood apart.
Evening in flight had dropped immortal flowers
Of sunset bloom. The quiet city lay
Like a pale gem beneath a night of stars,
And no sound rose.

                    Besought the Pharisee,
Beating his head upon the marble wall,
"God, God, I thank Thee for this bitterness;
I thank Thee that, in anguish, I am lift
Above my fellows, that Thou choosest me
For throes that rend no other, that Thou givest
An awful and peculiar agony
Such as ONE only bore. I thank Thee, God!"
Then as he prayed, he listened to the sobs
Heaving up from his soul, counted the tears
That burned upon his face, and held his woe
Supreme!

The other knelt, a Publican,
In sober dress and common attitude.
He prayed, "Ah, stern Jehovah, Thou dost take
My self-belief, my courage and my joy,
Even mine inmost treasure, secret love!
I bow to Thy decree. Mayhap Thy sword
Smites with like heaviness this desolate man
Beside me. We are brothers in despair.
Am I then isolate before Thy wrath?
Am I then all alone in agony?
Behold, Thy pitiless, ironic word
Brands us alike, the mighty Pharisee
And the poor blinded, weeping Publican!"

—Dorothy Landers Beall

HYMN: O PATIENT CHRIST

O patient Christ! when long ago
    O'er old Judea's rugged hills
Thy willing feet went to and fro,
    To find and comfort human ills—
        Did once Thy tender, earnest eyes,
        Look down the solemn centuries,
        And see the smallness of our lives?

Souls struggling for the victory,
    And martyrs, finding death was gain,
Souls turning from the Truth and Thee,
    And falling deep in sin and pain—
        Great heights and depths were surely seen,
        But, oh! the dreary waste between—
        Small lives, not base perhaps, but mean:

Their selfish efforts for the right,
    Or cowardice that keeps from sin—
Content to only see the height
    That nobler souls will toil and win!
        Oh, shame, to think Thine eyes should see
        The souls contented just to be—
        The lives too small to take in Thee.

Lord, let this thought awake our shame,
    That blessed shame that stings to life,
Rouse us to live for Thy dear name.
    Arm us with courage for the strife.
        O Christ! be patient with us still;

Dear Christ! remember Calvary's hill—
Our little lives with purpose fill![4]

—Margaret Wade Deland

THE RICH YOUNG MAN

It seemed so mad a thing to do—
To grieve so deep—to perish, too,
For men He never even knew!
A life so lonely, meek and bare!
I wonder why He made a prayer
For them that mocked and nailed Him there!
Vast wealth is mine; why do I see
My golden hoard without avail?
Why turns no man with love to me?
Why did He triumph, and I fail?
Poor and despised! how strange a thing
That mighty hosts, with worshiping,
Their homage to His name should bring!

Oh, 'tis a grievous mystery—
That mankind never looks to me
As to that spent and broken Christ
Who drooped on Calvary!

—Laura Simmons

SANDALPHON

Have you read in the Talmud of old,
In the Legends the Rabbins have told
   Of the limitless realms of the air,
Have you read it,—the marvelous story
Of Sandalphon, the Angel of Glory,
   Sandalphon, the Angel of Prayer?

How, erect, at the outermost gates
Of the City Celestial he waits,
   With his feet on the ladder of light,
That, crowded with angels unnumbered,
By Jacob was seen, as he slumbered
   Alone in the desert at night?

[4] From *The Master of Men*. Published by Harper & Brothers. Used by special permission of the author.

The Angels of Wind and of Fire
Chant only one hymn and expire
   With the song's irresistible stress;
Expire in their rapture and wonder,
As harp-strings are broken asunder
   By music they throb to express.

But serene in the rapturous throng,
Unmoved by the rush of the song
   With eyes unimpassioned and slow,
Among the dead angels, the deathless
Sandalphon stands listening breathless
   To sounds that ascend from below;—

From spirits on earth that adore,
From souls that entreat and implore
   In the fervor and passion of prayer;
From the hearts that are broken with losses,
And weary with dragging the crosses
   Too heavy for mortals to bear.

And he gathers the prayers as he stands,
And they change into flowers in his hands,
   Into garlands of purple and red;
And beneath the great arch of the portal,
Through the streets of the City Immortal
   Is wafted the fragrance they shed.

It is but a legend, I know,—
A fable, a phantom, a show,
   Of the ancient Rabbinical lore;
Yet the old mediæval tradition,
The beautiful, strange superstition,
   But haunts me and holds me the more

When I look from my window at night,
And the welkin above is all white,
   All throbbing and panting with stars,
Among them majestic is standing
Sandalphon the angel, expanding
   His pinions in nebulous bars.

And the legend, I feel, is a part
Of the hunger and thirst of the heart,
   The frenzy and fire of the brain,
That grasps at the fruitage forbidden,
The golden pomegranates of Eden
   To quiet its fever and pain.[5]

               —*Henry Wadsworth Longfellow*

[5] From *Longfellow's Complete Poetical Works*. Used by permission of and arrangement with Houghton Mifflin Company.

THE AGONY OF GETHSEMANE

THEY came unto a place which was named Gethsemane: and he saith unto his disciples, "Sit ye here, while I go yonder and pray."

And he taketh with him Peter and James and John, and began to be greatly amazed and sore troubled. And he saith unto them, "My soul is exceeding sorrowful, even unto death: abide ye here, and watch."

And he went forward a little and fell on the ground, and prayed that if it were possible, the hour might pass away from him.

And he said, "Abba Father, all things are possible unto thee; remove this cup from me: howbeit not what I will, but what thou wilt."

And there appeared unto him an angel from heaven, strengthening him.

And being in agony, he prayed more earnestly; and his sweat became as it were great drops of blood falling down upon the ground.

And when he rose up from his prayer, he came unto his disciples, and found them sleeping for sorrow, and said unto Peter, "Simon, sleepest thou? Couldest thou not watch one hour? Watch and pray, that ye enter not into temptation: the spirit indeed is willing, but the flesh is weak."

Again a second time he went away, and prayed, saying, "My Father, if this cannot pass away, except I drink it, thy will be done."

And he came again and found them sleeping, for their eyes were heavy. And he left them again, and went away and prayed a third time, saying the same words.

Then cometh he to the disciples, and saith unto them, "Sleep on now, and take your rest: behold, the hour is at hand, and the Son of man is betrayed into the hands of sinners."

"Arise, let us be going: behold, he is at hand that betrayeth me."[6]

✛

JESUS, A MAN OF PRAYER

By

Cynthia Pearl Maus

JESUS, the Son of God, was a Man of Prayer. He knew a secret garden of the soul, of which the Garden of Gethsemane, beyond the brook Kedron, is but a type. Into this secret garden of the soul He withdrew constantly, for to Him

[6] From *His Last Week*, pp. 40-41. By William E. Barton, Theodore G. Soares, and Sydney Strong. Published by the Hope Publishing Company, Chicago, Ill. Used by special permission of the publishers.

prayer was a very real, vital and spontaneous experience of searching for the *will* of God and of unifying His own will with that of His heavenly Father's. Jesus spent whole nights in prayer, before the choosing of the twelve, on the night of His betrayal and arrest. Indeed, prayer was so natural and vital a part of the Son of Man, that one day His disciples came to Him, saying: "Lord, teach us to pray, even as John taught his disciples," so that it will seem to us, as it does to you, that God is near, God hears, God knows, God understands.

And so Jesus taught them the prayer that is often referred to as the Lord's Prayer, but which is far more accurately called the Disciples' Prayer. To find the Lord's Prayer one needs to turn to the seventeenth chapter of the Gospel of John. This Disciples' Prayer has become the universal possession of all believing Christians through the intervening centuries, and is perhaps the most widely known and quoted portion of Scripture in the entire Bible.

A lover of stories has called our attention to the fact that even in the Disciples' Prayer there is the essence of a story—the story of the Fatherhood of God and the brotherhood of man. It is a selfless prayer-story, for does it not say: "Give us [not me] our daily bread; and forgive us [not me] our sins as we also have forgiven those who have sinned against us"?

The first half of this prayer-story emphasizes the universality of God's love and care for the children of men. All races of men in every country, clime, and condition are included in the "Our Father which art in heaven." The second half of this prayer-story emphasizes the selflessness of the Christian religion. The way to the heart of our Father in heaven, as Jesus conceived it, is not a "me and mine," but an "our and us," way. "Forgive us our trespasses as we forgive those who have trespassed against us."

In this prayer-story, Jesus not only taught His disciples how to pray, but He gave them the conditions under which prayer can and must be kept a vital sincere, personal experience of fellowship with God if it is to establish between the individual and his heavenly Father a unifying relationship.

In the preface to the Lord's Prayer or Disciples' Prayer as we find it in the Sermon on the Mount, Jesus says: "And when ye pray, ye shall not be as the hypocrites: for they love to stand and pray in the synagogues and in the corners of the streets, that they may be seen of men. Verily I say unto you, they have received their reward." Thus Jesus warns His disciples that praying overmuch in public places is a dangerous practice. Men and women are apt to think more about what they are saying, and how it is sounding in the ears of others than they are about the needs of God's world and their share in making it a better world.

Public prayer is necessary on certain occasions, but the individual who prays only in public, to be seen and heard of men, has missed and is missing the real experience of "aloneness with God" which Jesus knew; and which He taught His disciples to practice. "But thou, when thou prayest, enter into thine inner chamber, and having shut the door, pray to thy Father who is in secret, and thy Father who seeth in secret shall recompense thee."

Then, too, Jesus warns His disciples against the use of set words and phrases, "vain repetitions, as do the Gentiles," because it tends to destroy the fresh, vigorous searching of one's own heart; and to make of prayer instead a "give me, give me, give me" fetish.

There is a vast deal of difference between praying and saying a prayer. Real prayer is costly, for it means that one cannot ask God to do anything for him that he is not both ready and willing to attempt to do for himself. One may pray for health, but if one is constantly violating the laws of health, such a prayer cannot be answered with health. One may pray for peace, but if one cannot live harmoniously with those about him, such a prayer can be answered only in the negative. One may pray for the missionaries of the cross, and for God's needy children the world around; but unless the one who prays thus *gives generously* until he feels the pinch of it, and *serves sacrificially* with no thought of personal reward, he is using "vain repetitions" about which Jesus warned His disciples.

Prayer to be a real, vital, renewing experience of fellowship with God must be *unselfish*. Jesus said, "Your heavenly Father knows what things ye have need." One does not need to waste time begging God for a lot of things for oneself. And prayer must be *universal*, all-inclusive in its outreach for the needs of the children of men. One must submerge one's own *will* and *desires* in an honest heart-searching endeavor to discover *what* the *will* of the heavenly Father is for him.

All this and much more is included in the prayer-story found in the sixth chapter of Matthew and the eleventh chapter of Luke. It is only six verses long, yet it is at one and the same time one of the simplest and yet most profound of all Scripture passages, and there are times when hardly any follower of Christ can honestly pray it at all.

> Our Father which art in heaven,
> Hallowed be Thy name.
> Thy Kingdom come,
> Thy will be done on earth
> As it is in heaven.
> Give us this day our daily bread,
> And forgive us our debts,
> As we forgive our debtors.
> And lead us not into temptation,
> But deliver us from evil.
> For thine is the Kingdom,
> And the power and the glory,
> Forever. Amen.[7]

[7] See Burney's *The Poetry of Our Lord.*

SIFTING MEN'S HEARTS AND MOTIVES

WHEN we reached Capernaum Judas turned aside for no one. Though several men spoke to him he paid no heed to their greetings, but made straight for the house of Jesus. . . . And Jesus seeing him, spoke,

"You have just returned? You look very tired."

"I have somewhat to say to you," Judas answered.

"When did you last eat?" Jesus asked him, but Judas brushed the question aside, his mind so set on his purpose that he was regardless of his bodily weariness.

"I do not remember. This morning. What matter?" he said. "Where can we talk?"

"I was going to the other side of the lake. Come apart with me and rest awhile," said Jesus, and He put His shoulder to the gunnel of the boat, and I helping, we pushed her off. As she took the water I jumped in to steady her, and Judas followed. The other men would have clambered in, too, but Jesus put them aside, saying Judas would speak with Him alone, and so they gave it up, and when Jesus had got in, helped to push us off with oars. Whether it was that they thought I was joined with Judas on his business, or whether they were used to seeing me with Jesus, I know not, but they made no remark on my presence, and, indeed, the boat so quickly slid into deep water that I could not have got out of it if I would without leaving her guideless. So it came about that I heard what Judas had to say.

The wind was fresh, and Jesus and I set the sail. Judas did not help, but sat in the stern, silent and absorbed, while the boat raced across the blue lake to the other side. Here we landed and tied the painter to a great stone. Jesus brought bread and dates from the boat, and we climbed to the wide grassy plain above, but Judas would not eat.

"Later," he said, and for a time he lay face downward on the bleached grass as if he thought of what he had to speak. Then suddenly he sat upright, and turned his haggard face to Jesus.

"Master," he said, "I have preached the Kingdom as you told me. Throughout all Galilee I have found the same misery and slavery. Everywhere the hold of the Romans is tightening. Our statesmen do not care. They will never win us back our freedom. In a short time it will be too late."

His voice broke, and he covered his eyes with his hands. At the sight of his woe a lump came into my throat, and I turned away my head, but the tranquillity that lay in the eyes of Jesus did not waver. He sat patient, helping Judas with silence till he should recover himself.

In a moment Judas had mastered himself. He uncovered his eyes, and looked Jesus straight in the face.

"When I asked You before, You turned a deaf ear to me. But now I have seen the misery of the people, their oppression and starvation. Will You not listen? You alone can free them. You have but to lift Your hand, and thousands will flock to You. Never has there been such a ferment. The people will follow You anywhere, even to death."

His voice was hoarse with passion, and he pleaded as a man pleads for what he desires most upon earth.

"I cannot do it myself," he said. "The people will not follow me. I lack something. I have not the power to win men's hearts as You have, Master. And You care for them. You have seen their misery. Will You not help? Restore to us our nation."

A great compassion shone in the eyes of Jesus, and there was reverence in His voice as He answered,

"Judas, it is not the way. Listen. Once before this temptation came upon Me. When the message first came to Me, when I looked round on the world and saw men as they are, and God told Me to tell them what they might be, then I was driven into the wilderness, and there I fought with Devils. God gives the message. It is for the Messenger to learn how to deliver it. Your question was before Me, Judas, and to find an answer I wrestled with the powers of evil. All the kingdoms of this world and their splendor seemed to pass before Me, and a voice within Me said: 'These will all acknowledge your Kingdom and the rule of the God Who sent You. But You must first unite the people and drive out those who stop them from living as God would have them live. Then will God have the kingdom, the power, and the glory.' In My soul I pondered, and then I saw the meaning of the devil that spoke within Me, and I said, 'Oh, Satan, if I by your evil help drive out evil, then will you, not God, be Ruler. I will not fall down and worship you. For if I by force drive out force, will not the strong reign? And if I by cruelty drive out cruelty, will not the cruel be master?' I tell you, no, Judas, I will never hand this world over to the master of cruelty and force. It is not the way."

He ceased speaking. Judas did not answer. He sat silent, shaken, but not convinced; his body crouched together. Suddenly he looked up from beneath his pent brows, and said:

"Under our present rule the people starve. It is in Your power to give them liberty. If You will not have them fight for that high ideal, will you lead, that they may have bread?"

Jesus put the taunt aside, and answered, gently:

"That temptation, too, has been before Me. God has given Me power, but if I use My power to give bread only, I should be a traitor. Man does not live by bread alone, but by the breath of God within him. . . . No, Judas; neither is that the way. Men must seek first the Kingdom of God and His righteousness, and all these things will be added to them."

Judas was not vanquished. His head drooped on his chest, and with one hand he plucked restlessly at the turfs of grass beside him and, unseeing, flung them from him. After a moment he sighed and glanced at Jesus, and there was craft in his eye.

"God guards His servants," he said. "It is natural to shrink from sacrifice that seems too great to bear. But God would preserve His Messenger. Your power is great. You could escape."

Jesus met his look, and in His own there was so much of sadness and of pity that the cunning glint died out of the eyes of Judas.

"Judas," he said, "what I have taught shall I not stand by? God will not alter His laws to save even the most beloved servant. What a man sows that shall he also reap. If I, using My powers carelessly, trust to God to make a success of My failure, I am again in the power of the devil. Thou shalt not tempt the Lord, thy God."

There was silence. Judas frowned as if his mind was working hard, and suddenly, as if he abandoned his purpose, he rose to his feet.

"Master," he said, "if you will not lead in Galilee, will you go to Jerusalem?"

Jesus replied, "But, Judas, I have been to Jerusalem. Was it not in Jerusalem that I first met you?"

"You have never preached the Kingdom in Jerusalem," said Judas, and the lines of his face twitched and then hardened as if he sought to hide his thought. Jesus, still seated on the grass, searched his face, and Judas, bracing himself, met His eyes. A long look passed between the two, and then Jesus, too, rose to his feet and said:

"I will go to Jerusalem."

Judas stared at Him.

"You will go to Jerusalem?" he asked, as if amazed at his own success.

"I will go to Jerusalem," Jesus repeated, and half to himself He added, "It is not meet that a Prophet should die out of Jerusalem."

Judas caught the words and answered, hastily:

"You will not die. You will go to a triumph," and suddenly, as if seized with suspicion, he cried:

"You mean it? You have promised? You will not fail me?"

Jesus stooped and gathered up the bread and dates which Judas had rejected. Then He turned and said:

"I will never fail you, Judas."

And with that the talk ended.[8]

[8] From *By an Unknown Disciple*, copyright 1919. Reprinted by special permission of the author and the publishers, Harper & Brothers, New York City.

I NEED THEE EVERY HOUR

THIS great hymn of the church expresses, perhaps better than any other song, the most poignantly personal longing of every humble and devout follower of the Lowly Nazarene.

Its author, Annie Sherwood Hawks (1835-1918) was not present in any church nor engaged in any so-called religious service when the words of this great hymn came to her. Instead she was at her home in Brooklyn, New York, and engaged in ordinary, prosaic, household tasks.

On that particular morning, however, as she went about these homely household tasks, Mrs. Hawks says she was conscious of the nearness of her Master as she had not been before; and was wondering how anyone could get along without Him, whether in joy or in pain. Then into her mind flashed the words "I need Thee every hour." Immediately she seated herself near an open window through which the sunshine and balmy air of that June morning streamed, and pencil and paper in hand she quickly penned the lines of this great hymn almost as they are sung today. It was not until years later, when the shadow of a great loss fell across her own pathway, that she began to understand something of the comforting power which the words of this hymn have for others.

The verses she wrote that June day she later handed to her pastor, the Reverend Robert Lowry, who composed for them the tune "Need," adding the refrain to which this hymn is regularly sung.

The words were first published in a little pamphlet of hymns for use in the National Baptist Sunday School Convention held in Cincinnati, Ohio, in 1872. There is hardly a church hymnal of any communion in which this great prayer-hymn will not be found today.

I need Thee every hour,
Most gracious Lord;
No tender voice like Thine
Can peace afford.

Refrain

I need Thee, O I need Thee,
Every hour I need Thee,
O bless me now, my Saviour,
I come to Thee.

I need Thee every hour,
Stay Thou near by;
Temptations lose their power
When Thou art nigh.

Refrain

I need Thee every hour,
In joy or pain,
Come quickly and abide,
Or life is vain.

Refrain

I need Thee every hour,
Teach me Thy will;
And Thy rich promises,
In me fulfill.

Refrain

I need Thee every hour,
Most Holy One;
O make me Thine indeed,
Thou blessed Son.

Refrain

—*Annie Sherwood Hawks, 1872*

✝

SWEET HOUR OF PRAYER

To THE Christian who has really learned how to pray, and how to find release from the burdens and cares of this workaday world through prayer, there is no hymn of the Church that is more beautiful and meaningful than "Sweet Hour of Prayer," written by William W. Walford and sung to the tune "Consolation" composed by William B. Bradbury in 1859.

Jesus, the man of the Garden, found, in the hours He spent away from His disciples, and alone with His Heavenly Father, release from the stress and restless activity of His busy days of preaching, teaching, and healing. And He was able, through prayer, so to unify His own inmost thoughts and purposes with that which He felt to be the will of God for Him, that He came forth from these experiences filled with such peace, serenity, and harmony of body, mind, and spirit as enabled Him to "endure all things" for the Kingdom's sake.

Devout followers of Christ, through all the intervening centuries, whose deepest yearning has been to do what Jesus would have them do, have, through aloneness in prayer, been able also to experience something of the same joy, peace, and harmony of life that Jesus knew.

No Christian has discovered the "sweetness" of the "hour of prayer" who prays merely because he feels he ought to. Such a discovery is experienced only by those who deliberately seek aloneness with God through prayer because, more than anything else, that is what they *want to do*. Something of the *sweetness* and *joy* of such prayer experiences Mr. Walford is trying to express to us when we sing his great hymn, "Sweet Hour of Prayer."

> Sweet hour of prayer, sweet hour of prayer,
> That calls me from a world of care,
> And bids me at my Father's throne,
> Make all my wants and wishes known!
> In seasons of distress and grief
> My soul has often found relief,
> And oft escaped the tempter's snare,
> By thy return, sweet hour of prayer.
>
> Sweet hour of prayer, sweet hour of prayer,
> The joys I feel, the bliss I share
> Of those whose anxious spirits burn
> With strong desires for thy return!
> With such I hasten to the place
> Where God, my Saviour, shows His face,
> And gladly take my station there,
> And wait for thee, sweet hour of prayer.
>
> Sweet hour of prayer, sweet hour of prayer,
> Thy wings shall my petition bear
> To Him, whose truth and faithfulness
> Engage the waiting soul to bless:
> And since He bids me seek His face,
> Believe His word, and trust His grace,
> I'll cast on Him my every care,
> And wait for thee, sweet hour of prayer.
>
> *—William W. Walford*

✛

ABIDE WITH ME

THE passing of time is of vital concern to every mature person, because as the years go by comrades at our side pass to the great beyond and leave us lonely and desolate for their comradeship. Every passing year brings to us the consciousness that sooner or later, we, too, must pass through the gateway *death* into the great unknown.

Fortunately for Christians, our hymnology has for us constant and satisfying messages of cheer and comfort, because they endeavor to inspire faith and to envision for us something of the joy of heavenly experiences. Those who are nearing the end of this earthly life tend to ponder the glory of the world that is to be. Such is the message of the great Christian hymn, "Abide with Me: Fast Falls the Eventide."

This hymn was written by the Reverend Dr. Henry Francis Lyte, a native of Ednam, Scotland. After his graduation from Trinity College in Dublin he was jostled from one parish to another, and finally went to the little village of Brixham, England, as a curate. Here he gave his life fully and without stint to the fisher-folk and soldiers from the neighboring garrison.

One day his physician informed him that it would be necessary for him to seek a warmer and sunnier clime if he wished to add to his days on earth. Late one Sunday afternoon, after he had with difficulty preached his farewell sermon to his faithful parishioners that morning, Dr. Lyte went to his study and wrote the words of this beautiful and comforting hymn, "Abide with Me," which he handed to a relative when he came out of his study that evening.

The next day he started for Italy, but got no farther than Nice, France, where he died, November 20, 1847. He was buried in the English Cemetery at Nice.

Dr. Beecher introduced this hymn in America through his *Plymouth Collection*. With it appeared a note indicating that it was to be read, not sung. In 1861 it was published in *Hymns Ancient and Modern*, where it again appeared without a tune. Later, when the editors came together to review the manuscript, they discovered "Abide with Me" without a tune. Dr. William Henry Monk, a great musician and a member of the committee asked for the words. He read them carefully, and then, turning to the piano, he composed, in less than ten minutes, the tune to which "Abide with Me" is always sung.

Many followers of Christ like to repeat it at night before closing their eyes in sleep, because it is like feeling God's hand in benediction upon them. It was the last hymn sung by Edith Cavell before she was martyred in Belgium, October 12, 1915:

Abide with me: fast falls the eventide;
The darkness deepens; Lord, with me abide:
When other helpers fail, and comforts flee;
Help of the helpless, O abide with me.

Swift to its close ebbs out life's little day;
Earth's joys grow dim, its glories pass away;
Change and decay in all around I see;
O Thou Who changest not, abide with me.

I need Thy presence every passing hour;
What but Thy grace can foil the .tempter's power?
Who like Thyself my guide and stay can be?
Through cloud and sunshine, O abide with me.

I fear no foe, with Thee at hand to bless;
Ills have no weight, and tears no bitterness:
Where is death's sting? Where, grave, thy victory?
I triumph still, if Thou abide with me.

Hold Thou Thy cross before my closing eyes;
Shine through the gloom and point me to the skies;
Heaven's morning breaks, and earth's vain shadows flee;
In life, in death, O Lord, abide with me.

—Henry F. Lyte, 1847

✛

SUN OF MY SOUL, THOU SAVIOUR DEAR

SPEAKING of this great hymn, H. Augustine Smith in *Lyric Religion* says: "The years between 1820-1840 were stirring years in England. New intellectual forces were felt; English poetry was coming to its flowering; the spiritual awakening under the Wesleys and Whitefield was arousing the common people; and at Oxford, Newman and Keble, Faber and Manning, and others, were writing and preaching the *Tracts for the Times*.

"The *Tracts* are little read today. The intellectual and political freedom which was so strenuously debated then has long been accepted as a matter of course, but Keble's hymn remains, after a century of constant use in churches of all denominations, as fresh and inspiring and beautiful as when it was written in 1820."

The poet may have been watching the sun drop behind the clouds when he wrote this hymn, for he was a truly great lover of nature; and such a sight would remind him of the "Sun of Righteousness" which can only be hidden by clouds of sin. Or he may have had in mind a similar statement made by Tennyson. When he was asked by a friend during a walk through the garden what Christ meant to him, Tennyson paused beside a freshly opened flower, and then answered: "What the sun is to that flower, Jesus Christ is to my soul. He is the Sun of my soul."

This great hymn, "Sun of My Soul, Thou Saviour Dear," expresses a tenderness of thought which makes it one of the very great prayer-hymns of the Church. Canon Wilberforce, speaking of Keble's influence, said: "He gave to England's Church the learning of a deep divine, the love and trust of a loyal son, the labor of a devoted priest, and the pattern of a saint." As we sing the words of this great hymn we can but feel the truth of Wilberforce's statement.

The tune "Hursley," to which "Sun of My Soul" is regularly sung, bears the name of the parish in which Keble spent the closing years of his ministry, and where his body lies buried beneath the floor of the chancel. It was arranged by Dr. William H. Monk from a melody published in Vienna between 1744 and 1780.

Sun of my soul, Thou Saviour dear,
It is not night if Thou be near;
O may no earth-born cloud arise
To hide Thee from Thy servant's eyes.

When the soft dews of kindly sleep
My wearied eyelids gently steep,
Be my last thought, how sweet to rest
Forever on my Saviour's breast.

Abide with me from morn till eve,
For without Thee I cannot live;
Abide with me when night is nigh,
For without Thee I dare not die.

If some poor wandering child of Thine
Has spurned today the Voice Divine,
Now, Lord, the gracious work begin,
Let him no more lie down in sin.

Come near and bless us when we wake,
Ere through the world our way we take,
Till in the ocean of Thy love
We lose ourselves in heaven above.

—*John Keble, 1820*

✢

PURER IN HEART, O GOD

In this, one of the more modern hymns of the church, we find expressed the sentiment of which every devout follower of Christ feels the constant need. The words were written by Mrs. A. L. Davison and the tune by James H. Fillmore.

Try as best we may, every true and honest follower of Jesus of Nazareth is conscious of the smallness of his life as compared with Jesus, the Great Head of the Church. Every day, every hour, we fall short of the grace of the high calling in which we have been enlisted. Often neither the words of our mouths nor the meditations of our hearts are acceptable in His sight.

The need of our Saviour's sustaining grace in every hour of our lives is beautifully expressed in the words of this great hymn. We cannot live without Him in any true sense of the word "living." Such hymns remind us of this fact as its verses petition God for pureness of mind and heart and soul in everyday living.

Purer in heart, O God, help me to be;
   May I devote my life wholly to Thee.
Watch Thou my wayward feet, Guide me with counsel sweet;
   Purer in heart, help me to be.

Purer in heart, O God, help me to be;
   Teach me to do Thy will most lovingly.
Be Thou my Friend and Guide, let me with Thee abide;
   Purer in heart, help me to be.

Purer in heart, O God, help me to be;
   That I Thy holy face one day may see.
Keep me from secret sin, reign Thou my soul within;
   Purer in heart, help me to be.[9]

                                  —A. L. Davison

✢

STEAL AWAY TO JESUS

IF SLAVERY and poverty were the sorrow of the Negro in the antebellum days, religion and song were his consolation and refuge. If the present was hard to bear and seemed hopeless, the future, because of the simple and childlike faith of the Negro in a personal, living, loving heavenly Father, was rich in promise of fulfillment; for the ills of his life here on earth were to be richly compensated in the life to come.

To the Negro, religion has never been a hard and unyielding dogmatism. Neither has it been a rigid ethical system. Instead it has ever been primarily an emotional experience—an experience that naturally found its vent in spontaneous songs.

The best of these spirituals were born during the slave era, when heartstrings were taut, when in some sections all gatherings of slaves, even for religious purposes, were forbidden. And so in darkness and with secrecy and danger constantly lurking near they, if they worshiped at all, must 'steal away to Jesus.'

It was out of experiences like these that the beautiful, tender, heartsearching words of this great spiritual, which has comforted the hearts of so many searchers after God, was born.

          My Lord, He calls me,
          He calls me by the lightnin';
          The trumpet sounds within-a my soul,
          I ain't got long to stay here.

Refrain

          Steal away, steal away,
          Steal away to Jesus;
          Steal away, steal away home,
          I ain't got long to stay here.

[9] From *Hymns for Today*, No. 198. Published by Fillmore Music House, Cincinnati, Ohio. Used with permission.

Green trees a-bendin',
Poor sinner stands a-tremblin',
The trumpet sounds within-a my soul,
I ain't got long to stay here.

Refrain

Tombstones a-bursting,
Poor sinner stands a-tremblin'
The trumpet sounds within-a my soul,
I ain't got long to stay here.

Refrain

—A Spiritual

PART IV

JESUS, THE CRUCIFIED

CONTENTS

PART IV   SECTION I

HIS BETRAYAL AND ARREST

✣

"With his stripes we are healed."—ISAIAH 53:5

✣

HIS BETRAYAL AND ARREST

"Then cometh Jesus with them unto a place called Gethsemane, and saith unto his disciples, Sit ye here, while I go yonder and pray. And he took with him Peter and the two sons of Zebedee, and began to be sorrowful and sore troubled. Then saith he unto them, My soul is exceeding sorrowful, even unto death: abide ye here, and watch with me. And he went forward a little, and fell on his face, and prayed. . . .

"Then cometh he to the disciples, and saith unto them, Sleep on now, and take your rest: behold, the hour is at hand, and the Son of man is betrayed into the hands of sinners. Arise, let us be going: behold, he is at hand that betrayeth me.

"And while he yet spake, lo, Judas, one of the twelve, came, and with him a great multitude with swords and staves, from the chief priests and elders of the people. Now he that betrayed him gave them a sign, saying, Whomsoever I shall kiss, that is he: take him. And straightway he came to Jesus, and said, Hail, Rabbi; and kissed him. And Jesus said unto him, Friend, *do* that for which thou art come. Then they came and laid hands on Jesus, and took him. And behold, one of them that were with Jesus stretched out his hand, and drew his sword, and smote the servant of the high priest, and struck off his ear. Then saith Jesus unto him, Put up again thy sword into its place: for all they that take the sword shall perish with the sword. Or thinkest thou that I cannot beseech my Father, and he shall even now send me more than twelve legions of angels? How then should the scriptures be fulfilled, that thus it must be? In that hour said Jesus to the multitudes, Are ye come out as against a robber with swords and staves to seize me? I sat daily in the temple teaching, and ye took me not. But all this is come to pass, that the scriptures of the prophets might be fulfilled. Then all the disciples left him, and fled."—MATTHEW 26:36-39, 45-56

THE CORRUPTION OF JUDAS

By

Hermann Prell

(Interpretation)

THE artist who painted this challenging picture was born at Leipsic in 1854. He studied at the Dresden and Berlin Art Academies and later at Rome. He excelled in fresco work, in which he showed unusual skill. The original of this painting, "The Corruption of Judas," was painted in 1886 and bought in 1894 for the Dresden Art Gallery, where it now hangs.

There is something both repulsive and challenging in Prell's conception of the struggle which Judas underwent in this hour of temptation. One cannot look into the deep-set staring eyes of this haggard and rather unkempt person without being conscious of the struggle that is going on within his own mind.

The background of the picture adds much to the sinister struggle against evil influences that is so apparent here. Just where this scene may have occurred we do not know, but the painter, with true artistic instinct, has pictured for us a barren, solitary valley somewhere outside the city of Jerusalem. It is indeed a desolate and barren landscape with its rugged, wind-swept, rocky precipices and a tree or two in the background. The one near the edge of that abrupt rock is just tall enough for a man, who has already betrayed his inner best self, to suspend his body from.

Nor can you look into the faces of the three men in the foreground of this picture without being conscious that something evil is brewing here. Why should two such richly dressed personages be out here at this hour of night in this desolate, secluded spot laboring with this wretch who is evidently struggling with a fateful decision?

Far in the background at the left three tiny figures are approaching. It is evident that these richly gowned priests are anxious to bring Judas to a decision before they get near enough to discover who the conspirators are. Even the great Pascal moon, just rising over the rocky precipice peers at them as if it, also, suggested haste in consummating this bribe-taking conspiracy.

This painting is, indeed, a rich character-study in personalities. The two priests are the tempters, but the one on the left is the arch-schemer. He has furnished the brains and a good deal of the subtle acumen for carrying their plan through to its abhorrent conclusion. He, too, is the spokesman. From his outstretched claw-like fingers that even now are clutching at Judas' sleeve, we know that he has presented the preliminary argument that is influencing Judas to believe that this betrayal of his Friend will in the end prove a blessing to Israel. No doubt he has pictured in glowing terms the honor and prestige that will come to Judas if he can bring about the arrest of this troubler of his nation—honor, salutations in the market place and temple courts, the friendship of the rich and powerful, perhaps even a chief seat in the synagogue—are among the tempting awards offered. Yet we feel, as we look into the face of this priest of the Sanhedrin and observe his spidery outstretched hand, that he is a snake in the grass—the kind of a person who hires other men to do his dirty work and then forsakes them as soon as he has gained his evil ends. In such a priest's hands no man's honor is safe.

The crowning argument, however, is furnished by the rich old bearded priest in the right foreground, who holds in his outstretched hand the "thirty pieces of silver," while with the other he fingers additional coins in the money-bag at his side, ready, if necessary, to top the already extended bribe with one more coin for good measure. Yet not a silver piece more than is absolutely necessary to bind the bargain will be given to clinch this evil, unscrupulous deal. We shudder to think that priests, high in the service of the Jewish Sanhedrin, can be engaged in this villainy in the name of religion. The older man has just enough wit to let the money in his hand talk for him, and he holds it just near enough to the range of Judas' vision for him to be continuously, though subtly, influenced by it.

The contrast between the face of Judas and that of his conspirators is a marked one. This gaunt, unkempt "keeper of the treasury" for Jesus and His followers may not be above the part he is to play in this midnight arrest; but he is having the struggle of his life in making this wicked decision, now that the fateful hour is at hand. Which path, after all, will bring to him the largest gain—loyalty even unto death to Jesus and His little band, or union with these scheming, calculating priests who seek to bring about the arrest and trial of this One who has stirred up all Israel and yet will not declare Himself to be King, nor fight against the tyranny of hated Rome?

Whatever the exact nature of the struggle that is going on within, we know that Judas' suffering is in the nature of an Insurrection. Until he reaches out his hand to accept the fateful bribe we cannot be sure that he will actually become a partner to this nefarious scheme. And we find ourselves hoping against hope that he who walked and talked daily with the Master of Men will not stoop so low as to sell Him in this hour for "thirty pieces of silver," the price of a potter's grave.

We cannot feel that it was the silver alone that tempted Judas to perform this treacherous act. Perhaps, as one author assures us, Judas meant merely to force Jesus to assert His Messianic power and destroy his enemies rather than to let Himself and His kingdom be destroyed by them. If so, in this way, Judas might feel and think that he was rendering a real service to God's "kingdom of love."

Whatever the motive, which in the last analysis brought Judas to a final decision, it is inconceivable that one who, himself, had walked daily with the Master, who had preached repentance and the Kingdom of Heaven in com-

THE CORRUPTION OF JUDAS—*PRELL*

panionship with Jesus, who had, no doubt, cast out devils in His name, and who had followed His Master through perils and privations should in this fateful hour so utterly fail Him.

Yet, when we look deep within human nature, we know that concealed within our inner selves there is in all of us the possibilities for just such treacherous living. As we look into the stark-staring eyes of Judas and feel that the fateful moment is at hand when he will clinch the bargain for this fiendish deed, we feel like saying with Bunyan, "But for the grace of God, there goes John Bunyan." For by His grace are we all saved, "and that not of ourselves, it is the gift of God."

✛

THE KISS OF BETRAYAL

By

Casper Augustine Geiger

(Interpretation)

ONE cannot look at Geiger's "The Kiss of Betrayal" without realizing that one is looking at the world's greatest act of treachery. Judas, one of the twelve disciples who had been chosen by Jesus, who had become the keeper of the common treasury from which the wants of the whole group were supplied, and who had had every opportunity to know Jesus intimately, to learn His inmost ideals, and to walk with Him daily in all the relationships of personal friendship, by this one act of treachery makes of himself forever the most disloyal man of all times.

Today even the name of Judas is hated. No parents would think of naming their child Judas, because the name is a constant reminder of the jealous, penurious traitor whose treacherous act has branded that name for all time.

Geiger, in "The Kiss of Betrayal," has caught the very moment of this maliciously traitorous act. Only two persons are present in this painting, Jesus and Judas, yet it represents one of the greatest contrasts in all art. Although only a partial profile of Judas' face is shown, it is easy to tell who the betrayer is; for even this partial view of the traitor's face is marked by the evil influence of his inner thoughts.

For some time the Jewish leaders at Jerusalem, who hated the Master of Men, had been searching for a man that they could get to perform just such an act. No doubt they had been watching all of the twelve who so constantly associated with Jesus. They chose Judas because of an inner weakness of character that made him care more for the things he could grasp and hold with his hands, than for his ideals and loyalty to the Master.

No doubt there is hidden in the folds of his tunic at this very moment the thirty pieces of silver for which he was willing to sell his honor and integrity. You can almost hear the jingle of the coins as he steps forward to grasp and kiss Jesus, so that His enemies might take by force the right man. As you look at Judas' hands you have the feeling that they were in the habit of grasping and keeping everything that their owner might want. Judas had agreed to point Jesus out to the Roman soldiers that the Jewish religious leaders had brought with them on this midnight raid, by greeting his Master with a kiss. As you look at him in the midst of this cruel and treacherous betrayal, it seems as if he is almost trying to grasp Jesus as a possession to be sold.

In contrast with the cunning face and figure of Judas, look at the Master of Men, and note how the artist makes Him the center of interest in this picture. No halo is needed to tell us that this is the Divine Christ. His face shows neither fear nor anger. He will not denounce Judas as a traitor. He will not strike back at him for this treacherous act, vile and unmerited as it is. Notwithstanding the intuitive outward thrust of His hands, so expressive of the inner repugnance that even He must feel, we know that the love He bears this unworthy friend will triumph, and that He will "suffer all things," *even this,* for His Father's and the Kingdom's sake.

In spite of the fact that Judas has already dishonored the name "friend," we can almost hear Jesus saying to him, "Friend, do that for which thou art come." In the darkest hour of His life, and with full knowledge that this cruel betrayal marks the beginning of those last torturous hours which were to end His earthly career, Jesus, with a love that it is difficult for us, even yet, to fully comprehend, can and does speak of Judas as "friend."

I am glad that Geiger has called this picture "The Kiss of Betrayal," and not "Judas Betrays Christ" or some other title of similar content. In the familiar words of an unknown poet, the artist is saying:

> Still, as of old,
> Man by himself is priced.
> For thirty pieces Judas sold
> Himself, not Christ.

✠

PETER'S DENIAL

By

Count von Ferdinand Harrach

(Interpretation)

THE artist who painted this challenging picture of "Peter's Denial" was born at Rosnochau, Silesia, in 1832. He studied at the Weimar Art School, served in the wars of 1866 and 1870, lived one year in Italy, and then settled in Berlin. He was a member of the Berlin Academy in 1874 and thereafter. The

THE KISS OF BETRAYAL—*GEIGER*

PETER'S DENIAL—*HARRACH*

original of this beautiful picture was painted in 1879 and bought almost immediately for the museum at Breslau.

This painting is a graphic portrayal of one verse, "The Lord turned and looked at Peter," found in Luke's account of that hurried, early-morning trial of Jesus in the High Priest's palace. The scene is evidently the courtyard of the palace. Two soldiers of the guard, temporarily off duty, now that Jesus is being led into an inner chamber for questioning, have stacked their shields and spears against a near-by wall and thrown themselves down on a heap of straw on the flagstones while they warm themselves by an adjacent fire and discuss the circumstances attending the arrest of this unusual prisoner.

A serving-maid in the background has openly accused Peter of being one of Jesus' followers. He has three times denied the accusation, showing perhaps more feeling than the occasion seemed to warrant. Peter's vehement denial must have amused the maid, for she smiles as she points her accusing finger at him. Her words and actions have attracted the attention of the soldiers, for both of them have turned to stare at Peter's downcast face.

The cock on the grape vine above is just now in the act of crowing, and this vividly recalls to Peter's harassed mind not only his earlier declaration, "If all shall be offended in thee, I will never be offended"; but also the Master's prophecy, "This night, before the cock crow, thou shalt deny me thrice."

The cock on the grape vine above, greeting the dawn with his usual early-morning salutation, is entirely unaware of the bitter sorrow and humiliation that his crowing and the sympathetic look of Jesus have brought into the heart of this impulsive follower of the lowly Nazarene. Peter failed a good many times in following Jesus, but he, nevertheless, loved the Master with all the strength of his rich, impulsive nature.

John indicates that there was "another disciple" present who, in this tragic hour, secured entrance for Peter into the palace courtyard, but the artist has not seen fit to show him.

Peter must not be too harshly censured for this hasty, vehement betrayal of the Son of Man. He may have followed afar off, but at least he followed, and that is more than may be said of the other disciples, who on that night scattered like sheep when their Master was smitten.

No doubt that the throng of miscellaneous rabble had encouraged Peter to press in among them, to ascertain, if possible, what was to happen to his Lord and Master. And there in the courtyard he has remained after the mob dispersed. It took courage to do that, because he could not know that the arrest of the twelve men most closely associated with Jesus was not a part of the plans of the enraged priests. Then, too, had he not, just a few hours before, cut off the ear of one of the High Priest's servants? True, Jesus had healed the wound, but that might not exempt the perpetrator of the crime from arrest and trial.

Under the confusing circumstances of that ghastly night, this man whom Jesus likened to a "rock" deserves some credit for not having taken to his heels as did the others when the mob attacked Jesus in lonely Gethsemane.

In the midst of conflicting and confusing emotions the human heart often plays tricks upon us. None of us know just how strong or how weak we may be until the crisis arrives. Peter may have over-estimated his loyalty, but not his love. For when that noisy cock recalled to him the prophetic words of his Master, he went out in confused silence to weep bitterly that he had denied knowing his Master and Friend.

Speaking of this incident, Dr. Bailey says: "Peter's faithlessness belongs to a different category from that of Judas. There was no treachery in it, no pre-meditation, no active purpose to betray; only a temporary lack of nerve, a down curve of courage in the presence of personal danger, a recrudescence of the primitive instinct of self-preservation such as the recruit feels when first under fire. But the tears of repentance that followed washed out the guilt, and purged at the same time the elements of weakness that had prevented Simon from always being Peter. Henceforth Peter is all "Rock." Exceeding boldness, as at Pentecost, takes the place of fear, and upon Peter Christ may henceforth safely build his church."[1]

✛

"THEN THEY CAME, AND LAID HANDS ON JESUS AND TOOK HIM"

By

D. Mastroianni

(Interpretation)

THE solemn silence which reigned in the Garden of Gethsemane during Jesus midnight vigil with His Heavenly Father was broken by the tumult of the crowd accompanying the soldiers, that, led by Judas, the treacherous disciple, entered upon the stillness of that midnight hour.

Attracted by the noise, Jesus left the shadowy recesses by a narrow path to meet them, and it was there that Judas met and kissed his Master, revealing to the Roman soldiers by this act the man that they were to arrest. For Judas had said to the soldiers in advance of their arrival in the garden "Whomsoever I shall kiss that same is He, take Him and lead Him away safely" (Mark 14:44). No sooner had the traitor completed his nefarious treachery than Jesus said: "Judas, betrayest thou the Son of Man with a kiss?" But Judas, his act of treachery completed, stepped aside without an answer as the crowd pressed on.

Then Jesus said to the soldiers, "Whom seek ye?" and they replied, "Jesus of Nazareth." And Jesus answered, "I am He." And John indicates that no sooner had the Master uttered these words than "they went backward and fell to the ground (18:6).

[1] From *The Gospel in Art*, p. 331. Published by the Pilgrim Press. Used by permission of the author.

There was something in the supreme crisis through which Jesus had passed in the garden that has set upon Him heroic proportions. His purpose was fixed. He was ready to die. Yet the soldiers, unaware of the greatness of the One they had come to arrest, were so overwhelmed by His Divine Majesty that they would have failed in their duty had He not pressed the matter and offered Himself to them.

It is just this incident of "the soldiers falling backward on the ground" that Mastroianni, the Italian sculptor, has seen fit to portray in wax in this midnight arrest of the Master of Men. Observe the strength of character in Jesus as He stands before His captors. Here is no meek, frightened, fugitive from justice. Even the chief priests and Scribes seem to cringe and cower in the presence of the majestic dignity of the One who had so recently wrestled alone with God in the garden that He might discover and fulfill His Heavenly Father's will.

In the midst of this scene of dignity and power how futile seems the impulsive act of Peter, who, with his usual impetuosity, drew his sword and struck off the ear of Malchus, the High Priest's servant. It was at this time also that Jesus, healing the injury of this surprised servant of the High Priest, turned to Peter, saying: "Put up thy sword in its place; for they that take the sword shall perish with the sword. Thinkest thou that I cannot now pray to My Father, and He shall presently give Me more than twelve legions of angels?"

The Master of Men knew what He was doing. In that midnight vigil in dark Gethsemane He had, through prayer, clarified His own vision of what His Father's will was; and neither friend nor foe could shake his determination to drink the cup of His suffering to its bitterest dregs. Men must come to know what the living, loving, longing heart of God is like; and if the only way they could come to understand that fact was by His death on the cross by the cruelest method men knew how to devise, then Jesus was both willing and able to say, "Thy will, not mine, be done."

And they took Him and led Him away, while His disciples fled in fear; and He was as a lamb, dumb before its shearers; because deep in His own heart was the knowledge that only through the sacrifice of His own life's blood on the cross could the abundant life and love of His Heavenly Father ever get itself known to the sons of men.

We are indebted to Mastroianni, the great Italian sculptor, who has given us in this wax portrayal of the Son of Man, standing with quiet dignity in the presence of His friends and foes, the picture of a Man who has counted with joy the cost, and Who is not only ready and willing, but able to sacrifice Himself for the redemption of a world that knew not God.

"THEN THEY CAME, AND LAID HANDS ON JESUS AND TOOK HIM"
—MASTROIANNI

THE LAST SUPPER

Perhaps at first they talked of little things
At supper-time that evening in the spring—
The upper room was dim with candle-shine
As Jesus sat with twelve, remembering.
Then quietly He said, "There is one here
Whose kiss will bring betrayal by and by."
They did not look at Judas curiously,
But each man murmured, "Master, is it I?"

Each one looked inward, frightened lest he find
A shoddy place where he had dreamed of steel.
None placed the guilt on any other guest
Who had partaken of that gracious meal. . . .
When there are hungry on my little street,
When I see tears or hear a heart's hurt cry
Because some one has failed to keep high faith,
May I, too, murmur, "Master, is it I?"

—Helen Welshimer

GETHSEMANE

In golden youth when seems the earth,
A summer-land of singing mirth,
When souls are glad and hearts are light,
And not a shadow lurks in sight,
We do not know it, but there lies,
Somewhere veiled under evening skies,
A garden which we all must see—
The Garden of Gethsemane.

With joyous steps we go our ways,
Love lends a halo to our days;
Light sorrows sail like clouds afar,
We laugh and say how glad we are.
We hurry on; and hurrying, go
Close to the border-land of woe,
That waits for you, and waits for me
Forever waits Gethsemane.

Down shadowy lanes, across strange streams,
Bridged over by our broken dreams;
Behind the misty caps of years,
Beyond the great salt fount of tears,
The garden lies. Strive as you may,
You cannot miss it in your way.
All paths that have been, or shall be,
Pass somewhere through Gethsemane.

All those who journey, soon or late,
Must pass within the garden's gate;
Must kneel alone in darkness there,
And battle with some fierce despair.
God pity those who cannot say,
"Not mine, but thine," who only pray,
"Let this cup pass," and cannot see
The *purpose* in Gethsemane.[2]

—*Ella Wheeler Wilcox*

THIRTY PIECES OF SILVER FOR JESUS

(Judas Speaks)

"Which is in the sight of God a great price."

"I think you know, Annas, the price is low
    For such a man; there is not in Judea
So fair a face to rest your eyes upon,
    So smooth a breast to shatter with a spear.

"Besides, He's young, and has been well-beloved;
    There was a woman once who left the street,
And followed Him into a hostile house,
    And knelt and pressed her lips against His feet.

"He has no wealth, yet men have gone with Him,
    And left their homes and worldly goods behind,
Because His voice was gentle when He spoke,
    And when He looked at them His eyes were kind.

"Admit the price is low. For thirty coins
    One buys a plot of ground, a harlot's kiss,
A cask of wine, perhaps, a negro slave,
    But seldom such a comely man as this."[3]

—*Helene Mullins*

[2] From *Poems of Power*, published by W. B. Conkey Company, Chicago, Ill. Used by permission of the publishers.

[3] From *Earthbound*. Published by Harper & Brothers, New York City. Used by permission of the author and publishers.

THE LORD TURNED, AND LOOKED UPON PETER

The Saviour looked on Peter. Ay, no word,
　　No gesture of reproach! the heavens serene,
　　Though heavy with armed justice, did not lean
Their thunders that way! the forsaken Lord
Looked only on the traitor. None record
　　What that look was, none guess: for those who have seen
　　Wronged lovers loving through a death-pang keen,
Or pale-cheeked martyrs smiling to a sword,
Have missed Jehovah at the judgment-call.
　　And Peter, from the height of blasphemy—
"I never knew this man"—did quail and fall,
　　As knowing straight that God—and turned free
And went out speechless from the face of all,
　　And filled the silence, weeping bitterly.

—Elizabeth Barrett Browning

"WITH ME IN PARADISE"

If I had sat at supper with the Lord
　　And laid my head upon that saving breast
　　I might have turned and fled among the rest—
I might have been the one who left the board
To add the high priest's silver to his hoard.
　　Had our Redeemer stooped to wash my feet,
　　Would I have washed my neighbor's, clean and sweet,
Or thrice denied the Christ I had adored?

Long have I grieved that I was not Saint Paul
　　Who rode those seas and saw the tempest toss
The ships he sailed in when he heard the call
　　To preach the risen Christ and gain through loss.
Tonight I envy most among them all
　　That thief, who hung repentant on his cross.

—Alexander Harvey

YOUNG JESUS

"He steadfastly set his face to go to Jerusalem."—Luke 9:51.

They said that He was meek—they were not wrong,
  But He was more than meek!
The Christ I know was young and bronzed and strong,
  Clear-eyed, and tanned of cheek;
He wore His valor stoutly, as a shield
Borne to a bloody field!

And He was gentle—but the word falls short
  Of one lone Man who drove
The money-changers from the temple court;
  The Christ I know was brave!
What splendid courage made the knotted cords
More terrible than swords!

And He was patient—but His lips grew white,
  He spoke with God's own wrath,
Whose royal fury put the thieves to flight,
  And scourged them from His path.
The lash was light—it was their souls that bled,
They squealed like rats, and fled!

Lowly and meek and mild, they said of Him,
  Mocking Him as he died;
But He was firm of step and straight of limb,
  And tall, and level-eyed—
Young Jesus, turning gallantly to death,
This Man of Nazareth!

—Sara Henderson Hay

HE—THEY—WE

They hailed Him King as He passed by,
  They strewed their garments in the road,
But they were set on earthly things,
  And He on God.

They sang His praise for that He did,
  But gave His message little thought;
They could not see that their souls' good
  Was all He sought.

They could not understand why He,
   With powers so vast at His command,
Should hesitate to claim their rights
   And free the land.

Their own concerns and this world's hopes
   Shut out the wonder of His news;
And we, with larger knowledge, still
   His Way refuse.

He walks among us still, unseen,
   And still points out the only way,
But we still follow other gods
   And Him betray.[4]

                                        —*John Oxenham*

AN OLIVE TREE SPEAKS

That night in cool Gethsemane
Christ taught us immortality.
We heard Him pray beneath our boughs
And felt His wrestling spirit's vows
While high upon her ancient hills,
Jerusalem, walled in smugness slept
Nor guessed that her own Savior wept
Beyond the Kedron's full spring rills.

We trembled with His lonely woes,
We longed to crash on all His foes,
We saw His face when He arose—a Conqueror!

So for His sake we cannot die,
But from our gnarled, decrepit root
Send up a new young slender shoot
To tell His victory to the sky.
Before our old self bows to earth,
We give a scion olive birth
To witness what we learned that night
When Christ slew death within our sight
And to our hushed Gethsemane
Entrusted immortality.

                                  —*Madeleine Sweeny Miller*

[4] From *Gentlemen—The King*. Published by the Pilgrim Press. Copyright by the author. Used by permission.

JESUS AND GETHSEMANE

By

Elizabeth Stuart Phelps

It was not quite dark in Gethsemane, for a full moon, contesting with a stormy cloud, peered through. It was a still, cool spot, secure from disturbance; a favorite with Jesus. He had spent many solitary nights there. The place was dear to him; his feet turned to it instinctively. The eleven followed him, disturbed and subdued.

They fell back when he signified, by a gesture, his wish for the society of the three whom he preferred. They walked apart with Jesus into the most secluded portion of the olive garden. It was darker here, and strangely still. Jesus stretched out his arms with a groan. He Who had suffered so much and so long, and Who never complained of the worst that happened, suddenly appealed to them by the most piteous words:

"My soul is exceeding sorrowful . . . even to death. Tarry, and watch with Me!" Before any one of the three could reply, He had disappeared in the heart of the grove. . . . At the foot of the thick tree, with knotted hands, and with face upon the ground, a solitary figure sank.

Human endurance has gone to the limits of pain, shame, and death for all the causes that can torment the souls and bodies of men. . . . But here was a Man who carried a burden so isolate that the imagination almost refuses to hold it. . . . Here was a Man who believed that the salvation of the human race rested upon Himself. . . .

Gethsemane challenged it. Defeat, disgrace, and approaching death shook his convictions to the foundation. . . . He cried out against it:

"Father! Father!"

He was so young, so vigorous! The blood beat strongly in His being. He loved life, as all well souls and bodies do. Health throbbed in every artery, in every cell. Sickness had never weakened Him. No taint had ever marred Him. His system had never become the slave of His overstrained nerves. Even the torment of prolonged vigil had not conquered Him. He was alive to the last red drop in His fair, pure body; He was alive to the last energy of His unshaken brain. And His heart?—why, the life of His heart seemed something great enough to supply the forces and the fountains of the world!

Death!—at the top of vigor, at the brim of existence! Slow torture, and shameful—and tomorrow! *Unnecessary* death! . . .

The stillness startled Him. Smitten with a sudden sense of His loneliness, He staggered up and gazed about Him, looking for His friends. He had spent Himself in prayer, had shut Himself in to the society of God. Yet such a yearning for human sympathy rushed upon Him that it seemed as if He would drown in it. He pushed the olive branches apart, and called the names dearest to him—"Peter, and James, and John!"

But the tired men, sore with trouble, were all asleep. They turned stupidly at the sound of His voice. Peter sprang up. The lips of Jesus quivered: "Could ye not watch *one* hour with Me?" He said gently.

He went back to the thick olive trees; there on the ground He fell again. The drama of His life returned before Him, swiftly as scenery shot in flame and smoke. The devout docility of His childhood, the pure dreams of His boyhood, repassed; and the first surprise of His extra-consciousness. He heard the voice on Jordan when His kinsman, the prophet, baptized among the reeds. He listened to the message of the clouds that enveloped Him at Lebanon: *"My Beloved Son!"* What had they meant? What did they mean now? As slowly, as naturally, as the blossoming of character, His explanation of His own being had presented itself to Him. . . .

He had staked everything, He had suffered everything, on the conviction that He was in some supreme sense different from that which governed the personality of any other man, the Son of His God; chosen for a transcendent mission; destined to lift a world of men out of the doom of life. . . .

If this was not the most tremendous delusion which ever visited a human brain, then it was the grandest affirmation. For such was not the task of a man. It was the privilege of a Divinity. He had begun life by wondering why He was not like other men; He ended it by understanding. . . .

As naturally as manhood develops from infancy, so Christhood had developed from manhood. Gradually, quietly, He had come to perceive that it was His to live the divine life in human form. But this was not all. It was the conviction of Jesus that it depended upon Himself whether men should possess the privilege of personal immortality. He believed that He held in His Own hands the gift of eternal life to the human soul. He believed that upon the facts of His life, and upon the facts of His death, this solitary responsibility rested. In Gethsemane the whole load rolled upon His shaken frame. . . .

In Gethsemane it seemed to Jesus of Nazareth that He had achieved nothing. He was a defeated man. He had missed His Father's errand. Through the blind gates of death, in a few hours, He must be pushed, to hold up His trembling, empty hands and say:

"Father, I trusted Thee—but I have failed!"

There in the olive garden lay His poor friends, asleep again. Even they could not understand enough to give Him the little common, human sympathy that love saves for the emergency of the beloved. He stole out and watched them, and returned with His head sunken on His breast. . . . He had bared it to the night air for very anguish, and He perceived now that heavy drops were falling from His face and body and streamed upon His heart. He looked at them. In the faint light it could be seen that they were red. . . .

By the subtle law which may convert the most sacred private experiences into world-wide value, and which governed every event in the life of Jesus, there have been given to us certain records of an hour known only to Himself and God. The utterance of a prayer:

"Father, not as I will, but as Thou wilt!"

As His white lips framed these words, the olive branches stirred above His head, and there, as in the Jordan desert when His troubled life was at its morning, the mystical did visit Him. Men called that presence an Angel's, not understanding what an angel is. Gethsemane knew the secret of that comforting; but she holds it.[5]

✠

"HIS ENEMIES SHALL BE THOSE OF HIS OWN HOUSEHOLD"

JESUS was coming down the mountain-side, and we all went out to meet Him. When He was near, Peter hurried a pace or two in advance and burst into speech.

"Master! Judas would rid us of all oppressors."

There was a tranquillity on the face of Jesus and a light in His eyes as if He had looked upon things unseen. He turned to Judas, "What oppressors?" He asked, and sat down on a big stone to hear.

"The oppressors of our nation," said Judas. "You have seen the oppression of the poor and the violent perverting of justice and judgment in the province. The oppressors must be driven forth if the Kingdom is to be established. Seeing the power You have over the people, I have told them You will end the oppression."

"By driving forth the oppressors?" asked Jesus.

"Yes," cried Judas. "By thrusting them into the sea. By breaking their Empire in pieces, and humbling them so that they whisper out of the dust. . . ."

"Will that end oppression?" Jesus asked, and waited for a reply.

None came, for with the question we all, even Judas, fell silent, and after a space Jesus turned Him about, and we started again on our journey. . . .

Judas said: "Men will never use their minds. They prefer repose."

And Jesus cried out: "Do you think I am here to give repose to the world? I tell you no, but to cause division. I am here, not to cast peace but a sword on the earth. I came to kindle men's souls and to set the world on fire."

His face was radiant and His eyes shining.

"I tell you that now the Kingdom is being preached, men everywhere are

[5] From *The Story of Jesus Christ*. Published by Houghton Mifflin Company. Used by permission of the publishers.

forcing their way into it. It is God's will that men should have life and have it in greater fullness. Think you this will not cause division? If a man seek the Kingdom, his enemies shall be those of his own household, and even his old familiar friends, in whom he trusted, will turn against him. But I am here to teach men to be lawgivers to themselves, and he who is daunted by any man is not worthy of Me."

His passion woke passion in every man of us. It was as if a fire lit up in our souls and ran through our veins. Judas' eyes burned in his head, and Peter cried out:

"Master, tell us of the great deeds You said we should do."

Jesus looked at him and then at Judas, and a cloud came over the brightness of His face. The passion died out of His eyes, and there was a question in them as though He feared misunderstanding. He seemed to withdraw into Himself, seeking strength greater than His own, and when at last He spoke, it was slowly, as a man seeks for words to express a thing too great for words.

"All over the world, princes oppress their subjects, and the very men whom they enslave call them benefactors. The great exercise dominion over those who are weak, and everywhere men seek after power. But amongst you it shall not be so. For in the Kingdom of Heaven, whoever wishes to be great must serve, and he who strives to hold high place must be a servant. . . ."

Jesus went on, speaking as a man speaks of things long thought out.

"If a man would be a deliverer he must be ready to undergo much pain and to suffer. He will be rejected by his own generation. The councilors and the priests and the teachers will not listen to him. He will be spat on and despised; he will have contempt and scorn for his portion, and, at the last, it may be he will lose his life. . . ."

Again He was silent, and when He spoke, it was with balance and judgment, as a man speaks of something of which he has counted the cost.

"Through anguish and suffering men enter the Kingdom. He who wishes to be My follower must take up his cross and deny himself. If a man is not ready to lose his life for the Kingdom he will lose himself. Where is the profit if in gaining the world a man loses his soul? Can he earn aught of value equal to himself? I tell you that he who is ready to lose his life for My sake has found himself, and if a man endure to the end he shall find life, too. For it is by endurance that men win life."[6]

✣

GO TO DARK GETHSEMANE

In "Go to Dark Gethsemane" we have another of those older hymns of the Church that help us to understand, and to enter into, vicarious fellowship with the Master of Men, as He prepares His own inner life for the excruciating agony of the cross.

[6] From *By an Unknown Disciple*. Copyright, 1919. Reprinted by permission of the author and Harper & Brothers, publishers.

So much stress has been placed on the miraculous and the omnipotent power of Christ, that we forget sometimes that He was a man, God's Son in the flesh— a human being with a body that knew the agony of slow, torturing pain, even as we may know it.

To sing hymns that stress the pain, the humiliation, the suffering of God's sinless Son, helps us to appreciate, as we might not otherwise, the cost of human redemption, and to measure how great is God's love for the children of men.

This hymn was written by James Montgomery in 1820 and is usually sung to the tune "Gethsemane," composed by Richard Redhead, in 1853.

> Go to dark Gethsemane,
>   Ye that feel the tempter's power;
> Your Redeemer's conflict see;
>   Watch with Him one bitter hour;
> Turn not from His griefs away;
> Learn of Jesus Christ to pray.
>
> See Him at the judgment hall,
>   Beaten, bound, reviled, arraigned;
> See Him meekly bearing all;
>   Love to man His soul sustained;
> Shun not suffering, shame or loss;
> Learn of Christ to bear the cross.
>
> Calvary's mournful mountain climb;
>   There adoring at His feet,
> Mark that miracle of time,
>   God's own sacrifice complete:
> "It is finished!" hear Him cry;
> Learn of Jesus Christ to die. Amen.
>   —*James Montgomery, 1820*

✠

THOU DIDST LEAVE THY THRONE

THIS rich, challenging hymn was written by Emily E. S. Elliott in 1864. Its theme expresses the riches of glory in the heavenly home, which Jesus left that He might become "the abundant way of life" for the children of men.

The utter selflessness of Christ in leaving a heavenly throne and a kingly crown, that He might be born as the humblest of men in a borrowed stable in Bethlehem of Judea is the theme of the first stanza.

The music of the choir of angels that announced His birth to simple shepherds watching their flock on the hillside is the message of the second verse

The homelessness of Christ as compared with the foxes of the field and the birds of the air provides the motif for the third stanza; while the fourth verse emphasizes the "mocking scorn" with which Christ's gift of life abundant to men was received.

The last verse stresses the victory of Christ and the "room there must be" for Him in every human heart that would share in His ultimate victory.

The refrain, "O come to my heart, Lord Jesus," is particularly appealing to young people, as with joy they accept the challenge to abundant, victorious living through comradeship with Jesus.

Thou didst leave Thy throne and Thy kingly crown
  When Thou camest to earth for me;
But in Bethlehem's home was there found no room
  For Thy holy nativity;

Refrain

O come to my heart, Lord Jesus,
  There is room in my heart for Thee.

Heaven's arches rang when the angels sang
  Proclaiming Thy royal degree;
But in lowly birth didst Thou come to earth,
  And in great humility:

Refrain

The foxes found rest, and the birds their nest
  In the shade of the forest tree;
But Thy couch was the sod, O Thou Son of God,
  In the desert of Galilee:

Refrain

Thou camest, O Lord, with the living word
  That should set Thy people free;
But with mocking scorn, and with crown of thorn,
  They bore Thee to Calvary:

Refrain

When heaven's arches shall ring, and her choirs shall sing
  At Thy coming to victory,
Let Thy voice call me home, saying, "Yet there is room,
  There is room at my side for Thee."

Refrain

And my heart shall rejoice, Lord Jesus,
  When Thou comest and callest for me.

                    —*Emily E. S. Elliott, 1864*

'TIS MIDNIGHT; AND ON OLIVE'S BROW

THERE are no more poignantly beautiful hymns than those that center in those last, brooding, pain-racked hours of uncertainty that attended the betrayal and crucifixion of the Master of Men. Notwithstanding the fact that Jesus had tried on many occasions to prepare His disciples for the heart-breaking shock of His death on the cross, they could not comprehend that He, Who had raised others from the dead, was really to die.

After their farewell supper in the upper room, He took with Him to the Garden of Gethsemane His disciples. No sooner had He reached the garden, however, than He, with the three that were closest to Him in fellowship, separated themselves from the others and went on into the deeper recesses of the garden. Then bidding the three to "watch with Him for one hour," Jesus went on alone to the place to which He had often resorted for prayer, that He might unburden to the fullest a heart full to the breaking-point with its burden of woe.

Perhaps no other great hymn of the Church better expresses the dire loneliness and aloneness of that midnight hour in Gethsemane than " 'Tis Midnight; and on Olive's Brow," the words of which were written by William B. Tappan in 1822. And it helps us to "drink the cup of His sorrow" as we sing it, remembering the cost of Calvary.

'Tis midnight; and on Olive's brow
　The star is dimmed that lately shone:
'Tis midnight; in the garden now
　The suffering Saviour prays alone.

'Tis midnight; and from all removed,
　The Saviour wrestles lone with fears;
E'en that disciple whom He loved
　Heeds not his Master's grief and tears.

'Tis midnight; and for others' guilt
　The Man of Sorrows weeps in blood;
Yet He that hath in anguish knelt
　Is not forsaken by His God.

'Tis midnight; and from heavenly plains
　Is borne the song that angels know;
Unheard by mortals are the strains
　That sweetly soothe the Saviour's woe. Amen.

—*William B. Tappan, 1822*

LEAD, KINDLY LIGHT

(Interpretation)

"LEAD, Kindly Light, amid th' Encircling Gloom" is one of the most beautiful and appealing hymns in the English language. Occasionally you hear some one say that this hymn has no challenge for young people. The compiler of this anthology, however, has had opportunity to test this hymn out with thousands of young people in summer conferences, and has yet to find one who does not respond to its faith-assuring challenge.

This is due, no doubt, to the fact that this is one of the few hymns that ministers to the individual needs of young people during the stress and storm of later adolescence. During this period young people are completing their education and attempting to get into their lifework. At such a time they are often confronted with a certain amount of uncertainty. This hymn tends to steady them in their gropings and unsatisfied longings. It gives them confidence and courage because it assures them that God is leading them on.

John Henry Newman wrote this hymn while he was a young minister and at a time when he, himself, was passing through a period of illness, perplexity, and mental and spiritual unrest. He was facing one of the most important decisions of his life. The future seemed vague, uncertain, and baffling. As he tried to think his way through his problem, of only one thing was he assured, and that was that God had a work for him to do, and that His Heavenly Father was abundantly able to lead him through to victory.

This hymn was written on June 16, 1833 while its author was on the "becalmed straits of Boniface," at a time when he was anxious to get home to his native England. As we reflect on the verses of this hymn we may think of Newman, far from the land of his nativity, and in the midst of "th' encircling gloom" which surrounded him. He was conscious, nevertheless, of the "Kindly Light" that enables all those who follow in the Master's steps to walk in the light, because they follow a Friend and Leader Who never fails them.

Years later, when Dr. Newman had become a cardinal of the Roman Catholic Church, some one congratulated him on having written a universal hymn cherished by all believing Christians, and he modestly replied: "But you see it is not the words but the tune that has gained such widespread popularity." Undoubtedly the tune "Lux Benigna," to which this great hymn is always sung, does perfectly express the mood of the words so that the two have become inseparable. The words alone, however, will live always because they help all followers of Christ to a confident reliance upon God when storms assail and faith falters. We cannot sing the words of this great hymn without singing confidence and reverent assurance into our inmost souls.

Lead, Kindly Light, amid th' encircling gloom,
    Lead Thou me on;
The night is dark, and I am far from home;
    Lead Thou me on:
Keep Thou my feet; I do not ask to see
The distant scene—one step enough for me.

I was not ever thus, nor prayed that Thou
    Shouldst lead me on;
I loved to choose and see my path; but now
    Lead Thou me on.
I loved the garish day, and, spite of fears,
Pride ruled my will: remember not past years.

So long Thy power hath blest me, sure it still
    Will lead me on
O'er moor and fen, o'er crag and torrent, till
    The night is gone;
And with the morn those angels' faces smile,
Which I have loved long since, and lost awhile. Amen.
                    —*John Henry Newman, 1833*

✝

A BALLAD OF TREES AND THE MASTER

SIDNEY LANIER was born in Macon, Georgia, in 1842. He graduated from Oglethorpe College in 1860, where he remained as a tutor until the outbreak of the Civil War. As a student he had learned to play the flute. He joined the Confederate Army as a private soldier at the outbreak of the war, taking with him his prized silver flute.

After the war he taught school and then practiced law; but he never neglected his flute-playing or his study of literature and music. As a result he played the flute in a series of concerts with the Peabody Conservatory Orchestra in Baltimore; and in 1877 became a Lecturer in English Literature at Johns Hopkins University. He died in 1881. Besides his *Poems*, which were published after his death, he wrote *The Science of English Verse* and *The English Novel*.

A great religious poem becomes a hymn when it is set to music that is appropriate and worthy. This is preëminently true of the poem "A Ballad of Trees and the Master," written by Sidney Lanier in 1880. In two short verses there is portrayed the pathos of the struggle of Jesus during those midnight hours that preceded His arrest in the garden of Gethsemane, the beauty of nature, the love of the out-of-doors, and the hush of the Master's reverent devotion to the will of His Heavenly Father. If Sidney Lanier, the revered poet of the South, had written nothing else, his name and fame would live forever among the immortals.

It was not until as late as 1904 that the words of this beautiful poem were set to music by Peter C. Lutkin. It has grown steadily in appreciation and use among churches everywhere, doubtless because it associates both the life and the death of the Master of Men with the trees under whose shade He often rested, and which he sought out as a place of quiet meditation and prayer.

Into the woods my Master went,
Clean for-spent, for-spent;
Into the woods my Master came,
For-spent with love and shame.
But the olives they were not blind to Him,
The little gray leaves were kind to Him,
The thorn-tree had a mind to Him,
When into the woods He came.

Out of the woods my Master went,
And He was well content;
Out of the woods my Master came,
Content with death and shame.
When death and shame would woo Him last,
From under the trees they drew Him last,
'Twas on a tree they slew Him last,
When out of the woods He came. Amen.[7]

—*Sidney Lanier, 1880*

Words copyrighted by Mary D. Lanier and Charles Scribner's Sons. Used by permission.

CONTENTS

PART IV SECTION II

HIS TRIAL

✛

"And Pilate saith . . . unto them . . . I find no crime in him."—JOHN 19:4

✛

HIS TRIAL

"And they that had taken Jesus led him away *to the house* of Caiaphas the high priest, where the scribes and the elders were gathered together. But Peter followed him afar off, unto the court of the high priest, and entered in, and sat with the officers, to see the end."—MATTHEW 26:57-58

✠

"Now, when morning was come, all the chief priests and the elders of the people took counsel against Jesus to put him to death: and they bound him, and led him away, and delivered him up to Pilate the governor."—MATTHEW 27:1-2

✠

"Now Jesus stood before the governor: and the governor asked him, saying, Art thou the King of the Jews? And Jesus said unto him, Thou sayest. And when he was accused by the chief priests and elders, he answered nothing. Then saith Pilate unto him, Hearest thou not how many things they witness against thee? And he gave him no answer, not even to one word: inasmuch that the governor marvelled greatly. Now at the feast the governor was wont to release unto the multitude one prisoner, whom they would. And they had then a notable prisoner called Barabbas. When therefore they were gathered together, Pilate said unto them, Whom will ye that I release unto you? Barabbas, or Jesus who is called Christ? For he knew that for envy they had delivered him up. . . . And they said, Barabbas. Pilate saith unto them, What then shall I do unto Jesus who is called Christ? They all say, Let him be crucified."—MATTHEW 27:11-18, 21, 22

CHRIST TAKING LEAVE OF HIS MOTHER

By

Bernard Plockhorst

(Interpretation)

THE Gospels contain no more beautiful stories than those that cluster about Mary, the mother of Jesus, and her first-born Son. For while Mary did not always understand the actions of this gifted Child of Prophecy, she nevertheless treasured deep in her heart all of the marvelous sayings and prophecies about this Babe of Bethlehem; guided His childhood and youth, and followed Him with such a devoted love, even to the foot of the cross, that the world delights to honor her as the "perfect mother."

We know very little about the relations of Jesus with women, but we do know that during His entire ministry, including His cruel death on the cross and His glorious resurrection on Easter morn, that the women who loved Him were "last at the cross and first at the tomb on Easter morn"; and that among these women, Mary, His mother, was nearly always, if not always, present.

In Luke 8:1-3 we read: "And it came to pass soon afterwards, that he went about through cities and villages, preaching and bringing the good tidings of the Kingdom of God; and with him the twelve, and certain women who had been healed of evil spirits and infirmities: Mary that was called Magdalene, from whom seven demons had gone out, and Johanna, the wife of Chuzas, Herod's steward, and Susanna, and many others, who ministered unto them of their substance." We know also that this same band of women, including Mary, His mother, followed Jesus on his last journey to Jerusalem and according to Matthew (27:55-56) were at Calvary. We know also that Jesus was on affectionate terms with Mary and Martha and a frequent visitor in their home in Bethany.

The Master of Men also exemplified a sympathetic understanding of women, even of "women of the streets," as we read the Gospel story of the woman by the well in Samaria, and that other woman of the world who made her way unbidden into the house of Simon, the leper, bathing the feet of Jesus with her tears, as He reclined at meat, and drying them with the hair of her head. This latter incident is one of the most striking stories in the Gospel narratives, and one which, if tradition speaks truly, Jesus Himself commanded to be told wherever the Gospel was preached.

And there is no more poignantly beautiful incident in the entire life of Jesus than that moment when from the cross He said to his grief-stricken mother, "Woman, behold thy son"; and then, turning to his beloved disciple John, he said, "Behold thy mother." To John's lasting credit, the Gospel affirms, "And from that hour the disciple whom Jesus loved took Mary unto his own home."

CHRIST TAKING LEAVE OF HIS MOTHER—*PLOCKHORST*

We do not know where Mary, the mother of Jesus, stayed during that last Passover week in Jerusalem, but we do know that somewhere in that crowded city she found shelter, and doubtless saw her Son, at least from a distance, from day to day, as He cleansed the Temple, preached to the thronging multitude, and healed all manner of diseases.

Plockhorst, in his "Christ Taking Leave of His Mother," presents a tender and touching picture of their last embrace which probably occurred in the early evening before that last farewell supper with His disciples in the upper room in Jerusalem. Here, near one of the many arched entrances to the capital city of the Jews, Jesus stands facing His mother with one hand affectionately placed on the head of the woman who had always been first in His filial devotion, while with the other He clasps her left hand.

The eyes of each search the face of the other in the presence of impending disaster as if forever to indelibly imprint on memory's wall every line and feature. For days, with lessening expectation, Mary has watched, with the others, this gifted Son of hers. Like the other followers of Jesus, she has been expecting Him to proclaim His Messiahship and reinstate His kingdom on David's throne. She does not understand the delay, as day by day in the face of waning popularity she repeats to herself, "Not yet? Not yet?" Nevertheless, under the suspense of it all there is an undying trust and devotion to this uncrowned King and His purpose to reflect, not His will, but the will of God among the children of men.

With unsandaled feet they stand for a moment, these two, in the last farewell embrace that His earthly life is to know. Ahead of Him are hours of excruciating agony which will pierce her soul with incomprehensible pain. We feel, as we look into the eyes of Jesus searching His mother's face, that He would, if possible, spare her this, the deepest sorrow a mother can know— the unjust condemnation of her Son, the "only begotten of the Father."

In the background His disciples wait for Him to join them. John, the beloved, staff in hand, has turned to witness this fond embrace of a well-beloved Son and mother; while Peter, resting for a moment in a pensive mood by the stone arch, ponders over His Master's delay in proclaiming His Messiahship and reinstating His "Kingdom of God" on David's throne. Within a few hours, now, they will all be offended in Him, and smitten like sheep without the shepherding, understanding care of their Master and Friend.

"ECCE HOMO"

By

Antonio Ciseri

(Interpretation)

Antonio Ciseri was born at Ronco in Italian Switzerland in 1821. He was the son of a decorator. He studied at the Academy in Florence and early won distinction for his portraits. While still very young he was made professor in the Academy and for many years he conducted private schools of art in Florence. His historical paintings are nearly all religious and are remarkable for their color and somewhat theatrical composition. He died in Florence in 1891.

"Ecce Homo," or "Behold the Man," is a beautiful and striking picture, worthy to rank with any great historical painting of the last century with regard to technique, truthfulness, and insight. The original was completed shortly before Ciseri's death and is considered his masterpiece. It hangs in the National Gallery of Modern Art in Rome.

No one who has seen the original will ever forget it—the glowing sky, the brilliant Temple, the rich and archæologically accurate costumes, the "sea of upturned faces," the dramatic intensity of this moment when the turn of a hand determines the life or death of both the victim and the Jewish nation.

The term "Ecce Homo" usually suggests to our minds the tortured, upturned face of Christ wearing the crown of thorns. Ciseri shows us Pilate and his prisoner and the mob to whom his words are addressed. Undeniably the scene is well staged. Half the background and more is filled with the mass of the Temple, Egyptian in general motive, to suggest the permanence and dignity of the theocratic institutions on which the Jews prided themselves.

Between it and us rises a column of victory adorned with a spiral band of sculptures like that on Trajan's column in Rome. In the foreground where we are standing, tall pillars of the Roman mode indicate the palatial quality of Pilate's judgment-hall. Other symbols of his power are here. On the left, the bronze eagle of the legionary standard, the plumed bronze helmets of two soldiers of his bodyguard, and not the least the throne chair on its Greek-bordered base, cushioned with a leopard's skin—simple, but indicative of the judicial power of life and death which alone the Roman wielded.

Pilate's dignity is also shadowed in his friends. Note the self-possession and the power of that Roman patrician behind the chair, by his position and his pose a personal adviser to the chief. By the right-hand pillar stands a dark-haired man with the garb and beard of a philosopher, his roll still in his hand. He will doubtless charm Pilate's leisure by reading and discussing selections from Plato and Cicero and Epicurus. He loses none of his dignity when we learn that it is Ciseri himself.

Beyond the pillar two other Romans, an older and a younger, study intently the passions of the crowd. This is a new experience for one of them at least. Pilate's wife has turned her back on the bloody prisoner and the noisy mob, anxious for her husband and heartily sick of this wretched business, while her maid supports her hand with apparent sympathy. In their faces we see the only spark of feeling for Christ that the picture affords.

The prisoner stands near the balustrade, in full sight of all. He wears the thorns with which the soldiers crowned Him; His back is lacerated with their scourging; His hands are bound with a knotted rope, one end of which His keeper holds, a burly Gaul of gladiator build who also carries the reed with which they smote the King.

Christ is utterly wretched, yet He bears Himself like one who foresees the end and has prepared for it. Pilate, resplendent in royal robes, leans over and presents Him to his subjects. For the moment Pilate subordinates himself, effaces himself by pointing to Christ and addressing the people; his friends likewise efface themselves by giving their attention to the objects of Pilate's thought. There are, therefore, just two objects left for us to contemplate, the Man of Sorrows and the mob.

This is the real picture, these two. Over against one another they stand, the silent and bleeding Messiah and the howling crowd that was to constitute His Kingdom! Look at the faces through the balustrade and tell whether citizenship in a kingdom not of this world is for them! Look also at their dignified rulers who have climbed to the roof of their Temple and are undignifiedly waving their arms and hounding the crowd on to cry, "Crucify Him." The moment is big with decision.

A nation's fate is hanging in the balance. But clamor and hatred are tipping the beam, with direst consequences. The nation that rejects its heavenly King in favor of an earthly will ere long reject the earthly also, the white wonder of this Temple will dissolve in Titus' fervent heat, and forever they who would not have this Man to rule over them shall be a People of Dispersion, kingless, and homeless, because they knew not the time of their visitation. This is the insight Ciseri gives us—the Jewish nation is sealing its own doom.[1]

✢

CHRIST BEFORE PILATE

By

Michael (Mihaly) Munkacsy

(Interpretation)

MICHAEL (MIHALY) MUNKACSY (Moon-ha-chee) was born February 20, 1844, in the fortress of Munkacs in Hungary. His early life was one of hardships

[1] Adapted from *The Gospel in Art*, by Edward Albery Bailey. Published by the Pilgrim Press. Used by permission of the author.

"ECCE HOMO"—CISERI

CHRIST BEFORE PILATE—MUNKACSY

and struggles. His mother died soon after his birth; his father joined the army of Kossuth to fight Russia, and died in prison. Michael, the youngest of five orphans, was cared for by an aunt. Her house was plundered one night by marauders, and all but this boy Michael murdered. A poor uncle took him and apprenticed him to a carpenter, where he worked unremittingly for six years, growing in stature but with a blank mind. As he mastered his trade he developed a strong desire for education. Some students taught him to read and write, and he began to be interested in history and poetry. His first attempt at art was as a house-painter. He soon showed such skill in decorating trousseau chests that he gave up everything else for this, painting on them flowers, and later figures. Working from twelve to fifteen hours a day, his health soon broke down, and his uncle, who now had a small fortune, took care of him. On recovering he became acquainted with a portrait-painter, and knew, at last, what he wanted to do. He wanted to be an artist.

In 1863 he went to Pesth, where he made his living by drawing peasants, gypsies, etc. In 1866 he nearly went blind, and after some years of suffering finally landed in Munich with only ten dollars in his pocket. He continued to paint portraits and gradually acquired a market for his pictures. His first real commission was from an American, "The Last Day of a Condemned Man," which was exhibited in Paris in 1870 and soon made him famous. A little later he married a rich and titled widow of Luxembourg, and thereafter lived like a prince in Paris. In 1879 he won the Cross of the Legion of Honor.

For many years Munkacsy cherished the plan of painting this picture, and made many sketches of it. The final piece occupied a year's time and was finished in 1881. It was too late for exhibition at the Paris Salon of that year, but all Paris came to see it in the artist's studio. It was then exhibited in the various cities of Europe, where over two million people paid to see it. In 1886 it came to New York. It was later bought by John Wanamaker of Philadelphia, and is now in a permanent exhibition hall in that city.

Dr. Bailey says: "Munkacsy has conceived the incident of 'Christ before Pilate' as part of a great drama. It looks like Grand Opera, the closing scene when all the actors assemble for the impressive *finale*. The 'stage-princes' are here with their 'grand manner,' their exaggerated gesture, their consciousness of the audience; and the director has arranged the properties and grouped the personages so that the audience shall have an unobstructed view. The curtain has just risen.

"The scene is set for the Pretorium, or Judgment Hall, of Pilate. On the throne sits the Procurator himself. Below on benches are the various judges, who, to be sure, have no jurisdiction in a Roman court, but who represent the legal talent of the nation and lend dignity to the scene.

"To the left is the rabble that has pressed in to add the weight of its clamor to the evidence. Caiaphas is making a virulent speech: one can see that he is depending for his effect more on noise and gesture than on solid argument. He has the self-assurance of a Pharisee as well as a Pharisee's intolerance and obstinate prejudice. Notice the other Pharisees, for each character is a study.

Below Pilate are two: the farther one utterly malignant, the nearer one beginning to fear that a mistake has been made. Next to Pilate's hands is a judgment-warper who hopes to make Pilate look at him and take a tip on a point of law. Another stands up behind Caiaphas, his back against the wall, and looks down with curiosity and contempt on the prisoner.

"Under Caiaphas' raised arm three doctors of the law whisper about the case. Last and most impressive of these 'judges' is he on the front seat, a banker, self-complacent embodiment of the vested interests, a sort of Pharisaic 'Uncle Trusty' who believes that this innovator who has upset the money tables in the Temple has shaken the foundations of society! He is certainly a masterpiece.

"Let us look now at the minor characters. See the bunch of usurers behind Christ—very likely victims of his recent cleansing zeal. See the scoffer who leans over behind 'Uncle Trusty' in order to get a jeer squarely into the face of the prisoner. Another has climbed a bench and stretched out an arm toward his scoffing friend.

"On the left, held back by the soldier's spear-shaft, a fanatic throws up his arms in a hired paroxysm of zeal and shouts, 'Crucify Him!' Every face carries its message, gives its judgment of the prisoner, and that judgment is always unfavorable.

"Christ has only one friend here—that sweet-faced mother by the arch pier, a 'madonna lost in the Sanhedrin.' She is a foil to the chaos and the hatred of the mob, an embodiment of the Christian idea; powerless now, to be sure, but bearing in its heart the power that will regenerate the world. She will teach her little child to be a Christian, and through childhood the world will grow into righteousness.

"Pilate sits conspicuous against the background of his judgment seat. His robe is white and purple-bordered, the toga of a Roman senator. Behind him are the symbols of the power of Rome—the wreath and insignia that throughout the world proclaim the supremacy of the Senate and the Roman people.

"Pilate has a strong face, yet in this instance it is 'miserably full of indecision.' Mechanically he hears the arguments, but his thought is busy with the bearings of the case upon his personal fortunes: 'If I release, what trouble will these High Priests make for me? If I condemn, what about justice or a possible appeal to Cæsar?'

"His nervousness betrays itself as his fingers rise mechanically to keep count of the arguments in his brain. The politician, the trimmer, the time-saver, the responsibility-shirker, is here worming his way through the possibilities, while the *justice* of the Senate and the Roman people waits in the background.

"Christ stands in the center of composition, white against the background of His enemies. He is haggard from the physical strain and loss of sleep: yet with courage, dignity, calm forbearance, He looks His judge in the face and mutely demands justice. The loudly iterated charges of Caiaphas, the shouts of the mob, have no power to shake His sublime consciousness of His mission.

THE REMORSE OF IUDAS—ARMITAGE

Principles from which He will never swerve have brought Him here, and they will carry Him hence to an end that Pilate is powerless to change.

"His searching glance in reality reverses the relations that He and Pilate sustain—as Van Dyke has pointed out: He is in reality judge and Pilate is on trial. Pilate is measuring himself against a great ideal of law, which in spite of their faults the Romans had established throughout the circle of the lands; he is being weighed in the balances and found wanting. Of the Roman governor, like the traitor Judas, will be written 'GUILTY' on the judgment-rolls of eternity."[2]

Charles Nelson Page, in *Pictures That Preach*, tells this incident in relation to Munkacsy's "Christ before Pilate":

"A few years ago in Hamilton, Ontario, where Munkacsy's 'Christ before Pilate' was on exhibit, a rough sailor from one of the Lake boats accosted the woman who was in attendance at the door of the exhibit-hall with the blunt question, 'Is Christ here? How much to see Christ?'

"When he was told the admission fee, he growled out, 'Well, I suppose I'll have to pay it' and putting down a piece of silver he swaggered into the room. He sat down in front of the great picture and studied it a moment or two, and presently off came his hat. He gazed upon it a little longer, and then, leaning down, he picked up the description catalogue which he had dropped when he took his seat. He read it over and studied the painting anew, dropping his face into his hands at intervals. Thus he remained for a full hour. When he came out there were tears in his eyes, and suppressed sobs in his voice, as he said:

"'Madam, I came here to see Christ because my mother asked me to. I am a rough man sailing on the Lakes, and before I went on this cruise my mother wanted me to see this picture, and I came to please her. I never believed in any such thing, but the man who could paint a picture like that—he must have believed in it. And there is something in it that makes me believe in it too.'"[3]

✢

THE REMORSE OF JUDAS

By

Edward Armitage

(Interpretation)

EDWARD ARMITAGE was born in London in 1817. He studied in Paris under Delaroche and began exhibiting in the Paris Salon in 1842. In 1843 and 1847 he won first place in a competition for the decoration of the houses of Parlia-

[2] Adapted from *The Gospel in Art*, by Albert Edward Bailey. Published by the Pilgrim Press. Used by permission of the author.

[3] From *Pictures That Preach*. Published by the Abingdon Press, New York City. Used by permission.

ment. Following the second award he spent some time in historical paintings and frescoes for public buildings. During the Crimean War he went to the front in order to paint battle scenes. In 1860 and thereafter his subjects became largely Biblical. In 1872 he was elected to the Royal Academy. Being independent so far as means were concerned, he could work unhindered on his favorite themes. He died in 1896.

His "Remorse of Judas" was painted in 1886 and now hangs in the Tate Gallery in London. It ranks very high among his religious paintings. Its central theme may be found in Judas' desolate, terrifying cry, "I have betrayed innocent blood."

"The terror of this cry rings from the picture before us. Judas has come panting into the presence of these great ones with which he had made his nefarious bargain only a few hours earlier. The cords on his neck are swollen with the intensity of his effort, his mouth is open for breath as well as speech, his eye bulges and his cheek is haggard. His hand clutches the neck of the empty money-bag as if to strangle it from testifying against him, while with the other hand he thrusts the thirty pieces of silver into the faces of his one-time friends. The handle of the knife stuck in his girdle adds a suggestive threat of some desperate action. Judas is going mad. He cannot, it is true, save his victim, nor can he save himself, but he can at least lighten the torment of soul to the extent of the crushing weight of this ill-gotten silver. And so he reiterates: 'I have betrayed innocent blood! innocent blood!'

"But the raised hand and the imperturbable face of the Chief Priest put a chill even upon the fever of his remorse. Not so easily is the load rolled off. The deed has been done, the money has been earned; the irrevocable has arrived. Before the face of Judas yawns a great gulf fixed, so that those that would may not pass thence to the sweet heaven of virtue where the will is free. The priest stands for the eternal fixity of things done. . . .

"The other two priests represent the human side of this transaction. They are the 'great ones' whose friendship Judas was supposed to earn; they are the Sanhedrin whose word of praise was to enroll Judas on the rostrum of fame. Look at them now! In the face of one, scorn and loathing—half pity for the wretch who was so simple as to be caught with such cheap bait, and so moral that he can now suffer remorse. In the face of the other is that self-righteous and sublime unconcern that raises its brow and says, 'Depart from me. I never knew you.' Riches and power found and used their tool; now they cast it away. Its very name will be forgotten; the placid surface will close where it sank and smooth out every ripple. This enviable power of oblivion is attained at a great price; it is the supreme product of a life of selfishness. Such a life, if history is correct, lived Annas and all his house. So in this picture Caiaphas coldly turns his back on the creature that has gratified his dearest wish.

"There is a vulture in the sky beyond the wall. Do you see how the light, striking against the nose of Judas, has transformed it into a vulture's beak? So here are two vultures: one, that has preyed upon his own kind to his infinite undoing, is hurrying to his doom; and the other, who even now scents the carrion on the tree of hanging, is hurrying to the feast. Thus the dead bury their dead lest the whole world become corrupt.

"History has pilloried Judas as the archtraitor of the race. The heinousness of his sin, the absolutely unforgivable quality of it as far as man's sense of justice can see, is reflected in the punishment that Dante has meted out to him in the *Inferno*. In the lowest pit of hell, frozen into the lake of ice whose waters are the tears of humanity, is Satan, a huge shaggy monster with three faces and great batlike wings. In each mouth he crunches a traitor: Brutus and Cassius, traitors against the divinely appointed state, and Judas, traitor against God's Son, as Satan himself was traitor against God. Judas as chief of the three is placed in the central mouth, the one in the crimson face of hatred—for his sin was against love, and the little love he once had has now all reverted to hate. His head is mangled by the teeth of Satan in memory of the crown of thorns his treachery brought on Christ, and his back is lacerated by Satan's claws in repayment for the scourging. No other seer has produced so terrible a symbol of the enormity of the sin against redeeming love, and of the execration that has followed the traitor and will follow him through all eternity."[4]

✠

FROM BETHLEHEM TO CALVARY

From Bethlehem to Calvary the Saviour's journey lay;
Doubt, unbelief, scorn, fear and hate beset Him day by day,
But in His heart He bore God's love that brightened all the way.

O'er the Judæan hills He walked, serene and brave of soul,
Seeking the beaten paths of men, touching and making whole,
Dying at last for love of man, on Calvary's darkened knoll.

He went with patient step and slow, as one who scatters seed;
Like a fierce hunger in His heart He felt the world's great need,
And the negations Moses gave He changed to loving deed.

From Bethlehem to Calvary the world still follows on.
Even as the halt and blind of old along His path were drawn;
Through Calvary's clouds they seek the light that led Him to the dawn.
—*Meredith Nicholson*

[4] Adapted from *The Gospel in Art*, by Albert Edward Bailey. Published by the Pilgrim Press. Used by permission of the author.

THE NINTH HOUR

After the shameful trial in the hall,
  The mocking and the scourging, and the pain
  Of Peter's words; to Herod, and again
To Pilate's judgment-seat, the royal pall,
The cross itself, the vinegar and gall;
  The thieves close by, discipleship proved vain,
  The scoffing crowd, His mother's tears like rain,
There came one moment, bitterest of all.
Yet in that cry, when flesh and spirit failed,
  Last effort of the awful way He trod,
Which shook the earth, nor left the Temple veiled,
    In that exceeding great and bitter cry
    Was conquest. The centurion standing by
Said, "Truly this man was the Son of God."

                          —Caroline Hazard

JUDAS ISCARIOT

The disciple fled far from the one he betrayed,—
The blackest of traitors in scarlet arrayed.

Judas Iscariot looked at some land,
And fingered the blood money held in his hand;

This would he buy, and here would he live,
Gather his crops and—"Give, my son, give

"All that you have for the kingdom of God."
Something that glittered fell on the sod.

It was not hard silver that lay shining where
Judas was prostrate, offering prayer:

"Father, forgive me. Oh, what have I done?
I have betrayed Him, my Master, Thy Son.

"He loved me, His face when He gave me the wine
Was saddened with grieving for sin that was mine.

"I have betrayed Him—oh, was it for this
That I sold my Master—sold with a kiss?

"And shall I live while Jesus is slain?
The strands of the rope, Quick, knot them again . . ."

       ·   ·   ·   ·   ·

Golgotha in darkness, and Judas alone
Waiting the judgment before the White Throne.

Through paths of tall lilies that bend left and right
Christ comes to heaven, clothed all in light,

While stars sing together to welcome the Son,
He hears but the moans of the sorrowing one;

Deep merciful eyes on the penitent head—
"Father, forgive . . . he knew not," He said.

—*Catherine Cate Coblentz*

THE CROWD

Always He feared you;
For you knew Him only as the man of loaves and fishes—
The man who did marvelous things.
He who raised Lazarus,
Healed the lame, and made the blind to see,
Fleeing from you, He sought the solace of the garden.

He must have known
That you would cry, "Release unto us Barabbas!"
And fling your cruel words at Him
As He climbed to Golgotha alone.
Perhaps He knew
That some day you would build creeds about Him,
And lose Him in massive structures of stone,
With costly windows, dignified ritual, and eloquent preachers;
While outside He waited . . .
Sad . . . and alone.

—*Irene McKeighan*

WEDNESDAY IN HOLY WEEK

Man's life is death. Yet Christ endured to live,
  Preaching and teaching, toiling to and fro,
Few men accepting what He yearned to give,
  Few men with eyes to know
  His face, that Face of Love He stooped to show.

Man's death is life. For Christ endured to die
  In slow unuttered weariness of pain,
A curse and an astonishment, passed by,
  Pointed at, mocked again
  By men for whom He shed His blood—in vain?

—*Christina Rossetti*

HEROD PLANS

And so the Magic-worker comes at last!
Three years He's shown His wondrous might to men.
They say His touch has power, that fever flees
Before His fingers, even blind eyes see;
Today perhaps He'll show that power to me.
Youth slips from me, my body's growing old,
Older than my years warrant. I have lived
With wine and song and merry Roman girls
And merry Roman boys in Cæsar's house,
And now I pay the price. Perhaps this Man
Will touch me and will bring my youth again.
I'll try Him, seek a sign, and then I'll draw
Him close beside me, offer Him His freedom,
All He desires as well, if He will work
The miracle that brings me youth again.
He has His price, I'm sure, like any man.
Then Rome once more, while Cæsar stares agape
At my new strength—and nights of wine and song!

He stood and looked and answered not a word.
But, oh! how deep He looked within my soul
Past places where I had not looked for years.
Such men as He and John would drive me mad;
And so He goes to Pilate—and His end!

—William E. Brooks

PILATE REMEMBERS

I wonder why that scene comes back tonight,
That long-forgotten scene of years ago
Perhaps this touch of spring, that full white moon,
For it was spring, and spring's white moon hung low
Above my garden on the night He died.
I still remember how I felt disturbed
That I must send Him to a felon's cross
On such a day when spring was in the air,
And in His life, for He was young to die.
How tall and strong He stood, how calm His eyes,
Fronting me straight and while I questioned Him;
His fearless heart spoke to me through His eyes.
Could I have won Him as my follower,
And a hundred more beside, my way had led
To Cæsar's palace and I'd wear today
The imperial purple. But He would not move

One little bit from His wild madcap dream
Of seeking truth. What wants a man with "truth"
When He is young and spring is at the door?
He would not listen, so He had to go.
One mad Jew less meant little to the state,
And pleasing Annas made my task the less.
And yet for me He spoiled that silver night,—
Remembering it was spring and he was young.
—*William E. Brooks*

GOOD FRIDAY

Peter and James and John,
The sad tale runneth on—
All slept and Thee forgot;
One said he knew Thee not.

Peter and James and John,
The sad tale runneth on—
I am that one, the three;
Thus have I done to Thee.

Under a garden wall
I lay at evenfall;
I waked. Thou calledst me;
I had not watched with Thee.

Peter and James and John,
The sad tale runneth on—
By the priest's fagot hot
I said, "I knew Thee not."

The little maid spake out:
"With Him thou wentest about."
"This Man I never met—"
I hear the cock crow yet.
—*Lizette Woodworth Reese*

REMEMBERING CALVARY

Help me to suffer when I most would spare
  My human frame with pain and weakness spent;
Help me receive with open arms nor dare
  To flinch at pain, but count myself content,
And all that has been and that is to be
  Help me to bear,
    Remembering Calvary.

Help me to leash the hounds of my desire,
  Taming them to a more submissive will;
Help me to tune again a broken lyre
  And find that there is music in it still.
Help me to do these things all cheerfully,
    Nor count the cost,
        Remembering Calvary.

—Ethel Fanning Young

SIMON THE CYRENIAN

This is the tale from first to last:—
    Outside Jerusalem
I saw them lead a prisoner past
    With thorns for diadem.
Broken and weak and driven fast,
    He fell at my garment's hem.

There stood no other stranger by,
    On me they laid His load.
The Cross whereon He was to die
    I bore along the road.
I saw Him nailed, I heard Him cry
    Forsaken of His God.

Now I am dead as well as He,
    And, marvel strange to tell,
But Him they nailed upon the tree
    Is Lord of Heaven and Hell,
And judgeth who doeth wickedly,
    Rewardeth who doeth well.

He has given to me beacons four,
    A Cross in the southern sky,
In token that His cross I bore
    In His extremity;
For One I never knew before
    The day He came to die.

—Lucy Lyttelton

HIS LAST WEEK

(As Told by Mary, His Mother)

MOVED by common expectancy, great numbers of people flocked out from Jerusalem to meet Jesus as He was going into Jerusalem, and they called Him king, and made a great noise, and tore palm branches from trees, and stripped off their outer garments, carpeting His way as if on a triumphant march to a throne.

What is going to happen when He breaks into Jerusalem with tumultuous hosannas and enthusiasts swirling like waters in flood?

They swept on through the gates into the city. Down go the tables of the money-changers, their coins scattering on the pavement. Traders flee in fear before His uplifted scourge. Chaos reigns. Not one of them dares to say a word. Jerusalem is at His feet. Every kind of sickness goes out with a word or touch. Even the children are wild with excitement.

Has His hour come? The people have already proclaimed Him King. Will He acknowledge it? Will He proclaim Himself?

"The government shall be upon His shoulders and of His Kingdom there shall be no end," declared the prophet.

.   .   .   .   .

No, not yet, it seems; for at nightfall He went back to Bethany—without declaring Himself. We do not understand. How I longed to ask Him, but stood in awe.

.   .   .   .   .

He went back to Jerusalem today and repeated the work of yesterday. The crowds that had come in from everywhere want to see Him and we could not get near Him all day. Nothing else is talked of. All the people are with Him, except a few who perhaps are jealous.

Such a day as He had yesterday! But He went out to Bethany without declaring Himself King.

.   .   .   .   .

We are expecting the people to take Him by force when He goes to Jerusalem today. They did not. And He did not. The jealous ones are murmuring. Why does He not ascend the throne?

Salome and James and John are disappointed, but they are abiding His time with as much patience as they can. A day or two more may make His power so overwhelming that the Kingdom will come inevitably. He knows.

.   .   .   .   .

Salome rushed into my room with the news of His arrest. What! The
Messiah arrested! It cannot be. Angels in chariots protected Elisha and struck
his pursuers blind. They will do it again.

WAIT, my soul; at the extremity He will manifest Himself. What? They
are going to crucify Him! But they cannot. He is the Messiah of God. He is
to reign as a great King forever. Did not God send the angel to tell me so
before the Child was conceived? The miracle of miracles is at hand. He will
assert Himself.

.   .   .   .   .

They scourge Him! Can I believe my eyes! They play with His life and
mock at His pain and— He lets them! Gabriel, look! Descend with legions
of defenders, else Thy promise mocks us. Didst thou create hopes only
to crush them; promise redemption of Israel only to let it fail? If He die,
there is no redemption, the promise fails.

A great throng follows Him to the crucifixion—the same ones that yesterday shouted to make Him King. They have made up their minds that He
is not the Messiah, the King; for the Messiah would assert Himself, they
say, and triumph over them. O God, where art thou? Strike and they will
believe.

.   .   .   .   .

I flew to Him when He fell under His cross and Mary Magdalene and
Mary of Bethany were by my side, but the soldiers held us back.

When He saw us weeping helplessly, He said, tenderly,

"Weep not for me." But how could we help it?

"Assert thyself," I cried, but the soldiers crushed us back.

"Have patience," He said. "You shall see."

And the terrible march went on up Calvary's Hill.

.   .   .   .   .

He let them nail Him to the cross.

"Come down," they cry, "and we will believe."

"Come down," we cried. "Thou canst. Give the proof they ask. . . . Not
yet?"

"He saved others; let Him save Himself—and we will believe," they mock.

"Save yourself," we cried. "Thou canst. Accept their challenge and con-
found them. . . . No, not yet?"

His only answer was, "John, take care of mother; I am leaving her to
you."

John came to my side and helped me.

"Oh, John," I said, "is He to die? Is that what He means? The Messiah
die? What, then, meant the angel visits? O God, and Thine own voice speaking to Him out of the skies? Speak now. And the mighty works? Work now!
Let His extremity plead."

.   .   .   .   .

"What is it He cries, John . . . that He is forsaken of God? *God forsake HIM?* Is that what He says? Oh, John, is He to die? Tell me, have you hidden it from me? Mary, speak; they have hidden it from me? Have they conspired to hide it from me?"[5]

✠

JESUS, AS SEEN BY PILATE

By

Kahlil Gibran

MY WIFE spoke of Him many times ere He was brought before me, but I was not concerned. My wife is a dreamer, and she is given, like so many Roman women of her rank, to Eastern cults and rituals. And these cults are dangerous to the Empire; and when they find a path to the hearts of our women they become destructive.

Egypt came to an end when the Hyksos of Arabia brought to her the one God of their desert. And Greece was overcome and fell to dust when Ashtarte and her seven maidens came from the Syrian shores.

As for Jesus, I never saw the Man before He was delivered up to me as a malefactor and as an enemy of His own nation and also of Rome.

He was brought into the Hall of Judgment with His arms bound to His body with ropes. I was sitting upon the dais, and He walked towards me with long, firm steps; then He stood erect and His head was held high.

I cannot fathom what came over me at that moment; but it was suddenly my desire, though not my will, to rise and go down from the dais and fall before Him.

I felt as if Cæsar had entered the Hall, a man greater than even Rome herself. But this lasted only a moment. And then I saw simply a Man Who was accused of treason by His own people; and I was His governor and His judge.

I questioned Him, but He would not answer. He only looked at me. And in His look was pity, as if it were He who was my governor and my judge.

Then there rose from without the cries of the people. But He remained silent, and still He was looking at me with pity in His eyes.

And I went out upon the steps of the palace; and when the people saw me they ceased to cry out. And I said, "What would you do with this just Man?"

And they shouted as if with one throat: "We would crucify Him. He is our enemy and the enemy of Rome."

And some one called out, "Did He not say He would destroy the Temple? And was it not He who claimed the Kingdom? We will have no king but Cæsar."

---

[5] From *His Mother, A Story of Our Lord*, by G. M. Anderson. Published by the Bethany Press, St. Louis, Missouri. Used by special permission of the heirs and the publishers.

Then I left them and went back into the Judgment Hall again, and I saw Him still standing there alone, and His head was still held high.

And I remembered what I had read that a Greek philosopher said, "The lonely man is the strongest man." At that moment the Nazarene was greater than His race.

But I did not feel clement towards Him. He was beyond my clemency. I asked Him, then, "Are you the King of the Jews?"

But he said not a word.

And I asked Him again, "Have you not said that you are the King of the Jews?"

And He looked upon me. Then He answered with a quiet voice, "You, yourself, proclaimed me a king. Perhaps to this end I was born, and for this cause came I to bear witness unto *truth*."

Behold a man speaking of *truth* at such a moment.

In my impatience I said aloud, to myself as much as to Him: "What is truth? And what is truth to the guiltless when the hand of the executioner is already upon Him?"

Then Jesus said, with power, "None shall rule the world save with the *Spirit* and *truth*."

And I asked him, saying, "Are you of the Spirit?"

And He answered, "So are you also, though you know it not."

And what was Spirit and what was truth; when I, for the sake of the state, and they from jealousy for their ancient rites, delivered an innocent Man unto His death? No man, no race, no empire would halt before a truth on its way towards self-fulfillment.

And I said again, "Are you the King of the Jews?"

And He answered, "You, yourself, say this, I have conquered the world ere this hour."

And this alone of all that He said was unseemly, inasmuch as only Rome had conquered the world.

But now the voices of the people rose again, and the noise was greater than before. And I descended from my seat and said to Him, "Follow me." And again I appeared upon the steps of the palace, and He stood there beside me.

And when the people saw Him they roared like the roaring of thunder; and in their clamor I heard naught save, "Crucify Him! Crucify Him!"

Then I yielded Him to the priests who had yielded Him to me, and I said to them, "Do what you will with this just Man. And if it is your desire, take with you soldiers of Rome to guard Him."

And they took Him; and I decreed that there be written upon the cross above His head, "Jesus of Nazareth, King of the Jews." I should have said instead, "Jesus of Nazareth, a King."

And the Man was stripped and flogged and crucified.

It would have been within my power to save Him; but saving Him would have caused a revolution; and it is always wise for the governor of a Roman province not to be too tolerant with the religious scruples of a conquered race.

I believe unto this hour that Jesus was more than an agitator. What I decreed was not my will, but rather for the sake of Rome.

Not long after, we left Syria, and from that day my wife has been a woman of sorrow. Sometimes even here in this garden I see tragedy in her face. I am told that she talks much of Jesus to the other women of Rome.

Behold, the Man whose death I decreed returns from the world of shadows and enters into my own house.

And within myself I ask again and again, "What is *truth*, and what is not *truth*?" Can it be that the Syrian is conquering us in the quiet hours of the night?

It should not indeed be so. For Rome must needs prevail against the nightmares of our wives.[6]

✠

IN THE HOUR OF TRIAL

"In the Hour of Trial" is one of those great Christian hymns of the Church that seek to establish a relationship between the testing which Jesus and His disciples knew in the sad hours that preceded His death on the cross, and similar *testing* times which every devout follower of Christ in every age has experienced in one form or another.

In the hour of His trial Judas sold the Master for "thirty pieces of silver." In the hour of His trial Peter, the rock-man, denied with oaths that he ever knew His Lord. In hours of great temptation men and women in all ages have denied Christ in unusual ways and unexpected places.

James Montgomery, recognizing this common weakness of mankind, has given expression, in this beautiful hymn, to the self-searching appeal of every devout heart, that Jesus, knowing our frailties, will plead for us, His followers, when these testing times come to us.

> In the hour of trial,
>   Jesus, plead for me,
> Lest by base denial
>   I depart from Thee;
> When Thou seest me waver,
>   With a look recall,
> Nor for fear or favor
>   Suffer me to fall.
>
> With forbidden pleasures
>   Would this vain world charm,
> Or its sordid treasures
>   Spread to work me harm,

[6] From *Jesus*, by Gibran. Published by Alfred A. Knopf, New York City. Used by special permission of the publishers.

Bring to my remembrance
Sad Gethsemane,
Or, in darker semblance,
Cross-crowned Calvary.

Should Thy mercy send me
Sorrow, toil, and woe,
Or should pain attend me
On my path below,
Grant that I may never
Fail Thy hand to see;
Grant that I may ever
Cast my care on Thee. Amen.

—*James Montgomery, 1834*

✛

JESUS, LOVER OF MY SOUL

AMONG the great lyric hymns of the church, written by that prolific writer of hymns, Charles Wesley, none is more widely known or sung than "Jesus, Lover of My Soul."

In spite of the poverty and ever-present difficulties of Samuel and Susannah Wesley in the Rectory at Epworth, England, they found time to teach their children to sing. There is little doubt that the memories of those childhood days of Psalm-singing in the home helped to inspire the six thousand five hundred hymns which Charles Wesley wrote during his lifetime.

In spite of the strenuous life which both Charles and John Wesley lived, they were constantly on the move, preaching in open-air meetings, riding hundreds of miles each year on horseback, facing hostile mobs and organizing Methodist "societies"—yet in spite of all this feverish activity Charles Wesley found time to compose hundreds of hymns that continue to enrich the life of the Church to this day.

"Jesus, Lover of My Soul," which was written in 1740, is one of the really great hymns of the Church that has gone to the ends of the earth and has been translated into virtually all languages. It is cherished alike by saints and children; and men and women in all lands and in all conditions have found inspiration and spiritual refreshment in the words and music of this truly great Christian hymn.

It will live always because as literature it has the brevity, melody, intensity, and completeness of pure lyric poetry. The tune to which it is usually sung was composed by John B. Dykes in 1861.

Jesus, Lover of my soul,
  Let me to Thy bosom fly,
While the nearer waters roll,
  While the tempest still is high;
Hide me, O my Saviour, hide,
  Till the storm of life be past;
Safe into the haven guide;
  O receive my soul at last.

Other refuge have I none;
  Hangs my helpless soul on Thee;
Leave, ah, leave me not alone,
  Still support and comfort me.
All my trust on Thee is stayed,
  All my help from Thee I bring;
Cover my defenseless head
  With the shadow of Thy wing.

Thou, O Christ, art all I want,
  More than all in Thee I find;
Raise the fallen, cheer the faint,
  Heal the sick, and lead the blind.
Just and holy is Thy name,
  I am all unrighteousness;
False and full of sin I am,
  Thou art full of truth and grace.

Plenteous grace with Thee is found,
  Grace to cover all my sin;
Let the healing streams abound;
  Make and keep me pure within.
Thou of life the fountain art,
  Freely let me take of Thee;
Spring Thou up within my heart,
  Rise to all eternity.

—Charles Wesley, 1740

✦

I GAVE MY LIFE FOR THEE

WE ARE indebted to Frances R. Havergal for many beautiful hymns, all of which are more or less personal in their appeal. But among them all, none strikes a more responsive chord in the hearts of true followers of Christ everywhere than this one, "I Gave My Life for Thee."

Miss Havergal was the daughter of a minister, who was a poet and musician of more than ordinary ability; and she, herself, began to write verse at a very early age

In this hymn it is as though Jesus, Himself, was interrogating every human heart, by bringing to our attention the great love that our heavenly Father has for us, as shown by the gift of His only Son, Who left His Father's home and died an outcast on the cross that we might know life abundant here and life eternal hereafter. Its theme is the gift of salvation, but it emphasizes for our spiritual enrichment, the cost of redemption in love, in sacrifice, and in suffering.

I gave My life for thee,
  My precious blood I shed,
That thou might'st ransomed be
  And quickened from the dead;
I gave, I gave My life for thee.
  What hast thou given for Me?
I gave, I gave My life for thee.
  What hast thou given for Me?

My Father's house of light,
  My glory-circled throne,
I left, for earthly night,
  For wanderings sad and lone;
I left, I left it all for thee.
  Hast thou left aught for Me?
I left, I left it all for thee,
  Hast thou left aught for Me?

I suffered much for thee,
  More than thy tongue can tell,
Of bitterest agony,
  To rescue thee from Hell;
I've borne, I've borne it all for thee.
  What hast thou borne for Me?
I've borne, I've borne it all for thee.
  What hast thou borne for Me?

And I have brought to thee,
  Down from My home above,
Salvation full and free,
  My pardon and My love;
I bring, I bring rich gifts to thee.
  What hast thou brought for Me?
I bring, I bring rich gifts to thee.
  What hast thou brought for Me?

—Frances R. Havergal, 1858

I CANNOT THINK OR REASON

AMONG the newer hymns expressing the sentiment of the "Comradeship of
the Cross," none is more challenging to young people than this beautiful
hymn, "I Cannot Think or Reason," written by Willard Wattles in 1918.

It expresses youth's natural, spontaneous response to the call of Jesus to
sacrifice and service that the world may be lifted to new levels of living.

Young people find it easy to love Jesus. He, Himself, was a young Man.
Life with all of its richness was before Him to conquer and to enjoy; but He
sensed the deeper needs of the race for victory in the realm of things spiritual;
and He gave His life fully and freely that men might come to know and
appreciate these greater spiritual values which all must come to possess if
we are to live victoriously.

The spirit of comradeship with Jesus surges through every line of this
beautiful hymn-poem.

> I cannot think or reason,
>   I only know He came
> With hands and feet of healing
>   And wild heart all aflame,
> With eyes that dimmed and softened
>   At all the things he saw,
> And in his pillared singing
>   I read the marching law.
>
> I only know He loves me,
>   Enfolds and understands—
> And, oh, His heart that holds me,
>   And oh, His certain hands—
> The man, the Christ, the soldier,
>   Who from His cross of pain
> Cried to a dying comrade,
>   "Lad, we shall meet again."[7]

—*Willard Wattles, 1918*

✝

THE CRUCIFIXION

THE story of the Crucifixion of Jesus struck a responsive chord in the heart
of the Negro slave. He, too, had felt the sting of the lash; he knew the pain
of cords cutting into his thumbs or wrists as he was tied to the whipping-post.

[7] Words copyright by E. P. Dutton & Co., Inc. Used by permission.

He had heard the cries of agony of his fellows under torture or had given voice to them himself. Crucifixion to him was a frequent experience as he toiled and waited for a better day!

The poignant suffering of Love dying on the cross for men who didn't care surges through these songs of yearning that are the Negroes' way of picturing what the Master of Men suffered for you and for me. When one has heard these sung, as only Negroes can sing them, with pathos and deep appreciation of what the suffering love of God's only Begotten Son was like, he can never cease to be grateful for what the folk-songs of this once enslaved and forgotten race contributed to the enrichment of Christian worship.

Notice what these Negro bards have done with the story of the Crucifixion. These stories are always vividly colored. They not only tell it as it is, but they include in it their sense of the tragedy and pathos of it all.

> See how they done my Lord,
> And He never said a mumblin' word,
> See how they done my Lord,
> And He never said a mumblin' word.
> See how they done my Lord,
> And He never said a mumblin' word—
> My Lord, He never said a mumblin' word.
>
> They led Him into Pilate's hall,
> And He never said a mumblin' word.
> They led Him into Pilate's hall,
> And He never said a mumblin' word.
> They led Him into Pilate's hall,
> And He never said a mumblin' word—
> My Lord, He never said a mumblin' word.
>
> They put on Him a thorny crown,
> And He never said a mumblin' word,
> They put on Him a thorny crown,
> And He never said a mumblin' word.
> They put on Him a thorny crown,
> And He never said a mumblin' word—
> My Lord, He never said a mumblin' word.
>
> They put on Him a purple robe,
> And He never said a mumblin' word,
> They put on Him a purple robe,
> And He never said a mumblin' word.
> They put on Him a purple robe,
> And He never said a mumblin' word—
> My Lord, He never said a mumblin' word.

They nailed Him to the cross,
And He never said a mumblin' word;
They nailed Him to the cross,
And He never said a mumblin' word.
They nailed Him to the cross,
And He never said a mumblin' word—
My Lord, He never said a mumblin' word.

He suffered on the cross,
And He never said a mumblin' word.
He suffered on the cross,
And He never said a mumblin' word.
He suffered on the cross,
And He never said a mumblin' word—
My Lord, He never said a mumblin' word.

They pierced Him in the side,
And He never said a mumblin' word,
They pierced Him in the side,
And He never said a mumblin' word.
They pierced Him in the side,
And He never said a mumblin' word—
My Lord, He never said a mumblin' word.

He bowed His head and died,
And He never said a mumblin' word,
He bowed His head and died,
And He never said a mumblin' word.
He bowed His head and died,
And He never said a mumblin' word—
My Lord, He never said a mumblin' word.

—A Spiritual

CONTENTS

PART IV   SECTION III

HIS CRUCIFIXION

✠

"They took Jesus therefore; and he went out, bearing the cross for himself."—JOHN 19:17

✠

✠

HIS CRUCIFIXION

"So when Pilate saw that he prevailed nothing, but rather that a tumult was arising, he took water, and washed his hands before the multitude, saying, I am innocent of the blood of this righteous man; see ye *to it*. And all the people answered and said, His blood *be* on us, and on our children. Then released he unto them Barabbas; but Jesus he scourged and delivered to be crucified."—Matthew 27:24-26

✠

"And they set up over his head this accusation written, THIS IS JESUS THE KING OF THE JEWS. Then are there crucified with him two robbers, one on the right hand and one on the left. And they that passed by railed on him, wagging their heads, and saying, Thou that destroyest the temple, and buildest it again in three days, save thyself: if thou art the Son of God, come down from the cross. In like manner also the chief priests mocking *him*, with the scribes and elders, said, He saved others; himself he cannot save. If he is the King of Israel, let him now come down from the cross, and we will believe on him."—Matthew 27:37-42

✠

"Now from the sixth hour there was darkness over all the land until the ninth hour. And about the ninth hour Jesus cried with a loud voice, saying, Eli, Eli, lama sabachthani? that is, My God, my God, why hast thou forsaken me? And some of them that stood there, when they heard it, said, 'This man calleth Elijah.' . . . And Jesus cried again with a loud voice, and yielded up his spirit. And behold, the veil of the temple was rent in two from top to the bottom; and the earth did quake; and the rocks were rent; and the tombs opened."—Matthew 27:45-47, 50-52

✠

"And when even was come, there came a rich man from Arimathæa, named Joseph, who also himself was Jesus' disciple: this man went to Pilate, and asked for the body of Jesus. Then Pilate commanded it to be given up. And Joseph took the body, and wrapped it in a clean linen cloth, and laid it in his own new tomb, which he had hewn out in the rock: and he rolled a great stone to the door of the tomb, and departed. And Mary Magdalene was there, and the other Mary, sitting over against the sepulchre."—Matthew 27:57-61

THE CRUCIFIXION

By

Hermann Clementz

(Interpretation)

"Golgotha," or "The Crucifixion," by Hermann Clementz, a contemporary German artist, is one of the most challenging of all the modern paintings of the crucifixion scene. The original is now privately owned in Europe.

In this scene the two thieves between whom Jesus was crucified have already been bound to their rugged crosses, and these cruel instruments of death placed to await the slow and painful end that was to be their fate.

Between these two upraised figures, on the ground, another cross is being made ready for the Christ, who stands unabashed and unafraid in the foreground of this picture. At the head of the center cross stands Simon the Cyrenian, who was forced, when Jesus fell, to bear the weight of His heavy cross up the steep mountainside to Calvary. His task complete, he stands with folded arms. He does not understand what it is all about, but he cannot take his eyes from the face of this majestic Rabbi who is to die at the hands of a cruel and unjust mob.

At one side and behind the upraised crosses stand the Roman guards, and behind them the rabble that followed the High Priest and scribes to Calvary's summit, demanding the death of this "king of the Jews."

Directly behind Jesus stand Caiaphas and other prominent members of the Sanhedrin, some with folded hands as if in prayer, and others with outstretched arms as if invoking Jehovah's blessing on the death of this blasphemer Who claimed to be God's Son, and Who had said: "Destroy this temple, and I will build it again in three days."

Mingling with this group are certain of His friends and disciples who are helpless now to aid their Lord and Master in any way, while far away in the left-background a mounted captain of the Roman guard is gesturing as if to speed up the delay in placing this Jewish agitator on the remaining cross. The lowering sky gives every indication that a storm is brewing. Haste is imperative if the cruel edict of Pilate is to be fully consummated before sunset of the Jewish Sabbath.

In the immediate foreground on either side of Jesus are the women who loved Him, and who followed Him in helpful service throughout Galilee, and Samaria, even unto Jerusalem. Mary Magdalene at the right of Jesus is kneeling with upturned face as she implores the Master to save Himself from this cruel and unjust punishment. At the left, Mary, the mother of Jesus, unable longer to bear the anguish of that scene, has swooned away. Her head and shoulders rest against Salome, who is trying to comfort her.

CHRIST ON CALVARY—MUNKACSY

An almost blinding flood of light, as from clouds riven by lightning, floods the face and form of the Master, as He stands there in calm, majestic dignity, awaiting His destiny. His hands point downward toward the women who have followed Him in love and service; but His eyes are raised to His heavenly Father in prayer for their sakes. Even in this hour we feel that He is thinking of and praying for others rather than Himself.

On the preceding night He had won His own battle in that midnight wrestle with God through prayer in dark Gethsemane. Now He approaches His own cruel death on the cross with but little thought of Himself, but with real concern for these, His followers, whose hearts are broken by this tragedy which they must witness, and yet are powerless to alter or to understand.

For a few moments only He stands there supreme in His self-renunciation, free from the weight of His cross, and before the excruciating pain that is to attend His death on Calvary for the sins of men begins. "He has conquered the world ere this hour." With the raising of His body on the cross there begins that purging process that through the centuries is to blot out ignorance, bigotry, race prejudice, superstition, hatred, malice, and unbelief from the hearts of men. We can almost hear Him say: "Father, forgive them, for they know not what they do."

✛

CHRIST ON CALVARY

By

Michael (Milhaly) Munkacsy

(Interpretation)

THE scene of this picture is the little hill known as Golgotha, or Calvary, behind which lies Jerusalem. The interest centers upon the figure of Christ, whose cross stands in the right-hand portion of the composition, and whose figure is illuminated by a shaft of light from the dark, overhanging clouds. Close about the foot of the cross are gathered the friends of Jesus.

Near by are the crosses of the two malefactors who were crucified with the Saviour; the penitent thief at His right, the other at His left. Down the hill and running into the foreground to the left are Pharisees, Roman soldiers, scribes, and the rabble, kept back by the Roman soldiers.

The cross on which Jesus hangs rises high above everything else in the picture. The Redeemer is portrayed as a man of noble figure and sublime expression; the agony in His face is glorified by submission to the Divine will. The tension of His muscles shows extreme physical suffering. And the black clouds of an impending storm cover the sky. To this threatening sky above Him Jesus has just sent up the heart-rending cry, "My God! My God! Why hast Thou forsaken me?" and as if in answer there has come a momen-

of that crucifixion eve, only pain, deep, dull pain, and the hopelessness of unending despair. The Messiah, the Child of Promise, the Deathless One, was dead. What could life in the future hold for them?

Every devout Christian whose eyes rest on this magnificent painting as it hangs today in the Louvre, thanks God, from the depths of his heart, that there is yet another chapter in the story of the matchless life of Christ, which chapter was opened on that first Easter morn—a chapter that was to send these beaten and defeated followers of the lowly Nazarene out with deathless courage to finish, under the guiding Spirit of their risen Lord, that Kingdom of Love for which He lived and wrought and prayed and died. "Thanks be to God Who giveth us the victory through faith, even over death."

✠

DESCENT FROM THE CROSS

By

Peter Paul Rubens

(Interpretation)

THE original painting, "Descent from the Cross," constitutes the center panel of the altar-piece in the cathedral at Antwerp in Belgium. It was painted by Rubens in 1612. One has but to stand and gaze at it, as thousands do every year, to realize why it is included among the World's Twelve Great Paintings.

Speaking of the influence of this great picture, Dr. Bailey says: "Of all the religious paintings in the world, it has been one of the most admired. From a technical point of view it is well-nigh perfect. Its brilliantly lighted white center against the black-green background, together with the masses of dull red, are most impressive, even when gazed at from across the great cathedral. . . . The horrors of the crucifixion have passed away, and only the dull pain of memory mingles with the veneration due to the body of so precious a friend.

"The friends of Jesus are removing the body from the cross before nightfall, in order that the Sabbath may be unpolluted. Joseph of Arimathea, who begged the body of Pilate, stands halfway up the ladder on the left. On the right-hand ladder is Nicodemus. Two strong men have mounted other ladders and, having released the body, are now lowering it in a winding sheet. That the body is heavy is indicated by the strength exerted by the older man, who holds the cloth in his teeth while he braces himself against the crossbeam. John, too, who receives the body from below, finds that he is handling no phantom. In such details lies the realism of the picture; this is what actually took place.

"The body of Christ is a piece of masterly work. There is no doubt about Christ's being dead. All his members hang limp: the head drops heavily forward, the eyes are dead eyes, in the original the color is livid. And do

DESCENT FROM THE CROSS—*RUBENS*

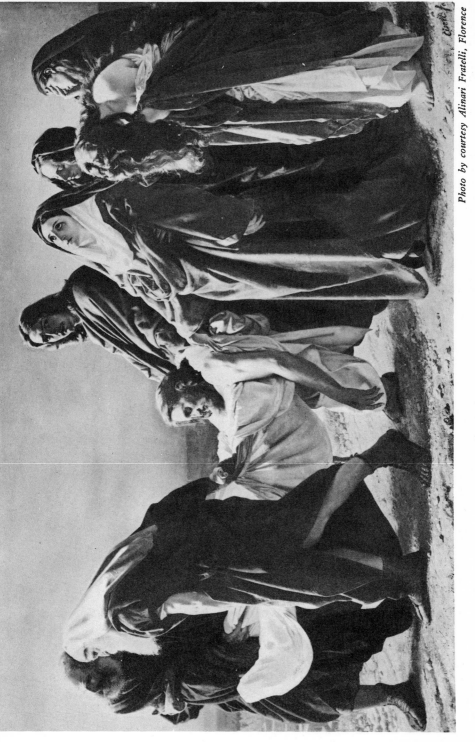

THE ENTOMBMENT—CISERI

you observe how the illusion of motion is created?—by the straight tensity of the upper part of the winding sheet that falls almost perpendicularly, merging by degrees into the folds and upturned portions below. The body has slid into the arms of John and the affectionate way in which all these mourners and helpers receive the burden shows how precious a burden it is.

"Among the three Marys it is easy to distinguish the Virgin because of her greater dignity and sorrow. She does not touch the body, but follows its every movement with a quick sympathy. Mary Magdalene receives the feet, as she does in so many pictures, just as in many of the crucifixions she embraces the feet. In this way the artists picture her passionate sorrow and her sense of unworthiness because of past sins. As in Rubens' 'Crucifixion,' the Magdalene is the most human, the most delicate, and the most beautiful portion of the picture.

"The religious value of such a picture lies in its power to revive personal memories. Death is one of the most solemn realities in the world; it is the door by which one passes from the seen and temporal into the more immediate consciousness of things unseen and eternal. Death is therefore a religious experience for him who dies and for those who follow with love the departing soul. No one who has performed the last rites for a loved one will fail to be touched by this pictured service or to feel again in less poignant form the solemnity of that hour. There are few spiritual lessons to be learned in the House of Mirth, but many and faithful are the counsels our hearts receive as we stand between the eternities and watch the iron doors close."[1]

✢

THE ENTOMBMENT

By

Antonio Ciseri

(Interpretation)

"The Entombment" by Antonio Ciseri was painted as an altarpiece for the Church of the Madonna del Sasso, in 1869. It represents the artist's commentary on Lamentations 1:12—"Is it nothing to you, all ye that pass by? Behold and see if there be any sorrow like unto my sorrow!"

Dr. Bailey in describing this picture says: "One golden afternoon in 1898 I wandered alone over the heights above Lake Maggiore, when I was attracted by an old monastery crowning a conical hill that rose some eleven hundred feet behind the city of Locarno. Straightway I became a pilgrim and began to climb the zigzag path, conspicuous from a distance by what looked like a

---

[1] From *The Gospel in Art*, by Albert Edward Bailey. Published by the Pilgrim Press, Boston, Mass. Used by permission of the author.

succession of white milestones of enormous size, but in reality were little shrines containing pictures of the Stations of the Cross. Crude though they were, they suggested the depth of piety that had constructed this laborious way and the monastery on the summit, dedicated to 'Our Lady of Sorrows,' and called now from the eagle's nest of her shrine, 'Our Lady of the Rock.' . . .

"The church itself was the climax of wonder, its inner walls covered with a thatch of votive offerings that wretched folk had left in hope of cure or in token of the same: chromos, faded flowers, ostrich eggs, samplers and mottoes in all kinds of stitches, models of ships, and what not, mirrors framed in gilt tinsel, tufts of hair, shreds of rag . . . each bit eloquent of suffering and release through the intercession of the Blessed Virgin. . . .

"Out of the mass of this holy bric-à-brac flamed Ciseri's glorious picture. The late sun streamed upon it, upon the pallid limbs of the Christ, upon the Virgin's upturned face of sorrow and her cerulean mantle; it kissed the bared shoulder of the Magdalene and lighted into a glory the golden stream of her hair that had fallen forward in the ecstasy of her passion. And it seemed then as if the picture were the final and perfect expression of that profound sorrow of the Mother that makes her eternally akin to every sorrowing heart. This is the Mary whom the poor can pity and love, the Mary who can pity and love in return. This is the embodiment of all the tender sympathy which man longs for in the Divine, but which a frigid and inexorable theology has driven from the heart of God. Finding only justice in the Father of the creeds, and only exalted perfection in the Son . . . the yearning heart of the world has turned toward Mary the eternal Mother, whose fellowship in its suffering makes her ever ready to pity and intercede. This is the true philosophy of the worship of Mary.

"The other figures in Ciseri's picture are only accompaniments of Mary and her Son. Yet they all enhance the beauty and interpret the sorrow of these central ones. One discovers that Ciseri has a feeling for the subtlety and suavity of line as well as for harmonious color: that he can express dignity as well as grace, the gravity of age as well as the charm of youth. Nicodemus, just past the prime of life, leads the sad procession, his face almost as ruddy as the orange under-robe he wears. Joseph of Arimathea shares with him the major burden, his snow-white beard contrasting so richly with his dull green mantle, and it in turn with the cream-colored head-cloth. The faces of these two have a strong portrait quality; they are full of character. John, who carries the shoulders of the Saviour, has the face of a poet—large eyes, full features now grief-stricken, and ruddy locks that hang upon the shoulder. Behind the Virgin walks Mary, the wife of Cleopas, and last of all Salome. And while the majestic bearing of Christ's mother makes us feel that the message of the picture is her grief, we almost forget her in admiration of the beauty of the Magdalene—the sunlight on the foot, on the white under-robe, on the mantle of old-gold and the rippling luster of her tresses.

"The head of Christ is the center of composition. While it follows somewhat the traditional features, we see in it a dignity and strength that few representations of Him possess. One feels that here was a great man, One absolutely worthy of the wealth of love that is being poured out; and this feeling in turn adds to our own sorrow that One so good and great should have been cut off in His prime. These feelings, you observe, are all modern rather than mediæval. There is positively no theology in this picture. This is not the entombment of the Second Person of the Trinity, with the Queen of Heaven for chief mourner; it is the burial of a beloved Son and the grief of a stricken mother."[2]

✢

HOLY SATURDAY

By

Eugene Burnand

(Interpretation)

I DOUBT if, in all the history of art, there is a finer portrayal of the stark tragedy that gripped the souls of the eleven men who were most closely associated with Jesus during His life and ministry, than this painting of "Holy Saturday" by Eugene Burnand, the great Swiss painter, who died as recently as 1921.

After the hurried interment of the body of their beloved Master in Joseph's new tomb, following Christ's cruel and unjust trial and crucifixion, during which time His disciples were scattered "as sheep without a shepherd," the few that remained near the foot of the cross hurried away to their more or less secret hiding-places in the great capital city of their race.

Notwithstanding the fact that Jesus had at various times and on many occasions, during those busy days that preceded His atonement on Calvary, told His disciples that He must be perfected through suffering they did not, could not, comprehend that it was to mean *death* on the cross. To the bitter end those who were near and dear to Him, expected the Master, Whom they had seen raise other men from the dead, to proclaim His royal Kingdom and to use His miraculous power to protect Himself from the scourge of death. This their beloved Teacher and Friend steadfastly refused to do; and to add to their bewilderment, even He, on the cross, had cried out: "My God! My God! Why hast Thou forsaken Me!"

Dazed with blinding sorrow, bewilderment, and confusion of mind and heart, Burnand, in his "Holy Saturday," portrays the eleven again in the upper room, where on Thursday night of that same week the Master had washed their feet, partaken with them of their farewell meal, and talked to them with a tender brooding sympathy.

It is probable that they gathered in this room again not by any previous planning, but driven, instead, by an inner compulsion to seek this hallowed place for quiet, repose, and undisturbed meditation and prayer on the meaning

[2] From *The Gospel in Art*, by Albert Edward Bailey. Published by the Pilgrim Press, Boston, Mass. Used by permission of the author.

HOLY SATURDAY—BURNAND

of the dreadful hours that had intervened since that farewell supper and the death of their beloved Teacher and Friend on Calvary's cross.

There is not a ray of hope on any face. Peter, at the end of the table, his agonizing brain resting heavily on his hands, can no longer think or talk; he can only weep and suffer in silence as he recalls his thricefold betrayal of his beloved Master in the courtyard of the High Priest's palace.

It is evident that John the beloved, who sits next to him, has been trying to comfort this impulsive friend; but words, mere words, are of no avail at such a time as this; because for Peter there was, as yet, neither the vision nor the hope of that later lakeside breakfast on the shores of blue Galilee, where he reaffirmed his faith in and love for the Master he had so vehemently denied, and secured forgiveness.

John doesn't understand any better than the others the tragic turn which recent events have taken; but he loves this impulsive fisherman friend, and cannot bear to see him suffer thus. The dull ache in his own heart has made him sensitive to the pain of others.

James sits at the other end of the table, his deep-set eyes peering into vacancy as he tries to recall the prophetic sayings of their dead Master, and to bring order out of the mental chaos in which he finds himself in this tragic hour.

Andrew, the quiet disciple, whose outstanding characteristic seems to have been his ability to bring others to Christ, stands with down-cast eyes and sorrowing face just behind Peter, his conscience-stricken friend.

The rest of the disciples are grouped about the three seated at the table, some watching with sympathetic faces the suffering Peter, their natural leader and spokesman, while others with downcast eyes stand idly by, lost in thoughts too deep for words, or hushed in silent interceding prayer.

What that "Holy Saturday" meant to these bewildered disciples in mental anguish, deep-seated longing, and unspoken sorrow, only those who have loved much and lost can ever know.

The Master of Men had His Gethsemane in the Garden on the night of His betrayal and arrest, while the three who were most closely associated with Him slept. Now these, His "sheep without a shepherd," are having theirs. They have lost the Messiah Whom they thought death could never claim; their dream of a restored Kingdom of God on David's throne has crumbled into dust before their pain-racked eyes; nothing but utter dejection and anguish of body, mind, and soul remains. The One Whom they had called the Messiah, and Who was to redeem Israel from the bondage of Rome is no more. The Master they had loved and with Whom they had lived in such happy, helpful associations for three years is *dead*; and with his death, *hope*, also, *died* in their hearts.

The good news so arrestingly sung by the poet in this striking contrast—

> But Calvary and Easter Day,
> Earth's blackest day, and whitest day,
> Were just three days apart—

had not yet become a reality to them. There was, as yet, no "whitest day";

instead, in the blackness of seemingly endless hours, they suffered on, unconscious of the passing of time.

This painting might well be called "The Death of Hope," because it pictures in all its stark tragedy the first stanza only of these challenging verses, called "Hope," from the pen of an unknown poet:

> He died!
> And with Him perished all that men hold dear;
> Hope lay beside Him in the sepulcher,
> Love grew corse cold, and all things beautiful beside,
>   Died, when He died!
>
> He rose!
> And with Him hope arose, and life and light.
> Men said, "Not Christ, but Death, died yesternight."
> And joy and truth and all things virtuous
>   Rose when He rose.

✛

BARABBAS

> By what strange whimsies is a man's fate swayed—
> I free to go, while He goes to His cross!
> I know His life; no evil has He done,
> For many a day in towns of Galilee,
> Have I stood in that crowd that swarmed Him round
> While His fingers healed the leper with their touch;
> Or at His word the devils fled away.
> And men know my life, all my evil fame—
> Now I stand free while He goes there to die!
> What was there to this Man that Annas feared,
> And that dull Roman with his oily face?
> He would be king? Nay, rather He would not!
> Such men as He would never bind with crowns
> And all the stiff seclusion of a throne
> Their right to mix with men. Some deeper thought
> Lay in that false priest's brain. Could it have been
> He feared the words He spake about High God,
> About men grown to stature of God's sons,
> One brotherhood that banished self from earth?
> No priest could gull a race that held such thoughts,
> Nor was there place for Pilate in such plan,
> Nor for Barabbas! No wonder Annas feared
> A world he could not mold for his own gain.
> And does He think to end Him with a cross?
>   —*William E. Brooks*

"Whom will ye that I release unto you?
Barabbas, or Jesus who is called Christ?"

THE MARTYR

And all the while they mocked Him and reviled,
And heaped upon Him words of infamy,
He stood serenely there, and only smiled
In pity at the blind intensity
Of hate; for well He knew that Love alone
Can cure the ills of men—of nations, too—
Though unregenerate mobs their prophets stone,
And crucify the gentle Christ anew.
So He but smiled, and drained with quiet grace
The bitter cup for lips too eloquent,
And dauntless, took the soul-degrading place
Designed for thieves—this Prophet heaven-sent!
And when the throng at length had hushed its cry,
Another cross loomed dark against the sky.

—*Natalie Flohr*

SIMON THE CYRENIAN SPEAKS

He never spoke a word to me,
    And yet He called my name,
He never gave a sign to me,
    And yet I knew and came.

At first I said, "I will not bear
    His cross upon my back;
He only seeks to place it there
    Because my skin is black."

But He was dying for a dream,
    And He was very weak,
And in His eyes there shone a gleam
    Men journey far to seek.

It was Himself my pity bought;
    I did for Christ alone
What all of Rome could not have wrought
    With bruise of lash or stone.

—*Countee Cullen*

CALVARY

I walked alone to my Calvary
And no man carried the cross for me:
Carried the cross? Nay, no man knew
The fearful load I bent unto;
But each as we met upon the way
Spake me fair of the journey I walked that day.

I came alone to my Calvary,
And high was the hill and bleak to see;
But, lo! as I scaled the flinty side,
A thousand went up to be crucified—
A thousand kept the way with me,
But never a cross my eyes could see.

—Author Unknown

I AM THE CROSS

I am the Cross of Christ!
I bore His body there
   On Calvary's lonely hill.
Till then I was a humble tree
   That grew beside a tiny rill;
I think till then
I was a thing despised of men!

I am the Cross of Christ!
I grew, sapped the water
   From that little stream;
I loved the sun and heard the winds
   And dreamed my humble dream.
And thus it was until
They took me to that pain-hurt hill.

I am the Cross of Christ!
I felt His limbs along
   My common, broken bark;
I saw His utter loneliness,
   The lightning and the dark;
And up till then
I thought He was as other men.

I am the Cross of Christ!
I crown the pointed spires
   Of man-made temples near and far.
I watch the rising and the setting
   Of each far-flung star;
All through the night I am
Eternal Sentinel for Man!

I am the Cross of Christ!
On my form they used to crucify
  The outcasts of the earth;
But on that lonely hill that day
  My kind received, in blood, new birth,
And ever till this day
A weary world bows at my feet to pray!

I am the Cross of Christ!
They say I tower "o'er the wrecks
  Of time." I only know
That once a humble tree
  This was not so. But this
I know—since then
I have become a symbol for the hopes of men.

—*William L. Stidger*

THERE IS A MAN ON THE CROSS

Whenever there is silence around me
By day or by night—
I am startled by a cry.
It came down from the cross—
The first time I heard it.
I went out and searched—
And found a Man in the throes of crucifixion,
And I said, "I will take You down,"
And I tried to take the nails out of His feet.
But He said, "Let them be
For I cannot be taken down
Until every man, every woman, and every child
Come together to take Me down."
And I said, "But I cannot hear You cry.
What can I do?"
And He said, "Go about the world—
Tell everyone that you meet—
There is a Man on the cross
Waiting for them to take Him down."

—*Elizabeth Cheney*

THE CROSS WAS HIS OWN

They borrowed a bed to lay His head
  When Christ the Lord came down;
They borrowed the ass in the mountain pass
  For Him to ride to town;

But the crown that He wore and the cross that He bore
  Were His own—
  The cross was His own.

He borrowed the bread when the crowd He fed
  On the grassy mountain-side,
He borrowed the dish of broken fish
  With which He satisfied.
But the crown that He wore and the cross that He bore
  Were His own—
  The cross was His own.

He borrowed a ship in which to sit
  To teach the multitude;
He borrowed a nest in which to rest—
  He had never a home so rude;
But the crown that He wore and the cross that He bore
  Were His own—
  The cross was His own.

He borrowed a room on His way to the tomb
  The Passover Lamb to eat;
They borrowed a cave for Him a grave,
  They borrowed a winding-sheet.
But the crown that He wore and the cross that He bore
  Were His own—
  The cross was His own.

—Author Unknown

A GUARD OF THE SEPULCHER

I was a Roman soldier in my prime;
Now age is on me and the yoke of time.
I saw your Risen Christ, for I am he
Who reached the hyssop to Him on the tree;
And I am one of two who watched beside
The Sepulcher of Him we crucified.

All that last night I watched with sleepless eyes;
Great stars arose and crept across the skies.
The world was all too still for mortal rest,
For pitiless thoughts were busy in the breast.
The night was long, so long, it seemed at last
I had grown old and a long life had passed.
Far off, the hills of Moab, touched with light,
Were swimming in the hollow of the night.
I saw Jerusalem all wrapped in cloud
Stretched like a dead thing folded in a shroud.

Once in the pauses of our whispered talk
I heard a something on the garden walk.
Perhaps it was a crisp leaf lightly stirred—
Perhaps the dream-note of a waking bird.
Then suddenly an angel burning white
Came down with earthquake in the breaking light,
And rolled the great stone from the Sepulcher,
And, lo, the Dead had risen with the day:
The Man of Mystery had gone His way.

Years have I wandered, carrying my shame;
Now let the tooth of time eat out my name.
For we, who all the wonder might have told,
Kept silence, for our mouths were stopt with gold.

—*Edwin Markham*

FOR ME

Under an Eastern sky,
Amid a rabble cry,
A Man went forth to die
   For me!

Thorn-crowned His blessed head,
Blood-stained His every tread,
Cross-laden on He sped,
   For me!

Pierced through His hands and feet,
Three hours o'er Him did beat
Fierce rays of noontide heat,
   For me!

Thus wert Thou made all mine.
Lord make me wholly thine,
Give grace and strength divine
   To me!

In thought and word and deed,
Thy will to do; oh! lead my feet
E'en though they bleed
   To Thee.

—*Author Unknown*

CRUCIFY!

Christ is walking through the streets,
Looking in each face He meets,
  Tenderly;
Not alone in church He stands,
Where suppliants kneel with folded hands;
Not alone in closet where,
He lifts the weight of human care;
But in the busy walks of life,
Amid the tumult and the strife,
Walks He with His bleeding feet,
Walks He where the people meet;
But they scorn Him, pass Him by,
And in their hearts they madly cry,
  "Crucify!"

Christ is walking through the shops;
By each workman meekly stops,
  Tenderly.
He would lift the heavy load.
He would clear the thorny road,
Smooth the wrinkles from each brow,
Wounds would heal and none allow.
Walks He with His bleeding feet,
Walks He where the people meet;
But they scorn Him, pass Him by,
And in their hearts they madly cry,
  "Crucify!"

Christ is walking through the slums;
With His cross and thorns He comes,
  Painfully.
Kneeling in each den of shame,
Seeing things too vile to name,
Yet with heart filled full of love,
Bids each sinner look above.
Walks He with His bleeding feet;
Walks He where the people meet;
But they scorn Him, pass Him by,
And in their hearts they madly cry
  "Crucify!"

Christ is walking everywhere,
With his face, deep scarred with care,
  Patiently;
But the people lift their eyes
Upward yonder toward the skies,
Knowing not that near them stands
Christ, the Lord, with piercèd hands,
Beckoning them toward His breast,
Where alone they may find rest.
Walks He with His bleeding feet,
Walks He where the people meet;
But they scorn Him, pass Him by,
And in their hearts they madly cry,
  "Crucify!"

—*William Reed Dunbar*

AND CHRIST IS CRUCIFIED ANEW

Not only once, and long ago,
  There on Golgotha's rugged side,
  Has Christ, the Lord been crucified
Because He loved a lost world so.
But hourly souls, sin-satisfied,
  Mock His great love, flout His commands,
  And drive nails deep into His hands,
And thrust the spear within His side.

—*John Richard Moreland*

HIS HANDS

The hands of Christ
  Seem very frail,
For they were broken
  By a nail.

But only they
  Reach heaven at last
Whom these frail, broken
  Hands hold fast.

—*John Richard Moreland*

THE EARTH WORSHIPED

A crown of thorns men gave to Christ,
  Who should have worn the bay,
The wreath lay gently on His brow
  And turned its points away.

"If thou be God," men mocking said,
  "Then show to us a sign."
They did not know the vinegar
  Changed at His lips to wine.

The very earth's foundations shook,
  High heaven veiled its face;
Within a tomb sealed with a stone
  Men made the Lord a place.

The stone rolled outward at His word,
  The linen cloths untwined,
Earth had more reverence than men
  For Him who saved mankind!

—Catherine Cate Coblentz

REVEALMENT

They planned for Christ a cruel death;
  Steel pierced His hands and feet and side;
They mocked His last expiring breath,
  And thought their hate was satisfied.

They wagged their heads and said, "Lo, He
  Would crush our temple and in three days
Restore its beauty. Come and see
  This boaster gone death's quiet ways."

They did not know that on that hill
  Eternal love was satisfied;
That Christ, who hung there, triumphed still.
  . . . And only cruel death had died!

—John Richard Moreland

CHRIST AND THE CEDAR TREE

YEARS ago in a forest near the city of the Great King, there lived a tiny cedar tree. The great cedars as they towered above loved that little cedar tree, and they whispered, "Come up higher! Come up higher!" And the little cedar sank its roots into the moist soil, it lifted up its head, it shot out its branches and it grew, and grew, and grew.

One night that little cedar saw a strange light in the sky, and it heard strange music the like of which no cedar tree had ever heard before; and it said to the tall trees that towered above, "What is the light and what is the music?" And the great cedars whispered back "that the angels of God on a distant hillside were talking to the shepherds of men; and that they were singing a song, and that it was all about a Child—a Child that was to be born near the city of the Great King."

And the little cedar wished it might see the angels of God as they talked to the shepherds of men; and again it sank its roots into the moist soil; it lifted up its head; it shot out its branches, and it grew until of all the young saplings, it became the pride and glory of the forest.

Years passed, and one day the Master of Men, now grown to manhood, came to that forest; and when He saw that young cedar tree, so straight, so strong and fine, He went up to it. He put His hands on its trunk; He touched its leaves; and immediately that young cedar felt the thrill of a strange life. And again it sank its roots into the soil; it lifted up its head; it shot out its branches and it grew until it towered among the mighty cedars of the forest.

Often after that the Master of Men came to that forest. Sometimes He sat beneath that cedar tree and He talked to His disciples, and the cedar tree observed that the Master was beloved by all men.

But one night He came alone, and His face was lined with sorrow. He knelt beneath that cedar tree, and He lifted up His eyes to the heavens, and He said, "Oh, Father! if it be possible let this cup pass from me. Nevertheless, not my will but thine be done."

Thrice He prayed like that, and thrice He went away. Then some cruel men came with swords and spears, and they bound the Master of Men and dragged Him away into the city of the Great King.

The next morning some woodsmen came with axes. They chopped down that young cedar tree, they trimmed away its branches, and they dragged it off to a distant hillside. And that night, when the wind came down from the city of the Great King to rustle the waves of distant Galilee, it paused in the forest long enough to whisper that that day it had seen upraised on Calvary, *a cedar cross,* and on its outstretched branches was the body of the Master of Men.[3]

[3] Adapted from *A Little Book of Profitable Tales*, by Eugene Field. In *Teaching the Youth of the Church*, Maus. Published by Harper & Brothers, New York City. Used by permission.

JESUS, AS SEEN THROUGH THE EYES OF ZACCHÆUS

By

Kahlil Gibran

You believe in what you hear said. Believe in the unsaid, for the silence of men is nearer the truth than their words.

You ask if Jesus could have escaped His shameful death and saved His followers from persecution.

I answer: He could indeed have escaped had He chosen, but He did not seek safety nor was He mindful of protecting His flock from wolves of the night.

He knew His fate and the morrow of His constant lovers. He foretold and prophesied what should befall every one of us. He sought not His death; but He accepted death as a husbandman, shrouding his corn with earth, accepts the winter, and then awaits the spring and harvest; and as a builder lays the largest stone in the foundation.

We were men of Galilee and from the slopes of Lebanon. Our Master could have led us back to our country, to live with His youth in our gardens until old age should come and whisper us back into the years.

Was anything barring His path back to the temples of our villages where others were reading the prophets and then disclosing their hearts?

Could He not have said, "Now I go east with the west wind," and so saying dismiss us with a smile upon His lips?

Aye, He could have said: "Go back to your kin. The world is not ready for Me. I shall return a thousand years hence. Teach your children to await My return."

He could have done this had He so chosen.

But He knew that to build the temple invisible He must needs lay Himself the corner stone, and lay us around as little pebbles cemented close to Himself.

He knew that the sap of His sky-tree must rise from its roots, and He poured His blood upon its roots; and to Him it was not sacrifice, but rather gain.

DEATH IS A REVEALER. The death of Jesus revealed His life.

Had He escaped you and His enemies, you would have been the conquerors of the world. Therefore He did not escape.

Only He who desires all shall give all.

Aye, Jesus could have escaped His enemies and lived to old age. But He knew the passing of the seasons, and He would sing His song.

What man facing the armed world would not be conquered for the moment that he might overcome the ages?

And now you ask who, in very truth, slew Jesus, the Romans or the priests of Jerusalem?

Neither the Romans slew Him, nor the priests. The whole world stood to honor Him upon that hill.[4]

✠

"BY HIS STRIPES WE ARE HEALED"

It was as Caiaphas predicted. Herod, who lodged in the old palace near the Temple, was flattered because Pilate had remitted the case of Jesus to him, but he made no attempt at judgment. His curiosity was gratified at the sight of Jesus and he asked Him many questions, hoping to stir Him to work a miracle, but Jesus was silent before him. Then Herod grew flippant, and hearing from Pilate's clerk that Jesus claimed to be King of the Jews, he sent for a gorgeous old robe and dressed Jesus in it, mocking Him, and amid much laughter ordered the King to be sent back to Pilate.

So the centurion brought Jesus back to the Prætorium. The place was again packed with people and again Pilate came out to the portico. He called the priests and rulers and the leading men in the crowd to the front and there addressed them reasonably, saying,

"You brought this Man before me charged with misleading your people, but when I examined Him I found no ground for the accusations brought against Him. Nor does Herod find Him to blame, for you see he has sent Him back to me. Jesus has done nothing deserving death. I will therefore give Him a slight punishment and release Him."

But the whole multitude burst into a shout:

"Away with this Man! If you release any, release Barabbas."

Pilate called out:

"Barabbas is a robber, but what harm has Jesus done?"

The mob would not listen, but with one accord cried out: "Crucify Him! Crucify Him!"

Pilate could not make his voice heard above the uproar. He stood patient outwardly, but with an ugly look in his eyes, and when at last the noise died away he said, with a bitter sneer:

"Would you have me crucify your King?"

And at that the uproar burst out worse than before, men crying in fury: . . .

"We want no king but Cæsar!"

Then Pilate, enraged, ordered Jesus to be brought into the portico, and Jesus, dressed in Herod's old robe, with His face covered with dust and blood, came forward and stood before the people. He was very tired, for He had been on His feet for hours, and the sight of His white face nearly broke my heart.

[4] From *Jesus*, pp. 119-121. Published by Alfred A. Knopf, New York City. Used with special permission of the publishers.

Pilate looked at Him in pity and, turning with contempt to the mob, said, savagely, "Behold your King!"

There was a storm of outcries and the mob, furious at Pilate's contempt of them, raged and yelled: "Away with Him! He is not our King. Crucify Him! Crucify Him!"

The tumult was beyond control. The guards moved nearer Pilate, but he waved them back and spoke to an attendant, and the man went and quickly returned, bearing a silver bowl and a towel. At Pilate's command he held these up, and the mob, marvelling, fell into silence. Then Pilate, in sight of all the multitude, washed and dried his hands and throwing the towel aside stepped forward and said to the crowd:

"I am innocent of the blood of this just Man. See you to it!"

And with loud shouts of triumph the people replied:

"His blood be on us and on our children."

The judgment seat was brought out again, and taking his seat Pilate delivered Jesus unto death. The centurion, whose duty it was to see the prisoners crucified, asked for the accusation that was put over the heads of the crucified, and the clerk brought Pilate's tablets, and he wrote. The priests crowded round to see what he had written, and Pilate in scorn read to them his writing:

"Jesus of Nazareth, King of the Jews."

Caiaphas remonstrated, saying:

"There is no accusation. People will not understand. Do not write 'King of the Jews,' but, 'He said I am King of the Jews.'"

But Pilate refused, saying, bitterly, "What I have written I have written." Then he gave orders for Barabbas to be released, and went away, and the centurion and his soldiers took Jesus and led him away. . . .

I did not see Jesus scourged. I could not bear it. I went down the gangway and into the courts of the Temple. My soul was numb. There was no feeling left in me, though I saw each object with such distinctness that they live in my mind to this day. I was still in this palsy when I saw Judas come across the court. He did not seem real to me, but like a figure seen in a dream, but, nevertheless, I called out:

"Judas! Is that you?"

He came nearer and I, still in a dream, said: "What is it, Judas? You look like death."

At that Judas came close to me and cried out, bitterly:

"Oh, man, can you not see what has happened to me? A door has opened in me and I have seen my own soul. What is there left for me but death? I have told them, yea, in their very sanctuary, that I have sinned, but they do not care. It is not their business, they said. No one cares save Jesus, and I have sent Him to His death. He trusted me, even though He knew I should betray Him. He risked his life and trusted, and I did betray Him.

"That is why I must die. I thought He didn't care, but He cares more than I. I thought He had no passion, and I have seen Him in the midst of it. What is there left for me but death?" And he tore his garment from me and went out.

And then suddenly my palsy left me and I could feel again. These things were really happening. Jesus would soon be dead. Judas was about to die, too, but my one thought was to see Jesus. Rising, distracted, I ran back to the steep stairway to the Antonia, and passing through the groups of waiting people I climbed rapidly to the gateway and entered the courtyard.

The soldiers were bringing Jesus out from the inner yard. They had dressed Him in His own clothes again, and two of them held Him by the arms, supporting Him. The Titulus that hung round His neck said in large white letters, "Jesus of Nazareth, King of the Jews." . . .

Several rough men waited in a corner, and when the centurion called out, asking if there were mates of the prisoners present who would bear their crossbars, two of them came forward and took up the bars of Gesmas and Dysmas. But Jesus had no mate. So Jesus steadied Himself, holding by the hand of a soldier, and the heavy bar was laid on His back, where His tunic covered the marks of the scourging. . . .

The sun was hot, and the sweat poured down the face of Jesus and He swayed now and then under the weight of the cross. A depression had fallen on the soldiers and they marched in silence and as if reluctantly. When some paces up the street, beyond the stairway, Jesus stumbled and lurched heavily, and Dysmas called out, sharply, "He's not strong enough to carry it." He was not rebuked, but Longinus halted the column and himself adjusted the heavy bar so that it set more easily on the shoulders of Jesus. . . .

A few yards further on Jesus reeled and fell. "Can't you see he's done?" Dysmas cried out. Again no man rebuked him . . . and Longinus looked round for help.

Beside me stood a big Negro who carried two market baskets full of vegetables. His black face and his blood-streaked eyes shone with pity, and when Longinus called to him he stepped forward willingly, but remembering his baskets, he paused and looked hesitatingly at me. I took the baskets from him and he went and lifted up the cross-bar as if it were a toy, and the soldiers, steadying Jesus, went on through the narrow streets and out by the Damascus gate.

Three posts stood ready by the roadside on a hillock where all men could see. The prisoners were offered drugged wine, but Jesus would not take it. So stripping Him again to the loin-cloth, they laid Him on the ground and stretching out His arms, they bound them with rope to the cross-bar and nailed His hands to the wood. Afterwards they did the same to the two thieves. When this was done they threw the clothing of the prisoners into a heap and diced for it.

Simon stood beside me with his market baskets. The tears rolled down his black cheeks, and from time to time he wiped them off with the back of his hand.

But the mob that lingered, looking on the agony of the crucified, had no pity, and sneered at Jesus, saying: "He wanted to save others. Let him save Himself if He is the Son of God." . . .

Dysmas, who hung to the right, had turned his head so that he could see the face of Jesus, and he said, "Do not forget me when you come into your kingdom."

And Jesus, His face drawn with pain, answered:

"This very day when this pain is over, we shall be together again." And the man, comforted, set his lips to endure to the end. . . .

As the day drew on a certain awe seemed to fall upon the crowd, and the mockers went and few were left save friends of Jesus. . . . Mary the mother of Jesus, and Mary of Magdala and the other women came and stood close to the crosses and no man ordered them away. Jesus opened His eyes and saw His mother standing there, and John, who had come up behind the women. He called out the name of John, who came closer, and Jesus said:

"You will take care of her, John?" and John, choked with tears, put his arm round the shoulders of Mary.

Jesus said to His mother:

"He will be your son." His lips were parched and He spoke with difficulty. The women wept aloud, and Longinus, to comfort the women, said, "He will not last long."

A thunderstorm was blowing up from the mountains and the clouds hid the sun. The women stood praying for Jesus and for the thieves, and the centurion leaned on the pike and was silent. Simon and the soldiers were silent, too. For a long time we stayed thus.

Suddenly Jesus opened his eyes and gave a loud cry. The gladness in His voice startled all who heard, for it seemed a shout of victory.

"It is finished," he cried. "Father, into Thy hands I commit My spirit."

And with that cry He died.

The centurion, turning away in awe, gave the pike back to the soldier from whom he had borrowed it. He stood silent for a moment and then said:

"Truly, this Man was a Son of God."

And Simon, the Negro, with a sob gathered up his baskets and went back into the city, but the women, weeping bitterly, stayed by the cross.[5]

✛

THE OLD RUGGED CROSS

AMONG the great hymns of the Church that center in the theme of the cross, none, perhaps, has had more widespread popularity than "The Old Rugged Cross," which was written by the Reverend George Bennard, and for which copyright was secured in 1913. It has been sung literally thousands of times

[5] From *By an Unknown Disciple.* Copyright 1919. Published by Harper & Brothers, New York City. Reprinted with special permission of the author and publishers.

as a solo, a duet, or quartette, and as a congregational hymn by vast audiences of people in this and other lands, and never fails to make a lasting appeal to human hearts.

This is due, no doubt, to the simplicity with which it portrays the story of what happened on the cross—the shedding of the blood of God's only begotten Son for the sins of the world—as He hung suspended there. For crucifixion, in the time of Jesus, was the most cruel and disgraceful method of killing that human skill knew how to devise, and the cross itself associated with all that was vile and unholy. Today the cross is cherished wherever Christianity has gone, because it became through the suffering of the sinless Son of God, the emblem of humanity's redemption from sin and degradation.

William L. Stidger, the poet, expresses what happened to the cross on that day, when Jesus hung suspended there, in this wise:

> I am the Cross of Christ;
> They say I tower "o'er the wrecks
> Of time." I only know
> That once a humble tree,
> This was not so. But this
> I know—since then
> I have become a symbol for the hopes of men.

When you use this great hymn as a solo, duet, or quartette, put into the singing of it something of the changed significance the cross, since Jesus' death, has come to have in human lives.

> On a hill far away stood an old rugged cross,
> The emblem of suff'ring and shame,
> And I love that old cross where the dearest and best
> For a world of lost sinners was slain.

Chorus

> So I'll cherish the old rugged cross,
> Till my trophies at last I lay down;
> I will cling to the old rugged cross,
> And exchange it some day for a crown.

> Oh, that old rugged cross, so despised by the world,
> Has a wondrous attraction for me,
> For the dear Lamb of God left His glory above,
> To bear it to dark Calvary.

Chorus

> In the old rugged cross, stained with blood so divine,
> A wondrous beauty I see
> For 'twas on that old cross Jesus suffered and died,
> To pardon and sanctify me.

Chorus

To the old rugged cross I will ever be true,
Its shame and reproach gladly bear;
Then He'll call me some day to my home far away,
Where His glory forever I'll share.[6]

Chorus

—*George Bennard*

✢

ALONE

GOSPEL songs and hymns become significant in their appeal to the human heart because of the rich and beautiful associations that cluster about them in relation to human experience. This is preëminently true with respect to such gospel songs as "Alone," the words and music of which were composed by Ben H. Price.

During the summer of 1935 I was crossing the Atlantic Ocean on the steamship *Britannic* with a delegation of four hundred and fifty church leaders en route to the Second World Convention of the Churches of Christ which was to be held at Leicester, England. Among these leaders were many of the finest choir directors, soloists, and accompanists that the Church in its ministry of music has developed. Mrs. Alice Burgess Zeiring, of Pittsburgh, Pennsylvania, was among this group of musicians.

I have heard many beautiful voices, but I think that never before had I heard anyone else sing this great gospel song "Alone" with greater feeling and reverence than did Mrs. Zeiring in connection with the Sunday church service out there on the billowing waves of the mighty Atlantic.

Nor shall I ever forget the heart-searching quality of this great song, portraying, as it does, the suffering and "aloneness of Jesus" during those last tragic hours that preceded His death on the cross. Simply, Mrs. Zeiring sang this gospel song in her deep, low, melodious contralto voice; and it seemed to that host of convention delegates that never before had we appreciated the cost of Calvary, as we did after hearing her sing for us this tragedy of suffering.

Mrs. Zeiring was so gracious and generous in the use of her magnificent voice for the glory of God, that her ministry of music in behalf of the churches of Christ will long be remembered. She died suddenly in the midst of a revival meeting in Kentucky during the fall of 1935, so that never again, this side of the great white throne, shall we hear her voice. She sings instead with the choir invisible about the Heavenly Father's throne.

[6] Copyright 1913 by Reverend George Bennard. Words and music now owned by the Rodeheaver Company, Chicago, Ill. Used by permission.

It was alone the Saviour prayed
In dark Gethsemane;
Alone He drained the bitter cup
And suffered there for me.

Refrain

Alone, alone,
He bore it all alone;
He gave Himself to save His own,
He suffered, bled, and died alone, alone.

It was alone the Saviour stood
In Pilate's judgment-hall;
Alone the crown of thorns He wore,
Forsaken thus by all.

Refrain

Alone upon the cross He hung
That others He might save;
Forsaken then by God and man,
Alone, His life He gave.

Refrain

Can you reject such matchless love?
Can you His claim disown?
Come, give your all in gratitude,
Nor leave Him thus alone.[7]

Refrain

—*Ben H. Price*

✠

THERE IS A GREEN HILL FAR AWAY

STRANGE as it may seem, this hymn, universally loved and sung by adults, was written by an Irish poetess as she sat by the bedside of a sick, feverish child.

Mrs. Cecil Frances Alexander (then Miss Humphreys) was tremendously interested in the Oxford Movement, and profoundly influenced by John Keble's *Christian Year*. Her first volume of poetry, *Verses for Holy Seasons*, written when she was twenty-one, was for the *Christian Year* for children.

Two years later her *Hymns for Little Children* was published. It attempted to cover in hymn-stories the items a child was supposed to have learned in the Church of England up to the time of confirmation. "There Is a Green Hill Far Away" was one of the hymns in this volume intended to explain and in-

[7] From *New Songs for Service*. Copyright 1914 by Homer A. Rodeheaver. Published by the Rodeheaver Company, Chicago, Ill. Used by permission.

terpret the words of the Apostles' Creed which read: "Suffered under Pontius Pilate, was crucified, dead, and buried."

Cecil Frances Humphreys Alexander (1823-1895) lived her entire life in Ireland. Her father was a large landowner in northern Ireland and had served with distinction in the Royal Marines. She learned, early, to express her thoughts in verses, and often supplied poems for a small weekly periodical which circulated only in the family circle.

When she was twenty-five she married the Reverend William Alexander, rector of Tyrone, who some years later was made Bishop of Derry and Raphoe. Mrs. Alexander was an ideal minister's wife and helpmate not only on his trips into the lonely country parish, but also as mistress of the bishop's palace.

Strange to say, Mrs. Alexander did not like to hear her poetry praised. Again and again when her husband would read to her words of lofty, impassioned commendation from men of genius or rank, she would listen without remark and then look up with a frown upon her face.

One day, however, her husband read to her a little tract by an English Non-conformist minister, telling of a great change in the heart and life of a very worldly man after hearing "There Is a Green Hill Far Away" beautifully sung. It awakened feelings and yearnings that became the starting-point for a new and changed life. When her husband finished reading those words of commendation Mrs. Alexander almost sprang from her chair as she said, "Thank God! I do like to hear that."

The music to which this great hymn-poem is usually sung was composed by George C. Stebbins in 1878 and published in *Gospel Hymns* No. 3, the first of the series of *Gospel Hymns* which Mr. Stebbins and Mr. Sankey edited.

> There is a green hill far away,
>   Without a city wall,
> Where the dear Lord was crucified,
>   Who died to save us all.
> We may not know, we cannot tell
>   What pains He had to bear;
> But we believe it was for us
>   He hung and suffered there.
>
> ### Refrain
>
> Oh, dearly, dearly He has loved,
>   And we must love Him too,
> And trust in His redeeming blood,
>   And try His works to do.
>
> He died that we might be forgiven,
>   He died to make us good,
> That we might go at last to heaven,
>   Saved by His precious blood.

There was no other good enough
To pay the price of sin;
He only could unlock the gate
Of heaven, and let us in.

Refrain

—*Cecil Frances Alexander, 1848*

✢

IN THE CROSS OF CHRIST I GLORY

"In the Cross of Christ I Glory" would forever remain one of the truly great hymns of the church, even if nothing at all was known of its author. But when we remember that the words of this hymn were written by one of the most outstanding English statesmen of his day, they take on deeper significance.

Sir John Bowring (1792-1872) was born at Exeter, England. He became the editor of the *Westminster Review* when he was only thirty-three, and was twice a member of the British Parliament, during which time he made notable contributions to prison reform. He served his country in many notable capacities, among which were Commissioner to France, as Consul at Canton, Minister Plenipotentiary to China, and Governor of Hong Kong. He was knighted for his unusual service in 1854.

At sixteen years of age he could speak and write Spanish, Italian, Portuguese, French, and German. Throughout his long life he was a student of literature, and published two notable volumes on the literature of peoples of other tongues. His *Specimens of Russian Poets* and *Danish and Norwegian Literature* brought to him merited recognition. Of his writings Dr. Duffield says: "He seems to have touched the very nerve centers of language, and to have comprehended by supreme instinct the essence of the poet's thought."

In a career so rich and varied, Sir John Bowring must have seen much of evil; and yet through it all he kept his faith in the Christ of the cross and in the glory and supremacy of the Christian religion. He had unusual opportunity to study the religion, philosophy, and literature of many races and peoples, and yet through it all he recognized the permanent and transcendent value of the cross and its message to human hearts.

The tune to which this great hymn is usually sung, "Rathbun," was composed by Ithamar Conkey in 1847, while he was organist and choir director for the Central Baptist Church at Norwich, Connecticut.

In the cross of Christ I glory,
Towering o'er the wrecks of time;
All the light of sacred story
Gathers round its head sublime.

When the woes of life o'ertake me,
Hopes deceive, and fears annoy,
Never shall the cross forsake me;
Lo! it glows with peace and joy.

When the sun of bliss is beaming
Light and love upon my way,
From the cross the radiance streaming
Adds new luster to the day.

Bane and blessing, pain and pleasure,
By the cross are sanctified;
Peace is there that knows no measure,
Joys that through all time abide.

—John Bowring, 1825

✣

WHEN I SURVEY THE WONDROUS CROSS

"WHEN I Survey the Wondrous Cross" is an old hymn, yet one of the best loved among all those composed by the great English writer of hymns, Isaac Watts, who is often referred to as the father of English hymnody.

Speaking of his ambition in the writing of hymns, Mr. Watts once said: "It was not my design to exalt myself to the rank and glory of poets; but I was ambitious to be a servant to the churches, and a helper to the joy of the meanest Christian."

As we read the words of this great hymn, "When I Survey the Wondrous Cross," and note its simplicity, its artistic and logical completeness, its deep solemnity, its religious fervor and passion, we cannot but agree with Matthew Arnold, who considered it the greatest hymn in the English language.

Isaac Watts was perhaps the most prolific hymn-writer of his day; and during his lifetime he practically ruled the sanctuary of music in the English Church. His hymns, and his only, were sung; and for many years nothing else, except Watts' hymns were sung throughout the English-speaking world. Even to this day a very large number of hymns composed by this great English hymn-writer of the seventeenth century (1674-1748) are included in all church hymnals.

The tune to which "When I Survey the Wondrous Cross" is sung, "Hamburg," came to us from the famous Gregorian Chants which date back to the days of Gregory the Great (540-604), who brought to completed form the High Mass of the Roman Church. In 1824 Lowell Mason, then organist for the Independent Presbyterian Church at Savannah, Georgia, arranged the present tune for this great hymn from one of the much earlier Gregorian Chants.

When I survey the wondrous cross
  On which the Prince of Glory died,
My richest gain I count but loss,
  And pour contempt on all my pride.

Forbid it, Lord, that I should boast,
  Save in the death of Christ, my God;
All the vain things that charm me most,
  I sacrifice them to His blood.

See, from His head, His hands, His feet
  Sorrow and love flow mingled down;
Did e'er such love and sorrow meet,
  Or thorns compose so rich a crown?

Were the whole realm of nature mine,
  That were a present far too small;
Love so amazing, so divine,
  Demands my soul, my life, my all. Amen.

—*Isaac Watts, 1707*

✤

BENEATH THE CROSS OF JESUS

As a child, in her home in Melrose, Scotland, Elizabeth Cecelia Douglas Clephane was fond of poetry, and she, with a younger sister, often held what they termed "literary seances." Elizabeth was blessed with an unusual imagination, which inspired her to write thrilling, breath-taking stories with hair-breadth escapes. She was gentle and generous; and among the poor and suffering of her native Scotland home was often referred to as "The Sunbeam," doubtless because she spent all her income, beyond her meager needs, for charity.

Miss Clephane will long be remembered for two significant hymns which have found a permanent and abiding place in the field of Christian hymnody—"The Ninety and Nine"—which was made famous by Ira D. Sankey through his use of it in the Moody-Sankey revival meetings in Scotland, 1873-1874; and "Beneath the Cross of Jesus," which appeared only a year before Miss Clephane's death at the age of thirty-nine.

There is little doubt that this latter hymn was written in the midst of her own pain and suffering, yet it breathes a spirit of confident trust and assurance which will make it live always. All the hymns composed by Miss Clephane were published by William Arnot in a book titled *Breathing on the Border*, the Introduction to which explains the caption by saying: "Written on the very edge of this life, with the better land fully in view, they seem to us footsteps printed on the sands of time, where these sands touch the ocean of eternity.

These footsteps of one whom the Good Shepherd led through the wilderness into rest may contribute to comfort and direct succeeding pilgrims."

The tune, "St. Christopher," to which "Beneath the Cross of Jesus" is sung, was composed by Frederick Charles Maker in 1881. He spent his entire life, eighty-three years, in one city, Bristol, England; and during seventy-five of these years was a singer and organist.

> Beneath the cross of Jesus
>   I fain would take my stand,
> The shadow of a mighty rock
>   Within a weary land;
> A home within the wilderness,
>   A rest upon the way,
> From the burning of the noontide heat,
>   And the burden of the day.
>
> Upon the cross of Jesus
>   Mine eye at times can see
> The very dying form of One
>   Who suffered there for me;
> And from my smitten heart with tears
>   Two wonders I confess—
> The wonders of His glorious love
>   And my unworthiness.
>
> I take, O cross, thy shadow
>   For my abiding-place;
> I ask no other sunshine than
>   The sunshine of His face;
> Content to let the world go by,
>   To know no gain nor loss,
> My sinful self my only shame,
>   My glory all the cross. Amen.
>
> —*Elizabeth C. Clephane, 1868*

PART V

CHRIST ALIVE FOREVERMORE

CONTENTS

PART V   SECTION I

THE RESURRECTION

---+---

"He is not here; for he is risen."—MATTHEW 28:6

---+---

---- ✛ ----

THE RESURRECTION

"Now on the first *day* of the week cometh Mary Magdalene early, while it was yet dark, unto the tomb, and seeth the stone taken away from the tomb. She runneth therefore, and cometh to Simon Peter, and to the other disciple whom Jesus loved, and saith unto them, They have taken away the Lord out of the tomb, and we know not where they have laid him. Peter therefore went forth, and the other disciple, and they went toward the tomb. And they ran both together: and the other disciple outran Peter, and came first to the tomb; and stooping and looking in, he seeth the linen cloths lying; yet entered he not in. Simon Peter therefore also cometh, following him, and entered into the tomb; and he beholdeth the linen cloths lying, and the napkin, that was upon his head, not lying with the linen cloths, but rolled up in a place by itself. Then entered in therefore the other disciples also, who came first to the tomb, and he saw, and believed. For as yet they knew not the scripture, that he must rise again from the dead. So the disciples went away again unto their own home.

"But Mary was standing without the tomb weeping; so, as she wept, she stooped and looked into the tomb; and she beholdeth two angels in white sitting, one at the head, and one at the feet, where the body of Jesus had lain. And they say unto her, Woman, why weepest thou? She saith unto them, Because they have taken away my Lord, and I know not where they have laid him. When she had thus said, she turned herself back, and beholdeth Jesus standing, and knew not that it was Jesus. Jesus saith unto her, Woman, why weepest thou? whom seekest thou? She, supposing him to be the gardener, saith unto him, Sir, if thou hast borne him hence, tell me where thou hast laid him, and I will take him away. Jesus saith unto her, Mary. She turneth herself, and saith unto him in Hebrew, Rabboni, which is to say, Teacher. Jesus saith to her, Touch me not: for I am not yet ascended unto the Father: but go unto my brethren, and say to them, I ascend unto my Father and your Father, and my God and your God. Mary Magdalene cometh and telleth the disciples, I have seen the Lord; and *that* he had said these things unto her."—JOHN 20:1-18

HOLY WOMEN AT THE TOMB

By

Axel Hjalmar Ender

(Interpretation)

THERE is perhaps no more striking and beautiful picture of that first resurrection morn than that painted by Axel Hjalmar Ender, the Norwegian artist, under the title, "Holy Women at the Tomb."

Ender was born near Kristiania, Norway, in 1853. He studied at the art school in Kristiania, in the Stockholm Academy of Art, and at Munich. He spent some time in Paris, but lived mostly in Kristiania, near the place of his birth. This painting of the "Holy Women at the Tomb" forms the altar-piece of the little wooden church at Molde, Norway, and is regarded as one of the artist's most attractive conceptions.

Molde is a city of fishermen and lies almost under the Arctic Circle. Here in a little wooden church in which the fishermen and native villagers come to worship hangs this marvelous picture of the "holy women," who came early to the tomb on that first Easter morn.

The artist has portrayed the sepulcher as a great cave into which the two Marys and Salome have come to anoint the body of the dead Christ. To their great amazement, they find the grave empty and the body gone, while sitting on the edge of the table where their Master had lain they see an angel of the Lord clad in robes of dazzling white.

The color effects in this painting are unusually attractive. Against the dull black background of the empty tomb is the shining-robed, flaxen-haired Norwegian angel, with upraised arm and glistening wings. The woman nearest the angel has on an undergarment of light salmon with a woven over-robe of terra cotta. Mary, the Virgin, who occupies the center, wears a dark-blue garment with a straw-colored head-dress, while the other woman, just entering, has on a terra-cotta skirt with an upper garment of blue and a straw-colored head-dress.

The golden light of that first Easter dawn streams through the archlike entrance casting its brilliance not alone on the women, but to a heightened degree on the shimmering white-robed angel who sits on the edge of the long marble slab on which had lain the body of the dead Christ.

You can almost feel the emotions that struggle for expression in the hearts of these women who came early to the tomb that they might anoint with oil and spices the body of their beloved dead. The Magdalene, half-bold and half afraid, stands nearest the angel. Mary, the Virgin mother, presses forward in her astonishment, eager to hear the angelic messenger's words; while Salome, near the entrance of the cave, is still occupied with her sorrow and unaware of the angel's presence.

On the lips of this deathless angel is the immortal truth which has been singing its way down through the centuries since that first Easter morn, "He is not here, He is risen! Behold the place where they laid Him." And because He lives, we too, we too, shall live.

No wonder this Norwegian artist, Ender, chose the resurrection for his theme. Year after year the fishermen and villagers who live in and about Molde see the unconquered sun burst forth from the underground, after its long night of winter, and day after day mount the sky till in the light of its radiance the ice of winter dissolves from the fjords and the flowers spring up in glad resurrection. For Easter means to the Northland the world's rebirth; the heralding of their brief but joyous, brilliant summer harvest.

✤

PETER AND JOHN RUNNING TO THE TOMB

By

Eugene Burnand

(Interpretation)

THE two fundamental things that mattered to Eugene Burnand were his faith and his art. He was born in 1850 at Moudon, a small town in the Canton Vaud, Switzerland. His artistic tastes appeared early in life, but his father, a colonel in the Swiss Army, wanted him to direct his gifts toward architecture rather than toward painting. He took the degree of architecture at the Polytechnic in Zurich, but during these years of training, his desire to become a painter instead of an architect grew. As soon as he had completed his training as an architect, he began to study painting, first at Geneva and later in Paris, where he worked passionately for several years.

He married in 1878 the daughter of the famous engraver, Paul Girardet, and settled in Versailles. But his love of nature and his desire to keep in touch with the artistic world of his time conflicted, and he changed his residence frequently, living first in Paris, then in Switzerland, and later in Italy. He died suddenly in Paris on February 4, 1921, but not until he had become recognized as one of the really great contemporary artists of his day.

For him his faith and his art were life-giving powers, and the source of all his development, the inspiration of all his work. His greatest desire was that those who saw his pictures should attain a closer fellowship with the living God.

Burnand's "Peter and John Running to the Tomb" is the artist's conception of what happened in John 20:1-10, where John, speaking of himself, says, "that other disciple outran Peter." This fact seems to be the theme of Eugene Burnand's now famous painting. Both Peter and John are running at top speed

HOLY WOMEN AT THE TOMB—*ENDER*

to see if the news which Mary Magdalene had brought to them is accurate. The brilliant dawn of the resurrection morn is left behind as they fly with eager feet toward the Sun of Righteousness, Who, according to Mary Magdalene, has "risen from the tomb."

Notice how the artist has produced the illusion of motion. John's hair ripples backward as his body bends forward against the wind. The folds of his white robe accentuate this. That Peter is the older and is losing out in the race is evident. His longer locks flare in the wind, his cloak tosses behind him, and his mouth opens to make labored breathing easier, while his hand presses back a heart that is well-nigh bursting with anticipated joy and sorrow.

John has youth in his favor. His hands are clasped together in front of his bosom, not for the purpose of making breathing easier, but rather as if in a prayer of gratitude over the astounding joy of seeing Jesus alive once more. He seems not to be conscious of the movement of his limbs, his thoughts are projected far ahead, and even his eyes are fixed on the gate of the garden wall that surrounds the tomb where Jesus lay.

Blundering Peter sees the little lead between himself and John widen as John forges ahead to see a vision that may not stay for him. The ecstasy of expected bliss and the fear that his lungs and heart will not be equal to the task of continued running are evident in the strong, rugged face of Peter.

Notice how the artist pictures the old Latin meaning of the word *anticipation*—the present experience of a future event, the reaching out and grasping of that which is not yet here. It is evident that these two disciples are reaching out with their *thoughts*. John, with his eyes fixed on the goal, strains them that he may not lose sight even for one moment of the spot toward which they are fleeing. On the other hand, Peter is running by faith—grasping the substance of things hoped for as he presses on toward the goal. In Peter's face there is a look arising not from the strain of running, difficult as that is, but rather from a fear that the report may not be true; or in the event that it is, of his own unworthiness to meet the Master face to face, after his cowardly denial with oaths in the courtyard of Caiaphas. The lines in his rugged face express his yearning to embrace the feet of Jesus as he exclaims, "Lord, Thou knowest all things, Thou knowest that I love Thee," even if and when my actions belie my words. Both are running with swiftness the race set before them as they envision a risen Christ.

Dr. Harold Frances Branch, in *Religious Picture Sermons*, says of this incident: "You ask me the secret of Peter's boldness as he preached on Pentecost. It is to be found in this wonderful moment when his soul awoke and stretched itself in its power and might. When he began to realize, for the first time, that this Saviour with whom he has companied was the mighty Son of God in very truth, the conqueror of death, who had stepped out triumphant from the sepulcher. Here is the emergence of power. Peter's soul is awakening. His ardor, his eloquence, his steadfast faith, were being born in that swift race to the tomb. He begins now, for the first time, really to understand the significance of his own declaration of faith in Christ, when he said, 'Thou art the Christ, the Son of the living God.' He begins to realize what kind of Master it was he had denied. . . .

"The greatest truths of life—love, honor, faith, purity, sacrifice—cannot be diagramed, they must be *experienced*! The pages of history have been made bright by the lives of those who have been transformed. All down the ages it has been men and women who have been touched, as these men were touched, who have lifted this old world nearer to Christ. They caught a vision, and followed it on steadfastly to the end, foregoing the things that other men counted dear, driving straight to a great self-sacrificing goal, spending themselves in service, proving themselves in love, wrapped around by the glory of a great ideal, driven on by the impulse of an irresistible urge, counting every day not a field to be sped over, but a garden to be cultivated in service for the King—such men it is who have blessed the world and lifted it. . . .

"The story is told of a woman who went to see Mr. Moody and to hear him preach. She was much interested in the psychology of the situation and wanted to study the man. Coming from the service she was asked what she thought of Mr. Moody. Looking up in surprise, she said, 'I forgot him in what he said. I went, intending to study him, but became so interested in his message that I forgot to study him. I lost Moody, but I found God.' "

That is what is happening to Peter and John as they race toward the empty tomb on that first Easter morning; they are losing their interest in the mere emptiness of the tomb, which Mary Magdalene had so tragically proclaimed, and running with expectancy to find a Risen Christ, who is indeed "the Son of the Living God." The eagerness of that *expectancy* is accentuated in every line of face and body.

Eugene Burnand was rewarded by having the state purchase two of his religious subjects for the Luxembourg Museum in Paris, the "Disciples at Emmaus" and "Peter and John Running to the Tomb." Both of these pictures illustrate the artist's genuine religious feeling, and his honest effort to humanize and make real the characters of these friends of Jesus'.[1]

✜

THE MORNING OF THE RESURRECTION

By

Edward Burne-Jones

(Interpretation)

OF ALL the great English artists of the last century, Burne-Jones was perhaps the most noted for his imagery and symbolism. He was born in Birmingham, England, in 1833. His mother died at his birth, and no child ever more literally hungered and thirsted after beauty than did this lonely half-orphan in his

[1] From *Religious Picture Sermons*. Published by H. M. Shelley, Philadelphia, Pa. Used with permission of the publishers.

PETER AND JOHN RUNNING TO THE TOMB—BURNAND

THE MORNING OF THE RESURRECTION—BURNE-JONES

dreary home in the grimy streets of Birmingham, one of England's oldest industrial cities.

He never saw a good picture until he was twenty-three years old. In 1855 he saw two pictures painted by Rossetti that set his heart aflame and made him determine to be an artist. He left Oxford University without a degree and went to London to study art under Rossetti. Later he was joined by William Morris and soon after these two formed the Wm. Morris Company for the production of stained glass, tapestries, etc. Many of the most exquisite stained glass windows in English churches, as well as some in America, are the work of his hands.

He made several trips to Italy for the purpose of studying art. In 1881 Oxford University gave him a degree, and in 1890 he received the decoration of Legion of Honor. Queen Victoria made him a baronet in 1894. He died in 1898.

His artistic creed, as stated in a letter written to a friend, reads as follows: "I mean by a picture a beautiful, romantic dream of something that never was, never will be, on a light better than any light that ever shone, in a land no one can define or remember—only desire." And as one looks at this painting by Burne-Jones one feels something of this intriguing beauty, mystery, and symbolism.

In "The Morning of the Resurrection" Burne-Jones is trying to express something of the mystery and awe that surrounded the solitary visit of Mary Magdalene back to the empty tomb of the Master, after that first hurried entrance of Peter and John following her tempestuous cry: "Our Lord is stolen from the tomb, and none to tell where He is borne away."

Mary, with her great cloak about her, has stolen back alone to this crude hollow in the rock, after the hurried departure of Peter and John. There she found two shining ones sitting "one at the head, the other at the foot of that stone table where the Lord had lain." In spite of them, and with eyes half-blinded from weeping, she entered the grotto and looked about her. These angelic messengers do not disturb her, not even by so much as the rustle of their great wings folded against the background of the empty sepulcher.

Suddenly another form falls across the threshold of the tomb's entrance. These angelic messengers seem almost to start as if to call Mary's attention from her sorrowing past to the reassuring present. Both angels raise a fold of their robes to their lips in token of their silent awe in the presence of One Whom they recognize to be above all powers and principalities. The one on the left raises his hand slightly and vaguely points, as Mary Magdalene turns a timid and startled gaze upon the face of this visitor who, at first, she imagines must be the keeper of the garden. Perhaps he has come to bid her to begone. With one hand she steadies herself against the low arch, while with the other she catches up her cloak, ready to flee at a moment's notice, if necessary.

The figure of the Presence seems to come nearer. For some strange reason she cannot take her eyes from His, as her heart falters between returning hope, fear, and courage. The Master stops and looks at her, and as His All-seeing eyes peer deeper and deeper into her inmost soul, her slumbering memory of that dear face begins to stir. Is she waking or dreaming? Is this the Master or just the garden's keeper? The moment is mystic and full of awe!

If it is the Master, why has He come? There can be but one answer to that question. He has come, answering the call of a great love that could not, would not, be comforted until she knew He was safe. This early-morning meeting, between the Master of Men and the woman last at the cross on that cruel crucifixion eve, and first at the tomb on His resurrection morn, is not a rebuff. It is, instead, the fulfillment of Mary's heart's desire, the assurance that He is alive and that she may continue to love Him world without end.

The vision that her tear-misted eyes behold will linger awhile longer, and as His deep-set eyes gaze into hers His lips will form her name, "Mary." The deepest joy of her overburdened heart will answer him with the cry, "Rabboni, Lord, my Lord, dear, dear Lord!" Then out of that grotto she will fly on the wings of the morning, bearing to his discouraged disciples and friends the good news that has since been ringing down the centuries: "I have seen the Lord! He is not dead! He is risen!"

The sun will rise, the angels vanish; the nearby city will awaken to its usual busy traffic; while along the dusty road a woman in white, her golden hair streaming behind her, runs, with the fleetness of a deer, along the hillside and outer walls of Jerusalem, bearing in her heart the conviction of a risen Christ, and a world transformed because "He is alive forevermore."

Something of all this Burne-Jones is trying to tell us as we gaze upon his painting of that first "Morning of the Resurrection."

✠

THE WALK TO EMMAUS

By

Eugene Girardet

(Interpretation)

EUGENE GIRARDET, the great Swiss painter, was born in Paris in 1853 of Swiss parentage. He studied under Gérôme, and became a famous painter of Biblical and Oriental scenes. His picture, "The Walk to Emmaus," was painted in 1904 and exhibited in the Paris Salon.

The incident of "The Walk to Emmaus" to which *two* only of the Gospels refer (Mark 16:12, 13, and Luke 24:13-35) has been a favorite with artists, but none, perhaps, has portrayed a more challenging picture of this event than Eugene Girardet.

It is still possible for pilgrims to walk from Jerusalem to Emmaus, for it is only threescore furlongs away; by foot it would be a journey of only about two and a half hours. One must follow the Jaffa road generally northwest for about fifty minutes and then break away from the carriage road and descend to the bottom of the valley below. The path from there winds

Photo by Braun et Cie. Courtesy E. S. Herrmann, New York City

through a narrow gorge, across terraces of rock on the slopes of which grow olive and pomegranate trees until it emerges on a lofty hill or plateau from which the Mediterranean Sea may be seen, shining in the sun. Near the junction of the ancient Roman roads, and on this direct route from the sea to Jerusalem, lies the ancient city of Emmaus toward which Cleopas and his friend, clothed in typical Syrian garb, are journeying as they converse earnestly with one another about the theme which is nearest to the heart of every disciple.

As they walk thus along this ancient pilgrim roadway, they are joined by a third person, who by the questions he asks, seems to indicate that he knows little of the tragic events that have so recently taken place in Jerusalem during the Passover.

In surprised wonder at his query: "What things?" Cleopas replies: "The things concerning Jesus, the Nazarene, who was a prophet mighty in deed and word before God and all the people; and how the chief priests and our rulers delivered Him up to be condemned to death and crucified. Moreover, certain women of our company amazed us, having been early at the tomb; and when they found not His body, they came, saying that they had also seen a vision of angels, who said that He was alive."

Much to their astonishment, this stranger that had joined them on the way began to talk eloquently and convincingly about Moses and the prophets, and interpreted to them all the Scriptures concerning the death and resurrection of Jesus.

It is just this portion of that incident that Girardet has so arrestingly portrayed in his "The Walk to Emmaus." Jesus walks a little behind the two men, who seem to be conversing between themselves rather than with Him. The shimmering white robe and somewhat vague outline of the Master may be the artist's way of suggesting that while they talked earnestly of these prophecies between themselves *vision* as to their hidden meaning was made clear by the shadowy spiritual Presence of this unseen traveler Who joined them along the way.

It is perhaps the artist's way of interpreting this incident in twentieth-century terms. He is trying to indicate that the appearance of Jesus was subjective rather than objective. Dr. Bailey speaking of Girardet's conception, says:

"Our eyes are usually holden to the true significance of events until some Providence or some prophet opens them for us. This is particularly true of our personal lives. We live mostly in the dark; we make our decisions, we suffer our defeats and failures, we move on to the next task as chance throws it in our way; we walk ofttimes through a land of thorns and briers, not knowing whither the trail issues. Then there falls a lightning flash of illumination, some simple happening that lights up the whole path we have been traveling, shows the reason of each detour and the lesson of each defeat; and we see how through it all God has been leading us by the hand. Sometimes it is a wise friend that points it out to us; sometimes it is a verse from the Good Book or a line from the poets that furnishes the Pisgah retrospect. But however and whenever it comes, our hearts burn within us as the panorama of life takes shape before our eyes, with its pathways running surely to their goals and the duties lying plain before our feet; and we know that it is good for us to be here. It is precisely this experience that Cleopas and his friend had. The darkness of the present dissolved in the light of a new insight; the tangled web of Scripture became a divine pattern; and the Kingdom, which they thought had vanished forever, now for the first time became possible of achievement because they had realized at last its true meaning. This is what we call inspiration; and whether or not we can visibly trace its source, it always comes from the Master of Life."[2]

✛

THE SUPPER AT EMMAUS

By

Rudolf Eichstaedt

(Interpretation)

AMONG all the contemporary artists of modern times who have attempted to paint the actual supper incident in the story of the walk to Emmaus, none have presented a more graphic and startling conception than that by Rudolf Eichstaedt, the German painter who was born in Berlin in 1856 and died in 1926.

The scene is the roof-top of an Oriental home overlooking the valley, the sea, and in the distance the faintly outlined rim of the setting sun, for the day was "far spent." At the left may be clearly seen the outlines of another Oriental home of remarkable beauty. A giant tree and a latticed grape-vine post balance the ends of this roof-top veranda, providing shade from the heat of the slowly setting sun. The outline of the outer wall of the house is clearly visible, while over it at the left end clusters of white clematis or wild roses appear, for it is spring.

Near the stool on which the shadowy form of the Master sits is the Oriental water-bottle and basin, used, no doubt, for bathing away the dust of the road from the sandaled feet of travelers, and over it a towel that would seem to suggest, at least, that it had been but recently used for that purpose with the guest-stranger in their midst.

The table is spread with a white cloth on which may be seen the plates and wineglasses containing the food and drink of this simple evening meal.

Unlike Eugene Girardet's painting of "The Walk to Emmaus," this Ger-

[2] From *The Gospel in Art*, pp. 405-406. Published by the Pilgrim Press, Boston, Mass. Used by permission of the author.

THE SUPPER AT EMMAUS—*EICHSTAEDT*

man artist has chosen to portray rather the supper scene of that same story. The stranger, Who had overtaken the two disciples on the way, has been constrained to "abide with us; for it is toward evening, and the day is now far spent." And He went in to abide with them that they might learn yet more of the hidden meaning of their Old Testament prophecies concerning the Son of Man.

Eichstaedt has undertaken to portray for us that portion of the story that has to do with the breaking of bread, which Luke tells in this wise: "And it came to pass, when he had sat down with them to meat, he took bread and blessed and breaking it gave to them. And their eyes were opened and they knew him; and he vanished out of their sight."

There was something in that reverent, beautiful custom which Jesus had taught His disciples of breaking and then blessing the bread and wine that revealed the personality of the Master to these two as nothing else could have done. How many times during those busy, happy years of fellowship with Him had they seen those same hands, at the end of a busy day of teaching and healing, break the bread and pour the wine, and then pause to ask the blessing of the Father upon their simple repast before He handed a portion of it to each of them.

Note how the older man's hands are clasped in startled adoration and prayer as he looks into the face of the Master which seems to be slowly dissolving into mist before his very eyes.

The younger man has fallen to his knees as with uplifted face and outstretched hands he gazes steadfastly at the face of his beloved Master, Who sits in misty dignity at the end of the table. Startled surprise, mingled with adoration, fear, and a desire to restrain, if possible, the form that is already slowly vanishing into mistiness is in the impulsive gesture of this younger man.

In a moment the beloved form of their Master will be no longer visible, and then they will say the one to the other, "Was not our heart burning within us, while He spake to us in the way, while He opened to us the Scriptures?"

And then with astounding joy they, like the women who came early to the tomb on that first Easter morning, will rise up and hurry back to Jerusalem to tell the other disciples that they, too, have seen the Master of Men *alive*, and "how he was made known to them in the breaking of bread."

The natural and the supernatural are here portrayed with remarkable beauty, skill, and artistry.

THE FIRST EASTER

Lonely in the house of John,
While others slept,
Sensing not cooling winds
Nor stars,
His mother wept—
Seeing alone
The wreathen thorns
About His head,
Hearing His words
Upon the cross,
Mourning Him dead.

Lonely in the house of John,
His mother lay,
Though birds cried
In the olive trees,
And all the east
Was gray.
Then—Light—
Light in the little room,
Wide arms,
An answering cry—
Light and His voice:
*"Be not afraid, O Mother,
It is I ——"*

—*Harry Lee*

CHRIST IS ARISEN

Christ is arisen.
  Joy to thee, mortal!
Out of His prison,
  Forth from its portal!
Christ is not sleeping,
  Seek Him no longer;
Strong was His keeping,
  Jesus was stronger.

Christ is arisen.
  Seek Him not here;
Lonely His prison,
  Empty His bier;
Vain His entombing,
  Spices and lawn,

Vain the perfuming,
Jesus is gone.

Christ is arisen.
Joy to thee, mortal!
Empty His prison,
Broken its portal!
Rising, He giveth
His shroud to the sod;
Risen, He liveth,
And liveth to God.

—*J. W. von Goethe*

CALVARY AND EASTER

A song of sunshine through the rain,
Of spring across the snow;
A balm to heal the hurts of pain,
A peace surpassing woe.
Lift up your heads, ye sorrowing ones,
And be ye glad of heart,
For Calvary and Easter Day
Were just three days apart!

With shudder of despair and loss
The world's deep heart is wrung,
As, lifted high upon His cross,
The Lord of Glory hung—
When rocks were rent, and ghostly forms
Stole forth in street and mart;
But Calvary and Easter Day,
Earth's blackest day, and whitest day,
Were just three days apart.

—*Author Unknown*

RESURGAM

It happened on an April day,
Bounded by skies so blue and still,
And olive trees all hushed and gray,
They led One up a skull-shaped hill
Followed by a crowd whose piercing cry
Was, "Crucify!"

It happened on an April morn,
  They nailed a Man upon a tree
Whose head was circled with sharp thorn,
  Lifted Him high that all might see
His agony, His heaving breath,
His awful death.

It happened on an April eve—
  The air was cut by one sharp cry
That wine nor gall could not relieve:
  "Eli . . . lama . . . Sabachthani!" . . .
Then lightning, thunder crack on crack,
The sun was black.

It happened on an April day
  They tombed a Man (the crowd had fled)
Sealed it; and set a watch that way
  To flout His words; to prove Him dead;
And show Himself He could not save
From the dark grave.

It happened on an April day. . . .
  A tremor shook the paling gloom,
A white flame tore the door away,
  Life came a victor from the tomb.
Love cannot die, nor truth betray. . . .
Christ rose upon an April day!

—John Richard Moreland

EASTER

Sing, soul of mine, this day of days,
  The Lord is risen.
Toward the sun-rising set thy face,
  The Lord is risen.
Behold He giveth strength and grace;
For darkness, light; for mourning, praise;
For sin, his holiness; for conflict, peace.

Arise, O soul, this Easter Day!
Forget the tomb of yesterday,
For thou from bondage art set free;
Thou sharest in His victory
And life eternal is for thee,
Because the Lord is risen.

—Author Unknown

MY EASTER WISH

May the glad dawn,
Of Easter morn
  Bring joy to thee.

May the calm eve
Of Easter leave
  A peace divine with thee.

May Easter night,
On thine heart write,
  O Christ, I live for Thee.

—Author Unknown

WHAT DOES EASTER MEAN TO YOU?

What does Easter mean to you?
Stately church with cushioned pew,
Where, Lenten season gone at last
And days of self-denial past,
Richly-clad, devoted throngs
Of worshipers unite in songs
Of praise in lily-scented air?
Is this what makes your Easter fair?

Does it mean the end of winter's reign,
Bright skies and welcome warmth again,
Singing of birds, budding of trees,
Sweet spring odors on the breeze
From daffodil and crocus bed
And balsam branches overhead?
Sad is the world and cold and gray
If this is all of Easter Day.

But if this blessed season brings,
A firmer faith in holy things;
Assurance of a living Lord;
A strengthening of the tender chord
Of love that binds us to the life to come
Where loved ones 'wait us in the heavenly home,
No pain or loss can e'er efface the bliss,
Dear friend of Easter, when it means all this.

—May Ricker Conard

"TELL THE DISCIPLES"

Into the tomb they took Him, sad of heart,
And rolled the stone, then turned aside apart
  To mourn each one the unfulfilled fair dream
To which their dead hopes could no life impart.

Back to the tomb they went at break of day.
The stone that sealed the tomb was rolled away!
  Frightened they looked, and heard the words of joy
"Fear not: for He is risen. Go your way.

"Tell the disciples." From the tomb they came,
Renewed in hope; with eyes alight, they bare
  Christ risen in their hearts, alive, not dead —
And, lo, He has been with them everywhere!

—*Author Unknown*

MY RISEN LORD

My risen Lord, I feel Thy strong protection;
I see Thee stand among the graves today;
"I am the Way, the Life, the Resurrection,"
  I hear Thee say.
And all the burdens I have carried sadly
Grow light as blossoms on an April day;
My cross becomes a staff, I journey gladly
  This Easter day.

—*Author Unknown*

IF EASTER BE NOT TRUE

If Easter be not true,
Then all the lilies low must lie;
The Flanders poppies fade and die;
The spring must lose her fairest bloom
For Christ were still within the tomb—
  If Easter be not true.

If Easter be not true,
Then faith must mount on broken wing;
Then hope no more immortal spring;
Then love must lose her mighty urge;
Life prove a phantom, death a dirge—
  If Easter be not true.

If Easter be not true.
'Twere foolishness the cross to bear;
He died in vain Who suffered there;
What matter though we laugh or cry,
Be good or evil, live or die,
If Easter be not true?

If Easter be not true—
But it is true, and Christ is risen!
And mortal spirit from its prison
Of sin and death with Him may rise!
Worth while the struggle, sure the prize,
Since Easter, aye, is true!

—*Henry H. Barstow*

✝

"HE IS NOT HERE! HE IS RISEN!"

The Testimony of the Women: First at the Empty Tomb
(Luke 23:55-56; 24:1-6, 9-11)

And the women, who had come with him out of Galilee, followed after, and beheld the tomb, and how his body was laid. And they returned, and prepared spices and ointment.

And on the sabbath they rested according to the commandment. But on the first day of the week, at early dawn, they came unto the tomb, bringing the spices which they had prepared. And they found the stone rolled away from the tomb.

And they entered in and found not the body of the Lord Jesus. And it came to pass, while they were perplexed thereabout, behold, two men stood by them in dazzling apparel: and as they were affrighted and bowed down their faces to the earth, they said unto them, Why seek ye the living among the dead? He is not here, but is risen.

And they returned from the tomb, and told all these things to the eleven, and to all the rest. Now they were Mary Magdalene, Joanna, and Mary, the *mother* of James; and the other women with them told these things to the apostles. And these words appeared in their sight as idle talk; and they disbelieved them.

Jesus Appears unto Two Disciples on the Walk to Emmaus
(Luke 24:13-21, 25-31, 33-35)

And behold, two of them were going that very day to a village named Emmaus, which is threescore furlongs from Jerusalem. And they communed with each other of all these things which had happened. And it came to pass, while they communed and questioned together, that Jesus himself drew near, and went with them. But their eyes were holden that they should not know him.

And he said unto them, What communications are these that ye have one with another, as ye walk? And they stood still, looking sad. And one of them, named Cleopas, answering said unto him, Dost thou alone sojourn in Jerusalem and not know the things which are come to pass there in these days?

And he said unto them, What things? And they said unto him, The things concerning Jesus the Nazarene, who was a prophet mighty in deed and word before God and all the people: and how the chief priests and our rulers delivered him up to be condemned to death, and crucified him. But we hoped that it was he who should redeem Israel.

And he said unto them, O foolish men, and slow of heart to believe in all that the prophets have spoken! Behooved it not the Christ to suffer these things, and to enter into his glory? And beginning from Moses and from all the prophets, he interpreted to them in all the scriptures the things concerning himself.

And they drew nigh unto the village, whither they were going: and he made as though he would go further. And they constrained him, saying, Abide with us; for it is toward evening, and the day is now far spent! And he went in to abide with them. And it came to pass, when he had sat down with them to meat, he took bread and blessed; and breaking *it* he gave to them. And their eyes were opened, and they knew him; and he vanished out of their sight.

And they rose up that very hour, and returned to Jerusalem, and found the eleven gathered together, and them that were with them, saying The Lord is risen indeed, and hath appeared to Simon. And they rehearsed the things that happened in the way, and how he was known of them in the breaking of the bread.

Jesus Appears to the Ten in the Upper Room
(JOHN 20:19-23)

When therefore it was evening, on that day, the first *day* of the week, and when the doors were shut where the disciples were, for fear of the Jews, Jesus came and stood in the midst, and said unto them, Peace *be* unto you. And when he had said this, he showed unto them his hands and his side. The disciples therefore were glad, when they saw the Lord.

Jesus therefore said to them again, Peace *be* unto you: as the Father hath sent me, even so send I you. And when he had said this, he breathed on them, and saith unto them, Receive ye the Holy Spirit: whose soever sins ye forgive, they are forgiven unto them; and whose soever sins ye retain, they are retained.

Jesus Appears unto Doubting Thomas
(JOHN 20:24-31)

But Thomas, one of the twelve, called Didymus, was not with them when Jesus came. The other disciples therefore said unto him, We have seen the Lord. But he said unto them, except I shall see in his hands the print of the nails, and put my finger into the print of the nails, and put my hand into his side, I will not believe.

And after eight days again his disciples were within, and Thomas was with them. Jesus cometh, the doors being shut, and stood in the midst and said, Peace *be* unto you. Then saith he to Thomas, Reach hither thy finger, and see my hands; and reach *hither* thy hand, and put it into my side: and be not faithless, but believing.

Thomas answered and said unto him, My Lord and my God. Jesus said unto him, Because thou hast seen me, thou hast believed: blessed *are* they that have not seen, and *yet* have believed.

Many other signs therefore did Jesus in the presence of the disciples, which are not written in this book: but these are written, that ye may believe that Jesus is the Christ, the Son of God; and that believing ye may have life in his name.

Jesus Appears to the Eleven on a Mountain in Galilee
(MATTHEW 28:16-20; MARK 16:19-20)

Then the eleven disciples went into Galilee, unto the mountain where Jesus had appointed them. And when they saw Him, they worshipped *him*; but some doubted.

And Jesus came to them and spake unto them, saying: All authority hath been given unto me in heaven and on earth. Go ye therefore, and make disciples of all the nations, baptizing them into the name of the Father and of the Son and of the Holy Spirit: teaching them to observe all things whatsoever I commanded you: and lo, I am with you always, even unto the end of the world.

So then the Lord Jesus, after he had spoken unto them, was received up into heaven, and sat down at the right hand of God. And they went forth, and preached everywhere, the Lord working with them, and confirming the word by signs that followed.

✛

THAT RESURRECTION MORN

By

Cynthia Pearl Maus

WHEN the darkness that followed the earthquake attending the death of Jesus had lifted from the land, the Nazarene was dead. "Strange," they said, "that He should so soon lose His mortal life." For among those who had watched His suffering there were some who were actually offended because His sensitive and exhausted frame could no longer support His torture. Even in death He robbed his tormentors of much of their frenzied satisfaction. Taking the quickest possible steps to make sure that He was really dead, they hurried to Pilate with their urgent request. "Give us a guard for the tomb," they said, "for this Galilean made strange statements that He would rise from the dead on the third day. So give us guards," they demanded, "that His friends may not steal away His body, thereby saving His reputation as a prophet, and maintaining His hold on the imagination of the people."

And Pilate, already disgusted and weary of the subject because of the chiding of his wife, granted their request; gave them guards, and ordered that His tomb be sealed with the imperial seal of Rome.

No sooner had His persecutors departed than Joseph of Arimathea, a prominent Jew who had always loved the Rabbi in silence, pushed his influential claims demanding the dead body of the Nazarene, and offered his own new tomb, which had never been occupied, as the burial-place. This eminent citizen achieved what His lowly disciples could not have accomplished.

With trembling fingers His chosen friends hurriedly drew the spikes out of his hands and feet, and with winding-sheets lowered His bruised and bleeding body to the ground. The tears of the woman who loved Him dashed upon his face as His head rested for a moment in the lap of His mother, while others of the more venturesome women lifted His bruised hands, that had healed and blessed but never harmed, to their lips. But His brow was so majestic in death that they could not intrude upon its now peaceful repose.

In the fast-fading light of the dying day they bore His body to the tomb with His beloved disciples as bearers and a few of the women following. Rudely they embalmed His body in such spices as could hastily be procured, and folding it into sweet, clean linen left it in the outer chamber of this new tomb because there was not time for the final interment.

Hurriedly they rolled the entry-stone into its place as the sun sank, and departed for their lonely and sad observance of the High Sabbath of Holy Week, just as the Roman guard supplied by Pilate came up to seal the tomb and begin their all-night vigil of this dead King of the Jews.

The watchers were brave men and accustomed to grave duties, but they were uncomfortable, for strange rumors about His majesty in suffering had already come to their ears. The intervening nights and day were long, there was no wind. They talked together concerning His hurried trial and crucifixion, while within the tomb, Jesus of Nazareth lay in state, awaiting the resurrection morn.

When the Sabbath night died away and early dawn began to pale the Eastern sky, the watchmen passed to and fro, as was their wont, coming together at the mouth of the sepulcher, where they stood guard. Suddenly the face of one of the watchers blanched in terror as he pointed with his spear and then fell. The stone that closed the tomb was moving!

The other guard sprang, with an oath, and struck at the stone with his sword, but it missed. The great disk continued to move in its groove and rolled slowly off to one side.

The moon was gone and the sun had not yet risen, yet the garden glowed with a strange, transcendent light as if aflame with a sky-born glory. The bolder of the guards turned faint, as had his mate, and dropped beside him, as a regal form clothed in glowing white emerged from the tomb into the garden that surrounded it, and disappeared in the misty light of that first Easter morn.

Later Mary, the Magdalene, came to the garden at Sunday's dawn. She had not slept, and she wondered why she could no longer weep. Somehow she thought of her miserable past without a pang. With wild joy she remembered what the Master had done for her. Other women had ministered unto Him, and loved him: let them continue to mourn! They had not suffered as she had. In that hour she felt as if she had outloved them all—as, indeed, she had outrun them all in her desire to come first to the garden of his tomb.

She crept up on tiptoe, as one does who hesitates to disturb a dear slumberer, but stopped abruptly. The guards were nowhere to be seen. The stone was rolled away from the mouth of the tomb, and the gapping sepulcher seemed open and empty. With her hands upon her heart, Mary gave one glance, then sped out of the garden and off to the lodgings of Peter and the other disciple whom Jesus loved, with her tragic message: "Our Lord is stolen from the tomb, and none to tell where he is borne away!"

Her breath was gone, and with it her courage also. She came back falteringly. She could not keep up with John and Peter, who ran on without noticing that she followed. When she reached the tomb they had already gone to share the tragic news of His disappearance with others who loved Him. Having no heart to go elsewhere, she loitered sadly about the deserted garden.

Meanwhile other women who had witnessed His tragic death came up more deliberately with their myrrh and spices, thinking to finish the burial preparations that their Sabbath law had interrupted, and to do for their Lord what should be done before it was too late. When they saw that the great stone had been rolled away, they put the myrrh carefully down on the ground and, stooping, crept into the open tomb. With shaking hands they reverently examined the grave-clothes, and the linen face-cloth folded so carefully by itself. "He is not here," they said. And they, too, hurried away to spread the sad news that His body had been stolen from the tomb.

Mary Magdalene, who had been weeping silently in the garden, was alone again. Wearily she approached the open sepulcher, and gathering her courage and strength she stooped down and looked into the tomb for herself. The marble slab, on which his body had lain in state, was bare. Beyond was the crypt in which they had meant to inter Him today. The morning sun streamed in. The sepulcher seemed empty! But was it! Look again! At the head and foot on that long white marble slab brilliant forms began to emerge, and she saw clearly through her tears the forms of two messengers clad in raiment of white.

Her tears ran into a sudden childlike smile as she said to them: "They have taken away my Lord, and I know not where they have laid him." Suddenly a shadow fell over her shoulder and entered into the tomb. It was the shadowy figure of a man. She thought it was the keeper of the burial garden and began to explain to Him how and why she was there.

Sobs racked her body now so that her words were hardly coherent or articulate and her eyes were blinded by tears she could not restrain. She did not recognize the Stranger while she tried to tell Him of her heart-breaking disappointment in finding the tomb empty, until He called her by her own name.

Then a cry of wild joy went up to the morning skies that arched the dome above the tomb—a cry of joy that has rung its radiant message down through the centuries:

"Rabboni; Lord! my Lord! dear, dear, Lord!"

She sprang toward him, crying and laughing, and her words fell from her in hysterical joy. "It is my dear Lord! *He is alive!*"

She fell at his feet and stretched up her arms to clasp Him, but he motioned her back, saying:

"Touch me not, for I have not yet ascended unto my Father and to your Father, unto my God and your God. But go yonder into Jerusalem, and tell my disciples that I go before you into Galilee, there shall ye see me, even as I have said. Mary! I am the Resurrection and the Life. He that believeth in me though he were dead, yet shall he live; and he that liveth and believeth in me shall never die!"

With unspeakable joy Mary Magdalene hurried away to bring her reassuring message to His disciples and to the world: "He is alive forevermore!"

✣

JOY COMETH IN THE MORNING

(As Told by Mary of Bethany)

"Weeping may endure for the night, but joy cometh in the morning."

THEY have buried Jesus and we are caring for the dear mother in our home in Bethany—in the room where Jesus often rested.

The disciples assembled this evening to close up their affairs. They looked at each other and spoke little, and in the silence the women wept.

"Weep on," said John; "it is all we can do. Hope is dead, but love lingers and hearts break. When Messiah comes what more could He do except to assert himself in the extremity?"

·   ·   ·   ·   ·

"I am going back home," said Peter, "back to my nets; we are nothing now. We shall not quarrel now about the chief offices. You and your brother may have them, John."

"It was a gorgeous dream while it lasted," exclaimed Thomas. "The awakening—well ——!"

They moved out into the night in ones and twos, and with eyes downcast passed through the streets like shadows and sought the seclusion of their rooms. Their ship had sunk; the waves and billows were sweeping over it; no courage in their hearts, no Master to save.

·   ·   ·   ·   ·

I tried to soothe the mother with stories about the beautiful things I had learned from Jesus. She wanted to know more about the precious pound of costly perfume I poured out on His feet, and I told her all that was in my heart.

"Did He say something about your doing it for His burial?" The words come faintly back to me, but how could they have any application to Him, I thought, and dismissed them from my mind.

"Yes, but I did not understand, either," I answered.

"I am so glad you did it while He was yet alive," she said. "Now let us try to adjust ourselves to a world with Him left out."

.   .   .   .   .

Mary Magdalene came running in this morning with the news that the body of Jesus had been stolen, the tomb was empty; but we kept it from the mother.

Peter and John were preparing to leave for their homes in Bethsaida, and when they heard it they ran to the tomb and found it true.

Peter and John have returned. Mary Magdalene has gone back to the tomb again.

.   .   .   .   .

Mary Magdalene has just burst into the room, crying:

"He is risen from the dead! I have seen Him. *He is the Messiah!* He is King!"

Kneeling by the mother's couch, she embraced and kissed her, exclaiming:

"You are the mother of the Messiah; He lives; they can kill Him no more, and of His Kingdom there shall be no end. Be of good courage; you will see Him—alive."

The mother put her arm around Mary Magdalene, saying:

"Poor child, thy love outruns thy reason. Lay down thy head upon my breast and be calm and sleep, lest thou go stark mad."

"No, no," she answered; "He lives; He is risen from the dead; I saw Him, I talked to Him. I was standing at the tomb, weeping, when He came up behind me. I knew there was somebody there, but thought it was the gardener. He spoke—just one word—my name—'Mary!' Could I ever forget the tone? And the cadence? It startled me. I turned and looked. There He stood—Jesus—risen from the dead. I know not what I did. He had to restrain me. When I came to myself I was prostrate at His feet, clinging to Him."

The mother stroked the hair of Mary Magdalene, saying, softly:

"Poor dear, He brought you up out of the depths and from that moment you have poured out the rich treasure of your life into His. Did your life go out with His? Rest now; time will heal. You and Mary of Bethany and I must live in each other's love and help each the other to adjust herself to a world with Him left out."

.   .   .   .   .

Strange stories are afloat about the disappearance of the body of Jesus. Rumors are that the disciples are blamed and are likely to be dealt with as their Master was. We are swayed by suspense, fear, and hope; but if Jesus has risen all will be well.

While the disciples were gathered together behind closed doors—and locked, for fear—Jesus appeared. We were terrified, supposing it to be a spirit.

"I am Jesus," he said. "A Spirit does not have nail marks and a spear-thrust as you see Me have. Look, feel for yourselves and doubt not."

We clung to each other in speechless awe, and bowed low and worshiped, hardly daring to believe, not understanding how it could be true.

Then the mother spoke,

"Truly, Son of God. We begin to understand. How much higher than ours the wisdom of God! His ways are past finding out. All is well.

"But, oh, we have lived an age since You were parted from us. Like lambs lost in the long, black night we cried for the Shepherd and the Shepherd was dead; and the little lambs huddled together and the howling of the wolves filled them with fear.

"But the Shepherd has come and the morning light, and with it life.

"Thou wilt never leave us more. We did not know You were to come into Your Kingdom through death. We looked for You to assert yourself in the extremity, and when You did not, but died instead—we—we—O Son of the Most High, I shudder yet! Our wisdom failed us. Teach us Thine."

. . . . .

"He vanished yesterday while we talked—vanished while the doors were locked—vanished with a thousand tremulous questions unanswered. We do not yet know what is coming; we just wait."

. . . . .

He appeared again today to some of the disciples and they asked Him if He was now going to establish His Kingdom; but He did not tell them. He told them instead to wait, that power was coming, and that they would do greater things than He had done.[3]

✛

"GOOD MORNING! CHRIST IS RISEN"

By

Dr. Raphael Harwood Miller

AND behold, Jesus met them, saying, "Good morning!" and they came and took hold of His feet and worshiped Him.

So the word was carried to the disciples, "The Lord is risen indeed." And that phrase became the password of the Fellowship of the Resurrection. Whenever Christians met one another the happy greeting was, "The Lord is risen." And the joyous answer came back, "He is risen indeed."

That was the identifying salutation and its appropriate response. It was

[3] From *His Mother, A Story of Our Lord*, by G. M. Anderson. Published by the Bethany Press, St. Louis, Mo. Used by special permission of the heirs and the publishers.

heard in the crowded streets of Corinth; in the midst of the many nationed throngs on the Temple hill at Jerusalem; among the merchants of Ephesus; from passing ships in the Mediterranean Sea; at the crossways of the desert; and among the servants of Cæsar's household.

"Good morning! Christ is risen."

That set men singing at their tasks; it gave meaning to daily living; it opened long vistas of exploration toward the truth; it brought courage to the suffering; it lightened heavy burdens; it sustained the martyr in his ordeal; it gave hope to the oppressed and made faith in spiritual purpose the answer to the unsolved mysteries of the universe.

The night after the crucifixion was the darkest night of the world. Death had held dominion over life until Christ came. The ancient world was haunted by the grave. Human thought and activity were never free from the specter of death's impending and awful finality. Life was lived in a tomb.

Intimations of immortality were but wandering fires that flared and sank to leave the darkness blacker yet. The death of Christ by itself only aggravated the tragedy and deepened the mystery. The most victorious Life the world has ever seen succumbed upon the cruel cross, and the grave enshrouded all His glowing deeds and bright promises.

Nothing could solve that riddle or redeem that tragedy but His resurrection.

Without Christ's resurrection life is a dream without substance, a progress without purpose, and a journey without destination. Before Christ's resurrection the thought of eternal life was considered too good to be true, but since the first Easter morning it is too good not to be true. We live in a world where what is good enough can be made true and where faith in the utmost grows from more to more.

"Good morning! Christ is risen."

Every fresh adventure of the human spirit; every new crusade against embattled wrong; every daring excursion across the frontiers of knowledge; every costly devotion to freedom's cause; every undaunted endeavor for a world of peace and good will; every tireless struggle for justice and equality; every heroic martyrdom for faith—all—all go forth under the cloudless resurrection morning whose sun shall stand still and whose light shall not fail until the work is done.

"Fear not. . . . I am the Living One; and I was dead, and behold, I am alive forevermore and I have the keys. . . . "

"I was dead." And when He died, the world died, with every human hope and every beautiful dream's fulfillment.

"I have the keys." He found His way through the darkest night that ever held the world in the black grip of horror, and He unlocked the tightest tomb ever sealed by human perversity and sin.

And He will find His way and ours through every night and out of every grave.

So we greet one another this Easter Day.

"Good morning! Christ is risen."

And the white-robed and joyous guests of God answer from heavenly places in Christ Jesus.

"He is risen indeed."[4]

✝

THE WALK TO EMMAUS

By

Elizabeth Stuart Phelps

IT WAS late afternoon of the first Easter, when two of the eleven, restless with sorrow, went out by the western gate of Jerusalem, for a country walk. They took the direction to a little place called Emmaus—a lovely village set over the hills in bloom and green. Life and light throbbed in the soft wind, in the gentle scenery. Thousands of birds were in the air. The soul of spring swayed by dreamily. But the hearts of the twain were as heavy as the clods of the grave. Their Lord was dead.

In the bewilderment of fresh bereavement, they talked drearily—of Him, of His great life, of His piteous death, of all that was precious and of all that was confusing to them in His history; of the failure of His purposes, of the ruin of their hopes and of His.

A Stranger joined them as they were walking—it seemed that He was one of the festive bands with which the suburbs of Jerusalem had been peopled the past week—and entered into their conversation. They thought Him a very ignorant man, though He had not that appearance, for He questioned them minutely about the life and death of their Rabbi. Was there a foreigner in Jerusalem who had not heard what had happened? They answered Him with a sort of surprised condescension, but they readily began to talk about their Lord; indeed, they could not speak of anything else. And as they strolled and talked, their feeling about the stranger underwent one of the swift transformations which simple minds experience in the presence of a superior. This was no ordinary tourist. This was a master of knowledge. He spoke of the Hebrew Messiah; of the meaning of ancient prophetic poetry; of the possibilities hidden in the scriptures of the race. He spoke of the recent events that had shaken Palestine—of the national hopes and of the national shame.

The two disciples felt deeply drawn to the stranger; their thoughts took a high turn; courage and faith swept back upon their despairing hearts like fire from heaven upon an abandoned altar. They clung so to the stranger that, when He would have left them and passed on up the country road, they could not, would not have it so. They begged Him, nay, they compelled Him, to accept their hospitality. So He indulged them, smiling, and went

[4] Minister, National City Christian Church, Washington, D. C. Used by permission of the author and *World Call*.

to supper with them in their simple house of entertainment. There it seemed the only right thing for Him to do to take the head of the table and serve; His hosts did not even wonder why. And it seemed to be wholly expected that He should ask the blessing of God upon the bread. Then it seemed not strange, in any way, when the two began slowly and quietly to understand who He was.

How did this recognition come about? Was it of the mind, or of the heart? Was it of the senses, or of the spirit? Had they been blinded or deafened? Had He changed, or was it they? The secrets of approach between the living and the dead were God's—were God's and *His*.

Like so much else that had been inexplicable, this, the utmost mystery, now yielded to His control. And they who loved and mourned a dead Christ, lifted their eyes and perceived that He was alive. . . .

Ah, the radiance! the rapture! The countenance that had been overstrained with suffering was blinding bright. His wan and wakeful eyes had taken on a look of rest which nothing could disturb again. His tormented body shone with such vigor that it seemed as if every nerve had forgotten that it had ever known a pang. His fine lips quivered—not with pain. When He smiled, it was as if the heart would break with joy to see Him. . . .

For forty days He whom Palestine had tortured and slain, trod her dust, elate and wonderful.

It pleased Him to reveal Himself on many occasions, and by the witness of many eyes and ears. It has been recorded that five hundred persons, at certain places and times, met with personal knowledge that the dead Nazarene lived again.[5]

✛

CHRIST THE LORD IS RISEN TODAY

In "Christ the Lord Is Risen Today" we have another of those grand, old Easter hymns of the Church composed by Charles Wesley in 1739; for Charles Wesley shares with David, the great psalmist of Israel, the honor of being among earth's noblest and most gifted writers of song.

It is another of those great hymns whose verses move to a triumphant climax; and should, therefore, always be sung in its entirety. The first verse rejoices in a risen Christ; the second verse in a living King; the third verse in the fact that the redeeming love of God has in Christ's resurrection accomplished its work; and the last verse stresses the joy and fellowship of Christians everywhere who exalt Christ above all else in their daily lives.

This great hymn is usually sung to a tune composed by J. Worgan in 1708, with the "Alleluia!" as a recurring refrain.

[5] From *The Story of Jesus Christ* by Phelps. Published by Houghton Mifflin Company, Boston, Mass. Used with special permission of the publishers.

Christ the Lord is risen today,
   Alleluia!
Sons of men and angels say
   Alleluia!
Raise your joys and triumphs high;
   Alleluia!
Sing, ye heavens, and earth reply,
   Alleluia!

Lives again our glorious King;
   Alleluia!
Where, O death, is now thy sting?
   Alleluia!
Dying once, He all doth save;
   Alleluia!
Where thy victory, O grave?
   Alleluia!

Love's redeeming work is done,
   Alleluia!
Fought the fight, the battle won;
   Alleluia!
Death in vain forbids Him rise;
   Alleluia!
Christ has opened Paradise.
   Alleluia!

Soar we now where Christ has led;
   Alleluia!
Following our exalted Head;
   Alleluia!
Made like Him, like Him we rise;
   Alleluia!
Ours the cross, the grave, the skies.
   Alleluia!

—Charles Wesley, 1739

✠

LIFT YOUR GLAD VOICES

No OTHER single occasion in the life of the Christ, save the birth of Jesus only, has been the inspiration of more joyous and beautiful music, both hymns and special numbers, than Easter, which commemorates the resurrection of our Lord from the dead.

For the most part all this Easter music is joyous and triumphant in character because of the new hope of victory over man's enemy, *death,* that Christ's resurrection brought into the hearts and lives of men everywhere.

Such a note of joy and gladness is to be found in this beautiful song, "Lift Your Glad Voices," the words of which were composed by Henry Ware, Jr. Each verse sings forth the glad note of triumphant joy which all followers of the lowly Nazarene find surging up in their hearts at each recurring Easter-time.

It is usually sung to the tune "Resurrection," composed by John Edgar Gould.

> Lift your voices in triumph on high,
>   For Jesus hath risen, and man shall not die;
> Vain were the terrors that gathered around Him,
>   And short the dominion of death and the grave.
>
> He burst the fetters of darkness that bound Him,
>   Resplendent in glory, to live and to save:
> Loud was the chorus of angels on high—
>   The Saviour hath risen, and man shall not die.
>
> Glory to God, in full anthems of joy;
>   The being He gave us death cannot destroy:
> Sad were the life we may part with tomorrow,
>   If tears were our birthright, and death were our end,
>
> But Jesus hath cheered the dark valley of sorrow,
>   And bade us, immortal, to Heaven ascend:
> Lift then your voices in triumph on high,
>   For Jesus hath risen, and man shall not die. Amen.
>   —*Henry Ware, Jr.*

✢

THE DAY OF RESURRECTION

"The Day of Resurrection" is an old, old hymn, whose authorship is attributed to John of Damascus of the eighth century. It was translated into English in 1862 by John M. Neale, and may be sung to either of two old tunes, "Lancashire" or "Rotterdam," both of which were composed in the last century, the first by Henry Smart in 1836 and the second by Berthold Tours in 1875.

In this great hymn the author describes the resurrection of Jesus from the dead as the "passover of gladness," and such, indeed, has it truly become in the life of the Church. For people who attend church at no other time of the year seem to be moved at Easter-time to be among the throngs who affirm their faith in God and in His living, triumphant Son, the Christ.

It helps us to grow in devotional fellowship with the saints of all the ages as we sing the words of this great hymn.

The day of resurrection,
  Earth, tell it out abroad;
The passover of gladness,
  The passover of God.
From death to life eternal,
  From this world to the sky,
Our Christ hath brought us over
  With hymns of victory.

Our hearts be pure from evil,
  That we may see aright
The Lord in rays eternal
  Of resurrection-light;
And, listening to His accents,
  May hear, so calm and plain,
His own, "All Hail!" and, hearing,
  May raise the victor-strain.

Now let the heavens be joyful,
  Let earth her song begin;
Let the round world keep triumph,
  And all that is therein;
Invisible and visible,
  Their notes let all things blend;
For Christ the Lord hath risen,
  Our joy that hath no end. Amen.

—John of Damascus

✠

CHRIST AROSE

"Christ Arose," although not among the older hymns of the Church, is distinctly challenging as an Easter hymn because of the contrast between the factual statements contained in the three brief verses and the note of victory in its affirmation refrain.

Both the words and music of this hymn were written by Robert Lowry, and its copyright bears the comparatively recent date of 1916.

Among the more recent Easter hymns of the Church, none has greater challenge for youth than this distinctly martial hymn of affirmation. You cannot sing the refrain, which follows with rapid tempo the slower movement of the verses, without feeling a surge of joy in your own heart over the fact that Jesus arose "triumphant o'er His foes," and that "He lives forever with His saints to reign."

Low in the grave he lay—
Jesus, my Savior!
Waiting the coming day—
Jesus my Lord!

Refrain

Up from the grave He arose,
With a mighty triumph o'er His foes;
He arose a Victor from the dark domain,
And He lives forever with His saints to reign.
He arose! He arose! Hallelujah! Christ arose! Amen.

Vainly they watch His bed—
Jesus, my Savior!
Vainly they heal the dead—
Jesus, my Lord!

Refrain

Death cannot keep his prey—
Jesus, my Savior!
He tore the bars away—
Jesus, my Lord![6]

—*Robert Lowry*

✚

WERE YOU THERE WHEN THEY CRUCIFIED MY LORD?

Not only did the Negro sing of his needs in these songs of the spirit (spirituals); but he sang the Bible stories, if not accurately, at least sincerely and heart-searchingly, as he knew them from the scattered and often inadequate Christian teaching that he had received at the hands of the white man.

The tragedy of Calvary and the triumph of Easter is dramatically portrayed with restraint and forcefulness in "Were You There?" This song is another example of the slave's response to the story of the Crucifixion. However, the unknown poet and musician does not stop with the horror and tragedy of Jesus' death on the cross; he sees beyond the grave the triumph of the Son of God over the cross, over death, and over the grave.

"Were you there when He rose from the dead?" and "Were you there when He ascended on high?" are expressions of the ageless and universal belief of the Negro in the immortality of human personality. For it is the slave's ability to get such a vivid mental picture that "causes him to tremble, tremble."

Associating this story of the suffering and death of Jesus with his own gives us this spiritual, which when sung with feeling, as the Negroes always sing

[6] Words and music copyright by Mary Runyon Lowry. Used by permission.

it, causes *us* to shudder and tremble. Its question-and-answer form makes it all the more poignantly personal.

Were you there when they crucified My Lord?
Were you there when they crucified My Lord?
Oh! sometimes it causes me to tremble, tremble, tremble.
Were you there when they crucified My Lord?

Were you there when they pierced Him in the side?
Were you there when they pierced Him in the side?
Oh! sometimes it causes me to tremble, tremble, tremble.
Were you there when they pierced Him in the side?

Were you there when the sun refused to shine?
Were you there when the sun refused to shine?
Oh! sometimes it causes me to tremble, tremble, tremble.
Were you there when the sun refused to shine?

Were you there when they laid Him in the tomb?
Were you there when they laid Him in the tomb?
Oh! sometimes it causes me to tremble, tremble, tremble.
Were you there when they laid Him in the tomb?

Were you there when He rose from the dead?
Were you there when He rose from the dead?
Oh! sometimes it causes me to tremble, tremble, tremble.
Were you there when He rose from the dead?

Were you there when He ascended on high?
Were you there when He ascended on high?
Oh! sometimes it causes me to tremble, tremble, tremble.
Were you there when He ascended on high?

—A Spiritual

CONTENTS

PART V   SECTION II

HIS ASCENSION

✠

"He parted from them, and was carried up into heaven."—LUKE 24:51

✠

HIS ASCENSION

"And he said unto them, These are my words which I spake unto you, while I was yet with you, that all things must needs be fulfilled, which are written in the law of Moses, and the prophets, and the psalms, concerning me. Then opened he their mind, that they might understand the scriptures: and he said unto them, Thus it is written, that the Christ should suffer, and rise again from the dead the third day; and that repentance and remission of sins should be preached in his name unto all the nations, beginning from Jerusalem. Ye are witnesses of these things. And behold, I send forth the promise of my Father upon you: but tarry ye in the city, until ye be clothed with power from on high.

"And he led them out until *they were* over against Bethany: and he lifted up his hands, and blessed them. And it came to pass, while he blessed them, he parted from them, and was carried up into heaven. And they worshipped him, and returned to Jerusalem with great joy: and were continually in the temple, blessing God."—LUKE 24:44-53

THE MISSION OF THE APOSTLES

By

Joseph Aubert

(Interpretation)

WE ARE indebted to Luke in his Gospel (24:50-53) and in Acts (1:1-11) for information as to what happened to Jesus and to the eleven disciples during the forty days following Christ's resurrection on that first Easter morn. We know that He was with His disciples frequently in various places and on many occasions, and that during these days He "opened their mind that they might understand the Scriptures." We know, also, that He bade them to tarry in Jerusalem following His ascension, until the power of the Holy Spirit should come upon them; after which they were to "go into all the world" and preach the good news of a risen Christ to men everywhere, who would live by faith and not alone by sight.

Joseph Aubert in his painting, "The Mission of the Apostles," has not attempted to emphasize the *ascension* as such, but rather a farewell scene on the shores of Galilee in which the Master gives them His farewell blessing, after charging them to continue steadfastly in prayer in Jerusalem as they there await the coming of His Holy Spirit, which is to continue to lead them into all truth.

We feel, as we look at this picture, that we can almost hear the Master say: "Behold, I send forth the promise of my Father upon you: but tarry ye in the city, until ye be clothed with power from on high." There is in the expression on the faces of these, His disciples, not only love and adoration, but *determination* to follow Him in faithful devotion, even unto death.

Note the out-stretched hand and foot of the one at the right. By both the expression on his face and the posture of his body he seems to be saying, "On this rock [faith in Jesus Christ] I shall build His Church, and the gates of Hades shall not prevail against it." The second on the right by his out-thrust foot and staff seems also to indicate that he will serve even until death for the Kingdom's sake. Peter, kneeling between the four on the right gazes steadfastly into the Master's uplifted face, as if to reaffirm his love and steadfast loyalty to the risen Christ forevermore. We feel that the "keys of the Kingdom" will be safe in his hands under the guiding influence of the Holy Spirit, which the Master is to send upon them with power not many days hence.

John the beloved, who is kneeling in the foreground with hands upraised in prayerful devotion, is, indeed, a far cry from the former "son of thunder" who would call down the wrath of God upon those who do not agree with him.

467

JOSEPH AUBERT
1899

THE MISSION OF THE APOSTLES — AUBERT

Photo by Braun et Cie. Courtesy E. S. Herrmann, New York City

THE ASCENSION—*BIERMANN*

There is no repetition of a gesture or expression; each of the eleven, in his own way, some through quiet meditative assent, others through prayerful devotion or aggressive gesture, are dedicating themselves to the cause for which Jesus lived and died—the building of God's Kingdom of Love into the life of a needy world—and in their inmost hearts they are pledging allegiance to this risen Christ, whose witnesses they are to be "both in Jerusalem, and in all Judæa and Samaria, and unto the uttermost part of the earth."

Following this, Christ's prayer of benediction upon them, His faithful eleven, He will lead them out until they are over against Bethany, which someone has picturesquely called "the home of His heart," and there while they stand gazing steadfastly at Him, He will be parted from them and carried away into heaven. And there, as Luke tells us, on the hillside near Bethany they will worship Him, and then return to Jerusalem to await with joy the coming of His Holy Spirit upon them. Throughout the days and nights that intervene they will be constantly seen in the Temple, praising God, through the risen Christ, to whom they have dedicated themselves in deathless devotion.

This more or less modern painting by the French artist, Joseph Aubert, who was born at Nantes, France, in 1840 and died in Neuilly in 1924, is unusually appealing, from the white-robed Christ whose hands are outstretched in blessing toward these, His faithful eleven, and the worshiping group in the near foreground of this rocky lakeside shore to the distant shore line of blue Galilee on which the Master had so often fellowshipped with them during His busy, active ministry. This picture is satisfying, for we like to feel that He left His disciples not a haggard, weeping, discouraged "sheep-without-a-shepherd" group; but with hearts aflame with love and eagerness to serve Him "even unto the uttermost ends of the earth."

✛

THE ASCENSION

By

Gottlieb Peter Biermann

It is difficult indeed to find a satisfactory picture of the ascension. Either there is too evident an effort on the part of the artist to make the event spectacular by over-emphasizing the supernatural, or there is too great an emphasis on the broken-hearted condition in which His followers are left when they see Jesus, the dearest of all their earthly friends departing from them to be seen no more on this earth, save with the eyes of the spirit.

Of all those that have attempted to portray the ascension, this one by the German artist, Gottlieb Peter Biermann, who was born in 1758 and died in 1844, is, to me, the most satisfying—not alone for the beauty of the form and face of the Master as He stands for a moment suspended in the clouds; but because of the significance in His downcast eyes and hands out-stretched in benediction upon the infant Church—that little group of disciples that witnessed, with yearning eyes, His home-going from the hills near Bethany.

For that little group of eleven men, with a few of the women who had followed Him in faithful service during His life on earth, really composed all there was of the embryonic Church. They were the only ones who belonged to it. It was an undiscerning Church that asked foolish questions: "Lord, wilt thou at this time restore again the kingdom of Israel?" (Acts 1:6). Nevertheless, it was to this infant Church that Jesus replied: "It is not for you to know the times and seasons which the Father hath put in His own power. But ye shall receive power after that the Holy Ghost has come upon you; and ye shall be witnesses unto Me both in Jerusalem, and in all Judæa and in Samaria and unto the uttermost part of the earth." And with these words, He lifted His hands in benediction as He parted from them. They were not to expect His reappearance, but to go on to Jerusalem and there await the coming of His Holy Spirit which was to guide them into all the fullness of truth.

Now and then we hear persons bemoaning the fact that Jesus is no longer visible on earth to human eyes. Yet when we think it through we know that when He was present in the flesh, He was bound as we are bound. If He was in Nazareth, He could not be at Bethany; and when He was in Galilee, He could not at the same time be in Jerusalem. Even after His resurrection He was limited, though not in so great a degree.

The gains of the ascension, after all, are tremendous, because since then His power is *universal*. He belongs now to all time and all ages. Jesus himself said (John 16:7): "If I do not go, the Comforter will not come; but if I go, I will send Him, who shall lead you into all truth." One has but to read E. Stanley Jones' book, *The Christ of the Indian Road,* to appreciate something of the marvelous influence of the Holy Spirit upon the hearts of the Indian natives. Dr. Jones says: "Nine years ago, Dr. John R. Mott was speaking in a fine hall in India to a non-Christian audience. In the midst of his address he used the name of Christ, and the audience hissed him. Nine years later we were in that same hall with one topic for six nights—'Jesus Christ and Him Crucified.' The audience increased every night until the last night they were standing around the doors and windows. I gave the invitation to those who would surrender themselves to Christ, leaving the question of baptism to their own inner convictions, to come and take the front seats. I felt at that time that if *one* would come I should be grateful, for William Carey had said if one of these high-castes should ever be converted, it would be as great a miracle as the raising of the dead. But that night between a hundred and a hundred and fifty came forward on that proposal."

Such scenes, that have been witnessed by missionaries of the cross in every land, could not have come to pass save through the influence of a universal Holy Spirit or Comforter, such as Jesus sent into the world on His return to His heavenly Father.

It is by the power of an ascended Christ that His Holy Spirit takes the word that is spoken, the song that is sung, the plans for Kingdom enterprises that are made, and makes them to come to pass somewhere in all the world for His Kingdom's sake. The Holy Spirit in all lands and under varying conditions and tremendous handicaps takes the frail human effort that we, His followers, make, and applies it directly and convincingly to the heart and conscience of individual hearers. These are the gains of an ascended Christ; these are the evidences of His Holy Spirit motivating the heart and lives of men and women in all lands.

All that may have transpired during that forty days of frequently personal appearances on the part of the Master of Men, following His resurrection, we can never know; but we do know that what He said and what He did opened the hearts of His followers to receive His revealed truth in a larger and fuller way than ever before. He became, not alone through His resurrection, but through these frequent intermittent visits and His final ascension to the right hand of the Father on High, not only a risen Saviour, but the Almighty, the all-Powerful Son of God, to whom their lives were dedicated in service throughout all time.

In his picture of "The Ascension" Gottlieb Peter Biermann has caught something of this all-powerful Christ in the act of ascending; but leaving behind Him as he goes a little band of men who were willing to "wait" for the promised "power from on high" with deathless devotion. The fact that we do not see the little group of followers on the hillside below, strengthens, rather than lessens, the picture's appeal. By leaving out a visible audience, the artist enables the ascending Christ to include among His followers on earth the faithful of all time, who live richly, from day to day, because of the power of the Holy Spirit in their lives.

✣

THE ASCENDING CHRIST

By

D. Mastroianni

(Interpretation)

AMONG the rich and beautiful portrayals of the life-story of the Son of God, none is more significant than the sixty-three scenes modeled in wax by the celebrated Italian sculptor, D. Mastroianni, which illustrate *The Life of Christ* by Reverend G. Robinson Lees. Two of these scenes are included in this anthology by special permission of Dodd, Mead & Company, the copyright owners.

Speaking of the ascended Christ, Reverend Lees says: "Those who hesitate to believe in the wonderful words of Jesus, who cannot reconcile their experience of life with His death and resurrection, stand face to face with the stupendous change He wrought in His disciples. From the depth of despair,

THE ASCENDING CHRIST—*MASTROIANNI*

when they saw Him die, they were roused to a pitch of enthusiasm which captured the world. This change occurred in a few weeks. Between the crucifixion and the first preaching of the great news of salvation—a gap of fifty days—something happened, a miracle so vast, a movement so vital, that it not only removed from these timorous and shrinking followers of Jesus the shadow of fear, but their characters were altered, and through them the whole history of the world changed.

"At His death the disciples . . . hid themselves behind closed doors for fear of the Jews. Fifty days later they stood in the midst of the multitudes who had witnessed the death of Jesus to proclaim the great fact of His resurrection. . . . The announcement of that fact ran like fire through the populace: a new light streamed into their minds, a new force moved their hearts, a new society, the Church, still existing, was begotten by the Spirit of God which came to reveal the truth of the life and death and resurrection of Jesus Christ, the Eternal Son of God. New life, new joy, the victory over sin and death, came through His triumph. Many people who had watched Jesus die believed all the disciples said about His resurrection.

"The Kingdom of God appeared in the hearts of men. It has never ceased to manifest itself wherever it has been proclaimed. Jesus is the King Eternal, as He is the Redeemer of mankind. And to those who find in Him their Saviour, accept him as their Lord, and look for His appearing, He vindicates His claim to be able to give them life forevermore."[1]

It was the result of this conviction in a risen, ascended Christ that caused John the beloved, years later, to write his book of Revelation to the seven churches in Asia. John the beloved disciple caught up in a vision wrote: "I heard a voice of much people in heaven saying, Alleluia" (Rev. 19:1). In his imagination John saw "a great multitude, which no man could number, out of every nation and of all tribes and peoples and tongues standing before the throne and before the Lamb, arrayed in white robes, with palms in their hands; and they cried with a great voice, saying, Salvation unto our God who sitteth on the throne, and unto the Lamb" (Rev. 7:9-10).

One of the elders, who with the angels was standing about the throne of God, answered John's unspoken inquiry as to who this multitude was, saying: "These are they that come out of great tribulation, and have washed their robes, and made them white in the blood of the Lamb" (Rev. 7:14).

It is just this incident of those who had "washed their robes in the blood of the Lamb," that Mastroianni has seen fit to portray, rising on the clouds with Jesus and the host of angels to their heavenly Father's throne on high, there to receive the reward of the faithful; and singing as they rise:

"Hallelujah; Salvation, and glory, and power, belong to our God: for true and righteous are his judgments. . . . Let us rejoice and be exceeding glad, and let us give the glory unto him; for the marriage of the Lamb is come,

[1] From *The Life of Christ*, Lees. Published by Dodd, Mead and Company, New York City. Used by permission of the publishers.

and his bride [the church redeemed] hath made herself ready" (Rev.
19:1-2, 7).

And as we study this masterpiece of the redeemed Church of the Living
God ascending with the Lamb to the Father on High, something of the
abounding joy which permeated the hearts of His faithful disciples in the
long ago is born anew in the lives of those who even unto this day follow
Him in faith and Christian devotion.

✠

THE ASCENSION

(The Testimony of Mary Magdalene)

In the gray dawn they left Jerusalem,
And I rose up to follow after them.
He led toward Bethany by the narrow bridge
Of Kedron, upward to the olive ridge.
Once on the camel path beyond the city,
He looked back, struck at heart with pain and pity—
Looked backward from the two lone cedar trees
On Olivet, alive to every breeze—
Looked in a rush of sudden tears, and then
Went steadily on, never to turn again.

Near the green quiets of a little wood
The Master halted silently and stood.
The figs were purpling, and a fledgling dove
Had fallen from a windy bough above,
And lay there crying feebly by a thorn,
Its little body bruisèd and forlorn.
He stepped aside a moment from the rest
And put it safely back into the nest.

Then mighty words did seem to rise in Him
And die away: even as white vapors swim
A moment on Mount Carmel's purple steep,
And then are blown back rainless to the deep.
And once He looked up with a little start:
Perhaps some loved name passed across His heart,
Some memory of a road in Galilee,
Or old familiar rock beside the Sea.

And suddenly there broke upon our sight
A rush of angels terrible with light—
The high same host the Shepherds saw go by,
Breaking the starry night with lyric cry—
A rush of angels, wistful and aware,
That shook a thousand colors on the air—

Colors that made a music to the eye—
Glories of lilac, azure, gold, vermilion,
Blown from the air-hung delicate pavilion.

And now His face grew bright with luminous will:
The great grave eyes grew planet-like and still.
Yea, in that moment, all His face, fire-white,
Seemed struck out of imperishable light.
Delicious apprehension shook His spirit,
With song so still that only the heart could hear it.
A sense of something sacred, starry, vast,
Greater than earth, across the watchers passed.

Then with a stretching of His hands to bless,
A last unspeakable look that was caress,
Up through the cortice of bright cherubim
He rose until the august form grew dim—
Up through the blue dome of the day ascended,
By circling flights of seraphim befriended.
He was uplifted from us, and was gone
Into the darkness of another dawn.

—Edwin Markham

RESURRECTION AND ASCENSION

He built a kingdom with His heart and brain,
    He knew hosannas and the psalms, till one
Played Judas for a paltry little gain,
    And in that hour His Kingdom was undone.
His spirit entering Gethsemane,
    Enduring bitter, bitter hours alone,
At last went staggering to Calvary,
    From thence to hell—and found a bed of stone.

But when the lilies flamed He breathed again,
    A man of scars, yet luminous and strange
With ecstasy unknown to other men—
    An ecstasy no Judas kiss may change.
The hosts who fled now worship from afar:
    They kneel before the beauty of a star.

—Earl D. Todd

THE SINGING SAVIORS

"Dead men tell no tales!" they chuckled,
  As the singing saviors died,
A few serene, and many shackled,
  Scourged, tortured, crucified.

Dead men tell no tales. . . . Is Shelley
  Dust blown dumbly over the ground?
Are Keats and Burns silenced wholly?
  Do Milton's stiff lips give no sound?

Is Shakespeare voiceless, Dante tongueless?
  And, in this black, protesting year
Is the dead Jesus wordless, songless?
  Listen! . . . They are all that you can hear!
                              —*Clement Wood*

THE GREAT WAGER

How is it proved?
It isn't proved, you fool! it can't be proved.
How can you prove a victory before
It's won? How can you prove a man who leads
To be a leader worth the following,
Unless you follow to the death, and out
Beyond mere death, which is not anything
But Satan's lie upon eternal life?
Well—God's my leader, and I hold that He
Is good, and strong enough to work His plan
And purpose out to its appointed end.

I walk in crowded streets, where men
And women, mad with lust, loose-lipped, and lewd,
Go promenading down to hell's wide gates;
Yet have I looked into my mother's eyes
And seen the light that never was on sea
Or land, the light of love, pure love and true,
And on that love I bet my life. . . .

. . . I bet life on beauty, truth,
And love! not abstract, but incarnate truth;
Not beauty's passing shadow, but its self,
Its very self made flesh—love realized.
I bet my life on Christ, Christ crucified,
Aye risen, and alive forevermore.
                              —*G. A. Studdert Kennedy*

ST. JOHN, THE AGED

I'm growing very old. This weary head
That hath so often leaned on Jesus' breast,
In days long past that seem almost a dream,
Is bent and hoary with its weight of years.
These limbs that followed Him—my Master—oft
From Galilee to Judah; yea, that stood
Beneath the cross, and trembled with His groans,
Refuse to bear me even through the streets
To preach unto my children. E'en my lips
Refuse to form the words my heart sends forth.
My ears are dull, they scarcely hear the sobs
Of my dear children gathered round my couch;
God lays His hand upon me—yea, His hand;
And not His rod—the gentle hand that I
Felt, those three years, so often pressed in mine,
In friendship such as passeth woman's love.

I'm old, so old I cannot recollect
The faces of my friends; and I forget
The words and deeds that make up daily life:
But that dear face, and every word He spoke,
Grow more distinct as others fade away,
So that I live with Him and holy dead
More than with living.

Some seventy years ago
I was a fisher by the sacred sea.
It was at sunset. How the tranquil tide
Bathed dreamily the pebbles. How the light
Crept up the distant hills and in its wake
Soft purple shadows wrapped the dewy fields.
And then He came and called me. Then I gazed,
For the first time, as from a window, shone
Divinity, looked on the inmost soul,
Broke on the silence of my heart and made
The whole world musical. Incarnate Love
Took hold of me and claimed me for its own.
I followed in the twilight, holding fast
His mantle.

O what holy walks we had,
Through harvest fields, and desolate dreary wastes,
And oftentimes He leaned upon my arm,
Wearied and wayworn. I was young and strong,
And so upbore Him. Lord, now I am weak,

And old, and feeble. Let me rest on Thee.
How strong Thou art. The twilight draws apace.
Come, let us leave these noisy streets and take
The path to Bethany; for Mary's smile
Awaits us at the gate, and Martha's hands
Have long prepared the cheerful evening meal.
Come, James, the Master waits; and, Peter, see,
Has gone some steps before.

    What say you, Friends?
That this is Ephesus? Aye, 'tis so, 'tis so,
I know it all; and yet, just now, I seemed
To stand once more upon my native hills,
The touch of His garments brings back strength
To palsied limbs. I feel it has to mine.
Up! bear me once more to my church. Once more
There let me tell you of a Saviour's love:
For, by the sweetness of my Master's voice
Just now, I think He must be very near—
Coming, I trust, to break the veil, which time
Has worn so thin that I can see beyond
And watch His footsteps.

    So raise up my head.
How dark it is! I cannot seem to see
The face of my flock. Is that the sea
That murmurs so, or is it weeping? Hush,
My little children. God so loved the world,
He gave His Son. So love ye one another:
Love God and man. Amen. Now bear me back.
My legacy unto an angry world is this:
I feel my work is finished. Are the streets so full?
What, call the folk my name? The Holy John?
Nay, write me rather Jesus Christ's beloved,
And lover of my children.

    Lay me down
Once more upon my couch, and open wide
The eastern window. See, there comes a light
Like that which broke upon my soul at eve,
When, in the dreary isle of Patmos, Gabriel came,
And touched me upon the shoulder. See, it grows,
As when He mounted toward the pearly gates.
I know the way. I trod it once before.
And hark! It is the song the ransomed sang
Of glory to the Lamb. How loud it sounds.
And that unwritten one. Methinks my soul
Can join it now. But who are these who crowd
The shining way? Say—joy! 'Tis the eleven,

With Peter first. How eagerly he looks.
How bright the smiles are beaming on James' face.
I am the last. Once more we are complete,
To gather round the Paschal feast. My place
Is next my Master. O my Lord, my Lord,
How bright Thou art, and yet the very same
I loved in Galilee. 'Tis worth the hundred years
To feel this bliss. So, lift me up, dear Lord,
Unto Thy bosom. There shall I abide.

—Author Unknown

HE DWELLS WITH US

Pray not "Abide with us." It need not be
We thus should pray on every land and sea,
For even now He dwells with you and me.

He is the essence of the perfumed flower,
He is the secret of the planet's power,
He is the beauty in the twilight hour.

We find Him in the vibrancy and vim
That sings to blossom on the apple limb,
Abide with us? We needs must learn of **Him.**

We find Him in the tears for mercy shed,
In every heart where hope and love are wed,
In loyal souls who for mankind have bled.

He holds the golden truth no age can dim,
He giveth life to life's full-measured brim,
He only grows who daily knows of Him.

It is His voice when loving words are said,
He sits with patient watchers by the dead,
When martyrs fall it is His blood runs red.

We must abide with Him. He is the light,
Without which mind were darkened as the night
And wrong a thing inseparable from right.

God lives in all things, even in the slime
And degradation of the streets of crime,
Equally in sot or saint sublime.

No single atom of the cosmic scheme,
No farthest ray of sunlight's golden gleam
But He controls and weaves into the Dream

God lives in human hearts, in thine, in mine;
We are the vessels of a life divine,
And every human breast a holy shrine.

—*Vincent G. Burns*

✠

JESUS ALIVE FOREVERMORE

or

The Testimony of the Eleven Upstairs

By

Charles A. McCalmon

"No-no-no," said Thomas, slowly and repeatedly but emphatically, shaking his head in all soberness, "I cannot and will not believe any such fantastic story. You may think that you saw Him; you may be honest as far as you know; but there is something wrong. When He was put into the tomb that was the end. People do not rise from the dead—at least not in these days when Romans crucify them and stick spears into them. Besides, how could He get into this room with the doors and windows locked and the shades drawn! It cannot be."

All eleven men were standing in a bare room containing only a rough table with a few scanty dishes over the top and a few rough table chairs scattered about. Some of the men were leaning on the backs of some of the chairs, others with one foot on them.

There was no floor covering. Not only were the window blinds drawn, but wooden pegs, driven into the casings here and there revealed the efforts of the occupants to prevent the exit into the outside world of even one ray of faint light from the flickering candle on the table. In the dim light the dubious but sincere Thomas apparently held the center of all attention. If an onlooker had been able to distinguish facial expressions and the revelation of inner thoughts, he would have discovered a blankness about the countenance of Thomas in comparison with the brightness and hopefulness of the others.

"It is not just our word that we ask you to believe; there is the testimony of High Heaven itself. You heard the group of women who went early to the tomb testify that they saw an angel at the open tomb who said, 'Fear not ye; for I know that ye seek Jesus which was crucified. He is not here; for He is risen as He said,'" said Bartholomew.

"Yes," replied Thomas. "They came running in that early morning, a week ago today, all out of breath. I admit they were filled with joy instead of fright as you would have supposed. But in the darkness about the tomb women are liable to see and hear almost anything—their imagination might carry them even beyond fear into joy."

James the Lesser stepped nearer to Thomas and directly in front of him, and said, "My mother was one of that group of women. As long as I can remember, she was never given to such impulsiveness. Besides, they went weeping, carrying spices and ointment for a corpse. Had it been imagination, they would have imagined something very different from that they did see. In imagination, you see what you expect; but they saw the opposite. The angel *himself* said to them, 'Why seek ye Jesus among the dead? He is not here! He is risen!"

"I—I don't believe in angels, anyway," stammered Thomas.

"You have to," insisted John. "Peter and I went to the tomb and confirmed just what the angel had told the women. All they knew was what the angels had told them. They told us; we ran to the tomb, Peter went in first and then I followed. There we found the clothes lying just as Jesus had left them, and the face-cloth lying in a separate place, indicating that they had been deliberately removed and laid aside. When accurate information comes through angels you cannot help but believe their message." John, youngster as he was, concluded as though the problem was settled beyond the shadow of a doubt. With a gesture of the hand, he indicated the finish of the argument as far as he was concerned and receded to the outside of the crowd—further disinterested.

"Why talk about angels, anyway?" impatiently asked James. "Mother and the other women that morning returning from the tomb *saw* Jesus himself. That is more important evidence than the angels' story, even though their testimony is true."

"Yes, and Jesus told them just as the angels had, that they should tell us about the risen Christ. That both Jesus and the angels thought first of us means most to me and ought to all of us," quietly put in Andrew.

Matthew cut Andrew off in his speaking: "Nobody surely could disbelieve Mary of Magdala. You remember, Thomas, the wretched piece of humanity she was that first time we saw her—the time she came into the banquet of Simon the Pharisee in Dalmanutha. Anyone who has changed as she has can never again be questioned for her truthfulness."

"I did not say that she was not truthful," explained Thomas. "Her very sensitive nature only makes her all the more susceptible to an overwrought imagination. I certainly would believe *her*—yes, but she *might be mistaken*, as she evidently *is* in this case."

"You surely could not say that about my cold-blooded father and Uncle [Dr.] Luke, would you, Thomas? I never knew either of them to get excited about anything. Besides the women's vision was only for a moment; but Jesus walked with father and uncle for some time along the road while it was still broad daylight—long enough to discuss the Scripture from Moses to Malachi. I suppose you think they only imagined that, too, do you?" Thaddeus ended, rather bluntly.

While Thomas was preparing to make reply to this question that really needed no reply, old Simon, grieved over the traitorous act of his own son, Judas, urged Thaddeus to continue by saying, "Didn't all of you see our Master at the supper table in the breaking of bread?"

"Yes," continued Thaddeus, "I suppose Thomas would call all of us filled with imagination. Mother, father, James, Dr. Luke and I were all there with this supposed Stranger who was talking to us about the Christ and the Scripture. He was different from anyone we had ever seen—you know, just something radiant about the way He spoke and acted—the accent of His voice and the certainty of His convictions. When we were ready to eat He blessed the bread just as Jesus used to do, and then we noticed that He was crumbling it into bits on His plate. Before we realized what was happening, He handed each of us five a piece. As we put them to our mouths, knowing nothing better to do with them, He vanished. The chair was vacant before we had time to worship Him."

"Don't you think that was real?" again questioned Simon, this time addressing Thomas.

But Thaddeus answered, "We know He was real for He had been with father and Dr. Luke for about an hour, and then with us in the home for another half-hour, and had eaten supper the same as the rest of us. There was no fake about that—nor the angels, either! It was Jesus. We knew Him as soon as we really looked at Him. We would have recognized Him sooner had we thought it possible and had looked straight at Him. It took His own familiar act of handing us the bread to make us look straight at Him and thus to see Him as He really was. We know, too, that He disappeared as all five of us looked at Him. No door opened, not a chair moved; but suddenly He was gone. We were not asleep, nor blinded; but all of us were looking in the same direction."

"That is like Thomas' trying to tell us that Jesus never suddenly appeared, nor suddenly vanished last Sunday evening right here in this room, when we all know that He did, for we were all here and saw it," urged Matthew.

"No, no, brothers, I cannot believe that, either," insisted Thomas. "I truly and honestly wish I could believe it, but I cannot. I tell you that it is against all reason."

"That depends upon how reasonable you are, Thomas," said Bartholomew. "Three years ago I could not have believed such things, either. I sympathize with your position. But from the time that Jesus told me about my being under the fig tree when I was absolutely sure that no one had seen me, I have been prepared to believe anything about Him. All things are possible with God, you know."

But Thomas replied: "Except I see with my eyes the prints of the nails and put my hand into the sword-thrust in His side, I will not believe."

"We did," sadly but fatherly said Simon.

"He will let you do just that," said Philip.

"He was as close and as real as He was that evening when we had our last supper together in this very room," said John, once more coming from his retirement and rather out of patience with the doubts of Thomas.

"Thomas," said Peter, who had been uneasily stroking his beard as he stood first on one foot and then on the other, and opening his mouth again and again as though he would speak—"Thomas, *I know.* I saw Him myself. Jesus and I talked for some time about things too intimate to report to even this group. You men are closer to me than any others in all the world—even my own family—but I cannot express even to you what He told me that first afternoon after His resurrection."

This solemn speech brought a lull and a quietness. Each man's heart burned within him—some with the assurance of the risen Lord, but Thomas with bitter disappointment that he, too, could not so hope and believe.

Then suddenly—a light! And lo! Christ stood in their midst. Thomas gasped as Jesus quietly and distinctly said, "Peace be unto you." And then to Thomas He said, "Reach hither thy finger, and see my hands; and reach hither thy hand, and put it into my side: and be not faithless, but believing."

"My Lord and my God!" gasped Thomas, as he threw his arms lovingly about the Master.

Epilogue

"And many other signs truly did Jesus in the presence of his disciples, which are not written in this book: But these are written, that ye might believe that Jesus is the Christ, the Son of God; and that believing ye might have life through his name.

"And there are also many other things which Jesus did, the which, if they should be written every one, I suppose that even the world itself would not contain the books that should be written. Amen."[2]

✝

HIS LAST DAYS ON EARTH

By

Cynthia Pearl Maus

Yes, Jesus was alive! And the most wonderful part of it all was that He seemed to care for the same things He had always loved before His cruel death on the cross—not only for the truths that He had taught and for the friends He had made but also for the places that His feet had known and trod.

Joyously He went into Galilee, to the haunts of His childhood and youth, and those busy, happy days with His disciples on blue Galilee. He had even sent word to His disciples by Mary Magdalene, saying, "I go before you into

---

[2] From *Jesus and Chums,* McCalmon. Published by the Cokesbury Press, Nashville, Tenn. Used by special arrangement with the author.

Galilee." And there on the shores of the lake He loved and from which He had called Peter and James and John, they found Him again.

When these puzzled fishermen came back to Galilee following the mystical resurrection of Jesus, and went back to their unsuccessful fishing, tired and a bit discouraged, He Who had so often put a new hope in their hearts during the old days, met them once again on the shores, prepared for them a breakfast, and ate with them. He cared for them with a strange and sympathetic kindness that at first they could not quite understand. When He called to them from the shore, Peter, as he was apt to do on any startling occasion, dashed headlong into the water and hurried longingly to his Master that he might reaffirm the love which his thricefold betrayal in the outer court in Jerusalem on the night of His trial had denied. It was on the shores of Galilee that that solemn and memorable conversation, which John tells us about in the twenty-first chapter of his Gospel, took place; where Jesus said to Peter for the third time, "Lovest thou Me," as if to purge forever from Peter's memory his threefold denial of his Lord.

It was Galilee, that had been less unkind to Him than any other province in Palestine, that received and kept the secret of His goings and comings throughout the nearly six weeks that followed His resurrection, during which time His friends and disciples saw Him frequently.

In these weeks He appeared and disappeared seemingly at will, but always peaceful and majestic. There was about Him a sort of mysterious joy in the fact that His Spirit after death might return again and again to the scenes that were best known and beloved by Him in life. Yet those who saw Him, and conversed with Him, and touched Him said: "It is not just a spirit; it is He."

What sacred and solemn delights and surprises came into the lives of His disciples and friends during that six weeks that intervened between His resurrection and His ascension. With the return of every daybreak these rugged men awoke with a strange, joyous and yet hushed expectancy. To one another they would say, "Will He come today?" and at nightfall they would say to one another: "Have you seen Him today? *Have you?*"

But there came a day when it was no longer possible for Him to be so constantly among just this chosen few. His destiny lay in the realm of the Spirit and with all time and ages. And so near the end of this six weeks of appearances to many persons and in many places, He bade His disciples and friends to come with Him to the hills. There He talked with them tenderly, directed their future, and glorified their souls with a living, loving faith, until they felt that to die for Him would be the happiest fate that could possibly befall them.

Then He made known to them that He would lead the way out of Galilee and toward Jerusalem, where they, His disciples, were "to tarry until they were clothed with power from on high." Mutely and without fully understanding what was to happen to Him and them, they followed Him. Near Bethany, where He had been so loved, He paused, as if He would come once again to the "home of His heart" before He departed from them in bodily form that He might remain with them always in spirit.

And there on the hillside near Bethany, He told them that they were to be His ministers even unto the ends of the earth, and that in turn He would be with them always in spirit, no matter where they were—"even to the uttermost parts of the world." And as He spoke to them, and while they gazed steadfastly at Him, His eye, His smile, His outstretched hands became remote. The air trembled between Himself and them. Mystery and mistiness began to blend in Him. Glory and ecstasy enfolded Him as His form rose slowly from earth toward heaven.

Somehow they could not entreat Him to stay. An expression graver than joy was in His eyes that seemed to follow them with wistful yearning. Ineffable love, understanding and sympathy were in His last look as it had been in the first that they saw upon His face. And out of that yearning, wistful look that shone from His eyes there was born in them such an unutterable response that it blinded for the time being all consciousness of other things. Slowly His form faded from their view; and the delicately tinted clouds enfolded Him.

Thus vanished from this earth Jesus of Nazareth, the only begotten Son of God. Evil had never touched His spirit. Corruption did not approach His body; and even His ashes were not permitted to remain in the soil that gave Him birth or the land that had crucified His precious body.

This Man of Galilee, who was born in denial of the known laws of life, and died in defiance of the accepted laws of death—He is Lord of both *life* and *death*. As the Master of both Life and Death He belongs to the ages; and to the ages He remains in spite of all criticism the one supreme Ideal of sacrifice and selflessness in service to the living—the one Magnificent Obsession of all men of all ages who believe that Spirit triumphs over death, that human life is *spirit* and *immortal*; and that through Jesus Christ, and Jesus Christ alone, we shall find the highway to abundant living here and throughout eternity.

✛

HANDEL'S "MESSIAH" AND "HALLELUJAH CHORUS"

By

Cynthia Pearl Maus

IF AMONG all the beautiful music in the world, the oratorio is the tone-cathedral, the record for achieving this masterpiece of musical architecture belongs to the master-musician-architect—George Frederick Handel, who was born at Halle, Lower Saxony, in 1685.

The middle and especially the latter part of Handel's life, however—the period during which most of his grand operas and oratorios were composed—was spent on English soil. Because of this the name of Handel is so much a household word among English-speaking people that he has come to be regarded almost as though he was of English nationality—even to his interment and monumental niche in the "Poets' Corner" in Westminster Abbey, thus definitely identifying his art-triumphs with British soil.

His "Messiah" was heard for the first time in London on March 23, 1843. The success and appreciation accorded to this—considered by many to be the grandest of all the oratorios—was instantaneous. This great oratorio was written in twenty-four days, for Handel was a prodigious worker. It was all original work except the choruses, "And he shall purify," "For unto us," "His yoke is easy," and "All we like sheep," all of which were adapted from a set of Italian duets that he had written in July of 1841. Although the original draft was written in such a short time, it is said that Handel spent more time in revising this, his masterpiece, than any of his previous oratorios.

While it has been nearly two centuries since this great oratorio was first written, it still occupies a place in the program of nearly every great musical festival in both Europe and the Western World. It is sung once a year, usually at Easter time, by almost every choral society.

Handel himself was a simple, direct, bluff, and masterful personality. In this his greatest masterpiece he took a few well-worn harmonies, sequences and points of imitation between the human voice and instruments, and put them together with an unerring sense of balance into mighty choruses, duets, and solos that have appealed for centuries to English-speaking peoples just because they are so direct, bluff, and masterful.

For Handel's "Messiah" is a tone-cathedral of which all the nations of the world may be justly proud, and for which humanity as a whole must ever be grateful. Mated with the mightiest of themes, this superb masterpiece has been compared to that music which will delight and exalt the human soul in its future redeemed and more blessed state of existence.

How wide and wonderful the influence of Handel's "Messiah" has been will, perhaps, never be fully known. It appeals to men and women and young people of all classes and grades of social and intellectual culture, and furnishes the most appropriate and impressive sacred Christmas and Easter music known. It has doubtless been heard by larger audiences and a greater number of people than any other sacred music ever composed.

If the oratorio itself is a favorite with music lovers everywhere, what can we say of the appeal of its magnificent angels' "Hallelujah Chorus"? Nearly every young person has at some time heard this mighty chorus from the "Messiah." Yet not all of them know what Scripture the composer of this marvelous chorus had in mind as he brought the "Messiah" to its grand and triumphant close.

Handel loved Bible stories, especially those that centered around the life of Jesus. He had heard them from early childhood, and as he grew to manhood he told these beautiful stories to others in musical form. The story of Jesus going to His heavenly home, after His resurrection from the dead, was particularly appealing to him. He thought about it a great deal.

He remembered that Jesus saw His friends and disciples many times after His resurrection. But as the spring passed into summer Jesus told these friends and His chosen disciples that He was going away soon to be forever with His heavenly Father; and that there He would make ready for them a far more beautiful heavenly home than might ever exist on this earth, lovely as it is. Handel remembered that Jesus had said to them in quiet serenity, "Let not your hearts be troubled. In my Father's house are many mansions, if it were not so I would have told you. I go to prepare a place for you; that where I am there ye may be also." "And while I am away preparing this heavenly home, you must 'go into all the world and preach the gospel to the whole creation, teaching them to observe all things whatsoever I have commanded you, and lo! I am with you always even unto the end of the world.'"

Handel remembered that one day Jesus led His disciples out of the city and along the road toward Bethany, and there, while they were gazing steadfastly at Him, he disappeared in the clouds from their sight.

Handel thought a great deal about that cloud of witnesses to which Jesus often referred, and which on that day parted Jesus from His friends and disciples. In his imagination he tried to picture what was happening behind that cloud. And in this musical story, the angels' "Hallelujah Chorus," he tells us what he thinks happened.

Handel believed that God sent His angels to meet Jesus, and to bring Him with songs of rejoicing into His heavenly home. He thought that other angels stayed by the Gates of Heaven to greet Jesus as He arrived. And he felt that these angels were so happy that they sang songs of joy while they waited.

One day Handel remembered a poetic psalm that he thought expressed the words which the angels must have been singing as Jesus returned to heaven after His resurrection. This poem is found in Psalms 24:7-10, and reads:

> Lift up your heads, O ye gates;
> And be ye lifted up, ye everlasting doors;
> And the King of Glory will come in.

If you will play, or have someone play, the "Hallelujah Chorus" for you, while you listen to the music you will hear the song the angels sang as they welcomed Jesus back to His heavenly Father's home. It will help you to hear if you will repeat this psalm softly as the music of this marvelous chorus is being played, beginning with the fifth measure through to the tenth.

Handel imagined that the angels at the gates, when they heard the other angels singing "Lift up your heads, O ye gates," answered, "Who is the King of Glory?" And that the angels who were accompanying Jesus replied:

> "The Lord strong and mighty,
> The Lord strong and mighty;
> The Lord mighty in battle."

The angels who were accompanying Jesus to His Father's home wished to have the gates wide open to receive Him, and so again they sang out in triumphant challenge:

> "Lift up your heads, O ye gates;
> And be ye lifted up, ye everlasting doors;
> And the King of Glory will come in."

And again the angels by the gates of heaven sang out with joy and gladness:

> "Who is the King of Glory?
> Who is the King of Glory?"

You can feel as well as hear the surge of joy in Handel's "Hallelujah Chorus" as the pianist plays these measures.

And again the angels who were with Jesus replied in an ever-increasing swell of assurance:

> "The Lord of Hosts, the Lord of Hosts,
> He is the King of Glory,
> He is the King of Glory!"

Then the angels who kept the heavenly entrance opened wide the gates, and Jesus, the King of Glory, passed through them into His Father's home.

To welcome Him, Handel imagined all the hosts of heaven sang a song of praise—the angels that were with Jesus and the angels that were by the gates, and the angels who were around the throne of God all sang praises to Jesus, the Friend and Redeemer of mankind. And the wonderful song that they sang, Handel makes the climax of his marvelous "Hallelujah Chorus."

The last words of that song of praise are,—"And He shall reign forever and ever. King of Kings and Lord of Lords. Hallelujah! Hallelujah! Hallelujah! Hallelujah!" Listen as the closing notes of Handel's "Hallelujah Chorus" are being played for you, beginning with the last note of the tenth from the last measure.

When you hear the mighty swell of this triumphant climax of the angels' chorus, you do not wonder that Queen Victoria, when first she heard Handel's "Messiah," laid aside her own crown and stood with her husband in recognition of that King of Kings who is above all, and who must reign supreme in every life that triumphs. Even to this day it is customary for audiences in English-speaking countries to stand throughout the singing of the "Hallelujah Chorus."

At Easter-time and especially on Ascension Sunday when we remember the joyous return of Jesus to His heavenly home, we should keep ringing in our own hearts the angels' "Hallelujah Chorus" as it has come down to us through the centuries in the "Messiah," and remember that our triumphant reunion with Him in His Father's home is conditioned on triumphant, creative living on our part as we continue to tell the story of His love to others everywhere.

I KNOW THAT MY REDEEMER LIVETH

THE words of this great hymn of assurance, "I Know that My Redeemer Liveth" were composed by Jessie H. Brown, one of the truly great hymn-writers of the Churches of Christ in America, and who after her marriage was lovingly known through years of devoted service as Jessie Brown Pounds.

Her own personal life was rich in poetic beauty and in devotion to the King of Kings, and that faith and devotion are nowhere more beautifully expressed than in this great hymn.

It is not infrequently sung as a duet or anthem; and is effective also as a solo or duet, with the congregation joining in on the chorus.

The music of this great hymn was composed by James H. Fillmore, of a family also prominent in the history of the Churches of Christ for the preachers, missionaries, and composers of music that it has contributed to the enrichment of the cause of Christ throughout the world.

I know that my Redeemer liveth,
    And on the earth again shall stand;
I know eternal life He giveth,
    That grace and pow'r are in His hand.

Chorus

I know, I know that Jesus liveth,
    And on the earth again shall stand;
I know, I know that life He giveth,
    That grace and pow'r are in His hand.

I know His promise never faileth,
    The word He speaks, it cannot die;
Tho' cruel death my flesh assaileth,
    Yet I shall see Him by and by.

Chorus

I know my mansion He prepareth,
    That where He is there I may be:
O wondrous tho't, for me He careth,
    And He at last will come for me.[3]

—*Jessie H. Brown*

[3] Copyright, 1893, by Fillmore Brothers. Used by permission of the Fillmore Music House, Cincinnati, Ohio.

LEAD ON, O KING ETERNAL

THERE is no more challenging processional hymn of the Church than this one, "Lead On, O King Eternal," the words of which were written by Ernest W. Shurtleff in 1888. It is sung to a tune familiar to all, "Lancashire," composed by Henry Smart in 1836.

The message of this beautiful hymn is triumphant. It is addressed to the "King Eternal," who through His death, resurrection and ascension has become the all-glorious, all-victorious Leader of men's hearts and minds through all the ages.

It expresses the Christian's cry of joyous devotion to the leadership of this King Immortal who is above all principalities and powers; and it affirms their pledge of allegiance until the kingdoms of this world shall become the kingdom of God.

There is a martial beat to the rhythm of the music of this great hymn that makes every follower of Christ stiffen his backbone and square his shoulders as he marches forward in the unfinished task of building in this world God's Kingdom of Love. One cannot sing such words in spirit and in truth without feeling a lift of courage and a joy of fellowship with Christ, the all-powerful, eternal King.

Lead on, O King Eternal,
   The day of march has come;
Henceforth in fields of conquest
   Thy tents shall be our home.
Through days of preparation
   Thy grace has made us strong,
And now, O King Eternal,
   We lift our battle song.

Lead on, O King Eternal,
   Till sin's fierce war shall cease,
And holiness shall whisper
   The sweet amen of peace.
For not with swords, loud clashing,
   Nor roll of stirring drums,
With deeds of love and mercy,
   The heavenly kingdom comes.

Lead on, O King Eternal;
   We follow, not with fears,
For gladness breaks like morning
   Where'er thy face appears.

> Thy cross is lifted o'er us,
>   We journey in its light;
> The crown awaits the conquest;
>   Lead on, O God of might. Amen.

> —*Ernest W. Shurtleff, 1888*

✝

CROWN HIM WITH MANY CROWNS

IT IS easy to feel with the author of this great hymn, "Crown Him with Many Crowns," written by Matthew Bridges in 1851, that we have in Christ Jesus a Leader worthy to be crowned King of Kings and Lord of Lords. It is sung to an old tune, "Diamemata," composed by George J. Elvey in 1868.

Over and over again in the recorded experiences of various mission fields, natives, when they have heard the story of God's great love for the children of men, as shown in the gift of His only Son, have acclaimed this Christ worthy of the many, many crowns about which the author writes with such joyous abandon in this hymn.

Worthy indeed is the lamb upon His heavenly throne to be crowned the king of life and light, of love and peace, for wherever the story of His matchless life is lived and told, those who hear the message are lifted to a new glory and grace.

Something of what we frail, stumbling, followers of Christ feel deep down in our inmost souls surges through every line of this great hymn. For we know that we can crown Him on His heavenly throne only as we enthrone the precepts for which He lived and died, as the dominating, controlling influence in all we think and say and do and are.

> Crown Him with many crowns,
>   The Lamb upon His throne!
> Hark how the heavenly anthem drowns
>   All music but its own!
> Awake, my soul, and sing
>   Of Him who died for thee,
> And hail Him as thy matchless King
>   Thro' all eternity.

> Crown Him the Lord of love!
>   Behold His hands and side,
> Rich wounds, yet visible above,
>   In beauty glorified.
> No angel in the sky
>   Can fully bear the sight,
> But downward bends His burning eye
>   At mysteries so bright.

Crown Him the Lord of peace,
  Whose power a scepter sways
From pole to pole, that wars may cease,
  And all be prayer and praise!
His reign shall know no end,
  And round His piercèd feet
Fair flowers of Paradise extend
  Their fragrance ever sweet. Amen.

—Matthew Bridges, 1851

✝

ALL HAIL THE POWER OF JESUS' NAME

"ALL Hail the Power of Jesus' Name" is one of those older hymns of the Church
that has been translated into many tongues; and which lives because it expresses the adoration of every humble follower of the King of Kings.

The words of this hymn were written by Edward Perronet in 1779, and it
is sung to the tune "Coronation," composed by Oliver Holden in 1793.

When Christians reflect on the matchless life of the Son of Man, and remember what He suffered that we might know life abundant here and life
eternal hereafter, we realize that Jesus is worthy not alone of our feeble praise
and adoration, but also of the devotion of God's angels of light and mercy
and life, who around the heavenly throne do always behold their Father's face.

We would be faithful to Him until men and women of every race and
tribe, the world around, bow in grateful acknowledgment, and in their own
lives "crown Him Lord of all."

All hail the power of Jesus' name,
  Let angels prostrate fall;
Bring forth the royal diadem
  And crown Him Lord of all!
Bring forth the royal diadem
  And crown Him Lord of all.

Let every kindred, every tribe
  On this terrestrial ball
To Him all majesty ascribe
  And crown Him Lord of all!
To Him all majesty ascribe
  And crown Him Lord of all!

Oh, that with yonder sacred throng
  We at His feet may fall,
Join in the everlasting song
  And crown Him Lord of all!
Join in the everlasting song
  And crown Him Lord of all!

—Edward Perronet, 1779

HARK, TEN THOUSAND HARPS AND VOICES

IN "HARK, Ten Thousand Harps and Voices," written by Thomas Kelly in 1804, we have another of those great hymns of the Church which emphasize the joy and gladness that abound in heaven, not alone because of the resurrection of Jesus from the dead, but, because of the glory of his *ascension* and *rulership* as King of Kings and Lord of Lords.

If Christianity had contributed no other gift to humanity save its redeeming hope of a resurrected life in the beyond, it would still be worth all it cost in sacrifice and suffering on the part of the Son of God. For by it Christ affirmed in man His faith that Spirit transcends flesh, and that immortality transcends mortality.

Jesus not only promised life abundant here to all those who follow Him in purity and devotion; but life eternal and immortal in the hereafter for that inner self or mind which we call soul or spirit. And in proportion as men and women come to understand that this inner selfhood is immortal, and that whether good or bad it abides eternally, in joy and happiness if goodness is the character we have written into it, or in desolation and distress if evil has been the intent of our heart in this life—they will seek to build spiritual temples in which they would be willing always to abide.

The music for this great hymn was written by the well-known composer, Lowell Mason, in 1840.

Hark, ten thousand harps and voices
　　Sound the note of praise above!
Jesus reigns, and heaven rejoices,
　　Jesus reigns, the God of Love;
See, He sits on yonder throne;
Jesus rules the world alone.

Refrain

Hallelujah! Hallelujah!
　Hallelujah! Amen!

Jesus, hail! whose glory brightens
　　All above and gives it worth;
Lord of life, Thy smile enlightens,
　　Cheers, and charms Thy saints on earth:
When we think of love like Thine,
Lord, we own it love divine.

Refrain

Saviour, hasten Thine appearing;
    Bring, O bring the glorious day
When, the awful summons hearing,
    Heaven and earth shall pass away.
Then with golden harps we'll sing,
"Glory, glory to our King!"

Refrain

—*Thomas Kelly, 1804*

PART VI

JESUS IS HERE

CONTENTS

PART VI   SECTION I

IN HIS BOOK AND HIS CHURCH

✛

"Every scripture inspired of God *is* also profitable for teaching."—II TIMOTHY 3:16

✛

499

IN HIS BOOK AND HIS CHURCH

"But abide thou in the things which thou hast learned and hast been assured of, knowing of whom thou hast learned them; and that from a babe thou hast known the sacred writings which are able to make thee wise unto salvation through faith which is in Christ Jesus.

"Every scripture inspired of God *is* also profitable for teaching, for reproof, for correction, for instruction which is in righteousness: that the man of God may be complete, furnished completely unto every good work."—II Timothy 3:16-17

✠

"The Bible is a many-sided book. Its historical value is beyond computation. As literature, it is without a rival, whether in prose or in poetry. As a book of authority in religion it has no peer. Its doctrinal value also puts it in a class by itself. Its appeal to the human imagination and its power to rouse the human intellect to loftiest efforts are best known to those who are the most faithful students of its pages.

"To read the Bible believingly, reverently, obediently, not being 'disobedient to the heavenly visions' which God gives to us through his word, is to begin here on earth that moral and spiritual transfiguration whose climax is the glorified image of Christ."
—J. H. Garrison

✠

"And Simon Peter answered and said, Thou art the Christ, the Son of the living God. And Jesus answered and said unto him, Blessed art thou, Simon Bar-Jonah: for flesh and blood hath not revealed it unto thee, but my Father who is in heaven. And I also say unto thee, that thou art Peter, and upon this rock I will build my church; and the gates of Hades shall not prevail against it."—Matthew 16:16-18

THE LAST SUPPER

By

Alois Lang

(Interpretation)

The Lord's Supper as it appears in Alois Lang's wood-carving for the church's chancel, with its simple setting and tragic sequence, has ever been one of dramatic interest to artists. No one scene in the life of Christ has been more often painted on canvas, carved in wood, or chiseled in stone than this particular scene; and many of these conceptions date far back in the early Christian centuries.

Of all that have painted this scene, two alone stand out supreme above all others—"The Last Supper" by Leonardo da Vinci, painted on the walls of the dining-room of a monastery in Milan, Italy, 1494-1496; and this remarkable wood-carving by Alois Lang of Bavaria, Germany (relative, not brother, of the Alois Lang who played the part of Christus in the 1930 and 1934 Passion Play at Oberammergau) which is the center altar-panel of St. Paul's Evangelical Church in St. Louis, Missouri.

In executing this new and more modern conception of The Last Supper, Mr. Lang had several purposes in mind, which must be known in order to correctly appraise and appreciate the value of this marvelous wood-carving.

As a decorative panel for chancel use in churches this Last Supper is viewed much of the time by most of its observers from a distance, yet there is a drawing power in the theme which impels in many a closer approach. Therefore, Mr. Lang, by detail of facial expression, has designed a panel that is equally pleasing in its spiritual appeal under close inspection with the strength of its shadow contrast when viewed from a distance.

The scene is the night of the Passover supper. In a small upper room in a house in Jerusalem, Jesus, surrounded by His disciples, is breaking the bread of their farewell meal.

Christ is the center of the composition. The lines of interest and action all converge toward Him. He has just said, "He, to whom I give the bread, he will betray me." Love, terror, grief and amazement find expression on the faces and in the cry of His disciples, "Lord, is it I?"

His statement startles the seated group and several hastily arise and draw nearer, and all, save Judas only, turn to the Master, anxious, yet afraid and reluctant to hear who the traitor may be.

Andrew and Thaddeus, at the extreme left end of the table, have risen, the one quietly curious, the other just raising his hand in protesting innocence.

Bartholomew, seated on the outer side of the left end of the table, is wondering who shall be given the bread.

Thomas, with hands folded as if in prayer; and James, the minor, with his right hand over his heart, both profess by look and gesture their loyalty.

John, the beloved disciple, seated nearest Jesus on the left and looking into his face, seems to be saying, "Master, Thou knowest it is not I who would betray you."

Peter and James, the major, nearest to Jesus on the right, both display grief and surprise in look and action over the Master's words.

Philip, the third figure on the right, with head slightly bowed, seems to say—more to himself than aloud—"Not I, Master?"

Matthew and Simon, at the end of the table on the right, have risen and seem to be saying: "Who can it be? Surely, not I."

There can be no doubt as to the real betrayer. Judas, at the outer side of the extreme right-hand end of the table, with his head bowed as if fearing to meet the Master's eye, is clutching in his left hand the money-bag, ready to rise and leave the table.

We are touched, in this wood-carving, by the face of the Saviour, kindly, submissive, forgiving, as though He were hopeful, even yet, that Judas might repent his action before it is too late. He that loveth much forgiveth much.

Mr. Lang has placed Protestant Christianity under lasting gratitude to him for this marvelous wood-carving of The Last Supper. No work of art could be more ideal as the center piece of the Church's chancel. Seated at worship, communicants may look constantly upon the table of Christ and His disciples in their farewell meal together; examine themselves, and through prayer and communion purge from their hearts every thought and motive that tends to deny Christ and to make ineffective in them His Kingdom of Love.

✠

JESUS AND THE BOOK OF BOOKS

(Interpretation)

WE SPEAK of the Bible as the word of God, and in a sense, of course, this is true. But in an even greater sense Jesus, Himself, is the living word of truth which the heavenly Father sent into the world that men might discover, in and through Him, what the *heart* and *mind* and *soul* of God are like.

John, the beloved, begins his Gospel story about Jesus with these significant words: "In the beginning was the Word, and the Word was with God, and the Word was God. The same was in the beginning with God. All things were made through Him; and without Him was not anything made that hath been made. In Him was life; and the life was the light of men" (1:1-4).

It is evident that the Word in this instance is being used as a symbol of *intelligence*. John is by this symbolic use of language trying to tell us that whatever of *intelligence* there is in the world, aye, much more of intelligence than man,

THE LAST SUPPER—LANG

with his finite mind has yet been able to discover, understand and appropriate, was in the beginning with the heavenly Father; and that everything that we see in this ordered world about us that gives evidence of thought, enlightenment, was made by the Word, the creative *intelligence* of God.

The Bible, therefore, is the *intelligence* of *God* expressed as best Godly men through the ages have been able to grasp the truth about God and to share it with others. But there came a time when greater knowledge and truth than men had yet been able to understand were needed, if man was ever to be redeemed from his own folly and lack of wisdom; and so John tells us that this "Word (or Intelligence) became flesh, and dwelt among us, and we beheld His glory, glory as of the Only Begotten from the Father, full of grace and truth" (1:14).

Those early followers of Jesus recognized Christ as the grace and truth of God; dimly, at first, it is true; but growing in conviction and significance in their lives, as they were led by His Holy Spirit into the fullness of understanding. For again we find John saying: "For the law was given through Moses; grace and truth came through Jesus Christ" (1:17).

And Jesus, referring to Himself, said, "I am the light of the world: he that followeth me shall not walk in the darkness, but shall have the light of life" (John 8:12). And again, "I am the way, and the truth, and the life. No one cometh unto the Father but by me" (John 14:6).

This picture of the open Bible with the face of Jesus shining forth from its pages is the artist's way of saying to us that Jesus is the center and core of the book which we call the Bible. For in a very real and true sense, the Old Testament or covenant was according to Paul a "schoolmaster to bring us to Christ." While the New Testament or covenant is the result of the efforts of men to put into words something of the richness of grace and truth that was incarnate in the Only Begotten Son of God.

Even His own chosen disciples recognized the difficulties and limitations of words when they tried to picture what Jesus was like; for does not John, the beloved, close his Gospel story about the Son of God by saying: "And there are also many other things which Jesus did, the which, if they should be written every one, I suppose that even the world itself would not contain the books that should be written" (21:25).

Jesus is greater than the Book. He transcends man's ability to confine within the pages of Holy Writ all of the grace and truth, the light and love, that was incarnate in God's Only Begotten Son. He can be truly known by men only as they endeavor in each and every life situation to live as much of His truth as they can in their own daily lives. For did not Jesus say: "He that doeth my will shall know the doctrine"? Therefore Dr. Rauschenbusch could truthfully say: "Only that much of the Bible [Word of God, Word of Truth, Word of Jesus] is yours that has become so through experience."

We are indebted to a present-day artist for this challenging picture of Hofmann's adult Christ as the center and core of all recorded truth about both God and man; for Jesus not only taught, but lived what God is like; saying to the disciples in answer to Philip's question, "Show us the Father, and it sufficeth us"—"Have I been so long time with you, and dost thou not know me? He that hath seen me hath seen the Father . . . the words that I say unto you I speak not from myself: but the Father abiding in me doeth his works. Believe me that I am in the Father, and the Father in me: or else believe me for the very works' sake" (John 14:8-11).

With the poet Richard Watson Gilder, the artist, in this picture, is saying to us:

> If Jesus Christ is a man—
> And only a man—I say
> That of all mankind I will cleave to Him
> And to Him I will cleave alway.
>
> If Jesus Christ is God—
> And the only God—I swear,
> I will follow Him through heaven and hell,
> The earth, the sea, and the air![1]

✠

CHRISTIAN SYMBOLS
(Interpretation)

THE picture on page 507 portrays the open Bible leaning against the cross, with lilies and lighted candles on either side. These are regarded as Christian symbols because they are constant reminders of the *light,* the *life,* the *love,* and the *truth* in Jesus Christ.

At the center is the cross, which in Jesus' time was considered an ignominious instrument of death but which became a beloved symbol to early Christians. They remembered the Master's words: "And I, if I be lifted up from the earth, will draw all men unto myself" (John 12:32). Jesus gave His life for the sins of the world, and for His sake the early Christians bore persecution courageously. The cross is the most universally accepted Christian symbol. More than four hundred various shapes exist, each with its special history.

The Latin cross, pictured here, is frequently seen in Protestant churches. On an altar or worship arrangement, it is always placed higher than any of the other symbols. Sometimes it is placed on three steps, which signify faith, hope, and love.

The use of lights in religious services began early in the history of the Church. Jesus Himself was, and is, the "Light of the world." The Gospel of John says of Jesus: "In him was life; and the life was the light of men" (1:4). Thus, lights became a symbol of the invisible presence of the Master of Men.

Jesus loved flowers and during His earthly ministry He spent much

---

[1] "The Song of a Heathen," Gilder. Copyright by Houghton Mifflin Company. Used by permission.

Photo by courtesy the VonTrotts, Philadelphia, Pa.

CHRISTIAN SYMBOLS

time in the out-of-doors. "Consider the lilies of the field, how they grow; they toil not, neither do they spin: yet I say unto you, that even Solomon in all his glory was not arrayed like one of these" (Matt. 6:28, 29). It is not strange that the early "followers of the way" associated Christ and His gospel with the flowers of the fields. The use of altar flowers has become an almost universal custom.

To His followers Jesus was also the Word of God made flesh. John, speaking of Him, says: "In the beginning was the Word, and the Word was with God, and the Word was God. . . . And the Word became flesh and dwelt among us (and we beheld his glory, glory as of the only begotten from the Father), full of grace and truth" (John 1:1, 14). John also has Jesus saying: "Know the truth, and the truth shall make you free" (8:32); and the Apostle Paul in Colossians 3:16 urges the followers of Christ to "let the word of Christ dwell in you richly; in all wisdom teaching and admonishing one another with psalms and hymns and spiritual songs, singing with grace in your hearts unto God." Inevitably the Bible, which is the Word of God, became a symbol early in Christian history, and it is frequently used today in worship arrangements, though properly speaking it is used on the pulpit or lectern rather than on the altar.

The monogram IHS appears in the picture both on the cross and on the front of the marble altar. There are several interpretations to this sacred Christian monogram. A popular one is that it comes from the Latin words *Iesus Hominum Salvator* (Jesus Savior of Men.) Others believe that it originated from the Latin: *In hoc signo* (In this sign, the cross, thou shalt conquer). Put simply, IHS means *Jesus,* and when the letters appear at the center of the cross they are there to remind us that the central teaching of the cross is that God's love and suffering for mankind is revealed in Jesus.

This arrangement of Christian symbols is depicted on the altar of the Overbrook Presbyterian Church in Philadelphia, Pennsylvania.

✙

EPWORTH-EUCLID METHODIST CHURCH, CLEVELAND, OHIO

(Interpretation)

MANY indeed are the marvelous examples of Christian architecture that have been inspired by the religion of Jesus Christ. Europe has its countless cathedrals and abbey churches, and the Americas are fast catching up with an ever-increasing number of fine church buildings.

A New World example of a beautiful Christian edifice is the Epworth-Euclid Methodist Church in Cleveland. Set in lovely parklike surroundings, the massive French Gothic styled stone structure becomes lighter as it rises from the ground. The exquisite heavenward spire soars up—reminding the world of higher things.

The stone sculptured figures over the various entrances of the church are of Old Testament prophets who prophesied the coming of the Messiah: Moses, Elijah, Amos, Hosea, Isaiah, and Jeremiah. These are complemented by representatives of the Christian faith that fulfill the ancient prophecies: St. Augustine, St. Chrysostom, John Wesley, Wycliffe, and Huss; there are also a few modern representatives of the Christian faith.

All of the appointments of the interior have been planned to remind the worshiper of Jesus and His teachings. Most outstanding examples of this are the "vine of life" carving at the communion rail, the golden onyx cross on the altar, and the subject matter of the various stained-glass windows.

The beautiful rose window above the altar, just back of the rood screen of the organ, is one of the really successful rose windows in America. Its rich colors: deep blue, with touches of jewel-red and green, are worthy of a French Gothic cathedral. The chancel windows are known as the "Singing Windows." The north chancel window contains the figures and symbols of the archangels Michael and Gabriel, and carries the words, "Who Is Like Unto God?" and "God Is My Strength." The words of "Gloria in Excelsis" also appear on this window. The south chancel window shows the archangels Raphael and Uriel, and the inscriptions, "God Is My Health" and "God Is My Light." The canticles inscribed on this window are "The Venite" and "Jubilate Deo." The borders of both of these windows include the "vine of life," the Rose of Sharon, and Singing Blue Birds. The four great windows of the nave and the clerestory windows picture events in the life, death, and resurrection of Jesus Christ.

Epworth-Euclid Methodist Church was designed by the late Grosvenor Goodhue, one of America's finest church architects. Mr. Goodhue was a frequent visitor to Europe and one of his favorite places, which he went to over and over, was the famed Mont Saint Michel in northern France. This unusual structure, built as an abbey church during the eleventh, twelfth, and thirteenth centuries, inspired Mr. Goodhue in designing the church in Cleveland. He wanted to show that the Gothic style still speaks today, and Epworth-Euclid Church illustrates this thesis admirably.

Even the architect's setting for the New World church is reminiscent of its elder sister, for, in approaching Mont Saint Michel, one drives out along the causeway of a peninsula. At high tide the ancient church and its cluster of buildings is surrounded by water. The graceful spire dominates the entire countryside as well as the local scene.

One who has visited both the Old World church of Mont Saint Michel and the New World Epworth-Euclid Methodist Church cannot help being struck by their similarity. Each has strong perpendicular lines, a graceful spire, and each is worthy of being called a "symphony in stone." The American church is lighter and warmer inside and out than the massive, heavy, and predominantly gray French church. Mr. Goodhue gave warmth, light, and

Photo by Cragg, Clevela

EPWORTH-EUCLID METHODIST CHURCH

Photo by Ernst Studios, Cleveland, O.

EPWORTH-EUCLID METHODIST CHURCH

color to his creation by incorporating many features of later French Gothic architecture, introducing richly colored stained-glass windows to lighten the interior.

Nearly a thousand years of Christian church architecture are spanned in these two churches—one in France and the other in America—dramatizing the long history of beautiful churches which have aided man in the worship of God as revealed by Jesus Christ.

✠

THE BIBLE

When I am tired, the Bible is my bed;
  Or in the dark, the Bible is my light.
When I am hungry, it is the vital bread;
  Or fearful, it is armor for the fight.
When I am sick, 'tis healing medicine;
Or lonely, thronging friends I find therein.

If I would work, the Bible is my tool;
  Or play, it is a harp of happy sound.
If I am ignorant, it is my school;
  If I am sinking, it is solid ground.
If I am cold, the Bible is my fire;
And wings, if boldly I aspire.

Should I be lost, the Bible is my guide;
  Or naked, it is raiment, rich and warm.
Am I imprisoned, it is ranges wide;
  Or tempest-tossed, a shelter from the storm.
Would I adventure, 'tis a gallant sea;
Or would I rest, it is a flowery lea.

Does gloom oppress? The Bible is a sun.
Or ugliness? It is a garden fair.

—Author Unknown

THE ANVIL—GOD'S WORD

Last eve I passed beside a blacksmith's door,
  And heard the anvil ring the vesper chime;
Then looking in, I saw upon the floor
  Old hammers, worn with beating years of time.

"How many anvils have you had," said I,
  "To wear and batter all these hammers so?"
"Just one," said he, and then, with twinkling eye,
  "The anvil wears the hammers out, you know."

And so, thought I, the anvil of God's Word,
  For ages skeptic blows have beat upon;
Yet, though the noise of falling blows was heard,
  The anvil is unharmed—the hammers gone.

—Author Unknown

FAITH

What if I say—
  "The Bible is God's Holy Word,
Complete, inspired, without a flaw"—
  But let its pages stay
Unread from day to day,
And fail to learn therefrom God's law;
What if I go not there to seek
  The truth of which I glibly speak,
  For guidance on this earthly way—
Does it matter what I say?

What if I say—
  That Jesus Christ is Lord divine;
  Yet fellow-pilgrims can behold
Naught of the Master's love in me,
No grace of kindly sympathy?
  If I am of the Shepherd's fold,
  Then shall I know the Shepherd's voice
And gladly make his way my choice.
We are saved by faith, yet faith is one
With life, like daylight and the sun.
Unless they flower in our deeds,
  Dead, empty husks are all the creeds.
  To call Christ, Lord, but strive not to obey,
Belies the homage that with words I pay.

—Maud Frazer Jackson

THUS SPEAKETH CHRIST, OUR LORD

Ye call Me Master and obey Me not,
Ye call Me Light and see Me not,
Ye call Me Way and walk not,
Ye call Me Life and desire Me not,
Ye call Me wise and follow Me not,
Ye call Me fair and love Me not,
Ye call Me rich and ask Me not,
Ye call Me eternal and seek Me not,

Ye call Me gracious and trust Me not,
Ye call Me noble and serve Me not,
Ye call Me mighty and honor Me not,
Ye call Me just and fear Me not;
If I condemn you, blame Me not.[2]

—*Anonymous*

THERE IS NO UNBELIEF

There is no unbelief;
Whoever plants a seed beneath the sod
And waits to see it push away the clod—
He trusts in God.

There is no unbelief;
Whoever says when clouds are in the sky,
"Be patient, heart; light breaketh by and by,"
Trusts the Most High.

There is no unbelief;
Whoever sees 'neath winter's field of snow,
The silent harvest of the future grow—
God's power must know.

There is no unbelief;
Whoever lies down on his couch to sleep,
Content to lock each sense in slumber deep,
Knows God will keep.

There is no unbelief;
Whoever says "tomorrow," "the unknown,"
"The future," trusts the power alone
He dares disown.

There is no unbelief;
The heart that looks on when the eyelids close,
And dares to live when life has only woes,
God's comfort knows.

There is no unbelief;
For thus by day and night unconsciously
The heart lives by that faith the lips deny.
God knoweth why![3]

—*Elizabeth York Case*

[2] Engraved on an old slab in the Cathedral of Lübeck, Germany.
[3] From the *Detroit Free Press*. Used with permission of the author.

STILL THOU ART QUESTION

We place Thy sacred name upon our brows;
   Our cycles from Thy natal day we score;
Yet, spite of all our songs and all our vows,
   We thirst and ever thirst to know Thee more.

For Thou art Mystery and Question still;
   Even when we see Thee lifted as a sign
Drawing all men unto that hapless hill
   With the resistless power of Love Divine.

Still Thou art Question—while rings in our ears
   Thine outcry to a world discord-beset:
Have I been with thee all these many years,
   O world—dost thou not know Me even yet?

—Author Unknown

I HAVE A RENDEZVOUS WITH GOD

I have a rendezvous with God!
Upon His blessèd day of rest,
To His loved house I go, and meet
With others on the Holy Quest;
Whose presence fills His holy place,
Our spiritual eyes behold
The radiance of our Father's face;
Then at the midweek hour of prayer
What strength flows down our need to meet,
As unto Him in prayer we turn,
United at the mercy seat!
How can I to my faith be true
If I keep not this rendezvous?

—Author Unknown

HE BUILDED HIS CHURCH

Within the hearts and souls of men
   Two thousand years ago
   He builded His Church.
He left no spires to reach the skies
   No stones piled high
   Into a great cathedral wrought.

No artisan—He shaped no cross
   Of fine carved wood or burnished brass.
   The only spires He built
Were shaped within the minds of men.
   Tall thoughts on which to later
   Build His Church.

The only Cross He left was in the
   Heart of man;
   And yet those spires, that cross—
Have towered down the centuries
   More stately, and more strong
   Than any tall cathedrals of our day.

More lasting, yet untouchable—
   For still with all the spires
   And crosses in our world
The one eternal spire remains unwrought
   Within the mind of man to challenge him,
   To lift his thoughts above.

HIS BUILDED CHURCH has but one
   cross within.
   No gold can yet compare with it,
Nor silver match its worth.
   His Church—its cross—undying lives
   Strong builded in the very heart of man.[4]

—Bernice Hogan

IS THIS THE TIME?

Is this the time, O Church of Christ! to sound retreat?
To arm with weapons cheap and blunt
The men and women who have borne the brunt
Of earth's fierce strife, and nobly held their ground?
Is this the time to halt, when all around
Horizons lift, new destinies confront
Stern duties wait the nations, never wont
To play the laggard, when God's will was found?

No! rather, strengthen stakes and lengthen cords,
Enlarge Thy plans and gifts, O Thou elect,
And to Thy Kingdom come for such a time!
The earth with all its fullness is the Lord's.
Great things attempt for Him, great things expect,

[4] From *The Bethany Guide*, December, 1954. Bethany Press, St. Louis, Mo. Reprinted by permission of the author and publishers.

Whose LOVE imperial is, whose POWER sublime
Fills all the earth, if we, who follow Him—
Build in this world, HIS CHURCH, unconquerable!

—Sumner Hoyt

GOD'S TEMPLES

I so love little churches!
  Vine-clad, of stone or brick,
Hid among elms and birches,
Time-hallowed, gentle places,
With welcome that embraces
  Both saint and heretic.

Blest are the country churches!
  I love their simple ways,
Their heartfelt hymns, that clearly
Soar up to God sincerely;
My heart remembers dearly
  Those bygone Sabbath days.

No carven pulpits gleaming,
  No wide and stately halls,
No brass and silver railing,
  Just shady porches, dreaming,
  And graceful ivy, trailing
Over the time-stained walls.

I sought God in cathedrals
  Vast aisles of white and gold;
Where waves of glorious music
  From the great organ rolled.
But God seemed high in Heaven.
  I could not sense Him there;
In all that pomp and glory
  There seemed no room for prayer.

Ah, give me little churches
  My happy childhood knew!
Time-hallowed, gentle places,
Hid among elms and birches,
Dear little country churches—
  I think God loves them, too!

—Edith D. Osborne

THE PARSON'S PRAYER

I do not ask
That crowds may throng the temple,
That standing room be priced:
I only ask that as I voice the message
They may see Christ!

I do not ask
For churchly pomp or pageant
Or music such as wealth alone can buy:
I only ask that as I voice the message
He may be nigh!

I do not ask
That men may sound my praises,
Or headlines spread my name abroad:
I only pray that as I voice the message
Hearts may find God!

I do not ask
For earthly place or laurel,
Or of this world's distinctions any part:
I only ask when I have voiced the message
My Saviour's heart!

—*Ralph S. Cushman*

THE BIBLE

We search the world for truth. We cull
The good, the true, the beautiful,
From graven stone and written scroll,
And all old flower-fields of the soul;
And, weary seekers of the best,
We come back laden from our quest,
To find that all the sages said
Is in the Book our mothers read.

—*John Greenleaf Whittier*

THE PSALM OF THE GOOD TEACHER

The Lord is my Teacher;
I shall not lose the way to wisdom.
He leadeth me in the lowly path of learning,
He prepareth a lesson for me every day.
He findeth the clear fountain of instruction—
Little by little He showeth me the beauty of truth.

The world is a great book that He has written,
He turneth the leaves for me slowly;
They are all inscribed with images and letters—
His voice poureth light on the pictures and the words.

Then am I glad when I perceive His meaning.
He taketh me by the hand to the hill-top of wisdom;
In the valley, also, He walketh beside me,
And in the dark places He whispereth in my heart.

Yea, though my lesson be hard, it is not hopeless,
For the Lord is very patient with His slow scholar.
He will wait awhile for my weakness—
He will help me to read the truth through tears—
Surely Thou wilt enlighten me daily by joy and by sorrow,
And lead me at last, O Lord, to the perfect knowledge of Thee.[5]

—Henry van Dyke

THE LOST CHRIST

Your skill has fashioned stately creeds,
But where is He, we pray—
The friendly Christ of loving deeds?
He is not here today.

With sentences that twist and tease,
Confusing mind and heart,
You forge your wordy homilies
And bid us heed your art.

But where is He—or can you tell?—
Who stilled the brother's strife,
Who urged the woman at the well
To live a better life?

[5] From *The Poems of Henry van Dyke*, copyright, 1920. Published by Charles Scribner's Sons. Used by permission.

Where is the Saint of Galilee,
    Crude Peter's faithful Guide;
The Man who wept at Bethany
    Because His friend had died?

We weary of your misty lore
    Behind dead walls of gray;
We want His loving words once more
    By some Emmaus way.

Give us the Christ who can bestow
    Some comfort-thought of death.
Give us a Christ our hearts can know—
    The Man of Nazareth.

                —*Thomas Curtis Clark*

WINDOWS OF THE SOUL

Let there be many windows in your soul,
That all the glory of the universe
May beautify it. Not the narrow pane
Of one poor creed can catch the radiant rays
That shine from countless sources. Tear away
The blinds of superstition. Let the light
Pour through fair windows, broad as truth itself,
And high as heaven. . . . Tune your ear
To all the wordless music of the stars,
And to the voice of Nature; and your heart
Shall turn to truth and goodness as the plant
Turns to the sun. A thousand unseen hands
Reach down to help you to their peace-crowned heights;
And all the forces of the firmament
Shall fortify your strength. Be not afraid
To thrust aside half-truths and grasp the whole.[6]

                —*Ella Wheeler Wilcox*

ALTAR FLOWERS

In chapel tonight
I suddenly became aware
of the flowers
on the altar
as I had not been aware

[6] From *Poems of Progress.* Published by W. B. Conkey Company, Chicago, Ill. Used by permission of the publishers.

of them
before.
There is nothing in my life
comparable to the beauty
of these humble blossoms
of red poinsettias.
What am I in the presence
of these exquisite tokens
of Thy divine artistry?
The shabbiness of my life
can offer Thee no worship
like unto the silent praise
of these flowers
on the altar.[7]

—Chandran Devanesen

✠

TWO THOUSAND MILES FOR A BOOK

By

Cynthia Pearl Maus

MANY, many years ago, when the Nez Percé Indians, who lived in that section of the great Northwest which is the source of the Columbia River, heard about the white man's Book of Heaven, they said it was the source of the white man's power. Traders had told them that some day missionaries would come from the country toward the rising sun with the white man's Bible and tell them all about this wonderful God; and so for years they waited and watched in vain.

Finally a tribal council was called and after much deliberation it was decided to send five of their braves, three old men and two young ones, on a long journey into the great unknown land beyond the Rocky Mountains in search of the white man's Book of Heaven.

One spring morning the five braves who had been chosen turned their faces eastward, but after two days of hard travel, one of the old men turned back, saying that he was too old to endure the hardships on the way. The others traveled for months, two thousand miles across mountains, hills, and plains until they reached St. Louis, Missouri, then but a small frontier post where a few hundred settlers made their home.

Early one October morning in 1882 these travel-worn Indians saw in the distance the houses of this little settlement. It was the first town they had ever seen; but if they were surprised, they gave no sign. Stolidly they pushed their silent way through the streets, looking to neither the right nor the left.

[7] From *The Cross Is Lifted* by Chandran Devanesen. Copyright, 1954, by Friendship Press, Inc., New York, N.Y. Reprinted by permission.

When General Clark, who was then in command of the barracks, heard that four strange Indians were without, he sent two officers to bring them in, thinking they had come to make a treaty of some sort. The Indians entered the barracks with calm dignity, and after greeting General Clark, took their seats in silence. Days passed and still these strange messengers said nothing as to the purpose of their journey; but at last they told the meaning of it all: "They wanted the white man's Book of Heaven. Would General Clark give it to them? They wanted to know God as the white man knew Him. Would General Clark tell them? They wanted a teacher who would go with them to the land of the Setting Sun, there to break to their people the 'bread of life'— would General Clark send one?"

General Clark hardly knew what to say. He told them all he thought they could understand about the white man's God, but he had no Bible printed in the language those Indians used, and he was not in command of missionaries; and so he could not fully satisfy their strange request.

All winter long the Indians waited and watched, hoping to learn more than had yet been told them of the white man's God. During that time General Clark planned amusements for them, and did everything he could to make their stay a pleasure. That winter the two old men, weakened by their long journey, sickened and died, and in the spring the two who remained indicated their desire to start again on the long journey back to their people.

General Clark heaped many rich gifts upon them in parting and on the night before their departure he gave them a great banquet in his own home. When the meal was over he asked Ta-wis-sis-sim-nim (No Horns on His Head) to address the company. And these are the words which that silent Indian spoke, as translated by a Wyandotte Indian who was present at the banquet and who acted as interpreter:

"I came to you over the trail of many moons from the land of the setting sun. You were the friends of my fathers who have gone the long way. I came to you with my eyes partly open for my people who sit in darkness. I go back with both eyes closed. How can I go back blind to my blind people? I made my way to you with strong arms through many enemies and strange lands that I might carry back to them the white man's Book of Heaven. I go back with both arms broken and empty. The two fathers who came with us were braves of many snows and wars. We leave them asleep here by your great river and tepees. They were tired in many moons, and their moccasins wore out.

"My people sent me to get the white man's Book of Heaven. You took me to where your women dance, as ours do not, but the Book was not there! You took me to where they worship the Great Spirit with candles, but the Book was not there! You showed me images of the Great Spirit and pictures of the Good Land beyond, but the Book was not among them to show me the way! I am going back the long trail to my people who sit in darkness. You make my feet heavy with gifts and my moccasins will grow old in carrying them, and yet the Book is not among them to show me the Way! When I tell my people in the big council that I did not bring the Book, no word will be spoken. One by one they will rise up and go out in silence! My people will die in darkness, and they will go on that long journey to other hunting-grounds. No white man will go with them, no white man's Book will make plain the way! I have no more words!"

The homeward journey was made as easy as possible for those two disappointed Indians. They were put on board a Missouri River steamer whose captain took the first fire-canoe that ever made that long journey of twenty-two hundred miles to the mouth of the Yellowstone River. Ta-wis-sis-sim-nim, who made that sorrowful speech at the banquet, died near the mouth of the Yellowstone, so that only one of the four was left to tell the story. He made his way back to his people with a message to cheer on his lips, even if there was a bitter, burning disappointment in his heart. He said: "A white man will be sent with the Book!"

And today, all over the United States, in Canada, aye, even in far-away Alaska, messengers of the cross are taking the white man's Book of Heaven to the Indians.[8]

✦

FOR SUCH AN AGE AS THIS!

By

Lynn Harold Hough

ONE day I rode from the railroad in the valley up to Jerusalem in an automobile of American manufacture. It seemed odd enough to go gliding toward the ancient city with the engine humming and the Syrian chauffeur with his clear, quick eyes and his steady hand at the wheel. One thought of those long-fled years when the ass was the carrier of powerful kings. One remembered that Jesus entered Jerusalem riding on an ass. He had a word of mastery for that ancient day. You still see camels with their burdens in Jerusalem. As you look at their awkward ease of motion you are tempted to think that they, too, represent the world of the prophets and of Jesus. You are tempted to think that the world of swift-moving cars—all the complicated world of modern machinery—has passed beyond His ken. Is it possible to think of Him as Lord of a world of moving wheels and bolts and softly-humming dynamos? Is the Bible best represented by lonely ivy growing upon a forgotten wall? Or is it like a tree of life yet continuing healing for the nations? Is it a memory of tragic loneliness? Or is it a power more potent than dynamos, more effective than great engines? Perhaps you look up at a passing airplane in Syria, and as you follow it with pursuing eyes to dim distances you wonder if it has made it impossible to see the bright shining of angels' wings. You think of all the vast steel structures in the world and you wonder if Bethlehem in Penn-

[8] From *Heralds of the Cross among Early Americans*, Maus. Published by the American Christian Missionary Society. Used with permission.

sylvania has taken the place of Bethlehem in Judæa. You enter a vast factory full of automatic workers—you see the power of the iron man in industry—and you wonder if the clear-eyed prophet of Nazareth can make Himself heard in all this din.

The situation is serious enough and you turn with a half-whimsical understanding to the foresight of the inhabitants of Samuel Butler's *Erewhon* who destroyed the machines before they became their masters. For all that you cannot go the full length of the suggestion of that great man, Mahatma Gandhi, and bring back the spinning-wheel and throw the dynamo into the rubbish heap. The problem of the machine cannot be solved by an executioner. It must be solved by a master. If modern civilization is likened to a high-powered automobile we may gaze at the great machinery with grave anxiety. But we will see, sooner or later, that we cannot meet the situation by destroying the machine. What we really need to do is to find a new driver. We will scarcely cease to produce machines. We must learn how to produce men who can be trusted to control and use the machinery for the purposes of moral and spiritual order, for the good of the world and the honor of God.

All fears that the Scriptures have become antiquated vanish quickly enough when we see that persons great enough and good enough to save civilization from a sort of mechanical suicide are the supreme need of the hour. The age which produces machines is not particularly skillful in producing persons. The ages which produced great persons must teach us how to produce the masters of our machines.

There is no literature like the Bible for teaching us how to produce men who are stronger than their own desires. Only the Man who rode into Jerusalem on an ass knows the secret of making men whose hands will be steady upon our high-powered machines. The safety of the world is in the hands of the driver. And it is the driver who can be provided by the Man of Galilee.[9]

✠

THE LEGEND OF THE PERFECT GIFT

In the heart of the city of Constantinople the great Church of Saint Sophia stands. And this is the legend of the way in which it received its name.

Long, long ago, back in the sixth century, the Emperor Justinian lived in the city of Constantinople. He was a great emperor and a great builder, and many were the things that he built for his people—public buildings, fortresses, and other things that would stand for years in the Empire. Finally he wanted to build something that would be his monument—something to be named for him, and that people for centuries would look upon and say, "Behold! this is the work of the Emperor Justinian."

[9] From *World Call*, July, 1932. Used with permission of the author and publishers.

Long he thought about it, and at last decided that he would erect a great church. No other hand, no other purse, was to be allowed to contribute to its construction. His was to be the decision in every detail—his the provision for every expense.

The last stone was lifted into place; the day of the dedication came; the crowd pressed close about the door, and Justinian drew back the veil. A shout of amazement burst from the crowd. For where the name of Justinian was to have been engraved, the name of an unknown woman stood!

"Who is this woman?" demanded the Emperor. "Hunt her out and bring her here!"

After a long search they brought her before the platform—a shrunken old woman, almost in tears. In broken sentences she sobbed out her story.

"I do not know how my name came to be written there. I have made no contribution to the temple: I am too poor for that. Only one day as the oxen went past my house, I saw how they were struggling under the load of heavy stones and I snatched a little straw from my mattress and held it up for them to eat."

That was all she had done—all that her poverty would allow her to do. But the angels who weigh the motives of men and women had written her name there instead of the Emperor Justinian's, because, having nothing else to give, she had given as her heart prompted her.

When you visit Saint Sophia chapel today, you will find the corner stone blank. You will be told that in due time the angels erased the name of this poor woman also, that the church might bear but one name, that of SOPHIA, which being translated means "divine wisdom."

But the memory of this woman lives though her name may be forgotten—lives forever in this legend of a perfect gift.[10]—*Anonymous*

✢

HE TOOK IT UPON HIMSELF

A MONK once lived in a rude stone hut on the mountain-side, where he could see from his window the village on whose streets he had played as a happy little boy. But it had been five years since he had left his home and the hillside where he had cared for the cattle.

Wearing the cross and a long robe fastened with a cord about his waist—the symbol of his order—he had entered into solitude, hoping to rid himself of the burden of the poverty, sin, and shame which lurked about him.

He had climbed the plateau, built his hut, and planted his garden, enjoying the sunrise and sunset as he listened to the birds and breezes. Ignorant of the

[10] From *The Pilgrim Elementary Teacher,* Pilgrim Press, Boston, Mass. Used with special permission.

world and the sufferings of others, he read and meditated and prayed. Thus he was content and thus he grew strong.

Then one day he fell asleep and dreamed. He had just finished reading the story of Calvary, and was so thrilled with that sad story of the cross, that he knelt in prayer, and as he prayed he fell asleep. As he slept he dreamed that he walked upon the road from earth to heaven. It was dark at first and hard to travel. But as he traveled on it grew lighter, and then beautiful with blossoming flowers.

At a turn in the road he met the Master. "O Master," he cried, kneeling at His feet, "why didst Thou leave us? We need Thee so sorely. Couldst Thou not have stayed?"

The Master answered, softly, "I finished the work I had to do."

"But the poverty and sin," said the monk, "are still with us. O Master, who can bear the burden of man's need?"

The Master smiled. "I share with those who love Me the burden of man's need. I left part of the burden for them."

"But, Master," cried the monk, in sorrow and in fear, as the Master looked deep into his soul, "what if they fail Thee?"

"Ah," said the Master of Men, "I am counting on those who *love Me,* and 'love never faileth.'"

The monk awoke. His dream had been so real, and the vision so clear, that he gazed for some moments about the tiny room, and then out into the moonlight. Later he sat down in silence to think. It had been so quiet, so comfortable; there had been time for worship and thought. But the dream disturbed him.

Again he fell upon his knees and prayed. Then he arose, took off his robe, and folding it neatly with the cross and beads laid it away. With mingled feelings of fear and hope he dressed in the clothes he had worn when, as a young student, he had left his father's house. "Now," he said, softly, "I am one of them—His friends on whom He is counting." Then he grasped his mountain stick firmly and started down the trail. And as he walked his look of fear changed to one of joy.

"I'm going back," he said aloud. "Back down into the midst of problems that must be met and solved—down where life is hard and men must toil; down into the thick of the battle with selfishness and greed; down into the midst of mad pleasure, where souls seek release and find it not—into homes where men and women struggle to be true and fail. The Master has finished His part. Now He works through me. I must not fail Him."—*Author Unknown*

THE STORY OF AN OLD, OLD BOOK

THE Holy Bible is a many-sided book, written by numerous "men of God" over a long period of years. Jeremiah 36:1-10 gives us a picture of how many portions of the Book of Books came to be:

And it came to pass in the fourth year of Jehoiakim the son of Josiah king of Judah, that this word came unto Jeremiah from the Lord, saying,

Take thee a roll of a book, and write therein all the words that I have spoken unto thee against Israel, and against Judah, and against all the nations, from the day I spake unto thee, from the days of Josiah, even unto this day.

It may be that the house of Judah will hear all the evil which I purpose to do unto them; that they may return every man from his evil way; that I may forgive their iniquity and their sin.

Then Jeremiah called Baruch the son of Neriah: and Baruch wrote from the mouth of Jeremiah all the words of the Lord, which he had spoken unto him, upon a roll of a book.

And Jeremiah commanded Baruch, saying, I am shut up; I cannot go into the house of the Lord:

Therefore go thou, and read in the roll, which thou hast written from my mouth, the words of the Lord in the ears of the people in the Lord's house upon the fasting day: and also thou shalt read them in the ears of all Judah that come out of their cities.

It may be they will present their supplication before the Lord, and will return every one from his evil way: for great is the anger and the fury that the Lord hath pronounced against this people.

And Baruch the son of Neriah did according to all that Jeremiah the prophet commanded him, reading in the book the words of the Lord in the Lord's house.

And it came to pass in the fifth year of Jehoiakim the son of Josiah king of Judah, in the ninth month, that they proclaimed a fast before the Lord to all the people in Jerusalem, and to all the people that came from the cities of Judah unto Jerusalem.

Then read Baruch in the book the words of Jeremiah in the house of the Lord, in the chamber of Gemariah the son of Shaphan the scribe, in the higher court, at the entry of the new gate of the Lord's house, in the ears of all the people.—JEREMIAH 36:1-10, A.V.

Through all the succeeding centuries men have at times remembered, and at times forgot to read the truths contained in the most widely known and published book in the world—the Holy Bible.

Every Christian, and many non-Christian, homes feel that they must have a copy of God's word in their own homes. Yet it often remains the least frequently read book of all that grace their homes or library shelves.

In bygone years the large family Bible, as it was called, was used as a sort of filing place for important documents, bits of poetry and prose, and family records. Not infrequently paper money was tucked away between its pages for safekeeping against a rainy day. Many of these old family Bibles provided blank pages in which the births, deaths and marriages of members of the household were recorded. Facsimiles of portions of such family records have been used frequently to establish the date and place of one's birth for important legal documents or in securing passports for travel to faraway places.

In bygone years this family Bible was used almost daily for worship, the father or mother reading aloud from its pages portions for the spiritual enrichment and guidance of members of the household. In the rush and turmoil of present-day living the reading of God's word is neglected, and a family Bible has almost entirely disappeared.

A smaller copy of the Book of Books is to be found in nearly every home, but it is often tucked away in a forgotten corner, rarely used, and dusted only when the minister is coming to call, or some saint in Israel is to be a guest in the home for a few days.

If your Bible and my Bible could talk, I wonder what story they would tell of our devotional habits? Some years ago the *Churchman Magazine* published an article entitled "The Diary of a Bible." It is a bit humorous and a bit outmoded *now;* and yet it reveals the habits of many present-day church members in relation to their Bible. It is included here to make you smile a bit, and *think*. If your Bible could talk, would it reveal a similar story?

The Diary of a Bible

January 15th:	"I've been resting quietly for a week. The first few nights after the first of the year my owner read me regularly; but now, he has forgotten me, I guess."
February 2nd:	"Cleaned up. I was dusted today, along with other things, and put back in my place."
February 22nd:	"My owner used me for a short time after dinner. Looked up a few references. Going to Sunday School 'tomorrow.'"
March 7th:	"Cleaned up. Dusted, and in my old place again. Have been down in the lower hall since my trip to Sunday School."
April 2nd:	"Busy day. My owner led a Christian Endeavor meeting and had to look up references. He had an awful time finding me, although I was right there in my place all the time."
May 5th:	"In Grandma's lap. She is here on a visit. Today she let a tear drop on Colossians 2:5-7."
May 6th:	"In Grandma's lap again this afternoon. She spent most of her time on I Corinthians 13, and the last four verses of the 15th chapter."
May 7, 8 and 9th:	"In Grandma's lap every afternoon now. It's a comfortable spot. Sometimes she reads me, and sometimes she talks to me."

May 10th: "Grandma's gone. Back in my old place again. She kissed me goodbye."

June 4th: "Had a couple of four-leaf clovers stuck in me today."

July 1st: "Packed in a trunk with clothes and other things. Off on a vacation, I guess."

July 7th: "Still in the old trunk."

July 10th: "Still in the old trunk, although nearly everything else has been taken out."

July 15th: "Home again and in my old place. Quite a journey, although I do not see why I went, for I was never taken out of the trunk."

August 1st: "Rather stuffy and hot. Have two magazines, a novel and an old hat on top of me. Wish they would take them off."

September 10th: "Cleaned up. Dusted and set right again."

September 22nd: "Used by Mary a few minutes today. She was writing a letter to a friend whose brother had died and wanted an appropriate verse."

October 1st: "Back in my old place again. Not even dusted this week. I seem to be used only for emergencies. Wonder why they bother with me at all?"[11]

✠

HOLY BIBLE, BOOK DIVINE

THERE is no more thrilling story in all history than the romance of the English Bible, and the price men have paid∙ to preserve its message for humanity. Through the centuries the Holy Bible has been a rich source of inspiration and comfort to people of every race, nation, and clime. Especially is this true of the period following immediately the Protestant Reformation. For centuries, during the Dark Ages, the Book of Books was chained in monasteries, where only a few privileged monks could have access to it. With the coming of the Protestant Reformation, however, it was liberated and men encouraged to read for themselves its priceless messages.

The invention of printing in the fifteenth century soon made the Bible available to the masses at comparatively moderate prices, so that this book soon came to be one of the most priceless possessions of men and women everywhere.

Something of what the Bible has meant and continues to mean to the hearts of men, the author, John Burton, has attempted to present in the words of his beautiful hymn:

> Holy Bible, Book divine,
> Precious treasure, thou art mine;
> Mine to tell me whence I came;
> Mine to tell me what I am.

[11] From *Churchman Magazine*. Used by permission of the publishers.

Refrain

Holy Bible, Book divine,
Precious treasure, thou art mine;
O thou holy Book divine,
Precious treasure, thou art mine!

Mine to chide me when I rove;
Mine to show a Saviour's love;
Mine thou art to guide and guard
Mine to punish or reward.

Refrain

Mine to comfort in distress,
Suff'ring in this wilderness;
Mine to show, by living faith,
Man can triumph over death.

Refrain

Mine to tell of joys to come,
And the rebel sinner's doom;
O thou holy Book divine,
Precious treasure, thou art mine.[12]

—John Burton

✛

O WORD OF GOD INCARNATE

THE power of the Word of God as an influence for good is universally recognized. The world's greatest leaders in all ages have been influenced by the Bible and its precepts. Christian leaders of today all agree that what this sin-sick world of ours needs most is the practice of the teachings of Christ as we find them recorded in the Book of Books.

The word of God deserves a place of respect and distinction in our hearts and homes, and in the educational curriculum of the church and church school, because the general education of all English-speaking people began with its translation in 1611.

James Bryce, one of the greatest of English ambassadors to our land, once said that no one could understand the history of man's progress during the past two thousand years without a knowledge of the Bible.

Something of the wisdom and guidance which the Bible contains for the children of men, William Walsham How has attempted to put into the words

---

[12] From *Hymns and Sacred Songs,* by E. O. Excell. Published by Hope Publishing Company, Chicago, Ill. Used with permission of the publishers.

of his great hymn, "O Word of God Incarnate," which was written in 1867.
It is usually sung to the tune "Munich," an old German chorale.

O Word of God incarnate,
  O wisdom from on high,
O Truth unchanged, unchanging,
  O Light of our dark sky;
We praise thee for the radiance
  That from the hallowed page,
A lantern to our footsteps,
  Shines on from age to age.

The Church from her dear Master
  Received the gift divine,
And still that light she lifteth
  O'er all the earth to shine.
It is a golden casket,
  Where gems of truth are stored;
It is the heaven-drawn picture
  Of Christ, the living Word.

It floateth like a banner,
  Before God's host unfurled;
It shineth like a beacon
  Above the darkling world;
It is the chart and compass
  That o'er life's surging sea,
'Mid mists and rocks and darkness,
  Still guides, O Christ, to thee.

O make thy Church, dear Saviour,
  A lamp of purest gold,
To bear before the nations
  Thy true light, as of old.
O teach thy wandering pilgrims
  By this their path to trace,
Till, clouds and darkness ended,
  They see thee face to face. Amen.

          —*William Walsham How, 1867*

✤

HOLY SPIRIT, TRUTH DIVINE

IN THIS great hymn, "Holy Spirit, Truth Divine," which was written by
Samuel Longfellow in 1864, we have another of those great hymns of the
church that stress the power and influence of the Holy Spirit as it is revealed
to us through the Word of God.

The extent to which Christians may claim the leadership of God's Holy Spirit in their lives is conditioned pretty largely on how familiar they are with the life and spirit of Jesus as revealed to us in the Book of Books. But the Bible is not a miraculous book that in some strange or unusual way implants itself on idle souls. It is a book of religious history to be read and studied, just as we would read and study any other book of a similar character.

The Bible differs from all other books in this respect, however, that to grow in one's understanding of its meaning, one must *live* its *teaching*. Not how much of it can you quote, but how much of the teaching of Jesus have you actually lived out in your everyday relationships with men and women. Jesus said "Know the truth and the truth shall make you free." As we seek His truth, and only to the extent that we seek His truth can we claim the leadership of His Holy Spirit in our lives. Something of this message we sing into our own souls as we sing this great hymn of the church.

Holy Spirit, Truth divine,
Dawn upon this soul of mine;
Word of God, and inward Light,
Wake my spirit, clear my sight.

Holy Spirit, Love divine,
Glow within this heart of mine;
Kindle every high desire;
Perish self in Thy pure fire.

Holy Spirit, Power divine,
Fill and nerve this will of mine;
By Thee may I strongly live,
Bravely bear, and nobly strive.

Holy Spirit, Right divine,
King within my conscience reign;
Be my law, and I shall be,
Firmly bound, forever free.

Holy Spirit, Joy divine,
Gladden Thou this heart of mine;
In the desert ways I sing,
"Spring, O Well, forever spring." Amen.

—Samuel Longfellow, 1864

I LOVE THY KINGDOM, LORD

"I Love Thy Kingdom, Lord" is not a new hymn. For more than a century it has contributed to the enrichment of Christian experience as men, women, and children have sung of their love for Christ, His Church and His Kingdom.

While this hymn expresses the heart-throb of Christians of all ages, I feel that it belongs in a peculiar way to childhood, for did not the Master of Men, Himself, say, "Of such are the Kingdom of Heaven."

Jesus not only "set the child in the midst" in the Christian religion; but He made the childlike mind and heart the badge of discipleship. We cannot hope to become or to remain children in His Kingdom of Love except as we become teachable, quickly forgetting and fully forgiving as does the little child.

Each time we sing this great hymn we need to remind ourselves that loving Christ, His Church and His Kingdom, makes service to "even the least of these" imperative in our daily behavior. For as we love, and in proportion to our love, we serve men, women, and children everywhere.

> I love Thy kingdom, Lord,
> The house of thine abode.
> The church our blest Redeemer saved
> With His own precious blood.
>
> I love thy Church, O God;
> Her walls before Thee stand,
> Dear as the apple of Thine eye,
> And graven on Thy hand.
>
> Sure as thy truth shall last,
> To Zion shall be given
> The brightest glories earth can yield,
> And brighter bliss of heaven.
>
> *—Timothy Dwight, 1800*

✠

THE CHURCH'S ONE FOUNDATION

In the long ago Jesus said, "On this rock I will build my church." It is of this rock, Christ Jesus, that the poet sings in this great hymn, "The Church's One Foundation." The words of this song were written by Samuel J. Stone in 1866. It may be sung to either of two tunes, "Aurelia," written by Samuel S. Wesley in 1864, or "Descant" composed by William Lester Bates in 1930.

This hymn with its more or less martial music provides one of the finest processional and recessional hymns that the Church knows. The tramping of the feet of millions of people who have found life abundant through the Church of Jesus Christ is in its rhythm and content. We feel, as we sing the words to this mighty hymn of affirmation, that the Christian hosts of all the ages are marching side by side in the task of building, through the Church, God's Kingdom of Love.

The Church is Christ's. "With His own blood He bought her," and that she might have victorious life, He died. Courage and high resolve are the motif of this great hymn. It strengthens our faith; it helps us to envision the greatness of the task to which we have been called as helpers. It glows with the joy of comradeship with Jesus in completing the unfinished task which He left to His Church in the world.

> The Church's one foundation
>   Is Jesus Christ her Lord;
> She is His new creation
>   By water and the word;
> From heaven He came and sought her
>   To be His holy bride;
> With His own blood He bought her,
>   And for her life He died.
>
> Elect from every nation,
>   Yet one o'er all the earth,
> Her charter of salvation
>   One Lord, one faith, one birth;
> One holy name she blesses,
>   Partakes one holy food,
> And to one hope she presses,
>   With every grace endued.
>
> 'Mid toil and tribulation,
>   And tumult of her war,
> She waits the consummation
>   Of peace forevermore;
> Till with the vision glorious
>   Her longing eyes are blest,
> And the great Church victorious,
>   Shall be the Church at rest.
>
> Yet she on earth hath union
>   With Father, Spirit, Son,
> And mystic sweet communion
>   With those whose rest is won;
> O happy ones and holy;
>   Lord, give us grace that we,
> Like them, the meek and lowly,
>   On high may dwell with Thee. Amen.

—Samuel J. Stone, 1866

CONTENTS

PART VI   SECTION II

IN THE BEAUTY OF NATURE AND IN HUMAN LIFE

---✝---

"Lo, I am with you always, even unto the end of the world."—MATTHEW 28:20

---✝---

535

✠

IN THE BEAUTY OF NATURE AND IN
HUMAN LIFE

"The heavens declare the glory of God;
  And the firmament showeth his handiwork.
Day unto day uttereth speech,
  And night unto night showeth knowledge.
There is no speech nor language;
  Their voice is not heard.
Their line is gone out through all the earth,
  And their words to the end of the world.
In them hath he set a tabernacle for the sun,
  Which is as a bridegroom coming out of his chamber,
  And rejoiceth as a strong man to run his course.
His going forth is from the end of the heavens,
  And his circuit unto the ends of it;
  And there is nothing hid from the heat thereof."

—Psalms 19:1-6

✠

"Consider the lilies of the field, how they grow; they toil not, neither do they spin; yet I say unto you, Even Solomon in all his glory was not arrayed like one of these. But if God doth so clothe the grass in the field, which to-day is, and to-morrow is cast into the oven; how much more *shall he clothe* you, O ye of little faith?"— Luke 12:27-28

"SUFFER THE CHILDREN TO COME UNTO ME"—SIMEONEY

"SUFFER THE CHILDREN TO COME UNTO ME"

By

A. Simeony

(Interpretation)

THIS comparatively modern painting of Jesus and the children by A. Simeony has unusual attraction because in it both Jesus and the children are intimately associated with the flowers, whose fragrant beauty is not unlike that of sweet, unspoiled childhood.

The artist, with consummate skill, has portrayed the Master sitting on a rock against the background of a flowering shrub, resting, no doubt, for a moment in a journey with His disciples from one place of healing and teaching to another. As He thus reposes, refreshing Himself in the glory and fragrance of one of nature's beauty spots, a mother and a group of children who have been gathering wild flowers among the rocks approach to pay their childish homage to the Children's Friend. It is easy to see that they all are anxious to share their precious "pretties" with the kind Teacher they have been taught to love and worship.

Children seem to have an intuitive knowledge about whom they can trust; and the Master of Men was the kind of person they found it easy to approach. The charm and beauty of these "little ones" beggar description, from the tiniest one snuggling against his mother's shoulder as he reaches out two chubby hands toward Jesus, to his more aggressive sister who is holding out toward the Master some of the lovely wild daisies her tiny hands have picked among the rocks.

That this Lover of Children is welcoming them with open arms is evident. His face shows a bit of weariness and His feet are no doubt travel-sore as He rests for a moment along the wayside; but His heart is being renewed with an inner sense of the worth-whileness of His task as He looks into the fresh, trusting, unspoiled faces of these human flowers in God's Kingdom of Love.

On more than one occasion the Master Who had said: "Consider the lilies of the field, they toil not, neither do they spin, and yet I say unto you that Solomon in all his glory was not arrayed like one of these," called the attention of His disciples, who thought they had bigger and more important things to do, to the needs of little children, saying: "It is not the Father's will that even the least of these should perish."

The disciples in the background do not quite see the importance of this delay, merely that the Master may, for a brief time, commune with little children and accept their simple gifts of wayside flowers. Judas in the near background clearly shows his irritation over so futile a waste of precious time. The other four are perhaps a bit more charitable—after all, children are important to the continued on-going of the race; but the Master of Men is in no hurry. He loves these children for themselves, for their artless grace, for their beauty of form and face, for the purity of their souls which under the right sort of environment and parental guidance will, in the years that lie ahead, become the "saviours of mankind." He knows all too well, "that as childhood goes, so goes the world."

The Master's words, "Suffer the little children to come unto Me, and forbid them not," have, through the centuries, become the Magna Charta of childhood. All the progress that has taken place during the intervening years with respect to their care, nurture, and education, dates back to the understanding heart of the Master of Men, who saw in the upturned faces of little children, as in the lilies of the field, the image of His heavenly Father.

Study each little face, for there is no repetition of expression or gesture; and your own heart will warm with gratitude to the artist who thus painted for us the children bringing their gifts of flowers to the Master as He sat resting by the wayside.

Flowers, sunshine, birds and the freedom of God's great out-of-doors should be the heritage of children everywhere; and you and I, His followers, each in his own community, must take up the crusade of "sins against childhood" until they are freed from every form of bondage that shackles even "the least of these" His little ones.

This is the message that the artist would have us feel as we look at this painting, "Suffer the children to come unto Me."

✤

THE GOOD SHEPHERD

By

Bernard Plockhorst

(Interpretation)

To REALLY appreciate the message of this great painting, "The Good Shepherd," by the German artist, Bernard Plockhorst, one needs to read, again and again, the Gospel story (John 10:1-16), because it was upon this incident, and the name "The Good Shepherd," which Jesus applied to Himself, that the artist based his picture.

We need to remember, as we study this great painting, that Jesus was a man of the out-of-doors. He loved wild nature, the sea, the sky, the mountains and hills of His native land. Probably no man in all Palestine spent more time tramping up and down the length and breadth of that little strip of country which we call "The Holy Land" than Jesus, during the brief years of His life and ministry among the children of men.

We need, also, to remember that Palestine is an Eastern country with customs that are prevailingly Oriental. It is a sheep-and-shepherd country. Even today it is not uncommon for visitors in Palestine to see the shepherds leading their flocks toward a common corral where they will be safe for the night, several flocks, belonging to different shepherds, often occupying the same sheepfold. In the morning each shepherd will call his own sheep, and without the slightest confusion, each flock will separate from the others as they withdraw from the corral, following their own shepherd, whose voice they know. The twenty-third Psalm is not only a beautiful, but an accurate, description of the custom that prevails, even today, among shepherds in folding their flocks for the night.

The sheep never make a mistake when they hear their shepherd's call, for as John says: "The sheep follow him, for they know his voice." Day and night the shepherd is with his sheep. One of the most familiar sights in Oriental countries is to see the shepherd leading his flock either to pasture or to the fold. Frequently there will be with him and the flock one or two large, fierce-looking dogs, strong enough to do battle with a wolf, or by their barking to give warning of the approach of thieves or other enemies.

The sheepfold, or corral, has, as a rule, only one opening, and at this opening the shepherd stations himself, counting the sheep as they enter, occasionally giving a thirsty one a bit of water, and watching for sores or bruised feet that must be anointed with healing oil. When all are within the fold the good shepherd stations himself directly in the opening to the inclosure for the night, thus becoming literally the door (entrance) to the sheepfold.

During the day, these shepherds are, for the most part, alone on the rocky slopes and in the canyons where the sheep graze. They have few companions other than the sheep, and this, of course, intensifies the comradeship that exists between sheep and the shepherd.

Around his shoulders the shepherd wears a cloth about seven or eight feet long and four feet wide, with a slit at each end through which his hands may be thrust, thus making it easy to grasp the shepherd's crook, or staff, in one hand, and at the same time have the other one free to rescue sheep from entangling briers.

Such a cloth may be seen about the Master's shoulders in Plockhorst's painting of "The Good Shepherd." It is a common thing also for the Oriental shepherd to gather into his arms one of the lambs, as Jesus is represented as having done in this picture, so that these little ones, ignorant of dangers lurking near, may not stray away from the flock.

Many of the followers of Christ are a good deal like sheep. Some follow near, and therefore enjoy the intimate fellowship that such close following brings; while others wander off into worldly enticements, where the perils are greatest and strength to resist least. Even the greatest of Christian leaders

THE GOOD SHEPHERD—*PLOCKHORST*

sometimes follow afar off. Peter was following Christ "afar off" when he strayed into the courtyard of the High Priest's palace on the night of Jesus' betrayal and arrest. He warmed himself by the enemy's fire, and ended with a thricefold betrayal of the Master whom he really loved.

The churches today are full of so-called Christians who follow Jesus, if at all, "afar off." And because they do not follow the Master closely in loving service, they drift into all sorts of by-paths and temptations, only to discover, in the time of great need or heartache, that they have forsaken the One whose companionship would mean most to them in time of peril and disaster, for the "hireling" who escapes when troubles come.

Notice the mother sheep of the little lamb that "The Good Shepherd" is carrying in His arm. She may not be able to see, as we can, the thorn in his leg; but she knows he has been hurt, and follows close to the shepherd, watching with a mother's anxious care the face of her little one.

Note also the wild, rugged beauty of the background of the picture—the narrow stony path between the rocks, the entangling thorns along the wayside, the lacy tree leaves, and the brook or pool's dim shore line in the distance.

The face of "The Good Shepherd," as with downcast eyes He fondles close to Him this injured lamb, is beautiful indeed. The tenderness of a mother is in the enfolding embrace in which He carries to safety even "the least of these."

✛

JESUS AND THE CHILDREN

By

Paul Hippolyte Flandrin

(Interpretation)

AMONG the modern paintings of Christ blessing the children, none, perhaps, is more homey and wholesome than this one, called "Jesus and the Children," by the French painter, Paul Hippolyte Flandrin, who was born in 1856. To me it is particularly attractive because it associates the Son of God with the great out-of-doors which He loved.

In this picture the tired Christ has no doubt stopped at some wayside home to rest, while a group of children of the everyday laboring class have gathered at His feet.

In the background is a mother quieting a fretful baby, while farther away, through an opening in the wall at her back, may be seen the spires of distant buildings.

This picture tells its own story. I have the feeling, as I look at it, that the flaxen-haired girlie whose chin Jesus is holding has perhaps made the little boy at the Master's side cry because she has been unwilling to share her toys,

JESUS AND THE CHILDREN—FLANDRIN

or because she may, with childish thoughtlessness, have monopolized some toy that belonged to him. Whatever the Great Teacher has just said to this straight-shouldered little girl with her hands clasped behind her, has arrested the attention of all the others, and they, too, have stopped their play to listen to what He is saying.

Even the dreamy-eyed, shy youth at His side has dried his tears and is both listening and thinking with the Master as He makes plain to these children the fact that thoughtlessness and selfishness bring happiness to no one and often cause misery and heartache.

I feel, too, that I would like to have been a member of this children's group near this wayside home as the Great Teacher tells them in His simple, direct, yet never-to-be forgotten way how to bring joy and happiness into the lives of others instead of tears and sadness.

One cannot look at Flandrin's "Jesus and the Children" without feeling that a story-lesson is going on, and to wish that "all the things that He began both to do and to teach" had somehow been preserved for the children of men. The quantity of choice teaching material that has been forever lost because "the books of the world would not begin to contain all of His wisdom," can never be measured. Enough truth is written, however, to enable us to both listen and follow with these children in the abundant way which the world's Great Teacher came to make plain.

As we gaze at the intense interest and attention in the rapt faces of these little children we have the feeling that whatever the problem may have been that has, for the time being at least, resulted in a lack of harmony, it will never again occur. For the Great Teacher not only taught adults, but children, with the authority of truth to which their own inmost hearts with joy responded.

The sturdy little play-horse in the background, which may have been the bone of contention, seems to be standing at attention also as if he knew that nothing, not even as nice a play-horse as he is, is worth quarreling about.

✛

CHRIST AT DAWN

By

Warner E. Sallman

(Interpretation)

"And in the morning, rising up a great while before day, He went out, and departed into a solitary place, and there prayed."—MARK 1:35, A.V.

THE artist who painted this picture, Warner E. Sallman, has become known around the globe for his beautiful pictures of the Christ. Mr. Sallman is not

CHRIST AT DAWN—*SALLMAN*

only a skilled artist, but he is also a devout Christian whose life manifests a very close communion with his Lord.

In "Christ at Dawn," the artist has captured the beauty and majesty of the dawn in all its splendor as it breaks upon a sleeping world. The landscape itself is a lovely background for the serene figure of the Christ who greets the dawn in fellowship with his heavenly Father.

The artist has portrayed for us the early morning mist rising up over the Sea of Galilee, for the rosy tints of the dawn are reflected in its blue waters. The calm and mirrorlike surface of the lake makes it difficult for us to imagine that at times severe and hazardous storms arise suddenly on this body of water, causing consternation and fear to the seafaring.

Across the lake is the city of Bethsaida, still sleeping. How symbolic this is of its attitude toward the Christ. Here it was that he had performed some of his mightiest works; out of it he had called three of his disciples, Philip, Peter, and Andrew. But its people were not awake to the great opportunity which was theirs—the opportunity of taking to their hearts the Saviour of the world, and accepting the new way of life which he offered.

Appropriately, Sallman has pictured sheep grazing on the hillside by the lake shore. What a picture of contentment! They want for nothing, for here are the green pastures and the still waters. They are unafraid for the Good Shepherd is here also.

The artist has painted the Christ wearing his red travel garment, but the blue of the early morning has transformed the red to purple, a symbol of his royalty. It is significant that the one who is King of kings found himself in need of prayer as he faced a new day of uncompleted tasks. His work was far from finished, his purpose had not as yet been accomplished. The road ahead was fraught with dangers and temptations. How was he to know the will of God in his life except the Father reveal it to him? How was he to continue his ministry among men, for whom he had a burning passion, unless the strength and power came from God?

"Thy will be done" were the words uttered by Jesus in the Garden of Gethsemane, but it is clear that he had learned to pray them long before that hour of crisis. That he on this occasion also had already made a complete dedication to his Father's will is evident.

Jesus was not permitted to remain long in the sanctuary of the hills, for crowds sought him persistently. He went on into towns and cities preaching, teaching and performing miracles. He met popularity and he met opposition but neither was able to sway him from his purpose. Regardless of circumstances, he sought always to do his Father's will.

After his crucifixion and resurrection, it was to Galilee he went again to walk the old familiar pathways. One of them, no doubt, led to his sacred place of prayer in the hills. Perhaps it was from this spot that he came down to the shores of the Sea of Galilee at dawn to greet a group of tired, discouraged disciples returning from an unsuccessful night of fishing, and had breakfast with them. For it was on the shores of the Sea of Galilee that Jesus turned to Peter with the searching question, "Lovest thou me?" Upon Peter's avowal of his love for the Master, thrice expressed, Jesus gave to him the command: "Feed my sheep."

Christ's ministry on earth was over. Very shortly he would return to his heavenly Father, but his unfinished work must go on. Down through the centuries that great commission has echoed. Today, nearly two thousand years later, the work is still going on. We, his followers, can be true to the task only by heeding the message of Sallman's "Christ at Dawn" in our own everyday lives.

The constant message of Sallman's "Christ at Dawn" is beautifully expressed in the poem "Strength through Prayer" written by F. Martin Bates:

> When worn by toils of busy days,
>   Christ found it always good to pray.
> In solitude He sought a place
>   To talk with God and seek His grace.
> So when I'm weary, worn and weak,
>   Continually His face I'll seek!
>
> In secret prayer, O blest retreat,
>   We need not ever know defeat.
> New strength for tasks both great and small,
>   Is promised those who on Him call,
> So when I'm weary, worn or weak,
>   Continually His face I'll seek![1]

✠

THE CONCERT

By

Imre Goth

(Interpretation)

THE POWER OF MUSIC IN NATURE AND IN HUMAN LIFE

PERHAPS better than any other picture, this painting by Imre Goth helps us to understand and appreciate the place and power of music in the natural world around us and in human life. Each face in the painting expresses a different type of response to the universal appeal of all great music. From the dreamy-eyed mother with her hands folded quietly in her lap to the aged husband and father in the rear, each person, in his own way, is feeling and responding to the message which the musician is executing with such consummate skill.

[1] This interpretation and the poem by Bates are from *Story of Sallman's Christ at Dawn.* Copyright, 1946, by Kriebel & Bates, Indianapolis, Ind. Reprinted by special permission of the publisher.

We feel, as we gaze upon this painting, that the older man in the background must, himself, be something of a musical artist. Note his alert attention to the skill with which the musician is interpreting for them some great classical composition. The father seems to be listening not alone with his ears, but also with his eyes and his hands.

Observe the thinker in the left foreground, his head resting on his half-closed hand. What strains of thought has this musical composition set surging through his mind and heart?

The closed eyes and still, almost deathlike expression of the daughter on the right indicate that she has been lifted into a new world of beauty, melody, and repose. As we gaze at her we are reminded that Beethoven once said: "He who can feel my music will be beyond the hurt of this world," and we can almost feel the repose of soul which all great music brings to the human heart.

The two brothers in the center are also lost in thought. One is blotting out the light from his eyes that he may more fully and completely receive through sound alone the message of the music. To him its beauty may be bringing surcease from a great sorrow, or the haunting refrain of "it might have been." The other brother, his eyes downcast, is lost in thoughts too deep for words. Upon his broad shoulders there may rest the burden of a great strain or heavy toil; but for the time being, at least, he has cast it off and is lost in the memory of this haunting, enchanting melody.

The mother's eyes are open, but they do not see—at least not the sights that are present to her senses at this moment. Her eyes are introspective: back, back into the dim, distant memories they look, as if to catch a moment of remembering joy that may never come again in just this way.

As we look at this great painting, "The Concert," we feel that the artist has caught all of his hearers up into some such thrilling ecstasy as the poet-musician experienced when she wrote:

> Seated one day at the organ,
>   I was weary and ill at ease,
> And my fingers wandered idly
>   Over the noisy keys.
>
> I know not what I was playing,
>   Or what I was dreaming then;
> But I struck one chord of music,
>   Like the sound of a great Amen.
>
> It flooded the crimson twilight,
>   Like the close of an angel's Psalm,
> And it lay on my fevered spirit
>   With a touch of infinite calm.
>
> It quieted pain and sorrow,
>   Like love overcoming strife;

It seemed the harmonious echo
From our discordant life.

It linked all perplexèd meanings
Into one perfect peace,
And trembled away into silence
As if it were loath to cease.

I have sought, but I seek it vainly,
That one lost chord divine,
That came from the soul of the Organ
And entered into mine.

It may be that Death's bright angel
Will speak in that chord again,
It may be that only in Heaven
I shall hear that grand Amen.

—Adelaide A. Procter

HE, TOO, LOVED BEAUTY

I who love beauty in the open valleys,
Tintings of sunset, and the swallow's flight,
Must breathe the air of squalid city alleys,
Shut from the cool caresses of the night.
Wistful of fragrance where the springtime dallies,
Sharing with sordid souls a city's blight.

He, too, loved beauty, but a city drew Him.
Flowers He found in little children's eyes;
Something of grace in lepers stumbling to Him;
Fragrance of spikenard spilt in sweet surprise;
Joy in forgiving men at last who slew Him;
Courage in service, hope in sacrifice.

—Edwin McNeill Poteat, Jr.

CHRIST WAS THE OUTDOOR SON OF GOD

My master was a Man, who knew
The rush of rain, the drip of dew,
The wistful whisper of the breeze,
Night's magic and its mysteries.

He was a Man of sun and stars,
He knew the Pleiades and Mars,
That star-trail called the Milky Way;
The crescent moon, the dawn, the day.

His feet were stained by dusty ways,
His cheeks were brown as autumn days;
His skin it had the look of one
Who knew the blazing balm of sun.

He walked alone upon the sea,
Spake peace to wave-washed Galilee;
All shores and seas were in His thought,
This Man, god-bred, star-led, sky-taught.

To Him there were no sweeter tones
Than water washing over stones;
To Him no splendid symphony
Like murmuring, blue Galilee.

His hair and heart were washed by showers;
He loved the wayside fields and flowers;
The sea and tree, the star and sod;
He was the Outdoor Son of God.

—*William L. Stidger*

OUT IN THE FIELDS WITH GOD

The little cares that fretted me
    I lost them yesterday
Among the fields above the sea,
    Among the winds at play;
Among the lowing of the herds,
    The rustling of the trees,
Among the singing of the birds,
    The humming of the bees.
The foolish fears of what might happen,
    I cast them all away
Among the clover-scented grass,
    Among the new-mown hay,
Among the husking of the corn,
    Where drowsy posies nod,
Where ill thoughts die and good are born—
    Out in the fields with God.

—*Author Unknown*

I SAW GOD WASH THE WORLD

I saw God wash the world last night
  With His sweet shower on high;
And then when morning came
  I saw Him hang it out to dry.

He washed each tiny blade of grass,
  And every trembling tree;
He flung His showers against the hills
  And swept the billowy sea.

The white rose is a cleaner white;
  The red rose is more red
Since God washed every fragrant face
  And put them all to bed.

There's not a bird, there's not a bee,
  That wings along the way,
But is a cleaner bird and bee
  Than it was yesterday.

I saw God wash the world last night;
  Ah, would He had washed me
As clean of all my dust and dirt
  As that old white birch tree!

—William L. Stidger

THE TEACHER AND THE LILIES OF THE FIELD

(Matthew 6:28-30)

He loved them well, those lilies of the field
That raised their little faces as He passed,
And smiled and nodded as He went His way.
They had been friends so long—since when a boy
He roamed the hillside fields of Nazareth,
To gather lilies gay for Mary's hands.

They watched Him growing year by year,
In wisdom, stature, and in favor fair
With man and God—His Father, too, and theirs.
And growing thus, He learned from bird and flower,
In Nature's wonder-book, His Father's world,

The lessons sweet of trust that knows no fear
Or anxious thought; thus the Great Teacher learned.

And when He heard that "voice without reply,"
That called Him to the task His Father planned,
These lilies cheered Him on His lonely way,
And spoke to Him of truth and life and love.

He loved and understood these flower friends,
Or else He could not thus have said the words,
That thrill us with their beauty and their truth
"Consider now these lilies of the field;
They toil not, neither do they spin;
And yet I say to you that Solomon,
Your boasted king, with wealth and glory crowned,
Was not arrayed like unto one of these."

Thus, from His Father's picture-book, He tried
With tree, and bird, and flower, and wheat, and tares,
And rock and sand, in plain and simple way,
To teach the truth so hard for men to see —
Whose eyes were blind with prejudice and sin.

The flowers unselfish grow where'er a hold
Is found for tiny rootlets in the earth
Or desert sands or mountain's lonely snows;
And in our gardens beautiful, the more
We gather, still the more they sweetly bloom.

And when the chilling frosts of autumn come,
They seem to glow and still more bravely smile,
As if to say, "Although we seem to die,
Our little flower souls still live, and we
Shall bloom again in spring's returning smile."

Dear Father of the flowers and souls of men,
And Jesus, lover to the death of all,
Help us to be unselfish, brave, and true,
And do our best to brighten life, and trust
That Thou dost understand and care;
Then when Thy call shall come for us to go
The journey that is but a step to Thee,
It will be well, and with the loved and lost,
Our souls shall blossom in eternal life.

—Ellie K. Payne

TIBERIAS AT DAWN

The muezzin's call throbs to the morning star,
  And shakes the velvet darkness of spent sleep.
Above the mosque, the moon's white scimitar
  Points to the purple hills beyond the deep.
There have been dawns in other lands, that came
  With painted banners flung across the sea;
There have been skies of blended pearl and flame,
  But this is spring and dawn—and Galilee!

In those grave hours when the Master's heart
  Ached with the bitter sorrows men have known,
Perhaps they slept, the while He walked apart,
  and braved the beauty of this dawn—alone.
Again there is a Presence on the sea —
The Master walks at dawn, by Galilee.

—Mary Brent Whiteside

GOD IS NOT FAR

God is not far from any one of us:
  The wild flower by the wayside speaks His love;
  Each blithesome bird bears tidings from above;
  Sunshine and shower His tender mercies prove,
    And men know not His voice:

God is not far from any one of us:
  He speaks to us in every glad sunrise;
  His glory floods us from the noonday skies;
  The stars declare His love when daylight dies,
    And men know not His voice!

God is not far from any one of us:
  He watches o'er His children day and night;
  On every darkened soul He sheds His light;
  Each burdened heart He cheers, and lends His might
    To all who know His voice.

—Thomas Curtis Clark

I HEARD GOD SPEAK

I heard God speak this day
Along an Alpine way.
'Twas where a mountain shower
Had washed a crimson flower
Nodding in the blue heights
When the rain was through.
It bent as if in prayer
Beneath the rain-washed air.
'Twas when the sun came out
I thought I heard God shout
With laughter down the seams
And crevices and streams.
I thought I saw His face
In one high, holy place
Up close against the sky
Where stars and planets fly;
Up where the clouds lie low
And wind tides ebb and flow;
From which I heard Him speak
In whispers of the wind
Some words supremely kind.
'Twas this I heard God speak
Through a flower and a peak.

—William L. Stidger

HE LEADETH ME

In "green pastures"? Not always; sometimes He
Who knowest best, in kindness leadeth me
In weary ways, where heavy shadows be.
Out of the sunshine, warm and soft and bright,
Out of the sunshine into darkest night,
I oft would faint with sorrows and affright,
Only for this: I know He holds my hand;
So, whether led in green or desert land,
I trust, although I may not understand.
Beside "still waters"? No, not always so;
Ofttimes the heavy tempests 'round me blow,
And o'er my soul the waves and billows go.
But when the storms beat loudest, and I cry
Aloud for help, the Master standeth by,
And whispers to my soul, "Lo, it is I."

Above the tempest wild I hear Him say:
"Beyond this darkness lies the perfect day;
In every path of thine I lead the way."
So whether on the hill-tops high and fair
I dwell, or in the sunless valleys where
The shadows lie, what matter? He is there.
And more than this; where'er the pathway lead,
He gives to me no helpless, broken reed,
But His own hand, sufficient for my need.

—*Henry H. Barry*

TO HIM ALL LIFE WAS BEAUTY

To Him all life was beauty. The sun upon the hills,
The sweeping shadows, and the winding lane.
Morning He loved, with dewdrops on the flowers;
Evening, with sunset and soft, warm April rain.
Friends He found in lepers stumbling to Him,
Love in those who hate, grace in sinners' eyes.
Dawn He saw with all earth's new-born glory,
Twilight and darkness, and hope in human sighs.
Youth was His, and springtime, and music in the trees;
Life was His, and sunshine, and the murmuring of the bees.
Joy in healing broken hearts; manhood's noble strife;
All the wonder and the beauty of a sacred human life.

.   .   .   .   .

He walked the common lanes, the city streets He trod,
And in His heart was beauty . . . the beauty born of God.

—*A.L.C.*

GOD'S AUTOGRAPHS

I stood upon a hill one night
And saw the great Creator write
His autograph across the sky
In lightning strokes, and there was I
A witness to this great event
And signature magnificent!

I stood one morning by a stream
When night was fading to a dream,
The fields were fair as fields may be
At spring, in golden mystery
Of dandelion—then God came on
And wrote His signature in Dawn.

One afternoon long years ago.
Where glacial tides had ebb and flow,
I found a cliff God's hand had smote;
I scanned its breast, whereon God wrote
With some great glacier for a pen
His signature for time and men.

One night I stood and watched the stars;
The Milky Way and ranging Mars,
Where God in letters tipped with fire
The tale of every tall desire
Had writ in rhyme and signed His name
A stellar signature of flame.

Creation's dawn was deep in night
When suddenly, "Let there be light!"
Awakened grass, and flower, and tree,
The starry skies, the earth, and sea;
Then to complete Creation's span
In His own image, God made man,
And signed His name, with stroke most sure—
Man is God's greatest signature!

—*William L. Stidger*

GOD

God is beauty,
God is love,
God is understanding,
God is quietness and rest,
God is peace. God is the song of ecstasy, that bursts in the springtime;
God is the blue of a calm day in summer.
God is the faith that comes where there is no reason for faith.
God is the voice of a bell, the peal of a trumpet.
God is timeless, spaceless.
God is all heights and all depths.
God is law and the maker of law,
God is beyond all and in all.
God is simplicity, enveloped by us in complexity.
God is perfection among imperfections.
God is a perfect poem,
God is God.

—*Catherine Cate Coblentz*

GOD MEETS ME IN THE MOUNTAINS

God meets me in the mountains when I climb alone and high,
   Above the wrangling sinners and the jangling devotees,
Up where the tapered spruce will guide my glances to the sky
   And canyon walls will mutely preach their mighty homilies
In hush so dense that I can sense—is it my pulses drumming?
   Or God's light footfall, coming through the silvery aspen trees?

Some way I seem to lose Him in the jostle of the street,
   But on a twisty deer trail, as I trudge along alone,
A mystic presence in the forest often stays my feet—
   No vision borrowed from a saint, but awesomely my own.
I feel it smite my spirit white, the prophet's taintless passion,
   As ancient as the fashion of the pine tree's rugged cone.

For me no school could give it life, as none can deal it death.
   Up through the pines' red pillars and across the snow and shale.
Where science and theology alike are but a breath,
   I follow marks that make the wisest book an idle tale.
Why should I squint at faded print to glimpse His timeworn traces?
   God walks the lonely places yet, where men first found His trail.

Where pines reach up the mountains and the mountains up the blue,
   And, tense with some expectancy, the lifting ledges frown,
The high desire of the hills is my desire too,
   For there my spirit laughs to fling its worldly duffle down
And, shaking free exultantly, calls to its great companion!
   God meets me in the canyon when I miss Him in the town.

—Badger Clark

AUTUMN

Today the peace of autumn pervades the world.
In the radiant noon, silent and motionless, the wide stillness rests like a tired
    bird spreading over the deserted fields to all horizons its wings of golden
    green.
Today the thin thread of the river flows without song, leaving no mark on
    its sandy banks.
The many distant villages bask in the sun with eyes closed in idle and languid
    slumber.
In the stillness I hear in every blade of grass, in every speck of dust, in every
    part of my own body, in the visible and invisible worlds, in the planets,

the sun, and the stars, the joyous dance of the atoms through endless time—
the myriad murmuring waves of rhythm surrounding Thy throne.

—Rabindranath Tagore

THE KISS OF A SUNBEAM

Flower, by the roadside small,
    If I could comprehend you,
All in all;
    I'd know the power
That in a sunbeam lies
    That makes you lift your face
Up to the skies;
    Seeking the kiss,
That in a sunbeam lies.[2]

—Cynthia Pearl Maus

MOONLIGHT REFLECTIONS

Looking out of my windows,
I have seen the moonlight
Shining on the tower.
The memory of Him
Has made me forget
My shadowland of earnest men.

. . . "Let not
        your heart
            Be troubled.". . .

And while my companions
Have passed thoughtlessly
Through this world;
I have intensely
Enjoyed my life
Hour by hour
Thinking of Him . . . !

. . . "I have
        overcome
            the world." . . .[3]

—José A. Franquiz

---

[2] Written on the Andalusian tour in Spain, 1956, on witnessing a tiny roadside flower twine its stem around a clod, and then turn its face directly up toward the sun.

[3] From *Puerto Rico in Pictures and Poetry* by Maus. Caxton Press, Caldwell, Idaho.

God never publishes His miracles. He improvises them before us. Because of this we never hear a tree grow, a flower open, a Spring come.

—*José A. Franquiz*

TWILIGHT SILHOUETTES

The sunset's glow is bright on far El Yunque,
    While waves thud softly on the near-by shore.
Silent upon the beach a lone fisherman standing,
    With gesture slow, flings out his line once more.

And something in his action stirs the soul
    With deep content, that simple things like these—
Twilight, and darkening shadows on the hills,
    Then night, a fisherman home-wending from the sea.

Such ancient, simple, and familiar things
    Bid us remember, past reason or regret
That Christ, Himself, is but a fisherman
    Who snares men's hearts with beauty for His net.[4]

—*Cynthia Pearl Maus*

✢

CHRIST AND THE SORRY THISTLE*

By

Gabriela Mistral

ONCE upon a time a lily in a garden—a rich man's garden—was asking the other flowers about Christ. The lily's master, passing by, had named Him while praising the newly opened flower.

A rose of Sharon, of vivid purple, answered:

"I do not know Him. He is perhaps a rustic, for I know all the prominent men."

"I have never seen Him, either," added a small, fragrant jasmine, "and no delicate spirit fails to breathe the perfume of my little flowers."

"Nor I, either," said the cold, impassive camellia. "He must be some clownish fellow. I have been worn on the breasts of handsome men and beautiful women."

The lily answered, "If He were, He would not be like me; and my master was reminded of Him when he looked at me this morning."

[4] From *Puerto Rico in Pictures and Poetry* by Maus. Caxton Press, Caldwell, Idaho.
* NOTE: "In a Monastery Garden," Kettleby, makes a fine musical accompaniment for this story.

Then said the violet, "There is one of us who has certainly seen Him; and that is our poor brother, the thistle. He lives by the roadside and knows everybody who goes by, and salutes them all, with his head covered with ashes. Although he is humiliated by the dust, he is sweet, since he bears a flower of my color."

"You have said one true thing," answered another tall lily of the field. "The thistle certainly knows Christ; but you make a mistake when you call him our brother. He has prickles and he is ugly like an evil-doer. He is one, too, for the wool of the lambs sticks to him when the flocks go by."

Then softening his voice hypocritically, he turned toward the road and called:

"Brother thistle, poor little brother of ours, the lily asks if you know Christ?"

And the voice of the thistle, weary, as if it were broken, came on the wind:

"Yes. He has passed along this road, and I have touched Him—I, a sorry thistle!"

"And is it true that He is like me?" asked the lily.

"Only a little, and that when the moon gives you an air of sadness. You carry your head too high. He carries His a little bent; but His mantle is as white as your cup, and you are happy enough to be like Him. Nobody will ever compare Him to the dusty thistle!"

"Tell us, thistle, what are His eyes like?"

The thistle opened another plant, a blue flower.

"What is His breast like?"

The thistle opened a red flower. "He goes with His breast like this," said the thistle, tearing the red flower until it bled.

"It is too crude a color," said the lily. "And what does He wear on His head for a wreath in spring?"

The thistle held up his thorns.

"That is a horrible wreath," said the camellia. "The rose is forgiven for her little thorns; but those are like the spines of the cactus, the bristly cactus that grows on the slopes."

"And does Christ love?" continued the lily, troubled. "What is His love like?"

"The love of Christ is like this," said the thistle, casting the tiny feathers of his dead corolla to fly upon all the winds.

"After all," said the lily, "I should like to know Him. How could that be, brother thistle?"

"To see Him pass, to get a glance from Him, become a wayside flower," the thistle answered. "He goes continually along the paths without rest. When He passed me He said, 'Blessed be you, because you blossom amid the dust and cheer the fevered glance of the wayfarer.' And He would not tarry in the rich man's garden even for the sake of your fragrance; because as He goes He scents in the wind another odor—the odor of the wounds of men."

But neither the lily that they called His brother, nor the rose of Sharon that He plucked as a child upon the hills of Nazareth, nor the twining honeysuckle, wished to become wayside flowers; and so, like the prominent men and worldly women who refused to follow Him over the scorching plains of self-sacrifice and service, they remained without knowing Christ.[5]

✠

THE LEGEND OF THE DOGWOOD TREE

"HELLO, folks: Has nature's garden a more decorative ornament than the flowering dogwood tree, whose spreading branches whiten the woodland borders and hillsides in May, as if an untimely snowstorm had come down upon them; and in autumn, painting the landscape with glorious scarlet, crimson, and gold, dulled only by comparison with the clusters of vivid red berries hidden among the foliage?

"According to the legend, in the time of Christ, the dogwood tree was supposed to have attained the size of the oak and other forest trees, and so strong and firm was the wood of this tree, that it was chosen as the timber for the cross.

"The trees were greatly distressed at having been chosen for such a cruel purpose, and Jesus, sensing their regret and pity for His suffering, made this promise:

" 'Never again shall the dogwood tree grow large enough to be used for a cross. Henceforth it shall be slender and bent and twisted, and its blossoms shall be in the form of a cross—two long and two short petals. And in the center of the outer edge of each petal there shall be nail prints brown with rust and stained with blood, and in the center of the flower will be a crown of thorns.

" 'All those who see it will remember, it was on a dogwood tree that I was crucified, and this tree shall not be mutilated nor destroyed, but cherished and protected as a reminder of my agony and death upon the Cross.'

"And so today, upon the hillsides, the dogwood tree grows as the legend promised, its branches slender, bent and twisted, bearing, each spring, its snowy blossoms, and each autumn its flaming berries.

"Sincerely, in the bond of friendship, WALTER W. FURNISS. WLW—Crosley Radio Corporation."[6]

[5] From *Some Spanish-American Poets*. Translated by Alice Stone Blackwell. Published by D. Appleton-Century Company, New York City. Used by permission of the author and publishers.

[6] A radio story. Used by special permission of the author.

THE MOST BEAUTIFUL WILL IN THE WORLD

THE last Will and Testament given below, expressing as it does not only an extraordinary love of mankind, but also an appreciation of the spiritual values in the world that money can never buy, has been pronounced by lawyers and laymen alike as the most beautiful and remarkable will ever made by man. It was left by Charles Lounsbury, adjudged insane, who died at the Cook County Asylum at Dunning, Illinois.

It is included in this anthology because the compiler of this anthology feels that the author of this will, even though he had been adjudged insane by men, had discovered God through his love of beauty as he found it all about him. With the Master of Men he had learned to commune with the "lilies of the field" and with beauty in every form as he found it in the great natural universe and in the hearts of men, women, and children. As he goes out into the great beyond, he goes blessing the children of men and bequeathing to them the rich heritage of the world's gifts which money alone can never buy.

KNOW ALL MEN BY THESE PRESENTS:

That I, Charles Lounsbury, being of sound mind and disposing memory, do hereby make and publish this, my last will and testament, in order as justly as may be to distribute my interests in the world among succeeding men.

That part of my interest which is known in law and recognized in the sheep-bound volumes as my property, being inconsiderable and of no account, I make no disposal of this in my will.

MY RIGHT TO LIVE, being but a life estate, is not at my disposal, but, these things excepted, all else in the world I now proceed to devise and bequeath:

ITEM I: I give to good fathers and mothers, in trust for their children all and every, the flowers of the fields, and the blossoms of the woods, with the right to play among them freely, according to the customs of children, warning them at the same time against thistles and thorns. And I devise to children the banks of the brooks, and the golden sands beneath the waters thereof, and the odors of the willows that dip therein, and the white clouds that float high over the giant trees. And I leave the children the long, long days to be merry in, in a thousand ways, and the night, and the moon and the train of the Milky Way to wonder at, but subject, nevertheless, to the rights hereinafter given to lovers.

ITEM II: To boys I devise jointly all the useful fields and commons where ball may be played; all pleasant waters where one may swim; all snow-clad hills where one may coast, and all streams and ponds where one may fish, or where, when grim winter comes, one may skate; to have and to hold the same for the period of their boyhood. All the meadows with the clover blossoms and butterflies thereof, the woods and their appurtenances, the squirrels and birds and echoes and strange noises, and all distant places which may be visited, together with the adventures there found. And I give to said boys each his own place at the fireside at night, with all pictures that may be seen in the burning wood, to enjoy without let or hindrance, and without incumbrance of care.

ITEM III: To lovers I devise their imaginary world, with whatever they may need; as the stars of the sky; the red roses by the wall; the bloom of the hawthorn; the sweet strains of music; and aught else by which they may desire to figure to each other the lastingness and beauty of their love.

ITEM IV: To young men jointly I devise and bequeath all boisterousness, inspiring sports of rivalry, and I give to them the disdain of weakness and undaunted confidence in their own strength, though they are rude. I give them the power to make lasting friendships, and of possessing companions, and to them exclusively I give all merry songs and brave choruses, to sing with lusty voices.

ITEM V: And to those who are no longer children or youths or lovers, I leave memory, and I bequeath to them the volumes of the poems of Burns and Shakespeare and of other poets, if there be others, to the end that they may live over the old days again, freely and fully, without tithe of diminution.

ITEM VI: And to our loved ones with snowy crowns I bequeath the happiness of old age, the love and gratitude of their children until they fall asleep.

Signed, CHARLES LOUNSBURY.[7]

✢

A PRAYER FOR THE SACRAMENT OF BEAUTY

Our Father, we thank Thee for the beauty of the world in which Thou hast placed us; for the universe whose vastness is revealed in the blue depths of the sky, whose immensities are lit by shining stars beyond the strength of mind to follow. We thank Thee for every sacrament of beauty; for the sweetness of flowers, the solemnity of the stars, the sound of streams and swelling seas; for far-stretching lands and mighty mountains which rest and satisfy the soul; the purity of dawn which calls to holy dedication; the peace of evening which speaks of everlasting rest. May we not fear to make this world for a little while our home, since it is Thy creation and we, ourselves, are part of it. Help us, like Charles Lounsbury, humbly to learn its laws and trust its mighty powers. Amen.

✢

THE LOST MELODY

THE shepherds were seated around their fire on one of the hills near Bethlehem. It was the night after the angel had appeared to them, and the heavens had been filled with other angels, singing "Glory to God in the highest, and on

[7] From *Services for the Open*, Mattoon-Bragdon. Published by the Century Company, New York City. Used with permission.

earth, peace and good-will toward men." Suddenly one of the shepherds said, "I can hardly believe it all happened!"

"It does seem like a dream," another said, "but the babe is still at the inn. I heard that wise men from the East came to see him after we left. They rode camels and brought gifts."

"What I am trying to remember," said the first one, "is that tune which came from the skies. The singers seemed very high up, but the night was still and clear. I remember the words they sang, but I cannot recall the tune."

"Nor can I," said a comrade. "I am pretty good at tunes, too; usually I can hum them right off after once hearing them. But this so affected me, I couldn't retain it. It was the grandest tune I ever heard. It was bright like a Spring morning, sweet like the laughter of a child at play, pretty as a girl's face when she looks at her lover and tells the story of her heart."

"You should have been a poet," said the shepherd next to him. And the others laughed. But none of them could remember the tune; so they talked of the babe they had found in the stable, and were glad they had knelt before its cradle in the yellow straw.

Presently a faint bleat came from far up the hillside. They all listened, then looked at each other. A lamb must have strayed from the flock, and they had not missed it!

The youngest shepherd among them sprang to his feet. "I'm going up to get that lamb!" he cried. The rest looked at him in surprise. Then an older shepherd said, "Do not go. There is a terrible field of briars up there . . . you cannot avoid them in the dark. The stones, too, are loose and slippery. You may fall to your death, if you go!"

"But," answered the youth, "wolves will get to the lamb. I cannot stay here with that frightened little creature up there. I'll be back soon." And he turned and ran up the dark hillside before the others could speak again.

The other shepherds waited a long time for the boy to return. To keep up their valor, each related what wounds he had received from briars and rocks and wolves in other days. Then, again, they talked of the lost melody, but none could recall it.

An hour passed, and another. At last they heard slow, stumbling footsteps approaching. They peered into the darkness, but could see nothing, for the night was filled with clouds and drifting mist. There was great anxiety in their voices when suddenly the boy shepherd came into the small circle of light cast by the fire. His body was bruised and bleeding. There was an ugly wound on his cheek, where he had fallen upon a rock. But in his arms he held the lamb!

"I have found the tune!" he cried; "it came to me just as I was picking up the lamb; and I could sing it!" exclaimed the boy in ecstasy. And as he stood there, bruised and bleeding, he sang the lost melody to the shepherds.

"That's it! You have it!" they all cried. And they tried to sing it, too, but could not get the tune right. So the boy became known as the singing shepherd.

Years passed. The babe born at Bethlehem had grown to manhood, and was known as a great prophet. One day, one of his followers came to him and said, "Master, there is a blind beggar at the gates, who sings the most beautiful song! Will you come with me and hear him?" So Jesus went.

The follower of Jesus touched the beggar on the arm and said, "The Teacher of Galilee would hear your song."

And so, the blind beggar sang and Jesus listened to the sweetness of the beggar's song. Then swiftly and gently he put his finger on the beggar's eyes.

The beggar leaped to his feet and cried out, "I see! I see again! God has touched me!" Then, looking upon Jesus, he said, "Who are you, Teacher of Galilee?"

Jesus smiled. "We have met before . . . long ago. I will tell you where, if you will tell me where you heard that song."

Then the beggar told Jesus how he had heard the angels sing over Bethlehem, and how the lost melody had come back to him while he was picking up the little lamb that was lost.

And Jesus replied, "It is a song of my Father's choir. They sang it the day I was born upon the earth. And because you have kept it alive upon the earth with your kind deed, I give you back your eyes."[8]

✛

ANOTHER YEAR OF SETTING SUNS

"ANOTHER Year of Setting Suns" is not a new hymn, for the words were written by John W. Chadwick in 1873; yet it is not as familiar to many people as other hymns that are both older and of more recent date.

It does present a definite challenge to us, however, to recall, each year, the many beautiful things which our heavenly Father has placed in the world around us for the enrichment and culture of our inner best selves.

God, in every generation, has not left the world without many witnesses of the beauty of His creative nature; for beauty and truth are both eternal; and inherent in the nature of the God in whose image the sons of men are made.

Every generation has known the beauty and challenge of seedtime and harvest-time; the invigorating beauty of spring, and the flaming scarlets, russets and browns of the harvest season.

It is of this continuous and never-ending testimony of the beauty of God as we find Him revealed in the great natural world of life and light about us that the poet sings in this beautiful nature-hymn "Another Year of Setting Suns."

The tune to which it is usually sung is called "Holy Cross" and was composed by James C. Wade in 1865.

[8] From *Sunshine Bookie of the Shepherd Boy*, published by the Sunshine Press, Litchfield Press, Litchfield, Ill. Used by permission of the publishers.

Another year of setting suns,
 Of stars by night revealed,
Of springing grass, of tender buds
 The winter's snow concealed;

Another year of summer's glow,
 Of autumn's gold and brown,
Of waving fields, and ruddy fruit
 The branches weighing down;

Another year of happy work,
 That better is than play,
Of simple cares, and love that grows
 More sweet from day to day;

Another year to follow hard,
 Where better souls have trod,
Another year of life's delight;
 Another year of God! Amen.

—John W. Chadwick, 1873

✚

FOR THE BEAUTY OF THE EARTH

THE Church will never be able to pay the debt of gratitude it owes to the poets and musicians of the world for the wealth of beauty and melody that has been their contribution to the enrichment of men's lives.

This hymn, "For the Beauty of the Earth" is among these rich and beautiful classics. I doubt if there is any other hymn, written for the purpose of extolling the blessings of God which surround us on every side, that is more greatly loved or more often sung than this one, the words of which were composed by Folliott S. Pierpont in 1864.

Each verse sounds forth its pæan of praise to God for some great gift to man from His Almighty Hand; and as we sing the words of this great hymn, we become conscious, as never before, of the wealth of blessings that our heavenly Father has bestowed on us, His earth children.

The melody to which this hymn is sung was arranged from "Treuer Heiland" by Conrad Kocher in 1838; and fits the message of the words in beautiful and dignified rhythm.

For the beauty of the earth,
 For the glory of the skies,
For the love which from our birth
 Over and around us lies;

Refrain

Lord of all, to thee we raise
This, our hymn of grateful praise.

For the wonder of each hour,
Of the day and of the night,
Hill and vale, and tree and flower,
Sun and moon, and stars of light;

Refrain

For the joy of human love,
Brother, sister, parent, child,
Friends on earth, and friends above,
For all gentle thoughts and mild;

Refrain

For thy Church that evermore
Lifteth holy hands above,
Off'ring up on every shore
Her pure sacrifice of love;

Refrain

Amen.

—Folliott S. Pierpont, 1864

✠

THIS IS MY FATHER'S WORLD

ONE who sings or reads this poem is led into a deeper appreciation of the natural world, for in it Maltbie D. Babcock (1858-1901) has glorified the common, everyday gifts from our heavenly Father in the field of nature. The complete poem consists of six verses, only three of which appear here.

Dr. Babcock was born in Syracuse, New York, and graduated from Syracuse University and Auburn Theological Seminary. While pastor of the Brown Memorial Presbyterian Church in Baltimore he became a great favorite with the students of Johns Hopkins University and in recognition of this was given a special room at the university for student consultations.

He later succeeded Dr. Henry van Dyke as minister of the Brick Presbyterian Church in New York. He died in Naples, Italy. After his death Mrs. Babcock published *Thoughts for Everyday Living,* a book including selections from the sermons, addresses and poems of Dr. Babcock.

The tune associated with Dr. Babcock's hymn-poem is "Terra Beta," an old English melody, arranged by Franklin L. Sheppard in 1915.

This is my Father's world,
  And to my listening ears,
All nature sings, and round me rings
  The music of the spheres.
This is my Father's world,
  I rest me in the thought
Of rocks and trees, of skies and seas—
  His hand the wonders wrought.

This is my Father's world,
  The birds their carols raise,
The morning light, the lily white,
  Declare their Maker's praise.
This is my Father's world,
  He shines in all that's fair;
In the rustling grass I hear Him pass,
  He speaks to me everywhere.

This is my Father's world,
  O let me ne'er forget
That though the wrong seems oft so strong,
  God is the Ruler yet.
This is my Father's world,
  The battle is not done;
Jesus who died shall be satisfied,
  And earth and heaven be one.[9]

—Maltbie D. Babcock, 1901

✛

SEEK NOT AFAR FOR BEAUTY

In "Seek Not Afar For Beauty" we have another of the more modern hymns of nature that poetic souls have written in praise of the beauty of God's great out-of-doors.

While neither the words nor the tune of this hymn may be as familiar to us as "For the Beauty of the Earth," it is, nevertheless, one with which both young people and adults should become acquainted, if for no other reason than to widen and enrich the range of nature-hymns which may be freely used in services of worship.

The words of this hymn were composed by Minot J. Savage, who was born in 1841 and died in 1918. The melody to which it is sung is known as "Willingham" and was composed by Franz Art in the latter part of the nineteenth century.

[9] Words copyrighted by Charles Scribner's Sons, from *Thoughts for Everyday Living*. Used with permission of the publishers.

Seek not afar for beauty: lo, it glows
　In the dew-wet grasses all about thy feet;
　In birds, in sunshine, childish faces sweet,
In stars and mountain summits topped with snows.

Go not abroad for happiness: for see,
　It is a flower blooming at thy door.
　Bring love and justice home, and then no more
Thou'lt wonder in what dwelling joy may be.

Dream not for noble service elsewhere wrought;
　The simple duty that awaits thy hand
　Is God's voice uttering a divine command,
Life's common deeds build all that saints have thought.

In wonder-workings, or some bush aflame,
　Men look for God and fancy him concealed;
　But in earth's common things he stands revealed,
While grass and flowers and stars spell out his name.[10]

Amen.
—Minot J. Savage

✢

DAY IS DYING IN THE WEST

AMONG the many beautiful vesper hymns that have been written through the years for the devotional enrichment of followers of the Christ, no other one is more widely known, loved, and used than this one, "Day Is Dying in the West," the words of which were composed by Mary Artemisia Lathbury in 1877.

The background of this lovely hymn for the eventide was Lake Chautauqua in western New York, where every year since 1873 hundreds of young people and adults have come apart for study, and the enrichment of their inner lives through inspiration, meditation, and prayer.

The lake and its beautiful surroundings, the rich devotional life of the conference, and the enriching fellowship with other Christians from many cities and states are all reflected in this great vesper hymn. Every verse gives expression to those rich devotional experiences which leaders and students alike feel as they gather by the lakeside as the "day is dying in the west" to worship, to meditate, and to pray.

And because this beautiful hymn was written, countless thousands of young people in all parts of the world still feel the challenge that surges through the

---

[10] Hymn No. 225 in *The New Hymnal for American Youth*, H. Augustine Smith. Published by D. Appleton-Century Company, New York City.

lines of this truly great vesper hymn, as by many lakes and mountain tops they gather together in summer young people's conferences and get-togethers of various sorts.

The tune always associated with this matchless vesper hymn is called "Chautauqua" and was composed by William F. Sherwin in the same year that the words of the hymn were written.

Day is dying in the west;
Heaven is touching earth with rest;
Wait and worship while the night
Sets her evening lamps alight
    Thro' all the sky.

Refrain

Holy, holy, holy, Lord God of hosts!
Heaven and earth are full of Thee;
Heaven and earth are praising Thee,
O Lord Most High;
Lord of life, beneath the dome
Of the universe, Thy home,
Gather us who seek thy face
To the fold of thy embrace,
    For thou art night.

Refrain

While the deepening shadows fall,
Heart of love, enfolding all,
Through the glory and the grace
Of the stars that veil Thy face,
    Our hearts ascend.

Refrain

When forever from our sight,
Pass the stars, the day, the night,
Lord of angels, on our eyes
Let eternal morning rise,
    And shadows end.

—*Mary A. Lathbury, 1877*

✠

TREES

I DOUBT if there is in the English language a more beautiful poem than "Trees," written by that comparatively young American poet, Joyce Kilmer, whose life was so tragically cut off by the First World War.

In the first place, nearly everyone has had the experience of seeing at some time or another a great tree in all the glory and strength of its maturity. Its symmetry, its poise, its shadowy lacing leaves and boughs, its deep-growing roots and sturdy trunk make it possible for the tree to provide not only a shady resting-place, but protection from heat and storm not alone for man, but also for the beast; and because of this the tree has become endeared to us in a closer way than almost any other single blessing that the wealth of nature provides for the comfort of men.

Something of what all of us feel, but are inarticulate to express, Joyce Kilmer has done for us in beautiful, well-chosen words that will live forever in our memory.

In 1922 this beautiful poem was set to music by Oscar Rasbuch. It may be secured in sheet-music form or found as No. 81 in *Services for the Open* by Mattoon-Bragdon, a splendid book of out-of-doors worship services published by the Century Company, New York City.

> I think that I shall never see
> A poem lovely as a tree.
> A tree whose hungry mouth is prest
> Against the earth's sweet flowing breast;
> A tree that looks at God all day,
> And lifts her leafy arms to pray;
> A tree that may in summer wear
> A nest of robins in her hair;
> Upon whose bosom snow has lain;
> Who intimately lives with rain.
> Poems were made by fools like me,
> But only God can make a tree.[11]

✢

GOD IS LOVE

ALL of us have made one or more radio friends because of particularly beautiful or challenging poems, hymns, or stories that have come out to us over the air waves during the past few years; yet no one program was more helpful and stimulating to me than that of the Cheerio Exchange through its many years of uninterrupted broadcasting history.

In the first place its "service to shut-ins purpose" was preëminently worth while; and the character of its program continued to be a never-ending source of inspiration.

I shall never forget hearing for the first time the beautiful hymn, "God Is Love," sung as a duet by Lovina Gilbert, soprano and Gerry Riegger, contralto of the "Cheerio" staff. It seemed to me, as I listened that spring

[11] Words used by permission of Aline Kilmer.

morning in 1936 to this duet, that the meaning of the Scripture "God so loved that He gave" took on an added significance. If the fundamental nature of God is *love* as the birds, the breeze and the sea affirm in the verses of this song, He could do little else than give His Only Begotten Son that men might know life abundant here, and life eternal hereafter.

The words of this beautiful hymn were written by Elsie Duncan Yale and the tune arranged by Alfred Judson from Beethoven's "Minuet." The song is No. 60 in *Cheerio's Favorite Hymns.*

Have you heard the whisper of the breeze?
"God is love, God is love!"
Have you heard the murm'ring of the trees,
  Singing softly, sweetly, "God is love"?

Chorus

Blessed song, echo on,
  Glad message sound forever;
Ringing 'neath the radiant skies above,
  "God is love, God is love!"

Have you heard the birds' exultant notes?
  "God is love, God is love!"
Down from distant heights the carol floats,
  Ringing gladly, clearly, "God is love!"

Chorus

Have you heard the singing of the sea?
  "God is love, God is love!"
Where the crested billows toss so free,
  Telling, telling ever, "God is love!"

Chorus[12]

—*Elsie Duncan Yale*

[12] Copyright, 1917, by Hall-Mark Company. Used by permission.

CONTENTS

PART VI   SECTION III

IN MOTHER LOVE

———————————————✠———————————————

"And his mother kept all *these* sayings in her heart."—LUKE 2:51

———————————————✠———————————————

IN MOTHER LOVE

"Honor thy father and thy mother, that thy days may be long in the land which Jehovah thy God giveth thee."—EXODUS 20:12

✠

"Hearken unto thy father that begat thee, and despise not thy mother when she is old."—PROVERBS 23:22

✠

"Can a woman forget her sucking child, that she should not have compassion on [her] son?"—ISAIAH 49:15

✠

"As one whom his mother comforteth, so will I comfort you."—ISAIAH 66:13
"And his mother kept all *these* sayings in her heart."—LUKE 2:51

✠

MOTHERS

What a wonderful thing
is a mother!
Other folks can love you,
But only your mother
understands;
She works for you—
looks after you—
Loves you, forgives you—
anything you may do;
And then the only thing
bad she ever does do—
Is to die and leave you.

—Baroness von Hutton

THE MADONNA OF THE SACRED COAT

By

C. Bosseron Chambers

(Interpretation)

AMONG all the modern Madonnas, none is more beautifully appealing than this one, "The Madonna of the Sacred Coat," painted by the American artist, C. Bosseron Chambers, the original of which hangs in the St. Ignatius Church, Chicago, Illinois.

This painting is a new idea in the portrayal of Mary, the Virgin Mother, for here she is represented as a young girl about eighteen years of age. She stands facing the spectator, in a very simple interior, clasping in her exquisitely beautiful hands a little brown tunic or coat. One really should see this picture in colors to appreciate to the fullest its beauty and charm.

According to tradition, Mary wove a seamless garment for Jesus when He was ready to discard His babyhood clothes, and this garment is supposed to have grown with Him, through the years.

The Jewish law prescribed the color and fashion for babes, youth, and manhood. Brown was usually the color worn by the poor, although white or red might be worn on festival days and for worship in the Temple.

This little garment which the Madonna Mother is clasping to her breast in this picture represents the "seamless robe" for which, according to St. John (19:23) the soldiers cast lots at the time of the crucifixion of the Christ.

"The Madonna of the Sacred Coat" has been called the "Madonna of the Home." In this painting she is the embodiment of gentle, refined domesticity. Standing in the living-room of her simple abode, looking down into the eyes of the beholder, she fondles the little brown baby garment to her breast as she remembers the soft, sweet charm of His childhood days.

Beside her on the table stand the simple viands of their daily repast—the fruits and vegetables which she will soon prepare for their evening meal.

According to sacred writers, the Virgin Mother must have been about fifteen years of age at the time the Angel Gabriel announced to her that she was to become the mother of God's "Only Begotten Son." In this portrait she is supposed to be about eighteen years old. About her there is every indication of youth and maidenhood. The appealing innocence that shines out of her saddened eyes, the stray locks falling from under the veil, her sweet, expressive mouth—all bespeak radiant, beautiful girlishness.

In her face and form there are also strength of character and refined dignity beyond the years of her girlhood; as there are mystery, calmness, and poise in the saddened yet steadfast gaze of her beautiful eyes. The feeling of deep

THE MADONNA OF THE SACRED COAT—*CHAMBERS*

THE MADONNA OF THE TEAR—*KAULBACH*

spirituality in the picture is accentuated by the sweeping, almost transparent veil that fits close to the head, with here and there a touch of blue in the shadows.

The shape of the Virgin Mother's head is beautifully outlined beneath the veil, while the deep folds at the sides of her lovely face tend to emphasize her cloistered, hidden spirit within. Then, too, the quiet repose of her young body, the ample draperies covering all contour and outline, enhances the spirituality of her charming girlishness.

The appeal of this painting, however, lies in the power of the eyes of the Virgin Mother, as she stands fondling the little empty coat that will never again feel the warmth of the baby God gave into her keeping. To our dull memories she recalls the love and suffering of the Madonna Mother of the Son of Man, who, always, when she did not and could not fully comprehend, still cherished "all these sayings, pondering them in her heart."

We would, if it were possible, take out of her eyes the look of unutterable sadness that empty arms mean to those who have been robbed, by death, of that which was dearer to them than even life itself.

Some one has beautifully said "God couldn't be everywhere and so he made mothers"; and the great mothers in every generation of the world's life are developed through pain and suffering so that their lives are more like the heart quality of God than are any other folk in the world.

Through the centuries these silent burden-bearers of the races of men go on making life happy and cheerful for others, filling their days with a thousand deeds of love; and healing the pain in their own hearts as in love they pour out their lives in service to others.

Something of what true womanhood and motherhood means to the enrichment and purifying of the race, Jesus, the Master, understood, as, dying on the cross, He turned to His mother and said, "Woman, behold thy son!" and to John the beloved, "Behold, thy mother." How glad we are that John's Gospel adds the sentence: "And from that hour the disciple took her unto his *own home.*"

✠

THE MADONNA OF THE TEAR

By

Hermann Kaulbach

(Interpretation)

THE conception and maternity of the Madonna Mother has been a favorite study on the part of artists through the centuries. Among the favored ones, "The Madonna of the Tear," by the German artist, Hermann Kaulbach, who was born in Munich July 26, 1846, ranks high. He was the son of Wilhelm

Kaulbach, a pupil of Piloty, and later went to Italy to continue his artistic education. He was awarded a medal in Vienna in 1873 and became an honorary member of the Munich Academy of Art in 1885.

From the conception of this embryonic Son of God there was a brooding mystery in the Madonna's mind and heart about everything that touched or affected this infant. The annunciation of the heavenly messenger at the time of His conception filled the Virgin Mary with alarm and confusion as well as with joy over the honor bestowed upon her. This confusion and alarm grew as the months of her travail went on, and especially when it looked for a time as though even her betrothed was to misunderstand and "put her away," thus leaving her to bear alone the shame attending the Virgin's conception of this, as yet unborn, Son of the Most High.

Mary was young, certainly not more than seventeen or eighteen when the responsibilities of mothering the Only Begotten of the Father fell upon her youthful shoulders. Her trip to Bethlehem with Joseph to be enrolled, preceding the birth of the Christ Child, was doubtless attended by much mental and physical anxiety and suffering, for was not this her first born? The refusal of the inn to make a place for them, and especially for her in the hour of her great need; the hurried preparation of an ox-stall in a near-by stable, with no bed save straw, and no attendants among her own kin save that of bewildered and inexperienced Joseph, was enough to strike fear to even an older woman.

The early-morning visits of the shepherds and later of the wise men from the distant East were frightening in their importance and significance. The pronouncements of the aged Simeon and of Anna, the prophetess, in the Temple at the time of the circumcision of this first-born son combined to increase the weight of responsibility that fell upon the shoulders of this young, inexperienced Jewish girl. The midnight warning of the angel to Joseph to take the young child and mother and flee into Egypt, thus escaping the jealous wrath of Herod the King; that long and wearisome journey on the part of Joseph, with Mary and the young Child on the back of their faithful donkey, through robber-infested lands, and later through seemingly never-ending desert to their new home among strange peoples and strange tongues— all these added to the sense of loneliness, confusion, and fear that attended the early life of this infant Son of the Most High God.

Something of all this loneliness and dread Kaulbach has painted for us in the deep-set eyes and tragic face of this young Jewish mother as she leans above her sleeping Child, the fingers of His little hand pressed against her lips. He is so sweet, so trustingly confident of her loving watch-care as He nestles for the first time in a bed at the end of weary days of traveling en route to Egypt, the land of strange peoples and customs.

Perhaps these lonely travelers had been subject to some strange new fright as they neared the land that was to shield this Holy Family from harm during the infant years of this Child of Promise. The tear speaks eloquently of relief from escape, while the far-away look in the deep-set eyes of the

Madonna indicates her desire to fathom the will of the heavenly Father in respect to this Son whose care has been given into her inexperienced hands.

The Baby may have become ill as a result of that long and perilous journey. We do not know. A sandstorm may have caused these weary, foot-sore travelers to miss the oasis with its spring of cool, refreshing water. Joseph, no longer young, may have felt the sting of a desert snake or scorpion and Mary, *remembering,* shrinks in alarm from the fate that may befall her and this new-born Son if they lose the protecting care of a husband and father. What the tragedy is that has befallen this Holy Family we may only guess; but the artist has not left us in doubt as to its influence on the mind and heart of this young mother. Fear, anxiety, a pleading unspoken prayer for guidance during the days and weeks that lie ahead are painted with consummate skill in the eyes and face of this young mother as she leans in brooding tenderness above her Child.

Motherhood is never without its anxieties, its heartaches, its cares. Perhaps it is just this that gives to mothers everywhere their unusual sympathy, insight and understanding. Certain it is that the circumstances attending the infancy of the Only Begotten of the Father were such as might well strike terror to the stoutest heart. But always the Madonna Mother, when she could not understand, prayed and kept buried deep in her own heart the anxieties and fears that beset her path in rearing this Child of Prophecy. Even during that last cruel week of expectation, despair, and agonizing grief His faithful mother followed Him in loving sympathy unspoiled by reproach to the fateful end. Gibran in his *Jesus the Son of Man* portrays Mary as standing at the foot of the cross, her right hand raised toward Him and saying through her tears: " 'My son, who is not my son, if this be of God may God give us patience and the knowledge thereof. And if it be of man may God forgive him forevermore.' And then turning to John and the other women, she said: 'Now behold, He is gone. The battle is over. The star has shone forth. The ship has reached the harbor. He who once lay against my heart is throbbing in space. . . .' And Mary returned to Jerusalem leaning upon John the young disciple. And she was a woman fulfilled."[1]

As we look into the tear-stained face and eyes of this young Madonna Mother, we know that God's way of making great women out of inexperienced girlhood is in the process, and deep in our own hearts we thank God for all the madonna mothers of the centuries.

[1] From *Jesus, the Son of Man,* by Kahlil Gibran. Used by special permission.

MARY, THE MORNING STAR MADONNA

By the

Italian-Japanese Painter

Signora Fulenia Picnet da Franchi of Siena

(Interpretation)

THIS striking picture was executed in 1919, at the request of Admiral Yama-moto, a convert to Christianity, and a former pupil of The Morning Star School (Catholic) in Tokyo.

The painting is symbolic, of course, representing as it does the Virgin Mary with the Christ Child lying close to her breast and surrounded by rays of light in the form of an eight-point star that hovers over a characteristic Japanese landscape.

In the foreground is E-no-Ura with its islets and promontories, and a plain, all in darkness, while in the background rises Fuji, the sacred mountain of Japan, whose snow-capped peak is just beginning to reflect the light of dawn.

Mary, the bright Morning Star, suspended in front of the crystal rays of light in the eight-point star, is giving Jesus, the Son of Justice, to shine sweetly upon the people of this pagan nation. Such, at least, is the conception of the Japanese-Italian artist, Signora Fulenia Picnet da Franchi, in "Mary, the Morning Star Madonna."

And while the flowing robes of the Madonna Mother may not be typically Japanese, there is about the oval face and head of the mother and the short black hair of the sleeping Child a suggestion, at least, of the charm and beauty of these artistic little people of the Sunrise Kingdom. We rejoice, at least, that a native Christian Japanese art is being developed that makes the Christ indigenous in the thought and adoration of the Orient.

✝

THE MADONNA OF THE BAMBOO

By the

Chinese Artist, Luke Ch'en

(Interpretation)

THIS painting is typically Chinese in its artistic conception and development, from the bamboo trees with their leafy foliage which adorn its beautiful and delicate background to the almond-eyed Chinese Madonna, who holds in her arms this young Chinese Baby-Saviour of her race.

MARY, THE MORNING STAR MADONNA—*DA FRANCHI*

THE MADONNA OF THE BAMBOO—*CH'EN*

It is said that the artist studied the New Testament for months in preparation for a series of paintings illustrating the Christian message in terms of Chinese imagery and ideals; and as a consequence of this study, he, himself, accepted Christianity in 1932 in preference to the older Oriental faiths of his native land.

One of the unique characteristics of the Christ and of the Christian religion is that it adapts itself to the culture and needs of every race and civilization. It is not difficult, therefore, to understand why and how each race and nation paints the Christ in terms of its own national and racial ideas and ideals.

No painting illustrates the universality of Jesus' appeal and teachings better than this comparatively modern picture of "The Madonna of the Bamboo." Christ is, indeed, the Christ of the Orient, for He, Himself, was an Oriental. And while the Occident, due to certain historical and political developments in human history, may have accepted Christ and His teachings more generally and perhaps a bit more readily than the Orient; nowhere do we find a greater compliment to the universality of Christ's message and appeal to all nations, races, and cultures, than in this remarkably beautiful conception of "The Madonna of the Bamboo" by the Chinese artist Luke Ch'en of Peking, China.

✠

A MODERN MADONNA

By

Roberto Ferruzzi

(Interpretation)

FERRUZZI, the Venetian figure painter, was born at Sebenico, a town in the province of Dalmatia in 1854. This province now belonging to the Austrian Empire was formerly a subdivision of the Venetian republic, and is still Italian in language and in manners and customs.

Roberto was the only son of his parents and when he was four years old they took him to Venice. Soon after the removal of the family to Venice, the father died, and the mother, who had devoted all her energies to the education of her gifted son, was obliged to take him back to Sebenico in order to look after the administration of the family property.

In 1868 he returned to Venice and became a pupil at the Liceo Marco Foscarini. Completing his studies there he entered the University of Padua, took the law course and received his degree. He had no serious liking for law, however, and never followed it as a profession.

Instead he began painting, not entering the Academy, but working by himself. He made rapid progress in art, and it did not take him long to master its technique. In 1883 he exhibited at Turin his first three pictures. His work met with favorable reception for all three of his pictures sold.

His "Madonnina," which did more than any other one picture to establish his reputation, was first exhibited in Venice in 1897, together with another painting entitled "Toward the Light." His "Madonnina" was purchased by the Fratelli Alinari of Florence. The type of face portrayed in this painting will be found among young girls in the Euganean hills near Padua.

This picture sometimes called "A Modern Madonna" and at other times "The Madonna and Child" is not a Madonna at all in the sense of being intended to represent the Virgin Mary. It is intended, instead, to represent the universal heart of young motherhood the world around of every age and race. This beautiful young girl holding in her arms the sleeping child is a sweet and gentle creature of our modern times. Her innocent young face awakens in all who gaze upon it an impulse to adore all young mothers who dedicate themselves to the high and holy task of mothering the children of men.

There is a meditative look on the face of this young mother as she gazes out over the head of her sleeping child that makes us think of the Virgin Mary pondering over the significant happenings in connection with the birth of her first-born child. The soft silken eyelids have already closed over the dreamy eyes of the child, and unbroken, restful sleep has already quieted his active young body into repose.

And the greatest rewarding compensation that mothers know is just to have sons and daughters who "rise up to call them blessed"; who make something of themselves of which mothers may be justly proud; and who, when their own mothers are no longer young, give them the same love and watch-care which was so generously bestowed on them during infancy and childhood.

Dr. Frank Crane, whose writings have been a constant source of challenge and inspiration to readers everywhere, wrote this beautiful testimonial on what the love of mothers should mean to the children of men.

MOTHER

She is my mother, said the young man, but I call her my baby. Old people are very much like babies, and we ought to love them, for of such is the Kingdom of Heaven.

I have an idea that life evens up things. When I was young and helpless she took care of me; now I take care of her. I am paying my debt. She never left me alone when I was an infant. Now I do not leave her alone.

She was patient with me then; now I am patient with her. She fed me; now I feed her. I clothe and keep her. She sacrificed her young life for me; and I am glad of every chance I have to sacrifice for her.

She loved me when I was ignorant, awkward, needing constant care, and all because I was hers, born of her body and part of her soul. Now every feebleness and trait of childishness in her endears her to me, for no other reason except that she is my mother.

By so much as she is a tax on my time, attention, and money, I love her.

A MODERN MADONNA—*FERRUZZI*

She shall not triumph over me in the day of judgment; for my tenderness shall equal hers.

She watched me until I grew up; I shall watch with her until she steps into Heaven.[2]

✚

LA VIRGIN COL FIGLIO

By

Bartolomé Esteban Murillo

(Interpretation)

MURILLO, the artist who gave us this charming painting, was born in Seville, Spain, in 1617. His parents died when he was eleven years old, and little is known of his earlier years, other than the fact that he studied art with his uncle and soon outdistanced him in ability. He had a desperate struggle with poverty during his adolescent years, and walked the entire distance from Seville to Madrid, where he was befriended by Velasquez, then court painter. For three years he grew in the mastery of art under the guidance of this renowned artist; and then returned to Seville where he obtained his first commission from a Franciscan monastery.

From then on his rise to fame and fortune was rapid and permanent. His time was fully occupied with orders from religious bodies and noblemen. He was admitted to the highest circle of society and worshiped by the common people.

In 1648 he married a lady of noble birth, and his home became a resort for the most distinguished personages of his day. Only once did he leave Seville till the time of his death in 1682.

This great artist was a devout Catholic, as all his art implies. He painted more than twenty different interpretations of the Immaculate Conception; and his madonnas are among the most beautiful in the world.

"La Virgin Col Figlio," the original of which hangs in the Pitti Palace in Florence, Italy, is regarded by many art critics as one of Murillo's best works. The features of both the Virgin and the Child are well-nigh perfect, and the flesh-white skin tones beyond compare. The Child possesses the physical beauty and charm of His exquisite mother, as He stands enshrined within her lovely arms.

In the eyes of both there is a dream, as yet unfulfilled. Mary's eyes question the future for this Child of destiny, whose coming is for the "healing of the nations"; whereas only childlike faith looks out at us from the eyes of this infant Son of God, whose future is as yet unknown and untried.

Note the matchless beauty and perfection of the hands of the Child and His mother; as well as the perfection and sweetness of mouth, nose, and

[2] Used by special permission of the author.

LA VIRGIN COL FIGLIO—*MURILLO*

chin. Faith, hope, and trust in God and in the future is the dominant message of this magnificent picture of the Madonna Mary and her infant Son. Storms may rise, persecution, heartache, and perhaps even defeat may prevail; but *now* Jesus is hers to love, to guide, to fondle, and to protect with the richness and unselfishness that mother love alone knows.

The appeal of this masterpiece draws one back again and again to view the canvas, and to ponder over the faith that God has in this Man and woman through whom, His Word affirms, "all nations shall be blessed."

✣

MOTHERHOOD

Mary, the Christ long slain, passed silently,
Following the children joyously astir
Under the cedrus and the olive tree,
Pausing to let their laughter float to her.
Each voice an echo of a voice more dear,
She saw a little Christ in every face.

Then came another woman gliding near
To watch the tender life which filled the place.
And Mary sought the woman's hand, and spoke:
  "I know thee not, yet know thy memory tossed
With all a thousand dreams their eyes evoke
  Who bring to thee a child beloved and lost.

"I, too, have rocked my little One.
  And He was fair,
Oh, fairer than the fairest sun,
And like its rays through amber spun
  His sun-bright hair!
Still I can see it shine and shine."
"Even so," the woman said, "was mine."

"His ways were ever darling ways"—
  And Mary smiled—
"So soft, so clinging! Glad relays
Of love were all His precious days.
  My little Child!
My infinite star! My music fled!"
"Even so was mine," the woman said.

And Mary whispered: "Tell me, thou,
  Of thine." And she:
"Oh, mine was rosy as a bough
Blooming with roses, sent, somehow,
  To bloom for me.

His balmy fingers left a thrill
Deep in my breast that warms me still."
Then gazed she down some wilder, darker hour,
    And said—when Mary questioned, knowing not,
"Who art thou, mother of so sweet a flower?"—
    "I am the mother of Iscariot."

                     —Agnes Lee

A TRIBUTE TO MOTHERHOOD

God made the streams that gurgle down the purple mountain-side—
He made the gorgeous coloring with which the sunset's dyed.
He made the hills and covered them with glory; and He made
The sparkle on the dewdrop and the flecks of light and shade;
Then knowing all earth needed was a climax for her charms,
He made a little woman with a baby in her arms.
He made the arching rainbow that is thrown across the sky,
He made the blessed flowers that nod and smile as we pass by;
He made the gladsome beauty as she bows with queenly grace,
But sweetest of them all, He made the love light in the face
That bends above a baby, warding off the world's alarms—
That dainty little woman with a baby in her arms.
A soft pink wrap embellished with a vine in silken thread—
A filmy, snow-white cap upon a downy little head—
A dress 'twould make the winter drift look dusty by its side—
Two cheeks with pure rose-petal tint, two blue eyes wonder wide,
And bending o'er—the mother face imbued with heaven's own charms,
God bless the little woman with a baby in her arms.

                 —Author Unknown

MOTHER'S LOVE

Her love is like an island
    In life's ocean, vast and wide,
A peaceful, quiet shelter
    From the wind, the rain, the tide.

'Tis bound on the north by Hope,
    By Patience on the West,
By tender Counsel on the South
    And on the East by Rest.

Above it like a beacon light
    Shine Faith, and Truth, and Prayer;
And through the changing scenes of life
    I find a haven there.

                 —Author Unknown

MARY AT THE WELL

I fill my jar
With drops that hold the colors of a star.
If I must walk at last, some darker way,
My heart shall hold this one immortal day,
And a Child's loveliness at play.
With seven sunbeams in His hair, my Jesus stands,
Pouring the drops like broken jewels through His hands.
With twenty sunbeams in His heart of gold,
He gives me little precious words to hold:
"When I am taller grown than all the sons of men,
I shall bring water so you do not thirst again—
Cold drops of crystal from a stream
Hidden in some white dream."

My heart within me is a cage of singing birds,
Keeping His lovely words.
His very thoughts are flower buds, tightly curled,
Until their day of blossoming through the world.
A little happier than other women are,
I bend as they, to fill my earthen jar,
With drops that hold the mysteries of a star.
                              —*Mary Brent Whiteside*

A BIRTHDAY

Did Mary make a birthday cake
For Christ when He was small,
And think the while she frosted it,
How quickly boys grow tall?

Did Joseph carve some foolish thing
From extra bits of wood,
An ox, a camel, or a bird,
Because the Christ was good?

Oh, sometimes years are very long,
And sometimes years run fast,
And when the Christ had put away
Small, earthly things at last

And died upon a wooden cross
One afternoon in spring,
Did Mary find the little toy,
And sit . . . remembering?
                              —*Helen Welshimer*

STARRY NIGHT

Like snowflakes on a window pane
   The stars lie scattered on the dome,
And Mary and Her Child look down
   At the shining speck that was their home.

Sweet Mary and her Child look down
   Through a silver casement in the night,
Remembering tears are in her eyes;
   He reaches out with young delight.

She leans and whispers in His ear:
   "I see the town of Bethlehem,
The shepherds on the very hills
   You traveled to Jerusalem.

Our God is good to let me hold
   My Baby still against my breast.
Oh, time is everywhere at once:
   I choose the moment I love best."

The stars no longer seem like flakes:
   The sky's a patterned coverlet
To tuck about the little feet
   Of Him who is her baby yet.

—Louise Ayres Garnett

A MOTHER

God sought to give the sweetest thing
   In His almighty power
To earth; and deeply pondering
   What it should be, one hour
In fondest joy and love of heart
   Outweighing every other,
He moved the gates of heaven apart
   And gave to earth a mother.

—Author Unknown

WALLS

Give me wide walls to build my house of Life—
   The North shall be of Love, against the winds of fate;
   The South of Tolerance, that I may outreach hate;

The East of Faith, that rises clear and new each day;
The West of Hope, that e'en dies a glorious way.
The threshold 'neath my feet shall be Humility;
The roof—the very sky itself—Infinity.
Give me wide walls to build my house of Life.

—Elinor Lennen

THE HOUSEWIFE

Jesus, teach me how to be
Proud of my simplicity.

Sweep the floors, wash the clothes,
Gather for each vase a rose.

Iron and mend a tiny frock
Taking notice of the clock,

Always having time kept free
For childish questions asked of me.

Grant me wisdom Mary had
When she taught her little Lad.

—Catherine Cate Coblentz

A PRAYER FOR A LITTLE HOME

God send us a little home—
To come back to when we roam—
Low walls and fluted tiles,
Wide windows, a view for miles;
Red firelight and deep chairs;
Small white beds upstairs;
Great talk in little nooks,
Dim colors, rows of books;
One picture on each wall;
Not many things at all.
God send us a little ground—
Tall trees standing round,
Homely flowers in brown sod,
Overhead Thy stars. O God—
Bless all the winds that blow
Our homes and all we know.

—Anonymous

KEEP SWEET

Amid the duties of today,
In all I think, and do, and say,
Whether I work, or rest, or play—
    Lord keep me sweet at HOME.

When household duties claim my care
And I seem needed everywhere—
Then tune my heart to praise and prayer,
    And keep me sweet at HOME.

No matter what the day may bring,
Or night—I pray in everything
My life may glorify my King—
    Especially at HOME.

—*Laura A. Barter Snow*

HYMN FOR A HOUSEHOLD

Lord Christ, beneath Thy starry dome
We light this flickering lamp of home,
And where bewildering shadows throng
Uplift our prayer and evensong.
Dost Thou, with heaven in Thy ken
Seek still a dwelling-place with men,
Wandering the world in ceaseless quest?
O Man of Nazareth, be our guest!

Lord Christ, the bird his nest has found,
The fox is sheltered in his ground,
But dost Thou still this dark earth tread
And have no place to lay Thy head?
Shepherd of mortals, here behold
A little flock, a wayside fold
That wait Thy presence to be blest—
O Man of Nazareth, be our guest!

—*David Henderson*

IRONY OF GOD

In vain
They shook their garments;
He did not hear the tinkling
Of little bells

On priestly hems;
Nor smell the smoky savor
Of slaughtered, burning life.

He did not see Jerusalem—
Nor Rome;
He passed by all "best families"
To dwell at last in Nazareth,
With Mary,
Mother of that Son
Who fraternized with fishermen;
Found heaven in little children;
And had a friend
Named Mary Magdalene.

—Eva Warner

THE MAIDSERVANT AT THE INN

It's queer, she said, I see the light
As plain as I beheld it then—
All silvery and calm and bright,
We've not had stars like that again.

And she was such a gentle thing
To birth a baby in the cold.
The barn was dark and frightening
This new one's better than the old.

I mind my eyes were full of tears
For I was young and quick distressed;
For she was less than me in years,
That had a Son against her breast.

I never saw a sweeter child—
The little one—the darling one.
I mind I told her when He smiled
You'd know he was his mother's Son.

It's queer that I should see them so—
The time they come to Bethlehem—
Was more than fifty years ago.
I pray that all is well with them.[3]

—Dorothy Parker

[3] Used by special permission of the author and *Bethany Guide*.

MARY, MOTHER IN HEAVEN TO THE MOTHERS ON EARTH

A Christmas Message

Oh, Mothers of the Earth today
  Whose hearts beat high this Christmas Morn,
In lowly homes beside the way,
  In palaces where kings are born,
My mother heart goes out to you
Whose little sons still climb and cling
About your knees. The years are few
Which time allots for mothering!
Your sons like mine will see ahead
The vision of the world's great need.
We mothers know the fear and dread
Which come when sons no longer heed
Our over-anxious worryings.
No longer fear! Take heart in this—
I gather up those precious things,
A trusting smile—a fragrant kiss—
A stumbling prayer—a tiny shoe,
And I, who know and understand,
On this, His Birthday, kneel with you
And offer up within my hand,
As gifts to lay before His feet,
Your mother love, that is pure gold—
Your mother prayers, as incense sweet—
Your mother tears, like myrrh of old—
These priceless gifts shall plead for them,
Your little sons, who climb and cling,
And my own Son of Bethlehem
Shall guard their eager visioning.[4]

—Sarah Palmer Colmore

THE PICTURE OF CHRIST

O, that the picture of the Christ
  Were painted clearly on the wall
Of every living room on earth,
  Where one could never fail at all
To see Him there—His gentle eyes
  Following one throughout the days;
Surely those eyes would influence
  A family's manners, words and ways.

[4] From *The Palm Branch,* December, 1954. Diocese of South Florida, Orlando, Fla. Reprinted by permission of the author and publishers.

O, that all parents of the earth
  Would feed their young the Bread of Life;
Give Living Water for their thirst.
  If every husband, every wife
Were so Christ filled that they could live
  His life for all the world to see;
If they would give their children Christ,
  How transformed this old earth would be![5]

—Grace Noll Crowell

✤

A MODERN MIDNIGHT MADONNA

By

Sarah Ashby Heassler

Do you have the picture of this present-day madonna in your home? It is as fine as any of the ancient ones. There is that fringe of darkness, the light and emphasis on the central figure of the mother and infant; yet there is just enough of the soft-toned ivory of crib and table to indicate that clean aloofness of the modern nursery. Crisp and clear are the lines of curtain and window-sash that form the frame for the midnight darkness outside the warm light of this room. There is brooding mystery in the purpled night with its dim street lights at a distance, and the tops of trees lumped against the staggered line of silhouetted houses. There is brooding mystery in the deep eyes of this young mother; her eyes are set under clear-cut brows over a mobile but definite mouth and chin. There is just enough disorder of shingled hair to give a soft tumbled line to the forehead and the one cheek away from the light. The hair has been severely pushed back behind the other ear so that it is boldly out-lined by the light.

From the posture and attitude of mother and baby, one can see that he has just drawn back his head from her breast, satisfied and replete. His head is thrown back almost horizontal with the table; the angle of light from the low-shaded lamp catches the baby's profile in rapt concentration on his mother's face. The mother's slanting gaze takes in the baby, quiet and relaxed, with her one arm circled about him, while the other arm rests lightly along the window sill, as the last of her look travels past him with yearning into the night.

Her face holds not the placid peasant gaze of some of our most famed mother-lore art. It is alert and intelligent, still, now, in its peaceful meditation, but with features all but sharpened by apprehension. There has been a struggle through to the peace of this room, not just placid and unmoved acceptance. In fact, the quietude is all the more striking because this pause is caught from out the unrest and turmoil of a steady stream of life's busy activity. The con-

[5] Used by permission of Mrs. Grace Noll Crowell, 719 Lowell Street, Dallas, Tex.

tentment on her features is that of glad service rendered and all things done for the instant. The groping in her eyes is now submerged in her glow of joy in her baby. As if loath to break the goodness and warmth of their content, both mother and child are resting in this moment of stability—a modern midnight madonna's moment caught up into the light of infinite love.[6]

✣

CHRISTMAS ON THE PLAINS

By

Cynthia Pearl Maus

IT WAS only a crude sod house on the plains of eastern Colorado, six miles from the nearest town. Only a lonely sod house with a thin volume of smoke issuing from its chimney, yet inside the *spirit* of *Christmas* was there. The yard was unadorned save for that four-room house with a half-in-the-ground lean-to in the rear for fruits and vegetables, a few scattered outbuildings here and there for cattle, hogs, chickens, and horses, and a dilapidated old well.

Inside, three half-grown girls, ranging from six to twelve years of age, were busily engaged covering, with striped paper sacks, a cross, crudely made of two lath, which was to serve instead of the proverbial Christmas tree of other years. One of the girls was cutting into strips the striped paper sacks, which their provident mother had carefully saved for them during the year, while another wound them tightly about the lath cross. The third and littlest girl was trying with her childish hands to pin together small paper funnels, which later were to be tied to the Christmas cross as containers for bits of candy— one for each member of this pioneer family, and one or two extra funnels for guests that might drop in on them from other ranches during the holiday season.

It was late afternoon on the day before Christmas, when a toil-worn mother, her basket on her arm, trudged into the yard and up to the door of that lonely sod house on the plains. Because her menfolk were away from home, working on an irrigation ditch some thirty miles distant, she had walked all the way to Sheridan Lake, her basket filled with eggs, butter, and milk, that she might exchange them for some popcorn, cranberries, sugar, oranges, and a bit of cheap candy and nuts with which to provide a meager treat for the members of her family on Christmas day.

Two years before they had landed on the plains of Colorado, coming from Iowa, with the purpose in mind of proving up their preëmption rights on at least two quarter-section ranches, so that the boys, now almost grown, might have at least a land-start in life. The first year had not been too hard, for they had brought with them enough potatoes, apples, canned fruits, vegetables, and smoked meat with which to live comfortably, even though the crops for the

[6] Used by special permission of the author. All other publication rights reserved.

first season in a virgin land were scant. These provisions, however, had long since been exhausted, and with drought killing their crops the first year, and hailstones as large as goose eggs razing the corn, then in tassel, to the ground during the second summer, the family were poor indeed.

A warm fire of crackling cow chips was burning away on the hearth and in the kitchen stove when this tired mother reached the little sod house, and setting her basket down on the table she called to the girls to come and help her with the evening chores. Soon the cows were milked, the chickens, hogs, and cattle fed, and the supper prepared.

After their meager evening meal the girls completed their last-minute decoration of the Christmas cross, while the mother popped some corn, which the girls strung on white thread, and this, interspersed with garlands of lovely red cranberries and a few tiny candles saved from other years, made this simple, cheery cross a happy reminder of the birthday of the King of Kings.

When the last funnel filled with tiny bits of candy had found its place suspended from the Christmas cross the three little girls sat on the floor in front of their handiwork and sang, with their clear, high, childish voices the old, loved hymns and carols of the Christmastide, which had been their heritage from infancy.

By the kitchen stove the tired, discouraged pioneer mother stood, remembering the happy Christmases of her own childhood home in Ohio; and suffering, as only mothers can, who know for the first time the pinch of dire poverty. There would be no toys or playthings of any sort for her little daughters this year. Every penny must be carefully guarded if the family was to have even food and clothing until another harvest-time rolled around, bringing the hope, at least, of abundant crops and funds with which to replenish the family's cash resources.

Now, tired and spent, after a day of weary labor in making her home on the plains scrupulously clean, preparation for a meager Christmas dinner, which somehow she had managed to scrape together, and her long twelve-mile trudge to and from the nearest town for the few scant things that must be purchased to replenish her larder, she stood by the stove and watched with tear-dimmed eyes the three girls, who, in spite of the poverty of their pioneer home on the plains, were singing joyously the well-loved Christmas hymns and carols as they watched with pleasure the tiny lighted candles on this crudely-made Christmas cross.

There would be nothing in the stockings they would later place by the fireside but an orange, an apple, a few nuts when they awoke on Christmas morning. True, her toil-worn hands had made for each girl a new fleeced nightgown, which they desperately needed, and a pair of yarn mittens for each of her menfolk; but beyond this there would be nothing with which to make glad the hearts of the ones she loved when Christmas dawned.

Tears flooded her eyes, and in spite of an effort to control herself, hard, dry sobs shook her weary frame. She busied herself by trying to punch up the fire so that the girls might not see her tears. But the eager eyes of the middle one had already sensed that something was wrong with mother, and, leaving the singing group for a moment, she scampered over to where her mother stood. Seeing her tears, she asked, in a childish whisper: "What are you crying about, mother, on Christmas Eve?" Getting no answer, she slipped her childish arms about her mother's waist and continued: "Are you thinking about the Baby Jesus and the cruel way in which men killed Him when He grew up?"

"Yes," answered the tired mother, drying her tears, "I am thinking about Him and the sorrow and heartache He later knew; but I am also thinking about my little girls for whom there will be no Christmas toys at all on the morrow. Old Santa Claus finds us too poor this year to help him make glad the hearts of even those we love, to say nothing of the other poor ranchers who are in desperate need."

"But, mother," answered this serious child, her dark, dreamy eyes filled with love as she looked earnestly into her mother's face, "we do not need any toys. We are well, we have *you,* and father and the boys are coming *home* to spend *Christmas* with us; so please don't cry any more."

Suddenly everything was all right again. Her tiredness was gone and her mother-heart released of its burden through the sympathetic understanding of a little child. She sat down on a near-by chair and called the girls to her. Then she lifted the littlest one in her arms, as she told them again the marvelous story of the birth of the Manger Child of the long ago.

When the story was finished they knelt at her knees for their good-night prayers, and then scuttled off to bed to sleep the dreamless sleep that only children know.

Quietly and quickly she wrapped in separate packages for each member of her little family the only Christmas gifts they were to receive. Then she filled the stockings of the little girls with oranges, apples, nuts, and a bit of candy, musing, as she worked, over the strange peaceful calm that had so suddenly come into her heart. The Master was right. He had said, "A little child shall lead them," and tonight her own little girl had, with intuitive insight, placed the emphasis where it ought always to be on this approaching birthday of the King. *Health, love* for *one another,* and *family togetherness*—these were the spiritual values that mattered, not gifts of things that one could buy or make. What was poverty, anyway, but a test of character. So long as they had health, mother and father, and the boys and girls together, they could and would weather every storm.

How long she sat alone in front of the fire, musing, after these last-minute tasks were done, she never knew; but suddenly she found herself humming that best-loved of all the Christmas hymns:

> Silent night, holiest night,
> Darkness flies, all is light;
> Shepherds hear the angels sing;
> "Alleluia! hail the King.
> Christ the Saviour is here,
> Jesus the Saviour is here."

The night was beautiful and calm. The soft snow that had fallen earlier in the day had frozen with the lowered temperature of nightfall, so that it sharpened every approaching sound. Suddenly she heard the creak of wagon wheels in the distance; then a cheery "Halloo!" She arose quickly and hurried to the door. Her menfolk were safe at home; and with their coming the Christmas melody of "peace on earth and good-will toward men" sang itself softly in the lonely mother-heart in that little sod house on the plains.

✠

THE ROPE OF LOVE

(The Indian's Version of the Twenty-third Psalm)

THE Indian language is not easily subject to translation, and in their intercourse with one another the various tribes use a sign language, more or less universal, which they have evolved. The following is a translation of the Twenty-third Psalm which can easily be interpreted by this sign language.

"The Great Father above is a Shepherd Chief. I am His and with Him I want not.

"He throws out to me a rope, and the name of the rope is LOVE.

"He draws me, and He draws me, and He draws me to where the grass is green and the water is not dangerous; and I eat and lie down satisfied.

"Sometimes my heart is very weak and falls down, but He lifts it up again and draws me into a good road. His name is Wonderful.

"Sometime, it may be very soon, it may be longer, it may be a long, long time, He will draw me into a place between mountains. It is dark there, but I will not draw back. I will not be afraid, for it is in there between these mountains that the Shepherd Chief will meet me, and the hunger I have felt in my heart all through this life will be satisfied.

"Sometimes He makes the love rope into a whip, but afterwards He gives me a staff to lean on.

"He spreads a table before me with all kinds of food. He puts His hands upon my head and all the 'tired' is gone. My cup He fills it till it runs over.

"What I tell you is true, I lie not. These roads that are 'Away ahead' will stay with me through this life; and afterward I will go to live in the 'Big Tepee' and sit down with the Shepherd Chief forever."[7]

[7] Extract from *The Missionary Review of the World*. Used by special permission.

THE PRINCE OF ILLUSION

By

John Luther Long

First, you must be told why and how he became a Prince for he was only a poor little boy living in a tenement.

The doctors had said that he would always be lame and blind, and that if he had no sorrows, no not one, he would almost certainly live ten years. But those who are born blind, the doctors warned his mother, are born with fancies, illusions. These must be made *real,* no matter how strange, how impossible.

Jack's familiarity with things of a princely nature came first through her reading to him; and presently she understood that he conceived himself to be a Prince. Then she resolved that he should be a Prince, an Emperor, if he wished, if it gave him pleasure.

Her room had only one window facing a wall, so that it gave no sunlight. All day the lamp burned, all day she sewed. A dun-colored curtain closed the opening to the outer room. In this room behind the curtain she lived his life of beauty and joy with him. Facing the door to the outer room was a dainty, white, canopied bed, frilled and chiffoned, with all its belongings immaculate. On the bed lay a boy some nine years old, but looking tragically older. Not a feature of his face was tolerable. He was hideously ugly.

One day, while she was sewing Jack called to her: "Mamma, are you there?"

"Yes, sweetheart," she answered, coming into the room.

Then he said: "Everything you have read me about, and told me about has been beautiful, gorgeous, splendid! Of course I'm glad; but, mamma dear, there must be something dreadful—ugly?"

"No sweetheart, the world is all beautiful."

"But mamma darling, isn't there one—just *one thing* in all the world that is dreadful? Sometimes I get tired of everything being beautiful, and I think ugly things would be nice for a change."

A great weariness was shown in her eyes, and a hunger for the truth that was so hard to quell. She didn't quite manage it today. "Yes—there is one thing in the world that is ugly."

"What is it, mamma?"

"*Death!*"

"*Death?* It doesn't sound *dreadful,* mamma dear. Is it sad?" For a long time he was silent, and then he said:

"Mamma dear, you have told me about everything in the world, but myself. Can it be that you are afraid to tell me? Am I *ugly* like death?"

"No, no darling! I suppose that is why I never thought to tell you, because you are so much a part of *all* that is *beautiful* in the *world.*"

"Oh, mamma, is it true? Am I beautiful like all the rest? For a moment I was afraid. If I were *ugly* like death, I should never wish to see."

"No, nor should I wish it."

"Go on, mamma dear, tell me about myself."

She looked long into the thin, elf-like face before her, and then she closed her eyes. She wished only to know the tender pressure of his small arms. "You have long and splendid locks, my darling—yellow, shining and silken."

"And my eyes?"

"They are blue; and there are long, curling lashes that lie upon your cheeks as you sleep. And your mouth, oh, Jack, my darling—your mouth is like a rose bud, and more sweet—more sweet to kiss."

"Mamma, darling, it is better than seeing to hear you tell about it . . . Sometimes I am almost glad I'm blind, when you tell me how beautiful I am."

Suddenly, resistlessly she sobbed.

"But why do you cry, mamma dear?"

"Don't you know, Jack, my sweet one?"

"No-o-o, mamma dear, I don't know much about crying, I have never cried. Maybe I don't know how."

"God grant that you may never learn. You never shall if I can prevent it. You shall be the happiest being that ever lived on this earth. You shall know no sorrow, regret or care—only *joy, joy, joy!*"

Jack's wants were modest enough. His mother managed to keep them so; but what she permitted him to need, he ordered royally.

"This morning I shall have nothing but fruit for my breakfast—an orange, banana and perhaps a pomegranate."

She went to a closet in the outer room, and opening the door so that he could hear it, she called, as if down a stairway:

"Donald, Donald!" She waited a moment, and then said: "You will bring the Prince a simple breakfast this morning—an orange and a banana will be sufficient, and hasten."

Quietly she procured a plate and the fruit from a shelf in the closet—waited a moment, and then said: "Thank you, Donald, you are very kind."

She closed the door of the closet so that Jack might know it, and took the fruit to the little boy.

"I like Donald, mamma. He always answers at once, and so very quietly. Tell him that he need not be afraid of me. For the moment I get back my sight he shall have a new suit of clothes, some money in a purse, and perhaps a ring. . . . And what does he say, mamma, dear!"

"He gives you his most humble service, and hopes that it will not be much longer until your highness comes to rule over his subjects."

One night under the glare of the electric lights by the side of the river, Jack heard his first orchestral music. The great orchestra was throbbing out the story of Siegfried's betrayal and death, when Jack gasped sobbingly and put his hands up to his eyes. His mother saw it, but he put his head under her arm, not like a Prince, but like a simple little boy; and she was reassured.

That night, as she watched him in his sleep, he seemed more pinched and shrunken than before; and *once* he sobbed; it was the *first* time. But then, as if some pent-up emotion had been loosed, he slept; and she was relieved.

The next day when they went out for a drive, he was very quiet. He asked no questions, and he kept his gaze straight ahead. When they returned home he seemed unusually tired. His mother noticed it and said:

"Jack, you are not going to be ill, are you? You are so brave. Fight whenever the illness comes. We have fought together for more than nine years. Don't abandon me *now,* fight with me."

They drove almost every day *now.* But Jack's eyes were always straight ahead, and often his head was tucked under her arm in that sweet new fashion. Often she took him to hear the music; and though he said it was beautiful, he always *listened* with his eyes *closed.*

One day Jack said: "Mamma darling, I'm tired today before we start. Let's not go out at all, but stay at home all the whole, long day. And you will talk to me softly, and I shall do nothing, but listen."

The next morning Jack was strangely, fearsomely ill. The cabman brought the doctor; and she held him on the stairs afterwards. The doctor said:

"What has happened to him?"

"Nothing," she answered.

"No shock? No heart-breaking disappointment?"

"No-o, he has been absolutely happy, and he will be to the end."

"But if he should pay for it with his life—doctors do not always know— Suppose he should regain his sight—it would be difficult for him to understand —to forgive. Think of his seeing everything, *himself,* yourself—" Then looking up at her, standing there like the white Goddess of the home, he added: "Ah, yes, *yourself*—seeing *you* that might mend it all."

She went back to the immaculate bed and put her arms around Jack, and he put his arms around her. For a long time they looked into each other's eyes—there were no tears—: Then she said:

"Oh, be brave my darling. . . . You have been a Prince all through—you have fought with me—fight *now."*

"I am brave, mamma darling." He paused for a moment, and then added softly, "So are you *brave,* mamma dear."

Suddenly terror and pity filled her soul, and silent God-sent tears flooded her eyes. And Jack forgetting, put up his little hand and tenderly brushed them away.

For a moment neither spoke, and then Jack said: "You will forgive me, mamma darling, will you not? I did not mean to tell you. I thought a Prince wouldn't do that way—not let you know—not hurt you."

"You are my Prince," she sobbed. "Oh, Jack, you are *my* Prince."

"I wished you would say that, mamma dear. I have not been blind since I *saw* the *music.* That was sixty-seven days ago. And, mamma darling . . . this I do not like to tell you. . . . I looked in the mirror, one night, when you were sleeping . . . and I *saw myself.* . . . But, first of all, mamma dear, I *saw you!* And all these sixty-seven days . . . I've seen you."

"Mamma darling, there is only one thing, in all the world—as *beautiful,* . . . Oh, more beautiful, than you said it was—and that is *you,* mamma darling."

Two tears, the first he had ever shed, came into his eyes; and then they lingeringly closed, looking into hers. The Prince of Illusion had entered God's kingdom of eternal love.[8]

✦

FAITH OF OUR MOTHERS

FOR years devout Christians of every nation, race, and clime have sung Frederick W. Faber's great devotional hymn, "Faith of Our Fathers, Living Still." It was not until as late as 1920, however, that Arthur B. Patten wrote a Hymn to Our Mothers to be sung to that same tune, "St. Catherine," to which we sing Faber's more universally known hymn.

Mother's Day is of comparatively recent origin as a special day in the life of the Church; but with its establishment on the second Sunday of May each year, there has arisen also the need of some great Mother's Day hymns appropriate to the occasion. Such a hymn Mr. Patten has provided in the challenging words "Faith of Our Mothers, Living Yet."

The theme of the four stanzas of this beautiful Mother's Day hymn emphasizes four qualities of motherhood's faith that are truly characteristic—*living, lavish, guiding,* and *Christian,* for such is the faith of all true mothers. It is a type of hymn that all of us may sing with genuine and reverent devotion.

> Faith of our mothers, living yet
>   In cradle song and bedtime prayer,
> In nursery love and fireside lore,
>   Thy presence still pervades the air.
> Faith of our mothers, living faith,
> We will be true to thee till death.
>
> Faith of our mothers, living faith,
>   The fount of childhood's trust and grace,
> O may thy consecration prove
>   The wellspring of a nobler race.
> Faith of our mothers, lavish faith,
> We will be true to thee till death.
>
> Faith of our mothers, guiding faith,
>   For youthful longings—youthful doubts,

[8] Abridged from *Century Magazine,* August, 1900. Copyright, 1900, by The Century Company, New York, N.Y. Used by permission of the publishers.

How blurred our vision, blind our way,
   Thy providential care without.
Faith of our mothers, guiding faith,
We will be true to thee till death.

Faith of our mothers, Christian faith,
   In truth beyond our man-made creeds,
Still serve the home and save the church,
   And breathe the spirit through our deeds.
Faith of our mothers, Christian faith,
We will be true to thee till death.

                          —*Arthur B. Patten, 1920*

✣

O BLESSED DAY OF MOTHERHOOD

THE Roman Catholic Church has for centuries emphasized the importance of motherhood by placing almost too much stress on the young, virgin mother, Mary, in its ritual and worship. So pronounced is this emphasis that it tends, at times, almost to overshadow the supremacy of Christ, and His death on the cross for the salvation of mankind.

On the other hand, to Jesus, more than to any other influence in the world, must go the credit for emancipating womanhood. It is a good thing, therefore, to note in these recent years the increased emphasis that Protestant Christianity is beginning to place on motherhood's contribution to the on-going process of building in this world God's Kingdom of Love. "As goes childhood, so goes the world"; and mothers, more than any other group in society, have the determining voice in the rearing of children, especially during the tender, impressionable years.

In his hymn, "O Blessed Day of Motherhood," Ernest F. McGregor has sought to emphasize the contribution which Christian mothers make, by a great hymn of praise to motherhood as a *blessed* day, a *sacred* day, a *precious* day, and a *wondrous* day.

O blessed day of motherhood!
   We lift our hearts in praise,
To thank thee, source of every good,
   Thy joy crowns all our days.
O God, our Father, bless this day,
   Enrich its golden store,
Of blessed mother love, and may
   Thy children Thee adore.

O sacred day of motherhood!
   Our faith, by thee increased,

Hath each alluring foe withstood;
  Our souls thou hast released.
O God, our Father, bless this day,
  Enrich its golden store
Of sacred mother love, and may
  Thy children Thee adore.

O precious day of motherhood!
  Teach us in thee to find,
The greater gifts of brotherhood;
  Bring peace to all mankind.
O God, our Father, bless this day,
  Enrich its golden store
Of precious mother love, and may
  Thy children Thee adore.

O wondrous day of motherhood!
  Thy love to all abound;
Beside the cross once Mary stood;
  Again let love be crowned.
O God, our Father, bless this day,
  Enrich its golden store
Of wondrous mother love, and may
  Thy children Thee adore. Amen.[9]

—*Ernest F. McGregor, 1925*

✢

UP TO ME SWEET CHILDHOOD LOOKETH

THIS is an old, old song, sometimes called the "Teacher's Hymn," because it emphasizes the influence which mothers and teachers have as a peculiar responsibility. It is sung to an old, old tune known as "Beecher," which may be found in almost any standard church hymnal.

The content of this hymn is in the nature of a prayer in which teachers, conscious of their great need, petition the heavenly Father for the *knowledge,* the *spirit,* and the *counsel* that they so sorely need, if they are to guide eager, alert minds into the fullness of truth.

It should be sung reverently as one would naturally voice a prayer.

The author of the words is unknown. It is one of those beautiful prayer songs that have come down to us through the years with no author's name associated with it; but which will live in the life of the Church because it expresses an ever-present need on the part of parents and teachers.

[9] Copyright by Ernest F. McGregor. Used by permission.

Up to me sweet childhood looketh,
　　Heart and mind and soul awake;
Teach me of Thy ways, O Father,
　　For sweet childhood's precious sake.
In their young hearts, soft and tender,
　　Guide my hand good seed to sow,
That its blossoming may praise Thee
　　Wheresoever they may go.

Give to me a cheerful spirit,
　　That my little flock may see
It is good and pleasant service
　　To be taught, O Lord, of Thee.
Father, order all my footsteps;
　　So direct my daily way,
That in following me, the children
　　May not stumbling, go astray.

Let Thy holy counsel lead me,
　　Let Thy light before me shine,
That they may not stumble over
　　Thoughtless word or deed of mine.
Draw us hand in hand to Jesus,
　　He who children ne'er forgot,
"Let the little ones come to Me,
　　And do thou forbid them not."

—Anonymous

✠

THERE IS BEAUTY ALL AROUND

THE English language contains no more beautiful word than *home,* for this simple word recalls to every person sacred memories, no matter where they were born or how humble their place of abode may have been.

Some years ago people were asked over the radio to list the ten most beautiful words. It is not strange that when the votes were tabulated most of these placed "home" at the head of the list.

And yet, as Edgar A. Guest indicates, "it takes a heap of living and a lot of lovin'" to make a house a home. Home can be a paradise on earth "when love shines in," or it can be a veritable hell with *love left out.*

Something of the richness and beauty that are always there when love is in evidence, John H. McNaughton has tried to put into the words of this beautiful song, "There Is Beauty All Around."

There is beauty all around,
   When there's love at home;
There is joy in every sound,
   When there's love at home.
Peace and plenty here abide,
   Smiling sweet on every side,
Time doth softly, sweetly glide,
   When there's love at home.

Refrain

Love at home, love at home,
   Time doth softly, sweetly glide,
When there's love at home. Amen.

In the cottage there is joy,
   When there's love at home;
Hate and envy ne'er annoy,
   When there's love at home.
Roses blossom 'neath our feet,
   All the earth's a garden sweet,
Making life a bliss complete,
   When there's love at home.

Refrain

Kindly heaven smiles above,
   When there's love at home.
All the earth is filled with love,
   When there's love at home.
Sweeter sings the brooklet by,
   Brighter beams the azure sky;
O there's One who smiles on high,
   When there's love at home.
       Refrain
          —*John H. McNaughton*

✛

SWING LOW, SWEET CHARIOT

THE exact origin of many of the Negro spirituals is unknown. Tradition says, however, that "Swing Low, Sweet Chariot," at least the chorus and melody, came directly from a tribe that inhabited the region of Central Africa that is near the great Victoria Falls.

When one of their chiefs, in the old days, was about to die, he was placed in a great canoe, together with the trappings that marked his rank, and with food for his journey; and then the canoe was set afloat in midstream, headed toward the Great Falls and the vast column of mist that rises constantly from them. Meanwhile his tribe on the shore sang its chant of farewell.

The legend is that on one occasion the chief was seen to rise in his canoe at the very brink of the Falls and enter a chariot, that descending from the mists, bore him aloft. This incident gave rise to the imagery and words, "Swing low, sweet chariot, coming for to carry me home."

The chorus, at least, and perhaps the melody also—we do not know—were later brought to America by African slaves of the long ago, modified and verses added as they came in contact with the Christian faith until this spiritual has come to have a universal Christian content and message.

Refrain

Swing low, sweet chariot,
  Coming for to carry me home.
Swing low, sweet chariot,
  Coming for to carry me home.

Verses

I looked over Jordan and what did I see,
  Coming for to carry me home?
A band of angels coming after me,
  Coming for to carry me home.

If you get there before I do,
  Coming for to carry me home,
Tell all my friends I'm a-comin' too,
  Coming for to carry me home.

I'm sometimes up and sometimes down,
  Coming for to carry me home;
But still my soul am heavenly bound,
  Coming for to carry me home.

—A Spiritual

CONTENTS

PART VI   SECTION IV

IN THE HEART OF CHILDHOOD

——————————————————✠——————————————————

"Suffer the little children to come unto me, and forbid them not."—LUKE 18:16

——————————————————✠——————————————————

613

✣

IN THE HEART OF CHILDHOOD

Lo, children are a heritage of Jehovah,
And the fruit of the womb is *his* reward,
As arrows in the hand of a mighty man,
So are the children of youth.

—PSALMS 127:3-4

✣

And he took a little child, and set him in the midst of them: and taking him in his arms, he said unto them, Whosoever shall receive one of such little children in my name, receiveth me: and whosoever receiveth me, receiveth not me, but him that sent me.—MARK 9:36-37

✣

And they were bringing unto him also their babes, that he should touch them; but when the disciples saw it, they rebuked them. But Jesus called them unto him, saying, Suffer the little children to come unto me, and forbid them not: for to such belongeth the kingdom of God. Verily I say unto you, Whosoever shall not receive the kingdom of God as a little child, he shall in no wise enter therein.—LUKE 18:15-17

✣

THE PRAYER OF A LITTLE CHILD

I do not kneel at night to say my prayers;
I think of spiders and I do not dare.
The splintered boards are rough, my knees are bare,
Besides the floor is cold out there,
And bed is warm; I'm safer here
Than in the outer darkness of a prayer.

But when the morning wakes up beautiful,
And sunshine makes our peach tree gloryful;
And God comes smiling down the garden walk—
I run and place my hand in His and talk.
I tell Him that I am a naughty lamb,—
He smiles, and says he made me like I am.

—*Kate Wisner McClusky*

ADER×DE×SMAA×BØRN×KOMME×TIL×MIG
×OG×FORMENER×DEM×IKKE×
HI×SAADANNE×HØRE×GUDS×RIGE×TIL

CHRIST AND THE CHILDREN—*HANSEN*

CHRIST AND THE CHILDREN

By

Aksel Hansen

(Interpretation)

THE picture on page 615 is a photograph of a relief by the Danish sculptor, Aksel Hansen. It hangs in the Glyptotek Museum in Copenhagen, and is particularly beautiful, arresting and lifelike. It portrays a group of Danish mothers bringing their little ones to Jesus that He may bless them.

You can almost hear the Master say in broken Danish dialect: "Suffer the small-born to come unto me, for of such is the kingdom of heaven," as He reaches out His hand to bless even the least of these.

The children in this relief are particularly beautiful. The expression of faces, hands, and bodies, is characteristic of the naive innocence of little children. Note how natural and lifelike is the expression of the two or three little tots that are peeking out and up at Jesus from under the form of this small infant that a fond mother is reaching out to the Master with extended arms. Look at the grace of that small up-raised hand in the foreground. The others may be a bit shy and timid, but she is ready now to be taken up and loved by this Friend of Children.

From the intense look of hope and expectancy on the mother's face we feel that this wee baby is perhaps ill and that Jesus is in the act of soothing away a dreadful fever with that compassionate right hand, while with the other He fondles the head of the tiny child behind Him.

The face of the Master of Men is strong and sensitive. A very sincere and deep appreciation of the cost of motherhood is expressed in the tenderness of His touch. These mothers have gone down into the valley of the shadow of death, that these sweet, innocent children might know life through their suffering. To them their children are more precious than gold, yea, than much fine gold; for they came into this world through the gateways of their homes.

To keep them well and strong, to help them to grow to clean, fine manhood and womanhood, is their daily task. As we look into the faces of these lovely, devoted Danish mothers, they represent not alone one race, but that quality of love and devotion which the word "mother" in every language implies. No sacrifice is too great for them to make where their children are involved. Their selfless, undying love is more like the love of God than any other love that humanity knows.

Their names may not be blazoned among the great preachers and professional leaders of the day, but they will teach their children to love God with a pure heart, and to serve Christ in filial devotion, and through this love, revealed not alone in words, but also in example, their children will share in building in this world God's Kingdom of Love.

"HALLELUJAH!"

By

J. C. Gotsch

(Interpretation)

THE nationality of the artist who painted this marvelously beautiful picture of the children singing their praises to the Christ they adore, is not definitely known. He was born in 1854; and the original of this, one of his greatest paintings, hangs in the Tate Art gallery in London, England.

The title of the picture is simply "Hallelujah," but one hardly needs a title to know that these children are singing a song of praise about Jesus, their Saviour, the words of which are very familiar to them. For while they hold in their hands scrolls on which are printed in tall letters the words of this chorus of praise, in one or two instances only has the artist pictured them as even looking at the scroll.

Instead, each child in her own girlish way is expressing through bodily posture, eyes, and hands the surge of joy which she is experiencing as she sings her "Hallelujah" to the King of Kings.

As we study this picture it seems as though each of these girls has, in meditation, been caught up into the glory of the presence of the Christ of Galilee, whose praises they have been so joyfully singing. It is evident that one or two have already become lost in meditative adoration as with hands upraised in prayer, they cease for a moment to sing words that they may commune in spirit with this Christ, who is "Lord of all" in their young hearts.

One or two, with downcast eyes, seem to be recalling in repentance some childish wrong they have done, the memory of which unkind act they would, if it were possible, purge forever from their hearts and lives.

The two in the front row at the right have clasped their hands in childish affection and comradeship as together they raise their voices in praise to this Friend of Children who, on earth, went about doing good.

The eyes of the girls in this painting are beautiful and natural to a remarkable degree. Note the second girl from the left end on the front row. She, too, is lost in meditative adoration on what it will be like to see and know Jesus face to face.

Some unknown art critic has said that for beauty of form, of face, of hair, hands, and eyes, this picture is worthy to live forever as a well-nigh perfect expression of the sincere and artless devotion of the children of every nation, race, and clime, singing their "Hallelujah" praises to the King of Kings, whom their young hearts adore with all the purity of love and devotion which children know.

No two expressions are alike. Each of them in her own sweet girlish way is

"HALLELUJAH!"—GOTSCH

Photo by courtesy Missionary Education Movement, New York City

THE HOPE OF THE WORLD—*COPPING*

both thinking and feeling the message which the singing of this great "Hallelujah Chorus" has inspired.

✠

THE HOPE OF THE WORLD

By

Harold Copping

(Interpretation)

WE ARE indebted to Harold Copping, a contemporary English artist, for this remarkably beautiful painting of the children of the races of earth gathered in the lap or about the knees of Jesus, the Children's Friend.

No more satisfying picture of Christ and the children has ever been portrayed than this one; from the nude black body of the little Negro lad, who watches the Master so intently from his position on the ground at His feet, to the demure and worshipful expression of the dainty little Indian lass, sitting so gracefully on the Master's knee, this picture is perfectly and entrancingly satisfying.

But, you say, there are no Japanese children in the painting? No, the artist is not trying to paint a picture representing the children of all the countries of the world; but rather a group of children, each one of which typifies one of the major races of the world—yellow, red, black, brown, and white. And the more you study the picture the more perfect and satisfying does its symbolic grouping become. For by it the artist is trying to tell us that Jesus is the *hope of the world* only in proportion as He can get Himself known to and enthroned in the heart and life of all the children of all the races of men.

The face of Jesus is a never-to-be-forgotten study, as He looks deep into the eyes of the little Chinese lad at His knee, who, with true Oriental, mystical wisdom may have asked the Master why His disciples have been so long in bringing the story of His life and love to China, with her many, many gods.

I recall, years ago, having the national Negro Superintendent of Religious Education for the Disciples of Christ, ask me about this picture. It hung in the conference room in which I was teaching from day to day in our first Negro Training School, held in connection with the annual International Convention of our Negro churches at Nashville, Tennessee. For a long time Patrick Henry Moss stood there studying this picture, and then he said: "Why is it, Miss Maus, that the only one of these children of the world who is not touching Jesus is the little black lad in the foreground?"

I thought for a long time, for up to that moment such a problem had not presented itself to my mind; and then I replied, honestly: "I do not know, Patrick Henry, perhaps because your race is one of the most backward of all the races of the children of men. But are you not glad that, at last, an artist has appeared with a sufficiently world-wide consciousness of what the 'Go ye' of the Master meant to include even the most backward child-race in 'The Hope of the World'?" For note that, next to Jesus, this little Negro lad occupies the most prominent place in the picture. You can't overlook him, or miss seeing the beauty and purity of his nude form, or his absorbing interest in what the Master of Men is saying in response to this hard-to-answer question that the Chinese lad has asked.

Note the delicate and sturdy racial beauty of each little child as he looks intently into the Master's face, waiting to understand. If you had the power so to do, you would not change a face, a form, a race, an attitude. The great arms of the Master as He encircles them all, His ample lap and strong and sturdy sandaled feet enhance the all-inclusiveness that is the message of this truly great painting, "The Hope of the World."

These children of the various races do not resent one another. There never is any racial prejudice in the heart of childhood until and unless it has been consciously or unconsciously sown there by un-Christian, pagan adults.

The Master of Men sits by the waysides of life, now, as He did centuries ago in Galilee, saying to us: "Suffer the children of all the races of the world to come unto me, and forbid them not"; for in them is the "hope of the world."

✠

CHRIST BLESSING THE CHILDREN

By

Rembrandt

ONE of the most human stories about Jesus is in Luke 18:15-17, which tells about Jesus and the children. Jesus had been preaching and teaching in parables. It had probably been a long and arduous day for him. His disciples realized that He was weary. When some of the mothers in the crowd pressed forward with their children for Jesus' blessing, the disciples rebuked the mothers.

Jesus' compassion extended especially to women and children; thus He could say, "Let the children come to me, and do not hinder them; for to such belongs the kingdom of God. Truly, I say to you, whoever does not receive the kingdom of God like a child shall not enter it" (RSV).

This tender and compassionate incident is appealingly pictured in "Christ Blessing the Children" by Rembrandt, or School of Rembrandt, as some critics insist. Whether the painting came entirely from Rembrandt's brush does not matter, for the message is clear to us. [As this revised edition is being plated word comes from the National Gallery, London, that this painting has recently been attributed to Nicolas Maes, one of Rembrandt's leading pupils.—The Publisher]

It is a Dutch setting—these are Dutch folk, villagers who have brought their

CHRIST BLESSING THE CHILDREN—*REMBRANDT*

children with them to hear and see Jesus. It was the custom, in the seventeenth century, Rembrandt's time, to put Biblical scenes in familiar settings. Few if any people had traveled to Palestine to learn what kind of clothing was worn there. Being deeply religious folk, the Dutch believed that the familiar Bible teachings applied to them as much as to anyone else. Thus their artists painted pictures as though the incident had occurred in their own period. Hence the caps, kerchiefs, and other details are plainly Dutch.

One immediately senses the deep interest and eagerness of the people. By their expressions and gestures they reach out to Jesus. The women are typical of mothers the world over, wanting the best for their children. One of them has asked her husband to lift the child high up over the heads of the crowd so that he may see and so that Jesus may bless him. Another extends the baby in her arms. One mother has pushed her little one to within reach of Jesus, and there she stands, timid, peering anxiously at her mother, and not quite knowing what all this means. The child has an orange or ball in her left hand and a finger of her right hand is in her mouth. Her reaction is typical of a child two years old, indicating that the artist must have loved and understood children.

The face and figure of Jesus is very beautiful and spiritual. Radiance, deep love, and compassion are all evident. Even the hands are tender as they gently reach to hold and bless the child. Rembrandt has pictured Jesus as one who loves children with His whole heart.

Rembrandt lived from 1606 to 1669. He is an example of a truly great artist who spent much of his life painting scenes from the Bible. He was so fascinated by the character of the Jewish face that he lived the declining years of his life in the Ghetto of Amsterdam.

Rembrandt was not one who cared for popular acclaim. He painted because he felt impelled to and because he believed in his art. Love, human relationships, and understanding of the Bible are all embodied in his Biblical paintings, as they are in this example, "Jesus Blessing the Children."

The common people understood and loved Rembrandt's art. He preferred to include them as models rather than those who were noble or wealthy.

To the fine art of painting, Rembrandt's chief contribution was that of *chiaroscuro:* the effects of light, particularly of light as contrasted with darkness. Rembrandt had a "magic touch" with his brush, a touch which illuminated the most important portions of his scene with warm, mellow, radiant light. It is a light which seems to come from within an object or person, rather than from without as a floodlight does. This marvelous *chiaroscuro* technique illumines the faces in "Jesus Blessing the Children," particularly the face of Jesus, and gives the entire composition an unmistakable spiritual tone.

Rembrandt used no halos; no studied effects. His was a simple, human, appealing, and spiritual art.

CARITAS

By

Abbott Handerson Thayer

(Interpretation)

ABBOTT HANDERSON THAYER, one of America's great portrait painters, was born in Boston, Massachusetts, August 12, 1849, and died May 29, 1921. He spent his boyhood in New Hampshire, where an open air life was favorable to the development of a tendency toward the scientific exactitude inherited from his father.

As a young artist, trained at the Academy of Design, his first ambitions were those of an animal painter. He went to Paris in 1875 and entered the atelier of Gérôme where he gave his time largely to painting French landscapes and flowers, in which fields he attained unusual skill.

The revelation of the painter's genius, however, came some years later when he began to pour into his work not only artlessness and spontaneity, but also the deeper qualities of his inmost soul. He painted portraits superbly, especially those of women of many kinds and types. His portrayals were more than just pictures of beautiful women; they were portrayals of great truths—love, purity, devotion, and service shining through women's faces.

So spiritually beautiful are his women that one is tempted to call them madonnas, yet nothing could be further from the truth. His "Caritas" in the Boston Museum of Fine Arts is a splendid illustration of his ability to portray spiritual qualities in human form. A kindred composition in the Freer Gallery at Washington, D.C. is called "The Virgin." In the Gellatly collection in New York is another entitled the "Virgin Enthroned," which is characterized by the same spiritual qualities of virtue and truth in the form of beauty.

Many, for which his daughter posed, suggest the religious paintings of the early Florentine masters. This deep religious feeling comes out strongly in "Caritas" which, freely translated, means *charity*. It symbolizes the championship of the oppressed as well as the protecting care of the weak. This painting brings to mind these lines by Elizabeth Barrett Browning:

> Do you hear the children weeping, O my brothers,
>   Ere the sorrows come with years?
> They are leaning their young heads against their mothers,
>   And that cannot stop their tears.
>
> But the young, young children, O my brothers,
>   They are weeping bitterly;
> They are weeping in the playtime of the others,
>   In a country of the free.

CARITAS—*THAYER*

This instinctive tendency of true motherhood and womanhood to protect the weak is beautifully expressed in this titian-haired "Caritas" who stands with downcast eyes and arms outstretched in protection of those who are being denied childhood's birthright to love, care, light, laughter, sunshine and adequate food, play and rest.

The chief message which the pictures of this great American painter of the nineteenth century suggests is the spiritual quality of love and beauty lavishly bestowed in service to others. This same ideal is beautifully embodied in the life of the Madonna—mother of the Christ of Galilee.

✠

JESUS AND THE DOCTORS

By

Edouard von Gebhardt

(Interpretation)

EDOUARD VON GEBHARDT (1838-1925), the German artist who gave us this painting, once said: "My whole art groups itself around the life of Jesus." Out of his total of eighty-five finished pictures, sixty-four are drawn from this theme. In his sixty-two years of unremitting toil he displayed an ability both as an artist and seer that quite overshadowed his contemporaries in religious painting.

We must always remember Gebhardt's basic practice of translating scripture into a German setting. The landscapes, architecture, costumes and types are German, or peasant races akin to German, and the epoch so represented is the age of Martin Luther. That was the age when Germany was more genuinely religious than it ever was before or has been since. Gebhardt said: "We read the Bible in Luther's language; why not portray Biblical events in the attire of Luther's time."

Most painters misinterpret scripture inexcusably. They make the boy Jesus a judge, or a preacher, or a supernatural revelation, or a conceited youth. According to Luke, Jesus was not Deity teaching; he was a boy, hearing the doctors and asking them questions as any bright adolescent would do. We must credit Gebhardt with having read his Bible.

This scene presents the sacristy or chapter-house of a medieval country church. Everything is substantial to match the dignity and apparent wealth of the learned ones. . . . Study each face carefully for they are wonderfully graphic. Beginning on the right, number one is a kindly old man who listens courteously. Number two, evidently the leader in the discussion, stops reading, takes off his glasses and beneath his shading hand looks at the boy with searching eyes as if he could hardly credit such spiritual understanding in a mere youth. Number five has a keen face and is so wholly absorbed in what the boy is saying that he can hardly keep his seat. The other men are deeply impressed,

JESUS AND THE DOCTORS—*VON GEBHARDT*

all but the two at the extreme left. The stout old man evidently hasn't heard very well and the younger man is repeating to him what has been said. Every man in the room is strongly individualized and worthy of the position he occupies.

In the figure of Jesus, Gebhardt has carried realism to the limit. The boy is unmistakably a Jew. We know he was historically a Jew, but for an artist to give Christ Semitic features is dangerous. Adolf Menzel tried it in 1857, using Polish Jews for types; Zimmermann did it in his version of the story in 1879, and produced a most appealing picture. Max Liebermann tried it in the same year. But most of these attempts were not well received by the religious world because they cut too roughly across traditional idealization, and practically no artist has tried it since. Christ as a nineteenth-century Jew is sure to arouse a sense of incongruity. It is impossible to find our spiritual ideal in a racial type that is so easily caricatured. Nevertheless in this picture Gebhardt has largely escaped the danger, partly because he has put into the slight figure such an intense sincerity and spirituality. Somehow as you look at this boy you feel in him all the concentrated moral earnestness of the Jewish race, their keenness of intellect, their readiness of speech. This lad cannot sit on his chair. In his eagerness to know he edges forward till his toes touch the floor, and he holds out a questioning finger to his teacher as if he demanded that all wisdom be compressed into the next answer. Here is a boy who cannot be fooled or bluffed. His soul is athirst for God, and he knows what he wants to know.

One sees where the boy gets his earnestness, as well as his features, when one looks at his mother. She bursts unceremoniously into the room. When she finds her humble son conversing with the great ones who are to her as gods, she throws up her hands and exclaims in good round German, "Gott in Himmel!"

Gebhardt, in this picture, has captured the essence of the situation; Jesus at twelve years was a spiritual genius searching in his boyish way for reality. He is going to find it in spite of Doctors of Divinity.[1]

✠

THE CHILD'S APPEAL

I am the Child.
All the world waits for my coming.
All the earth watches with interest to see what I shall become.
Civilization hangs in the balance,
For what I am, the world of tomorrow will be.

[1] Abridged from *Christ and His Gospel in Recent Art* (pp. 26-28) by Albert Edward Bailey. Copyright 1935-48 by Charles Scribner's Sons, 597 Fifth Avenue, New York 17, N.Y. Reprinted by permission of the publishers.

I am the Child.
I have come into your world, about which I know nothing.
Why I came I know not;
How I came I know not.
I am curious; I am interested.

I am the Child.
You hold in your hand my destiny.
You determine, largely, whether I shall succeed or fail.
Give me, I pray you, those things that make for happiness.
Train me, I beg you, that I may be a blessing to the world.

—Mamie Gene Cole

NAZARETH DAYS

What days of loveliness He had—
Jesus, the little lad!
His hours, on their dovelike wings,
What singing things!
He saw dawn come in beauty, and a breath
Of color and song, to ancient Nazareth,
And rested, when the evening shadows fell,
By Mary's well,
Dropping one day, a crown of lilies, and again,
Of fragile cyclamen.

He found pomegranates, that would bleed
Rose-jewel seed,
And sweet, ripe almonds, smooth and cool,
As pebbles shining in a pool.
Beauty He knew in field and hilltop place,
And in His mother's face.

Quaint lore He had, of all the birds that fly,
And for His books were earth and air and sky;
A fountain's rim where little ripples start,—
And Mary's heart.

—Mary Brent Whiteside

A CHILD'S CHRISTMAS SONG

Lord, I am just a little boy
    Born one day like You,
And I've got a mother dear
    And a birthday, too.
But my birthday comes in spring,
    When the days are long,

And the robin in the tree
  Wakens me with song.
Since the birds are all away,
  Lord, when You are born,
Let Your angels waken me
  On Your birthday morn.

Lord, I'm just a little boy,
  Hidden in the night:
Let Your angels spy me out
  Long before it's light.
I would be the first to wake
  And the first to raise
In this quiet home of ours
  Songs of love and praise.
You shall hear me first, dear Lord,
  Blow my Christmas horn;
Let Your angels waken me
  On Your birthday morn.

—T. A. Daly

CHILDHOOD

To be Himself a star most bright
To bring the wise men to His sight,
To be Himself a voice most sweet
To call the shepherds to His feet,
To be a child—it was His will
That folk like us might find Him still.

—John Erskine

BOYHOOD

And, oh, was Jesus once a little boy, a little boy like me?
I wonder if His mother told Him tales of sailors and the sea,
And let Him go while He was still a child to look at Galilee?

And did He have a little boat like mine, as real as boats can be,
And let it sail and float upon the waves and play that it was free;
And did He choose the roundest, smoothest stones and skip them, just like me?

And did He love to look across the blue to places you can't see,
And did His mother hug Him close, like mine, and call Him, Honey Bee;
And on His birthday did they make Him gifts and light a Christmas tree?

I hope when Jesus was a little boy that He was just like me.[2]

—Louise Ayres Garnett

[2] Set to music by the author, and published by Oliver Ditson Company, Boston, Mass. Used by permission of the author.

IN BED

When evening comes
  And I'm in bed
    And mother sits and sings
And holds my hand
  And strokes my head,
    I think of all the things
That I have heard—
Can they be true?
  That children just like me
Are cold and lost and hungry, too,
  In lands across the sea.

They say they wander in their fright
  All numb with cold and dread;
And when I think of them at night
  I want to hide my head
Upon my mother's gentle arm
  That holds me close and still,
And seems to promise that no harm
  Can ever come, or ill.

And then I hear my mother's voice
  So tender in a prayer,
"Dear God, may all the girls and boys
  Who wander over there
Be brought for kindly sheltering
  To those who crave to give,
And they who mourn shall learn to sing
  And they who die shall live."

And when the prayer is done I sleep
  So still without a sound,
And dream no little child shall weep
  And all the lost are found!
                —Corinne Roosevelt Robinson

PERHAPS

Dear God, I wonder, when You climbed
  The hill of Calvary—
Where were the children that You used
  To take upon Your knee?
Where were they? In among the crowd?
  And did they, too, not care

What happened to You, God, dear God,
　　But only came to stare?
Where were the children that You loved?
　　They do not seem to be
Around as You begin to climb
　　The hill of Calvary!

O God, I wish that I had been
　　A child that day! I might
Have done some little things for You
　　To make the cross more light!
I might have given You a glass
　　Of water on the way—
"I love You," whispered, as You passed,
　　"I love You so today!"
I might have done this—and yet—O!
　　Perhaps I would have hid
Among the people and done just
　　What other children did.

　　　　　　　　　　　　—*Mary Dixon Thayer*

"Herein is our love made perfect."

THE TEACHER

Lord, who am I to teach the way
　　To little children day by day,
　　So prone myself to go astray?

I teach them knowledge, but I know
　　How faint the flicker and how low
　　The candles of my knowledge glow.

I teach them power to will and do,
　　But only now to learn anew
　　My own great weakness through and through.

I teach them love for all mankind
　　And all God's creatures, but I find
　　My love comes lagging far behind.

Lord, if their guide I still must be,
　　Oh, let the little children see
　　The teacher leaning hard on Thee.

　　　　　　　　　　　　—*Leslie Pinckney Hill*

PATTY—POEM

She never puts her toys away;
Just leaves them scattered where they lay—
I try to scold her, and I say
"You make me mad!"

But when to bed she has to chase,
The toys she left about the place
Remind me of her shining face,
And make me glad.

When she grows up and gathers poise
I'll miss her harum-scarum noise,
And look in vain for scattered toys—
And I'll be sad.[3]

—*Nick Kenny*

TWO PRAYERS

Last night my little boy confessed to me
Some childish wrong;
And kneeling at my knee,
He prayed with tears,—
"Dear God, make me a man
Like Daddy—wise and strong;
I know You can."

Then while he slept
I knelt beside his bed,
Confessed my sins,
And prayed with low-bowed head.
"O God, make me a child
Like my child here—
Pure, guileless,
Trusting Thee with faith sincere."[4]

—*Andrew Gillies*

[3] From *Poems That Touch the Heart* by A. L. Alexander. Copyright, 1941, by Doubleday & Company, Inc., Garden City, N. Y. Reprinted by permission of the publishers.
[4] *Ibid.*, pp. 35-36. Reprinted by permission of the publishers.

GRACE FOR THE NOONDAY MEAL

Dear Lord, we bow our heads to pray
At noontime of this happy day.
Thus far Thy love has kept us true
Half of this wondrous daytime through.

We thank Thee for the food we eat
And for our happy homes so sweet;
For all of those who love us so,
For all adventuring ways we go.

For cloud and sun and wind and showers,
For grass and trees and birds and flowers;
For clothes to wear and tasks to do
This whole glad happy daytime through.

Be with us all this afternoon,
And may we ever keep in tune
With all Thy love and all Thy ways,
Through all these happy, happy days.[5]
                                        Amen.

—William L. Stidger

GRACE BEFORE THE EVENING MEAL

Father, we thank Thee for this day
For food, for fun, for life, for play;
And as the evening shadows fall,
We bring to Thee, dear Lord, our all;
And as we pray, we ask Thy grace
Upon this happy, happy place.[5]
                                  Amen.

—William L. Stidger

[5] From *I Saw God Wash the World* by William L. Stidger. Copyright, 1934, by the author. Published by the Rodeheaver Hall-Mack Company, Winona Lake, Ind. Reprinted by permission of the author.

A TRIBUTE TO CHILDHOOD

By

George W. Rideout

WHEN God made the child He began early in the morning. He watched the golden hues of the rising day chasing away the darkness, and He chose the azure of the opening heavens for the color of childhood's eyes, the crimson of the clouds to paint its cheeks, and the gold of the morning for its flowing tresses. He listened to the song of the birds as they sang and warbled and whispered, and strung childhood's harp with notes now soft and low—now sweet and strong.

He saw little lambs among the flock romp and play and skip, and He put play into childhood's heart. He saw the silvery brook and listened to its music and He made the laughter of the child like the ripple of the brook. He saw angels of light as upon the wings of love they hastened to holy duty, and He formed the child's heart in purity and love.

And having made the child, He sent it out to bring joy into the home, laughter on the green and gladness everywhere. He sent it into the home and said to the parents, "Nourish and bring up this child for Me." He sent it to the church and said, "Teach it My love and My laws." He sent it to the state and said, "Deal tenderly with it and it will bless and not curse you." He sent it to the nation and said, "Be good to the child. It is thy greatest asset and thy hope."

✛

THE CHILDREN'S MAGIC CHRISTMAS TREE

ONCE, in the long ago, there was a magic Christmas tree exactly in the center of the world. It was exquisitely decorated with tinsel, gifts, and ornaments, and when all the candles were lighted the children came running to see this beautiful Christmas tree.

In those far-away days the known world was small, and all the children could come quite easily, except that some little girls had bound feet and stumbled; and other tiny married ones were shut up in dark houses. Others bore heavy burdens, and still others worked all day in mines and mills. Nevertheless, crowds of happy, care-free children were there.

Then the One who gave the tree, looking about as if searching for some one He missed, said, "Where are the others?" The children who had come were quiet, until one of the littlest said, "Why, they couldn't come. Too bad! Poor little things, they will miss seeing this beautiful tree."

Then another replied, "They wouldn't care much about a Christmas tree"; and one of the boys called out, "We need all these presents for ourselves; there aren't enough even now to go round."

"That's right," said a selfish little girl. "They are horrid little children, not one bit clean, nice, and well dressed. We do not want them. This tree is ours."

Then the One who gave the tree said, "But I wanted all the children, every blessed little one, high and low, rich and poor, clean and soiled."

Now when the children saw how disappointed He was, they ran fast and everyone brought some one else who couldn't come alone. The boys went down into mines and mills and called to the others; and the little girls hurried away to find tired little ones doing up Christmas packages in stores and delivering them at homes. Some found those in China with bound feet, and others the tiny ones shut up in dark rooms in India; and together they all came running to see the magic Christmas tree.

Then the magic Christmas tree grew bigger and brighter, its candles sparkled like stars, and there were presents for everyone. And all the children of the world stood under its branches and sang carols to the King of Kings. The shining angel on the top of the tree sang, too, but the One who gave the tree was happiest of all, for He knew that the *real Christmas could only come* when all the children of the world shared in its happiness and rejoicing.—*Author Unknown.*

✠

THE SPIRIT OF CHRISTMAS

By

Evelyn Norton

IT WAS only an old log cabin in the midst of a lonely cotton-field. Only an old log cabin with a thin volume of smoke issuing from the remnant of its chimney, and one lone pine tree near the door through which the wind whistled cheerlessly. And yet the *spirit* of *Christmas* was there.

Inside, an old Negro mammy sat huddled before a poor little fire. Side by side on her lap leaned two little woolly heads. Four much-worn shoes were stretched toward the fire as the owners sat on the rough boards of the floor, and listened with their black eyes full of wonder at the story of the Christ Child.

"Yas sir, He was bawn in a stable, jes' a plain, ole cow-stable."

"Oh no, granny, not Marse Jesus! Shooly you'se mistookin'."

"No, I ain't mistookin'. Ain't I been knowin' 'bout Marse Jesus since befo' yo' was bawn? Now don't yo' go fer to interrupt yo' ole granny."

"No'm, we ain't. Go on, granny, tell some mo'."

"Well, sir, 'way back befo' de war; when dere wasn't no Santa Claus, no Christmas, no nuffin' dere was a little Baby bawn one night in a stable in

Bethlehem of Judæa. And jes' de ve'y minute He was bawn, de black clouds of darkness all passed away; an' de light shined and de angels from Heaven come down and sung tunes—Marse Gabriel and Marse Peter an' all de rest of 'em. And dat little Baby He jus' lay dere in His mother's arms and He smile, like little babies does when de mammies says dey's seein' angels. An' dat night ev'rybody loved ev'rybody else. An' dere warn't no mo' lyin' an' stealin' an' swearin' er badness in de whole wide world—an' de world's been bettah ev'ry since."

Here granny came to a full pause, for she had exhausted all her little store of knowledge of the Christ Child.

"Go on, granny, tell some mo'; please do?"

"No, no honeys. Not ternight. Marse Santa Claus'll be comin' along hyeah putty soon, an' den what yo'all gwine to do?"

Soon the two little pickaninnies were tucked in bed snug and warm; and as granny stood above them, looking down on their little kinky heads and their shining black faces, she whispered: "God bless deir little *white hearts* in deir little *black bodies,* an' may de dere Marse Jesus alwuz tooken keer of His little black lambs."

Then there was silence in that old log cabin in the midst of the lonely cotton-field. The dying firelight cast strange flickering shadows on the rough walls and floors and upon the faces of those three peaceful slumberers. Outside, a low, wintry moon hung in the sky, and the wind whistled softly through that old pine tree. But who shall say that the *spirit* of *Christmas* was not there?

✠

IF HE HAD NOT COME

By

Nan F. Weeks

IT WAS Christmas Eve, and after Bobby had carefully hung his stocking by the fireplace he went off to bed. Usually Bobby did not like to go to bed early, but tonight he was eager to get to sleep so as to be sure to wake up early to see his gifts.

For their daily Bible lesson that day Bobby and his father had read Jesus' own words to his friends found in John 15:22. Five words had stayed in Bobby's mind, and he kept saying them over and over again until he fell asleep. They were the words, "If I had not come."

It seemed as if he had not been asleep any time when a cross, harsh voice said: "Get up, get up, I tell you. It's time to get up."

Thinking about the skates he wanted and the flashlight and the motor and the books for which he'd been wishing, Bobby got up and hurried into his clothing and went downstairs. But all was still. No one was there to greet him; no stocking hung beside the fireplace; no wreaths were in the window, no splendid tree was there.

Hurrying to the door, Bobby looked down the street. The factory was open and he could hear the rumble of the machinery. He grabbed his cap and sweater and raced down the street to the factory door, and there stood a grim-looking foreman.

"What's the factory running for on Christmas?" asked Bobby.

"Christmas?" asked the man. "What do you mean? I never heard that word. This is one of our busy days, so you clear out of here."

Filled with wonder, Bobby hurried on down the street toward the stores, and to his amazement he found them all open. The grocer, the dry-goods man, the baker, each one was busy and cross, and each said in reply to his question, "Christmas? What's Christmas?"

When Bobby tried to explain, "It's Jesus' birthday," and that the first part of the word "Christmas" means "Jesus," he was gruffly ordered to move along, as this was a very busy day.

Going round the corner, he thought: "I'll go to church, our own church, for there's to be a Christmas service there." All at once Bobby stopped short before a big vacant field, and he mumbled to himself: "I guess I'm lost. I was certain our church was here. I know it was." Then he noticed a signboard in the center of the big vacant lot, and on going nearer to it he read the words, "If I Had Not Come."

Suddenly the meaning of it all dawned on the puzzled boy, and he said, "Oh, I know, 'If I Had Not Come'—that's why there's no Christmas day nor any church."

He was wandering along in a gloomy way, when he thought of the box of toys and games his class had sent to the Orphans' Home, and he said, half aloud, "I guess I'll go up to the Home and see the children get their presents." But when Bobby reached the place, instead of seeing the name of the Home over the gateway, he read these same five words, "If I Had Not Come," and beyond the archway there was no fine building.

Seeing an old man, feeble and ill, by the roadside, Bobby said: "I guess you're sick, mister. I'll run to the hospital and tell them to send an ambulance for you." But when he reached the grounds no splendid building was to be seen, nothing but signs and posters bearing the words, "If I Had Not Come."

As Bobby hurried back to the corner where the Rescue Mission had been he said, "I'm sure they'll take the poor old man in there, anyway." But men with angry faces were gambling and swearing and over the door Bobby saw, instead of the name of the mission, the same words, "If I Had Not Come."

Thinking still about the poor old man, Bobby hurried home to ask his father and mother to help him. On his way across the living-room he waited to look up in a Bible these words, "If I Had Not Come." Turning past the pages of the Old Testament, he found that there was no new part. After Malachi all the pages were blank, and as he held them up to the light on each one he could see a faint outline of the words, "If I Had Not Come."

With a sigh Bobby said, "Oh, what a terrible world this is—no Christmas, no churches, no homes for little orphan children, no hospitals, no rescue missions, no almshouses, nothing but jails and gambling-houses and police patrols and sickness and wrong and——"

Just then there came the sound of bells. The chimes were playing. Bobby listened, and sure enough it was his favorite hymn "Joy to the world, the Lord is come," and then he heard his mother's cheery voice saying, "Merry Christmas, Bobby!"

With a joyous bound Bobby was out of bed, and kneeling down, he said, "O Lord Jesus, I thank You that You did come, and I'll show You how thankful I am by always trying to be the kind of boy You want me to be."[6]

✠

THE ANGEL WHO REFUSED TO SING

(A Christmas Story)

By

J. Chapman Bradley

"And suddenly there were with the angel a multitude of the heavenly host, praising God and singing. . . ."

THIS is the story of the little angel who refused to sing on the night when Christ was born. It began in heaven where the angels of the heavenly choir were rehearsing for the earth's first Christmas carol service. They had practiced for eons, for as you know there is no night there, and a thousand years are as but a day. The heavenly concert had been polished to the last minutia of perfection, and was about ready to be released into time so that mortal ears could hear its beauteous haunting refrain all through the ages of man. All was in a state of preparation in heaven; earth was about to receive her saviour-king. All was ready—save one thing—

There was in the heavenly chorus a tiny angel with the sweetest voice ever heard throughout the spheres. It was high as the mountain air, yet soft as the summer dew upon the flowers. It was strong as a mother's love and as true as a homing pigeon. The fluted melody of his song stilled the melody of the birds, causing them to wonder and delay their flight that they might hear more. The blossoms all beamed when this little angel sang, the moon lifted her haughty head to hear, and the stars left their courses to cluster 'round his pathway.

But the tiniest angel in the heavenly choir was the problem child of heaven. He had barely missed being an imp, but his enchanting voice and his engaging personality caused the saints who made up the committee on examinations to lift their eyebrows and admit him, for he answered every question with a song.

[6] In Keystone Course IV, Part I. Copyright, the American Baptist Publication Society. Used by permission.

His love of mischief, however, had thrown heaven into an uproar upon more than one occasion, and his frankness and independence of thought had been a source of frequent embarrassment to the saints. He was a cosmopolitan angel as may be inferred from his name: Mulforaj (Mulforage), O'Brien, Antonio, Chiang, Koussowitsky, McTavish, Stackpole, Goldberg, Smith.

Now being a cosmopolitan angel, Mulforage Smith had a mind of his own. While the saints in glory were busy praising God around the great white throne, he was frequently to be found stretched out under the tumtum trees lost in pensive thought. While the four and twenty elders were busy burnishing their gleaming crowns, Mulforage Smith was likely to be found engaged in earnest conversation with Gabriel, the choir-master, and the Father's chief messenger. When the rest of the heavenly family agreed to accept a certain decision or when personally asked to do something, the tiniest angel in heaven invariably asked "why?" (Gabriel patiently explained that this was because his name had McTavish in it!) And there were certain saints in the Ladies Circle of Light who had intimated that they had heard it said that Mulforage was a secret admirer of the dread Lucifer, whom the Father had dismissed from heaven many light years before! It must be admitted that Mulforage had been known to appear at one concert of the heavenly choir with a black Saturnic circle around his ethereal eye. But this story that he was a "fellow-traveller" of Lucifer seemed utterly without foundation, because while Mulforage Smith was a mischievous angel, a questioning angel, an independent angel, there was no trace of wickedness in him.

I

The last rehearsal of the heavenly chorus was about over. Gabriel tapped upon his trumpet for order. He was about to call for a repetition of the great Amen, when Mulforage Smith, who had been behaving like a perfect lamb for centuries, suddenly and calmly announced,

"I am sorry, Master Gabriel, but I cannot do it."

"Cannot do what? Sing the Amen? Nonsense!"

"No, Master Gabriel. I simply cannot sing at all in the concert tomorrow night. I positively refuse to sing!"

Gabriel put down his trumpet and stared in stupefaction. A quick gasp went up from all over the alabaster rehearsal room, followed by excited buzzing. Finally Gabriel spoke, as though he were not sure his ethereal ears had heard correctly.

"You . . . refuse . . . to sing? But why? Don't you feel well?" (Gabriel should have known better than to ask this question, because there is no pain nor suffering in heaven. Yet he couldn't think of anything else and said the first thing that came into his mind.)

"Of course not, Master Gabriel. The trouble is I have been doing a great deal of thinking about this concert, and I have conscientious objections to participating in it."

"*Conscientious objections!* Well, of all your peculiar notions this is the strangest yet. Come now, is this another of your jokes? By this time heaven has had ample cause to be aware that your name is Mulforage O'BRIEN Smith; but this is a poor time for your fine Irish wit to display itself. Explain yourself, sir."

"No, Master Gabriel, I am not joking. I confess I have never been more serious. I am objecting to the sentiment of the song we are supposed to sing tomorrow night. 'Peace on earth, good will toward men,' indeed! The trouble with a lot of you saints is you do not keep up with things. Look down there at that place called earth! Look at it! Look what a mess it's in! 'Peace on earth' —forsooth. Have any of you been over to Celestial Square recently to read the planetary bulletins as recorded by the moving finger? I thought not. Through bloody fighting Egypt and Spain have been annexed to the Roman Empire; the bearded Drusus and his brutal brother, Tiberius, have conquered all the wild peoples of the Rhine and the Elbe—which will afterwards come to be known as Germany and produce one of the most war-like races in history. Look down there at your precious Jerusalem. Before three quarters of this very century has passed, Titus will come along, tear that city apart and destroy its temple. Look at the Middle East—the Kenva Dynasty is fighting for its life against the Andhra Dynasty which will eventually overthrow it. And what's happening in the Far East? That little country of Japan has just passed an edict stressing the importance of ship-building owing to the difficulty of land transport. The beginning of an empire, and you know what that means. 'Peace'? All you angels are singing 'peace, peace' when there is no peace. There never was, and there never will be!"

"Have you quite finished with your historical dissertation, Master Smith? I am sure this is all very interesting, but I'm afraid it is a little late to think of these matters. Even now Mary and Joseph are winding up the hills toward Bethlehem."

Gabriel was a very patient angel, but this time he was annoyed. Part of his annoyance was because he had no very clear explanation to the matter under discussion. His lips drew firmly together.

"Either you sing, Master Smith—or we will excuse you!"

Sadly the little angel who refused to sing sighed a deep sigh. Then, because his name was also Goldberg, he raised his hands in a characteristic and expressive gesture of despair, as though to say, "What's the use of trying to explain how I feel about that song?" and unhappily he left the rehearsal room.

Gabriel soon had the chorus singing again; its melodies ringing throughout the spheres. For after all, gifted as the little angel was, the heavenly chorus was not dependent on any one voice—and the angels sang with the passion of those who love to sing, and the beauty of those who can. Mulforage, downcast heart and all, thrilled as he listened, shuffling along the path to the tumtum forest— hands in the pockets of his robe and scuffing his sandals kicking at the loose stones as he went.

The chorus sang as never before. Every angel striving to make up for the little angel's strange behavior. But heaven had witnessed its first walkout in all eternity.

II

And it came to pass, as the city of David, the little town of Bethlehem lay wrapt in deep and dreamless slumber, that "angels from the realms of glory" were winging "their flight o'er all the earth." Shepherds, in the fields abiding, were watching o'er their flocks by night—

"And, lo, the angel of the Lord came upon them, and the glory of the Lord shone round about them; and they were sore afraid."

"And Gabriel said unto them, 'Fear not: for, behold I bring you good tidings of great joy, which shall be to all people.

" 'For unto you is born this day in the city of David a Saviour, which is Christ the Lord. And this shall be a sign unto you; Ye shall find the babe wrapped in swaddling clothes, lying in a manger.'

"And suddenly there was with the angel a multitude of the heavenly host praising God and singing, 'Glory to God in the Highest, and on earth peace, good will toward men.' "

And this is the way in which

It came upon the midnight clear, that glorious song of old,
From angels bending near the earth, to touch their harps of gold;
"Peace on the earth, good-will to men, from heaven's all-gracious King."
The world in solemn stillness lay to hear the angels sing.

"Hark," cried the shepherds, no longer fearful,

Hark! the herald angels sing, "Glory to the new-born king;
Peace on earth, and mercy mild, God and sinners reconciled!"
Joyful all ye nations, rise, join the triumph of the skies;
With the angelic hosts proclaim, "Christ is born in Bethlehem!"

And the angels sang more beautifully than they had ever sung before. The wondering world turned over in its slumber and thought that it must have died—so moving was the song. And God heard the song, and was well pleased. But in heaven there was one little angel who had refused to sing. The one with the sweetest voice of them all.

III

And it came to pass that after the angels were gone away from the shepherds into heaven; and God walked in the tumtum garden in the cool of the heavenly day . . . Suddenly, Mulforage, the tiniest angel of them all, felt the presence of God—as he lay stretched out on his flowery bower, lost in pensive thought. And the glory of the Lord shone round about him—but he was not afraid. He stood up respectfully, with his curly little head bowed in the presence of the Lord of all the Universe.

And the Lord said unto him: "What doest thou here, Mulforage? The heavenly chorus sang more beautifully than ever before. Yet I missed one voice in all the rest. Thine, my child. Why art thou here?"

"My Father, I could not sing. How can I cry 'Peace, peace on earth' when there is no peace. To do so, seemed to me, but to proclaim a lie."

"Who art thou, Mulforage, to question the everlasting word of God! Stubborn little one—the song does not say that peace *is* upon the earth. The song proclaims that because of Him who is born this day, that *one* day peace *shall* be upon the earth, and that one day in the fullness of time, good will shall reign among ALL men. I, the Lord, have spoken it!"

The righteous glory of God was more dazzling than the brightness of ten million noon-day suns; and Mulforage fell upon his face before that light.

"Forgive me, my Father, I have been wrong to question Thy Law."

"Behold, thou art forgiven. Knowest thou who is born in the city of David this day? It is my Son, Mulforage; the Prince of Heaven and of Peace; my only begotten Son—in whom I am well pleased. Look now through the obscuring clouds of history. What seest thou?"

"I see a cross, my Father, and the form of one hanging upon it."

"Aye, a cross. And on that cross the Prince of Glory shall die. But only for a moment. For from the earthly bonds of death He shall rise again—with healing for the nations in his wings. He shall live eternally and shall be born again and again in the hearts of men throughout all time. A cross—the emblem of human tragedy and sacrifice, the emblem of suffering and shame—but he shall feel no shame. Lifted up he will draw all men unto him as the sun draweth the rain. Kings shall come to the brightness of his rising; till that day when every knee shall bow and every voice shall own him Lord of lords and King of kings. In that day his kingdom will be finally established in the hearts of men and war shall be no more."

And it came to pass that after the Lord had gone away from him that Mulforage decided to go to Bethlehem to worship the Christ child. He hailed a cruising star and skyrocketed to earth. Magi in the distant East saw the star and began their toilsome journey till, later, they, too, came to the place where the young child was.

Mulforage told the star-driver to shut off his meteor and wait for him, then he stole cautiously into the stable. The ox and the ass saw him and stood still. Joseph was there, but he saw him not, nor Mary. But the infant stirred upon his mother's breast and listened.

"I will sing you my sweetest song, baby Jesus. Hearken well. For 'the hopes and fears of all the years are met in thee tonight.' I bring to you the gift of the singing heart. No matter how great your discouragements, your heart shall never know recoil. For you will know men at their worst, and yet see in them their best possibilities. Guard well, baby Jesus, this gift of the singing heart. For by its power, you can transform despair into hope and turn tragedy into glory."

And while Mulforage was singing, the grass forgot to grow; the sun tarried in his course; the birds dared not twitter. For though the world heard it not, the creatures of God all heard it. And from heaven there resounded an answering shout: "Glory to God in the highest, and Glory be to His Son on earth, the Prince of Peace!"

The Babe sighed upon his mother's breast and turned to sleep. The eternal "WORD" of God had become flesh, and dwelt among men.[7]

✠

HOW STRONG AND SWEET MY FATHER'S CARE

THIS old, old hymn, the words of which are by an unknown author, is one that children in every generation love to sing in their high, clear, sweet, childish voices.

Children have a good many fears and worries about which adults know little. Perhaps that is the reason why there is something particularly attractive to little children in the sentiment expressed in the words of this hymn.

Most of these little ones have been taught by loving mothers, and faithful church-school teachers that their heavenly Father not only knows what they do, but that He cares for them and watches over them, as do their own parents.

They find joy, therefore, in expressing, through song, their confident belief that this heavenly Father, whom they cannot see, not only loves them, but that His spirit is round about them all the time in loving watch-care.

The teachings of Jesus would seem to support the fact that God watches over these little ones in a peculiar way, for does not Jesus say, speaking of the children, "their angels do always behold the face of My Father who is in heaven"? (Matthew 18:10).

This, the children's hymn, is usually sung to the tune "Eudora," composed by J. R. Murray.

> How strong and sweet my Father's care,
> That round about me, like the air,
> Is with me always, ev'rywhere,
>   He cares for me.
> O keep me ever in Thy love,
> Dear Father, watching from above;
> And let me still Thy mercy prove,
>   And care for me. Amen.

—Anonymous

[7] Adapted from a story printed in the December, 1943, *Presbyterian Tribune*, now combined with the *Presbyterian Outlook*, 1. N. 6th St., Richmond 19, Va. Used by permission of the author J. Chapman Bradley, % Hotel Pearson, 190 East Pearson St., Chicago, 11, Ill., and the publishers.

PRAISE HIM, PRAISE HIM

IT IS impossible to estimate or number the countless thousands of children who, through the years, have raised their young voices, in the words of this old, familiar hymn, "Praise Him, Praise Him," to their heavenly Father in gratitude for His love and watch-care over them.

Each verse enables the children to express their appreciation to God for all His love and kindness to them in a different way. In the first verse they sing forth His praises; in the second they express the love of their young hearts to God, the Giver of all good and perfect gifts. In the third verse they are given opportunity to express, through song, their thanks to God for His never-to-be-exhausted goodness to them; and in the fourth verse they are able to avow the desire of their young hearts to "serve Him" in grateful appreciation for all His love and care of them.

No one can visit a beginners' or primary department of the Sunday school, and there hear a group of happy, wholesome children singing this lively praise song, without rejoicing in his own heart that hymn-writers have not forgotten entirely the devotional needs of little children for vehicles through which they may pour out their heart-felt thanks to God, through songs.

> Praise Him, praise Him, all ye little children,
> God is love, He is love;
> Praise Him, praise Him, all ye little children
> God is love, He is love.
>
> Love Him, love Him, all ye little children,
> God is love, He is love;
> Love Him, love Him, all ye little children;
> God is love, He is love.
>
> Thank Him, thank Him, all ye little children,
> God is love, He is love;
> Thank Him, thank Him, all ye little children;
> God is love, He is love.
>
> Serve Him, serve Him, all ye little children,
> God is love, He is love;
> Serve Him, serve Him, all ye little children,
> God is love, He is love. Amen.

—Anonymous

TELL ME THE STORIES OF JESUS

ALL the world loves a story. Yet no single group is more quickly interested, held and educated through stories, than are the children of the church and church school.

This hymn, "Tell Me the Stories of Jesus," is one of those truly beautiful children's songs that seem to have come as a spontaneous response to the urgent demand of children everywhere—"tell me a story."

As we read the verses of this great children's hymn, we feel, indeed, that if Jesus were here in person today, boys and girls would cluster about His knees as they did in the long ago to listen to His stories.

Their youthful minds are full of questions now, as they were then, that they would like to ask of this Friend of Children. Each verse of this hymn suggests a number of things that happened during the life of the Master on this earth, about which the children would like to ask questions.

And if He could be here again in person, as He was in the long ago, we feel that He, too, would seek the children out, that His own inner life might be refreshed by their naïve interest in all the beautiful things which the Master said and did.

The words of this favorite children's hymn were written by Mr. W. H. Parker and the tune by F. A. Challinor.

Tell me the stories of Jesus
I love to hear;
Things I would ask Him to tell me
If He were here;
Scenes by the wayside,
Tales by the sea,
Stories of Jesus,
Tell them to me.

First let me hear how the children
Stood round His knee;
And I shall fancy His blessing
Resting on me;
Words full of kindness,
Deeds full of grace,
All in the love-light
Of Jesus' face.

Into the city I'd follow
The children's band,
Waving a branch of the palm tree
High in my hand;

One of His heralds,
  Yes, I would sing
Loudest hosannas!
  Jesus is King.

Tell me in accents of wonder,
  How rolled the sea,
Tossing the boat in a tempest
  On Galilee!
And how the Master,
  Ready and kind,
Chided the billows,
  And hushed the wind.[8]

—W. H. Parker

✠

A LOVE MESSAGE OR THE WHISPER SONG

AMONG the beautiful songs written particularly for little children and with the motive of giving them opportunity to share the message of God's love with other children, none is more appealing than this one, "A Love Message," the words of which are by an unknown author. It is often referred to as "The Whisper Song," since the children in singing it like to make believe they are whispering this secret of God's love to all the children of other nations and races the world around.

There is no better time than during the impressionable years of childhood for parents and teachers to build into the inner life of little children a love and appreciation of all of God's family of every race and clime; and songs like this one, help these little ones to think of all the children of the world as a part of God's earth family. It is well named "A Love Message," for such indeed it becomes, when sung in the high, clear, melodious voices of children of the Western World to other children whose faces they may never see, and whose names they may never know.

The music for this delightful children's hymn will be found on page forty-three of *Melodies for Children's Voices,* published by the Leyda Publishing Company, Wapello, Iowa.

I want to send a whisper song,
  Across the waters blue . . .
And say to all the children there,
  "Jesus loves you, loves you."

[8] Used by permission of the Sunday School Union.

If they should not quite understand,
They'll wonder if it's true; . . .
But I will keep on whisp'ring still,
"Jesus loves you, loves you."

—Anonymous

✛

HEAVEN

THE immediate temporal needs of the Negro have always been few; and especially was this true in the days of slavery. A hut, enough clothes in which to be warm, food, and a chance to worship and work with his fellow creatures constituted his greatest needs.

But these were not always adequately provided. The crude log-cabin huts in which the slaves lived were not always warm, their clothes for the most part were of the coarsest kind of materials or represented the cast-off, out-worn clothes of their Master's family. Their food was often not only inadequate, but painfully monotonous. To complain usually meant the whipping-post or other punishment equally hard to bear.

And so in the spiritual "Heaven" you will note that they sang in each verse of what they wanted but could not have until they got to heaven.

A few were allowed to peek in, now and then, when there was a party or festive occasion going on at the "big house," and when this happened they were amazed at the beauty of the glistening silks and satins, the shining slippers and other evidences of wealth and luxury.

Because of the Negro's innate passion for music they were thrilled with the sweet strains of the harp and other instruments that they heard in the "white man's house." Of course, they never could expect to own such luxuries as these on earth; and so in their childlike faith in the untold riches of their heavenly Father, they sang about the joys and blessings that would be theirs when they got to heaven.

I've got a robe, you've got a robe,
All-a God's chillun got a robe.
When I get to heaven goin' put on my robe,
Goin' to shout all over God's heav'n.

Refrain

Heaven, heaven! Everybody talkin' 'bout heaven
Ain't goin' there; Heaven, heaven,
Goin' to shout all over God's heav'n.

I've got a crown, you've got a crown,
All-a God's chillun got a crown.

When I get to heaven goin' put on my crown,
Goin' to shout all over God's heav'n.

Refrain

I've got a harp, you've got a harp,
All-a God's chillun got a harp;
When I get to heaven goin' to play on my harp,
Goin' to play all over God's heav'n.

Refrain

I've got a song, you've got a song,
All-a God's chillun got a song.
When I get to heaven goin' to sing a new song;
Goin' to sing all over God's heav'n.

Refrain

I've got a shoes, you've got a shoes,
All-a God's chillun got a shoes;
When I get to heaven goin' to put on my shoes;
Goin' to walk all over God's heav'n.

Refrain

—*A Spiritual*

CONTENTS

PART VI   SECTION V

IN YOUTH'S RESPONSE TO ALTRUISTIC SERVICE

"Remember also thy Creator in the days of thy youth."—Ecclesiastes 12:1

---✢---

IN YOUTH'S RESPONSE TO ALTRUISTIC SERVICE

"Rejoice, O young man, in thy youth, and let thy heart cheer thee in the days of thy youth, and walk in the ways of thy heart, and in the sight of thine eyes; but know thou, that for all these things God will bring thee into judgment. Therefore remove sorrow from thy heart, and put away evil from all thy flesh, for youth and the dawn of life are vanity."—Eccᴌᴇsɪᴀsᴛᴇs 11:9-10

✢

"Remember also thy Creator in the days of thy youth, before the evil days come, and the years draw nigh, when thou shalt say, I have no pleasure in them."—Eccᴌᴇsɪᴀsᴛᴇs 12:1

✢

"Let no man despise thy youth; but be thou an ensample to them that believe, in word, in manner of life, in love, in faith, in purity."—I Tɪᴍᴏᴛʜʏ 4:12

✢

THE TALENTS—*BURNAND*

THE TALENTS

By

Eugene Burnand

(Interpretation)

AMONG the many challenging and beautiful stories which the Master shared with His disciples during His lifetime on earth, none is more significant or far-reaching in its implications than this parable of the Talents (Matthew 25:14-30) on which Eugene Burnand, the great Swiss artist of the nineteenth century, has based his painting of that name.

Confronting the three men in this picture stands the master whose servants they are. He has just returned from a visit into another country. Before his departure he had delivered to each of these men a portion of his goods, giving to one five talents, to another two, and to the other one, to each according to his several abilities, Matthew tells us.

The two in the front are clear-eyed and eagerly expectant. They have not been idle or slothful about their master's trust. In their hands they hold not only the original talents that he, the master, had so graciously given them, but also the increase that through wise use they had been able to accumulate.

With benign face the master stands, one hand upon the head of his faithful, much-loved dog, the other open and ready to receive the gifts they bring as they come to give account of their stewardship. It seems that we can almost hear the master say to them: "Well done, good and faithful servants: thou hast been faithful over a few things, I will set thee over many things: enter thou into the joy of thy lord."

In the background, his empty hands folded in complacent idleness, is the unfaithful servant. He has idled away both his own time and opportunity, as well as his master's talent, in slothful, unprofitable living; and now comes to explain his *nothingness* with the trumped-up excuse that he knew his lord to be a "hard man, reaping where he did not sow, and gathering where he did not scatter," and because of this he went away in fear, digged in the ground, and hid his master's talent. He will end, we know, by trying to excuse his lazy, incompetent selfhood with the remark, "Lo, thou hast here thine own."

Some one has likened this story of the Talents to the "kingdom of abundant personality." To each and every one of us the Lord of Abundant Life has given, as did the master in this parable, one, two, or five talents or abilities, to each according to our capacity for development. Many of us, like the unfaithful servant in this parable, wrap our talents or abilities up in the napkin of "let George do it," and as a result we go through life mediocre in ability, with talents undeveloped that might have been used to the glory of God, to our own personal enrichment, and to the lifting of the whole social stratum of our times.

Others, like the two faithful servants whom the master is praising in this picture, put their abilities, no matter how meager they may be, out to usury in the marts of the busy world in which they live; and when life's harvest-time comes for them, and the "Master of all Good Workmen" calls for an accounting, they will come with alert, self-respecting eagerness to present, not just the one, two, or five talents which were entrusted to them, but other talents also and in addition characters rich in development through creative living. To these the Master of Abundant Personality can truly say: "Thou hast been faithful" and "Enter into the joy of abundant living."

This picture is the artist's way of saying to each and every one of us:

> What you are is God's gift to you,
> What you make of yourself is your gift to Him.

There are comparatively few *one talent* people in the world. To most of us God has given many, many capacities, all, of course, in an undeveloped, embryonic state. This life on earth, this world in which we live, with its rich and constantly varying stimulation, is our opportunity for growth and development. We may be faithful to *little* and become *much,* or we may be unfaithful to *much* and become *little*. Our destiny is not with others, but within ourselves.

✣

THE WISE AND FOOLISH VIRGINS

By

Etienne Azambre

(Interpretation)

SOME unknown writer has fittingly called the story of "The Wise and Foolish Virgins" the *Parable of Preparation* or *Readiness*; for such, indeed, is the emphasis of this incident as told by Jesus in Matthew 25:1-13.

And strange as it may seem, the world today, as in the time of Jesus, seems even yet to be fairly equally divided into the same two classes—those who see to it in advance that they are prepared to meet almost any emergency or occasion, and those whose life-habit it is to put off until tomorrow everything that just doesn't have to be done today.

Clearly the emphasis of Jesus in this story of "The Wise and Foolish Virgins" is that the foolish must of necessity bear the penalty which their own lack of wisdom and energy has produced. They are to miss the joy and fellowship of entering into the feast of good things, which the bridegroom has made ready, for no other reason than that they are *unprepared,* and that because of their own folly.

THE WISE AND FOOLISH VIRGINS—*AZAMBRE*

ETIENNE AZAMBRE

It is just this moment when the midnight cry, "Behold, the bridegroom! Come ye forth to meet him," arose that the French artist, Etienne Azambre, has chosen to portray in his painting of "The Wise and Foolish Virgins." In the foreground the five *wise virgins,* their lamps trimmed and lighted, have already formed the procession for a forward march to meet the bridegroom and his happy party. While against the friendly pillars in the background three of the foolish virgins may be seen—one still asleep, another, her arms upraised in a prolonged yawn, has evidently just awakened, while a third sits dreamily on the steps, too indolent even to seek oil for her empty lamp from the wise virgins ahead.

Only two of these foolish virgins seem to have enough concern even to beg oil of the wise virgins, who prepared in advance for a prolonged wait or even delay on the part of the bridegroom. That their request is fruitless is evident from the expression on the faces of the two wise virgins on the left-hand side of the processional. Why should they jeopardize their own preparedness for these foolish virgins who had had the same opportunity to get ready for the bridegroom's coming as had they?

The artist means to tell us that life itself is here portrayed in this parable of "The Wise and Foolish Virgins." Those who are ready in any time of emergency or opportunity always enter in; while those who are unprepared are, by virtue of their own unpreparedness, left out.

In other words, there is a law of compensation in human life and relationships, which may not be violated without penalty. To those who are prepared life provides opportunities to utilize that preparedness. To those who are too foolish, weak, undiscerning, or lazy to prepare in advance so that they may be ready when the "great day," the "great guest," or the "great occasion" arises, disappointment, frustration, hopelessness prevail as a direct and natural result. No individual or group may sin away its day of opportunity and then expect the reward of the faithful, the alert, the prepared. This is the message which Azambre, the French artist, has thus graphically portrayed for us in this midnight scene of "The Wise and Foolish Virgins."

✠

THE LIGHT OF THE WORLD

By

Holman Hunt

(Interpretation)

WILLIAM HOLMAN HUNT was one of three artists in London (Hunt, Rossetti, and Millars) who inaugurated a movement in art known as the pre-Raphaelite

Movement, the aim of which was to improve the art then being produced, by studying nature itself and by taking as a model the work of painters who preceded Raphael, endeavoring to follow the idealism of design and execution that marks the work of these old masters.

Of the three, Hunt alone held to the original purpose of the new school and developed it into what Dolores Bacon calls, "a truly great school." In estimating Hunt's work, Miss Bacon says: "There is not one false note that shocks us, or makes us feel that, after all, the story is affected and artificial. They are sincere, truthful pictures that speak to the mind as well as to the eye."

In getting the truth of detail Hunt experienced many hardships in travel, and spent infinite pains in painting types, costumes, and scenery in Palestine and elsewhere, to gain the historic truths of his Scriptural scenes. He has studied, as have few others, to gain the true and literal setting for every subject, never allowing himself to paint a picture whose scene is laid in a foreign country without first visiting it and learning the truth regarding accessories. This picture, "The Light of the World," so often reproduced, is spoken of by John Ruskin as "one of the very noblest works of sacred art ever produced."

"Behold, I stand at the door and knock: If any man hear My voice and open the door, I will come in to him, and will sup with him, and he with Me." This is the Scripture visualized in Holman Hunt's great masterpiece, "The Light of the World," of which there are two originals, one in Keble College, Oxford, England, and one in St. Paul's Cathedral in London. Both are indeed marvelous paintings done with exquisite coloring and minute attention to detail.

There is in this picture a mystery of color and a blending of light and shade that move the soul to devotion and worship. It is evangelistic in its appeal. It portrays the moment when human destiny hangs in the balance, when Divine Love patiently waits upon human reluctance. Here is the perpetual issue between heaven and earth—*choice*. Here is the continual challenge of Christ to men. Here we see the ever-present appeal of love to lethargy. It is a *call* to *decision* done in oil and color.

On this canvas Holman Hunt has portrayed the door of the human heart, barred with nails and hinges rusty. It is knitted and bound to the stanchions by creeping ivy. A bat, a creature of the night, hovers near. The threshold is overgrown with brambles and wild grass. Jesus approaches in the night-time. He is garbed as a prophet, priest, and king. The white robe denotes His prophetic office, the breastplate His priesthood, and the crown of gold intertwined with thorns proclaims His royalty.

He brings a twofold light. The lantern in His hand represents the light of conscience. It reveals sin. Its fire is red and fierce. Within its radiance fall the door, the weeds, an apple—a symbol of man's first sin. The other light is from Christ's face. It proclaims the hope of salvation. It is an illumination both subdued and sublime. His expression is as appealing as the tenderness of God. Thus He stands at the door of each and every man's heart, asking admittance.

> O Jesus, Thou art standing
>   Outside the fast-closed door;
> In lowly patience waiting
>   To pass the threshold o'er:
> Shame on us, Christian brethren,
>   His name and sign we bear,
> Oh, shame, thrice shame upon us
>   To keep Him standing there.

When Jesus dined with Zacchæus something wonderful came into the life of that despised publican as a result of that visit. His whole attitude toward life and property changed because Jesus came into his heart.

When Jesus sat at Simon's banquet, something happened. Ere the meal was ended such words were spoken to Simon as he had never heard before. Something happened to a woman also when Mary Magdalene, the harlot, washed His feet as He reclined at the table and wiped them with her lovely hair.

Jesus was welcomed into the home of Lazarus, Mary, and Martha, and they yielded to Him their love and devotion and received in return "that better part that passeth not away" with the years.

Even the good man who furnished Him an upper room for the Passover feast discovered shortly that His guest had become the host, for that supper sacrament and the room marked the birthplace of the Christian Church.

And even today, as in the long ago, when Jesus enters into human life something wonderful happens. He has power to sanctify each room, to beautify each activity, to glorify each duty, and to turn the water of our commonplace experiences into the wine of spiritual refreshment and enjoyment.

The message of this wonderful painting is—

> There's a stranger at the door.
>   Let Him in.
> He has been there oft before.
>   Let Him in.
>
> Let Him in ere He is gone,
>   Let Him in, the Holy One.
> Jesus Christ, the Father's Son,
>   Let Him in.

THE LIGHT OF THE WORLD—*HUNT*

"COME UNTO ME" —BURNAND

"'COME UNTO ME'"

By

Eugene Burnand

(Interpretation)

IN THE painting "'Come unto Me,'" by the Swiss painter Eugene Burnand, we have one of the most stimulating conceptions of the universal challenge of Jesus to the youth of every age.

In this picture it is as though Jesus and John the beloved had stopped along the wayside to greet and talk with a group of alert, serious-minded young people. That the one in the right foreground, whose hand is clasped in the Master's, had just made a major life decision is evident. Every line of his slim, straight young body seems to indicate that "he has counted the cost" and will be worthy and faithful no matter where his decision may lead him.

The girl at his side—whether sister or sweetheart we do not know—also has reached an epoch-making choice. These two, we feel, have both heard and accepted the Master's challenge of "Come unto Me," and "Go ye into all the world."

This group of eager-eyed, expectant young people is symbolic of youth in every age, some of which always choose the "hard right as over against the easy wrong."

The deep-set eyes of the Master are searching the soul of this lad whose hand He holds so firmly in His own. The decision this youth has just made to follow Christ may mean that his strong young body will, one of these days, provide a sporting feast for lions in the arena at Rome while Nero fiddles and the stupid populace applaud. Or it may cause him to be among those heroic Christians of the first century whose bodies became the torch-lights of a new religion of love that has swept round the world. In far-away India, China, or among the savage hordes of Northern Europe, these two may yet bear on their bodies the marks of martyrdom.

For the "Come unto Me" of the lowly Nazarene has always carried with it also the "Go ye into all the world." He does not call youth in any age to a life of smug, easy, complacent living. His message to men in every age is "Go, sell all that thou hast, give to the poor, and come and follow Me." Everything that keeps us from single-hearted devotion to Christ and His cause must go before the "Come unto Me," and the "Lo, I am with you always, even unto the end of the world" have any great significance.

The message of Christ to young people in every age is beautifully expressed in Kipling's "Explorer":

> Something's hidden, go and find it,
> Go and look behind the ranges.
> Something's lost behind the ranges—
> Lost, and waiting for you—Go!

And the testimony of all those in every age who have "left all," who have both "come" and "gone" is a pæan of praise as to the worth-whileness of the constant challenge of the living, victorious Christ.

The barren mountains in the distant background in this picture symbolize that world of hardship, of sin, of unrighteousness into which all those who "love the Lord" must go, there to build the portion of the wall of His Kingdom that is nearest to them.

The flowers in the foreground are symbolic of the vital, life-renewing quality which youth in the blossom-time of life in every generation bring to the glorious task of building in this world God's Kingdom of Love.

Close against the breast of the girl at the side of this lad to whom Jesus has just spoken is the Book of Books—the Master's words which in every age lead all those who seek into the fullness of truth.

The faces of these eager, serious-minded young people have a haunting, mystical quality. The two in the foreground have made their decision and for them it is unalterable. Study the faces of those "who follow in their train." Each, in its own way, is expressing his response to the challenge the Master has given. There is in the eyes of the second lad, whose Bible is held firmly in his closed hand, a look almost of fear that Jesus will think he is too young to follow "even until death" the challenge which his more mature friend has just accepted.

Behind him is the half-hidden face of another dreamy-eyed youth, who within himself seems to be weighing the issue as to whether or not he is strong enough to bear the loneliness of separation from all those whom he holds dear, if he, too, should make a similar decision.

Farther down the incline in shadowy outline are the faces of two more girls and a lad, each weighing the cost of discipleship in his or her own way. Will it pay? Am I strong enough to be true even unto death? Yet they come, irresistibly drawn by this "Stranger of Galilee," who in every age challenges youth to high resolve, and to heroic living and serving for His kingdom's sake.

> I heard Him call,
> "Come follow." That was all.
> My gold grew dim,
> My soul went after Him,
> I rose and followed.
> That was all.
> Who would not follow
> If he heard Him call?

"THE NAZARENE"—*TODD*

"THE NAZARENE"

By

H. Stanley Todd

(Interpretation)

CHARLES HADDON BLOOM, writing of a recently painted picture of the Christ, which the artist, Henry Stanley Todd, calls "The Nazarene," says:

"Last night I heard the artist, in simple and beautiful words, tell a great audience in one of our churches how he came to paint his conception of Jesus. Colonel Todd is an outstanding American, a courtly gentleman of the old school. He has painted many of the masters among men: princes and noblewomen. He greatly desired, through many years, to put on a canvas his heart picture of the Master of all men. Then came the World War. His part in it was the Red Cross in Belgium and France. His spirit was stirred at the tragedy. His heart bled, especially for the hordes of children. The sorrows of the outraged and helpless became his personal sorrow. Far beyond the limits of his office and instructions he went to attempt to alleviate them. All the while the Christ was growing within him, the hope of a glory to come to light.

"He read and reread the New Testament. He called upon all that was within him: all his knowledge of men splendid and true; all his innate love of manliness; all of his artistic skill; all that the long years of preparation and technical mastery had brought to him; and then, one summer, came the day of the white heat of creative composition. That which had been forming in his soul was transferred to canvas. A new and different Christ had joined the list of artistic immortals in the field of Christian art."

Soon after its completion this great painting was placed on exhibition in the Newhouse Galleries in New York City for several days. Then the artist graciously granted the use of it to the churches in Greater New York, asking the New York Federation of Churches to superintend its journeys from church to church. It was unveiled in Dr. Ralph Sockman's church on Christmas Sunday morning, at evening a great audience saw it at the Broadway Temple. Following its exhibition in the larger churches of the five boroughs of New York City, it went, under the direction of the Federation Council of Churches, to several of the larger cities of America, and finally to the Hall of Religion, Century of Progress World's Fair, in Chicago. It will in all probability find a permanent home in some religious atmosphere and surroundings, as the gift of the artist to the Church at large.

The following appraisal of this painting by E. C. Sherburne, a New York art critic, under the head, "An Original Conception of Christ in a Painting," gives some conception of its reception by the world of art. He says:

"I have recently seen Colonel H. Stanley Todd's painting of the Christ. . . .

Always the conventional Christ in pictures has been the Man of Sorrows, that pathetic, drooping, and sad type epitomized in Italian or Spanish art according to the nationality of the artist. . . . Here we have THE TRIUMPHANT CHRIST. . . . He was to be crucified, but also to rise again and survive eternally as an idea of the unconquerability of righteousness. . . . We are the disciples of such a Christ. . . . This is an upstanding Christ . . . the One who drove the money-changers from the Temple; He who faced the accusers of the Magdalen. . . . In harmony with this theme of triumph is the joyous color scheme, a harmony of white, bluish green, and gold.

"The upper part of the figure is His own, as if the Nazarene were standing on a hillside, glowing against the cloud of dappled sky, as He might have appeared during the Sermon on the Mount, with the listeners just out of sight. . . . By omitting any specific audience, Colonel Todd has included everybody, past, present, and future, who has been willing to heed the teaching of the Christ.

"With the Christ in art so often depicted as a Latin type, Colonel Todd's painting is startling at first in its divergence from convention. . . . This Nazarene has golden hair and blue eyes. In this, the artist has complete support in the histories of Biblical times, for there were blond tribes of Israel. . . . We are startled by this new aspect of Christ, startled, but far from being dubious. We accept it as logical to itself, and consistent with the triumphant nature of the portrait. . . . HERE is, not merely hope, but certainty, and serene joyfulness that sees all the sons and daughters of men singing together in unity.

"Having this quality of vision, of completeness in its trinity of mental, emotional, and spiritual appeal, the picture has that spontaneity that results only from a firm plan and an unwavering intent, supported by a ripeness of technical experience. No fumbling or uncertainty got in the way of the artist's expression in this painting, of what we like to call 'THE TRIUMPHANT CHRIST.'"

The Rev. Dr. Ralph W. Sockman, pastor of the Madison Avenue M. E. Church of New York City, says:

"One day recently . . . I entered a darkened room where, in solitary impressiveness hung Colonel Todd's picture of the Galilean Christ. The figure so arrestingly modern, with its light hair and blue eyes transported me into another world . . . a world of noisy men made quiet, a world of worried men made calm, of sinful men made pure, of hopeless men made confident. And when I came out again into the confusion of the New York streets it was not quite the same as when I entered."

And Frank S. Fry, pastor of the Reformed Church on Staten Island, inspired by looking at this picture, wrote the poem, "The Nazarene."

> I am looking at Thy face, O Nazarene,
> And wond'ring what it is that holds me fast;
> What charm is in Thine eye that will not let me go,
> That seems to say, "Dear one, I love thee so."
>
> I am thinking of Thy love, O Nazarene,
> And pond'ring deep the marks that love hath cast:

What grace is on Thy lips, which oft to me doth say,
In dulcet note, "Dear one, I love thee so."

I am musing on Thy word, O Nazarene,
And asking why it draws my soul to Thee;
What merit hast Thou found, or grace, that to my heart anew
Thy Word doth say, "Dear one, I love thee so."

Thy love is in Thy face, O Nazarene,
Thy love is on Thy lips; its light is in Thine eye.
My answer is "Thyself." Thy living, dying love
To me hath said, "Dear one, I love thee so."

And as we study this new and arrestingly modern conception of Christ, His followers the world around respond also with the words of the poet, "Dear One, we love Thee so."

✠

BOY AND ANGEL

By

Abbott Handerson Thayer

(Interpretation)

PEOPLE often asked Abbott Handerson Thayer why he painted wings on so many of his figures. The artist would reply, "To symbolize an exalted atmosphere. I want to show a quality beyond the casual."

"Beyond the casual"—that is the crux of Thayer's art. Certainly this quality is admirably displayed in his "Boy and Angel," where the great, spreading angel wings symbolize an atmosphere of inspiration.

In this painting, the artist portrays a youth, on the threshold of adolescence. Like other boys of his age, this lad is looking to the future. His finely modeled face, straightforward, dignified, serious mien, clearly indicate that he is a person of character. He is quietly fearless and seems aware of a guidance that surrounds and upholds him as he tries to glimpse the world of living that lies ahead.

The angel who stands behind the youth is pictured as a noble woman, clad in a golden garment. Her crown and halo, together with her wonderful wings, show that she is meant to represent the inspiration of spiritual things. She enfolds and protects the young lad, and, at the same time, directs his gaze upward. Notice that this angel does not actually touch or in any way push the boy. It is as though the lad, having made his choice, feels the assurance, direction, and protection of all that is good and true. It would seem that this is the message of "Boy and Angel," especially in the light of Abbott Handerson Thayer's personal life.

BOY AND ANGEL—*THAYER*

Born in Boston on August 12, 1849, Abbott Thayer reached his own cross-roads when, as a lad of sixteen, he decided to make painting his profession. It was not an easy decision, for his parents had other plans for him. But, like the boy that he was to create on canvas when he was much older, he made his decision and ever after walked with the assurance of one who has "a guardian angel." He was able to meet poverty and personal sorrow in the manner of those whose life has a steadying purpose.

The first years of his artistic career were spent painting animals. He gained a national reputation as a painter of birds and animals. His deep interest in nature led him to become a fine amateur ornithologist and this avocation lasted throughout his life.

However, early in his career he directed his talents to figure painting, concentrating especially on women and children. Thayer idealized women and this explains why he so often put wings on them. Throughout his life he was preoccupied with painting angels. He always had some canvas under creation which had a beautiful angel in it. His "Caritas," his beautiful "Stevenson Memorial," and many others are among the examples of paintings of angels.

These women-angels are fine, noble, virginal, pure, strong, and possessed of great character. They are truly symbolic of all that is good. And their wings! They are always great golden or white wings that bear them up and infuse the entire painting with strength and spirituality. Thayer married again following the death of his first wife, and both of his wives were unusually fine women. It is clear that his idealization of these two women is reflected in his art.

Thayer's paintings also speak of his love and understanding of children. The death of two of their boys greatly saddened the Thayers. Though they had other children whom Thayer often used as models, he never forgot those two little boys; they brought him close to other children and youth. We can see this warm, sympathetic portrayal of children in "Boy and Angel."

Abbott Handerson Thayer was an accomplished and widely recognized artist. He studied and traveled abroad and was known in art circles of Paris as a fine draftsman.

In America, he always had all the commissions he could take care of. Leading art dealers and museums sought him for paintings for exhibition.

It is said that Thayer understood and was able to portray the essential spirit of man and the divine significance of life in a way that few other artists have been able to do. He has always been admired for his symbolic figures which are possessed of great beauty and dignity. His friends often spoke of him as an idealist who practiced what he preached.

Abbott Thayer left a great heritage to American art when he died in 1921. The Metropolitan Museum of Art in New York showed seventy-eight of his drawings and paintings at a large memorial exhibit the year following his death. Today, he is represented in most of America's leading art galleries and museums.

YOUTH

Youth am I!
I am a skylark on the wing,
Alive, alert to joy and spring,
No valleys tempt me; peaks allure—
Long flights my quivering wings endure;
And only he who seeks the height
Of great adventure, views my flight
Toward the light.

Youth am I!
I seek new ways beneath the blue;
I take far flights unknown to you—
Yet do I need your faith in me,
For though I seem so wild and free,
When comes the storm and darkened sky,
I would you had climbed as high
As skylarks fly.

Youth am I!
Since you were young it is so long
That you forgot life's morning song,
And do you doubt my loyalty
To ideals high; or can you see
Beneath my shining, morning face
The semblance of an inner grace,
High heaven's trace?

—Alice G. Moore

EVERY YOUTH

Every Youth has a quest to make,
  For life is the King's Highway,
And a joyous heart is the script we take,
  On the road of Everyday.

Every Youth has his gifts to guard,
  As he fares to a far-off goal;
A body pure, and a mind unmarred,
  And the light of a lovely soul.

Every youth has a task of his own,
  For the Father has willed it so.
Youth seeks the way, and He alone,
  Can show him the path to go.

Every youth has a lovely Guide,
From the vale to the mountain crest;
For the Unseen Friend who walks beside,
Is the Way and the End of the Quest.

—Mary S. Edgar

GOD'S DREAMS

Dreams are they—but they are God's dreams!
Shall we decry them and scorn them?
That men shall love one another,
That white shall call black man brother,
That greed shall pass from the market-place,
That lust shall yield to love for the race,
That man shall meet with God face to face—
Dreams are they all,
  But shall we despise them—
  God's dreams!

Dreams are they—to become man's dreams!
Can we say nay as they claim us?
That men shall cease from their hating,
That war shall soon be abating,
That the glory of kings and lords shall pale,
That the pride of dominion and power shall fail,
That the love of humanity shall prevail—
Dreams are they all,
  But shall we despise them—
  God's dreams!

—Thomas Curtis Clark

WHO HAS KNOWN HEIGHTS

Who has known heights and depths, shall not again
  Know peace, not as the calm heart knows
  Low, ivied walls, a garden close,
  The old enchantment of a rose.
And though he tread the humble ways of men,
He shall not speak the common tongue again.

Who has known heights, shall bear forevermore
  An incommunicable thing
  That hurts his heart, as if a wing
  Beat at the portal, challenging:
And yet, lured by the gleam his vision wore,
Who once has trodden stars seeks peace no more.

—Mary Brent Whiteside

CHRIST OF THE HIGHWAYS—A PRAYER

Christ of the highways up and down
  Through ancient Galilee,
Be Thou the Christ of the highways still,
  They have such need of Thee—
Highways athrong with lonely boys
  Their home-doors closed, their bread
The bitter crust that beggars share,
  The highway's rest, their bed;
O walk again the weary roads,
  Be comforter, we pray,
Of the despair that cries along
  The sad highways today.

—*Grace F. Guthrie*

HOLY THURSDAY

You've heard of Holy Thursday, Easter week? . . .

I work as waitress in a restaurant,
And Sunday all of us work extra hard
And extra long, with no time off at all;
But I get Thursday off—the other girls
Get other days, because of Sunday work.
I was brought up with Sundays very strict;
My mother would be shocked if she could know
The way I spend 'em now . . . and yet, perhaps
She'd understand about my Thursdays.
                                        You
Seem like you'd understand—I've never told
Anyone else—it seems so sort of queer.

I call it Holy Thursday to myself.
There isn't any church, but I go out
To Forest Park; I take my Testament
And some good book, and read, all by myself.
The lady at the library would help me
Just at first, to choose the books; but now
I pick 'em out myself—not stories—lives
Of folk that did big things when it was hard.

And books on places I won't ever see
And such as that. On rainy days I go
Down to the library, or read at home;
And winter days, sometimes, I read in bed

(My room's not very warm). Sometimes I sew
For the Red Cross, or charities, that give
The patterns to you, and the cloth, and you
Just give your work. Sometimes I get the kids
That live there in our building, and don't know
What to do next, with not much place to play,
And tell 'em stories—just 'most anything
I think the Lord would like to have me do.

I don't feel right about this Sunday work,
And yet, this job was all that I could get;
So I have Holy Thursday, just for me.
It makes me feel good—gives me a new start
For a new week, like Sunday used to do.
Some folks have Saturday—I guess the day
Isn't the thing—it's how you feel that counts,
Yet it seems sort of silly, telling it. . . .

Does it sound queer? . . . I wish I hadn't told.[1]

—*Dorothy Brown Thompson*

CHOICE

Ask and it shall be given.
Ask—ask.
And if you ask a stone
Expect not bread;
And if the stone flitter like a caught star,
And shine on a warm, soft breast,
And you have tossed your soul away
To see it in that nest,
Yet it is still a stone—not bread.

Seek and you shall find.
Seek—seek.
And if you go to the crowded street
Look not to find the hills;
And if the shops sit gay along the way,
And laughter fills the air,
Still—you have lost the hills.

Knock and the door shall open.
Knock—knock.
Two doors are there. Beware!
Think well before you knock;
Your tapping fingers will unlock
Your heaven or hell.

—*Ellen Coit Elliott*

[1] From *The Christian Advocate*. Used with permission of the author and publisher.

IF YOU WILL

If God can make—of an ugly seed,
  With a bit of earth and air,
And dew and rain, sunshine and shade—
  A flower so wondrous fair;
What can He make—of a soul like you,
  With the Bible and faith and prayer,
And the Holy Spirit—if you do His will,
  And trust His love and care!

—*A. D. Burkett*

NOT THE CHRIST IN THE MANGER

Not the Christ in the manger,
Not the Christ on the cross,
But the Christ in the soul
Shall save that soul
When all but love is lost.

—*Katherine Lee Bates*

COME CLEAN!

When the game is on and your friends about,
And you could put your rival out
By a trick that's mean but wouldn't be seen,
Come clean, my lad, come clean!

When exams are called and you want to pass,
And you know how you could lead your class,
But the plan's not square, you know it's mean;
Come clean, my lad, come clean!

With the boss away, you've a chance to shirk,
Not lose your pay—not have to work,
He'll neither fire you nor vent his spleen;
Come clean, my lad, come clean!

When you're all alone and no one about,
And not a soul could find it out,
And you're tempted to do a thing that's obscene;
Come clean, my lad, come clean!

For a home awaits, and a girl that's true,
And a church and state have need of you,
They must have your best—on you they lean,
Come clean, my lad, come clean!

—Author Unknown

YOUTH PRAYS FOR PEACE

Lord, we are the Youth of every land,
    Pleading for peace;
We are the ones who will be sacrificed
    Unless wars cease;
We are the ones elected, Lord, to pay
    A price too high.
You gave us life, and it is not Your will
    That we should die.

Open the blind eyes of our leaders, Lord,
    In every land;
Open their hearts and minds and make them wise
    To understand
That war is sad and horrible and wrong,
    And useless quite;
That we, the clean, strong Youth of earth,
    Have the good right
To life and love and happiness and peace.

We would not be
Killers of men—we want to walk the earth
    Clean-handed, free
From war with all its horrors, lust, and greed,
    Its dark despair.
Lord, may there never be another war—
    This is our prayer.

—Grace Noll Crowell

WHERE ARE YOU GOING, GREAT-HEART?

Where are you going, Great-Heart,
With your eager face and your fiery grace?—
    Where are you going, Great-Heart?

"To fight a fight with all my might;
For Truth and Justice, God and Right;
To grace all Life and His fair Light."
    Then God go with you, Great-Heart!

Where are you going, Great-Heart?
"To lift Today above the Past;
To make Tomorrow sure and fast;
To nail God's colors to the mast."
  Then God go with you, Great-Heart!

Where are you going, Great-Heart?
"To break down old dividing lines;
To carry out my Lord's designs;
To build again His broken shrines."
  Then God go with you, Great-Heart!

Where are you going, Great-Heart?
"To set all burdened peoples free;
To win for all God's liberty;
To 'stablish His Sweet Sovereignty."
  Then God go with you, Great-Heart.

—*John Oxenham*

WHO WANTS THE BOYS AND GIRLS?

God wants the boys, the merry, merry boys,
The noisy boys, the funny boys,
  The thoughtless boys;
God wants the boys with all their joys
That He as gold may make them pure,
And teach them trials to endure,
  His heroes brave
    He'd have them be.
  Fighting for truth
    And purity,
  GOD WANTS THE BOYS!

God wants the happy-hearted girls,
The loving girls, the best of girls,
  The worst of girls;
God wants to make the girls His pearls,
And so reflect His holy face,
And bring to mind His wondrous grace,
  That beautiful
    The world may be,
  And filled with love
    And purity.
  GOD WANTS THE GIRLS!

—*Anonymous*

THE CROSS AT THE CROSSWAYS

See There!—God's signpost, standing at the ways
    Which every man of his free will must go—
Up the steep hill—or down the winding ways—
    One or the other every man must go.

He forces no man, each must choose his way,
    And as he chooses so the end will be;
One went in front to point the Perfect Way.
    Who follows fears not where the end will be.

To every man there openeth
A Way, and Ways, and a Way,
And the High Soul climbs the High Way,
And the Low Soul gropes the Low,
And in between on the misty flats,
The rest drift to and fro.
But to every man there openeth
A High Way and a Low,
And every man decideth
The Way his soul shall go.

                                        —*John Oxenham*

✠

STRADIVARIUS

In GEORGE ELIOT's poem, "Stradivarius," Naldo has been discussing with
Stradivarius the occupation of making violins. The reply of Stradivarius, the
great maker of violins, shows something of his appreciation of the feeling
of fellowship which service and cooperation with God bring to the inmost heart
of man.

        But God be praised,
Antonio Stradivarius has an eye
That winces at false work and loves the true,
With hand and arm that play upon the tool
As willingly as any singing bird
Sets him to sing his morning roundelay,
Because he likes to sing and likes the song.

•   •   •   •   •

When any master holds
'Twixt chin and hand a violin of mine,
He will be glad that Stradivarius lived,
Made violins, and made them of the best.
The masters only know whose work is good:
They will choose mine, and while God gives them skill
I give them instruments to play upon,
God choosing me to help Him.

.   .   .   .   .

'Tis God gives skill,
But not without men's hands: He could not make
Antonio Stradivarius' violins
Without Antonio.

—George Eliot

✠

THE TALKING PICTURE

HE WAS a little large for his age, and yet he was only a boy; but he was going away from home, away to a distant city to live and to work. His mother could hardly bear to see him go alone, not even sure that he was consciously taking God with him, although she had tried, as best she could, to lead the boy to Him.

When he came home one evening, a few days before he was to start, his mother said to him: "John, I want you to go down to the art gallery tomorrow and see a picture that hangs there."

"Oh, mother," said the boy, "I don't care anything at all about pictures; and anyway I haven't got the time."

"Son," replied his mother, "in a little while you'll be a long way from home, where I'll not be asking you to do things to please me. I want you to do *this* for *me?*"

"Well," answered the boy, "if you put it that way, of course I'll have to go." And so on the morrow, he went.

He was directed to the room where the picture hung, and he walked down a long corridor and opened the door to enter; but on the threshold he paused. On the platform at the far end of the room a man was kneeling in prayer, so he closed the door and waited. After a few moments he opened the door again, and seeing the man still at prayer, he closed it again and waited. Four or five minutes passed, and when he opened the door again, and saw the man kneeling, he entered to investigate. And then he saw that the man at prayer was the picture.

It was a life-size painting of Christ in Gethsemane, wonderfully lighted and framed in black velvet. He walked eagerly forward to study a picture that could thus have misled him. What a wonderful face it was! And yet why that look of worry and care? His mother had always taught him that Christ was not afraid to die; then why that look of worry on His brow?

For a long time he stood looking at the picture, and then he went out. But he wanted to see it again; he wanted to ask some questions about it. That evening he said to his mother, "I should like to see that picture again. Will you come down with me tomorrow and we'll look at it together?" And with a glad heart the mother went to the gallery with her boy.

This time the boy, hat in hand, entered the room reverently, and the two walked quietly down toward where the picture hung. For a long time he stood looking at it: and then he turned to his mother and said: "Mother, you've always taught me that Jesus was not afraid to die, that He had done no wrong. Then why that look of worry on His face, and why do His hands seem to be pleading so?"

"Son," answered his mother, with a silent prayer in her heart for guidance, "He had only been a teacher for three years and there was so much that He wanted to teach and to do. But now, on the 'tomorrow' He was to die and leave it all undone. I think He was worried with the fear that those whom He loved and trusted would forget and leave the work undone, for even *now* the three that He had asked to watch with Him for one hour were lying asleep at the entrance to this garden. I think that He was afraid that all through the centuries His followers would forget and leave undone the work that He, in going, could not do. I think that this might have caused that look of worry on His brow."

For a long time the boy stood looking at the picture, his face sinking lower and lower as his eyes looked steadily into the face of the man at prayer. Then he raised his head and straightened his shoulders as he said, "Oh, Man of Galilee, if there is anything that You have left undone, anywhere, that I can do, You can count on me."

And he went out, away to that distant city to work, and to live a Christ-guided life.[2]

✢

THE HALL OF HEROES

HAVE you ever thought how many different kinds of heroes there are in the world? In every land there are names of people who lived long ago that are still kept in loving memory and honor because those who bore them performed heroic and noble deeds. Some of them risked their lives to find out how to

[2] Adapted from a longer story, author unknown, in *The Use of the Story in Religious Education*. Published by Harper & Brothers. Used with special permission.

conquer disease and to help bring the blessing of health to the world. Some suffered and died for the truth. Some fought against enemies of their country and gave their lives on the field of battle. All these are true heroes, and we are glad to give them praise and honor; but there are others who deserve higher honor than any of these. Let me tell you a story that I have read. It was a vision, perhaps, that some unknown author had of a Hall of Heroes. This is the way his story described it:

"Suddenly I found myself standing before a great building. There was a wide entrance, approached by a long flight of broad steps, at the top of which in the shadow of a great doorway stood a man. When I went up to him and asked, 'Will you please tell me what this building is?' He answered very graciously:

" 'This is the Hall of Heroes. Would you like to see through it?"

" 'Thank you very much,' I said and followed him in.

"When we entered I found myself in the center of a magnificent hall, around the inside of which ran marble staircases leading to the different floors. All was silent, and when my guide spoke to me, his voice was echoed along the high wall and balconies like the soft deep notes of a cathedral organ. 'Here we enshrine,' said he, 'the memories of all heroes from the least unto the greatest. Let us go in.'

"Turning, I saw opposite me an open door; and over the door was written, 'Heroes of Battle.' I think that you would be able to tell the names of a great many whom I saw there as I walked slowly down the long aisles of that great chamber. Men who had fought and won great victories, men whose defeat had been glorious because they had all their wounds in front. Leonidas, who fell at Thermopylæ; Horatius, who kept the bridge; Nelson, with his armless sleeve; and Gordon, without a weapon. There, I saw, too, heroes of the World War, many of whom I had known, and I was overwhelmed with a feeling of sadness as I thought of the sacrifice of so many young lives lost in battle. I saw that the face of my guide was shadowed with sorrow, too, as we came to the end of the room and passed out into the great hall.

" 'Let us go to the next floor,' he said. 'Some day the nations of the world will learn to love each other and then "Men will beat their swords into plowshares and their spears into pruning-hooks, and nation shall not lift up sword against nation, neither shall they learn war any more." '

" 'I wish that were true today,' I said.

" 'It will surely be true some day,' he answered. 'And you can help to bring it to pass if you will.'

" 'I will do all that I can,' I promised, and my guide's face brightened as he turned to me and smiled.

"When we reached the landing at the top of the stairs, I saw before me a door over which was inscribed 'Heroes of the Lonely Way.' Here were the pioneers—men who had cut their way through the jungles of dark continents, who had scaled unconquered mountains, crossed waterless deserts, discovered the source of rivers, sailed over unknown oceans, and pushed their way along the very rim of the earth. I felt ashamed that I knew so few out of that brave multitude; but I knew Columbus and a few others, and my guide stopped me every now and then, and told me stories of deeds of courage and faith and endurance which have done more for the world than all the conquests of the sword.

"As we ascended the second flight of steps my guide pointed to an open door before us, over which was written 'Heroes of Truth.' Then he spoke as I had never heard man speak before of the glory and beauty of truth; of the conflict that is waging between truth and error, and of the certainty that truth will triumph in the end. With my heart aflame at his words I entered the room, and saw the hosts who had stood bravely for the truth in places where error was powerful and had many followers. Socrates was there, with the cup of hemlock in his hand; and Luther was there who defied the Pope as he nailed his thesis to the door; and all the noble army of martyrs was there from Stephen to Margaret Wilson, who was tied to the stake in Solway Firth and drowned by the rising tide because she refused to deny what she believed to be true.

"I could have stayed a long time in that glorious chamber, but my guide led me on, and we came to the last staircase of all. It was broader than all the others, and was made of something which hushed every footstep into silence. On the steps were written the words, 'Greater Love Hath No Man Than This, That a Man Lay Down His Life for His Friends.' Over the door which opened for us into this gallery was inscribed, 'Heroes of Love.' My guide did not enter this room in front of me as he had done each time before, but standing at one side, motioned with his hand that I should pass in.

"I found that this room was the great dome crowning the building which I had seen from the outside; but it was bigger and higher than I could ever have thought. At first I imagined it was empty, but it was the marvelous light that blinded my eyes. Then, in the very center, I saw a cross, with a man crucified upon it. A moan escaped from my lips. 'Jesus!' I whispered half to myself. As I grew accustomed to the light, I found that the room was not empty; indeed, it was the fullest of all; for the walls seemed to stretch away in the distance, and the dome seemed to rise into mist, and all the mighty space was filled. Slowly I began to distinguish faces: I saw David Livingstone, who gave his life for the people of Africa; I saw James Chalmers, who gave his life for the savages of New Guinea; I began to see quite plainly the multitude that cannot be numbered of the Heroes of the Cross. Then I caught the sound of music. It came up from the bottom of the huge building, as if every kind of hero, from the least to the greatest, was joining in one mighty chorus. It filled the room in which I stood. I heard the words at last, 'Blessing, and glory, and wisdom, and thanksgiving, and honor, and power, and might, be unto our God forever and ever. Amen.'

"I felt I could endure it no longer. I turned and left the room, and ran down the staircase with the music ringing in my ears and a great throbbing in my heart. In the hall at the foot of the staircase my guide was waiting for me. He walked with me to the great entrance, and said in the kindliest voice, 'You will be here some day?' I stopped in astonishment.

" 'I?' I answered, 'I, a hero?'

" 'Why not?' he answered, smiling. I looked into his face. He seemed to know the great longing in my heart, and with infinite tenderness read and answered my unspoken question.

" 'How can you? "Ask, and it shall be given unto you; Seek, and ye shall find; Knock, and it shall be opened unto you; for everyone that asketh, receiveth; and he that seeketh, findeth; and to him that knocketh it shall be opened." I am sure you will be with us some day.'

"We stood outside the door. He held out his hand to me to say good-by. I thought it had the print of a nail in it. He said, 'On which floor would you like us to prepare a place for you?' And through me, He asks it again of you, and of you, and of you."

—By an author who prefers to remain "unknown"

✛

THE STORY OF THE VIOLIN SERMON

AMONG the beautiful stories that have had their inception in music, none is more lively than the one by Robert Freeman, the former versatile pastor of the Pasadena, California, Presbyterian Church. Dr. Freeman came to America from Edinburgh in 1896 when he was eighteen years of age. He studied in Alleghany College and later graduated from Princeton Theological Seminary.

Music is one of Robert Freeman's recreations. Frequently he would be found playing the tower chimes in his great church. This church owns its own broadcasting apparatus, thus making it possible for thousands of people in southern California to "listen in" on the inspiring sermons and uplifting music of his services.

Robert Freeman's favorite hymn is "O Love That Will Not Let Me Go," by George Matheson, the blind preacher, partly because of the sentiment which this hymn contains and its particularly suitable tune; but more largely because its author was a blind fellow-Scotsman whom Dr. Freeman heard once and has seen many times.

In his parable, "The Violin Sermon," Dr. Freeman says: "Music is a kind of inarticulate, unfathomable speech which leads us to the edge of the infinite and lets us for a moment gaze into that." He bases his story of "The Violin's Sermon" on the text "Making melody in your heart unto the Lord" (Ephesians 5:19). He selected the violin for this parabolic sermon rather than the harp, because from his point of view, the violin with its four strings represents four great departments of the common life of man, each string necessary to the instrument, but each string useless unless tuned to an accepted standard and kept perfectly tuned in relation to the other three.

Dr. Freeman says: "There is, first, the deep bass 'G' string of *work*. The obligation to work is a law of God. He who carefully prescribed rest on one day in the week was as careful in the Decalogue to prescribe work on the six remaining days of each week. 'I must work,' was one of the mottoes in the life of Jesus. No one, who is unwilling fairly to contribute by work to the world's wealth, whatever his contribution may be, whether by creation, distribution, or inspiration, has any right to live and to expect support from society. Labor is a law of life. No legacy justifies leisure. No income exculpates one for failure to show an output. Any man can earn a rest, but no man can inherit one. 'I must work' is God's own law for Himself. Surely, He is rich enough to quit, for the silver and the gold are His, and the cattle on a thousand hills! . . . 'Establish thou the work of our hands upon us,' sings the psalmist. The habit of sloth is disastrous to mind and body; but work, whatever be the tools or materials, is making the workman. God has linked happiness with duty and health with labor. 'My meat is to *do* the will of Him that sent me, and to accomplish His work.'

"This 'G' string of *work*, then, must be tuned. There is no melody issuing from the heart of the slacker and the loafer, no development for the parasite who is unfortunate enough to have his sustenance provided without his personal effort. 'Produce! Produce!' cried Carlyle. 'In God's name produce, though it be but the pitifulest, infinitesimal fraction of a product.'

"Second, there is the mellow 'D' string, that I think of as the symbol of pleasure. There can be no doubt that there is such a string on life's instrument. 'All work and no play makes Jack a dull boy.' The only problem is that of tuning this indispensable string. When is the string of pleasure in tune? is the question with which we who are teachers are continually faced. . . .

"We know that pleasure contributes, as does labor, to the development of individual character. Perhaps it makes an even greater contribution since the teacher is much more beloved. . . . But youth is not sent to college for athletics or dramatics or forensics, delightful as they may be, these are subordinate. When fraternity parties and class fights and intercollegiate games assume primary consideration, then the player has lost sight of the goal and is traveling across the field. When pleasures become a necessity they cease to be of value and become, instead, the enemies of the soul. You never hear a violin solo played on the 'D' string—there are more important strings on each side of it.

"Pleasures are only incidental trip-hammers in the framing of an ironclad character. The ultimate, and not the immediate, is the consideration—not of a single note, but of the whole concerto. Pleasures must pull toward perfection. If in this they fail, in this they condemn themselves and destroy their value.

"Then, there is the 'A' string of friendship running up and down the scale of our affections from casual acquaintances up to that incomparable experience to be envied by all and known to most when two lives merge into one, pledged until death.

"The 'A' string is probably more played upon than any other. Its brilliant notes are continually interwoven, whether the composition seeks the higher or the lower ranges. It is the mezzo-soprano of the instrument. It is the strong tone by which all the others are tuned; if it is out of tune, all is out of tune.

"I covet for all of you the richest experiences of human love, the joy of un-sullied and unwavering admiration and affection yielded by that one whose regard is your chiefest desire. But there will be no such happiness unless the string of love be in tune. Impurity, irregularity, faithlessness, habitual selfish-ness while the strings are yet in the tuning will wreck the whole symphony. On the other hand little acts of self-denial and habitual kindness and thought-fulness will contribute to a life of melody.

"The fourth string gives us our highest notes—notes that penetrate to the heart like the song of the nightingale. It is the 'E' string of *Religion*. There they are—love of work, love of pleasure, love of friends, and love of God. I am not urging my personal religious convictions upon you; but I am urging the necessity of the religious life. Worship is an art. Religion is life, it is the life of God in the soul of man—the life that continually takes God into considera-tion. Neglect this string and you are cut off from all the higher reaches of which your instrument is capable. Let this string remain untuned to the great spiritual standards and values in the world, and you become the discordant note, while others swell together in a diapason of faith, and victory. For with-out religion all the other cultivations of life but cry for the lost chord. Religion is the crown and glory of the hardest worker, the gayest player, and the most devoted lover.

"John Philip Sousa, in a weird tale called 'The Fifth String,' tells of a Tuscan virtuoso named Angelo Diotti, who played upon a violin with an additional string made up of extra lengths of the other four woven together. This fifth string was forbidden to the artist. All of his playing must dodge about it without the silken bow's ever falling upon it. The penalty of failure or disobedience was death. We, too, have a fifth string. As Diotti must not play upon his, so we cannot play upon ours. As his was the string of death, so ours is the string of suffering. It, too, gathers up all the ends of the other strings, and what they are determines whether music and sweetness or discord and harshness shall issue forth from this string. For it has no key by which to screw up to pitch, and so only when work and play, love and worship, are in tune can tuneful notes come from suffering. Christ was made perfect by suffering, and for that end does it come to us all. It is friction that tells the tale. Rubbing and pulling and snapping discovers what is in the violin. Simi-larly, the frictions of life, the petty inconveniences and the great trials make audible the melody or discord of the heart. It is not the calm ease of an hour in church on Sunday, but the pressure and the inconveniences and the irking personalities about us on Monday that discovers what is in us.

"One may readily fancy the plea of many, 'Mine is such a poor second-rate violin of life that there is little music to be gotten out of me.' Yet Paganini, when his own instrument had been taken away, faced the crowd with a cheap substitute in his hands, saying 'I will show you that the music is not in the violin, but in Paganini himself.' Mozart composed his immortal 'Requiem' on a broken-down spinet in a garret in Vienna. A master can play on anything; your Master can. So go forth praying God to help you tune the strings devoted to your labor, your leisure, your love, and your Lord—to work, to play, to friendship and to worship—praying God, too, Himself, to so play upon those strings that you shall know the joy of a melodious heart, and the world shall be glad for your music; Himself to play till the last string breaks its quivering strands and the instrument is ready for the new strings and for an honorable place in the greater orchestra of eternity."[3]

✠

THE TYRANNY OF RICHES

When I had gone forward some distance I saw a group of men and some mules in the distance, and made for them. When I reached them I saw that Jesus was not one of them, and that they disputed together. A young man in silk raiment stood in the middle, and urged something upon some other men, who, rougher in manner and clad in coarser garments, withstood him. Some paces behind them stood two servants, holding three mules, one of which had saddle-cloths of finely woven wool, and stirrups of silver. . . .

So Peter led the way up a steep hillside, and the young man went behind him with his servants and the mules close to his heels. I followed with John.

"We shall find Him in the highest place, where He can see over all the earth," said John as we climbed; and it was near the top that we came upon Jesus. By this time the sun was beginning to set, and a great peace lay upon the land. Jesus sat gazing over the wide country that lay before Him, but He turned when He heard our footsteps. Peter went up to Him.

"Master, these two rich men have come to speak to You," he said. "John thought You would wish to see them."

"John was right. I would turn none away. What do they need?" asked Jesus.

The young man stepped forward, and with great courtesy knelt down. "Master," he said, "I have come to ask You what I can do to inherit eternal life?"

Jesus regarded him for a moment, and His eyes went to the menservants and the mules, and He looked at them before He answered. Then he said:

"You have been brought up in the Commandments of Moses. Keep these."

"I have observed them all," said the young man.

"There is one further," said Jesus. "Thou shalt love thy neighbor as thyself."

"This, too, have I done," said the young man. "What else do I lack?"

For a moment there was silence, and then Jesus said, and His eyes searched the young man as he spoke:

"There is still one thing lacking. Go and sell all that thou hast and give to the poor, and then come and follow Me."

[3] From *Music and Religion*, edited by Stanley Armstrong Hunter. Published by the Abingdon Press. Used with permission of the author and publishers.

The young man rose to his feet and stood silent, his eyes cast on the ground. The servants moved uneasily, and one of them scratched his head, as if the answer pleased him not. Jesus spoke again:

"How is it you say you love your neighbor as yourself? Is not your house full of goods, while around you your brothers, also sons of Abraham, are clad with dung and dying of hunger? Goeth there aught at all from out your house for them?"

The young man made no answer. He did not raise his eyes, and after a moment he turned aside. The servants turned also, and they all began to go slowly down the hill. Jesus watched them go. Then He said, and His face was tired and discouraged, and His eyes clouded:

"How hard it is for the rich to enter the Kingdom of God. I tell you, Simon, that it is easier for a camel to enter through the eye of a needle than for a rich man to come into the Kingdom."

Simon was astonished.

"Who, then, can be saved if the rich cannot?" he asked.

"God is the Awakener of man. With Him all is possible," said Jesus, and he turned to me.

"Good Master—" I began, but he stopped me.

"Do not call me 'good.' No one is good but God," He said, and suddenly His eyes lit up and he questioned:

"Did I not see you at Simon's yesterday? Why have you come?"

"I, too, would live," I said, and my eyes met His.

He watched me for a moment, and then He smiled. "The other would not believe, so he went away," He said.

"So will not I," I answered.

"What! though you, too, have riches?" he said, and there was mirth in His eyes as if he mocked a little, even while He loved.

"All that I have is yours," I replied, and then He rose up and kissed me, and from that day He was my friend.[4]

✢

AN INTERNATIONAL DINNER

By

Elsie Ball

SNIP! Snip! Snip!

Agnes carefully trimmed the black-paper figures of a girl and a boy carrying a pail.

"Jack and Jill went up the hill," she repeated. "I only have to paste these on, and my lantern will be ready."

"It's just lovely!" Dorothy cried, admiringly. She turned the bright golden lantern around carefully. "This side is Mary and her lamb, and this is Old Mother Hubbard and her dog, and here is Simple Simon, fishing in a pail. Oh, it's so cute, Agnes! You'll be sure to get first prize."

"I don't think I'll go to the lantern parade," Agnes said, slowly. "Miss Hopkins says I have to walk with Mary Lee."

"That Chinese girl?" exclaimed Dorothy in a shocked voice. "Oh, Agnes, I don't blame you for not wanting to be in the parade! My mother says they ought not to let a Chinese girl go to our school."

"I wish all those foreigners would stay in their own countries and not bother us," Agnes said. "We could get along without them."

"I'm afraid we'd miss a good many things if we had to get along without any help from other countries," Mrs. Simpson observed.

"I wouldn't care; I'd be glad to miss them," said Agnes.

"Very well," her mother replied. "You shall have a chance to try it."

Dinner time came, and Agnes took her seat at the table eagerly.

"I'm so hungry!" she said.

"I knew you would be," her mother observed, "so I opened a can of salmon for you. There are plenty of potatoes, and you may have all the salt you want."

Agnes stared in astonishment.

"Why can't I have dinner like the rest of the family?" she asked.

"I don't see anything here you'd care for," her father replied. "The roast lamb is really Asiatic, like Mary Lee. Of course, this particular lamb grew up in America, and came from European stock, but the original home of all sheep was in Asia."

"May I have some peas?"

"But peas were first raised in China. Possibly some of Mary Lee's ancestors first sold them to Europeans."

"Can't she have any salad?" Brother Jack asked, looking concerned.

"Lettuce first came from Greece," Mrs. Simpson said. "And there's olive oil in the salad; olive trees came from Asia. Apple trees were brought to this country from Europe. Walnuts originated in Asia. The salad is quite too foreign."

"Anyway, she can have some bread and butter," Jack said.

"The hard wheat that was used to make the flour for the bread was probably raised in Minnesota," Mr. Simpson said. "But we Americans got the seed from Russia, and we should have no butter if the Asiatic people hadn't domesticated cows, long before America was discovered."

"The foreigners taught us how to make bread, too, as well as raise the wheat," Mrs. Simpson said. "The people in Egypt and in China made loaves like ours thousands of years ago."

Little sister Jean was listening with great interest. "Agnes can't even have a glass of milk," she said, "because it came from a Jersey cow!"

Everyone laughed, even Agnes, who was beginning to look a bit serious.

"I shouldn't have said what I did about the foreigners. I didn't know what I was talking about," she said.

"Not many people in any country realize what they owe to other lands," answered her father. "The fact is, we all need one another; and the more we help one another the happier we all shall be."

The day before the lantern parade Agnes came home looking so happy that her mother asked, "Did your lantern win a prize?"

"I got honorable mention," Agnes replied. "Mary Lee's lantern won first prize. It looks like a beautiful big flower. And, oh, mother, Mary Lee has to sit in the judges' stand while the other children march, and they let her choose some one to sit with her, and she chose me! It's true, as father said," Agnes continued, "that the more we help one another the happier we all shall be."[5]

✤

I WOULD BE TRUE

IN THIS simple three-verse hymn, "I Would Be True," written by Howard Arnold Walter in 1917, we have another of those newer hymns of the Church that have an instinctive appeal and challenge to young people. Probably no other one song is more often requested by youth, or sung with greater appreciation and power, than this great character-making hymn.

In the deepest recesses of their own inmost selves young people long to be, as this song so poetically expresses it, *true, pure, strong,* and *brave;* and youth's oft-repeated singing of this great hymn helps to reinforce in everyday living the constant challenge of these much-to-be-desired virtues.

Young people are conscious also of their need of friends and passionately desire to be helpful friends to others. The second verse of this great hymn enables them to voice not only their longing for the ability to be true friends; but also their desire to be self-giving, humble, and to be able to "look up, and laugh, and love and lift."

The tune "Peek," to which this song is regularly sung, was composed by Joseph Yates Peek in 1911.

> I would be true, for there are those who trust me;
> I would be pure, for there are those who care;
> I would be strong, for there is much to suffer;
> I would be brave, for there is much to dare.
> I would be brave, for there is much to dare.
>
> I would be friend of all, the foe, the friendless;
> I would be giving, and forget the gift;
> I would be humble, for I know my weakness;
> I would look up, and laugh, and love, and lift,
> I would look up, and laugh, and love, and lift.

[5] From *Friends at Work,* by Elsie Ball. Copyright, 1934. Published by the Methodist Book Concern. Used with special permission of the publishers.

I would be learning, day by day, the lessons
  My heavenly Father gives me in his Word;
I would be quick to hear his lightest whisper,
  And prompt and glad to do the things I've heard.
And prompt and glad to do the things I've heard. Amen.

—Howard Arnold Walter, 1917

✠

JUST AS I AM, THINE OWN TO BE

AMONG the newer hymns written during the latter part of the nineteenth century, none is more appealing to young people than the splendid words "Just As I Am, Thine Own to Be," written by Marianne Farningham of England. One feels, as one sings these words, that Miss Farningham must, herself, have been a youth to write four brief verses each of which expresses the deepest longing of every devout Christian young person.

And how much better these newer words fit the experience of the young people of today than do the words of that other older hymn, "Just As I Am without One Plea," to which tune these newer words are usually sung.

Then, too, these newer words sung as a solo to the tune of Nevin's "My Rosary" provides an unusually attractive special number in programs of worship for young people. Such an adaptation makes it necessary to repeat the last phrase of each verse of this hymn, if the words to "Just As I Am, Thine Own to Be" are to fit Nevin's melody; but so slight a change may easily be made by anyone familiar with the tune of "My Rosary."

Just as I am, Thine own to be,
Friend of the young, who lovest me,
To consecrate myself to Thee,
  O Jesus Christ, I come.

In the glad morning of my day
My life to give, my vows to pay,
With no reserve and no delay,
  With all my heart I come.

I would live ever in the light,
I would work ever for the right,
I would serve Thee with all my might,
  Therefore, to Thee I come.

Just as I am, young, strong, and free,
To be the best that I can be
For truth and righteousness and Thee,
  Lord of my life, I come. Amen.

—Marianne Farningham, 1887

O JESUS, I HAVE PROMISED

IN THIS hymn, "O Jesus, I have Promised," the words of which were written by John E. Bode in 1868, we have another of those great and challenging hymns of the Church that emphasize the call of Jesus to a life of service.

This hymn has a distinct appeal to young people, and especially to those who have accepted Jesus as their personal Saviour and as their ideal in living the abundant, creative life.

Youth's constant need to feel the spirit of Christ above the clamor of the world's demands is beautifully expressed in the lines of this hymn. There is an ever-present need on the part of young people in every generation to hear the words of the Master clear and strong above the storms of their own passions and self-wills.

This hymn is usually sung to the tune "Angel's Story," composed by Arthur H. Mann in 1883, although it will be found in some hymnals also to a tune composed by J. W. Elliott.

> O Jesus, I have promised
> To serve Thee to the end;
> Be Thou forever near me,
> My Master and my Friend;
> I shall not fear the battle
> If Thou art by my side,
> Nor wander from the pathway,
> If Thou wilt be my Guide.
>
> O let me feel Thee near me;
> The world is ever near.
> I see the sights that dazzle,
> The tempting sounds I hear;
> My foes are ever near me,
> Around me and within;
> But, Jesus, draw Thou nearer,
> And shield my soul from sin.
>
> O let me hear Thee speaking
> In accents clear and still,
> Above the storms of passion,
> The murmurs of self-will.
> O speak to reassure me,
> To hasten or control;
> O speak, and make me listen,
> Thou Guardian of my soul.

O Jesus, Thou hast promised
To all who follow Thee,
That where Thou art in glory
There shall Thy servant be;
And, Jesus, I have promised
To serve Thee to the end;
O give me grace to follow,
My Master and my Friend. Amen.

—John E. Bode, 1868

✠

NOW IN THE DAYS OF YOUTH

THIS great hymn, "Now in the Days of Youth," popular with young people in both England and America, was written by Reverend Walter J. Mathams of London, for use in Christian Endeavor and Sunday school conventions. It was introduced to America by Grace Wilbur Conant in her *Worship and Song,* a well-known Church-school hymnal published by the Pilgrim Press in 1913.

The theme of this hymnal has to do with the dedication of young life, in all its freshness and purity to Jesus, the "White Comrade of the Way." The ancient Old Testament exhortation "Remember also thy Creator in the days of thy Youth" (Ecclesiastes 12:1) is felt throughout the lines of this hymn, as is that other equally familiar New Testament passage from Paul's letter to the Church at Corinth: (I Cor. 16:13) "Watch ye, stand fast in the faith, quit you like men, be strong."

The central thought in the first verse of this hymn is the commitment of one's life to God through Jesus Christ. The second verse expresses the thought of surrender to God's will and of getting one's marching orders from Him. The third stanza embodies the idea of courageous living, and the fourth an appeal to Jesus to impart His spirit, thus insuring "larger years to come."

The tune "Diademata," to which this hymn is most frequently sung, was composed by Sir George Job Elvey in 1868. He was born at Canterbury, England, and educated at Oxford, which college later honored him with the degree of Doctor of Music. He was knighted in 1871 for eminent services to his country, and died in 1893. He was buried just outside the West front of St. George's Chapel at Windsor, England.

Now in the days of youth,
When life flows fresh and free,
Thou, Lord of all our hearts and lives,
We give ourselves to Thee;
Our fervent gift receive,
And fit us to fulfill,
Though all our days, in all our ways,
Our heavenly Father's will.

Teach us where'er we live,
  To act as in Thy sight,
And do what Thou wouldst have us do
  With radiant delight;
Not choosing what is great,
  Nor spurning what is small,
But taking from Thy hands our tasks
  To glorify them all.

Teach us to love the true,
  The beautiful and pure,
And let us not for one short hour
  An evil thought endure.
But give us grace to stand
  Decided, brave and strong,
The lovers of all holy things,
  The foes of all things wrong.

Spirit of Christ, do Thou
  Our first bright days inspire,
That we may live the life of love
  And loftiest desire;
And be by Thee prepared
  For larger years to come;
And for the life ineffable,
  Within the Father's home. Amen.[6]

—*Walter J. Mathams, 1913*

✠

GOD, WHO TOUCHEST EARTH WITH BEAUTY

AMONG the newer hymns that have been written especially for youth, none is more beautiful or makes a greater appeal than this one, "God, Who Touchest Earth with Beauty," written by Mary S. Edgar of Toronto, Canada.

Youth is the "blossom time" of life. At no other time in life does a love of the beautiful make a greater appeal than during the middle and later periods of adolescent maturation. That is the reason, no doubt, why this hymn is so appealing and attractive to young people. Their own natures, newly sensitized by the baptism of power that comes with adolescence, instinctively respond to beauty as they see it reflected in the great natural world about them.

Youth would, indeed, be as beautiful as the flowering earth in springtime, as crystal pure as the waters that trickle down the mountain-side, as glad and free as the merry dancing waves, as lofty in their thoughts and ideals as the

[6] From *Worship and Song,* Winchester and Conant. Published by the Congregational Publishing Society, Boston, Mass. Used with permission of the publishers.

arching skies, as strong and as true as human nature can be when it responds
only to the higher calls of truth and beauty.

In the five brief verses of this hymn youth finds opportunity to express its
own deepest heart-yearnings. This hymn is usually sung to the tune "Geneva,"
written by C. Harold Lowden.

> God, who touchest earth with beauty,
>   Make me lovely, too,
> With Thy Spirit re-create me,
>   Make my heart anew.
>
> Like Thy springs of running waters,
>   Make me crystal pure;
> Like Thy rocks of towering grandeur,
>   Make me strong and sure.
>
> Like Thy dancing waves in sunlight,
>   Make me glad and free;
> Like the straightness of the pine trees,
>   Let me upright be.
>
> Like the arching of the heavens,
>   Lift my thoughts above;
> Turn my dreams to noble action,
>   Ministries of love.
>
> God, who touchest earth with beauty,
>   Make me lovely, too;
> Keep me ever by Thy Spirit,
>   Pure and strong and true. Amen.

—*Mary S. Edgar*

✠

THE PRAYER OF THE QUEST

THIS more or less recent "Prayer-of-the-Quest" challenge to young people was
written by Miss Eleanor B. Stock for the purpose of setting forth especially
the Christian Quest idea, which has been so popular among young people,
and which was first used at the Lake Geneva International Council Camp
Conferences for Older Boys and Girls in 1927. The song was later published
in *Singing Pathways* to the tune "Loeschorn," arranged by Mary Stevens Dickie,
the author of this volume.

The message of this splendidly devotional prayer-song for young people is
that of an intimate personal petition to Jesus, the Friend and Comrade of
youth, to guide them *first* in their quest for *beauty* of body, mind, and soul;

second, in their quest for *knowledge* which will lead them into all truth; and *third,* in their quest for *service* in the spirit and name of their "White Comrade of the Way." The last verse is a sort of climax to the other three in its petition for the guidance of Christ "all along life's far pathways."

The music for this attractive prayer-song for young people will be found in *Singing Pathways,* and also on page 65 of *Worship and Hymns,* published by the Bethany Press, St. Louis, Missouri.

> Take us on the Quest of Beauty,
> Poet Seer of Galilee.
> Making all our dreams creative,
> Through their fellowship with Thee.
>
> Take us on the Quest of Knowledge
> Clearest Thinker man has known!
> Make our minds sincere and patient,
> Satisfied by Truth alone.
>
> Take us on the Quest of Service,
> Kingly Servant of man's need,
> Let us work with Thee for others,
> Anywhere Thy purpose leads.
>
> All along our Quest's far pathways,
> Christ our Leader and our guide,
> Make us conscious of Thy presence,
> Walking always at our side.[7]

—Eleanor B. Stock

✠

HAVE THINE OWN WAY, LORD

"Have Thine Own Way, Lord," is one of the older, devotional hymns of the Church; but its message never fails to be a challenge alike to young people and adults, probably because it is intimate and personal in its appeal.

Three types of hymns seem to appeal in a peculiar way to young people; (1) those that express an intimate, personal relationship with Christ; (2) those that have a social message, such as "Stand Up, Stand Up, for Jesus" or "Jesus Calls Us"; and (3) those that express the idea of the lure of the far-away. Under this latter classification come nearly all the great missionary hymns of the Church.

[7] Arrangement copyrighted in 1929 in *Singing Pathways,* by Mary Stevens Dickie. Powell & White, Edwards Bldg., Cincinnati, Ohio, publishers. Used by permission of E. B. Stock and M. S. Dickie.

This one, "Have Thine Own Way, Lord," is decidedly individualistic in its appeal. It is in the nature of a prayer to the Master to "take our wills and make them Thine." It recognizes the struggle that all of us have to make to bring our will under subjection to the will of God for our lives; and as a result it voices a heartfelt need in the life of every true follower of the Christ of Galilee.

Have Thine own way, Lord!
　Have Thine own way!
Thou art the Potter;
　I am the clay.
Mold me and make me
　After Thy will,
While I am waiting,
　Yielded and still.

Have Thine own way, Lord!
　Have Thine own way!
Search me and try me,
　Master, today!
Whiter than snow, Lord,
　Wash me just now,
As in Thy presence
　Humbly I bow.

Have Thine own way, Lord!
　Have Thine own way!
Wounded and weary,
　Help me, I pray!
Power—all power—
　Surely is Thine!
Touch me and heal me,
　Saviour divine!

Have Thine own way, Lord!
　Have Thine own way!
Hold o'er my being
　Absolute sway!
Fill with Thy Spirit
　Till all shall see
Christ only, always,
　Living in me! Amen.

—Anonymous

O JESUS, YOUTH OF NAZARETH

AMONG the newer and more modern hymns which the young people of today are learning to sing with real devotion and appreciation is this one, "O Jesus, Youth of Nazareth," by Ferdinand Q. Blanchard, former minister of the Euclid Avenue Congregational Church, Cleveland, Ohio.

According to Mr. Blanchard there was no unusual incident attending his writing of this poetic hymn, other than a desire one Christmastime for a new hymn that would express something more than the conventional delight of the angels and wise men over the coming of the "Child of Lowly Manger Birth." For this hymn was originally written as a Christmas hymn, although the first stanza which definitely connects it with the birthday of the King of Kings is usually omitted.

Since the other four verses express the ever-present and all-the-year-round longing in the heart of Christian youth, Mr. H. Augustine Smith, in including it in his *New Hymnal for American Youth,* asked permission to omit the first verse, thereby making this hymn suitable for use at all times.

It is usually sung to a tune composed by George W. Chadwick in 1888.

> O Jesus, youth of Nazareth,
>   Preparing for the bitter strife,
> Wilt Thou impart to every heart,
>   Thy perfect purity of life?
>
> O Christ, whose words make dear the fields
>   And hillsides green of Galilee,
> Grant us to find, with reverent mind,
>   The truth Thou saidst should make us free.
>
> O suffering Lord on Calvary,
>   Whom love led on to mortal pain,
> We know Thy cross is not a loss
>   If we Thy love shall truly gain.
>
> O Master of Abundant Life,
>   From natal morn to victory's hour,
> We look to Thee; heed Thou our plea;
>   Teach us to share Thy ageless power.[8]

—Ferdinand Q. Blanchard, 1906

[8] Used with permission of the author and publisher.

I KNOW NOT HOW THAT BETHLEHEM'S BABE

THIS Harvard Prize hymn, written by Harry Webb Farrington, is one of the finest of all the hymns of today. Speaking of the occasion which inspired the writing of it Dr. Farrington says: "As a first-year graduate at Harvard in 1910, I entered the competition for the prize Christmas hymn. My words were so simple that I hesitated to submit them. To my surprise they were awarded the prize, and afterward Professor George Herbert Palmer spoke of it as 'a perfect poem.'"

It took Dr. Farrington only thirty minutes to write it. The words came to him from the deep well of his boyhood experience of conversion, when as a lad of eleven he knelt at the altar in sincere and tearful repentance in an old-fashioned revival service in the Methodist church at Darlington, Maryland.

Carl Price, the eminent critic and hymn-writer, named this hymn, "I Know Not How That Bethlehem's Babe," as one of the ten great hymns of the last hundred years. Others have pointed out the fact that it is a perfect Christology, presenting as it does in three brief verses the *incarnation, atonement,* and *resurrection* of Jesus.

John N. Burnham, the blind organist of the Epiphany Lutheran Church of New York City, composed the tune, appropriately called "Veritas." This hymn has been translated into many languages.

> I know not how that Bethlehem's Babe
> Could in the Godhead be;
> I only know the Manger Child
> Has brought God's life to me.
>
> I know not how that Calvary's Cross
> A world from sin could free;
> I only know its matchless love
> Has brought God's love to me.
>
> I know not how that Joseph's tomb
> Could solve death's mystery;
> I only know a living Christ,
> Our immortality.[9]

> *—Harry Webb Farrington, 1910*

[9] From *Valleys and Visions.* Copyright by Harry Webb Farrington. Used by permission of Mrs. Harry Webb Farrington.

O BEAUTIFUL FOR SPACIOUS SKIES

"O BEAUTIFUL for Spacious Skies" was written in its original form at Colorado Springs, Colorado, during the summer of 1893, while Miss Bates was teaching in a summer school there. On her way out she had visited the Chicago World's Fair, where she was greatly impressed by the symbolic beauty of the White City. She spent three weeks or more under the purple range of the Rockies and enjoyed many trips to Pike's Peak and other scenic points of interest. When she left Colorado the four stanzas were penciled in her notebook, together with other memoranda in verse and prose of the trip.

No further attention was paid to those verses until during the second summer following, when they were copied and sent to *The Congregationalist,* where they first appeared July 4, 1895. The hymn attracted an unusual amount of attention and was almost at once set to music by the eminent composer, Silas G. Pratt, and republished in his *Famous Songs.*

After several years, during which time this hymn had run the gauntlet of criticism, Katherine Lee Bates changed the wording of the opening quatrain to the third stanza. A copyright of this revised version was obtained, not from the motive of money-making, but to protect it from misprints and conscious alterations. It has been sung to a great many tunes, the one most generally accepted being "Materna," composed by Samuel A. Ward in 1882.

This great hymn, perhaps the most beautiful of all those that emphasize our country's heritage, has gone into reform schools and prisons, settlements, men's clubs, the councils of the Boy Scouts and Girl Scouts; the Jewish Women's Council, and rites of the Camp Fire Girls. The Australian Christian Endeavorers have adopted it, substituting the word "Australia" for "America" and setting it to music of their own. It is sung in Canada with the refrain "O Canada"; and in Mexico with the refrain "Mi Mejico."

This hymn is especially suitable for community singing, for Memorial Day, Washington's birthday, Lincoln's birthday, Fourth of July, patriotic mass meetings, and school-day flag-raisings. The Young Men's Christian Association, the Young Women's Christian Association, as well as missionaries of all Protestant churches, have carried it to the ends of the earth.

Miss Bates said: "That this hymn has gained, in less than twenty years, such a hold as it has upon our people, is clearly due to the fact that Americans are at heart idealists, with a fundamental faith in human brotherhood."

> O beautiful for spacious skies,
>   For amber waves of grain,
> For purple mountain majesties
>   Above the fruited plain!
>   America! America!
>   God shed His grace on thee

And crown thy good with brotherhood
From sea to shining sea!

O beautiful for pilgrim feet,
Whose stern, impassioned stress
A thoroughfare for freedom beat
Across the wilderness!
America! America!
God mend thine every flaw,
Confirm Thy soul in self-control,
Thy liberty in law!

O beautiful for heroes proved
In liberating strife,
Who more than self their country loved,
And mercy more than life!
America! America!
May God thy gold refine
Till all success be nobleness
And every gain divine!

O beautiful for patriot dream
That sees beyond the years
Thine alabaster cities gleam
Undimmed by human tears!
America! America!
God shed His grace on thee
And crown thy good with brotherhood
From sea to shining sea.[10]

—Katharine Lee Bates, 1893, 1904

[10] Words copyrighted by the estate of Katharine Lee Bates. Used by permission.

CONTENTS

PART VI   SECTION VI

IN THE FELLOWSHIP OF PRAYER

--✠--

"My house shall be called a house of prayer."—MATTHEW 21:13

--✠--

✛

IN THE FELLOWSHIP OF PRAYER

"And Jesus entered into the temple of God, and cast out all them that sold and bought in the temple, and overthrew the tables of the money-changers, and the seats of them that sold the doves; and he saith unto them, It is written, My house shall be called a house of prayer: but ye make it a den of robbers."—MATTHEW 21:12-13

✛

"And when ye pray, ye shall not be as the hypocrites: for they love to stand and pray in the synagogues and in the corners of the streets, that they may be seen of men. Verily I say unto you, they have received their reward. But thou, when thou prayest, enter into thine inner chamber, and having shut thy door, pray to thy Father who is in secret, and thy Father who seeth in secret shall recompense thee. And in praying use not vain repetitions, as the Gentiles do: for they think that they shall be heard for their much speaking. Be not therefore like unto them: for your Father knoweth what things ye have need of, before ye ask him."—MATTHEW 6:5-8

✛

"I exhort therefore, first of all, that supplications, prayers, intercessions, thanksgivings, be made for all men; for kings and all that are in high place; that we may lead a tranquil and quiet life in all godliness and gravity."—I TIMOTHY 2:1-2

✛

"Pray without ceasing; in everything give thanks: for this is the will of God in Christ Jesus to you-ward."—I THESSALONIANS 5:17-18

CHRIST IN GETHSEMANE

By

Hermann Clementz

(Interpretation)

THAT which Matthew set forth in the words, "He went a little further, and fell on his face, and prayed, saying, O my Father, if it be possible, let this cup pass from me: nevertheless, not as I will, but as thou wilt," Hermann Clementz, the German artist, has attempted to set forth in paint on canvas. Before such a scene one is silent. The soul is hushed in the presence of this cry of suffering. A mystery broods over this midnight scene in the Master's life. Those who have been called to enter some such Garden of Gethsemane and there have fallen under the crushing weight of some unbearable woe find fellowship in this picture that others cannot appreciate.

Let us withdraw into the shadows and consider its meaning. Let us meditate, not upon its message of sorrowing, but on its call to heroic service. Back of every supreme achievement is a supreme endeavor. Great achievements are wrought by those who have the capacity, the patience, the courage, to go a "little further" than anyone else has yet ventured.

In this picture our Divine Master goes a "little further" in rendering the supremest endeavor in the supremest realm in the accomplishment of the world's supremest achievement—the expressing of God's personality in human character.

Just as the toilers who have it in their hearts to render a surpassing service find themselves gradually separated from the multitude, so Christ in His desire to redeem the world leaves the crowds that throng Him on every side, leaves the Temple area with its worshipers, leaves the city streets with their traffic and travelers, leaves the group that followed Him with confidence, leaves the daylight where eyes peer and curiosity is awake—leaves all, that He may, with the chosen few, take a path from the city gate, across a brook, into a garden where silence broods and the stars alone keep vigil. Then leaving even this group of His intimates, He goes forward with the three who knew Him best, but who are also soon left as He, Himself, "went a little further"— falling on His face, crushed with the world's woe, heartbroken for humanity's sin, *alone, alone,* crying out: "If it be possible. . . . Yet not *my will,* but THINE be done!"

Many had wrought works of righteousness for the world's redemption before Christ came. The vision of God's holiness and purity had flashed before one generation after another. Moses had seen the glory, and came from Sinai as an interpreter of the moral law. Prophets again and again gave utterance to the high ideals of a *spiritual kingdom*. Martyrs to the truth had died, seeing its triumph afar off.

But there was needed some one who in this spiritual realm of moral integrity was able to go "a little further"—further than the lawgiver, than the prophet, than the martyr, than the philosopher, than the priest, than the king. There was needed a SAVIOUR who, in the supremest offering of Himself, in a sacrifice unlike that which man could offer, would lift the standard of character to its highest pinnacle; One who, being the brightness of God's glory, the express image of the Divine, nevertheless would stoop so low as to get His fingers under the bottom of the world's *sin* and *misery,* and lift that burden so high that it was placed penitent and believing at the feet of God.

The constant challenge of "Christ in Gethsemane" to every follower of the lowly Nazarene is to "go a little further." Crowd close to the Master. Go a little further in your devotion to Him. Get under the interests of His spiritual Kingdom of Love with all of your resources. Go a little further in your loyalty, a little further in prayer, a little further in church-attendance, a little further in coöperation, a little further in helping people to actualize in their own lives Christ's Kingdom of Love.

The chief point in Clementz' picture is the emphasis it lays on the loneliness of Jesus. "The first law of all heroism is the courage to go on when others are left behind." The artist wisely has given to his Hero a regal aspect as of an uncrowned King, for so He was. The light about His head is the artist's way of saying what Luke says, that an angel from Heaven strengthened Him. It was His filial trust and His knowledge of His father's approval, which never deserted Him through it all. With His Father's approval of His heroic struggle, He came out from the olive grove "well content with death and shame," and walketh henceforth through His remaining passion with the mien of a conqueror.

The sight of this solitary sufferer in Gethsemane has been and will continue to be, as long as art remains, one of the mightiest redemptive forces in human life. It made sin seem a new thing. The sin that caused such suffering could not henceforth be looked upon lightly. Gethsemane is the best corrective of the theory that sin is only "involuntary error." Men became conscious of sin as never before, when they looked at it through the eyes of the stainless Christ. Such a sight supplies the strongest motive to keep men from sin. Show a man the suffering that his sin imposes on an innocent wife or child, and this motive operates, when all others have failed.

Gethsemane is a challenge to all men to be heroic. The trial question it puts to every man is whether he will follow Jesus in His Gethsemane. "You cannot," says Ruskin, "save men from death but by facing it for them; nor from sin by resisting it for them. That is the final doctrine, the inevitable one, not of Christianity only, but of all heroic faith; and the first trial question of a true soul to itself must always be—Have I a religion, have I a country, have I a love that I am ready to die for?"

Jesus left eight of His disciples at the outer gate of the olive garden. A little

CHRIST IN GETHSEMANE—*CLEMENTZ*

later He parted from Peter, James, and John also. He is left alone. Who can follow in His train?

When Charles Kingsley was *hissed at* in a workingman's meeting by those to whom his heart went out, he burst into tears. Then he tramped off twenty miles through the night, and at daybreak wrote his poem, "The Three Fishers." That was Kingsley's Gethsemane. No man can understand Jesus in the olive garden, and, like Jesus, no man can be a hero or a Saviour until he has a Gethsemane of his own.[1]

·   ·   ·   ·   ·

"To stand, with a smile upon your face, against a stake from which you cannot get away—that, no doubt, is heroic. True glory is resignation to the inevitable. But to stand *unchained,* with perfect liberty to go away, held only by the higher claims of love and duty, and let the fire creep up to the heart— that is heroism."—F. W. ROBERTSON.

·   ·   ·   ·   ·

"The so-called heroes of this world have conquered by the shedding of other men's blood; but this man [Christ] by the shedding of His own." H. B. RIDGEWAY.

✛

PRAYING HANDS

By

Albrecht (Albert) Dürer

(Interpretation)

ALBRECHT DÜRER, the artist, who painted "Praying Hands," was the son of a Hungarian goldsmith who was born in Nuremburg, Germany. He was obliged to work at his father's trade while he was a young boy, because of a very large family and lack of money. Always he wanted to draw and paint. Finally he was allowed to leave home and to go away and study with a great artist. Because he was very poor, it was hard for him to study and make a living at the same time. During these days of struggle Albrecht (Albert) Dürer found a friend, a man somewhat older than himself, who also had a desire to become a great artist. The two of them decided to live together, and one day when the struggle to earn enough food had discouraged both of them almost to the point of giving up their dreams, Albert's friend made a suggestion.

"This way of working and trying to study," he said, "is intolerable. We

---

[1] Adapted from *Pictures That Preach,* by Charles Nelson Page. Copyright, 1924. Used by permission of the Abingdon Press.

are neither making a living nor are we mastering our art. Let us try another way. One of us could make the living for us both while the other continues to study. Then when the paintings begin to sell, the one who has worked may have his chance."

"True," answered Albert, thoughtfully, "but let me be the one to work."

"No, I must be the one to work, because I have already a place to work in the restaurant. I am older, and I have not so much talent. You must not waste your years. Let it be as I say."

So the older man had his way. Albert Dürer worked faithfully to master his art while his friend worked at any kind of labor he could find to buy them food and to pay for their mean little room. He served in the restaurant, washing dishes, and scrubbing floors to add to the small sum he was paid. His hours were long and the work was menial and hard, but he did it cheerfully because he was helping his young friend and looking forward to the time when he would be able to use his brush again.

At last the day came when Albert Dürer came home bringing the money which he had received for the sale of a wood-carving. It was sufficient to buy food and to pay their rent for a considerable length of time.

"Now," he said, "the time has come when I will be the breadwinner, and you shall go to your paints, my good friend. You need no longer work, but I will care for both of us."

So his good friend left his serving and dish-washing and scrubbing, and took up his brush. But something had happened in those days during which he had worked so hard with his hands. The hard work had stiffened his muscles, enlarged his joints, and twisted his fingers so that they could no longer hold the brush with mastery and skill. He worked long and hard, only to find that his art would have to be sacrificed forever.

When Albert learned what had happened to his friend, he was filled with a great sorrow. Of course he would always care for him and give him a friend's love, but he could not give him back his skill. One day Albert returned to his room unexpectedly and heard the voice of his friend in prayer. He entered softly, and seeing the work-worn hands folded reverently, a great thought came to him.

"I can never give back the lost skill of those hands," he thought; "but I can show the world the feeling of love and gratitude which is in my heart for his noble deed. I will paint his hands as they are *now*, folded in prayer, and the world shall know my appreciation for a noble, unselfish character. It may be that when people look at the picture they will remember with love and devotion all hands that toil for others and like me express in some beautiful way their appreciation for such beautiful service."

As we look at the picture I think we can read the story. Look at these toil-worn hands. You can see evidences of the hard labor that earned the living for both artists. Notice the broken finger nails and the enlarged joints. Yet in spite of these disfigurements, are they not beautiful hands? Let us think silently of other toil-worn hands the world around that have labored to make things

PRAYING HANDS—*DURER*

THE OMNIPRESENT—ROSENKRANZ

easier for others as we look at Dürer's picture of "Praying Hands," and try to feel as the artist must have felt when he decided to paint the hands of his friend at prayer.[2]

✠

THE OMNIPRESENT

"O, GOD, OUR HELP IN AGES PAST"

By

Arild Rosenkranz

(Interpretation)

DURING the summer of 1935, it was the privilege of the compiler of this anthology on *Christ and the Fine Arts* to both recruit and dean the Youth Sessions of the Second World Convention of the Churches of Christ, which convention was held in DeMontfort Hall, Leicester, England.

Following that rich and compensating experience a group of sixteen convention delegates enjoyed a motor-bus trip through the British Isles. It was known as the Cathedral-Castle tour, and included stops at most of the great cathedrals and castle cities, particularly of England and Scotland.

Among the many places visited was the ancient city of Chester in Northwest England, one of the oldest and earliest cradles of Christianity in the British Isles. The present cathedral is perhaps the third or fourth building to occupy this site, and even its structure dates back to the ninth or tenth century. In early English history Chester was a walled city, and portions of the old Roman wall, in an excellent state of preservation, may yet be seen along the side and rear of the cathedral.

In this quaint old cathedral at Chester it was the author's privilege to see, for the first time, a large, colored picture of "The Omnipresent," by Arild Rosenkranz. It was framed on an inclined standard in the center aisle of the great cathedral, about a third of the way from the rear entrance to the steps of the Angel Choir; and in such a position that the glowing rays of the dying sun cast a brilliantly beautiful light on it through the large rose window over the west entrance of the cathedral.

One of our party asked the significance of this picture, and Bishop Frank Selwyn Macaulay Bennett, who personally conducted us through the great cathedral, replied: "Well, that picture means many things to many people, but it certainly says to every devout follower of Christ what Jesus in the long

---

[2] Adapted from "Praying Hands," *Christian Worship for American Youth*, by Laura Armstrong Athearn. Published by the Century Company, New York City. Used with special permission of the publishers.

ago once said to His disciples: 'God is Spirit, and they that worship Him must worship Him in spirit and truth.'"

To really appreciate to the fullest the beauty and meaning of this great masterpiece of religious art it must be seen in colors. It is evident, however, that the artist is trying to say to us that it doesn't make any difference where one is—in God's house, out in the open overlooking a great ravine as are these men, in the home, or in the busy marts of business and industry—wherever Christ's followers may be, if they are *in the spirit,* they may consciously pour out the deepest needs of their hearts to God in prayer; and He will hear, and in His own good time and way answer them.

Some one has indicated that this great painting emphasizes three attitudes of prayer typical of men in all ages. The man on the extreme left, his hands open and upraised to God in prayer, typifies the person that finds access to God through communion of spirit with Spirit, easy, spontaneous, and natural. The second man, his head bowed and his hand slightly raised, represents that vast majority of the followers of Christ who are conscious that they do not follow very close or very well. They seek the guidance of the Divine Will occasionally and usually when they have made a mess of things by following the dictates of their own unguided wills. The third man, kneeling at the extreme right of the picture, his head bowed in deep contrition as the weight of his own unworthiness overwhelms him, typifies the man or woman who has never really found God through conscious obedience to and fellowship with Christ. He, too, in the tragic hours of need, like the publican Jesus referred to, "Will not even so much as lift up his eyes to heaven," but prostrates himself upon the ground as he raises his voice in petition for release from the weight of his self-imposed burden.

For it is a well known fact that all men pray, believers and non-believers alike, in times of emergency. Christians ought to pray habitually; and if they pray *in the spirit* as did Jesus, seeking not their own will, but to discover the will of God for their lives, they, too, will find it increasingly easier, as the years go by, to harmonize their wills with the will of their Heavenly Father.

In this great painting the artist is trying to tell us that God is "omnipresent," always present everywhere. He is in His world in spirit to be contemplated and understood by the children of men of every race and class, the world around, as in reverence and true humility we seek to "worship [worthship] Him in spirit and in truth."

CHRIST CLEANSING THE TEMPLE—*KIRCHBACK*

CHRIST CLEANSING THE TEMPLE

By

J. Frank Kirchback

(Interpretation)

IN THIS painting of "Christ Cleansing the Temple" by the English painter, J. Frank Kirchback, we have a vivid portrayal of one of the rare incidents in the life of Jesus when His righteous indignation flamed into active anger.

According to the Mosaic law, every Jewish pilgrim to the Holy City, save women, slaves, and children, must pay into the Temple treasury at Jerusalem, as Temple dues, a half-shekel or Galilean shekel (equal to about one shilling and twopence). Inasmuch as these Jewish pilgrims came from all lands, they naturally brought with them the money used in the land from which they came. This foreign money nearly always had carved on it the heads of kings or emperors, gods and goddesses; and was classified by the priests under the head of graven images, which made the offering of it, of course, a violation of the Second Commandment. Such coin could not be used as Temple dues or for the purchase of sacrifices to be used in the Holy Place.

For the service of changing these foreign coins into Galilean shekels, the money-changers not only charged a fee of about twenty per cent of the coin's value, but often an additional amount if these foreign coins were worn or not of full weight. These over-charged pilgrims would refuse, often with oaths, to be thus robbed, so that around the tables of the money-changers there arose constantly the noise of shrill voices bickering, disputing, and arguing, sometime even swearing in the very precincts of the Holy Place where the Jews believed the presence of Jehovah resided.

In the days preceding the Passover feast these money-changers often made a profit of between eight and nine thousand pounds in exchange on Temple dues alone. Most of it was wrung from hard-working men and peasant people; and all in the name of the worship of Jehovah. These travel-stained pilgrims were often exasperated to the point of fury, but were powerless to defend themselves against the system of graft that the high priest, the merchants and money-changers, had built up.

The Greek mason, the small farmer from Cyprus, and the lawyer from Alexandria were often unable to bring with them the lamb or doves needful for the Temple sacrifice, which meant that they must buy them in the Temple court of the Gentiles. To avoid endless wrangling with these dove and sheep merchants because of their foreign money, they must first change still more of it into shekels, thus making it possible for the money-changers to make an even greater profit. It was not uncommon practice to charge these foreign pilgrims as much as fifteen shillings for two doves, whose price in the open market was a silver denarius (or about twopence). And if they did not buy of the Temple merchants, whose sheep and doves had already been examined by the priest, their sacrifice, which must be without spot or blemish, would not be accepted at the altar. Thus the Temple merchants had a practical monopoly on the sale of doves and lambs and worked hand in hand with the priests and money-changers in the system of Temple graft.

It was into some such scene as this that Jesus came, four days before the Passover feast. A wave of pity and wrath swept through Him as He saw poor people being robbed at the very time they were coming to pay their vows to God—pity for these simple, honest pilgrims, who with the sweat of many a hard day's work had earned the money needful for this annual pilgrimage to the city of their God; and wrath over the injustices of these swindlers who, under the cloak of the sale of sacrifices to the living God, virtually stole money from the people.

No less than a hundred thousand animals were sold in a single week for the sacrifices of these pilgrims who came from all parts of the world. So that in Jesus' time the sacrifice to the worship of Jehovah, who had said "I will have justice and mercy," had grown into a colossal graft system, at the expense of the poor, in the very Temple courts around the Holy of Holies.

These booths of the money-changers and sacrifice merchants were often referred to as the Booths of the Sons of Annas; for Annas, the High Priest, in his princely palace on the hill, and Caiaphas, his son-in-law in his palatial home, literally raked in millions of shekels as controllers of the Temple market. The avarice and corruption, the licentious luxury, gluttony and oppression of the High Priest and his family, were bywords among the people.

As a lad Jesus had seen His own father laboring in the carpenter's shop, His friends driving the plow, His mother patching clothes and stinting food at home that they might save first one denarius then another until the Galilean shekel was bought and put away for the Temple dues. All this robbery of the people in the name of Jehovah, the just and merciful, and in His Holy Temple rose up before Jesus as He strode into the Temple court. The hour had come to cleanse this place from such merchants and money-changers.

Stooping, He picked up stray pieces of cord that the merchants had dropped and twisted them swiftly into a whipcord; as He cried out across the marble courtyard: "Away with you. This is My Father's House. It is written: 'My house shall be called a House of Prayer; but you have made it a den of robbers.' With swift passion He gripped a money-changer's table and sent it whirling into space. The money went clanging across the marble stones. Panic seized the other money-changers and merchants in the presence of His righteous fury. Other tables were overturned by these swindlers fleeing from such a demonstration of righteous wrath as the Temple courts had never before witnessed. Even the animals and their drovers took flight into the open court beyond. Meanwhile the pilgrim multitude shouted with joy at the courage of this one man putting to flight the grafters who had fleeced them.

The Temple authorities in the right foreground of this picture are furious;

but they know that it is dangerous to attempt to lay hands on this Prophet of the people. Their fingers itch to destroy Jesus, but for the present, at least, they must bide their time in silence.

Such is the scene that the English artist, Kirchback, has portrayed for us so strikingly in his "Christ Cleansing the Temple." It is indeed a masterpiece in lights, shadows, and contrasts—a study of reverence on the part of the devout; in admiration on the part of the less courageous; and of hate and envy on the part of those who had made of His Father's house "a den of robbers."

This robbery of the poor in the very name of Jehovah was more than Christ's sense of justice and righteousness could endure; and before the white heat of His anger those enmeshed in this system of religious graft fled in terrifying fear.

✢

THE CHRISTUS

By

Bertel Thorvaldsen

(Interpretation)

This magnificently beautiful statue, "The Christus," by the Danish sculptor Bertel Thorvaldsen, is re-created in marble in the Court of the Christus in Forest Lawn Memorial-Park in Glendale, California. Thorvaldsen lived more than one hundred years ago, and the original statue is in the Church of Our Lady in Copenhagen, Denmark.

Christians throughout the world offer their prayers to Christ, God's Only Begotten Son, who loved each one of us so much that he died that we, through him, might have everlasting life. That is why so many artists and sculptors have chosen Christ as the subject of their works.

On the face of "The Christus" one sees the love and mercy of Jesus of Nazareth as he appeared to his Apostles after his resurrection from the dead, with the simple greeting: "Peace be with you."

This masterpiece is a fitting re-creation for the Court of the Christus, a place of meditation and prayer. In front of the majestic sculptured figure is a prayer bench where all who will may kneel and voice their own prayer of thanksgiving for the gift of God's Only Begotten Son, and his redeeming contribution to the children of men.

With both arms extended, "The Christus" invites all who are troubled and tired and distraught to "come unto me" that they may find peace, and rest, and release from the stresses of present-day problems and living. With the unknown poet, their hearts sing:

THE CHRISTUS—*THORVALDSEN*

He rose!
And with him hope arose, and life and light,
Men said, "Not Christ, but Death, died yesternight."
And joy and truth and all things virtuous
Rose when He rose.

✠

PRAYER

Prayer is like a spirit
  Hovering near our heart
With its joy upsoaring,
  Soothing every dart.

Prayer is like a sunset
  Which impels the eye,
Opening such vastness
  That we outward fly.

Prayer is like a mountain
  Towering and steep—
Only by hard climbing
  May our vision sweep.

Prayer is like the ocean,
  Fathomless to sound,
But yields to patient searching
  Of its depths profound.

Prayer is like a painting
  Grand in line and hue—
Before it long we linger
  Import to construe.

Prayer is like sweet music
  Faint, then crashing near,
Swelling into meaning
  To the yearning ear.

Prayer is life and motion
  Catching step with God—
Weaving mighty patterns
  On our earthly sod.

—Sarah Ashby Heassler

MY FOURFOLD PRAYER

For the gift of strength and health
And for friendship's boundless wealth,
For the power to think aright,
And for religion's guiding light—
  We give Thee thanks.

—Anonymous

PROOF

If radio's slim fingers
  Can pluck a melody
From night, and toss it over
  A continent or sea;

If the petaled white notes
  Of a violin
Are blown across a mountain
  Or a city's din;

If songs, like crimson roses,
  Are culled from the thin blue air—
Why should mortals wonder
  If God hears prayer?

—Ethel Romig Fuller

PRAYER

I asked for bread; God gave a stone instead.
Yet, while I pillowed there my weary head,
The angels made a ladder of my dreams,
Which upward to celestial mountains led.
And when I woke beneath the morning's beams,
Around my resting-place fresh manna lay;
And, praising God, I went upon my way.
  For I was fed.

God answers prayer; sometimes, when hearts are weak,
He gives the very gifts believers seek.
But often faith must learn a deeper rest,
And trust God's silence when He does not speak;
For He whose name is Love will send the best.
Stars may burn out, nor mountain walls endure.
But God is true, His promises are sure
  For those who seek.

—Author Unknown

TALKING WITH GOD

More things are wrought by prayer
Than this world dreams of. Wherefore, let thy voice
Rise like a fountain for me night and day.

For what are men better than sheep or goats
That nourish a blind life within the brain,
If, knowing God, they lift not hands in prayer
Both for themselves, and those who call them friend?
For so the whole round earth is every way
Bound by gold chains about the feet of God.[3]

—Alfred Tennyson

CLEAN HANDS, CLEAN WORDS, CLEAN THOUGHTS

O God, our Father, give me clean hands, clean words, clean thoughts;
Help me to stand for the hard right against the easy wrong;
Save me from habits that harm;
Teach me to work as hard, and play as fair in Thy sight alone as if all the
world saw;
Forgive me when I am unkind; and help me to forgive others who are unkind
to me;
Keep me ready to help others at some cost to myself;
Send me some chances to do a little good every day, and to grow more like
Christ. Amen.

—William DeWitt Hyde

PRAYERS BY TOYOHIKO KAGAWA

I

I want to be ever a child
I want to feel an eternal friendship
 for the raindrops, the flowers,
 the insects, the snowflakes.
I want to be keenly interested in everything,
 with mind and muscle ever alert, forgetting my troubles in the next moment.
The stars and the sea, the ponds and the trees,
 the birds and the animals, are my comrades.
Though my muscles may stiffen, though my skin may
 wrinkle, may I never find myself yawning
 at life.

II

Take Thou the burden, Lord;
I am exhausted with this heavy load.
 My tired hands tremble,
 And I stumble, stumble,
 Along the way.
Oh, lead with Thine unfailing arm
 Again today.

[3] From *The Idylls of the King.*

Unless Thou hold me, Lord,
The road I journey on is all too hard;
Through trust in Thee alone
Can I go on.

Not for self thus do I groan;
My country is the load I bear.
Lord, hear my prayer:
Make Thy strong hand
Strike off the chains of my loved land.
God, draw her close to Thee![4]

—trans. by Lois Erickson

A PRAYER

Give me work to do;
Give me health;
Give me joy in simple things.
Give me an eye for beauty,
A tongue for truth,
A heart that loves,
A mind that reasons,
A sympathy that understands;
Give me neither malice nor envy,
But a true kindness
And a noble common sense.
At the close of each day
Give me a book,
And a friend with whom
I can be silent.

—Author Unknown

AN EVENING PRAYER

If I have wounded any soul today,
If I have caused one foot to go astray,
If I have walked in my own willful way—
    Dear Lord, forgive!

If I have uttered idle words or vain,
If I have turned aside from want or pain
Lest I, myself, should suffer through the strain—
    Dear Lord, forgive!

[4] From *Songs from the Slums,* Kagawa. Copyright, 1935. Published by Cokesbury Press, Nashville, Tenn. Used by permission of the author and publishers.

If I have craved for joys that are not mine,
If I have let my wayward heart repine,
Dwelling on things on earth, not things divine—
    Dear Lord, forgive!

Forgive the sins I have confessed to Thee;
Forgive the secret sins I do not see;
For which I know not, Father, teach Thou me—
    Help me to live.

—G. Maude Battersby

A MORNING PRAYER

Let me this morning do something that shall take
    A little sadness from the world's vast store,
And may I be so favored as to make
    Of joy's too scanty sum a little more.
Let me not hurt, by any selfish deed
    Or thoughtless word, the heart of foe or friend;
Nor would I pass, unseeing, worthy need,
    Or sin by silence when I should defend.
However meager be my worldly wealth,
    Let me give something that shall aid my kind—
A word of courage, or a thought of health,
    Dropped as I pass for troubled hearts to find.
Let me tonight look back across the span
    'Twixt dawn and dark, and to my conscience say—
Because of some good act to beast or man—
    "The world is better that I lived today."[5]

—Ella Wheeler Wilcox

HE PRAYED

He prayed for strength that he might achieve;
He was made weak that he might obey.
He prayed for health that he might do great things;
He was given infirmity that he might do better things.
He prayed for riches that he might be happy;
He was given poverty that he might be wise.
He prayed for power that he might have the praise of men;
He was given weakness that he might feel the need of God.
He prayed for all things that he might enjoy life;

[5] From *Poems of Power*, Wilcox. Published by W. B. Conkey Company, Chicago, Ill. Used by permission of the publishers.

He was given life that he might enjoy all things.
He had received nothing that he asked for—all that he hoped for;
His prayer was answered—he was most blessed.

—Author Unknown

PRAYING HANDS

Those praying hands! What saint of old didst raise
In some far, dim-lit cell, those hands in prayer,
With uplift face in solemn vesper hour?
No soul of feeble spirit could these claim
For writ upon their lines is strength indeed;
And love of art and beauty is portrayed
In grace of slender fingers that are held
So reverently together as they pray.
A saintly monk's, these praying hands may be,
Kneeling in dawning light the bare gray stones
Upon—in ancient monastery,
Pouring with fervent heart his matins forth,
Thereby refreshment gaining for his soul.

But, ah! Those hands! Those praying hands do speak
So much that stirs my heart, that I could think
They are the very hands of Christ Himself.
Can we not see their gentleness as they
On heads of little children soft were laid?
Their strength as clasping hand of friend
They sent Love's thought pulsating to His heart?
And reaching out to cleanse and heal and bless,
They found in service here their purest joy?
Did He not lift them even so to God
When in Gethsemane alone He prayed?
Cannot we read in them the strain that brought
Those drops of sweat upon His suffering brow?

O praying hands! I kneel here—for they call
My soul to worship in so strange a way
That I can only see them as Thy hands
And where the cruel nails pierce them through.

O Lord, teach us to pray as Thou didst pray,
And only let us go when we have learned.[6]

—Gertrude B. Walker

[6] From "The Churchman Afield," *Boston Saturday Transcript.* Used by permission.

A ROAD PRAYER-SONG

These to be thankful for: a friend,
A work to do, a way to wend,
And these in which to take delight;
The wind that turns the poplars white,

Wonder and gleam of common things,
Sunlight upon a sea gull's wings,
Odors of earth and dew-drenched lawns,
The pageantry of darks and dawns;

Blue vistas of a city street
At twilight, music, passing feet,
The thrill of spring, half joy, half pain,
The deep voice of the autumn rain.

Shall we not be content with these
Imperishable mysteries?
And jocund-hearted take our share
Of joy and pain and find life fair?

Wayfarers on a road where we
Set forth each day right valiantly,
Expectant, dauntless, blithe, content,
To make the great experiment.

—Author Unknown

MY PRAYER

In the clear morning
I have climbed the hill.

Smoke from the factories
Rolls west to east
Across the huge red sun.

A train puffs past
Through tiny, far-off fields.

Bright buds are everywhere.
  God of the hills,
  The smoke,
  The sun,
  The growing grain,
I cannot word my prayer.

God . . . green things . . .
Green things . . . God . . .
Lord of each little leaf
  On every tree
Lord of the clouds that drift
  Far out to sea,
  I thank Thee
That Thou hast shown
  Jesus
  To me.

God,
I pray
That Thou wilt take
Evil away. Amen.[7]

—Toyohiko Kagawa

[7] From *Songs from the Slums*. Copyright, 1935. Published by Cokesbury Press, Nashville, Tenn. Used by permission of the author and publishers.

SOME ONE HAD PRAYED

The day was long, the burden I had borne
  Seemed heavier than I could longer bear,
And then it lifted—but I did not know
  Some one had knelt in prayer.

Had taken me to God that very hour.
  And asked the easing of the load, and He
In infinite compassion, had stooped down
  And taken it from me.

We cannot tell how often as we pray
  For some bewildered one, hurt and distressed,
The answer comes—but many times those hearts
  Find sudden peace and rest.

Some one had prayed, and Faith, a reaching hand,
  Took hold of God, and brought Him down that day!
So many, many hearts have need of prayer—
  Oh, let us pray.

—Grace Noll Crowell

JIS' BLUE

"Jis' blue, God
Jis' blue.
Ain't prayin' exactly jis' now, tear-blind, I guess,
Can't see my way through.
You know those things
I ast for so many times—
Maybe I hadn't orter repeated like the
    Pharisees do;
But I ain't stood in no market place;
It's jis' 'tween me and You.
And You said, 'Ast' . . .
Somehow I ain't astin' now and I hardly
    know what to do.
Hope jis' sorter left, but Faith's still here—
Faith ain't gone, too.
I know how 'tis—a thousand years
Is as a single day with You;
And I ain't meanin' to tempt You with
    'If You be . . .'

And I ain't doubtin' You.
But I ain't prayin' tonight, God,
Jis' blue."

—Etta Oldham

GOD OF ALL NATIONS

God of all nations,
We pray for all the peoples of the earth,
For those who are consumed in mutual hatred and bitterness,
For those who make bloody war upon their neighbors,
For those who tyrannously oppress,
For those who groan under cruelty and subjection.
We pray Thee for all those who bear rule and responsibility,
For child races and dying races,
For outcast tribes, the backward and down-trodden,
For the ignorant, wretched, and the enslaved,
We beseech Thee, teach mankind to live together in peace,
No man exploiting the weak, no man hating the strong,
Each race working out its own destiny,
Unfettered, self-respecting, fearless.
Teach us to be worthy of freedom,
Free from social wrong, free from individual oppression and contempt,
Pure of heart and hand, despising none, defrauding none,
Giving to all men in all the dealings of life
The honor we owe to those who are thy children,
Whatever their color, their race, or their caste.[8]

—Anonymous

AND WHAT SHALL YOU SAY?

"Many that are first shall be last, and the last first."

Brother, come!
And let us go unto our God.
And when we stand before Him
I shall say—
"Lord, I do not hate,
I am hated.
I scourge no one,
I am scourged.
I covet no lands,

[8] From a *Book of Prayers* for use in an Indian college.

My lands are coveted.
I mock no peoples,
My people are mocked."
And, brother, what shall you say?[9]

—Joseph S. Cotter, Jr.

A PRAYER FOR THE POOR AND OUTCAST

God of love,
We pray Thee this day for the poor and outcast of this land:
For those who from year's end to year's end
Never have enough for their body's need:
For those who live perpetually on the bitter edge of starvation:
For those whose lot is continually shame and oppression,
Who, for no fault of their own, are loathed and spat upon:
For those who labor constantly,
In heat and thirst, for a miserable reward:
For those who are driven through want to shame and sin:
For those who have no hope in this life or beyond:
For those who labor helplessly for cruel masters:
For those who are bound fast by dark superstition and horrible dread:
For those who lack bitterly Thy light and Thy life:
For all these, O our Father, we beseech Thy grace.
And we ask thee for a share of Thy spirit,
That we may give ourselves, gladly and generously,
In the constant endeavor to rescue and to emancipate
These, the needy and helpless ones of our nation—
These without whom she cannot be saved.

—J. S. Hoyland

A HYMN FOR THE NEW AGE

O Master of the modern day,
   Our hearts are kindled as we know
Thou walkest still along life's way
   As in the ages long ago!
And by the magic of Thy will
New worlds Thou art creating still.

We thank Thee that the truth moves on
   With wireless wave and healing ray;
That yester's noon was but the dawn
   Of brighter glories in our day.
And now by faith, in holy dream
We glimpse tomorrow's grander gleam.

[9] From *The Book of American Negro Poetry*, by James Weldon Johnson. Published by Harcourt, Brace and Company, Inc. Used by permission.

We thank Thee that Thou rulest still
This goodly orb on which we dwell—
That Thou dost still reveal Thy will
To those who would the dark dispel—
That upward o'er the peaks of time
Thy plan unfolds in form sublime.

Help us to keep Thee as our guest
While speeding o'er the highways grand,
Or cleave the air at Thy behest
To give some soul a helping hand!
Thy tireless Spirit leads the way
To heal the woes that throng our day!

Enlarge our minds to grasp Thy thought,
Enlarge our hearts to work Thy plan,
Assured Thy purpose faileth not
To put Thy spirit into man!
God of the present age and hour,
Thrill us anew with holy power!

—William Steward Gordon

A TROPICAL MOON ON GOOD FRIDAY

(A 1940 Good Friday meditation from the mountainside worship shrine
at McLean Conference Grounds, Puerto Rico)

Tropical moon, how you glow tonight,
High o'er the mountains, luminous, bright,
Telling earth's children, from near and afar,
God watches o'er them like yon evening star.

This is Good Friday, and years, years ago
In a land that's far distant
Your mellow light glowed on a cross
That was empty and naked, where He,
The world's blessed Saviour,
Once hung on a tree—

Dying that men might forevermore know
God's love, like the moonlight, steadfastly
Does glow on all of His creatures—
The high and the low, the rich and the naked,
The sick and the well, the saint and the sinner—
Christ died for them all,
Shedding His life's blood as suspended
He hung, there on Golgotha
Till Black Friday was done.

Luminous moon, as you shine tonight
O'er earth's weary children in lands near and far,
May your silver beams teach this strife-ridden world
His calmness, serenity, patience and love—
Love that will sheathe every sword in the land
And make of men, brothers, whose hearts understand
The hearts of each other, and who answer the call
Of the Christ—"That they all may be one, as we,
Father, are one," in the *unity* of *spirit,*
And in the bonds of peace and love.[10]

—Cynthia Pearl Maus

✛

THE MUSIC IN A REST

"THERE is no music in a rest, but there is the making of music in it. In our whole life-melody the music is broken off here and there by *rests* and we foolishly think we have come to the end of the theme. God sends a time of forced leisure, sickness, disappointed plans, frustrated efforts, and makes a sudden pause in the choral hymn of our lives; and we lament that our voices must be silent, and our part missing in the music which ever goes up to the ear of the Creator. How does the musician read the *rest?* See him beat the time with unvarying count, and catch up the next note true and steady, as if no breaking-place had come between.

"Not without design does God write the music of our lives. Be it ours to learn the tune, and not to be dismayed at the *rests.* They are not to be slurred over, not to be omitted, not to destroy the melody, not to change the keynote. If we look up, God Himself will beat the time for us. With the eye on Him, we shall strike the next note full and clear. If we sadly say to ourselves, *there is no music in a rest,* let us not forget *there is the making of music in it.* The making of music is often a slow and painful process in this life. How patiently God works to teach us. How long He waits for us to learn the lesson."— *John Ruskin.*

We cannot say too much for silence—and entering into the silence. Some one reminds us that silence is "like the sleeping seas. It gathers to itself calmness and strength. It rests upon peace and beauty. It is the whisper of endless time. It is the purifier of men's souls. It is the mighty force that bears human souls to the realms of greatness." Not only should we enter into the silence. The silence should enter into us.

If chosen men had never been alone,
In deep mid-silence open-doored to God,
No greatness ever had been dreamed or done.

[10] From *Puerto Rico in Pictures and Poetry* by Maus. Caxton Press, Caldwell, Idaho.

But greatness that is born of silence is not for itself. It is related to achievement. It is but a pause—whether momentary or prolonged—and it stands in measured relation to the music in which it is set.—*Dean Gresham.*

And so I come for deeper rest to this still room;
    For here, the habit of the soul
Feels less the outer world's control,
    And from the silence, multiplied
By these still forms on every side,
    The world that time and sense have known
Falls off and leaves us, God, alone.

—John Greenleaf Whittier

✠

THE ADVENTURE OF PRAYER

PRAYER is being with God. You can't choose at all about it except just in choosing to be with Him. Perhaps He will take you onto a mountain with Him. Perhaps He will take you into the night with Him, or into the mist where you will not be able to see Him. Perhaps you will be with Him in pain, or in exaltation, or in happiness, or in tiredness.

He just says: "Come unto me"; and you say: "I will," or "I will not."

You make no stipulations, that is not your part; you know that He wants you, and you know what *kind* of *wanting* that is by the *manger* and the *cross.*

You know that if you say you will not come, He does not leave off wanting you; and so you imagine what that means.

You know that if you come to Him He will ask you to help Him about the Kingdom, and that in the end He will give you that work for it that no one else can do.

You know that He will bring you into the fellowship of His friends, and that you will be allowed to bring Him into the fellowship of your friends.

But, of course, you will go with Him before His enemies; and the things that they say about Him will be said about you.

And you will also go among people who don't care, whom He is trying to arouse to a sense of His love.

Quite often He and you will be left desolate with the doors locked before you, and the people on the other side scornful or amused.

You will find that He will ask you to do things that you can only do if you forget about yourself and the sort of person you thought you were, or He may ask you to face death or complete shame as He, Himself, does.

And all the time you will fail Him so often that by and by you will have no self-confidence left, only a growing confidence in Him instead, because *He* does not fail *you.*

And prayer must be *fearfully difficult,* because it isn't easy to be with God, although it is simple. It means that some things must go, like pride, unkindness, self-indulgence, and self-importance.

But all the same it is a choice which the best part of you wants, so that the most glorious souls of all the ages do choose the Adventure of Prayer, revealing, costly, difficult as it is, for it is the pathway to the Father heart of God.[11]

✝

A SHEPHERD IN SOUTH LEBANON

By

Kahlil Gibran

IT WAS late summer when He and *three* other men first walked upon that road yonder. It was evening, and He stopped and stood there at the end of the pasture.

I was playing upon my flute, and my flock was grazing all around me. When He stopped, I rose and walked over and stood before Him.

And He asked me, "Where is the grave of Elijah? Is it not somewhere near this place?"

And I answered Him, "It is there, Sir, underneath that great heap of stones. Even unto this day every passerby brings a stone and places it upon the heap."

And He thanked me and walked away, and His friends walked behind Him.

After three days Gamaliel, who was also a shepherd, said to me that the man who had passed by was a prophet in Judea; but I did not believe him. Yet I thought of that man for many a moon.

When spring came Jesus once more passed by this pasture, and this time He was alone. I was not playing on my flute that day for I had lost a sheep and I was bereaved, and my heart was downcast within me.

And I walked towards Him and stood still before Him, for I desired to be comforted.

And He looked at me and said, "You do not play upon your flute this day. Whence is the sorrow in your eyes?"

And I answered, "A sheep from among my sheep is lost. I have sought her everywhere but I find her not. And I know not what to do."

He was silent for a moment. Then He smiled upon me and said: "Wait here awhile and I will find your sheep." And He walked away and disappeared among the hills.

After an hour He returned, and my sheep was close beside Him. And as He stood before me, the sheep looked up into His face even as I was looking. Then I embraced her in gladness.

And He put His hand upon my shoulder and said, "From this day you shall

[11] By Margaret Cooper. Published by *The Challenge Unlimited,* 92 Russell Street, W.C.1, London, England. Used by special permission of the publishers.

love this sheep more than any other in your flock, for she was lost and now she is found."

And again I embraced my sheep in gladness, and she came close to me, and I was silent.

But when I raised my head to thank Jesus, He was already walking afar off, and I had not the courage to follow Him.[12]

✝

HIS WAY

By

Gladys Payne Shafer

THE boy Jesus as he bent over the bench in the yard, laying away his tools for the night, wondered at the fragrance which floated out from his mother's kitchen.

All afternoon she had been busy—too busy to come out and sit by his bench as was her habit, nor had she even inquired from the doorway how his work progressed. Now he knew that a cake, delicious mixture of choice oil-of-olives, dates, almonds, and meal, blended by the careful hands of his mother, was baking.

It was not often that a cake found its way to the table of this humble family of Nazareth. What special occasion could this be, the boy asked himself. Then suddenly his face brightened, as he remembered that it was his own birthday!

Not strange that he had forgotten its approach, for since the day Jonas had hired him to build the doors and frames for his new stable, Jesus had been intent on his work with little thought for anything else. Proudly the lad looked at the pile of frames, finished now, each one fashioned by his own hands. Tomorrow, Jonas would come for them and then Jesus would begin to make the doors.

The boy thrilled in anticipation of this work—the most important that he had ever undertaken. They must be sturdy, well-made doors that Jonas would be proud to place in the new stable. And they would be well-made doors— Jesus knew how to make them. Had he not watched and helped Joseph build doors for every new building that had been erected in the village since he, Jesus, had been scarcely taller than the work-bench itself?

So this was his birthday. He might forget, but his mother had always remembered. It was then that Mary came to the door-way and looked at him half-reproachfully.

"This is your birthday, my son. Have you forgotten?"

"I had forgotten until the smell of the baking cake came to me. Then I knew that it was an especial day—my birthday!"

[12] From *Jesus the Son of Man* by Kahlil Gibran. Copyright, 1928, by Kahlil Gibran. Published by Alfred A. Knopf, Inc., New York, N.Y. Reprinted by permission of the publishers.

Suddenly Jesus turned to his mother. "Mother, this is David's birthday, too."

"David?"

"David, the lame boy, who sells figs and dates in the village. I have told you of him."

"Yes, I remember. Last year you told me that your birthdays came on the same day."

Mary's son nodded thoughtfully. "David has no mother. His birthday is the same as other days. Never has he had the taste of a cake such as you make, Mother. A cake made with the very figs and dates that he sells."

Quickly Mary replied: "Then, my son, ask David to come to supper tonight. He shall have cake on his birthday."

Sadly the boy Jesus shook his head. "David is not able to climb the hill. He might have climbed it a year ago, but he cannot now."

Mary's face brightened with a happy thought. "Then you must take a large piece of your cake to David."

Again Jesus shook his head. "No, Mother, not that. Do you not see? Never has David, who is as old as I am, had a gift of any kind. Never has he known that something was made for him alone. Never has he had the gift of a whole cake. Mother, do you not understand?" Hopefully Jesus searched his mother's face. And Mary, looking into the kindly eyes of her young son, said that she understood.

So it was that a little later Jesus went down the steep hill carefully bearing a wonderful birthday cake to David.

Back of Mary's house there was a rounded knoll, commonly called "The mountain" by the boys and girls of the village. When he returned from his errand, it was here that Jesus bounding easily up the path, found his mother. He stopped suddenly as he saw her. All beauty gave him a deep sense of joy, so poignant it might almost be pain, and now as he beheld the calm loveliness of her face while she looked out toward the shadowing hills, he thought her the most beautiful mother he had ever seen.

Mary turned and saw Jesus. "You were away a long while, my son," she said. "Did you stay with David to enjoy the cake with him?"

"No, I left it with David and his father. It made them very happy, Mother."

"And you—"

"On the way home I met Ruth walking the street again, trying to find her children. They had wandered away, as they so often do. Ruth looked very weary so I told her to go home and rest while I looked for the little ones."

"Did you find them?"

"Yes, I found them. They were farther from home than they should have been. They are like sheep—one strays and the others follow. They need a shepherd."

"You were already tired, Son."

"No, I have found that when the heart sings one does not tire at any task. It is the unhappy heart that drags and makes one weary."

Jesus sat down beside his mother on a great rock and together they looked out across the valley where occasional gray masses moved slowly through the dusk.

"See," said the boy, pointing to a thin spiral of smoke which rose like an amethyst pencil from the plain, "yonder is Thomas' evening fire. His flock is settling there for the night. The flock to the south is John's."

"How do you know, my lad, at this distance, whose flocks we see?"

"It is simple. John has a white dog—see him flash among the sheep as he rounds them up? Thomas' dogs are brown, so they are not visible through the dusk."

The youth moved closer to his mother and spoke confidingly. "Often have I thought I'd like to be a shepherd."

"Yes, my son, I know."

"You know? You have seen this?"

"Yes, Son. Many, many times I have seen that you have the way of a shepherd."

A long silence fell between Mary and her son. A star that had appeared first as a pale spark in the sky, gradually brightened until it far outshone the others. As the two watched the star, Mary at last said, "Some day I shall tell you of a beautiful, great star which was seen one night some years ago."

"Oh Mother! Will you not tell me now?"

"I cannot tell you, yet."

"Was it in this countrry? Did you see the glory of it?" the boy eagerly asked.

The mother hesitated. "No, I was not—where I could see the sky that night. I did not see the star, but I felt it."

While the lad sat thinking of the wondrous star, Mary's thoughts returned to the little lame boy and the birthday cake. It had been a beautiful cake. She was glad that the cake had made David happy. She was glad, too, that her son had been happy to give his cake to David. But Mary sighed. Then she spoke: "It was a strange way to observe your birthday—giving your cake away."

Jesus looked up at the radiant star. "Mother," he said whimsically, "if I were a king, and the whole world celebrated my birthday today, this is the way I would have it: that each person who wished to do me honor would give some treasured thing to someone who needed it more than he. *That would be my way.*"[13]

---

[13] The following Christmas story is based upon "Meditation of a Long-Ago Christmas Night" by Gladys Payne Shafer, published in *The Elementary Magazine*, December, 1936. Reprinted by permission of the author and publishers.

NEARER, MY GOD, TO THEE

THIS great Christian hymn, "Nearer, My God, to Thee," was composed by Mrs. Sarah Flower Adams, an English girl of rare charm and poetic ability; and was suggested by the story of Jacob's vision as found in Genesis 28:10-22. It was first published in 1841, and although it met with some favor, it was not until 1860 that Dr. Lowell Mason's beautiful and sympathetic musical setting "quickened it into glorious life" and gave it a permanent abiding-place in the hearts of people everywhere.

In the great Peace Jubilee held in Boston, Massachusetts, in 1872 this hymn was sung by nearly fifty thousand voices. Dr. Mason, then in his eightieth year, was present and was delighted and moved by the fervent singing of this matchless melody.

Many interesting stories are told in connection with the usefulness of this hymn, which has been an inspiration wherever the Christian religion has gone. It was the favorite hymn of our martyred President McKinley and of Helen Gould, whose wholesome and noble charity made her one of the best-loved women in America.

It is almost universally used in connection with memorial services for honored dead in both the army and navy; and it is not unusual to hear it sung by students and groups of native Christians in many tongues the world around.

> Nearer, my God, to Thee, nearer to Thee!
> E'en though it be a cross that raiseth me;
> Still all my song shall be, nearer, my God, to Thee,
> Nearer, my God, to Thee, nearer to Thee.
>
> Though like a wanderer, the sun gone down,
> Darkness be over me, my rest a stone;
> Yet in my dreams I'd be nearer, my God, to Thee,
> Nearer, my God, to Thee, nearer to Thee.
>
> There let the way appear, steps unto heaven;
> All that Thou sendest me in mercy given;
> Angels to beckon me nearer, my God, to Thee,
> Nearer, my God, to Thee, nearer to Thee.
>
> Or if on joyful wing, cleaving the sky,
> Sun, moon, and stars forgot, upward I fly,
> Still all my song shall be nearer, my God, to Thee,
> Nearer, my God, to Thee, nearer to Thee. Amen.

—*Sarah F. Adams*

THE BEAUTIFUL GARDEN OF PRAYER

THE words to this comparatively new prayer hymn of the church were composed by Eleanor Allen Schroll and dedicated to Miss Mary Kelly, who gave thirty-four years of her rich Christian life and love in service as a missionary teacher and superintendent of the Girls' School at Nanking, China.

The message of the song was inspired by the rich and beautiful prayer-life that Miss Kelly through her long years of service in far-away China developed within her own personality. This great prayer song is very much beloved by young people the world around, and is often sung as a solo or duet in young people's gatherings, because it voices a heart-felt need of youth everywhere.

There's a garden where Jesus is waiting,
　There's a place that is wond'rously fair,
For it glows with the light of His presence,
　'Tis the beautiful garden of pray'r.

Refrain

O the beautiful garden, the garden of pray'r,
O the beautiful garden of pray'r;
There my Saviour awaits, and He opens the gates,
To the beautiful garden of pray'r.

There's a garden where Jesus is waiting,
　And I go with my burden and care;
Just to learn from his lips words of comfort
　In the beautiful garden of pray'r.

Refrain

There's a garden where Jesus is waiting.
　O can aught with His glory compare;
Just to walk and to talk with my Saviour,
　In the beautiful garden of pray'r?[14]

Refrain

—*Eleanor A. Schroll*

[14] From *Hymns for Today*. Published by Fillmore Music House. Used by permission.

ERE YOU LEFT YOUR ROOM THIS MORNING

DID YOU THINK TO PRAY?

THIS old prayer-hymn is definitely associated in my mind with Mrs. Arlene Dux Scoville, whom I heard sing it in many International Conventions of the Disciples of Christ after 1912 as a special contribution to the Foreign Society Day program and work.

There is something about the *artistic rendition* of a poem, a hymn, or a story that tends to definitely associate it in one's mind with the poet, the singer, or the story-teller who first made it live for one in beautiful, rugged simplicity. No one who has ever heard Mrs. Scoville sing this hymn, "Ere You Left Your Room This Morning" in her marvelously clear, lyric soprano voice, can ever forget the experience. Through the years, as she has sung this great prayer-hymn in our international conventions as well as in hundreds of revival meetings, she has moved countless thousands to seek the "secret garden of the soul" in solitude, as did the Master in the long ago, there to pour out the deepest yearnings of their lives to God in prayer.

The words of this beautiful song were composed by Mrs. M. A. Kidder, and the tune by W. O. Perkins. Every verse of it contains a distinct challenge to the Christian, for he cannot hope to follow Christ, in the fullest way, without constant daily prayer and intercession.

Ere you left your room this morning,
    Did you think to pray?
In the name of Christ, our Saviour,
Did you sue for loving favor,
    As a shield today?

Refrain

Oh, how praying rests the weary!
    Pray'r will change the night to day;
So when life seems dark and dreary,
    Don't forget to pray.

When you met with great temptation,
    Did you think to pray?
By His dying love and merit
Did you claim the Holy Spirit
    As your guide and stay?

Refrain

When your heart was filled with anger,
    Did you think to pray?
Did you plead for grace, my brother,

That you might forgive another
Who had crossed your way?

Refrain

When sore trials came upon you,
Did you think to pray?
When your soul was bowed in sorrow
Balm of Gilead did you borrow
At the gates of day?[15]

Refrain

—Mrs. M. A. Kidder

✣

'TIS THE BLESSED HOUR OF PRAYER

WILL CARLTON, himself a writer of popular verse, truthfully said: "All over this country, and, one might say, the world, Fanny Crosby's hymns are singing themselves into the hearts and souls of people. They have been doing his for many years, and will do so as long as our civilization lasts. There are today used in religious meetings more of her inspired lines than of any other poet, living or dead. . . . Her sacred lyrics have been translated into several languages. She is easily the greatest writer of hymns, and will always occupy a high place among authors."

Although blind from birth, she was unusually alert mentally, and composed during her lifetime more than five thousand hymns, sometimes writing as many as seven a day. Yet she never entered upon the task of composition without a prayer that her efforts might be used to the glory of God and the uplift of humanity.

" 'Tis the Blessed Hour of Prayer" is one of the really great prayer hymns of the Church, and will live always in the hearts of followers of Jesus, who, like the Lowly Nazarene, have discovered the secret and power of high-minded living through constant and frequent prayer.

'Tis the blessed hour of prayer, when our hearts lowly bend,
And we gather to Jesus, our Saviour and Friend;
If we come to Him in faith, his protection to share,
What a balm for the weary! O how sweet to be there!

Chorus

Blessed hour of prayer, blessed hour of prayer,
What balm for the weary! O how sweet to be there!

[15] From *Favorite Hymns*. Standard Publishing Company, Ninth and Cutter Streets, Cincinnati, Ohio. Used by permission.

'Tis the blessed hour of prayer, when the Saviour draws near
With a tender compassion His children to hear;
When He tells us we may cast at His feet ev'ry care,
What a balm for the weary! O how sweet to be there!

Chorus

'Tis the blessed hour of prayer, when the tempted and tried
To the Saviour who loves them their sorrow confide;
With a sympathizing heart He removes ev'ry care;
What a balm for the weary! O how sweet to be there!

Chorus

At the blessed hour of prayer, trusting Him, we believe
That the blessing we're needing we'll surely receive;
In the fullness of this trust we shall lose ev'ry care;
What a balm for the weary! O how sweet to be there! Amen.

Chorus

—Fanny Crosby

✛

INTO MY HEART

THERE is perhaps no more popular prayer benediction among Christian youth than the simple yet sincere words of "Into My Heart," which were composed by Harry D. Clarke in 1924.

The Scripture portion which was the author's inspiration for this beautiful song, bearing the subtitle "My Prayer," is found in Revelation 3:20, where John puts these significant words into the mouth of the Saviour: "Behold, I stand at the door, and knock: if any man hear my voice, and open the door, I will come in to him and will sup with him, and he with me."

Some years ago, as the Pioneer Young People's Superintendent for the Disciples of Christ in America, it was my privilege to secure permission from Mr. Clarke to include both the words and the music of this personally appealing prayer-song in the *Songs for the Sing* which is used in all of the Youth conferences of this communion. From that year on, this prayer-song has been regularly used as the sung benediction in connection with the Chapel periods and "closing friendship circle" in these conferences by countless thousands of young people all over America and the world.

One of the conferees in one of our summer conferences a few years later, wrote the lines for a second verse "Out of My Heart," sung to the same tune, and it, too, is growing in popularity. Then the first world-gathering of the youth of the Churches of Christ, meeting in Leicester, England, in 1935, added a third verse "Going with Thee." These three verses were used as a processional from the "closing friendship circle" of the youth sessions to De Montfort Hall, where the young people occupied the center section of that great auditorium, and five young people from the Youth group took charge of the Saturday evening session of the World Convention, bringing to the general convention the results of their deliberations.

This benediction will live always in the hearts of young people because of its intensely personal appeal. The words only are reprinted here; the music will be found on page 10 of *Songs for the Sing*; and as song No. 144 in *Glad Tidings,* published by Robert H. Coleman, Dallas, Texas. It should always be sung as a prayer.

> Into my heart, into my heart
> Come into my heart, Lord Jesus;
> Come in today, come in to stay,
> Come into my heart, Lord Jesus.
>
> Out of my heart, out of my heart,
> Shine out of my heart, Lord Jesus;
> Shine out today, shine out alway,
> Shine out of my heart, Lord Jesus.
>
> Going with Thee, going with Thee,
> We're going with Thee, Lord Jesus;
> To work and to play, to serve and to pray,
> We're going with Thee, Lord Jesus.[16]
>
> —*Harry D. Clarke, 1924*

✠

I COULDN'T HEAR NOBODY PRAY

"I Couldn't Hear Nobody Pray" is another of those spirituals that picture for us in a few brief verses the misery and utter loneliness of heart which was the Negro's portion as a result of the cruelty inherent in the slave-trade, that *inhuman* traffic in *human lives* that often separated husbands and wives, and sons and daughters from mother and fathers, as they were put on the block and sold to slave-owners from distant states, some never again to see the faces of the ones they loved.

Many, of course, of the slave-owners of the ante-bellum days were devoutly religious and made it possible for their slaves to have a place of worship of their own, either in the gallery of churches in which they themselves worshiped, or in a small church near the Negro quarters of their own or some neighboring plantation.

Others were without distinctly religious bent themselves, and therefore felt

[16] Copyright (first verse only) by Harry D. Clarke, 1924. Used by permission of the author.

no responsibility whatever for making it possible for the slaves they owned to meet in worship with Negroes from other near-by plantations. For such as these their lot was lonely indeed.

And since the religion of the Negro is distinctly a *heart* religion—a cry for fellowship and friendship with all of God's children—he naturally poured out the utter loneliness of his heart and soul in never-to-be-forgotten words like these:

Refrain[17]

I couldn't hear nobody pray,
I couldn't hear nobody pray;
I was way down yonder by myself,
And I couldn't hear nobody pray, O Lord.

Verses

In the valley, I couldn't hear nobody pray,
On my knees, I couldn't hear nobody pray;
With my burden, I couldn't hear nobody pray,
And my Saviour, I couldn't hear nobody pray.

Refrain

Chilly waters, I couldn't hear nobody pray,
In the Jordan, I couldn't hear nobody pray;
Crossing over, I couldn't hear nobody pray,
Into Canaan, I couldn't hear nobody pray.

Refrain

Hallelujah! I couldn't hear nobody pray,
Trouble over, I couldn't hear nobody pray;
In the Kingdom, I couldn't hear nobody pray,
With my Jesus, I couldn't hear nobody pray.

Refrain

—*A Spiritual*

✠

STANDIN' IN THE NEED OF PRAYER

"And the publican standing afar off, would not lift up so much as his eyes unto heaven; but smote upon his breast, saying, God be merciful to me a sinner."— LUKE 18:13.

---

[17] In all Negro Spirituals the refrain should be sung at the beginning and following each of the verses.

THE Bible itself was the main source of material for a great many of the Negro spirituals. Many of the Bible stories and incidents gave the slaves, especially the song-leaders, or bards, opportunity to develop their descriptive powers.

In this song the slave pictures the publican as a lowly person like himself, one who must surely not be as good as God wants him to be, or else he would not be undergoing the hardships that are his lot. Thus he likens himself to the publican to whom Luke refers in the Scripture above—a sinner, one who needs to pray and to be prayed for, and so he sings:

Refrain

It's me, it's me, O Lord,
Standin' in de need of prayer.
It's me, it's me, O Lord,
Standin' in de need of prayer.

Verses

It's not my sister nor my brother,
But it's me, O Lord,
Standin' in de need of prayer.
It's not my sister nor my brother,
But it's me, O Lord,
Standin' in de need of prayer.

It's not my mother nor my father,
But it's me, O Lord,
Standin' in de need of prayer.
It's not my mother nor my father,
But it's me, O Lord,
Standin' in de need of prayer.

It's not my elder, nor my deacon,
But it's me, O Lord,
Standin' in de need of prayer.
It's not my elder, nor my deacon,
But it's me, O Lord,
Standin' in de need of prayer.

—A Spiritual

CONTENTS

PART VI   SECTION VII

IN THE "INASMUCH" OF SERVING

——————————————————————✠——————————————————————

"Inasmuch as ye did it unto one of these my brethren . . . ye did it unto me."—MATTHEW 25:40

——————————————————————✠——————————————————————

IN THE "INASMUCH" OF SERVING

"But when the Son of man shall come in his glory, and all the angels with him, then shall he sit on the throne of his glory; and before him shall be gathered all the nations: and he shall separate them one from another, as the shepherd separateth the sheep from the goats; and he shall set the sheep on his right hand, but the goats on the left.

"Then shall the King say unto them on his right hand, Come, ye blessed of my Father, inherit the kingdom prepared for you from the foundation of the world: for I was hungry, and ye gave me to eat; I was thirsty, and ye gave me drink; I was a stranger, and ye took me in; naked, and ye clothed me; I was sick, and ye visited me; I was in prison, and ye came unto me.

"Then shall the righteous answer him, saying, Lord, when saw we thee hungry, and fed thee? or athirst, and gave thee drink? And when saw we thee a stranger, and took thee in? or naked, and clothed thee? And when saw we thee sick, or in prison, and came unto thee? And the King shall answer and say unto them, Verily I say unto you, Inasmuch as ye did it unto one of these my brethren, *even* these least, ye did it unto me.

"Then shall he say also unto them on the left hand, Depart from me, ye cursed, into the eternal fire which is prepared for the devil and his angels: for I was hungry, and ye did not give me to eat: I was thirsty, and ye gave me no drink: I was a stranger, and ye took me not in; naked, and ye clothed me not; sick, and in prison, and ye visited me not.

"Then shall they also answer, saying, Lord, when saw we thee hungry, or athirst, or a stranger, or naked, or sick, or in prison, and did not minister unto thee? Then shall he answer them, saying, Verily I say unto you, Inasmuch as ye did it not unto one of these least, ye did it not unto me. And these shall go away into eternal punishment: but the righteous into eternal life."—MATTHEW 25:31-46

AMONG THE LOWLY—*L'HERMITTE*

AMONG THE LOWLY

By

Léon Augustin L'hermitte

(Interpretation)

THERE is a peculiar fascination in this comparatively recent painting, "Among the Lowly," by the contemporary French artist, Léon Augustin L'hermitte, who was born at Mont-Saint-Tere, in 1844 and died in 1925. The charm of this picture lies in its simplicity. Jesus, Himself, was a man without a home, and therefore found delight in the hospitality of the humble, peasant cottages of His day.

In this picture L'hermitte has painted Jesus in the act of blessing the simple, frugal meal of this lowly peasant family. In the doorway of the cottage stands the father, who has just come in as thanks is being offered to the heavenly Father for the food which His bounty makes possible. One of the littler children has run to meet him, and the father has lifted her in his arms as he stands, hat in hand, in the doorway with his head bowed.

On the right of the Master are the old grandparents, their hands folded in prayer on the table, while near them another child, too small to understand what it is all about, has turned with a smile to welcome the return of her work-aday daddy.

To the left of the mother stands the older daughter, her hands behind her as she listens reverently to the words that fall from the Stranger's lips. In the mother's lap, a babe in arms is nursing, while just behind her another childish face peeks around as if to inquire what the Strange Man is doing.

The son of the family has evidently just opened the door to the cottage for his father, and stands with his hand on the door, watching the reverent, hat-in-hand attitude of his father.

On the table is the simple repast of this lowly peasant home, consisting, no doubt, of a pitcher of water or wine, a glass or two, a bowl of thick soup or porridge, and two or three dishes from which portions will be served to the Guest and older members of the family first and then to the others later.

The Master of Men is, of course, the center of interest, as He stands just behind the table with one hand resting on it, and the other upraised in blessing on the food and this humble home that has made Him its welcome guest.

One has the feeling, as he studies this picture, that, after all, only a few things are essential to happiness in this life. The emphasis in this painting is not on material riches, but on the spirit of gratitude to the giver of all good things, for health, home, food, and the love that binds families together.

We feel, as we look at this toiler and his family, much as John Murdock, the tutor of the Burns children, expressed himself, when he said of the thatched-roof cottage in which Robert Burns was born and reared: "In this mean cottage, of which I myself was at times an inhabitant, I really believe there dwelt a larger portion of happiness and content than in any place in Europe."

Wealth and the material things that may be purchased with it are often not synonymous with either *health, happiness,* or *content.* One must possess the deeper spiritual values to which Jesus referred when he said to Martha, "Mary hath chosen the good part, which shall not be taken away from her," if one is to enjoy real happiness and contentment in this life. We can all be troubled and over-anxious about material things, or we can cultivate an appreciation for the things of the spirit, knowing that our heavenly Father knows the temporal things of which we have need and will supply them adequately for all those who toil.

Better a humble cottage with Christ as guest, simple furnishings and frugal meals; than a palace royal in which greed, and avarice, irreverence and discontent abound. This is the message of the artist's "Among the Lowly," the original of which hangs in the Metropolitan Museum of Art in New York City.

✛

CHRIST MOURNS OVER THE CITY

By

Paul Hippolyte Flandrin

(Interpretation)

JESUS' message of the social gospel has no finer, stronger ally than that portrayed by the French painter, Paul Hippolyte Flandrin, in his "Christ Mourns over the City." And no interpreter of religious art has given us a finer exposition of the social message of this picture than Dr. Albert Edward Bailey, whose interpretation is included herein by permission of the author. He says:

"No one but a modern could have conceived this picture, and none but moderns can understand it. It is an expression of the social Gospel, the translation of Christ's lament into terms of industrialism, materialism, and greed, the arraignment of civilization before the bar of conscience.

"Christ stands on Olivet and with the vision of a Seer looks down the vistas of time. The Jerusalem of Caiaphas lying before Him has dissolved in mist, and in place of the frowning city wall rises a compact tier of tenements. The dark flats are crowded like the rabbit-warrens of old Jerusalem, only there is no bright and wind-swept housetop for any family but the topmost one. Behind, where the Temple of the Living God once stood, there is a murk of smoke and a reek of steam, and through the gloom come the pulse-beats of trip-

CHRIST MOURNS OVER THE CITY—*FLANDRIN*

hammers and the sudden spurts of white-hot flame from furnace doors. Some new god is being worshiped here, some

> Moloch, horrid king, besmeared with blood
> Of human sacrifice, and parents' tears.

"You can see the hosts assembling to serve him, the myriads of men who all day feed the flames and pour the metal; myriads of little children driving their task from dawn till sunset amid the rattle and roar of looms and gears. Once the Seer holds out His arms and cries, 'Suffer the little children to come unto me!' But His voice is lost in the din of ravenous machines.

"Above, where Herod's palace should have lowered, he sees the domes and towers of great cathedrals. But they stand deserted. No lights gleam from them; if there is organ music rolling through the lofty aisles, no ear hears it but God. There may be priests at the altar, but the people are not thronging thither for the Bread of Life; they are still tending their fires and their hammers, still fighting for the bread that perishes, still hating one another like the monsters of a pre-Adamic age. . . .

"Meantime God's daylight dies, and the pall of night settles down unrelieved by stars. But still the Seer stands motionless above the city, His hands clasped in contemplation, His sad yet fascinated face still poring on the sights and sounds that strike upon His soul. Where are His disciples? Have they given up in despair the task of preaching love and good will? Is there no one to say, 'See that ye despise not these little ones?' No one to throw down the altars that smoke to Mammon and Belial? No one to repeat the old commandment, 'Thou shalt worship the Lord, thy God, and him only shalt thou serve'; or that greater one, 'Thou shalt love thy neighbor as thyself'? Yes, thank God, we know that there are some down there in the great city who care; there are a few who wrestle with Boards of Trade for a square deal, who clean up Bowerys and East Sides, who plead with Senators to pass child-labor laws in order that God's little ones may have a day of sunshine before they go to grind in the prison house; who preach an honest day's work for a day's pay, and no dynamite for the open shop. Yes, there are a few who care—after two millenniums of the Gospel! But the artist who painted this picture has not shown them.

"This is Paul Flandrin's judgment on Christianity in 1904. Had he painted the picture between 1914 and 1918, he would have filled the air with bursting shrapnel, he would have wrecked the cathedral dome, piled the foreground with shattered bodies of men, and pierced with bayonets a newly crucified Christ. And a fair maiden with stars in her hair would crouch behind the cross and hug a bag of gold!"[1]

---

[1] From *The Gospel in Art*, Bailey. Published by the Pilgrim Press, Boston, Mass.

"IF THOU HADST KNOWN"

By

William Longstaff

(Interpretation)

THE story of the painting of the picture, "If Thou Hadst Known," is an exceptional one. In the summer of 1931 a man, who by his own preference wished to be known as Mr. Nobody of London, walked into the studio of the artist, Mr. William Longstaff, after making an appointment by telephone. He wanted the artist to paint a picture of Christ that would suggest world kinship and rulership. This rulership, however, was not to express imposing authority, but to be rather wistfully appealing, spiritually impelling, and to be entitled "If Thou Hadst Known."

Having left this strange commission, this man vanished, calling several times to observe progress and finally to pay for it in bank notes and to cause it to be sent to the City Temple, London, England, as a gift from Mr. Nobody to Dr. F. W. Norwood, its minister.

The painter, Mr. William Longstaff, to whom this strange commission was given, is a great artist; yet among the many pictures he had hitherto painted, none had been on a religious theme. Naturally he would have to find his inspiration for this strange commission in the New Testament. He must clearly interpret not only the Judæan Christ, but the Christ of the centuries, who by His own choice would not be merely a King of the Jews or of a temporal kingdom.

As the artist read and studied the life of Christ, he saw Him entering Jerusalem in triumph. His people had long endured national humiliation, qualified only by the hope that one day a Deliverer would come. Just now they believe that He has come. Their joy knows no bounds. Christ is borne along on the wings of popular rejoicing.

But this Christ of Galilee is Himself far-seeing. He knows that while His claims are admitted, His Spirit is rejected. They would enthrone Him in state because they have misunderstood His Spirit. They would have a King in Jerusalem, but they have no intention of attuning either Jerusalem or their hearts to the sacrificial motif of His reign.

Therefore the Christ is more utterly alone amid their hosannas than when in the wilderness the wild beasts had supplied the accompaniment to His meditation.

As we look at Him in this picture we see that His wide universal mind is embracing the whole world. Jerusalem is but a transitory landmark in a growing cycle. It is already doomed. His soul has long since envisaged its overthrow.

There might have been recovery had there been repentance. But the hour has passed. Repentance is not rung in amid a fanfare of hosannas. Jerusalem will fall as its precursor. Only slowly, after many crucifixions, will His own Spirit pervade the wide world.

The soul of Christ as we see it in this picture is lonely though regal. He is in this hour rejected, though not self-denied. He has no anger, but a vast compassion. He sees the inevitability of it all. "They know not what they do." The strong walls of Jerusalem, the white marble and glittering gold of the Temple move Him to tears. The great weight of human ignorance burdens His Spirit, but does not crush His hope.

It is all so clear to Him, but so hidden from them. They have a zeal for righteousness, but not according to knowledge. The law is against them, and none can do aught against the law. Men must blunder till they discover its meaning and fully obey.

The soul of Christ is strong in the truth, but full of compassion. His own fate is merely accidental. He has seen it approaching, and opened His arms to receive it. But the pity of it; ah! the pity of it! "If thou hadst known in this thy day, even thou, the things which belong unto peace, but now are they hid from thine eyes."

The artist pondered the words, "If Thou Hadst Known." The face of Him who speaks is not accusing, it is not supercilious. It is the face of One who sees the hard truth in its white brilliance, but pities profoundly the fluttering, moth-like men who dash themselves against it with their tinted wings. Yet there is no trace of cynicism. *Truth* is greater than momentary triumph or momentary pain. It will win, at last, and its light will be mellowed and life-giving.

The face in this picture is the face of an idealist, but not of a visionary. He is the Son of Fact, but facts have a soul, and in the deep center of them is the *love of God*. He is but thirty-three years of age, but He has seen deep into the will of the Ancient of Days. His lips are firm, but His eyes are smiling through a haze of tenderness.

The great world swims in space within His soul's orbit. The mist envelops it, the clouds drift athwart it, but the mists are clearing and the clouds are passing. His hands are not mailed fists. They are sensitive, though strong. They seem to be hiding the wound-prints in their palms, while they point upward to the throne of God which is encircled by judgment and mercy. The truth is there. It is firm and strong and sweet, though hidden in this hour. It is like a peal of bells, the sound muffled while the storm is raging, but clear as silver chimes whenever the winds are lulled. Meanwhile the other ears hear them not.

"If Thou Hadst Known," these words have the cadence of an infinite regret. Perhaps it is only through regret that we learn. We have to go on sometimes until, looking back, we see the "might-have-been" rising like a vision above the grim actualities. Then we either despair or repent.

Slowly, through the centuries, that vision has been and is rising above the fog. If men had known the things that belong unto peace, how different the history of the race in every land might have been.

But there is a Spirit which is eternal, and though oft crucified, still rests its upward-pointing hands upon the cloud-encompassed world, abating not its claim. It is the Christ-Spirit, gallant and dauntless. Time is nothing to it, for time is on its side. In varying ages it waxes and wanes, but never is quenched. It has its triumphs and defeats, but it never surrenders. It is as true today as at the time of His entry into Jerusalem that the kind of throne we are ready to give Him is not the kind that He can accept. We still entangle together cannon and the cross.

Only time can justify His claims. The Christ goes on His way. The cross does not halt Him. Time and experience must do their work. Every great iniquity must be weighed in the scales of Fate till it is found wanting. Each generation has its special testing. For us the hard lesson is WAR. It may destroy our civilization, but it will not destroy humanity. Those who most effectively repudiate it will reach the topmost place. They who refuse to "put up the sword" will perish by the sword.

The revelation of Judæa two thousand years ago remains valid forever. For that is the meaning of Christ. He has no magic wand wherewith to banish human woes, only a magnetic pull which is never relaxed. He can make a scourge of cords or bare His back to the scourging; but in the end men will come His way or be cast out of the Temple.

He claims the world because the world cannot do without Him. To serve Him is difficult, but to fall away from His orbit is to lament when the light is clear, that we had not known the things that belong to our peace.

The artist who painted this picture, "If Thou Hadst Known,"[2] said that he had never before painted such a theme. Then he added, "Nothing I ever painted took so much out of me as this."

It is always so. The way of Christ is the most difficult way of all, but it is, in the end, the only way to great things and to permanent peace.

So long as this picture abides may it bear witness to the Eternal Spirit which wills redemption but will not grant it for low triumphs, but only for the growth of the soul into the fuller life of the divine.[3]

[2] Photolithic reproductions in rich coloring of the picture, "If Thou Hadst Known," are obtainable from the City Temple, London, England, for six shillings.

[3] Adapted from the sermon, "If Thou Hadst Known," by Dr. F. W. Norwood, D. D., pastor of the City Temple, London, England. Published by Pety & Company, printers, S.E.5, London, England. Used with the special permission of the author.

"IF THOU HADST KNOWN"—*LONGSTAFF*

THE HEALER

By

Harold Copping

(Interpretation)

No PAINTER in the field of modern religious art has more truly caught the spirit of the Christ as it shines forth in the deeds of kindness and mercy of His followers, than the English painter, Harold Copping, in his "The Healer," which is reprinted here by permission of the London Missionary Society.

Into the heart of Africa, the "dark continent," these medical missionaries of the cross go with their ministry of healing for both sick bodies and sin-sick souls. In the right background of this picture the artist shows low grass-thatched roofs of typical African huts half hidden in the profusion of trees and grasses of its luxuriant tropical climate.

In the foreground is the medical missionary kneeling, with his small metal box of already-prepared medicines beside him on the ground, ready for the numerous calls for his healing ministry that each day brings forth. On the ground, also, may be seen an open leather case of small medical instruments, which all these itinerant physicians carry with them on these trips to remote jungle homes in the forest. A low stool and two earthen vessels, probably filled with clean water, stand near by for the cleansing of wounds and sores; while in his hand the kneeling medical missionary holds a cooling draught of water or healing medicine for this fever-stricken lad.

Directly in front of the doctor is the naked form of a boy, too ill to even sit up. His scantily-clad mother must raise him in her arms so that the doctor may place this glass of water or medicine to his fever-parched lips.

In the near background at the right side of the picture stand the half-clad forms of two children of the forest, watching with absorbing interest this medicine man in the act of performing what to their primitive minds seems nothing less than a miracle. Note the look of grinning happiness on the face of the sick lad's brother as he sees the one who has been too ill even to raise his head from the grass mat open his eyes and smile wanly into the doctor's sympathetic face as the already administered medicine begins to take its effect.

Behind this kneeling servant of mankind stands the shadowy outline of the Great Physician, who went about throughout all Galilee, Judæa and Samaria, preaching, teaching, and "healing all manner of diseases." His half-shadowed arm is outstretched as if in the act of blessing the work of this, His faithful servant, in far-away, pagan Africa. We can almost hear Him saying: "Lo, I am with you always, even unto the end of the world."

This modern masterpiece, "The Healer," by Copping, is representative of the spirit of that army of physicians that as medical missionaries have gone to the ends of the earth in their ministry of sympathy, love, and mercy for even the most backward of races. "These are they who have washed their robes in the blood of the Lamb," and who throughout the whole earth have interpreted, perhaps more fully and truly than any other servants of the Master of Men, the spirit and teachings of the world's greatest Teacher, Preacher, and Servant of the race. As we gaze upon this painting we rejoice that one of our present-day artists has so truly caught the spirit of these "soldiers of the cross" who minister for us and for Christ in the far-away places of the world.

✛

CHRIST, THE UNIVERSAL SAVIOUR

By

Hsu San Ch'un

(Interpretation)

THE compiler of this anthology has purposely included in it reproductions of two or three paintings by artists other than those of the Western World; because in this way the universality of Christ's appeal to men and women of all races and nations may be better shown.

C. M. Yocum, speaking of the universal appeal of Christ, says: "When an Italian paints Christ, he portrays Him as a Southern European. The Ethiopian picture of the 'Babe of Bethlehem' represents a dark-skinned infant in the arms of an Abyssinian Madonna. Jesus is portrayed as an Oriental by His worshipers in the East and as an Occidental by those of the West; as a blond by the Nordic, and as dark-skinned by the sons of Ham. Recently we have seen hanging on our walls the fair-haired, blue-eyed Christ by H. Stanley Todd. When a Western artist paints Buddha, he is always an Oriental. Mohammed is ever a man of Asia. Pictures of Abraham Lincoln seen so often in the Orient always present a man of the West. But, strange as it may seem, Jesus is an Oriental or an Occidental, light or dark, according to the skin of the artist who paints Him. Why?

"Is it not because Jesus is timeless and raceless, classless and ageless, and is it not inevitable that each should think of Him as blood Brother? Each artist, identifying Christ as a member of his own racial family, seeks to interpret Him, not simply to present a view; seeks to reveal His character, not merely to expose His striking characteristics.

"And because Jesus is a universal Saviour, the twentieth century finds no incongruities in Him who lived in the first century. The Orient sees in Him the mystical, contemplative Christ, spending long hours in solitary prayer, while the West hears a practical reformer shout, 'I must work the works of Him that sent Me while it is day.' Children respond to Him as a King and gentle Friend; young people accept His challenge to great adventure; maturity loves Him for

THE HEALER—*COPPING*

CHRIST, THE UNIVERSAL SAVIOUR—*HSU SAN CH'UN*

His strength and courage; and age leans upon Him as One infinitely patient, enduring, and full of hope. All humanity claims Him."[4]

The picture of Christ the Universal Saviour is splendidly illustrative of the appeal that the Master of Men makes to the hearts of men and women of all nations and races. This scroll, painted by Hsu San Ch'un, has as its title "Eternal Life Spring Source"; and the text which in the original scroll is written in Chinese characters above the mountain in the background reads: "Jesus said, 'All who drink of this water certainly will thirst again, but whoever drinks of the water I give through all eternity will never thirst again.'"

One cannot study this picture painted by a native Chinese artist without coming to understand and appreciate something of the world-wide hold that Jesus, the Son of God, has on the hearts and minds of the races of men the world around.

✛

JESUS CHRIST—AND WE

Christ has no hands but our hands
    To do His work today;
He has no feet but our feet
    To lead men in His way;
He has no tongue but our tongues
    To tell men how He died;
He has no help but our help
    To bring them to His side.

We are the only Bible
    The careless world will read;
We are the sinner's Gospel,
    We are the scoffer's creed;
We are the Lord's last message
    Written in deed and word—
What if the line is crooked?
    What if the type is blurred?

What if our hands are busy
    With other work than His?
What if our feet are walking
    Where sin's allurement is?
What if our tongues are speaking
    Of things His lips would spurn?
How can we hope to help Him
    Unless from Him we learn?

—Annie Johnson Flint

[4] March, 1936, *World Call*. Used by permission of the author.

LIVE CHRIST

Live Christ!—and though the way may be
   In this world's sight adversity,
He who doth heed thy every need
   Shall give thy soul prosperity.

Live Christ!—and though the road may be
   The narrow street of poverty,
He had not where to lay His head,
   Yet lived in largest liberty.

Live Christ!—and though the road may be
   The straight way of humility,
He who first trod that way of God
   Will clothe thee with His dignity.

Live Christ!—and though thy life may be
   In much a valedictory,
The heavy cross brings seeming loss,
   But wins the crown of victory.

Live Christ!—and all thy life shall be
   A High Way of Delivery—
A Royal Road of goodly deeds,
   Gold-paved with sweetest charity.

Live Christ!—and all thy life shall be
   A sweet uplifting ministry,
A sowing of the fair white seeds
   That fruit through all eternity.[5]

—John Oxenham

OBEDIENCE

I said, "Let me walk in the field."
   He said, "No; walk in the town."
I said, "There are no flowers there."
   He said, "No flowers, but a crown."

I said, "But the skies are black,
   There is nothing but noise and din."
And He wept as He sent me back.
   "There is more," He said; "there is sin."

[5] From *Quotable Poems*. Used by special permission of the author.

I said, "But the air is thick
  And fogs are veiling the sun."
He answered, "Yet souls are sick,
  And souls in the dark undone."

I said, "I shall miss the light,
  And friends will miss me, they say."
He answered, "Choose tonight
  If I am to miss you, or they."

I pleaded for time to be given.
  He said, "Is it hard to decide?
It will not seem hard in Heaven
  To have followed the steps of your Guide."

I cast one look at the fields,
  Then set my face to the town;
He said: "My child, do you yield?
  Will you leave the flowers for the crown?"

Then into His hand went mine;
  And into my heart came He;
And I walk in a light divine,
  The path I had feared to see.

—George MacDonald

THE LOOM OF LIFE

Children of yesterday, heirs of tomorrow,
What are you weaving? Labor and sorrow?
Look to your looms again; faster and faster
Fly the great shuttles prepared by the Master.
  Life's in the loom. Room for it! Room!

Children of yesterday, heirs of tomorrow,
Lighten the labor and sweeten the sorrow;
Now while the shuttles fly faster and faster,
Up and be at it! At work with the Master.
  He stands at your loom. Room for Him! Room!

Children of yesterday, heirs of tomorrow,
Look at your fabric of labor and sorrow,
Seamy and dark with despair and disaster,
Turn it and, lo! the design of the Master.
  The Lord's at the loom. Room for Him! Room!

—Mary A. Lathbury

CHRIST OF THE EVERYWHERE

Christ of the Andes, Christ of the Everywhere.
  Great Lover of the hills, the open air,
And patient Lover of impatient men
  Who blindly strive and sin and strive again,—
Thou Living Word, larger than any creed,
  Thou Love Divine, uttered in human need,—
Oh, teach the world, warring and wandering still,
  The way to Peace, the footpath of Good Will![6]

—Henry van Dyke

THE TRIMMED LAMP

I dare not slight the stranger at my door—
  Threadbare of garb and sorrowful of lot—
Lest it be Christ that stands; and goes His way
  Because I, all unworthy, knew Him not.

I dare not miss one flash of kindling cheer
  From alien souls, in challenge glad and high.
Ah, what if God be moving very near
  And I, so blind, so deaf, had passed Him by?

—Laura Simmons

BARTIMEUS

God, grant to us Thy blessed Gift again,
To walk with us, as once in Galilee—
Talking of pebbles, and of birds o'erhead;
Of little children, and our daily bread—
To us, Thy lowly fisher-folk! Make plain
The shining wonder of Himself again
That we may touch the seamless garment's hem,
And be made whole of selfishness and sin;
Behold, the hearts made humble and contrite—
Lord, that we may at last receive our sight!

—Laura Simmons

[6] From *The Poems of Henry van Dyke.* Copyright, 1920, by Charles Scribner's Sons. Used by permission.

THE IDEAL CITY

O you whom God hath called and set apart
To build a city after His own heart,
Be this your task—to fill the city's veins
With the red blood of friendship: plant her plains
With seeds of peace: above her portals wreathe
Greeting and welcome: let the air we breathe
Be musical with accents of good will
That leap from lip to lip with joyous thrill;
So may the stranger find upon the streets
A kindly look in every face he meets;
So may the spirit of the city tell
All souls within her gates that all is well;
In all her homes let gentleness be found,
In every neighborhood let grace abound,
In every store and shop and forge and mill
Where men of toil their daily tasks fulfill,
Where guiding brain and workmen's skill are wise
To shape the product of our industries,
Where treasured stores the hands of toil sustain,
Let friendship speed the word and share the gain,
And thus, through all the city's teeming life,
Let helpfulness have room with generous strife to serve.

—Washington Gladden

WAIT

If but one message I may leave behind,
One single word of courage for my kind,
It would be this—Oh, brother, sister, friend,
Whatever life may bring, what God may send,
No matter whether clouds lift soon or late,
Take heart and wait.

Despair may tangle darkly at your feet,
Your faith be doomed, and hope, once cool and sweet,
Be lost; but suddenly above a hill,
A heavenly lamp, set on a heavenly sill,
Will shine for you and point the way to go.
How well I know.

For I have waited through the dark, and I
Have seen a star rise in the blackest sky

Repeatedly—it has not failed me yet.
And I have learned God never will forget
To light His lamp. If we but wait for it,
It will be lit.

—Grace Noll Crowell

THE SOUL OF JESUS IS RESTLESS

The soul of Jesus is restless today;
Christ is tramping through the spirit-world,
Compassion in His heart for the fainting millions;
He trudges through China, through Poland,
Through Russia, Austria, Germany, Armenia;
Patiently He pleads with the Church,
Tenderly He woos her.
The wounds of His body are bleeding afresh for the sorrows
    of His shepherdless people.
We besiege Him with selfish petitions,
We weary Him with our petty ambitions,
From the needy we bury Him in piles of carven stone,
We obscure Him in the smoke of stuffy incense,
We drown His voice with the snarls and shrieks of our disgruntled bickerings,
We build temples to Him with hands that are bloody,
We deny Him in the needs and sorrows of the exploited—
    "least of His brethren."
The soul of Jesus is restless today,
But eternally undismayed.

—Cyprus R. Mitchell

IF JESUS CAME BACK TODAY

If Jesus came back today
What would the people say?
Would they cheer Him and strew the way
With garlands of myrtle and bay
As they did on that distant day
When He came to Jerusalem?
What would America say
If Jesus came back today?

I think without shadow of doubt
When He'd traveled and spoken about
In church and school and street
And clubs where the rich men meet,

His quiet, fearless smile
At our godless greed and guile
Would raise our wrath and bile.

When we heard those firm lips speak
In accents serene and meek:
"I have come to protect the weak
From the plunderer and the knave,
I have come to free the slave,
To lift the poor from the slime
Of need and disease and crime,
To break the grip of gold
On my brothers, young and old;
To throw the prisons wide
And put the rich sinners inside
With those who have made the law
By the rule of fang and claw. . . ."

We would take Him and ride Him out
Like a renegade on a rail,
Or throw Him in the county jail
As a dangerous, radical Red
Who was probably off His head.
"Away with this common lout!"
With derisive laughter and shout
We would mock His daring dream.
"Love?" we would fairly scream,
"Why, what does the madman mean?
This talk is O.K. with rubes,
Or idealistic boobs,
But we are men of knowledge
Who have graduated from college.
Look at the things we own:
Look at our books and inventions,
Our schools, our clubs, our conventions.
We have more goods and gold
Than our mansions and homes can hold.
We have all we can eat and drink,
To the poor we freely give.
Does this fanatic think
He can teach *us* how to *live?*"

O doesn't it shame the dead
And break your heart as mine
That He who broke the bread
And offered His life's new wine
To serve the Cause divine,
That He who suffered and bled
That the hungry might be fed,

That the workman might be free,
That the blinded eyes might see,
That the captive might lose his chains
And the rich his ill-gotten gains . . .
To think while we mouth His name
(Does it not bring a blush of shame?)
We so callously scorn His star
And go hoarding and whoring afar
Where the follies and fleshpots are?

We fashion great churches and creeds,
But the heart of the people still bleeds
And the poor still rot in their needs.
We display with pride His cross
In the midst of our pagan life
While we hug to our hearts the dross
Of our selfishness and strife.
What sacrifice have we made
To live the love He prayed?
What willing blood have we shed
To do the deeds He said?
To be popular and well-fed
We forsake the way He led
And follow a ghost instead!

—Vincent G. Burns

WANTED—A MESSENGER

The Lord Christ wanted a tongue one day,
  To speak a message of cheer
To a heart that was weary and worn and sad,
  Weighed down with a mighty fear.
He asked for mine, but, 'twas busy quite,
With my own affairs from morn till night.

The Lord Christ wanted a hand one day
  To do a loving deed;
He wanted two feet on an errand for Him,
  To run with gladsome speed,
But I had need of my own that day;
To His gentle beseeching I answered, "Nay."

So all that day I used my tongue,
  My hands, and my feet as I chose;
I said some hasty, bitter words
  That hurt one heart, God knows.
I busied my hands with worthless play,
And my willful feet went a crooked way.

While the dear Lord grieved, with His work undone,
  For the lack of a willing heart!
Only through men does He speak to men,
  Dumb must He be apart.
I do not know, but I wish today,
I had let the Lord Christ have His way.

                    —Author Unknown

I SHALL NOT PASS THIS WAY AGAIN

The bread that bringeth strength I want to give,
The water pure that bids the thirsty live:
I want to help the fainting day by day.
I'm sure I shall not pass again this way.

I want to give the oil of joy for tears,
The faith to conquer crowding doubts and fears.
Beauty for ashes may I give alway.
I'm sure I shall not pass again this way.

I want to give good measure running o'er,
And into angry hearts I want to pour
The answer soft that turneth wrath away.
I'm sure I shall not pass again this way.

I want to give to others hope and faith,
I want to do all that the Master saith;
I want to live aright from day to day.
I'm sure I shall not pass again this way.

                    —Author Unknown

THE DISCIPLE

I could not leave Thee, Christ! For when I tried
To leave Thee for alluring ways aside
From Thine own way, Thy power withheld me, kept
My feet from wandering too far, inept
And aimless, down a dwindling path that led
Through mazed confusion to the house of dread.

I could not leave Thee, Christ! For when I yearned
With passionate intensity and burned
With fiery torment to assuage my thirst
For freedom by a turbid stream that burst
In gushing torrents from a naked hill—
Thou ledst me back to waters deep and still.

I could not leave Thee, Christ! For when I sought
To fling aside Thy counsel when I thought
That in my crazy freedom I should find
Some way of life for body, soul, and mind
Better than Thou didst teach, I heard Thee say,
"Come back to Me, for thou hast lost thy way."

I would not leave Thee, Christ! For I am lame
From wandering, and the consuming flame
Of passion has gone out and left my soul
A smoldering ember, and the criss-crossed scroll
Of life ends as it started with the line,
"I cannot leave Thee, Christ! For I am thine."

—Dwight Bradley

THY NEIGHBOR

Who is thy neighbor? He whom thou
    Hast power to aid or bless,
Whose aching heart or burning brow
    Thy soothing hand may press.

Thy neighbor? 'Tis the fainting poor
    Whose eye with want is dim.
Oh, enter thou his humble door
    With aid and peace for him.

Thy neighbor? He who drinks the cup
    When sorrow drowns the brim;
With words of high sustaining hope
    Go thou and comfort him.

Thy neighbor? 'Tis the weary slave,
    Fettered in mind and limb;
He hath no hope this side the grave.
    Go thou and ransom him.

Thy neighbor? Pass no mourner by.
    Perhaps thou canst redeem
A breaking heart from misery.
    Go share thy lot with him.

—Author Unknown

AMERICA FIRST

America first, not only in things material,
But in things of the spirit.
Not merely in science, invention, motors, skyscrapers,
But also in ideals, principles, character.
Not merely in the calm assertion of rights,
But in the glad assumption of duties.
Not flouting her strength as a giant,
But bending in helpfulness over a sick and wounded world
    like a Good Samaritan.
Not in splendid isolation,
But in courageous coöperation.

Not in pride, arrogance, and disdain of other races and peoples,
But in sympathy, love, and understanding.
Not in treading again the old, worn, bloody pathway which ends
    inevitably in chaos and disaster,
But in blazing a new trail along which, please God, other nations will follow
    into the new Jerusalem where wars shall be no more.

Some day, some nation must take that path—unless we are to lapse into utter
    barbarism—and that honor I covet for my beloved America.
And so in that spirit and with these hopes, I say
    with all my heart and soul, "America First."

—G. Ashton Oldham

"A MAN MUST LIVE"

"A man must live!" We justify
Low shift and trick to treason high;
    A little vote for a little gold,
    Or a whole Senate bought and sold,
With this self-evident reply—
        "A man must live!"

But is it so? Pray tell me why
Life at such cost you have to buy.
In what religion were you told
A man must live?
There are times when a man must die!
There are times when a man will die!
Imagine for a battle-cry
From soldiers with a sword to hold,

From soldiers with a flag unfurled,
This coward's whine, this liar's lie,
  "A man must live!"

The Saviour did not *live!*
He *died!*
But in His death was life—
Life for Himself and all mankind!
He found His life by losing it!
And we, being crucified
Afresh with Him, may find
Life in the cup of death,
And, drinking it,
    Win life forevermore.[7]

          —Charlotte Perkins Gilman

I KNOW A NAME

I know a soul that is steeped in sin,
  That no man's art can cure;
But I know a Name, a Name, a Name
  That can make that soul all pure.

I know a life that is lost to God,
  Bound down by the things of earth;
But I know a Name, a Name, a Name
  That can bring that soul new birth.

I know of lands that are sunk in shame,
  Of hearts that faint and tire;
But I know a Name, a Name, a Name
  That can set those lands on fire.

Its sound is a brand, its letters flame,
  Like glowing tongues of fire.
I know a Name, a Name, a Name
  Of which the world ne'er tires.

          —Author Unknown

YOU—AN ANSWER TO PRAYER

You can be—yes—you—
An answer to prayer.
There is work to be done;

[7] The first two verses by Charlotte Perkins Gilman. Published in a book called *In This Our World* (now out of print). The last verse was added later by some unknown author.

A field is to be won;
And millions are praying—
Hands lifted, hearts saying:
O Lord, yet how long
Until right conquer wrong?
You can answer that prayer—
You—answer that prayer.

Be an answer to prayer—
You—an answer to prayer:
By performing the task
God and Right of you ask;
By your courage, your smile;
Fortitude under trial;
By the faith songs you sing;
By the good cheer you bring;
You can be—yes—you—
An answer to prayer.

Be an answer to prayer—
You—an answer to prayer:
By doing your part
Everyday from the heart
As for Christ; everywhere
Gladly doing your share.
Money, service you give,
Life, love—nobly live
And you truly will be—
You—an answer to prayer.

—*A. D. Burkett*

A MANHATTAN CHRISTMAS EVE

You have heard the beautiful story
Of the blessed Saviour's birth,
How a choir of heavenly glory
Sang of peace, good will on earth—
How the shepherds and wise men gathered
From their fields and lands afar
To discover the lowly manger
Underneath the shining star.
Sometimes it seems only a story,
Bethlehem is so far away,
But what would you say if I told you
It happened right here today?

Down in the East Side of the city,
  Where the Jewish people live,
I was bringing the Christmas baskets
  Which our kindly people give
To the sick and the poor and needy,
  And I trudged through sleet and snow
While the lights of the great black city
  One by one began to glow
And spangle the gathering darkness
  Like fairy stars in the sky,
When piercing the noise of the city
  There was heard a baby's cry.

Then a moment later a chorus
  Sang the sweet "O Holy Night"—
I could tell they were children's voices
  But in the deceptive light
I could see but a disordered crowd
  Where alleyways leave a wall—
Some happening gripped their attention
  Men, women, children and all.

I saw as I came somewhat nearer
  A sight I shall never forget—
A few humble household belongings,
  A mattress ragged and wet,
And on it a babe and its mother
  There in the snow and the sleet,
In the rainy and grimy gutter
  Of a filthy East Side street.

A man standing near me whispered to me:
  "Thrown out for not paying rent!
Poor folks are having hard times this year!"
  I nodded a grim assent.
I knew that throughout this land of ours
  Were many cases like this—
Destitute souls who had lost the road
  To prosperity's mocking bliss.

The mother was pitifully smiling
  But filled with tears were her eyes,
Her facing this crowd was a trial,
  Stabs of pain her baby's cries.
A little lad laid his overcoat
  Over the poor woman's form,
A girl wrapped the baby in her shawl
  And tucked him in tight and warm.

A rough workman pushed his way forward,
  And offered the father a job—
The man was struck dumb with excitement,
  His reply a heart-rending sob.
I went up and laid my basket down
  With goodies, fruits, and honey,
Another man passed his hat around
  Till it brimmed over with money.

The kindly heart of that city crowd
  Was a stirring thing to see—
Their quick response to a brother's need
  Was a miracle to me.
I will always see that mother's tears,
  The father near her kneeling—
The baby clapping its little hands,
  The children sweetly singing.

The Christmas tale was here once more:
  The angels were singing children
The shepherds the crowd that gathered,
  The gift-givers the Wise Men.
As I wended my long way homeward
  My heart was thrilled through and through
With a strange, deep sense of God's nearness
  For I knew that this was true:

The Holy Family is these three—
  Father, mother, little son:
Wherever human love is set free
  There God's holy will is done.
Wherever a little child is born,
  And a mother smiles through pain:
There is the eternal Christmas morn
  And the miracle wrought again.
Wherever in woe and want and need
  Some soul lifts a gift of grace
To lend a hand where stricken hearts bleed
  There our God unveils His face.

—*Vincent G. Burns*

DEDICATE YOUR LIFE

See families wrecked by liquor;
  For their sakes—dedicate your life.
See soldiers marching to kill;
  For their sakes—dedicate your life.

See church members indifferent
    and careless;
For their sakes—dedicate your life.
See children dying from hunger;
For their sakes—dedicate your life.
See girls selling their bodies
    for dollars;
For their sakes—dedicate your life.
See share-croppers living in shanties;
For their sakes—dedicate your life.
See rich men groping in the dark;
For their sakes—dedicate your life.[8]

—*Samuel F. Pugh*

✠

WHAT IF THEY HAD QUIT?
(A Dream)

YEARS ago I dreamed a dream, and in my dream five men—Peter, Andrew, Matthew, John, and Paul—were seated on a hillside, looking out over the Sea of Galilee. It was twenty years after the Day of Pentecost, and they had met by appointment to talk over a crisis in the lives and programs of three of their number.

The work was going hard with them. Paul had suffered the loss of all things; Peter had left all to follow Christ, and was finding it hard to support his family; and Matthew had just had a flattering offer at a large salary and an interest in the business to return to his old place in the customs house.

Peter, as usual, opened the discussion. He said: "My wife's mother has opened a boarding-house in Capernaum; it will cost us almost nothing to live with her while we are getting started again, and I have a chance to buy back my interest in the fishing business. I can make a good living and a little more by fishing five days in the week, and I will have all my Sundays for evangelistic work in the cities around the lake. I am getting along in years and am afraid I can't stand the pace at which I have been working. And then, too, I need the money."

Paul said: "Aquilla and Priscilla have been greatly prospered in the tent-making business in Ephesus, and have offered me a position at a good salary to open a branch business in Philippi, and from there to work out and establish and supervise the business of the principal cities in Macedonia. I can do this work; it will not be any harder for me than the care of all the churches, and I will have all my Sundays for Christian work, and can lay by a little something for the rainy day, which I can see is coming."

[8] From *Between-Time Meditations.* Copyright, 1954, by the Bethany Press, St. Louis, Mo. Reprinted by permission of the author and publishers.

Matthew said: "My story of the life of Christ is having a large sale, and is bringing me in enough to pay my expenses, but my business experience tells me that I ought to have a larger margin. Persecution may come and sales would fall off. I have a chance now to take my old position, and I know that I can make enough out of it not only to support myself and family, but to take care of the rest of you if you should get into trouble. And then, too, I will have more leisure for writing and can probably help the cause more in this way than by traveling about the country."

Andrew said: "Peter, do you remember the day when you thought that you had lost your wife's mother? Do you see that sand beach over there? That is the very spot where we beached our boat after the miraculous haul of fish, and where we quit the fishing business, and where the Master said, 'Fear not; from henceforth thou shalt catch men.' How long a time is 'henceforth'? Do you see that hillside over there? That is where the Master fed the five thousand, and I can see the very spot where that lad stood when I asked him to give up his lunch for the Lord to multiply. Don't you remember the look of compassion and longing on the Master's face when He looked out over the multitude and asked us to pray that laborers might be thrust forth in His harvest? If we are going to continue to pray that other men may rise up, leave all and follow Him, can we do less?"

John, who was leaning against Peter, felt a big tear drop on his hand, and looking over at Paul, he saw his jaw set, the old fire come back into his eye, and the old war-horse look into his face, as he quietly said: "Men, I don't think we need to talk about this any more; let us pray."

And as they prayed, the things of time and sense receded; a light breeze rustled in the near-by tree-top, reminding them of that "rushing mighty wind" on the day of Pentecost and of the marvelous power with which Peter had preached the gospel on that day. They seemed also to see the Master himself standing on the shore just a few rods away, and to hear Him saying to them again, "Launch out into the deep and let down your nets for a draught," and "Fear not, from henceforth thou shalt catch men."

They looked, and the evening caravan for Tyre was just swinging into sight. "Good-by," said Paul. "I must catch the next boat for Ephesus, and I will get Aquilla to put up the money for a campaign in that old city that will shake the whole of Asia."

"Good-by," said Peter. "Andrew and I will just say good-by to the folks, and we will have time to join the midnight caravan for Babylon, and may go on East as far as the land of Sinim."

"Good-by," said Matthew. "There is a group of publicans down in Jerusalem who were going in with me on this tax-gathering proposition; but I will get them to join me in financing a five-year campaign in Egypt and up the Nile as far as Ethiopia. I have heard from the Ethiopian treasurer that practically the whole country is open to us, and he believes that all Ethiopia will soon stretch out its hands to God."

"Good-by," said John, and he sat there alone till the stars came out and the waves on the beach, impelled by the rising wind, sounded like the voice of many waters, and he said to Him that stood by: "Lord, do not charge this thing against them. I have felt that way myself at times, as Thou knowest; and I would have left this work but for the fact that Thou didst prevent and strengthen me. They, too, are ready to live and to die for Thee, as I am.

"I thank Thee for Andrew, for his deep life and steady faith. If it please Thee, let him stay and work with Peter, and then the one who can chase a thousand shall put ten thousand to flight.

"And now, Lord, let us see Thee ever before us, ever to hear Thy voice and walk and work with Thee, and we will not fear what men can do unto us."

A sudden storm broke over the lake and I awoke. And as I thought upon the dream I heard the voice of a modern John calling to me out of his rich experience:

> "Go labor on, spend and be spent,
>   Thy joy to do the Father's will;
> It is the way the Master went.
>   Should not the servant tread it still?

> "Go labor on, 'tis not for naught;
>   The earthly loss is heavenly gain;
> Men heed Thee, love Thee, praise Thee not,
>   The Master praises. What are men?

> "Go labor on while yet 'tis day;
>   The world's dark night is hastening on.
> Speed, speed Thy work, cast sloth away.
>   It is not thus that souls are won."[9]

✛

GOD'S MAN IN AFRICA

or

"Practicing Christianity"

A CONCERT crowd thronged the Abbey, one afternoon not long ago, to hear a man named Schweitzer play the organ. They, too, were awed and hushed; awed by the artistry of the greatest organist in Europe; hushed by the golden melody that streamed from his finger tips. He swept them out of themselves, up and out of the grinding, fighting world outside the Abbey doors, held their hearts in moments of high ecstasy, set them dreaming and forgetting and exulting. He stirred again the tender memories of the past, set them marching in dim troops across their minds. . . . The artist was playing from the Preludes of Bach. Bach! In Westminster! At the hands of a master of Bach! . . .

[9] By C. K. Ober. Reprinted with permission from *The Missionary Intelligencer*, by request.

Now this man had just come running out of Africa, to play a few concerts, raise a little money, and go running promptly back again. He could have stayed in Europe and enjoyed it. Musical Europe, at least, would be glad to sit at the feet of Albert Schweitzer and revel in his Bach. He is an organist famous wherever organs are known. He is the authority par excellence on the life and work of composer Sebastian Bach. As few other men, he makes Bach live beautifully again as he touches his organ keys.

He is a theologian known and marveled at wherever there is theology. His pen has produced a dozen deep and learned volumes of religious subjects that many a famous scholar might well wish he could have written.

He is a surgeon and physician whose skill is worshiped in Africa as the magic of God.

He is, according to Bishop Barnes of Birmingham, one of the world's three greatest living men.

And he refuses to be anything more than "a poor Negro's doctor," with his office and operating-room in the deep jungles of French Equatorial Africa.

Why does a man like this toss over his shoulder the worship and honor of the West, and go trotting off to the tropics of another world?

Thrilled as a boy by stories of the missionary heroes, the "missionary complex" had probably been working in this youth all across the years. Coupled with that admiration of the missionary was his reverence "for all who live and breathe," his loathing of suffering in any form, his entire subjugation of himself to the will of God. But all his brooding and meditation and debate were suddenly ended by a statue—by the sculptured figure of a Negro at the foot of the statue of Admiral Bruat by Bartholdi—the same Bartholdi who gave us our Statue of Liberty in New York Harbor. Walking in the Champs de Mars, at Colmar, young Schweitzer caught a glimpse of that stone face and it burned its way into his soul. The infinite sadness of the eyes, the everlasting tragedy, and the eternal hope that rested on that black brow went to his heart like a knife. Waking and asleep, he could not drive from his mind the figure of this black man against the sky. It came over him that "We are all Dives, while out there in Africa sits wretched Lazarus, the colored folk. . . . We sin against the black man at our gate. . . . I resolved to study medicine and to put my ideas to the test out there."

He told his friends. They were horrified. They raved, they pleaded, they stormed, they argued, they wept. But Albert Schweitzer stood with God against the world—and went back to school again. In four years he graduated, a doctor of medicine. And in 1913, with a trained nurse who was also his wife, he set his face toward darkest Africa.

Schweitzer is there now. He made a flying trip to Europe in 1931 for "rest"; during his vacation he worked on another book and raised more money for the hospital. They tried to keep him home: Prague and St. Andrews Universities made him an honorary Doctor of Philosophy; the city of Frankfort presented him with their Goethe Prize, which is awarded for distinguished service to humanity. Westminster called him again, and he played. Ramsay MacDonald sent for him to come to Downing Street and talk. But they couldn't hold him. Just before Christmas, that year, he went back. Schweitzer will die in Africa. For he cannot die happily anywhere else on earth. We are sure of that, because Oganga of the Forest, as Africa knows him, has given us this confession of his faith from his own lips: ". . . . For years I have been preaching about Christianity. But inwardly I was longing to be practising Christianity silently. This I do now, or I try to do it."[10]

✛

THE POET OF THE PEOPLE

In one of America's more conservative magazines a few months ago there appeared an article entitled "The World's Ten Living Christians," and Edwin Markham's name was in that group.

Markham is a Christian because he loves Christ and lives the Christ life by the severest test; and that is, he does without things. He lives in a manner that will astonish the world when it discovers the facts.

I can remember that, when I have taken him to some hotel or club for a rather luxurious meal, he has been uneasy all through it. I have noted his uneasiness. One day I asked him what bothered him, and he said, as simply as a child: "I cannot bear to be sitting down to this wasteful meal when I think of the thousands of people on earth who do not have enough to eat. Why do we not eat in some more moderate place and save the money for others? I do not believe, if we are followers of the lowly Nazarene, and take Him seriously, that we have any right to eat more than necessity requires."

It has always been difficult for me to get the poet to ride in Pullman cars. Only in extremely long jumps will he take a sleeper. He sits up. He says that he does it for two reasons—to save the extra expense and to ride with the common people. And I know him well enough to realize that there is no melodrama about either reason he offers. When I greet an ordinary lecturer, or visiting genius, I go to the Pullman car steps; but when I go to meet the greatest living poet America has today, I know that I shall find him climbing down from a day coach after the night's ride. . . .

He dresses simply, even poorly, because he does not have fine clothes. An old battered hat, an old overcoat that some friend has given him, whether it fits or not—that is the picture we who love him have of him, and shall have to the end of time. I doubt if he ever willingly indulged in luxury on his own account.

He lives simply in his own home, as simply as a peasant, and yet he is glowingly and gloriously happy in his simplicity. His sympathy for the hungry of the earth has never been blotched by luxurious living. Is it more than mere theory? It is a part of his very life. . . .

[10] By Hubert W. Peet, in *The Christian Herald*, March, 1931. Used with permission.

Then there is the miracle of the Markham youth. Approaching eighty, this man walks and lives and talks as a man of thirty. Where most men are burned out at his age, he still has glowing within him the fires of youth.

He will start out on a three months' trip through ten states from New York to Texas by himself, making often two or three speaking engagements a day, sleeping in day coaches at night, picking up meals where he can; laughing, shouting, exuberant, boyish; making friends on every train, at every wayside lunchroom, in depots, hotel lobbies; giving himself to every human being he meets with an overflowing, expansive personality such as I have never seen in my life.

He overflows like a great Nile River and enriches the soil of humanity with his physical and spiritual buoyancy. He is the most abundant human being, physically and spiritually, I have ever met. He emits sparks and electrical power with every handshake. His eyes and his fingers spit fire. When he comes into a room he brings an electrical atmosphere like a summer thunder-storm. He is Dawn, he is Youth. . . .

I write of the miracle of Markham because I consider him to be the great pioneer of the social gospel in America. When Walter Rauschenbusch, Harry Ward, and Bishop Francis J. McConnell are forgotten in dust; when humanity no longer remembers these names or what these men did or said, the name and the fame of "The Man with the Hoe" will go thundering down the eons. Before these men were heard of, "The Man with the Hoe" was preaching the social gospel and beating down the rotten foundations of oppression, injustice, and monarchy in Europe.[11]

✛

THE HEALER COMES

THE sun was setting over the far-off cluster of date palms as Sindano, the brown African boy, trudged along the narrow path in the high grass toward the village where he lived. . . .

The house in which Sindano lived was one of the round thatched huts whose tops he could see far beyond the palm trees. It was dark and stuffy, for there was no opening but the door, which had to serve as window and chimney as well. He used to sleep stretched out on a grass mat, his neck resting on the low pillow made out of sticks. He ate the corn porridge that his mother made every day, using his hands as a spoon. Sometimes he used to set traps to catch birds and fish to eat with the porridge.

Sindano was only ten years old, so he did no very hard work yet. Sometimes he herded the village cattle or watched the crops, but he spent a lot of his day playing games with the boys of the village—swimming in the river near by, sleeping in the hot sun, hunting for food, or listening to the talk and stories

[11] Wm. L. Stidger in *Zion's Herald*, February 25, 1931. Used with permission.

that were told under the council tree in the middle of the village or by the fires in the huts.

Often he was happy enough, but he remembered evil days when some one in the village fell ill and when the terrible witch-doctor, with his ugly cap and his necklace of thorns, was called to cast out what he believed to be the evil spirit in the sick man. Sometimes the witch-doctor would cut a hole in his patient to let the spirit out. Sometimes he only made a great noise or gave him some evil-smelling medicine to drink and charms to wear. But if the patient died it was said that some man or woman had cast a spell over him, and the witch-doctor would accuse the murderer and demand that he should die a dreadful death. Then, even the strong men of the village shook with fear lest they should be accused. Sindano thought sadly about his own little brother who lay in the hut at home, very thin and miserable with illness. The witch-doctor had done *him* no good.

When he reached home he found the whole place astir with excitement. As he sat down by the big porridge-pot with his father he heard scraps of the news about which everyone was talking. Early that morning a man in strange clothes with a white skin had come into the village. He had spoken for a long while to the present Chief Mushidi about his son who was ill and cried out with pain day and night. At first Mushidi had been suspicious, but the stranger spoke kindly to him and said he would make his son well again. Then a strange thing happened, for the white man went to the place where Mushidi's son lay, touched him with a strange bright charm,[12] and gave him something to drink. And after a while the sick boy had ceased his crying, for the stranger by his magic had taken the pain away.

"Then," said Sindano's father, "Mushidi and the whole village came to listen to the words of the stranger. He spoke to us concerning the spirits we worship and of the Only Great One, who is far away. He said: 'The Spirit of the Only Great One is kind and good. He does not wish us to suffer.' The stranger told us that he, too, worshiped Him, that he knew His laws, and would teach them to us. Many new things he told us concerning the Only Great One of whom we know but little. And when Mushidi asked how he had come to know these things, he spoke of One named Jesus, who had lived many years ago, and who taught them to men. Mushidi asked the stranger to stay and tell us more, but he was going on a journey and could not. Yet he promised to send a teacher to tell us more, and that he himself would come back and heal those that were sick in the village before many days were past." Sindano listened to all this with wide-open eyes. He was anxious to see the stranger, and to hear the story of Him who told men about the Only Great One. He lay awake that night, thinking about it. . . .

Three months later Sindano sat on the ground with a dozen other boys and tried to learn the things the new teacher taught him. Every day he and the others took their places under the shelter of a big tree and had their "school." They were learning to write on the earth with pointed sticks—to make strange

[12] It was a thermometer, but, of course, the Africans did not know that.

marks with meaning to them—"hiding words in strokes," Sindano called it. The new teacher taught them to read, too, and to say words and sentences after him altogether in a loud sing-song voice. And every day he taught them some of the laws of the Only Great One. The new teacher was as brown as Sindano, and he had the same woolly hair and white teeth. But he wore a clean white cloth instead of the dirty rags the villagers had, and there were no charms hanging round his neck to frighten away evil spirits such as Sindano's people wore. He was strong and kind and the boys liked him, though he was very angry if they stole or told lies.

This is the way the new teacher told the boys the story of Jesus—part of it every day. . . .

"Once, many, many years ago, there lived a great Chief of His tribe. The tribe had had many chiefs before Him, some of whom had led their people into battle against their enemies, some who had ruled them well and made them happy, and from one of these rulers this Chief was descended. He was truly their chief although they did not know it, for another and a stronger tribe ruled over them.

"Now this Chief went through His country doing kind and merciful deeds to all the people. To those who were blind He gave back their sight. Those who were sick with fever He healed. Those who were lame and paralyzed He made strong. And when they thanked Him for His kindness He would say, 'Even so is the Only Great One kind. He looks on all men and loves them and desires that they should be kind to one another. I speak His message, and it is by His power that I heal you.' . . .

"Now, it happened," continued the teacher, "that some of the chief men of that tribe were jealous, and they were angry with the Good Chief because many followed Him. So they brought false charges against Him and bribed witnesses to tell lies and deceived the stronger tribe that ruled over them, saying that the Good Chief was plotting to fight against them and take away their power. And having done all this, they put Him to a cruel and shameful death."

Sindano gasped with horror. "They killed their Chief," he said. "They were an evil people. Did not His spirit come back and take vengeance on them? Did He not curse their grain and their cattle and their sons and daughters?"

The teacher paused and looked at the circle of boys who sat with wide-open eyes in front of him.

"Truly He came back," he said, "but not to take vengeance. He was full of sorrow because of the wickedness of His people; because they knew not the laws of the Only Great One and because many of them were in pain and trouble. Therefore He appeared to His friends and spoke thus: 'Go now unto My people and unto all the tribes of the earth whom the Only Great One loves, and speak the words I spoke whilst I was with you, and do also the deeds I did. And behold My spirit shall be with you always and with all those who follow Me.' "

Then the little boy with the lame foot who sat next to Sindano said, "They did not build a hut for His spirit, such as we build for our chief."

"There was no need," said the teacher. "He would not dwell there; but wherever His followers obey His words and do deeds of kindness and mercy the Spirit of the Good Chief is with them. The Shinganga [doctor] who healed Mushidi's son is one of His followers, and I, too, follow Him." . . .

Sindano waited while the others went back to their homes. "Teacher," he said, "I also would become one of His followers and keep His words. The Good Chief shall be my Chief."[13]

✛

THE DOCTOR HAS COME!

"Shinganga has come! The doctor has come." The news traveled like lightning through every hut in the village. The missionary doctor had pitched his tent under the council tree with Mushidi in his best robes of leopard skin, and Mushidi's son on one side of him, and the teacher whom the doctor had sent on the other. Mushidi's command was, "Let all those who have any sickness or disease come before the Shinganga and be healed." The crowd stood round and jostled one another to see what the Shinganga did, and Sindano stood as near as he could.

He watched them lead Katela's wife out of her dark hut through the bright sunshine to where the doctor stood. She turned her head from side to side as if in pain and moaned. But when the doctor's strong, cool hands touched her she became quiet. Sindano saw the doctor take something out of a box and put it on her eyes and wind a bandage round her head. He gave something to the women who brought her and told them what they must do to make her eyes well. Then a man limped up to him with a sore foot, and the Shinganga dressed that, too. One by one the others followed. One had a wound made by the claws of a leopard on his arm, and the doctor bound it up. Then came two men carrying a third in a blanket slung on a pole.

When the doctor saw that man he shook his head. "I cannot heal him here," he said. "He must come to the Chipatala [hospital]. It is many miles away, but it is his only chance."

He turned to look at a tiny black baby that an African mother had brought to him, and then took some medicine from the box that was near. The woman who stood near Sindano uttered cries of surprise and joy. "Wonderful! Wonderful!" she said. "He drives out the evil spirits at a touch."

The woman with the baby came back through the crowd, her face lit up with joy. As she came she threw down on the ground a horn-shaped charm that she had used to find the things she wanted. She had found what she

---

[13] Adapted from *Sindano Stories*, by Vera E. Walker. Published by the Livingstone Press, London, England. Used with permission of the publishers.

wanted now, and she did not need this any more. The other woman joined her, and they went back to the huts. Then Sindano saw his own mother come toward the doctor, carrying in her arms his little brother. She laid him down on the grass before the Shinganga, and at a sign from him put her arm around him and lifted him up, for he was too weak to move. A look of pity came over the doctor's face.[14] He poured something into a glass, and gave it to the little boy. There was no sign at first. Then Sindano's brother slowly opened his big eyes and smiled.

"See! see!" said the man with the bandaged arm to Sindano, "he lives! What new witchcraft is this?" Sindano leaned forward with sparkling eyes.

"The Shinganga is a follower of the Good Chief who went through the land healing all those who were in pain," he exclaimed. "He died, but behold, these His followers keep His words and do even as He. His spirit dwells in no house that men build, but wherever His followers do deeds of kindness and mercy there is the Spirit of the Good Chief Himself with them."

That night at sunset the missionary gathered all the people round him and spoke to them again of the Good Chief whom he followed. Then the teacher called together his boys to sing their hymn. Clear and strong Sindano's voice rose above the rest:

> "The great good Doctor is here,
>   His name is Jesus,
> He shows us compassion,
>   Hear the words of Jesus.
>
> Take up the glad song,
>   The song of the name of Jesus,
> The greatest Name,
>   Of Jesus—Our Chief."

"Come again," said Mushidi to the Doctor. "Come many times again. And leave us with a teacher that we may learn more about this new teaching."

Will the doctor come again? In the scattered villages of Africa—in the million villages of India and in the towns and hamlets of China hundreds of thousands of people are asking that question. They suffer untold pain and misery, and they know nothing of the story of the Good Chief Who sent out His followers to preach, to teach and to heal the sick.

Sometimes there is only one doctor for hundreds of miles of wild country. How often can he visit the people?

"Can they not come to the hospitals," you ask? "Yes, if there were enough hospitals. But every hospital is full, and each needs doctors, and nurses and a big supply of medicines and bandages."

We call ourselves followers of the Good Chief. What are we going to do about it?[15]

[14] See Harold Copping's picture, "The Healer," on page 756.

[15] Adapted from *Sindano Stories*, by Vera E. Walker. Published by the Livingstone Press, London, England. Used by permission of the publishers.

"CHALLENGE"

THIS great hymn, "Challenge," or "Are Ye Able?" as it is sometimes called, was written for a consecration service at the Boston University School of Religious Education by Earl Marlatt in 1926. It had its inception, however, in the classroom of the late Marcus D. Buell of Boston University School of Theology, where Mr. Marlatt was a student from 1919 to 1922.

Speaking of the forces that contributed to its composition, Mr. Marlatt says: "Jesus always threw out a challenge. When Salome asked for her sons a place in His kingdom, Jesus knew that just ahead of Him was Jerusalem and possibly crucifixion. He wondered if these young 'sons of thunder' as he was accustomed to call them, had courage enough to follow Him that far. So he said to them, 'Are ye able to drink the cup that I shall drink of and to be baptized with the baptism that I am baptized with?' They said unto Him, 'Lord, we are able.'"

Two years later Mr. Marlatt went to Oberammergau to see the Passion Play. The most significant scene in the Passion Play is the Crucifixion, and the most moving moment in that scene is the one where the thief turns to Jesus and says, "Remember me when thou comest into Thy kingdom." And Jesus, seeing both his faith and penitence, replies, "Today shalt thou be with Me in paradise." As Anton Lang said those words, Mr. Marlatt says, "immortality suddenly became as real to me as the sunlight, and I knew that nothing, nothing could ever shake my faith in that vision.

"Somehow those two moments got together when I was asked to write a hymn of self-dedication for the School of Religious Education. The words came so spontaneously to the music of a tune which Harry Mason had already written that the text seemed to write itself. I sang it to myself as I crossed the Boston Common one evening, and by the time I had reached my room on top of Beacon Hill the song was finished. I needed only time to transcribe it for the quartet and congregation which sang it in Pilgrim Hall three days later."

"Challenge" was later adopted as one of the school songs of Boston University School of Theology, where Mr. Marlatt is now a faculty member, and has been carried by his students out into their ministries all over the world. One of his former students, serving as a chaplain in Sherborn Prison for Women, wrote Mr. Marlatt that she had used this hymn in a Sunday vesper service at the prison. Two hours later she was called to the cell of one of the so-called "incorrigibles," who said: "I suppose you were surprised to have me call for you. I don't wonder. I've never done much with religion. If I had I wouldn't be here, probably. That song we sang tonight made me see what the things you believe can mean to people like me. Please tell your friend, who has never seen me, that he wrote that third verse for me." And she repeated it from memory. "Just thank him, please, and tell him I'll try to remember and be different."

"Are ye able," said the Master,
"To be crucified with Me?"
"Yea," the sturdy dreamers answered,
"To the death we follow Thee."

Chorus

Lord, we are able, Our spirits are Thine,
Remold them, make us, like Thee, divine.
Thy guiding radiance above us shall be,
A beacon to God, to faith and loyalty.

"Are ye able to relinquish
Purple dreams of power and fame,
To go down into the garden,
Or to die a death of shame?

Chorus

"Are ye able to remember
When a thief lifts up his eyes,
That his pardoned soul is worthy
Of a place in Paradise?

Chorus

"Are ye able, when the shadows
Close around you with the sod,
To believe that spirit triumphs
To commend your soul to God?

Chorus

"Are ye able?" still the Master
Whispers down eternity,
And heroic spirits answer
Now, as then, in Galilee.[16]

Chorus

—*Earl Marlatt, 1926*

[16] Copyrighted by the author, used with his permission.

O MASTER, LET ME WALK WITH THEE

OF ALL the beautiful hymns that have come down to us through the years, there is perhaps no one that is more appealing than this great devotional hymn which was written by Washington Gladden in 1879. It was almost immediately associated with the tune "Marydon," which had been composed a few years earlier, in 1874, by Henry Percy Smith.

This hymn, "O Master, Let Me Walk with Thee," has been sung by literally millions of people of every race and clime, and has gone to nearly every country where the Christian religion is known. It expresses perhaps better than any other hymn of the Church the rich fellowship which all true followers of Christ experience when they walk close to the Master in loving, helpful service to others.

While not written primarily for young people, this great hymn of the Church has a strange mystical appeal for them, and is frequently used by them in planning services of worship in young people's conferences, Christian Endeavor meetings, and city and state-wide get-togethers.

> O Master, let me walk with Thee
> In lowly paths of service free;
> Tell me Thy secret; help me bear
> The strain of toil, the fret of care.
>
> Help me the slow of heart to move
> By some clear, winning word of love;
> Teach me the wayward feet to stay,
> And guide them in the homeward way.
>
> Teach me Thy patience; still with Thee
> In closer, dearer company,
> In work that keeps faith sweet and strong,
> In trust that triumphs over wrong.
>
> In hope that sends a shining ray
> Far down the future's broadening way;
> In peace that only Thou canst give,
> With Thee, O Master, let me live.

—Washington Gladden, 1879

WHERE CROSS THE CROWDED WAYS OF LIFE

IN THIS great Christian hymn, "Where Cross the Crowded Ways of Life," written by Frank Mason North in 1903, we have another of these more modern hymns of the Church that call our attention to the busy marts of our great cities where people of all races and nationalities are crowded together in a heterogeneous mass; and of their need for fellowship with the Christ.

When the compiler of this anthology on *Christ and the Fine Arts* wrote Mr. North for permission to include in it this great hymn with a brief story as to its message, he graciously replied: "This hymn has but one mission in the world, and that is to help men of all races and conditions better to understand the person and meaning of Jesus Christ. I shall be glad to have you use it if it serves this purpose."

One can neither read nor sing the lines of this great hymn-poem without feeling the conviction in the heart of its author that men shall be made better only as they come to know, to love, and to serve the Christ, who in spirit still walks the highways of the world in helpful service to mankind.

Where cross the crowded ways of life,
  Where sound the cries of race and clan,
Above the noise of selfish strife
  We hear Thy voice, O Son of Man!

In haunts of wretchedness and need,
  On shadowed thresholds dark with fears,
From paths where hide the lures of greed,
  We catch the vision of Thy tears.

From tender childhood's helplessness,
  From woman's grief, man's burdened toil,
From famished souls, from sorrow's stress,
  Thy heart has never known recoil.

The cup of water given for Thee
  Still holds the freshness of Thy grace;
Yet long these multitudes to see
  The sweet compassion of Thy face.

O Master, from the mountain-side,
  Make haste to heal these hearts of pain;
Among these restless throngs abide,
  O tread the city's streets again;

Till sons of men shall learn Thy love,
  And follow where Thy feet have trod;
Till glorious from Thy heaven above,
  Shall come the city of our God. Amen.[17]

—Frank Mason North, 1903

✣

RISE UP, O MEN OF GOD

IN THIS great Christian hymn, one of the most challenging of the more recent hymns of the Church, we find strongly expressed the idea of human brotherhood.

Speaking of the occasion which called it forth, Reverend William P. Merrill, former minister of the Fifth Avenue Brick Church of New York City, says: "I was asked to write a *brotherhood hymn,* and this one seemed just to come of itself. The wide use that has been made of it has been a matter of very deep satisfaction to me."

In these days of racial prejudice and misunderstanding, and of class hatred and strife, we need, more and more, to recognize and emphasize this thought of the brotherhood of mankind; and to stress those great humanitarian elements and interests in which all must share alike.

We can feel the throb of human brotherhood in every verse of this great Christian hymn which represents the best thought of Christianity today.

It is usually sung to a much older tune, "St. Thomas," composed by Aaron Williams in 1763.

Rise up, O men of God,
  Have done with lesser things,
Give heart and soul and mind and strength
  To serve the King of Kings.

Rise up, O men of God.
  His Kingdom tarries long;
Bring in the day of brotherhood
  And end the night of wrong.

Rise up, O men of God
  The Church for you doth wait,
Her strength unequal to her task;
  Rise up, and make her great.

---

[17] Words copyrighted by Frank Mason North. Used by permission.

Lift high the cross of Christ,
    Tread where His feet have trod;
As brothers of the Son of man,
    Rise up, O men of God.[18]

—William P. Merrill, 1911

✛

WE'VE A STORY TO TELL TO THE NATIONS

AMONG the great missionary hymns of the Church, perhaps none has a greater appeal than this one, written by Colin Sterne in 1896, "We've a Story to Tell to the Nations." It is usually sung to the tune "Message" as adapted from an earlier melody by H. Ernest Nichol.

This is the type of hymn which should be sung in its entirety, because each verse stresses a different thing that Christians have to share with the people of all nations and races. The first stanza emphasizes the *story* we have to tell; the second the *song* we have to sing; the third the *message* we have to bear; and the fourth the *Saviour* we have to show. As a hymn it moves naturally to a climax in the last stanza, and to omit one or more of its verses in singing it is to spoil the beauty and effectiveness of its message as a whole.

We've a story to tell to the nations,
That shall turn their hearts to the right,
A story of truth and mercy,
A story of peace and light.
A story of peace and light.

Refrain

For the darkness shall turn to dawning,
And the dawning to noonday bright,
And Christ's great Kingdom shall come on earth,
The Kingdom of Love and Light.

We've a song to be sung to the nations,
That shall lift their hearts to the Lord;
A song that shall conquer evil
And shatter the spear and sword,
And shatter the spear and sword.

Refrain

We've a message to give to the nations,
That the Lord who reigneth above
Hath sent us His Son to save us,
And show us that God is love,
And show us that God is love.

[18] Words copyrighted by William P. Merrill. Used by permission.

Refrain

We've a Saviour to show to the nations,
Who the path of sorrow has trod,
That all of the world's great peoples
Might come to the truth of God,
Might come to the truth of God.

Refrain

—*Colin Sterne, 1896*

✠

IF I COULD BUT TELL ALL THE GLORY

Among the many beautiful hymns that have found their way into the newer hymnals of the Church is one called "If I Could But Tell All the Glory," written by Eleanor Allen Schroll, on which copyright was secured by the Fillmore Brothers Company in 1920.

This evangelistic song first appeared in sheet-music form; and is remarkably beautiful when sung as a duet (soprano and alto), the audience or congregation joining in on the refrain.

The theme of its three verses all emphasize telling, first of the *glory*, second of the *goodness*, and third of the *saving grace* of the Saviour, while the refrain to be sung following each verse stresses the fact that "better than telling is *living* a life ever faithful and true."

This splendid new hymn will be found on pages 127-128 of *Hymns for To-day*, published by the Fillmore Brothers Company, Cincinnati, Ohio.

If I could but tell all the glory
    That shines in my soul day by day,
Or if I could tell of the Saviour,
    Till echoes would ring it for aye,
I'd shout it aloud from the mountain,
    I'd sing it o'er valley and plain;
I'd tell it and tell it and tell it,
    Till millions would hear the refrain.

Refrain

But better than telling is living
    A life ever faithful and true;
Then souls that are waiting in darkness,
    Will see Jesus' love shining through.

If I could but tell of His goodness,
    His love, and His infinite care;
Or if I could show you the vision,
    I see when I meet Him in pray'r;

Or if I could tell the old story
　　Till others would feel He was near,
I'd tell it and tell it and tell it,
　　All nations His praises would hear.

Refrain

If I could but tell you of Jesus,
　　Of how I was saved by His grace,
Or if I could paint the compassion
　　I see in the dear Master's face,
I'd sing till the far-away echoes,
　　Would ring from the earth to the sky,
I'd tell it and tell it and tell it,
　　In praises that never would die.[10]

Refrain

—Eleanor A. Schroll

✠

THE STRANGER OF GALILEE

MANY new, and remarkably beautiful sacred songs have established for themselves a permanent place in the musical literature of the Church during the
decades that have intervened since the close of the First World War.

Among these newer hymns, none is more appealing in the simplicity of its
message than "The Stranger of Galilee," the words of which were composed
by Mrs. C. H. Morris, and the music by Mabel Miller Sturgis.

This song is unusually effective when sung as a solo, and is obtainable in
sheet-music form for high, medium, and low voices. It is also published as
an anthem for mixed men's and women's voices, and as a duet for high and
low voices in "G."

It is one of those songs that tell a story of the rich and varied service which
the Stranger of Galilee rendered to the children of men; and is evangelistic
in the individual appeal it makes to the human heart to "love Him forever"
and to claim Him as a personal Saviour.

In fancy I stood by the shore, one day,
　　Of the beautiful murm'ring sea;
I saw the great crowds as they thronged the way
　　Of the Stranger of Galilee.
I saw how the man who was blind from birth
　　In a moment was made to see;
The lame were made whole by the matchless skill
　　Of the Stranger of Galilee.

[19] Words reprinted by permission of the Fillmore Music House, 528 Elm Street, Cincinnati, Ohio.

Chorus (to be sung after the first and second verses)

And I felt I could love Him forever,
 So gracious and tender was He!
I claim'd Him that day as my Saviour,
 This Stranger of Galilee.

His look of compassion, His words of love,
 They shall never forgotten be,
When sin-sick and helpless He saw me there,
 This Stranger of Galilee.
He showed me His hand and His riven side,
 And He whispered "It was for thee!"
My burden fell off at the piercèd feet
 Of the Stranger of Galilee.

I heard Him speak peace to the angry waves
 Of that turbulent, raging sea;
And lo! at His word are the waters still'd,
 This Stranger of Galilee.
A peaceful, a quiet, and holy calm
 Now and ever abides with me;
He holdeth my life in His mighty hands,
 This Stranger of Galilee.

Chorus (to be sung after the third and fourth verses)

Oh, my friend, won't you love Him forever,
 So gracious and tender is He!
Accept Him today as your Saviour,
 This Stranger of Galilee.

Come ye who are driven, and tempest tossed,
 And His gracious salvation see;
He'll quiet life's storms with His "Peace, be still!"
 This Stranger of Galilee.
He bids me to go and the story tell
 What He ever to you will be,
If only you let Him with you abide,
 This Stranger of Galilee.[20]

—Mrs. C. H. Morris, 1928

[20] Copyrighted by Standard Publishing Company, Cincinnati, Ohio. Published by the Boston Music Company. Used by permission of the publishers and copyright holders.

Index of Art and Art Interpretations by Artists and Titles

The *Italics* show the page on which the picture will be found; the Roman figures refer to the interpretation of the picture.

ACKNOWLEDGMENTS

ACKNOWLEDGMENTS are here made for the generous co-operation of authors and publishers in the compilation of this anthology (revised and enlarged in 1959).

The author-compiler has made every effort to trace the ownership of all copyrighted pictures, poetry, stories, and hymns through the public libraries, art galleries, art agencies, and publishers; and to the best of her knowledge has secured all necessary permissions from authors (some of whom are now deceased) or their recognized agents or from both. Should there be any question regarding the use of any picture, poem, story or hymn included without permission having been secured, regret is hereby acknowledged for such unconscious error. The compiler, upon notification of such oversight, will be pleased to make proper acknowledgment in future editions of this anthology.

Besides such acknowledgments as may appear throughout the volume the compiler wishes to express her sincere thanks to Mr. Abbott Book, 140 Arbor Dr., Piedmont 10, Calif., for his co-operation in loaning to her prints of works of art together with permission to include these with interpretations in this anthology. Also to Mrs. Rose Page Welch of Chicago, Ill., for the assistance she rendered in interpreting the Negro spirituals. Thanks are also expressed to Mrs. John W. Geller of Indianapolis, Ind., for her assistance in interpreting the hymns in Parts I, II, and III.

Sincere thanks are also due to the following publishers and individuals for their co-operation in allowing the use of poems, stories and pictures:

PICTURES

The Abbott Book Library of Art, 140 Arbor Dr., Piedmont, Calif., for permission to include reproductions of "The Concert" by Goth and "Caritas" by Thayer.

Alinari Fratelli, 8 Via Nazionale, Florence, Italy, for permission to include reproductions of the following pictures: "The Sistine Madonna" by Raphael; "Christ and the Tribute Money" by Van Dyck; "The Magdalene" by Guercino; "The Wedding at Cana" by Veronese; "Ecce Homo" and "The Entombment" by Ciseri; and "A Modern Madonna" by Ferruzzi.

American Seating Company, Grand Rapids, Mich., for permission to include a reproduction of "The Last Supper" by Lang.

Albert Edward Bailey, % Pilgrim Press, 14 Beacon St., Boston 8, Mass., for permission to include five art interpretations from *The Gospel in Art,* as follows: "Repose in Egypt" by Merson; "Ecce Homo" and "The Entombment" by Ciseri; "The Remorse of Judas" by Armitage; "Descent from the Cross" by Rubens; and "Jesus and the Doctors" by Von Gebhardt; also brief paragraphs quoted in connection with these and other art interpretations.

The Challenge Limited, London, England, for permission to include the picture "Christ and the Children" by Hansen.

Dodd, Mead and Company, 432 Fourth Ave., New York 16, N. Y., for permission to include two Mastroianni art reproductions, "The Ascending Christ" and "Then They Came, and Laid Hands on Jesus and Took Him," from Lees' *The Life of Christ.*

Epworth-Euclid Methodist Church, Cleveland, Ohio, for permission to include photographs of the interior and exterior of the Epworth-Euclid Methodist Church.

Forest Lawn Memorial-Park, Glendale, Calif., for permission to include a reproduction of "The Christus" by Thorvaldsen.

A. Giraudon, 9 Rue des Beaux Arts, Paris, France, for permission to include reproductions of the following pictures: "The Immaculate Conception" by Murillo; "Christ on the Cross" by Rubens; "Descent from the Cross" by Rubens; "Christ Mourns over the City" by Flandrin.

Gramstorff Brothers, Inc., Malden, Mass., for permission to include reproductions of "The Ascension" by Bierman; "The Corruption of Judas" by Prell; "Holy Women at the Tomb" by Ender; "Praying Hands" by Dürer; "Christ Cleansing the Temple" by Kirchback.

Edward Gross Company, Inc., 118-120 E. 16th St., New York 3, N. Y., for permission to include "The Madonna of the Sacred Coat" by Chambers.

E. S. Herrmann, 385 Madison Ave., New York 17, N. Y., for permission to include the following reproductions: "Jesus and the Children" by Flandrin; "The Mission of the Apostles" by Aubert; "The Flight into Egypt" and "The Walk to Emmaus" by Giradet; "The Wise and Foolish Virgins" by Azambre; "The Arrival at Bethlehem" and "Repose in Egypt" by Merson; "The Arrival of the Shepherds" by Lerolle; and "Peter and John Running to the Tomb" by Burnand.

House of Art (no longer in business) for permission to include reproductions of the paintings: "Christ Blessing the Children" by Plockhorst; "Christ in Gethsemane" by Hofmann; "The Kiss of Betrayal" by Geiger; "The Madonna of the Tear" by Kulbach; "The Omnipresent" by Rosenkranz; "Christ and the Fishermen" by Zimmermann.

Kriebel & Bates Company, 4125 N. Keystone Ave., Indianapolis, Ind., for permission to include the picture "Christ at Dawn" by Warner E. Sallman, together with an abridged interpretation from the booklet story published by Kriebel & Bates Company.

Kuntsverlag-Trowitsch & Sohn, Frankfurt (Oder), Germany, for permission to include reproductions of the following paintings: "Healing the Sick Child" by Max; "Christ Going through the Wheat-Fields" by Wehle; "Christ the Welcome Guest" by von Uhde; "The Boy Christ in the Temple," "Christ and the Rich Young Ruler" and "The Crucifixion" by Clementz.

Rudolf Lesch Fine Arts Co., Inc., 225 Fifth Ave., New York 10, N. Y., for permission to include reproductions of the following pictures: "Christus and Nicodemus" by von Uhde; "Raising the Daughter of Jairus" by Repin; "Christ Have Mercy Upon Us" by Deitrich.

Livingstone Press, 42 Broadway, Westminster, London S. A., England, for permission to reproduce the picture "The Healer" by Copping.

The Metropolitan Museum of Art, Wolfe Fund, Fifth Ave. and 82nd St., New York 28, N. Y., for permission to include a reproduction of "Among the Lowly" by L'hermitte.

Missionary Education Movement (Friendship Press), 257 Fourth Ave., New York 10, N. Y., for permission to include a reproduction of "The Nazarene" by Todd, with interpretation material which H. Stanley Todd provided; for permission to include a reproduction of "The Hope of the World" by Copping.

The National Gallery, Trafalgar Square, London, England, for permission to include "Christ Blessing the Children" by Rembrandt.

Rev. E. W. Norwood, City Temple, London, England, for permission to reproduce the picture "If Thou Hadst Known" by Longstaff.

Review Pictures, Takoma Park, Washington, D. C., for permission to include reproductions of the following pictures: "Triumphal Entry," "Christ Taking Leave of His Mother," and "The Good Shepherd" by Plockhorst; "Christ Tempted by Satan" by Cornicelius; "The Lost Sheep" by Soord; "The Transfiguration" by Raphael; "Peter's Denial" by Harrach; and "The Morning of the Resurrection" by Burne-Jones.

The Swiss Society for the Diffusion of Religious Art, Winau, Switzerland, for permission to reproduce the picture "Come Unto Me" by Burnand.

Taber-Prang Art Company (no longer in business) for permission to include a reproduction of "The Son of a Carpenter" by Lafon.

The Trustees of the Tate Gallery, Millbank, London, S. W. 1, England, for permission to reproduce the following pictures: "Ecce Ancilla Domini" by Rossetti; "The Annunciation" by Hacker; "Christ Washing Peter's Feet" by Brown; "The Remorse of Judas" by Armitage; "Hallelujah!" by Gotsch.

H. Stanley Todd (now deceased) for permission to reproduce his picture, "The Nazarene." (Write Friendship Press, 257 Fourth Ave., New York 10, N. Y.)

The Von Trotts, Philadelphia, Pa., for permission to reproduce the photograph of "Christian Symbols."

John Wanamaker, Inc., Philadelphia, Pa., for permission to reproduce the paintings: "Christ before Pilate" and "Christ on Calvary" by Munkácsy.

POETRY AND HYMNS

Abingdon Press, 201 Eighth Ave., S., Nashville 2, Tenn., and Toyohiko Kagawa for permission to include the poems "My Prayer" and "Prayer" from *Songs of the Slums* by Toyohiko Kagawa.

Appleton-Century-Crofts, Inc., 35 W. 32nd St., New York 1, N. Y., for permission to include the poem "Praying Hands" by Gertrude B. Walker.

Asia Magazine (no longer in business) for permission to include the poem "Autumn" by Rabindranath Tagore.

Henry H. Barry for permission to include the poem "He Leadeth Me."

The Estate of Katharine Lee Bates, % Woman's Press, 425 Fourth Ave., New York 16, N. Y., for permission to include nine poems from *The Pilgrim Ship*.

Boston Music Company, Boston, Mass., for permission to include the words of the hymn, "The Stranger of Galilee" by Mrs. C. H. Morris.

Walter Russell Bowie, 119 Windsor Rd., Alexandria, Va., for permission to include the poem "The Continuing Christ" from *The Master of Men* compiled by Thomas Curtis Clark.

Dwight J. Bradley, 485 Columbus Ave., Boston, Mass., for permission to include the poem "The Disciple" from *The Master of Men* compiled by Thomas Curtis Clark.

W. E. Brooks, The Manse, First Presbyterian Church, Morgantown, W. Va., for permission to include the poems "Herod Plans," "Pilate Remembers," and "Barabbas."

Vincent G. Burns (now deceased) for permission to include the poems "He Dwells with Us," "If Jesus Came Back Today," "Like Jesus," "A Manhattan Christmas Eve," and "Out of Nazareth" from *I'm in Love with Life*.

Witter Bynner and Alfred A. Knopf, Inc., 501 Madison Ave., New York 22, N. Y., for permission to include the poem "A Poet Lived in Galilee."

Chautauqua Press, Chautauqua, N. Y., for permission to include the words of the hymn "Break Thou the Bread of Life" by Mary A. Lathbury.

The Christian Century, 407 S. Dearborn St., Chicago 5, Ill., for permission to include poems by W. E. Garrison, Thomas Curtis Clark, Elizabeth Cheney, Lucy Lyttleton, Thomas S. Jones, Jr., Raymond Kresensky, Irene McKeighan, Eva Warner, Theodosia Garrison, Gladys Latchaw, Phyllis Hartnoll, Celia Thaxter, and William Hurd Hillyer.

Badger Clark, Custer, S. D., for permission to include the poem "God Meets Me in the Mountains" from *Sky Lines and Wood Smoke*.

Thomas Curtis Clark (now deceased) for permission to include the following poems: "The Lost Christ" and "Song of Christian Workingmen" from *Quotable Poems* (Vols. I and II); "God's Dreams" from *A Book of Worship;* "Questions" from *Christ in the Poetry of Today;* "God Is Not Far" from *Hymns of Worship*. Also for permission to include the poems "My Master's Face" by William Hurd Hilmer and "To Him All Life Was Beauty" by A. L. C. from *The Master of Men* compiled by Clark. Address communications to Mrs. Thomas Curtis Clark, 242 Marshall Ave., Bellwood, Ill.

Catherine Cate Coblentz, 2737 Macomb St., Washington N. W., D. C., for permission to include the poems "Judas Iscariot" and "The Housewife" from *The Master of Men* compiled by Thomas Curtis Clark; also, "The Earth Worshipped" and "God" from *Quotable Poems* (Vol. I), compiled by Thomas Curtis Clark.

Mrs. Sarah Palmer Colmore for permission to include the poem "Mary, Mother of Heaven, to Mothers on Earth," reprinted from *The Palm Branch,* Diocese of South Florida, Orlando, Fla.

W. B. Conkey Company, Chicago, Ill., for permission to include three poems by Ella Wheeler Wilcox from *Poems of Power* and *Poems of Progress.*

Grace Noll Crowell, 719 Lowell St., Dallas, Tex., for permission to include the poem "The Pictured Christ."

Margaret Deland, "Ships Cabin," Marblehead, Mass., for permission to include the poem-hymn "O Patient Christ."

Chandran Devanesen, % Friendship Press, 257 Fourth Ave., New York 10, N. Y., for permission to include the poem "Altar Flowers" from *The Cross is Lifted.*

E. P. Dutton & Company, 300 Fourth Ave., New York 10, N. Y., for permission to include the poem "Obedience" by George MacDonald.

Doubleday & Company, Inc., 575 Madison Ave., New York 22, N. Y., for permission to include two poems from *Poems That Touch the Heart* by A. L. Alexander, as follows: "Two Prayers" by Andrew Gillies and "Patty-Poem" by Nick Kenny.

Mary S. Edgar, Apt. 6-a, Wychwood Park, Toronto, Ontario, Canada, for permission to include the words of the hymn "God, Who Touchest Earth with Beauty," and the poem "Every Youth."

Ellen Coit Elliot, 756 Santa Enez, Stanford University, Palo Alto, Calif., for permission to include the poem "Choice" from *The Christian Century.*

John Erskine, 130 Claremont Ave., New York 27, N. Y., for permission to reprint the poems "The Shepherd Speaks," "Kings and Stars," and "Childhood."

Evangelical Publishers, 241 Yonge St., Toronto, Ontario, Canada, for permission to include the poem "Jesus Christ and We" by Annie Johnson Flint.

Fillmore Music House, Cincinnati, Ohio, for permission to include the words of two hymns by Eleanor A. Schroll, "If I Could But Tell All the Glory" and "The Beautiful Garden of Prayer."

Natalie Flohr, 118 Ashland Ave., River Forest, Ill., for permission to include the poem "The Martyr" from *The Master of Men* compiled by Thomas Curtis Clark.

Florida Christian Endeavor News for permission to include the poem "Who Wants the Boys and Girls?"

Mary Dillingham Frear, "Arcadia," 1434 Punahou St., Honolulu, T. H., for permission to include the poems "Fishermen" and "The Young Workman."

Mrs. (Agnes Lee) Freer, 81 East Elm St., Chicago, Ill., for permission to include the poem "Motherhood" from *The North American Review.*

Ethel Romig Fuller, Poetry Editor for *The Oregonian,* 2366 West Burnside St., Portland, Ore., for permission to include the poem "Proof" from *Kitchen Sonnets.*

Louise Ayres Garnett, 1226 Judson Ave., Evanston, Ill., for permission to include three poems, "Boyhood," "Song of a Little Child," and "Starry Night," previously published by the Oliver Ditson Company.

Grace F. Guthrie, Hereford, Tex., for permission to include the poem "Christ of the Highways—A Prayer."

Molly Anderson Haley, 906 Plandone Rd., Manhassett, N. Y., for permission to include the poem "Miracles."

Harper & Brothers, 49 East 33rd St., New York 16, N. Y., for permission to use the poems "Wait" and "Some One Had Prayed" from *Light of the Years* by Grace Noll Crowell; the poem "The Great Wager" by G. A. Studdert-Kennedy; and the poem "Simon the Cyrenian Speaks" by Countee Cullen (permission also of Countee Cullen, now deceased).

Alexander Harvey, North Hackensack, N. J., for permission to include the poem "With Me in Paradise."

Herbert Seymour Hastings (now deceased) for permission to include the poem "His Cradle."

Sara Henderson Hay, The Woman's Press, 425 Fourth Ave., New York 16, N. Y., for permission to include the poem "Young Jesus."

Sarah Ashby Heassler, 5221 North Illinois St., Indianapolis, Ind., for permission to include the poem "Prayer" from *World Call.*

Bethany Press, 2640 Pine Blvd., St. Louis 3, Mo., and Mrs. Bernice Hogan, 629 Roundtree, Hillsboro, Ill., for permission to include the poem "He Builded His Church" from *Bethany Guide.*

Houghton Mifflin Company, 2 Park St., Boston 7, Mass., for permission to include a hymn and a poem by Katharine Lee Bates, "O Beautiful for Spacious Skies" and "Not the Christ in the Manger," from her *Selected Poems;* the poem "Music" by Ralph Waldo Emerson; two poems, "Sandalphon" and "Blind Bartimeus," and a hymn "I Heard the Bells" from *Longfellow's Complete Poetical Works.*

Alfred A. Knopf, Inc., 501 Madison Ave., New York 22, N. Y., for permission to include the poem "A Poet Lived in Galilee" by Witter Bynner.

Kriebel & Bates, 4125 N. Keystone Ave., Indianapolis, Ind., for permission to include the poem "Strength through Prayer" by F. Martin Bates, in connection with the art interpretation of "Christ at Dawn" by Sallman.

Elinor Lennen, 2879 Sunset Pl., Los Angeles 5, Calif., for permission to include the poem "Walls" from *Psychology Magazine.*

The Living Church, Church Literature Foundation, 407 E. Michigan St., Milwaukee 2, Wis., for permission to include the poem "Remembering Calvary" by Ethel Fanning Young.

Edwin Markham (now deceased) for permission to include the poems "The Consecration of the Common Way," "A Guard of the Sepulcher," and "The Ascension." Address communications to his son, Virgil Markham, 92 Waters Avenue, New Brighton, Staten Island, N. Y.

Cynthia Pearl Maus, 2619 Wilshire Boulevard, Apt. 810, Los Angeles 57, Calif., for permission to include "The Kiss of a Sunbeam" and three poems from *Puerto Rico in Pictures and Poetry,* compiled and edited by Maus, published by Caxton Press, Caldwell, Idaho, as follows: "A Tropical Moon on Good Friday" and "Twilight Silhouettes" by Maus, and "Moonlight Reflections" by José A. Franquiz.

Madeleine Sweeny Miller, The Arlington, Aiken & Centre Ave., Pittsburgh 32, Pa., for permission to include the poems "An Olive Tree Speaks" (permission also of *The Christian Advocate,* 41 E. 42nd St., New York 17, N. Y.) and "How Far to Bethlehem?"

Margaret P. Montague, 2110 Grove Ave., Richmond, Va., for permission to include the poem "The Christmas Street."

John Richard Moreland, Spottswood Manor, Norfolk, Va., for permission to include the poems "And Christ Is Crucified Anew," "Resurgam," "Revealment," and "His Hands."

Helene Mullins, 559 Fifth Ave., New York 17, N. Y., for permission to include the poem "Thirty Pieces of Silver for Jesus" from *Earthbound,* published by Harper & Brothers.

Meredith Nicholson, % American Legation, Caracas, Venezuela, for permission to include the poem "From Bethlehem to Calvary" from *Poems,* published by Bobbs-Merrill Company.

Novello & Company Ltd., 160 Wardour St., London W. 1, England, for permission to reproduce the words of the hymn "O Love That Wilt Not Let Me Go" by George Matheson.

John Oxenham (now deceased) for permission to include the following poems: "The Inn of Life" from *Selected Poems;* "Live Christ" and "The Pilgrim Way" from *Quotable Poems* compiled by Thomas Curtis Clark; "He—They—We," "Like Other Boys," and "The Cross at the Crossways" from *Gentlemen—The King;* and "Where Are You Going, Great-Heart?" from *The Master of Men* compiled by Thomas Curtis Clark. (Address correspondence to Miss Erica Oxenham, Heather Lane, High Salvington, Worthing, Sussex, England.)

Dorothy Parker and *Bethany Guide,* 2640 Pine Blvd., St. Louis 3, Mo., for permission to include the poem "The Maidservant at the Inn."

Pilgrim Press, 14 Beacon St., Boston 8, Mass., for permission to use the words of the following hymns: "O Master Workman of the Race" by Jay T. Stocking; "We Would See Jesus" by J. Edgar Park; and "Now in the Days of Thy Youth" by Walter J. Mathams from *Worship and Song* by Winchester and Conant.

Edwin McNeill Poteat (now deceased) for permission to include the poem "He, Too, Loved Beauty." Address all communications to Mrs. Edwin McNeill Poteat, 2643 Park Lane Circle, Apt. D., Birmingham 9, Ala.

Samuel F. Pugh and The Bethany Press, 2640 Pine Blvd., St. Louis 3, Mo., for permission to include the poem "Dedicate Your Life" from *Between-Time Meditations* by Samuel F. Pugh.

Elizabeth Woodsworth Reese (now deceased) for permission to include the poems "Good Friday" and "His Mother in Her Hood of Blue."

The Rodeheaver Hall-Mack Company, Winona Lake, Ind., for permission to reprint the words of the following hymns: "The Old Rugged Cross" by George Bennard; "Alone" by Ben H. Price; and "God is Love" by Elsie D. Yale, from *Cheerio's Favorite Hymns.*

Charles Scribner's Sons, 597 Fifth Ave., New York 17, N. Y., for permission to include the poems by Sidney Lanier, Henry van Dyke, and Maltbie D. Babcock.

Charles M. Sheldon (now deceased) for permission to include the poem "Jesus the Carpenter" from *Quotable Poems* (Vol. I), compiled by Thomas Curtis Clark.

Laura Simmons, 120 Charles St., Boston Mass., or 303 29th St., New York 1, N. Y., for permission to include the following poems: "The Rich Young Man," "Bartimeus," "The Way," and "The Trimmed Lamp."

Hilda W. Smith, West Park, N. Y., for permission to include the poem "Barley Bread."

Standard Publishing Company, 9th and Cutter Sts., Cincinnati, Ohio, for permission to include the words of the hymns "Ere You Left Your Room This Morning" by Mrs. M. A. Kidder and "The Stranger of Galilee" by Mrs. C. H. Morris.

William L. Stidger (now deceased) for permission to include the following poems: "God's Autograph," "I am the Cross," "I Heard God Speak," "I Saw God Wash the World," "Judean Hills are Holy," and "Christ Was the Outdoor Son of God" from *I Saw God Wash the World.* Also for "Grace for the Noonday Meal" and "Grace before the Evening Meal." Address communications to Mrs. William L. Stidger, 120 Oxford Rd., Newton Centre, Mass.

Eleanor B. Stock for permission to include the words of the hymn "The Prayer of the Quest" from *Singing Pathways* by Dickie.

Mary Dixon Thayer, % Mrs. Maurice Fremont-Smith, 12 Hereford St., Boston, Mass., for permission to include the poem "Perhaps."

Dorothy Brown Thompson, 6435 Pennsylvania Ave., Kansas City, Mo., for permission to include the poem "Holy Thursday" from *The Christian Advocate.*

The University of Chicago Press, 5750 Ellis Ave., Chicago 37, Ill., for a paragraph defining poetry from *Finding God through the Beautiful* by Theodore G. Soares.

Helen W. Welshimer for permission to include the following poems: "The Last Supper" from *Good Housekeeping Magazine* and "A Birthday" from *World Call.* Address communications to Rev. P. H. Welshimer, % First Christian Church, Canton, Ohio.

Mary Brent Whiteside (now deceased) for permission to include the following poems: "Mary at the Well," "Nazareth Days," "The Carpenter," "The Song of Joseph," "Tiberias at Dawn," and "Who Has Known Heights."

Helen Slack Wickendon, % The Woman's Press, 425 Fourth Ave., New York 16, N. Y., for permission to include the poem "The Door."

Clement Wood, for permission to include the poem "The Singing Saviors."

World Call, 222 S. Downey Ave., Indianapolis 7, Ind., for permission to include the following poems: "Prayer" by Sarah A. Heassler; "America First" by Bishop G. Ashton Oldham; "Youth" by Alice G. Moore; "Jis' Blue" by Etta Oldham; "A Prayer for the Poor and the Outcast" by J. S. Hoyland; and "Christ of the Everywhere" by Henry van Dyke.

Ethel Fanning Young (now deceased) for permission to include the poem "Remembering Calvary."

STORIES

Abingdon Press, 201 Eighth Ave., S., Nashville 2, Tenn., for permission to abridge the story interpretation of "Christ in Gethsemane" from *Pictures that Preach* by Charles Nelson Page; "The Story of the Violin Sermon" by Robert Freeman, and other paragraphs from *Music and Religion;* the story "His Way" from the 1936 *Elementary Magazine.*

Henry Altemus Company, 24 S. Orianna St., Philadelphia, Pa., for permission to include the story "The Star" by Florence M. Kingsley.

American Baptist Publication Society, 1701 Chestnut St., Philadelphia 3, Pa., for permission to include the story "If He Had Not Come" by Nan F. Weeks, from the Keystone Graded Lessons.

The Heirs of G. M. Anderson, % Bethany Press, 2640 Pine Blvd., St. Louis 3, Mo., for permission to include the following five stories from *His Mother, A Story of Our Lord:* "His Last Week," "Jesus, the Miracle Man," "Joy Cometh in the Morning," "Strange Happenings to the Young Child," and "The Virgin's Story."

Appleton-Century-Crofts, Inc., 35 W. 32nd St., New York 1, N. Y., for permission to include two stories by Laura Armstrong Athearn, from *Christian Worship for American Youth,* and one story by Mattoon-Bragdon, from *Services for the Open.*

The Atlantic Monthly, 8 Arlington St., Boston 16, Mass., for permission to brief the story "When Christmas Comes" by Joseph Fort Newton.

Alice Stone Blackwell, compiler, and Gabriela Mistral, author, for permission to include the story "Christ and the Sorry Thistle" from *Some Spanish-American Poets,* published by Appleton-Century-Crofts, Inc., 35 W. 32nd St., New York 1, N. Y.

J. Chapman Bradley, Hotel Pearson, 190 East Pearson St., Chicago 11, Ill., and *The Presbyterian Outlook,* 1 North 6th St., Richmond 19, Va., for permission to include the story "The Angel Who Refused to Sing."

The Century Magazine (August 1900), published by The Century Company, New York, N. Y., for permission to abridge the story "The Prince of Illusion" by John Luther Long.

The Challenge Limited, London, England, for permission to include the story "The Adventure of Prayer" by Margaret Cooper.

The Christian Herald, 27 East 39th St., New York 16, N. Y., for permission to include the story "God's Man in Africa" by Hubert W. Peet.

Robert Freeman for permission to include "The Story of the Violin Sermon" from *Music and Religion* compiled by Stanley A. Hunter, published by Abingdon Press, 201 Eighth Ave., S., Nashville 2, Tenn.

Walter W. Furniss, % WLW (Crosley Radio Station), Cincinnati, Ohio, for permission to include the story "The Legend of the Dogwood Tree."

Harper & Brothers, 49 East 33rd St., New York 16, N. Y., for permission to adapt one story from *Ben Hur* by Lew Wallace (permission also of Lew Wallace, Jr.); and for six abridged stories from *By an Unknown Disciple* (permission also of A. P. Watt, London, England); also two stories from *The Little Boy of Nazareth* by Edna Madison Bonser.

Sarah Ashby Heassler, 5221 North Illinois St., Indianapolis, Ind., for permission to include her hitherto unpublished story "A Modern Midnight Madonna."

The Hope Publishing Company, Chicago, Ill., for the composite Bible story from *His Last Week* by William E. Barton and others.

Houghton Mifflin Company, 2 Park St., Boston 7, Mass., for permission to include three stories from *The Story of Jesus Christ* by Elizabeth Stuart Phelps.

Alfred A. Knopf, Inc., 501 Madison Ave., New York 22, N. Y., for permission to abridge four stories from *Jesus, the Son of Man* by Kahlil Gibran as follows: "Jesus, As Seen by Mary Magdalene," "Jesus, As Seen by Pilate," "Jesus, As Seen through the Eyes of Zacchaeus," and "A Shepherd in South Lebanon."

Livingstone Press, 42 Broadway, Westminster, London S. A., England, for permission to include two stories from *Sindano Stories* by Vera E. Walker.

Rev. W. Russell Maltby (now deceased) for permission to include two story-letters entitled "Jesus, As Seen by Johanan, Collector of Taxes at Magdala," and "Jesus, As Seen by Zacchaeus, Commissioner of Taxes at Jericho."

Edwin Markham (now deceased) for permission to include brief paragraphs from the introductory pages of *The Book of American Poetry,* Markham. Address communications to his son, Virgil Markham, 92 Waters Avenue, New Brighton, Staten Island, N. Y.

Charles A. McCalmon, % Abingdon Press, 201 Eighth Ave. S., Nashville 2, Tenn., for permission to include the story of "Jesus Alive Forevermore" from *Jesus and Chums.*

Meigs Publishing Company, Indianapolis, Ind., Mrs. Phoebe A. Curtiss and the Heirs of Washington Gladden, for permission to include the story "The Shepherd's Story" by Washington Gladden from *Christmas Stories and Legends* by Phoebe A. Curtiss.

Methodist Publishing Company, 150 Fifth Ave., New York 11, N. Y., for permission to include the story "An International Dinner" from *Friends at Work* by Elsie Ball.

Rev. Raphael E. Miller (now deceased) for permission to include the story-sermon "Good Morning, Christ Is Risen" from *World Call,* 222 S. Downey Ave., Indianapolis, Ind.

Joseph Fort Newton (now deceased) for permission to brief his story "When Will Christmas Come?" from *The Atlantic Monthly.* Address communications to Estate of Joseph Fort Newton, 529 Heath Road, Merion, Pa.

Rev. F. W. Norwood, City Temple, London, England, for the sermon-interpretation of the picture "If Thou Hadst Known" by Longstaff.

Fleming H. Revell Company, 316 Third Ave., Westwood, N. J., for permission to include two stories from *Far above Rubies* by Agnes Sligh Turnbull.

Mrs. Gladys Payne Shafer, Longbranch, Wash., for permission to include the story "His Way," formerly published in *The Elementary Teacher,* Abingdon Press, 201 Eighth Ave. S., Nashville 2, Tenn.

Mabel F. Shelley and the late H. M., publishers, Philadelphia, Pa., and Harold F. Branch, the author, for paragraphs from *Religious Picture Sermons.*

Theodore G. Soares, Box A, Dana Point, Calif., for permission to use a paragraph from *Finding God through the Beautiful.*

Eleanor B. Stock for permission to include the stories "Sister" and "The Hill Road" from *The Classmate,* published by Methodist Publishing House, 201 Eighth Ave., S., Nashville 2, Tenn.

H. Stanley Todd (now deceased) for permission to use story-interpretation material on his picture "The Nazarene." (Write Friendship Press, 257 Fourth Ave., New York 10, N. Y.)

Agnes Sligh Turnbull for permission to include two stories, "The Mother of the Lad with the Loaves and Fishes" and "The Miracle of Cana," from *Far above Rubies.*

John C. Winston Company, 1010 Arch St., Philadelphia 7, Pa., for permission to abridge the article "The Use of Pictures in Teaching" from *Great Pictures as Moral Teachers* by Henry E. Jackson; and also to use the interpretation of Guercino's "The Magdalene" from the same volume.

World Call, 222 Downey Ave., Indianapolis 7, Ind., for permission to include the story "For Such an Age As This" by Lynn Harold Hough.

Zion's Herald for permission to include the story "The Poet of the People" by William L. Stidger (now deceased). Write Mrs. William L. Stidger, 120 Oxford Road, Newton Centre, Mass.